THE AMERICAN AND EUROPEAN
REVOLUTIONS, 1776-1848

PROCEEDINGS OF THE SECOND
(BICENTENNIAL) CONFERENCE OF
POLISH AND AMERICAN HISTORIANS
IOWA CITY, IOWA, U.S.A.
29 SEPTEMBER–1 OCTOBER 1976

THE AMERICAN AND EUROPEAN
REVOLUTIONS, 1776–1848:
SOCIOPOLITICAL AND IDEOLOGICAL ASPECTS

Edited with Introduction by
Jaroslaw Pelenski

UNIVERSITY OF IOWA PRESS
1980

University of Iowa Press, Iowa City 52242

The preparation of this volume was made possible (in part) by a grant from the Program for Research Tools and Reference Works of the National Endowment for the Humanities, an independent Federal agency.

Library of Congress Cataloging in Publication Data

Conference of Polish and American Historians, 2d, Iowa
  City, 1976.
  The American and European revolutions, 1776-1848.

  Includes bibliographical references and index.
  1. United States—History—Revolution, 1775-1783—
Congresses. 2. United States—Relations (general)
with Poland—Congresses. 3. Poland—Relations
(general) with the United States—Congresses.
4. Revolutions—Europe—Congresses. 5. Europe—
History—1789-1900—Congresses. I. Pelenski, Jaroslaw,
1929-   II. Title.
E204.C66 1976   301.29'73'04   79-22599
ISBN 0-87745-097-8

CONTENTS

ILLUSTRATIONS

PREFACE

The studies published in this volume were originally presented at the Second Conference of Polish and American Historians, an American Bicentennial event, entitled "The American and European Revolutions, 1776-1840s: Sociopolitical and Ideological Ramifications," which took place at the University of Iowa, Iowa City, Iowa, on 29 September-1 October 1976 under the joint auspices of the Committee of Historical Sciences of the Polish Academy of Sciences, the Institute of History of the University of Warsaw, and the Department of History of the University of Iowa. Various other institutions both in Poland and in the United States cooperated in this initial endeavor, and Professors Stefan Kieniewicz (Chairman of the Committee of Historical Sciences, Polish Academy of Sciences) and Jaroslaw Pelenski (University of Iowa) served as its coordinators. Participants included scholars both from the three sponsoring institutions and from other American and Polish universities.

A similar meeting, the First Conference of Polish and American Historians, had been held in Nieborów, Poland, two years earlier, in May 1974, the first such exchange between Polish and American historians. The proceedings of the first conference, entitled *State and Society in Europe from the Fifteenth to the Eighteenth Century,* and also edited by Jaroslaw Pelenski, will be published by the University of Warsaw Press simultaneously with this volume.

The Second Conference of Polish and American Historians was the only Bicentennial event of its kind that involved scholars from an East European country. It was only appropriate that such an event should be conducted in cooperation with Polish historians, for of all East European countries, it was Poland with whom the emerging United States had the closest ties during the revolutionary era. It was also Poland with whose people the Americans had close contacts and relations throughout modern history; a nation from whose people have come a great many American citizens. Thus, far from being an either accidental or contrived event, the Bicentennial historical conference involving Polish and American historians was a natural event that corresponds well to the nature of things, to the historic friendship and ties between the people of Poland and the United States, and to the special relationship between the two countries.

The editor wishes to express his appreciation to the National Endowment for the Humanities for its generous research grant toward support of the Iowa Bicentennial Conference and the preparation of its proceedings for publication, and for its special subvention to partially defray the publication costs of this volume. Thanks are also due to the

ix

International Research and Exchanges Board for its Collaborative Projects Grant in aid of the conference. The assistance of the following institutions, which made the success of the conference possible, should be acknowledged: the Polish Academy of Sciences for its contributions, the University of Iowa for hosting the conference, and the U.S. Department of State for other arrangements.

Many individuals, including the editor's colleagues and friends, contributed significantly to the congeniality of the occasion; among them President Willard L. Boyd, Vice President Duane C. Spriestersbach, and Professor Laurence Lafore, all of the University of Iowa, ought to be singled out for their particular help and hospitality.

The editor is especially indebted to his Polish and American colleagues for consenting to participate in the conference and for agreeing to publish their papers in this volume. The editor's appreciation extends as well to Margaret B. Ševčenko for editing, and to Mary E. Strottman for meticulously typing the final manuscript, and to his student, Janusz Duzinkiewicz, for proofreading the galleys and for preparing the index. And, finally, as always, the editor wishes to express his deep gratitude to his wife, Christina Pelenski, for her never failing assistance in the preparation both of the conference and of this volume.

J. P.
Iowa City, Iowa
April 1979

INTRODUCTION

Revolutions figure among the great events of human history and among the perpetual concerns of their practitioners and students. Political thinkers, ideologues, historians, and social scientists of all persuasions have attempted to solve the riddles of the etiology and taxonomy of revolutions with the aim either of discovering why and how they constantly recur, or of integrating the varieties of forms they assume into a meaningful theoretical framework. In spite of the many contributions to the study of revolution that have appeared in the last three decades, the subject still suffers from confusion, in part because of the devaluation, banalization, and vulgarization of the concept of revolution in our times,[1] in part from the ambivalence, at least among some historians, toward the various theories of revolution advanced by social scientists, often in response to contemporary political and social problems. Although few would deny the validity of trying to integrate the accumulated knowledge or to formulate new scholarly paradigms, those theories of revolution that have been promulgated over the last quarter-century often appear to be in need of reevaluation, of questioning, and of revision; some should even perhaps be abandoned altogether.

Reexamining the established theories of revolution has become mandatory, especially in view of recent tendencies in the humanities and social sciences to remain no longer satisfied with only one, or a few, dominant schools of thought in any given discipline. A genuine discomfort among the students of revolution regarding the established periodizations, classifications, and categorizations has led to study of neglected historical phenomena, submerged political orientations, and ideological subcurrents and subgroups within the revolutionary movements, particularly those which, for one reason or another, were not crowned by success. Similarly, neglected or forgotten authors who also contributed to the analysis of revolution, either as contemporaries or *ex post facto,* are now being brought to light.

Until recently, the study and evaluation of revolutions were considerably influenced by "modernist" and future-oriented theories of history, which emphasized dramatic ruptures, fundamental transformations, rapid changes, and, ultimately, "progress," and were closely connected with an interest in the origins of modernity and the foundations of the modern world. They began with a very distinguished intellectual tradition centered on one of the more influential revolutionary models: the French Revolution—sometimes in combination with the American one—which was viewed as the dramatic opening phase in the history of modern times. Scholars who were engaged in the study of the emergence and the evolution of the very concept of revolution and of its related sociopolitical and cultural terminology were inclined to connect it very closely with the notion of modernity.[2]

As a result, scholars tended either to extend the notion of modernity to the present or arbitrarily to select a specific revolution, such as the Russian Revolution of 1917-20, the Chinese Revolution of the late nineteen forties, or some other revolution or revolutions in the developing world, and to analyze it in the context of historical modernity without being too concerned with the degree to which its referential context was applicable in any given case. Many simply neglected to probe into the question of what modernity means when it is applied to the French, or the Russian, or even the Fascist revolutions. The appeal of the modernist approach lies in its being a historiographic reflection of the attractive and influential theory of modernization which is supposed to resolve, or at least to explain, the complexities of the contemporary world.

Only recently have scholars begun to feel uncomfortable with the chronological delimitations of the history of revolution imposed by the modernist or modernizing approach and cautiously to inquire into the problem of revolution in early-modern Europe.[3] At least a tentative beginning has been made regarding the applicability of the concept of revolution to developments prior to the French Revolution, but no attempt has been undertaken, to the best of my knowledge, to bring up the question of whether or not the revolutions that have taken place between the late eighteenth century and the mid-twentieth form some kind of unity. Would such a unity stand up to scrutiny if we used as a measure the presence or absence of fundamental changes in property relations, for example? Such a criterion would greatly modify the present classification of revolutions by bringing the American and French revolutions into a closer relationship to the so-called early-modern revolutions of the seventeenth century, particularly those in which political and constitutional questions were overriding. At the same time it would separate the French Revolution from the Russian and the Chinese revolutions. In spite of all the charisma and canonical importance which the revolutionaries of the radical Left attached to the French Revolution, their own revolutions would have to be placed in quite a different category.

An even more complicated problem has been posed for historians by the new theories of revolution formulated by social scientists. Their broad generalizations and conceptual theorems have generated a great deal of interest,[4] especially those that are the products mainly of American social scientists and depend on economic, psychological, political, or sociological explanations (the last variety could also be referred to as politico-sociological, with some authors emphasizing behavior, and others stressing structure).[5] Of the four approaches, the political and politico-sociological theories have had the greatest influence. The theory of revolution provided by the social scientist Chalmers Johnson,[6] for example, develops a useful typology by classifying revolutions into six basic types: (1) jacquerie, (2) the millenarian rebellion, (3) the anarchistic rebellion, (4) the Jacobin-Communist or "great" revolution, (5) the conspiratorial coup d'etat, and (6) the militarized mass insurrection. At least parts of Johnson's typology have been questioned by various historians, but no one in the past fifteen years has been able to propose a better solution, in part because of the reluctance most historians—including those who work with quantitative methods—display toward engaging in theoretical inquiries at all. By and large, historians continue to adhere to what they regard as traditional humanistic inquiry. As a result, the field of the theory of revolution has been preempted by social scientists, who claim to be more rigorous in their handling of empirical data, to be better able to apply theory, models, and ideal types, and to be better equipped to undertake comparative studies.[7]

The new theories of revolution that have resulted cannot be accepted without reservation, however. With few exceptions,[8] social scientists who have advanced theories about revolution have conducted little in the way of bona fide empirical research. Instead, they have been inclined to rely on the results obtained by historians without being able to verify these results. Some of their findings, particularly those of the psychologists, have been marred by conceptual ambiguities and constant diversions into broader and even more questionable theorems and by the subordination of the concept of revolution to such general notions as "civil strife" and "violence."[9]

Significant questions can also be raised regarding the methodology of comparative studies of revolution, or comparative history in general. A number of comparative studies have been undertaken by authors whose empirical research is limited to a single country, a single system, a single society, a single narrowly defined period, a single set of data, often in a single language, and exposed to a single mode of theoretical inquiry. It is a paradox of the contemporary academic condition that narrow specialists embark with the greatest of ease on comparative and pluralist research endeavors, while researchers with a variety of skills and broad theoretical backgrounds shy away from them.

The historian studying social-science literature pertaining to the theories of revolution is astonished by the ease with which the social scientist moves across centuries and historical periods and among social groups, movements, and ideologies. Even those historians who are partial to the social sciences are not quite comfortable with the complete rejection of the fundamental assumptions of historicism that an event, a social or political movement, or a theory ought to be judged in its own historical context. Social scientists have no qualms about applying the concept of revolution, or any other concept for that matter, to any period in history and any sociopolitical framework, while the historian agonizes over whether or not he is justified in applying the concept of revolution to, say, the early-modern period, or the notion of ideology as a comprehensive system of ideas, beliefs, and assumptions about man, society, the universe, and their mutual relationship to the sixteenth century, even if he has familiarized himself thoroughly with the social-science approach to the theoretical connotations of the term "ideology."[10]

The response of historians to this sort of problem is usually either dutifully to accept the theoretical tools suggested by the social scientists and the integration of the results of their work into the already prescribed theorems, which quite often have been formulated independently of any empirical data, or to resign themselves to the idea that history, after all, has become the servant of the social sciences and must therefore abandon its lofty theoretical and scholarly concerns to them. This pessimism, however, does not seem entirely warranted. A close and simultaneous reading of both the historical and social-science literature on revolution produced during the last thirty years reveals that advances in social-science studies on the theory of revolution have often followed the appearance of some new imaginative historical contribution, while the theoretical interests of social scientists have similarly awakened the formulation of new concerns and the opening of new fields in history. It would be difficult to decide which currents are the more preponderant both in quantitative and qualitative terms.

What, then, are the tasks of the historian? Historians ought to be able not only to embark upon new avenues in their own discipline, but to respond to new societal concerns which they can partially explain on the basis of historical experience. Such a statement would have been met with scorn only a few years ago by the more exclusive social scientists. At present, however, we seem to be witnessing a return to the past, albeit not for any very inspiring reason, but simply because of the general crisis that appears to be besetting our contemporary world. Since revolution, a classical theme of history, has been one of the principal historical mechanisms by which crises have been resolved, we are perhaps justified in wishing to revisit the classical age of revolutions, particularly in conjunction with the American Bicentennial, from the perspective of new scholarly and societal concerns.

This brief discussion of contemporary scholarship on revolutions, particularly the theoretical literature, should serve as a background for the sixteen studies presented in this volume. These studies, written by scholars of different methodological schools and theoretical persuasions, fall into four general groups: (1) those dealing with the experiences of the American Revolution; (2) with Polish-American relations in the revolutionary era; (3) with the political and social aspects of the French Revolution; and (4) with the revolutionary traditions in East Central Europe.

In two of the studies in the first group the authors integrate new scholarly and societal concerns into the framework of American revolutionary history. The study by Stow Persons explores the origins and the early phase of ethnic interaction in eighteenth-century Pennsylvania and problems arising from the relations between Anglo-Americans and one of the first European immigrant groups, the Germans, and their resolution through "Anglo-Americanization." Linda Kerber deals with the emergence of political consciousness among American women and the vexing question of their politicization in the American Revolution. From the methodological point of view, both use a traditional approach, a careful survey of the documentation pertaining to the problems, and both conclude their contributions with cautious summations of their findings. The two studies offer an appropriate introduction to selected problems in fields that have only recently begun to develop their own methodology and have a limited historiographic tradition. The theme of religion and the American Revolution, or church and state in American history, already has an established tradition in historical scholarship. Sydney V. James proposes modifications and refinements to those accepted views on the evolution of the relationship between the civil authority and the various Protestant denominations during the colonial and revolutionary periods and provides new insights into the establishment of generalized Protestantism as a national faith. These studies are representative of the main stream of American historiography; in a paper on revolutionary consciousness in America and Europe written from a Marxist perspective, Jerzy Topolski, has undertaken an innovative venture by combining the Polish version of creative Marxism with the conceptual findings by leading Western historians up to the early nineteen seventies, leaving the theoretical problems of revolution posed by Western social-science literature for another discussion.

The contributions devoted to Polish-American interactions in the revolutionary period and to Polish-American relations in post-revolutionary times by Piotr S. Wandycz, Anna M. Cienciala, and M. K. Dziewanowski should open a new phase in the historiography of those subjects. All three papers revise the established canons of national iconographic historiographies. Their authors have carefully reexamined the sources, established reasonable criteria for the new approach to these relations, and transformed their discussions from the realm of mythology and wishful thinking to the level of hard and reassuring realities.

A revisionist bent, although of a different sort, is also evident in the three studies devoted to the sociopolitical aspects of the French Revolution. In particular, the essays on the "new" French elite and the sociopolitics of the French Restoration, in which the distant consequences of the Revolution considerably influenced the realities of the new state, reconsider established assumptions, including in one case some of those previously held by the author. Robert Forster shows that the Revolution was not a significant break in the history of the French social elite and by implication in French social history. Alan B. Spitzer underscores the survival of political and ideological attitudes formed during the Revolution in a nonrevolutionary sociopolitical setting. The contributions pertaining to the history of the French Revolution, including the one by Bogusław Leśnodorski, reveal the influence of Braudel on political and sociocultural history in general.

Five studies in this volume have been devoted to the revolutionary developments in East Central Europe during the classical period of revolutions—a field with a venerable tradition in the national historiographies of that region. The introductory study concerns itself with the Ukrainian *haidamak* insurrections and their challenges to the old regimes. In it Jaroslaw Pelenski has departed from the established tradition of viewing the *haidamak* insurrections as jacqueries or primarily antifeudal peasant movements and has proposed a new interpretation based on an analysis of their social composition with emphasis on the role of the Cossack leadership groups.

The Polish contributors address themselves to three problems in East European revolutionary history of particular interest to the historian of revolutionary movements: Jerzy Skowronek deals with the models of revolution formulated by East European revolutionary groups in the Napoleonic period; Andrzej Walicki with the theories of revolution developed by the Polish revolutionaries between the insurrections of 1830–31 and 1848–49; and Stefan Kieniewicz with the revolutionary populations, specifically the Russian Decembrists and the Polish revolutionaries, during the Restoration era. Together the three studies provide an introduction to the present state of research on revolutions in Poland. This group of studies closes with a reassessment of the opening, reformist phase of the Hungarian "lawful" Revolution of 1848–49 by Istvan Deak. No doubt, both this reassessment and the author's recent work on the Hungarian Revolution of 1848–49[11] will open a new round of scholarly debate on this grand topic of Hungarian history.

The concluding study in this volume, on art and politics in the revolutionary age, falls into a somewhat different category. In it Jan Białostocki relates art to sociopolitical change and shows how contemporary history is integrated into the art of a revolutionary age.

In spite of their obviously diverse views on the problem of revolution, the authors of the studies presented here attempt to strike a balance between the traditional and basically historicist approach, which avoids the pitfalls of excessive contemporary relevance, and the revisionist approach, which stresses the need to challenge the established assumptions and to propose new conceptualizations based upon well-grounded research. This endeavor has resulted in the emergence of a preponderant view—which can be considered as its single most important contribution to the study of revolution—that in spite of revolutions, fundamental sociopolitical changes take place rather slowly, that historical, cultural, and social conditioning has been in itself a powerful force, and that revolution, and especially its consequences, in a considerable number of cases should not necessarily be regarded as a prologue to modernity but can equally well be viewed as an epilogue to the past. Obviously, such a viewpoint, more than any other, emphasizes historical continuity, a greater reliance on, and longevity of, established patterns and models, and the value of history itself.

Jaroslaw Pelenski

NOTES

1 For a thought-provoking but somewhat one-sided assessment of these developments, see J. Ellul, *The Autopsy of Revolution* (translated from the French) (New York, 1971), especially chap. 4.

2 For a penetrating, and still the best traditional analysis of the concept of revolution, confer K. Griewank, *Der neuzeitliche Revolutionsbegriff* (Weimar, 1955; 2nd ed., Frankfurt a/M, 1973). Griewank was preceded by E. Rosenstock-Hussey, "Revolution als politischer Begriff in der Neuzeit," in *Festgabe für Paul Heilbron zum 70. Geburtstag* (Breslau, 1931) (Abhandlungen der Schlesischen Gesellschaft für vaterländische Cultur, Geisteswissenschaftliche Reihe, Issue 5), who, however, restricted himself to its political aspects. For the more recent accounts and emendations, see P. Zagorin, *The Court and the Country* (London, 1969), chap. 1; M. Foisil, *La révolte des nu-pieds et les révoltes normandes de 1639* (Paris, 1970), pp. 136–38; R. Mousnier, *Reserches sur les soulèvements populaires en France de 1485 à 1787: Questionnaire*, Centre de Reserches sur la Civilisation de l'Europe Moderne, Paris, n.d., p. 6; F. Gilbert, "Revolution," *Dictionary of the History of Ideas*, ed. P. Wiener (New York, 1973).

3 Three contributions should be mentioned, although their authors have not abandoned the modernist approach altogether: J. H. Elliott, "Revolution and Continuity in Early Modern Europe," *Past & Present* (1969), no. 42: 35–56; R. Forster and J. P. Greene, eds., *Preconditions of Revolution in Early Modern Europe* (Baltimore and London, 1970); and P. Zagorin, "Prolegomena to the Comparative History of Revolution in Early Modern Europe," *Comparative Studies in Society and History* 18, 2 (1976): 151–74.

4 For a summary and evaluation of this vast literature, see L. Stone, "Theories of Revolution," *World Politics* 18, 2 (1966): 159–76; the collection of essays on various theories of revolution in C. J. Friedrich, ed., *Revolution, Yearbook of the American Society for Political and Legal Philosophy*, Nomos 8 (New York, 1967); I. Kramnick, "Reflections on Revolution: Definition and Explanation in Recent Scholarship," *History and Theory* 11 (1972): 26–63; P. Zagorin, "Theories of Revolution in Contemporary Historiography," *Political Science Quarterly* 88 (1973): 23–52; T. R. Gurr, "The Revolution—Social-Change Nexus: Some Old Theories and New Hypotheses," *Comparative Politics* 5 (1972–73): 359–92; G. P. Meyer, "Revolutionstheorien heute; Ein kritischer Überblick in historischer Absicht," in H. -U. Wehler, ed., *200 Jahre amerikanische Revolution und moderne Revolutionsforschung, Geschichte und Gesellschaft*, Zeitschrift für Historische Sozialwissenschaft, Sonderheft 2 (Göttingen, 1976), pp. 122–76.

5 Kramnick's systematization of the literature (see above, note 4) is quite useful for our discussion.

6 The two principal studies to be mentioned in this connection are: *Revolution and the Social System*, Hoover Institution Studies, no. 3 (The Hoover Institution on War, Revolution, and Peace, Stanford University, 1964) and *Revolutionary Change* (Boston and Toronto, 1966).

7 Concerning a discussion of the relationship of historical scholarship and the social sciences, see D. S. Landes and Ch. Tilly, eds., *History as Social Science* (Englewood Cliffs, N.J., 1971).

8 For one example, see Ch. Tilly, *The Vendée* (Cambridge, Mass., 1964).

9 Among the numerous examples is T. R. Gurr's, *Why Men Rebel* (Princeton, 1970). For additional discussion of this approach, and the relevant literature on the subject, see Ch. Tilly, "Revolutions and Collective Violence," in F. I. Greenstein and N. Polsby, eds., *Handbook of Political Science*, vol. 3: Macropolitical theory (Reading, Mass., 1975), pp. 483–555.

10 For a thoughtful but debatable assessment of the applicability of the concept of "imperial ideology," see G. Stökl, "Imperium und imperiale Ideologie-Erfahrungen am Beispiel des vorpetrinischen Russland," in *Vom Staat des Ancien Regime zum modernen Parteienstaat, Festschrift für Theodor Schieder zu seinem 70. Geburtstag*, eds. H. Berding, K. Düwell, L. Gall, W. J. Mommsen, H. -U. Wehler (Munich-Vienna, 1978), pp. 27–39. He discusses J. Pelenski's *Russia and Kazan: Conquest and Imperial Ideology (1438–1560s)* (The Hague–Paris, 1974) and other studies.

11 I. Deak, *The Lawful Revolution: Louis Kossuth and the Hungarians, 1848–1849* (New York, 1979).

PART I

EXPERIENCES OF THE AMERICAN
REVOLUTION AND THE PROBLEM OF
REVOLUTIONARY CONSCIOUSNESS IN
AMERICA AND EUROPE

RELIGION AND THE AMERICAN REVOLUTION: THE DEVELOPMENT OF THE FEDERAL STYLE IN THE RELATIONS BETWEEN RELIGION AND CIVIL AUTHORITY

Sydney V. James, University of Iowa

The topic, religion and the American Revolution, has had a venerable history. Yet, while many have written about it, it is nevertheless still in need of some further thought and discussion. Fortunately, within recent years, four scholars of diverse backgrounds have encouraged that endeavor by offering some fresh ideas on the subject: Sidney E. Mead, a specialist (if that term applies to him) in both history and religion; William G. McLoughlin, a historian; Mark D. Howe, a lawyer and legal historian; and Robert N. Bellah, a sociologist.[1] They have reopened old questions and reconstructed the categories of analysis. They have also—or so one hopes—finally disposed of the old notion that the Revolution divorced church from state and inaugurated an era of strictly secular government. And finally, they have, though in rather different formulations, pointed out the ways, mainly extralegal, in which government and religion have kept a liaison ever since—and to some extent as a consequence of—the Revolution. Their ideas suggest several lines along which analysis could be continued and several subjects on which detailed research needs to be done.

Appreciating the accomplishments of these four scholars requires an acquaintance with the historiographical background of their work. Before they reinterpreted the revolutionary period, the prevailing view for many years had been that in the Revolution the people of the United States, in a fever of idealism, veered sharply away from the old practice of establishing a church and toward a complete freedom of religion. By the Constitution and its First Amendment they erected a beacon toward which state policies sooner or later steered their course. The conventional analysis of the states' actions after 1776 interpreted events in some places as holding the colonial course of freedom of religion and in other places as coming about and heading toward disestablishment. The climactic event in these discussions was the contest resulting in Virginia's adoption of the Act for Establishing Religious Freedom in 1786. Triumph in this struggle was treated as the key victory of progress over traditionalism, after which other laggard states simply fell into line, while the country discovered, and overcame, a long series of secondary problems that cropped up along the way in implementing the basic policy. Historians generally found religious developments in the revolutionary period to be grounds for national self-congratulation. The culmination of this line of scholarship, the massive work of Anson Phelps Stokes, was presented almost explicitly as an offering on the altar of American nationalism.[2]

One important variant on these standard ideas appeared in J. Franklin Jameson's *American Revolution Considered as a Social Movement.* Jameson organized the subject of religion and the Revolution in a way that remained influential for several decades. He accepted the common view that religious zeal had declined during the revolutionary period as public attention turned to political concerns and as Americans took to the rationalism and Enlightenment that had been imported from Europe. He added to that explanation the impact of the sheer physical damage to church property occasioned by the Revolution itself and the disruption within ecclesiastical organizations arising from independence. He also drew attention both to the labors of reconstruction and the reconstitution of the major denominations after 1783. Churches formerly dependent on European hierarchies had to find ways to make do on their own; in the process they acquired local bishops for the first time and instituted national systems of organization. Even denominations without such compelling reasons set up national structures. To do so, the several communions resorted to written constitutions providing for representational schemes of one sort or another. So the Revolution led to a vital period of rearrangement intended to bring organized religion into harmony with national independence and, perhaps without conscious design, into congruity with national political institutions as well.[3]

Reassessments of the record by Mead, McLoughlin, Howe, and Bellah have not stopped at conclusions that the wall separating church from state supposedly erected by the Revolution was less solid than had previously been thought; rather, they have gone on to investigate the nature and meaning of religion in public affairs in subsequent years. Their principal formulations have concerned phenomena at the national, rather than the state, level:[4] Mead posited a "Religion of the Republic" with the public schools as the established churches; Howe pointed out the evangelical conception of separating church from government and how that view guided policy even more than did the better-known rationalist conception; McLoughlin discussed the formation of what he called the Protestant Establishment—the unofficial but influential classification of several rather traditional types of religion as being standard for citizens of the United States and the inclusion of the teachings they had in common into education, political rhetoric, and other aspects of public life; Bellah propounded the concept of a civil religion, a body of principles linking piety to national loyalty in a rather deist fashion as enunciated in the Declaration of Independence, but evolving in public utterances of high officials on ceremonial occasions toward a Christian tone during the nineteenth century, when public observances were added to allow active participation by the citizens at large.

While these ideas obviously differ in many ways, they share a premise that most of the people in the United States concurred on certain basic religious principles that had begun to take shape in the revolutionary period and had undergone important modifications after the religious upheaval that occurred around 1800. The predominant set of beliefs fell something short of a consensus because it excluded various strands of Christianity, such as the Catholic, and relegated others to the sidelines.

Bellah's concepts are particularly stimulating, but he has not developed them to throw light on all the events of the revolutionary period. His theory of a civil religion has no direct bearing on the welter of controversies and shifts of policy on the state level from which came much that characterizes the social and legal position of churches in the United States as a whole. An understanding of the revolutionary period must make sense out of what happened in the states.

The plausibility of a national civil religion does suggest, however, that there may be complementary formulations applying to the states. If a civic cult was created at the federal level without an institutional connection to any church, the age-old fusion of civic and salvational elements in Christianity was dissolved. The personal or individual functions of religion became the concern of the states. Yet this distribution of the components of Christianity was not made all at once following the promulgation of the Declaration of Independence. Rather, the states within their own jurisdictions for varying lengths of time tried to readjust both the civic and private elements of religion to the new circumstances.

Looking at events in this light facilitates the understanding of much that took place. Those states attempting to maintain institutional connections with a church—or, as several tried, with an assortment of churches—failed to devise a means to achieve their objective in the face of the great, and increasing, diversity of denominational affiliations among their citizens. If the genius of Jefferson and Washington guided them to foster an initially noninstitutional religious underpinning for federal authority, it was the sad fate of the states to struggle hopelessly in the effort to adapt customary institutional forms for the same purpose. Moreover, state experiments in securing religious backing kept foundering precisely because certain age-old assumptions about the civic value of religion—ones that had given meaning to institutional establishment—had all but died out, leaving the personal or salvational component more heavily stressed than ever in the existing denominations.

Using these propositions, I shall now proceed to an analysis of developments at the state level, after a brief review of what the ideas about the social functions of religion were which immigrated to the English colonies in the seventeenth century and how they were implemented there. Attention will then be given to state action in the revolutionary period and to the climate of thought that influenced public policy.

I

The influence of events in the colonial years on ecclesiastical changes during the revolutionary period needs careful consideration. Overlooking what happened before 1776 leaves mysterious both the vulnerability of church establishments in the late colonial years and the widespread interest in multiple establishment during the revolutionary period. In the seventeenth century, no colony created a system of institutions that gave any church the place it had had in the mother country around 1600. One colony, Virginia, presumably expected to create such a system but deviated from the traditional plan through force of circumstances. Other colonies deliberately refused to establish anything like the European relation between church and state, while still others created a variant on it along Puritan lines. By the early eighteenth century, however, even though several more colonies officially established the Church of England, all were turning away from the traditional connections between secular and ecclesiastical authority. Religious diversity advanced everywhere. In addition, old convictions about the social utility of the church—convictions based on a belief in the corporate or organic nature of the body politic—were giving way to ideas that treated religion as serving the community simply by dint of shaping its citizens' behavior.

The European ideas that the earliest English colonists brought with them were the ideas that these new Americans used in making their communities, whether by accepting them, modifying them, or opposing them. Traditional thought, in one form or another, stressed several points. Political and ecclesiastical loyalties ought to coincide; neither the solidarity of the community nor the safety of the realm could be assured in the presence of religious disagreement. The church should unite a community in a single mode of worship and should inculcate fidelity to all the duties attached to the various individual roles, whether determined by rank, occupation, age, sex, or kinship. The clergy should teach honor to secular authority and dignify government by suitable ceremonies. The church should exercise a discipline by various means to restrain wrongdoing. The state should protect the institution of the church and help preserve its doctrinal purity. The state needed the assistance of the church to achieve secular welfare. Because the body politic existed as a corporate entity in the eyes of God, not only would the aggregate of individual sins and the virtues or wickedness of the rulers affect the collective prosperity by regulating the flow of divine blessings or chastisements, but the presence or absence of uniformity in faith and practice would also influence God's providence. Traditional Christianity, moreover, made the institution of the church in many ways a counterpart of the structure of society and government, an arrangement that provided mutual reinforcement for the two systems.

The clearest case demonstrating the importance of English traditions was Virginia. There the Church of England was brought in at the outset without hesitation or even much thought about how it should operate. The Anglican ecclesiastical system, however, was introduced only incompletely. The parishes became important centers of power, preserving their autonomy rather than submitting to a bishop's authority. The two churchwardens and the other vestrymen, a panel of laymen that ordinarily filled vacancies by cooption, controlled the parish and all its business. After some early difficulties, the vestries halted formal induction of ministers into possession of the parish temporalities and instead hired clergymen on annual salaries, to the persistent annoyance of English prelates.[5]

Lay control was never undercut. After an early plan to appoint a Virginia bishop had collapsed, opinion in the colony hardened against any semblance of episcopal authority in the hands of a local official, no matter what title he might sport. The jurisdiction in Virginia of the Bishop of London was never fully defined, although attempts were made, and he had no more than a customary and informal role in certifying men as ministers or teachers for the colony and in serving as a channel by which their complaints could be taken to imperial officials.[6] He appointed a representative with the title of commissary, beginning in the late seventeenth century; but that official never overcame lay opposition to his exercise of jurisdiction, and he remained only the unofficial captain of the clerical team. He had influence chiefly by virtue of enjoying the ear of officials in England.[7]

Nevertheless, the Virginia Anglicans kept some of the main features of the traditional partnership of church and state. Law and custom gave the parishes a curious assortment of civil duties, less important in sum than the parallel functions of the Church of England at home. Vestries in Virginia saw to the poor and orphans, for instance, and some of the work of caring for roads, but they lacked exclusive power in either of these fields. Nor did the church in the colony acquire any of the jurisdiction of ecclesiastical courts in England. Neither in Virginia nor in any other colony was anything of the sort established. Churchwardens could, and did, present malefactors to secular tribunals for trial and punishment.

The colonial legislature protected and regulated the church, sometimes in effect assuming episcopal powers, and gave it monopolistic privileges as it was politically feasible to do so. Statutes enacted in the early 1660s provided basic laws that remained the foundation of the ecclesiastical system for over a century. The legislature created new parishes as needed. Various measures restrained dissent. Puritans were frozen out of the colony in the seventeenth century, but Quakers, though harassed by the authorities, remained in small numbers. Under pressure from England, Virginia began in the eighteenth century to extend toleration to Dissenters a few steps behind the mother country. By the middle of that century, immigration and the religious revival known as the Great Awakening created substantial religious minorities, claiming between them over half the population by the outbreak of the American Revolution.

Until then, the Anglican Church in several ways approximated its traditional role: the territorial parish went unquestioned; worship united high and low, except for the majority of blacks, while dramatizing and defending gradations in rank; the ministers taught social harmony and the ancient virtues; the gentry staffed the vestries and therein exerted a suitable array of powers over the parishes and carried out a number of civil functions akin to those of ecclesiastical officials in England. Religious ceremonies provided as much beautiful mystery as the parish could afford in order to impress the laity, while the clergy connected up the whole proceedings with support of the throne.

Yet the church served only in minimal ways to uphold secular government within Virginia. There was no cathedral at which governors assumed office; they received no anointment. They enjoyed a suitably honorific seat in the local parish church, but no ecclesiastical hierarchy lifted their authority on its shoulders. The Church of England in Virginia existed as a congeries of parishes operated by boards of laymen. Congregational autonomy could scarcely go further.

Outside Virginia, the Anglican establishments were thinner still and were created after 1690 at great cost in local strife. By the end of the colonial period, solidly established churches existed in and near New York City and in Charleston, South Carolina. The parishes of Maryland, in most respects like Virginia's, enjoyed almost the same support. But in the bulk of the Carolinas and Georgia, the Church of England was weak or even hard to find. Toleration laws had been ample from the start; outside Virginia, Anglicans were always a minority. The Bishop of London had the same undefinable responsibilities; commissaries generally served in each of these other colonies, although local opposition and the ill-conceived policy of a Bishop of London brought an untimely end to the position in South Carolina.[8] Anglican laymen successfully fought any form of ecclesiastical jurisdiction, and in many places local resources were so short as to need supplementary funds from the great missionary organization, the Society for the Propagation of the Gospel in Foreign Parts, better known as the S.P.G.

Where the Church of England was established outside Virginia, it failed to develop most of its traditional social functions. It could not bring together the whole population of a parish, either physically or doctrinally. Dissenters went their own ways, and the Anglicans doggedly resisted inclusion of blacks, especially slaves, in spite of efforts by S.P.G. missionaries to convince owners that sound religion would make their human property more docile and industrious.[9] Doubtless the point can be exaggerated; yet in the eighteenth century, religion was stratifying, social superiors generally embracing the Church of England, while lesser folk frequently resorted to whatever communions they found congenial.

The Puritans who founded Massachusetts and Connecticut implemented their own version of traditional English ways. They did so with surprising success in the seventeenth century, considering their liturgy and church polity. They opposed a clerical hierarchy and formal connections between congregations, so they wanted no pyramid of prelates to help elevate the power of a magistrate. Parish ministers, like their churches, wielded no temporal authority in their ecclesiastical capacities. Worship consisted of prayers, sermons, psalms, and the sacraments of baptism and communion, all conducted in an austere public building. In theory, the churches recognized only two inborn ranks among human beings: the predestined elect and the damned.[10]

Within these constraints, the New Englanders demonstrated extraordinary virtuosity in adapting the traditional ways to fit their institutions. The clergy constantly taught respect for earthly rank and lent support to the secular officials, giving them advice on request in matters of law and policy. Ministers dignified every election and public event with sermons and prayers and promulgated an elaborate political theory to justify the civil authority. The government in turn combated religious dissidence. Although technically it did so only when the civil peace was in jeopardy, by seventeenth-century reckoning virtually any dissent on a serious point was a threat to secular tranquillity.

The corporate conception of the body politic flourished. No people have excelled those of early New England in using collective ceremonies of repentence and thanksgiving as a branch of statecraft. If Plymouth could break a drought, Massachusetts could win a war by timely application of the correct appeal to heavenly power.[11] Associated with collective acts of abasement and rejoicing went a hypothesis, particularly important in Massachusetts, that the people as a whole enjoyed a special relationship with God, a national covenant on terms unavailable to any other nation since the ancient Hebrews.

Puritans in the New World kept the traditional territorial parish, although they allowed communion—the touchstone of church membership—to a dwindling proportion of the population. So the ecclesiastical system simultaneously had to be universal or national and exclusive. Restricting church membership implied consigning the excluded to their own wicked ways, unrestrained by pastoral care. This the Puritan immigrants did in form, though not altogether in substance. Public laws required all to attend services for worship, even if only the members would receive the benefits of communion, discipline, baptism for their children, and (if they were male) rights to vote on ecclesiastical business. The effect of this arrangement was not glaring in Massachusetts so long as the devout were prevalent and all adults could join a church if they understood and accepted the doctrines upheld in the pulpit and had managed to avoid a scandalous course of life. Within a few years, however, the churches generally adopted the policy of accepting only the "converted," those who had undergone a spiritual crisis that left reasonable hope of predestination to heaven. When this change had wrought its effects, the church members became a minority within a parish, giving rise to institutional peculiarities distinctive to the region.[12]

In broad terms, the New England parish was regulated by two overlapping deliberative bodies: the male inhabitants who qualified for the vote in local government and the men who were church members. The larger assemblage, often called the society of the parish, voted on such subjects as levying taxes for support of the church, on the minister's salary, and on other aspects of managing the parish temporalities. The male church members (for these purposes called the church) determined questions about the spiritual affairs of the parish, including selection of a minister. In effect, church and society had to agree on a candidate to fill the pulpit because no man would accept a call without assurance of a salary. By the eighteenth century, the cumbersome ecclesiastical system had become firmly embedded in the regional culture. It is hard to avoid the conclusion that the prolonged disputes it facilitated gave a welcome intensity to life. The imperfect division of responsibilities between church and society, for all the trouble that ensued, seemed to express basic realities, and, in a roundabout way, it did tie the nonmembers to the ecclesiastical structure.

In its odd fashion, the New England parish kept the ancient tradition of unifying the community under the influence of the church. Ostensibly, it separated the putative elect from the rest along a line drawn arbitrarily by divine power and totally unrelated to rank or wealth. Yet all were obliged to attend services and learn the doctrines preached from the pulpit. The inside circle of members often coincided roughly with the roster of the most respected and prosperous people in the community. Communal solidarity and custom reconciled the age-old territorial parish with the corollaries of predestination in a way that neither law nor logic could describe, let alone justify.

In several colonies, no church was established by law. These included most of New York and all of Rhode Island, New Jersey, Pennsylvania, and its appendage that was later named Delaware. In each of them, various persuasions were prominent, although diversity was the norm. The most interesting local configuration was that in Pennsylvania, where Quakers, for all their thoroughgoing opposition to ecclesiastical establishment, regarded themselves as holding a leading position. Even after they ceased to amount to a majority of the population, they continued to include the largest share of rich and prominent citizens, many of whom won election to the colonial legislature in districts where Quaker voters were sparse. The Friends regarded the province as theirs, a place where they would properly hold the principal public offices, where other people would be welcome but would be morally obliged to refrain from obtruding their wishes on the policies set by Quakers. These policies, of course, included an absence of public financial support of any religion, absence of a requirement to take an oath to hold office or give testimony in court, and an absence of compulsory military service and, insofar as possible, any other warlike measures. The fact that the religion of the Friends called for policies that prevented usual kinds of action rather than starting alternatives camouflaged, but did not alter, the Quakers' determination to have the government in harmony with their faith. In sum, they saw themselves as rightfully having some of the traditional privileges of an established church.[13] Their neighbors, of course, grew increasingly bold in disputing this view.

By rejecting a traditional connection between church and state, Rhode Island and the Middle Colonies (except New York in part) chose to do without certain social benefits that the connection had been expected to yield. Sometimes the choice was unwitting: unrealistic hopes for unity in belief, once coercion was removed, beguiled several leaders at the outset. Roger Williams and a few others, however, deliberately set a voluntary faith and church ahead of any conceivable social benefits to be gained by attempts at forced unanimity, and they chose to treat government as a purely secular affair of interests and rational deliberations. Public officials need not be sustained by mystery and clerical unction. Civic ceremonial, such as the engagements used in Rhode Island instead of an oath, would allude only to the promise of the candidate to serve the people in accord with the law.[14] Modest additions, in the form of civic processions or ritual reading of a charter, might lend dignity to government without any taint of priestcraft.

A church, then, had to be regarded as dealing directly with no institution larger than the family and as providing social benefits mainly by improving individual conduct. The religious fellowship could carry on the accustomed business of helping the family, maintaining the roles within it, carrying forward the moral instruction of the young, and shepherding them into marriages within the fold. This conception of the social function of the church, only part of the traditional complex of functions, had begun as one suited to dissident sects struggling to survive in the shadow of a national church; but in America the concept was linked with a strictly secular understanding of the state. The alteration of context made a great difference in the long run, although it probably seemed small at the outset.

Religious fellowships created without ties to secular authority took a variety of forms; but whatever the ecclesiastical polity, it usually needed a way to control property, and for that reason, if for no other, it sometimes sought a form of recognition by the civil government. The traditional mode had been the ascribed corporate status enjoyed by the Church of England, which put ownership of ecclesiastical temporalities into an abstract rather than a personal form. English law and policy favored giving comparable privileges only to Anglicans in the colonies. A grant of incorporation, properly an act of the sovereign, was to carry out purposes endorsed by the crown, such as organizing parishes of the king's church.

The fundamental assumptions appeared with increasing clarity during a succession of controversies in New York. An act of 1693 provided for public support to Anglican churches in and near New York City. The publicly elected vestry prescribed by the law had the initiative in selecting the rector, and Dissenters chosen to that board appeared bent on naming a Dissenter. The governor prevented them by strenuous use of his power and a few years later issued a charter in the name of the king, making the rector and communicants in Manhattan a body politic. A Dutch church had just been incorporated, although of course without access to tax money. Presumably this lesser award of privileges was intended to divert the main element among the Dissenters trying to control the Anglican vestry. (In later years, after several more such incorporations had been allowed to Dutch Reformed congregations, but not to other applicants, the discrimination was justified by the terms of the surrender of the province to the English in the seventeenth century.) When the New York City Presbyterians obtained a minister and built a meeting house, they tried several times after 1719 to obtain a charter of incorporation. Each time they were denied it because of the governor's opposition or pressure from Anglican Trinity Church. In time, British policy hardened in determination that only Anglican congregations should enjoy the benefits of incorporation.[15]

Unable to use the traditional legal device, Dissenters in localities where an established church held sway, like all sects where one did not, had to find a method for putting ownership of property in safe hands. The problem was complicated for those who regarded any legal recognition as a stain on the purity of the church. Quakers used a series of increasingly intricate trust agreements by which a group of Friends as private citizens held title to meeting houses, burial grounds, or property owned to bring in income.[16] Rarely did any inconvenience result. Baptists in Rhode Island blithely put their property in the name of one or several of the brethren, had the deed recorded, and forgot about it.[17] Anglicans, where they lacked special legal standing, could vest property in English units of the church that enjoyed corporate capacities, such as the S.P.G. Such arrangements served as long as ecclesiastical property had little value and voluntary contributions remained reliable for its upkeep—and for Quakers much longer.

If churches without standing in law had limited means of gaining legal safeguards for their property in the ordinary course of events, they could get highly effective aid from the courts when challenges appeared. Deeds of trust and related instruments often included terms that were widely understood, even if they had no reference to an ecclesiastical polity known to law—phrases on doctrinal tenets, or even mere descriptive language to identify an incumbent pastor or the location of a meeting house. Judges took these clauses seriously as evidence of intent in the transactions and thus gave the substance, if not the form, of legal recognition to nonestablished churches. In an extreme case, the civil authority in Rhode Island upheld a somewhat strained interpretation of ambiguous clauses in a will so as to sustain the claims of a Baptist congregation to the income from certain property bequeathed in trust.[18]

For all the reassurance that judicial recognition gave, incorporation remained an attractive way to end uncertainty. Toward the end of the colonial period, a few colonies granted charters to religious bodies of Anglican and other denominations. William Penn's rights in Pennsylvania included that of erecting corporations, and his successors incorporated Lutheran and Calvinist bodies as well as Anglican.[19] Perhaps emboldened by this example, the government of Rhode Island began granting charters of incorporation in 1769, first to an Anglican church, later also to Congregational and Baptist ones.[20]

Developments in colonies without establishments foreshadowed much that happened in places with them. Various immediate causes operated, but underlying them were two basic changes: advancing religious diversity and weakening belief in a collective fate influenced by unity or difference in faith. Perhaps the two were opposite sides of the same coin. Certainly it became hard to insist that unison in worship was needed to win a divine smile on earthly undertakings when variety flourished without bringing chastisement. Nothing could restrain the progress of heterogeneity, especially after the British monarchy began requiring toleration of dissent and after non-English immigration set in heavily.

The importance of heterogeneity to changing thought is further suggested by the record in the old Puritan colonies, where traditional ideas died conspicuously slowly and where undeniable diversity spread less rapidly than elsewhere. Legal concessions to Dissenters, and thereby a sort of recognition, began in Connecticut and Massachusetts during the middle of the colonial period. Under pressure from London usually, the legislatures extended toleration inch by inch, writing laws to prescribe methods by which Anglicans, Baptists, and Quakers could gain exemption from taxes to support the established churches or "Standing Order." All these Dissenters found fault with the statutes; nevertheless, the laws did admit into civil cognizance the basic attributes of three kinds of congregation outside the Standing Order and also prescribed administrative devices to determine their adherents.[21]

To be sure, divisions had existed all along within the New England Standing Order. Disagreement had raged over issues that often seemed momentous to insiders if not to outsiders. The opposing sides could insist that they were united on essentials, however, and by upholding congregational autonomy could avoid formal schisms for many years. The Great Awakening strained the system, publicizing quarrels among the clergy, shattering congregations, and often driving schismatic elements into forming churches outside the Standing Order.

During the eighteenth century, dissent rushed in upon the Anglican establishment in Virginia, the only colony where the Church of England had ever embraced the bulk of the population. Non-English immigrants arrived who kept their faiths; then the Great Awakening stimulated native dissent. Law gradually accommodated heterogeneity. In the middle of the eighteenth century, the colony grudgingly gave Presbyterians the right to have ministers licensed to preach. This concession was grounded partly on interpreting a statute of 1699 to mean that Virginia had adopted the English Act of Toleration. The Anglican clergy tried to fight this infringement on its monopoly but could not counterbalance the pressure brought by Baptists and Quakers on both sides of the Atlantic. Still, even after other setbacks, the position of the established church was not greatly impaired either in law or prestige.[22] Nevertheless, licensing implied that the officials granting licenses had standards to use, whether based on doctrine, polity, or credentials; so the standards indirectly made such attributes of a dissenting body matters of law.

In the other places where the Church of England was established, toleration of dissent was routine. Yet in New York and in the South, eighteenth-century immigration brought Dissenters who were different in new dimensions. The few Jews and Catholics may have posed the most puzzling legal problems on the technical level; yet the great influx of non-English peoples did far more to change the practical meaning of heterogeneity. Scots, Irish, Germans of several kinds, Swiss, and Africans from various lands—all arrived in great numbers, bringing a profusion of faiths. Often the religious affiliation in the New World became an ethnic one as well. The old polarity of Church and dissent among the English lost its simple clarity when colonial governments faced requests for legal rights or privileges from a bewildering assortment of foreigners with unfamiliar ecclesiastical practices. Official response to immigrant religions took no systematic pattern before the end of the colonial period. Rather, governments granted favors to some especially welcome newcomers, such as the French, and ignored others as long as they were content to live in communities of their own.

Well before 1776 the flow of events had rendered irrelevant the seventeenth-century conceptions of a body politic that needed unity in worship to assure its happiness. What remained, barring the increasingly artificial devices of establishment, was something close to a consensus on how government should uphold what nearly all Christians thought was good. Commonly overlooked in the dissection of toleration laws were the statutes giving legal support to Christianity, or to all forms of it with a few exceptions of minor importance. Even Rhode Island had laws against profaning the Sabbath, and it kept them in the face of protests by the citizens who were Seventh Day Baptists and who thought they should keep Saturday sacred and labor on Sunday.[23] All colonies had such laws, as they had laws against blasphemy. Most had laws against Catholicism, and many forms of oaths included doctrinal points at variance with the convictions of assorted varieties of Christians as well as Jews. And, of course, much of the criminal law had been designed to punish what Christians regarded as sin.

II

The Revolution brought dramatic changes in the states where the Church of England had been established, less obvious ones where it had not. The foregoing review of colonial developments, however, points out circumstances that affected what happened after the Declaration of Independence. Seventeenth-century convictions about the organic nature of a society in its relation to God had weakened drastically; as a result, institutional ties between government and churches lost a serious part of their justification. Legal recognition in various fashions had been extended to dissent, blurring the practical distinction between the official church and the others. Several colonies had got along rather well without a partnership with any church, belying age-old wisdom that regarded such a tie as essential.

Events in the eighteenth century were proceeding toward multiple establishment quite as much as toward religious freedom and separation of church and state. In fact, a comprehensionist outcome was achieved in some places during the Revolution. In others, the two policies competed for legislative favor. To some degree, even, the two could be seen as virtually the same. A great part of the reasoning for religious liberty could also support a wide-spectrum multiple establishment, and, so long as few questioned laws to repress sin or to exact doctrinal tests or repudiation of papal authority as qualifications to hold civil office, the distinction between the two policies was easy to belittle. Moreover, while the prevailing opinion continued to regard statutory recognition, especially grants of corporate standing, as badges of official approval properly reserved to an official ecclesiastical organization, extension of legal blessing in this form would be widely understood as adoption into the privileged family of establishment. Yet, sooner or later, multiple establishment fell into disfavor for ideological or practical reasons. The disconnection of church and state had scarcely been achieved, however—not even the disconnection of religion from the state. Rather, connections were made, but they were not entirely the traditional ones.

During the revolutionary period, the Americans who were determining policy for the states and the federal government held similar views on some general points but disagreed on what those views implied for governmental treatment of religion and the churches. Most men concurred on a few fundamentals. There should be no secular power in the hands of the clergy as such, nor any single official church, and above all, none with ties to a foreign power (London or Rome) that might impair political loyalty to the state or to the United States. Further, there should be no involuntary adherence to any persuasion, although there might be strong encouragement. Many, however, wanted public support of churches, the most attractive proposal being to require each taxpayer to choose which one would get his money or, if he rejected all affiliations, to use his tax for a general religious fund or for the poor. In places where the Church of England had been established, the officials commonly advocated eradicating what they regarded as objectionable features of the establishment, although they took different sides on what ones ought to be salvaged or extended. New Englanders, however, ordinarily wanted to preserve the Standing Order with only such changes as expediency and a modicum of liberality required.

In all states, a number of seemingly vital points hardly entered the discussion. Few seriously considered the possibility that laws to enforce a Christian Sabbath or punish profanity smacked of establishment. Fewer still perceived the growth of a concept of standard or respectable Christianity, a concept that merely widened the range of sects on which public policy should smile. This idea can be seen in retrospect in phenomena such as the choice of clergymen from an assortment of denominations to open legislative sessions with invocations or in laws altering forms of oaths or affirmations to accommodate Quakers and others while often repelling Catholics. To explore the incoherent record of actions within the states and the diverse, sometimes discordant, ideas that lay behind them, a few examples will be sufficient.

In South Carolina, the state attempted a sort of multiple establishment and expressed some interesting views in its constitutions. The organic law of 1778 declared that "the Christian Protestant religion shall be deemed, and is hereby constituted and declared to be, the established religion of this State." The document, however, neither prescribed nor proscribed taxation to support churches; it only stated that nobody should "be obliged to pay towards the maintenance and support of a religious worship that he does not freely join in, or has not voluntarily engaged to support." Then it contained a list of doctrines to which all must agree in order to receive the blessing of the civil authorities. The list included belief in one eternal God and in heaven and hell, belief in the duty to perform public worship, belief in Christianity as the one true religion, acknowledgment of divine inspiration of both Testaments, and conviction that the Bible alone gave the rules for the faith and practice of Christians. If they agreed to these tenets, any fifteen adult males might obtain incorporation as a religious society, regardless of what other points they might deem essential or what liturgy they might prefer. The constitution, however, required that incorporated religious societies (except those of the Church of England already in existence) should choose their ministers by majority vote and that clergymen must subscribe to a long declaration, closely derived from the Anglican *Book of Common Prayer,* on doctrines and pastoral duties.[24]

This plan was no establishment by some standards, although it contained traditional features and in some respects favored the Anglicans. It laid down several points in doctrine, but none in liturgy. At the same time, however, it prescribed one crucial feature of ecclesiastical polity: choice of ministers by majority vote of the men who formed the legally recognized religious society. This provision had an element of kinship with revolutionary political principles, but it ran against the practices of several denominations. Moreover, the notion of allowing taxation to support the churches, although nobody should be compelled to pay involuntarily, belied both the idea of taxation and the traditions of establishment. In statutory implementation, the scheme could scarcely avoid offending the principles of some otherwise acceptable denominations. Under analysis, the South Carolina plan seems hopelessly impractical, which is easy to say since it was abandoned in 1790. It was then that a new constitution forbade all "discrimination or preference" in treating religions, although it guaranteed the rights of those societies incorporated under the earlier one.[25] Thereafter, Catholics and Jews ceased to be Dissenters, the churches could choose their ministers as they saw fit, and the legislature faced the task of determining what religious bodies should receive legal recognition in the future.

Virginia, too, flirted with multiple establishment after the Declaration of Independence. Although the dalliance came to naught, it was an important part of the complicated search for a durable policy. The first state constitution contained a "Bill of Rights" that guaranteed to the citizens the "free exercise of religion," yet for several years this statement was regarded as an announcement without legal force. The legislature continued to treat the Anglican churches as remaining established.[26] Dissenters naturally objected and kept state policy on ecclesiastical affairs a lively topic for nearly two decades. Deliberation in the autumn of 1776 revolved around several points. One of them, a proposal for a "general assessment," a tax on all ratable citizens for support of the churches in the state, was deferred then; and while it was subsequently reconsidered in various forms, it was clearly a lost cause by 1785.

At the outset of the Revolution, Virginia began reducing legal support of the Anglican Church. The legislature repealed colonial statutes requiring attendance at Anglican services and punishing the expression of dissenting views. Further, it excused Dissenters from taxation for support of the Anglican parishes and suspended the law requiring Anglicans to pay such taxes. After the suspension had been extended several times, it was made permanent in 1779.[27] The next year the legislature enacted a law purporting to give all ministers the authority to join couples in marriage, but the statute clearly stipulated that no more than four clergymen of a dissenting denomination might have this authority in any one county, that they should be selected by the county court, and that their authority (unlike that of Anglican ministers) was to be valid only inside the county.[28]

Substantial though these changes were, they did not level the special position of the Anglican parishes. The endowments and other property, to some extent acquired with tax money, remained in the control of the vestry. The parish continued to have obligations to care for the poor and could tax all the residents for that purpose. The social, and hence political, preeminence of the old church was also hardly reduced. Dissenters organized to advance their opinions. Finally, in 1784, they won laws ending invidious distinctions among clergymen in the authority to solemnize marriages and transferring the duty to aid the poor from the vestries to secular overseers.[29] For any further gratification, the Dissenters had to wait longer.

For the time being, deliberation on state policy turned to revising the position of the Anglican Church, known by then as the Episcopal Church, although it still had no bishop. The clergy wanted several measures. The first of these was an act of incorporation to assure continued ownership of parish property by granting each parish corporate status and prescribing methods for the election of vestrymen. Next was the repeal of old statutes requiring clergymen to have ordination by an English bishop and to "subscribe to orders of the Church of England." And finally, there was a proposal to give the clergy unprecedented influence in the church by authorizing them to sit as a convention to make canons and bylaws for the whole state and to act as an ecclesiastical court with sole power to pass sentences removing ministers from office.[30]

The clergy, in 1784, obtained much of what it sought. Detachment from the Church of England was hardly controversial. Dissenters objected to the incorporation bill as an alliance between the state and the Episcopal Church and were not mollified by the inclusion of clauses allowing other churches to have incorporation upon request to the legislature. Laymen in the Episcopal fold saw to the alteration of the provisions on the clerical convention, amending them to require inclusion of one lay delegate from each parish.[31]

The new legislation did not last long. The incorporation act was repealed after three years, returning some of the basic problems of policy to their previous unsettled condition. After a ruling by the state Court of Appeals in 1793 that the Virginia "Bill of Rights" was part of the constitution and that all statutes contrary to it were void, the legislature confirmed this stand by formally repealing all the questionable laws and declaring that the civil power had no authority to prescribe "any species of ecclesiastical or church government in lieu of [the formerly established Church of England]." Thereafter, in 1802, the state began to take the final steps to reduce the Episcopalian parishes to a par with the other churches. Under an act of that year, the glebe lands, being regarded as endowments granted by the public partly for the support of the poor and partly for the support of Anglican worship, were to be sold and the proceeds devoted to the poor or for other secular purposes as soon as an incumbent minister ceased to officiate in any parish. The process of divesting the parishes of their glebes, what with litigation and the longevity of some rectors, took until 1840.[32]

Well before that date—in fact, at the time when the proposal to incorporate the Episcopal Church was under consideration—the strongest attempt had been made to create a system to support religion by a general assessment. Various plans had been proposed, each resembling the South Carolina method. In one way or another, the Virginia proposals called for the following features: Christianity should be declared the established religion; a few rudiments of doctrine should be prescribed; everyone should pay a religious tax, although some versions stipulated that those unwilling to choose a church to support could have their tax money spent on some secular purpose, such as relief of the poor, that formerly had been in the province of the Church. The last form of the plan was narrowly defeated in 1785 after the Presbyterians ceased wavering and joined the Baptists and other denominations in opposition. The Baptists saw clearly that conceding legislative power to enact a general assessment plan implied conceding power to determine which denominations would qualify for support, and this concession in turn would imply two more: that the secular authority could prescribe church polity to the denominations or that it could define as acceptable the form used by one denomination only, thus making a single established church by manipulating a law ostensibly passed to support many.[33] As in the case of South Carolina, it is easy to see that the proposals in Virginia were rather impractical. If Baptist objections reflected undue fear, they also pointed to some fundamental flaws.

In the aftermath of defeat for general assessment, Dissenters joined the churchmen who had wanted separation of church and state all along and won the legislature's support for a "Bill for Establishing Religious Freedom." This measure called for totally voluntary adherence to organized religious bodies, freedom to hold and express any religious opinion whatever, safety against penalties for embracing minority views, and removal of religious tests for the exercise of civil office. Passed on the heels of the incorporation act, the new law had surprisingly little effect; what effect it had was more to strengthen toleration than to create freedom. Probably it served mainly to allay Dissenters' fears that the law favoring the Episcopal Church was potentially a step back to the colonial establishment.

Ironically, even this celebrated statute of 1786 had theological premises. The preamble, beginning with "Almighty God hath created the mind free," sketched a statement of belief about the fallibility of human understanding and the significance of religion to secular life. The legislature deleted a phrase that Jefferson had written in the bill, saying that God planned religion "to extend . . . its influence on reason alone," and thus refrained from a full commitment to rationalism.[34] If Dissenters and a sufficient number of Episcopalians were willing to take the formulations in the preamble, either they did so to gain passage for the rest of the bill or because they found the premises to their judgment. Whatever the case, the rationalist tone and implications won their resentment in the nineteenth century. By then the erstwhile Dissenters no longer needed the alliance with rationalists in the Episcopal fold.[35]

Multiple establishment, in the eyes of some who enjoyed its favor, was practiced in the New England states other than Rhode Island.[36] Connecticut did not write a new constitution during the revolutionary period; it kept the charter of 1662 as its organic law and made minor alterations to cover the severance of ties with royal authority. No great changes were needed in ecclesiastical law for several years.

Massachusetts, however, wrangled over the basic connection between church and state until it accepted the constitution of 1780 and then wrangled over implementing the clauses in that document. In the Declaration of Rights preceding the constitution, Article III laid down the principles on which the state tried to act for some time. This article authorized the legislature to require towns or other jurisdictions functioning as parishes to choose Protestant ministers and raise taxes to support public worship. It also authorized laws to require attendance at services. In both points, the article delicately indicated the latitude that would be permissible. Religious taxes would be universal, but any Dissenter from the Standing Order might have his money ''applied to the support of the public teacher or teachers of his own religious sect or denomination, provided there be any on whose instructions he attends.'' Likewise, church-attendance laws must allow Dissenters liberty to attend services of their choosing or to stay home if there was none on which they could ''conscientiously and conveniently attend.''[37]

These constitutional provisions required little change in colonial law and less in ordinary behavior. Religious taxes and church attendance had been evaded in various ways, sometimes through the lassitude of the officials. The new constitution protected individual rights to attend any worship desired, or none at all. Further, it made eligible for tax support any minister, not just those of the Standing Order and the three recognized dissenting denominations—or at least it seemed to. Advocates of the new constitution thought these changes were all that reasonable people could desire. The Massachusetts plan appeared so sensible that it was used with a few modifications, such as elimination of the equivocal provisions on church attendance in the New Hampshire constitution of 1784. Vermont, in its constitution, endorsed complete religious liberty but set no barrier against statutes prescribing public support of town ministers by those without conscientious scruples about paying.[38]

Attractive and practical as the Massachusetts plan seemed, it gave rise to countless difficulties. Several sources of trouble may be seen, including opposition to what appeared to be state policy, uncertainty among the officials as to what the laws truly meant or should mean, persistent determination to protect the Standing Order, and the legacy of institutional adjustments in the late colonial period. For many years before the Revolution, the parishes or precincts had been treated as incorporated, perhaps by analogy to the parishes of the established church in England or by derivation from towns in the colony, with which parishes had at first been coterminous. The first of these possibilities was in discord with English policy; the second had little foundation in law, especially after towns were divided into multiple parishes. During the eighteenth century, the legal nature of the precinct was treated with studied vagueness, both to avoid antagonizing royal officials and to avoid entangling civil authority in disputes among the devout over theology and worship. As a result, the provincial legislature chose to make the parishes virtually autonomous, even from its own control. It could do nothing when the Dissenters, who formed the majority in a few towns, chose Baptists or Quakers as parish ministers. It refused to intervene even when towns asked adjudication of their quarrels, whether over choice of a minister or location of a meeting house. Secular power thus almost foreswore the old obligation to define and protect orthodoxy against challenges.[39]

Controversies in parishes, together with increasing heterogeneity in the province, eventually inspired expedients that in some measure clarified the legal position of the Standing Order, though mainly to safeguard ecclesiastical temporalities. To solve quarrels in some places, the legislature made bands of dissidents into "poll parishes," entities having the same powers as territorial parishes, although composed of people living in several such units. In 1755, to clarify ownership in perpetual succession of property donated for pious ends, the legislature enacted a statute incorporating the deacons in each parish and the churchwardens in each Anglican vestry so that they might hold such property *ex officio* and defend it in court. The same law authorized churches to tax owners of pews and to sell these facilities if the tax was not paid. Shortly thereafter, various groups within Standing Order churches, ones facing an actual or imminent dissenting majority within their parishes, began seeking incorporation of trustees or other such officers to hold temporalities. So far, incorporation was to protect property for Standing Order churches.[40]

With this background in practice, Massachusetts after the Revolution continued to regard incorporation as a device to aid the state-favored religious order. The state gave such privileges to trustees for certain churches and then to whole societies. In effect, the corporate nature of the old-fashioned parish was being detached from its territorial base.[41]

Public policy, however, had not been clarified. Controversy arose over the implications of the new state constitution. The Supreme Judicial Court in 1785 ruled that tax money could not be levied for religious societies unknown to the law, so the apparent meaning of Article III of the Declaration of Rights was a delusion. Only incorporated societies could receive funds raised on public authority, and only Standing Order precincts could be considered to have corporate status, regardless of the implied recognition of dissenting congregations in the constitution and several statutes. As most Standing Order parishes had no explicit grant of corporate standing, the legislature went to their rescue in 1786 by reenacting the law of 1755 and declaring that "the inhabitants of each respective parish and precinct" constituted "a body corporate" with ample power. The high court did not adhere consistently to its own position but wavered between it and more liberal views until 1811, when the legislature decided that religious taxes might be devoted to churches without corporate standing and that unincorporated societies might choose trustees who would have power to hold and improve donations for the benefit of the religious body.[42]

While uncertainty prevailed, dissenting groups began asking for charters. After 1789, the legislature generally granted them whenever requested. Some Baptists, however, refused to ask, regarding a charter of incorporation as a link to civil authority that would pollute the church. To the Standing Order, tax support remained the crucial point, and the legislature ordinarily tried to sustain it. The effort to preserve the remains of the old establishment did not fail until the Unitarians in eastern Massachusetts gained majorities in so many parishes that the Trinitarians decided to join the Dissenters in seeking a legal separation of church and state by which the churches would forego tax resources.[43] This coalition won its victory in 1833. Multiple establishment had finally lost its last base.

Only two or three of the states where churches formerly had been established failed to give serious consideration to a comprehensionist plan. These were New York, Georgia, and perhaps North Carolina. Their first constitutions set a policy of religious freedom. A general assessment plan, though not enacted, was authorized by the Maryland constitution of 1776 and ardently advocated during the late eighteenth century.[44]

It did not follow, however, that these states and those that had never established a church disavowed all connection with religion. In various ways they imposed religious tests for voting or holding office, frequently against Catholics or non-Christians or atheists, less often against Christians who rejected the doctrine of the Trinity or the divine inspiration of the two Testaments.

Policies of religious freedom, toleration of dissent, or multiple establishment did not in themselves determine how ecclesiastical property might be held or what meaning should be attached to such methods as were allowed by law. The ultimate solution, statutes permitting any denomination to seek incorporation on terms it found good, was still controversial.

New York proceeded as quickly as any to what became the general plan. When revolutionaries there wrote a state constitution in 1777, they refused special standing to any denomination. This they did by a direct assertion and also by abrogating the force of all statutes of the province or of England and any element in common law that could sustain a preference for one communion.[45]

These decisions were implemented only after the British occupation of New York City had ended in 1783. Then the state not only abolished the special privileges of the Church of England, particularly the tax powers of a few Anglican vestries, but also tried to create a new basic relation between religious bodies and civil authority. The legislature adopted a measure "to enable all the religious denominations in this State to appoint trustees, who shall be a body corporate, for the purpose of taking care of the temporalities of their respective congregations." After the fashion of South Carolina's attempt to impose a single mode of choosing ministers, New York stipulated that the men in each congregation or religious society had to elect the trustees. This arrangement suited some, but it offended both the Dutch Reformed and the erstwhile Anglicans. They agitated for legal provisions that would suit their ecclesiastical polities and won them within a few years.[46] No religious organization, to be sure, was required to appoint trustees who would qualify as a body corporate and take ownership of ecclesiastical property. In New York and the other states after the Revolution, religious bodies could and did continue to make whatever arrangements they saw fit to vest title to property in the hands of clergymen or members of their flocks. So Jews and Catholics, for example, were able to conduct their ecclesiastical affairs without recourse to the provisions of any statute.

On one plane, the revolutionary disestablishment in New York accomplished very little. It ended the superiority of a few Anglican churches, expressed legally in their tax powers; it made poor relief a secular responsibility in those parishes; and it extended on uniform terms the possibility for any ecclesiastical body in the state to enjoy legal security and perpetual succession in ownership of property it held. This last in intent, if not in form, was similar to privileges given to several Dutch Reformed congregations in the colonial period.

On another plane, to be sure, the change was greater. The preeminence of the Anglicans had been symbolic to an important extent and fell with the repudiation of the king. The decision to enact a general statute enabling any religious body to avail itself of a standard form of legal standing, while it provoked objections in two denominations, expressed a rather new conception of the relations between church and state. In the past, statutes (as distinct from creeping recognition through the judiciary) had treated one claimant for favor at a time, bringing each individually and on its own initiative and political backing into the sunshine of explicit legal definition—that is to say, recognition, or in the estimation of the time, approval. The general statute of

1784 required no showing of merit for enjoyment of recognition. The question of merit was relegated to polar opposites of reckoning: the statute implicitly argued that all denominations had a value the state should sanction and aid; at the same time, the state had so little concern with what they were, or what polity or tenets or liturgy they endorsed, that it would extend its blessing on no condition other than willingness to abide by certain legal formalities and to choose trustees by the prescribed method.

Some other states followed approximately the same course. Rhode Island, which had already begun granting incorporation to any religious society that sought it, continued to do so after the Revolution but for some time wrote no general incorporation law. Through charters, this state went surprisingly far in giving legal force to the ecclesiastical polity and to the internal decisions of those groups that obtained incorporation.[47] North Carolina, in 1796, passed "An Act to secure property to religious societies or congregations of every denomination."[48] In 1789, Georgia began incorporating churches with charters for a Baptist and an Episcopalian church.[49]

Conspicuously, these states and New York were all places where religious freedom had been adopted early as a basic policy or where the Church of England had been thinly established. Moreover, in a general way they often adapted the institutional peculiarities of the New England Standing Order when extending legal recognition to churches: ordinarily, the legislature refrained from conferring legal standing on a church as such—it was left an autonomous spiritual institution—and instead conferred legal standing on a related institution set up to manage temporalities, which in Massachusetts was usually called the precinct or society. A state, by granting powers to a board of trustees or to a religious society under that designation, could deal almost exclusively (or at least, primarily) with the secular affairs of a church and avoid taking cognizance of, let alone endorsing, its doctrines, discipline, or internal constitution. The trustees or the society thus became a convenient placental institution between a religious fellowship and the civil state.

This cursory review of events in the states leads to several observations. Curiously, the federal government had scarcely affected what happened. Further, there was no landslide movement in the states toward thoroughgoing religious freedom. Although each state followed its own path, all continued, or even expanded, uncontroversial measures such as Sabbath laws, criminal statutes against sin, or religious qualifications for voting or holding office. Where public policy aroused controversy, it centered on the connection of the state with the church and was little concerned with religion. Liberty for the citizens to believe as they would was hardly an issue.

III

Following the twists and turns of state action in great detail will not lead to an understanding of the outcome unless the thinking of the revolutionary period is taken into account. Traditional interpretations offer little except backwardness or greed to explain opposition to religious freedom. If the end of the story is not defined as the inevitable victory of virtue, the ideas of the actors obviously gain importance, and they were ideas having many shared assumptions and varying within a fairly well-defined range of possibilities. In broad terms, everyone endorsed the importance of religion to society, especially if the government was to take a republican form, but the benefits were to arrive by the route of individual deportment rather than as a result of divine delight over unity in worship.

The founders of the federal government, how deliberately no one knows, avoided from the start all the current snarls in relations between church and state. Instead of seeking an articulation of institutions, they promulgated a simple noninstitutional faith. As Robert Bellah pointed out, the "civil religion" was at first deist in tone and overt principles, although the content nevertheless was derived in a serious way from the Puritan concept of the national covenant and carried an implicit call for a kind of conversion. Eventually, the evangelical inner message reached the surface and tinctured the public language with a distinctly Christian hue. The civil religion, launched by Jefferson's words in the Declaration of Independence and carried forward most obviously in the ceremonial pronouncements of presidents, imparted a religious quality and fervor to patriotism.[50] In this far-sighted way the federal government achieved the traditional goal of summoning the aid of a general faith while avoiding an entangling alliance with a church.

By comparison with the states, legal arrangements at the federal level were of minor importance, although they have been analyzed to extract portentous conclusions. The Articles of Confederation were almost silent on religion. One passage in Article III bound the states to join in common defense whenever any was attacked "on account of religion, sovereignty, trade, or any other pretence whatever." The ratificational paragraph at the end credited "the Great Governor of the World" with inclining "the hearts of the [state] legislatures" to authorize the delegates to Congress to ratify the document. The Articles, however, scrupulously avoided allusions to oaths.[51] The United States Constitution of 1787 contained only the clause requiring that officers of the states and the United States "shall be bound by oath or affirmation, to support this Constitution; but no religious test shall ever be required as a qualification to any office or public trust under the United States."[52]

Viewed from a later age, this formulation appears internally contradictory. What is an oath but a religious test? What is an affirmation but a variant on an oath? To make sense of this clause, it is necessary to read it in the light of prevailing ideas when it was written, when a religious test meant avowing adherence to a doctrine or creed upheld by a known religious organization and rejected by others. So the Constitution was written to forbid confining public office in the federal government to those belonging to some preferred denomination. In this sense, the document ruled out a partnership between the government and one church or a cluster of favored churches. If this was policy, it was also political expediency.

Likewise, the First Amendment to the Constitution had a meaning specific to the time of its ratification. By this addition, the Constitution contained the statement, "Congress shall make no law respecting an establishment of religion, or prohibiting the free exercise thereof."[53] Plainly these words forbade legislation by the United States establishing a church or tampering with state laws that established one. While this provision has been taken as determining a national policy, which to some extent it may have done, its primary function was to guard the states against federal interference. Once again, political expediency as well as ideals may be discerned in the wings. No state or region wanted its local ways overthrown by congressional statutes. The price of autonomy for the states was a fairly strong flavor of the secular in the national government, which pleased those who favored rationalism in religion or rejection of all establishments.[54] The First Amendment also served to keep the federal government away from linkage with the churches. Serenely, Washington could write, "It is now no more that toleration is spoken of, as if it was by the indulgence of one class of people, that another enjoyed the exercise of their inherent natural rights."[55] He addressed citizens of Rhode Island to assure them that the federal government had no intention of dabbling in plans for an establishment.

By refusing to attempt a connection with ecclesiastical organizations, the federal government perhaps unwittingly took to itself a manageable form of civil religion, one of Christianity's components since the time of Constantine, and left the states to do as they saw fit. Many of them tried to preserve a means of gaining support from the customary institutional alliance with a church but found it vexatiously difficult to do so. Others looked to a multiplicity of churches. The intentions may have been traditional, but the circumstances and the thinking about the alliance were not. The social benefits of the churches were expected to come from the cultivation of individual virtue. Thus, the common understanding of the case directed state concern to what was much less the civic component of historic Christianity than its other, the personal or salvational. Broad though the consensus may have been on how religion worked for secular happiness, controversy raged both on how to implement what all believed and on a few disputed points. A few examples will illustrate the range of thought.

Conspicuously, the most prominent views on the social importance of religion claimed that piety was useful to the general welfare by its control of individual conduct; much less importance was given to collective action or morality, let alone liturgy, in determining the tenor of divine providence toward a nation. The Massachusetts constitution, which provided for a species of establishment, justified the provision by asserting that "the happiness of a people, and the good order and preservation of civil government, essentially depend upon piety, religion and morality" and that "these cannot be generally diffused through a community, but by the institution of the public worship of GOD, and of public instructions in piety, religion and morality." The same document also contained the declaration:

> It is the right as well as the duty of all men in society, publicly, and at stated seasons, to worship the SUPREME BEING, the great creator and preserver of the universe. And no subject shall be hurt, molested, or restrained, in his person, liberty, or estate, for worshipping GOD in the manner and season most agreeable to the dictates of his own conscience; or for his religious profession or sentiments; provided he doth not disturb the public peace, or obstruct others in their religious worship.[56]

An influential commentary on an earlier Massachusetts constitution, which was rejected, had clarified the prevailing view on conscience. The "Essex Result" of 1778 analyzed the natural rights of mankind and classified the "rights of conscience" as unalienable. "We have duties, for the discharge of which we are accountable to our Creator and benefactor, which no human power can cancel. What those duties are, is determinable by right reason, which may be, and is called, a well-informed conscience. What this conscience dictates as our duty, is so; and that power which assumes a controul over it, is an usurper; for no consent can be pleaded to justify the controul, as any consent in this case is void."[57] The author of the "Essex Result" was Theophilus Parsons, who later as a judge forcefully upheld the laws underpinning the Standing Order.

The dominant concepts in Massachusetts combined two elements that were roughly compatible with one that seems discordant. The obligations of conscience were absolute, and the state could only forbid any exercise of them that might hurt other people. This view could harmonize with the belief that churchgoing promoted attitudes and conduct beneficial, or even essential, to the welfare of the secular community. Yet the state proposed to authorize compulsory taxation for the support of religion and nearly compulsory attendance at divine worship. Presumably the professed atheist was not to be deemed credible, for all men were considered under conscientious obligation to worship God. So the rights of conscience were simultaneously unalienable and in a limited way subject to the determination of the state's body politic as a whole when it approved a constitution declaring what must be true of any well-informed conscience. To make sense of this discord, it is necessary to assume that the existence of God was considered proven past dispute, and, more important, that the social well-being varied according to the average level of virtue and morality prevailing among the citizens. Obviously, there was only the faintest echo of the seventeenth-century conviction that the body politic as a whole must be united in doctrine and liturgy.

In Virginia, approximately the same ideas were expressed in surprising quarters even before the Revolution. The general premises in a public controversy concerning the established church, beginning in 1771, had been derived from William Warburton, Bishop of Gloucester, who had written in England earlier in the century. A latitudinarian and Whig, Warburton had boiled down the state's legitimate demands in religion to three essentials: belief in God, divine providence over human affairs, and the absolute distinction between good and evil. The state needed assurance of belief in these points in order to give credence to an oath. Otherwise, the state, being founded on a civil compact for secular ends, could be indifferent to doctrine. Yet religion had a wider social utility in fostering behavior conducive to secular happiness and also had its source in divine will outside, and prior to, any civil society. Therefore, conscience and organized churches had to be utterly free from legal restraint.

The Anglican clergymen who promulgated these views in Virginia, on one occasion in a sermon to the House of Burgesses, provoked a devout layman to argue for a more positive purpose to link church and state. That gentleman, Robert Carter Nicholas, had no intellectually powerful arguments for his position; he favored a "friendly and amiable Alliance between Church and State, which the best and ablest Divines have thought essential to the Prosperity of both," and he thought that an Anglican minister should strive to demonstrate the "superiour Advantages of our Establishment, and the various and striking Beauties of our Liturgy," in order to encourage the faithful and win converts.[58]

If these were the terms on which establishment was discussed by dedicated Anglicans just before the Revolution, the thoughts of Thomas Jefferson expressed a short time later were less completely radical than has often been assumed. In a famous passage in his *Notes on the State of Virginia,* Jefferson argued:

The error seems not sufficiently eradicated, that the operations of the mind, as well as the acts of the body, are subject to the coercion of the laws. But our rulers can have authority over such natural rights only as we have submitted to them. The rights of conscience we never submitted, we could not submit. We are answerable for them to our God. The legitimate powers of government extend to such acts only as are injurious to others.

So far the reasoning would have won the applause of Theophilus Parsons and other friends of the New England Standing Order. Jefferson deviated from their views when he continued:

But it does me no injury for my neighbor to say there are twenty gods, or no god. It neither picks my pocket nor breaks my leg. If it be said, his testimony in a court of justice cannot be relied on, reject it then, and be the stigma on him. Constraint may make him worse by making him a hypocrite, but it will never make him a truer man . . . . Reason and free inquiry are the only effectual agents against error. Give a loose to them, they will support the true religion, by bringing every false one to their tribunal, to the test of their investigation. They are the natural enemies of error, and of error only.[59]

His deviation lay in the argument that belief in twenty gods or none was a matter of no concern to the state and that reason (not reason plus revelation) gave the human being an understanding of true religion.

Jefferson also departed from many state lawmakers in his indifference to a belief in divine providence, future rewards in heaven and hell, and the duty of public worship. Yet he obviously believed in one God, as did advocates of the establishment, and only by implication outdid them in an inclination to dismiss the importance of liturgy. Conspicuously—and it was probably the most inflammatory of his views—he set no great store on the social benefits of mere churchgoing.

The Pennsylvania constitution of 1776, one ordinarily held up as an example of establishing (or, in this case, continuing) religious liberty, barely approached Jefferson's position. The document asserted "That all men have a natural and unalienable right to worship Almighty God according to the dictates of their own consciences and understanding." It then went on to promise that "Laws for the enforcement of virtue, and prevention of vice and immorality shall be made and constantly kept in force." It further declared that all existing religious or educational societies should continue to enjoy the property and privileges they had previously held. It made belief in God a prerequisite to exercising the rights of citizenship and stipulated that those who took public office must also believe that both Testaments were written by divine inspiration and that God created and governed the universe, rewarded the good, and punished the wicked. This formulation was liberal for the time in that it posed no obstacle to civil rights for Catholics, even if it did for atheists, Universalists, and all non-Christians. The barrier against non-Christians was removed in 1790, but otherwise little was changed for many years.[60]

Numerous other examples might be offered to illustrate American thinking on the social value of personal religion during the revolutionary period, yet these few should indicate clearly enough the spectrum of disagreement. The few radicals argued that reason, unaided by revelation, would ascertain the truth of a few basic points, notably the rudiments of virtuous conduct and the truth of one God being the creator of the universe. Discovery of these fundamentals was within the intellectual reach of anyone and would make the discoverers good citizens, which was a desirable result in itself and all that civil authority could rationally ask. Many more people believed that fear of hell and acknowledgment of divine revelation were needed to produce good conduct and that regular attendance at worship was the only reliable way to increase the likelihood of virtuous behavior. From that point opinion split on the value, or indeed the legitimacy, of civil authority shepherding the citizens to church and charging them for the benefit they received. But even those who wanted churchgoing positively encouraged—nobody spoke in favor of coercion—proposed no more than an official church to which all should go unless attached to some other or, failing this plan, taxation to support an assortment of Protestant denominations. All in all, the range of disagreement was narrow, and widely held ideas were used about as often to support connections between church and state as to oppose them. Everyone advocated leeway for the dictates of conscience; the only question was whether there was some limit to what conscience might honestly dictate.

Throughout the discussion of the significance of personal religion in the revolutionary period ran the assumption that, in deliberating on government's relations to it, only secular considerations should be determinative. The relation was not viewed as a question of what religious thought required of government. Nobody proposed that constitutions and laws should be written to embody divine principles, regardless of what human reason might deem preferable, or that the conduct of public business should be done with an eye to preventing God's wrath or responding to his warnings resulting from failings in collective behavior. Above all, nobody considered the arrangement of powers within a government or the ratification of a constitution to have an affinity with a single faith or ecclesiastical polity, as James I had linked monarchy to episcopacy. At most, as shown in the South Carolina constitution of 1778, a state might prescribe a choice of pastors by the votes of their flocks, which was giving the rules of secular to ecclesiastical government, rather than the other way around, and define an establishment beyond that only by a few doctrinal points intended to gain the approval of the respectable forms of Protestant Christianity. This was as close an approach as one can find to articulating a concept of McLoughlin's Protestant Establishment, which took form unofficially on the national scale in the nineteenth century. As overt legal policy regulating ecclesiastical institutions, it could be attempted only at the state level, where it proved unworkable.

In the states, the vague and general connections between law and Christianity remained uncontroversial and in a sense persisted as the basis for future policy. Agreement prevailed that criminal law was to enforce Christian definitions of virtue and that the teachings of the churches would curb crime while also fostering virtues highly valuable to civil society, such as neighborliness, elevated standards of justice, and a disposition to set public ahead of private interests. Therefore, there was no necessary conflict between law and religion except on minor points where Christians differed, such as what was essential to observance of the Sabbath. Nobody proposed that unity in faith and liturgy was needed for the welfare of the state. At most, a state might require individuals to express their acceptance of a few basic beliefs in order to vote or hold office. These simple religious tests were not considered religious tests at all. Even Quakers, whose experience with civil disabilities resulting from their refusal to take public oaths had left them with a raw nerve on this subject, sought (and won) only permission to substitute an affirmation. The climate of opinion in the late eighteenth century thus framed a choice among public policies that seemed vitally different, yet rested on the same general convictions about human life.

Differences there were. A few would discard revelation, traditionally paired with reason as the means for discovering true religion. Rationalism, however, proposed no great departure from the Christian code of behavior; Jefferson would merely cast away supernatural justifications. People who rejected rationalism nevertheless argued over the importance of churchgoing, debating its utility to civil government. Even Massachusetts, which proposed to tax everybody to support public worship, offered citizens the liberty of staying away. To a considerable extent, the controversy over public policy in the states dwelt on expediency, on how to secure the widest possible influence of sound religion on the citizens. Some thought voluntarism would work better than coercion; when it did, they exulted in their triumph and attributed their choice to divine preference. If religious liberty was God's will, separation of church and state was a concept deprived of its ancient pugnacity, and the concept of one true church lost its force. Distinctions between denominations had more to do with personal taste than with access to heaven.[61]

The prevailing views of the revolutionary period also for the time being relegated to minor consideration traditional expectations that religion would bind high and low together in worship while defending the differences in rank. Most seriously, the social distinctions based on color and servitude were left with greatly impaired ecclesiastical support. Some churches might justify slavery, for instance, and might also expect owners to take their slaves to divine services or provide occasions to teach them the rudiments of Christianity; but other churches left black people to develop their own institutions, and still others denounced slavery as incompatible with the Gospel. American religion spoke with no single voice on slavery but on the whole tended to encourage black people to devise their own forms of Christian devotion. Among white people, the likelihood of denominational choices conforming to social position increased rapidly. Divisiveness and certain kinds of social irresponsibility seemed to be the results of voluntary religion, and the widely held opinions about the social benefits of Christianity found nothing drastically wrong with these effects.

Concealed within the general opinions of the revolutionary period, however, were tendencies toward what William McLoughlin labeled the Protestant Establishment, an unofficial comprehensionist establishment of traditional Trinitarian and usually evangelical churches. Based first on the widely shared estimation of the social utility of religion and the virtual unanimity on the meaning of virtue and justice, second on the belief in unfettered obedience to conscience or reason in the choice of denomination, endorsement became possible of a broad range of Protestant communions as equally serviceable to the nation. It was an easy step from saying that a citizen could choose any denomination to saying that everybody ought to embrace one. The predominant Protestant views, if somewhat watered down, came to be regarded as the functional equivalent of a national faith binding together the citizens reasonably well, for all their diversity in other respects. The national "civil religion" came implicitly rather than avowedly to rely for its underpinnings on this national Protestant near-consensus during the nineteenth century, although the common faith operated in the realm of personal religion.[62]

The creation of this generalized Protestantism as a national faith was the outcome of the deliberations and experiments in institutional arrangements during the revolutionary period. As the process moved toward completion, it facilitated a revision in thinking about the legal standing of churches. Incorporation for all that wanted it, whether in charters granted by a legislature upon petition or bureaucratized under the terms of a general statute, eventually lost its connotations of conferring endorsement. The usual view has been that routine incorporation allowed the state to give churches security in their property without implying approval of, or imposing rules upon, their internal polity or teachings. Equally, however, routine incorporation at first left undisturbed the older assumption that a charter was a manifestation of public favor. Under the reasoning that expected a social benefit from churchgoing, regardless of the church attended, and even more under the informal partnership between generalized Protestantism and the nation, the government began to confer corporate standing on all churches, since most of them, at least, merited it; and the rest had to be given it anyway because the informal establishment was considered by its beneficiaries to be legal freedom of religion.

NOTES

1 S. E. Mead, *The Lively Experiment: The Shaping of Christianity in America* (New York, 1963); W. G. McLoughlin, "The Role of Religion in the Revolution; Liberty of Conscience and Cultural Cohesion in the New Nation," in *Essays on the American Revolution,* ed. S. G. Kurtz and J. H. Hutson (Chapel Hill, 1973), pp. 197–255; M. D. Howe, *The Garden and the Wilderness: Religion and Government in American Constitutional History* (Chicago, 1965); R. N. Bellah, "Civil Religion in America," *Daedalus* 96 (Winter 1967): 1–21; idem, *The Broken Covenant: American Civil Religion in Time of Trial* (New York, 1975). The discussion has been vexed by disagreement over what falls into the category of religious. Some scholars put under that rubric everything pertaining to what sociologists classify as "values" and everything pertaining to beliefs or to the abstract concept of the morally approved. As a result, political principles and patriotism have been lumped together with theologies, creeds, and churches. Surely there is insight to be gained from considering the supraindividualistic commitments of a people in one framework. Just as surely, however, much clarity of thinking is to be lost by discarding traditional categories, such as religious, political, etc.

2 A. P. Stokes, *Church and State in the United States,* 3 vols. (New York, 1950); for Stokes's explanation of his purpose, see especially vol. 1, pp. xlv–liv.

3 J. F. Jameson, *The American Revolution Considered as a Social Movement* (Princeton, 1926), pp. 143–58. Although the date of publication is 1926, the text was composed for delivery as a set of lectures in 1895 and underwent only minor alterations for the lectures given thirty years later that comprise the book. See A. M. Schlesinger, Introduction to *The American Revolution Considered as a Social Movement* (Beacon Edition, Boston, 1956), pp. ix–x. Surprising to see, Jameson's analytical categories were used by S. E. Ahlstrom in *A Religious History of the American People* (New Haven, 1972), chap. 23.

4 McLoughlin is an exception. His masterful *New England Dissent 1630–1833: The Baptists and the Separation of Church and State,* 2 vols. (Cambridge, Mass., 1971), treats Massachusetts, Connecticut, New Hampshire, and Vermont with awe-inspiring thoroughness. Yet this work and his comprehensive essay are somewhat loosely related.

5 This paragraph and the five following are based, except as noted, on W. F. Craven, *The Southern Colonies in the Seventeenth Century* (Baton Rouge, 1949); B. Bailyn, "Politics and Social Structure in Virginia," in *Seventeenth-Century America: Essays in Colonial History*, ed. J. M. Smith (Chapel Hill, 1959), pp. 90–115; G. M. Brydon, *Virginia's Mother Church and the Political Conditions Under Which It Grew*, 2 vols. (Richmond, Va., 1947; Philadelphia, 1952); and W. H. Seiler, "The Anglican Parish in Virginia," in *Seventeenth-Century America*, pp. 119–42.

6 A. L. Cross, *The Anglican Episcopate in the American Colonies* (New York, 1902), pp. 1–138, 277–308.

7 Brydon, *Virginia's Mother Church*, vol. 2, pp. 56–57.

8 Cross, *Anglican Episcopate*, p. 87.

9 W. D. Jordan, *White Over Black: American Attitudes Toward the Negro, 1550–1812* (Chapel Hill, 1968), pp. 180–87.

10 The remarks in this paragraph and the four that follow are based, with exceptions as noted, on P. Miller, *Orthodoxy in Massachusetts, 1630–1650* (Cambridge, Mass., 1933); idem, *The New England Mind: The Seventeenth Century* (Cambridge, Mass., 1939); idem, *The New England Mind: From Colony to Province* (Cambridge, Mass., 1953); E. S. Morgan, *Visible Saints: The History of a Puritan Idea* (New York, 1963); and many other writings by these scholars and their students.

11 Miller, *New England Mind: From Colony to Province*, pp. 19–21.

12 Morgan, *Visible Saints*, passim.

13 The remarks on Quakerism and places where it figured significantly are mostly drawn from S. V. James, *A People Among Peoples: Quaker Benevolence in Eighteenth-Century America* (Cambridge, Mass., 1963); idem, *Colonial Rhode Island—A History* (New York, 1975); G. B. Nash, *Quakers and Politics: Pennsylvania, 1681–1726* (Princeton, 1968); and R. N. Lokken, *David Lloyd, Colonial Lawmaker* (Seattle, 1959).

14 See, e.g., J. R. Bartlett, ed., *Records of the Colony of Rhode Island and Providence Plantations, in New England*, 7 vols. (Providence, 1856–62), vol. 1, pp. 441–42.

15 H. Hastings [and E. T. Corwin], eds., *Ecclesiastical Records, State of New York*, 7 vols. (Albany, 1901–16), vol. 2, pp. 1074–79, 1114–15, 1136–65, 1178–79; vol. 3, pp. 1563–66, 2173–76; vol. 6, pp. 4046–48, 4067, 4081, 4083–84, 4095–96, 4098–99; vol. 7, p. 95n.

16 E.g., Portsmouth Land Evidence Records (MS, Town Hall, Portsmouth, R.I.), vol. 1, p. 435; vol. 2, pp. 623–24; vol. 4, pp. 83–84; vol. 5, pp. 175–78; vol. 9, pp. 465–66.

17 E.g., the deeds of land for Seventh Day Baptist meeting houses in Westerly, Westerly Town Council Records (MS, Town Hall, Westerly, R.I.), vol. 1, p. 95; Westerly Land Evidence Records (MS, Town Hall, Westerly), vol. 5, p. 217.

18 To understand the wrangle in Rhode Island, one must piece together the following: the will of John Clarke, in Middletown Town Council Records (MS, Town Hall, Middletown, R.I.), vol. 3, pp. 248A–254A; Newport Town Council Records (MS, Newport Historical Society, Newport, R.I.), vol. 3, pp. 242, 250; vol. 4, pp. 27–31, 41, 45, 46; vol. 5, pp. 25, 34–39, 54, 150, 174; Rhode Island Colony Records (MS, State Archives, Providence), vol. 4, pp. 202–10, 272–74; and Papers of John Wanton, et al., v. Jeremiah Weeden (MS, General Court of Trials file papers, Office of the Clerk of the Superior Court in Newport County, Newport, R.I.), Box 1721.

19 Draft of charters for Anglican churches in Philadelphia and covering letter from Thomas Penn, London, 15 March 1765, to John Penn, Thomas Penn Letterbook

Number 8 (MS, Historical Society of Pennsylvania, Philadelphia), pp. 236–41; Thomas Penn, London, 14 December 1765, to John Penn, Thomas Penn Letterbook Number 8, p. 331.

20 Bartlett, ed., *Records of the Colony of Rhode Island,* vol. 6, p. 573; vol. 7, pp. 20–21, 32–33, 41, 198, 271, 272.

21 McLoughlin, *New England Dissent,* chaps. 5–28, passim. Use of the term "Standing Order" needs an explanation. Much learned opinion opposes calling the New England system an establishment because the churches were independent of one another and the government meticulously refrained from prescribing their doctrines, polity, or liturgy. It may be pointed out that the Massachusetts legislature accepted the Cambridge Platform of 1648 and at various times called on the clergy to resolve questions of practice, if not of faith, while the Connecticut legislature adopted the "Saybrook Platform" of 1708. Actually, the question of whether the New England system was an establishment or not seems rather a quibble. It was obviously at least a functional equivalent of an establishment, with the usual alliance between the dominant elements in society and the clergy, and it varied from European models chiefly in respects determined by local beliefs and practices. As disagreements between New England ministers were frequent and sometimes led to opposing sides forming within the clergy and the faithful, nobody can claim that a shimmering harmony embraced all the churches. For this reason, it is convenient to employ the term "Standing Order," which was commonly used in the eighteenth century, to designate the swarm of churches enjoying public support by taxes and other marks of favor. For a lawyer's argument that this system was not an establishment, see Howe, *Garden and the Wilderness,* pp. 34–36.

22 Stokes, *Church and State,* vol. 1, pp. 209–15; Brydon, *Virginia's Mother Church,* vol. 2, chaps. 7, 8, and 17.

23 Bartlett, ed., *Records of the Colony of Rhode Island,* vol. 3, pp. 30–32; vol. 5, p. 339.

24 F. N. Thorpe, ed., *The Federal and State Constitutions,* 7 vols. (Washington, 1909), vol. 6, pp. 3255–57; Stokes, *Church and State,* vol. 1, p. 434. The skeletal doctrines prescribed by South Carolina strongly resemble the civil religion analyzed by Bellah in "Civil Religion in America," pp. 8–10.

25 Thorpe, ed., *Federal and State Constitutions,* vol. 6, p. 3264.

26 Stokes, *Church and State,* vol. 1, pp. 380–81.

27 Ibid., pp. 381–83.

28 Brydon, *Virginia's Mother Church,* vol. 2, pp. 409–10.

29 Ibid., pp. 411–12, 449.

30 Stokes, *Church and State,* vol. 1, pp. 384–86; Brydon, *Virginia's Mother Church,* vol. 2, pp. 444–47.

31 Ibid., pp. 441–43, 447; Stokes, *Church and State,* vol. 1, pp. 384–86.

32 Ibid., pp. 394–95.

33 Ibid., pp. 387–92.

34 J. P. Boyd, et al., eds., *The Papers of Thomas Jefferson* (Princeton, 1950–), vol. 2, pp. 545–53, contains an authoritative text of the act and of the bill as drafted by Jefferson, as well as critical commentary on surviving texts.

35 Mead, *Lively Experiment,* pp. 27–37, 45–52.

36 E.g., Timothy Dwight, *Travels in New England and New York,* 4 vols., ed., B. M. Solomon (Cambridge, Mass., 1969), vol. 1, p. 6; cf. McLoughlin, *New England Dissent,* vol. 2, p. 864.

37 O. Handlin and M. F. Handlin, eds., *The Popular Sources of Political Authority: Documents on the Massachusetts Constitution of 1780* (Cambridge, Mass., 1966), p. 443. Article III was the most controversial part of the Constitution. Reports of opinion in the various towns reveal the wide range of objections to it. For a digest of them, see the Handlins's introduction, pp. 29–33. Quite likely, Article III did not get the required popular vote, but the Constitutional Convention manipulated the town reports so as to reach the conclusion that the whole document had been approved.

38 McLoughlin, *New England Dissent*, vol. 2, pp. 795–97, 844–46; Thorpe, ed., *Federal and State Constitutions*, vol. 4, p. 2454; vol. 6, pp. 3740, 3752. The New Hampshire and Vermont constitutions derived many of the phrases in their clauses on religion from the Pennsylvania constitution of 1776 rather than the Massachusetts constitution; see Thorpe, ed., *Federal and State Constitutions*, vol. 6, p. 3082.

39 K. G. Alliman, "The Incorporation of Massachusetts Congregational Churches, 1692–1833; The Preservation of Religious Autonomy" (unpublished Ph.D. dissertation, University of Iowa, 1970), chaps. 1 and 2, passim.

40 Alliman, "Incorporation of Massachusetts Congregational Churches," pp. 119–38, 140–50; *The Acts and Resolves, Public and Private, of the Province of Massachusetts Bay*, 21 vols. (Boston, 1869–1922), vol. 3, pp. 778–79. The law of 1755 said that the "ministers of the several Protestant churches, of whatever denomination," would "be deemed capable of taking, in succession, any parsonage land" or other land granted for the use of the ministry, and of suing for it in court or alienating it under certain conditions. The rest of the statute contained nothing further on this subject but instead expanded on the conditions relating to the Standing Order or the Anglican churches.

41 Alliman, "Incorporation of Massachusetts Congregational Churches," pp. 150–71.

42 Ibid., pp. 180–86; McLoughlin, *New England Dissent*, vol. 2, p. 1002; J. D. Cushing, "Notes on Disestablishment in Massachusetts, 1780–1833," *William and Mary Quarterly*, 3rd ser., vol. 26 (1969), pp. 169–90.

43 Alliman, "Incorporation of Massachusetts Congregational Churches," pp. 191–210; McLoughlin, *New England Dissent*, vol. 1, pp. 647–49, 680–83; vol. 2, pp. 706, 816–26, 859–60, 1088, 1189–1262.

44 N. W. Rightmyer, *Maryland's Established Church* (Baltimore, 1956), pp. 117–18; T. O. Hanley, *The American Revolution and Religion: Maryland* (Washington, 1971), pp. 60–68.

45 Thorpe, ed., *Federal and State Constitutions*, vol. 5, pp. 2635–37.

46 *Laws of the State of New York* (Albany, 1886–), vol. 1, pp. 532–35, 597–98, 613–18, 646–49, 661–62; Hastings, ed., *Ecclesiastical Records, State of New York*, vol. 6, pp. 4316, 4321, 4331, 4339, 4341, 4343, 4346.

47 E.g., copy of the charter and amendment in Minutes of the Newport Six Principle Baptist Society (MS, Newport Historical Society, Newport, R.I.), pp. 1–6.

48 H. Potter and B. Yancey, eds., *Laws of the State of North Carolina*, 2 vols. (Raleigh, 1821), vol. 2, pp. 811–13.

49 R. Watkins and G. Watkins, *A Digest of the Laws of the State of Georgia* (Philadelphia, 1806), pp. 409, 410.

50 Bellah, *Broken Covenant*, pp. 27–28, 45–46, and passim.

51 W. C. Ford et al., eds., *Journals of the Continental Congress, 1774–1789*, 34 vols. (Washington, 1904–37), vol. 19, pp. 214, 221.

52 Article VI, section 3; see Thorpe, ed., *Federal and State Constitutions*, vol. 1, p. 27. Some members of the Constitutional Convention offered the opinion that the absence

of powers over religion in the list of those given to Congress further prevented federal intrusion into this field. See Stokes, *Church and State,* vol. 1, pp. 531–37, 549–50.

53 Amendments, Article I; see Thorpe, ed., *Federal and State Constitutions,* vol. 1, p. 29.

54 Stokes, *Church and State,* vol. 1, pp. 560–61. Only much later, when the Fourteenth Amendment was interpreted as extending the First over state governments, did the First become a barrier against a religious establishment by an individual state.

55 J. C. Fitzpatrick, ed., *The Writings of George Washington,* 39 vols. (Washington, 1931–44), vol. 31, p. 93n.

56 Handlin and Handlin, eds., *Popular Sources of Political Authority,* p. 442.

57 Ibid., p. 330.

58 M. Quinlivan, "From Pragmatic Accommodation to Principled Action: The Revolution and Religious Establishment in Virginia" (paper read at the meeting of the Organization of American Historians in St. Louis, 8 April 1976), pp. 5–7, 11–15. Quinlivan drew the quotations from Nicholas's argument in Purdie and Dixon's *Virginia Gazette,* Supplement, 20 May 1773.

59 Thomas Jefferson, *Notes on the State of Virginia,* ed. W. Peden (Chapel Hill, 1955), p. 159.

60 Thorpe, ed., *Federal and State Constitutions,* vol. 5, pp. 3082, 3091, 3100, 3113, 3121.

61 Mead, *Lively Experiment,* pp. 65–66, makes this point in a somewhat less irreverent tone.

62 Bellah, "Civil Religion in America," pp. 1–21.

AMERICAN ETHNICITY IN THE REVOLUTIONARY ERA

Stow Persons, University of Iowa

Scholars have long been interested in the history of immigration to the United States and in the subsequent struggles of the newcomers to secure a foothold in an unfamiliar society. Often themselves descended from the nationality whose immigrant history they have described, they have provided sympathetic accounts of the hardships, accomplishments, and contributions of their forebears. Some are historical accounts; others, quite distinct from these, are the ethnic studies by sociologists and social psychologists that began with Thomas and Znaniecki's *Polish Peasant in Europe and America* (1918–20). While the sociological studies tend to be conceptually much richer than the work of the historians, they also often tend to slight the historical dimension. It is to be hoped that ethnic history in the future can combine the virtues of both approaches.

Two major phases of American ethnic history can be distinguished: the earlier period of Europeanization, extending from the first colonial settlements to the closing of unrestricted immigration following the First World War, and the more recent twofold process of integration and the stabilization of ethnic pluralism, which has involved native Indian, African, and Asiatic peoples, as well as Europeans. The period of Europeanization excluded the native Indian population and fashioned a caste status for unfree African labor. Within the European population, the struggle for ethnic mastery resulted in the dominance of the Anglo-Americans through ethnic assimilation, although accomplished in a manner not anticipated by contemporaries. One should emphasize the spontaneity of these processes. Only in retrospect do they take on the role of epochal decisions. The character of the period of Europeanization was not firmly established until the end of the revolutionary era, and then only as the unanticipated outcome of nearly a century of ethnic interaction.

Ethnic integration of a different kind is only now beginning. There is mounting evidence to suggest that the assimilation process among many ethnic groups stops short of complete amalgamation, and that public policy as well as the will to survive will assure the perpetuation of ethnic distinctions for a long time to come. A stable ethnic pluralism requires equal access to opportunities and services without regard to these distinctions, and the laws upholding integration policies now guarantee that access.

The English colonizers of continental North America, in contrast to the Spanish in Mexico, did not conquer and incorporate the native Indian tribes into their colonial societies. The Indians were too few in number and too unsettled in their way of living to be useful as a source of labor. Although Englishmen were not averse to enslaving captives of wilderness warfare whenever the opportunity arose, relatively few Indians were enslaved except in the Carolinas, where a substantial export trade in Indian slaves flourished briefly in the 1670s. Most of the English colonial ventures were commercial in purpose and did not include plans for military conquest; the consequent weakness of the early settlements resulted in a permanent state of confrontation between colonials and Indians in which the colonials gained the upper hand only gradually, as they grew in numbers and power over the ensuing century or more.[1] Although at first there was some uncertainty as to whether the Indians should be incorporated into European colonial society, or excluded from it, exclusion eventually prevailed. Indian tribes were customarily dealt with by treaty, that is, as foreigners; only a small minority lived in settlements of their own within white society, according to the pattern of segregation later to be known as the reservation system.[2]

Under these circumstances, the early reactions of Europeans to Indians were based on ethnic differences and reflected their prevailing cultural concerns. No fact loomed larger than that these strangers were non-Christians, spoke unknown languages, and observed unfamiliar customs. The first impulse of the Europeans was to relate the Indians to the world they knew by attributing their descent to one of the Ten Lost Tribes of Israel, or to some other origin that would reaffirm their common humanity. Differences of color figured among the various ethnic distinctions without at first being of particular significance.

The Christianizing of heathen aborigines was everywhere a feature of the official rationale for colonial settlement, to be taken more or less seriously according to the degree of Protestant sectarian radicalism of the settlers. The English Quakers and German Mennonites of Pennsylvania were notable for their determination to live at peace with the Indians, scrupulously adhering to their terms of land purchase, and refusing to demoralize them by using liquor or firearms in trade for furs. Similarly, the Puritans of New England, although concerned primarily with perpetuating the truth among "the spiritual seed of Abraham" (i.e., themselves), made at least sporadic efforts to convert the Indians.[3] In 1633, the Massachusetts General Court decreed that Indians who had become civilized and Christianized should receive grants of land comparable to those made to English settlers, and, where sufficiently numerous, they might also be organized into townships.[4] These provisions suggest that at the outset the Puritans were not averse to contemplating the same prospects for assimilating the Indians that would later apply to Europeans. Several "Praying Indian" villages formed a kind of buffer zone between the coastal settlements and the less tractable "salvages" of the interior.

But whatever the original intentions of the colonists, the realities of trade and land hunger inevitably precipitated conflict. The Indian wars in Virginia in the 1620s and 1640s established a pattern of pushing the Indians back and stabilizing the new boundary—at least temporarily—by treaty. A similar pattern prevailed in New England following King Philip's War in 1676. The fear and hatred engendered by border warfare nurtured simpler and less ambiguous attitudes among the white settlers toward Indians and their culture. Indians were now considered to be a lesser order of beings, destined to permanent exclusion from white society, if not to eventual extermination. At the same time, ironically enough, a painful realization slowly spread among the white settlers that the wilderness and its savage way of life exercised a fascination that some whites were unable to resist. Instances were not uncommon of whites being freed from Indian captivity, only to turn their backs on civilized society, preferring the life of savage liberty to the ordered restraints of colonial community life. Unable to withstand the superior military technology and organization of the whites, the Indians were nevertheless able to maintain an unconstrained way of life which for two centuries would continue to be a tempting avenue of escape for the dominant whites, even if more in fantasy than in fact.[5]

Slavery underwent a comparable process of definition during the early colonial period. For many years following the introduction of African labor in 1619, distinctions between permanent chattel slavery and indentured servitude for a specified number of years were not clearly drawn, although it was generally agreed that religious distinctions were crucial: Christians could not be enslaved; heathens captured in warfare, as well as "strangers"—which in practice meant Indians or Africans—could be. Everywhere the practice of slaveholding preceded the enactment of a legal framework for the institution, often by many years, so that the origins of the practice in many areas remain in considerable obscurity. In Massachusetts, for instance, although there is some evidence for the presence of slaves as early as 1639, the laws make no reference to slavery prior to 1696.[6] Throughout most of the seventeenth century, heathenism and savagery, rather than race and color, remained the principal justifications for enslavement.

During the eighteenth century, the ambivalent attitudes toward Negroes that have characterized American society up to the present day began to take shape. Quakers and, to a lesser extent, New England Puritans began to speak out against slavery on both religious and moral grounds. But, at the same time, prejudice associated with servile status and skin color had also begun to appear. Nor were these always divergent tendencies: hostility to slavery could occasionally be found combined with an anti-Negro prejudice that was expressed in laws prohibiting the importation or manumission of slaves, or laws regulating the conduct of free Negroes.

Antislaveholding sentiment spread rapidly among the Quakers after 1750. It was focused initially on slave trading and later on the ownership of slaves by the Friends themselves. Because of the Quaker principle of action by consensus, a generation of agitation was needed before the Friends were persuaded to abandon the practice; but by the end of the Revolution, they were substantially free of it. Their arguments fused the natural-rights tradition of liberty with the radical sectarian Christian concern for the poor and downtrodden.[7] Thus, in Rhode Island, a colony in which Quakers were numerous, a statute of 1774 prohibiting the importation of slaves noted the inconsistency of men engaging in a struggle to preserve their own rights at the same time they were denying those rights to others.[8]

The most important ethnic debate of the revolutionary era was conducted, not in religious terms, but in terms of the social and political values of the Enlightenment. One consequence of the ethnic revolution now under way has been a closer look by historians at the paradox of enlightened thinkers in America promulgating life, liberty, and the pursuit of happiness while countenancing slavery and often owning slaves themselves. The affirmation of natural rights—radical enough in the countries of Western Europe sharing a common cultural heritage—faced a far more awkward test in America with its African and native minorities. When the American revolutionaries spoke of the inalienable rights of all men, what kind of rationalization were they making that excepted these minorities? Although Thomas Jefferson, for one, was acutely aware of the paradox, many others were less so, perhaps because they had not yet arrived at our own vivid sense of a worldwide political community. Europe, together with its colonial extensions, was still in some sense their entire political world, and when one spoke of "the rights of men" one was thinking of Europeans. To that extent, the politics of Enlightenment was geographically and ethnically conditioned.

Another extenuating circumstance, recently noted by Edmund Morgan, was the close association in the enlightened mind between political liberty, personal independence, and private property.[9] Only a truly independent person could be free, and that independence could be assured only by the possession of property. Free laborers were dependent upon their employers, and in Virginia in particular the planters recalled with alarm the threat posed by the mobs of landless, unemployed whites who had joined in Nathaniel Bacon's rebellion of 1676.

The threat had been ended by the substitution of black slaves for white labor, since blacks could be more firmly controlled and had neither hope nor expectation of bettering their lot. Because of this, it was inconceivable to men like Jefferson that freed slaves in appreciable numbers could be allowed to remain in the country—the natural-rights philosophy in America was firmly contained within the barriers of class and caste.

So much attention has recently been focused on these contradictions and on the inability of slaveholders to bring their practices into accord with their principles that one is tempted to overlook the enormous contribution the Enlightenment made to the advancement of the antislavery cause. Thanks to the influence of enlightened ideas, the notion conceived by a few radical Protestant sectarians that slaveholding was a sin became transmuted into a broader civil condemnation of the denial to any individual of his natural rights. The institution of slavery was everywhere thrown upon the defensive, and, most important, among the continental Anglo-American colonies and revolutionary states the abolitionist movement was inaugurated. By 1804, provision for the elimination of slavery had been made everywhere except in the staple-crop regions of the South.[10] The revolutionary ideology took such deep root in America as to initiate a strain for consistency between ideology and social practice; the effects of that tension are still being felt.

Although the revolutionary era properly may be credited with inaugurating the movement for the abolition of slavery, it did not come to grips with the more profound problem of ethnic social equality. This became the task for our own generation. The appearance of a small free Negro class in the early eighteenth century exposed the depths of the prejudice against blacks that had already formed in the minds of white Americans. Several colonies enacted laws forbidding interracial marriage and miscegenation in the belief that mulattoes inherited the undesirable traits of their black parents.[11] Other restrictive legislation reflected the fear that free Negroes were "an idle, slothful people" liable to become public charges.[12] The process of assimilation of European peoples culminating in the prospect of amalgamation through intermarriage, which was to become the common expectation of Americanizers during the nineteenth century, thus explicitly excluded Negroes. Why it did not also exclude Indians remains something of a problem. But in many parts of the country Indians were increasingly remote and invisible; perhaps, too, the widely held view that they were deficient in sexual vigor and therefore no threat to white racial purity diverted attention from the intermarriages and illicit unions that were not uncommon wherever Indians and whites were in close contact.

Eighteenth-century Pennsylvania provides a convenient microcosm to explore the issues of ethnic interaction during its first phase, because the settlement of Germans in Pennsylvania in large numbers prior to 1750 precipitated controversies that were to reflect the characteristic American concerns about immigration for the next century and a half. From the beginning, although Americans of British origin were everywhere dominant in the English colonies, settlers from other countries were welcomed or at least tolerated. Their labor was needed, and opportunities were abundant—land was the principal resource, and most newcomers were peasant farmers. In 1739, in order to attract more settlers, Parliament had provided for the naturalization of foreigners, granting them all the rights of native-born Englishmen.[13] William Penn, the Quaker founder of Pennsylvania, had deliberately sought out and encouraged settlement by radical Protestant sectarians from the Continent whose religious and social principles were similar to those of the Quakers. The promise of religious freedom, exemption from military service, and a liberal land-distribution policy brought substantial numbers of Mennonites, Dunkards, Schwenkfelders, and other sectarians; they settled in compact agricultural communities in eastern Pennsylvania. An oath or affirmation of allegiance to the Crown and of fidelity to the proprietor was sufficient to assure the right of political participation to anyone who could also satisfy Pennsylvania's nominal property and residency requirements.

The sectarians were followed after 1720 by increasing numbers of Lutherans, German Reformed, and Moravians. Lieutenant Governor Thomas estimated in 1755 that there were over 100,000 Germans in the colony, constituting nearly three-fifths of the population. More recent arrivals were alleged to include many convicts, paupers, and other undesirables swept up by the shipping companies for sale as indentured servants (similar complaints were to remain the standard litany of immigration opponents for two hundred years). The influx of Scotch-Irish settlers from Ulster after 1717 offset the German immigration and equalized the British and non-British portions of the population, but it failed to stem the growing concern for the future of English society and culture in the colony.[14]

The Anglo-Americans of Pennsylvania developed what would in time come to be known as the theory of "Americanization." In reality a theory of "Anglo-Americanization," it asserted the desirability of Anglo-American cultural traits and proposed methods for perpetuating them. Its central expectation was that non-English elements of the population would come to adopt Anglo-American traits, assuring that the person thus assimilated would live according to the norms and practices of the dominant group.

The Anglo-Americans found an influential spokesman in Benjamin Franklin, who both publicly and privately expressed his fears that the

Germans would come to dominate Pennsylvania and that German culture would prevail there. While admitting that the Germans were excellent farmers, industrious and frugal, who contributed greatly to the economic development of the country, he also claimed that they were willing to settle for lower wages and a lower standard of living, and could consequently undersell the English colonists, thus in effect driving them out of the colony.[15] In 1753, Franklin informed Peter Collinson of London, who in turn was expected to alert Parliament, that the Germans were an ignorant, stupid lot, unaccustomed to English liberty and unable to comprehend it. Although at first they had avoided politics, more recently they had been drawn into it, only to be manipulated by demagogues. Franklin was particularly concerned with the durability and persistence of German culture in America. Rather than learn English and Americanize themselves, they had patronized their own German-language printers and established a newspaper. Advertisements were printed in both languages, as were street signs in German neighborhoods; courts were obliged to accept wills and deeds executed in German. In a few years, Franklin gloomily predicted, it would be necessary to provide interpreters in the legislature so that one half might know what the other half were saying.[16]

The anxiety created by these local problems may be better understood when it is recalled that the imperial struggle with the French was about to be resumed; the menace of invasion on the western frontier transformed a general ethnic hostility into suspicions regarding the loyalty of the Germans to their country. Franklin noted their sectarian refusal to bear arms, and he repeated the widespread rumor that French agents had circulated among the Germans threatening them with reprisals should they aid the British in the military defense of Pennsylvania.[17]

Franklin's proposed solution to the German problem took the form of a series of legislative measures looking toward the assimilation of the Pennsylvania Germans into Anglo-American culture. The most important of these in the long run, Franklin thought, would be the provision of free English schools for German children; in the meanwhile, he would disqualify for any public post of trust, honor, or profit anyone who could not speak English, and he would require all bonds, deeds, and wills to be rendered in that language whenever possible. But he would not suppress German printing houses or forbid the importation of German books, because the forces of Americanization would soon make that unnecessary. While he would prohibit the immigration of any more Germans to Pennsylvania, he had no objection to their settling in other English colonies, as he believed that the more widely dispersed the minority, the more readily it would be assimilated.[18]

Franklin's views toward ethnic relations were to comprise the prevailing attitude of Anglo-Americans for the following two centuries. He located the problem in the dynamic context of social process, advocating only such positive measures as seemed necessary to permit the forces of assimilation to bring about a spontaneous resolution. Among these, the most important place was assigned to formal education. The proposal that incentives be provided to encourage ethnic intermarriage seemed to him artificial and unnecessary.

Franklin candidly confessed to an abiding racial prejudice, associated primarily with skin color. In the concluding paragraph of his *Observations on the Increase of Mankind* (1751), he noted that the number of white people in the world was comparatively small: all Africa was black, Asia was mostly "tawny," the native Indians were red, and, among the Europeans, the Spanish, Italians, French, Russians, and Swedes were "swarthy." So also were the Germans, except for the Saxons, who, with the English, comprised the principal body of white people. It seemed only natural to Franklin that he should share a universal prejudice in wishing to increase the number of his own kind wherever the opportunity afforded, as it did in America. It saddened him to reflect that instead of capitalizing on this opportunity, the Americans were "darkening" themselves with the black and swarthy races.[19]

Support for Franklin's educational proposal was vigorously promoted in England by William Smith, a Scottish Anglican protégé of the Archbishop of Canterbury who came to the colonies in 1751 and, after a few weeks in Pennsylvania, had become alarmed at the cultural and political threat represented by the unassimilated Germans. Returning to England in 1753, Smith sought to persuade the Society for the Propagation of the Gospel in Foreign Parts to establish free English schools in the German settlements of Pennsylvania. His proposal was motivated by both cultural and political concerns. Frontier life posed the familiar threat of degeneration into "wood-born savagry," while the English liberties with which the newcomers had been generously endowed were simply an invitation to license in the hands of those unequipped to appreciate them. Smith reminded his readers of Montesquieu's maxim that freedom demands education. At the same time, he was fully aware of the assimilative function of education. As German youths acquired English speech and manners, ethnic distinctions would be forgotten, and intermarriage would result in ultimate amalgamation. Special attention should be paid to the civic purposes of education. If citizens were too pacific, as Smith believed some Americans—notably the Quakers and the German sectarians—were, they could be educated to a better appreciation of the necessity for self-sacrifice in the defense of their liberties. The primary educational objective in Pennsylvania should be to make good citizens rather than good scholars, since "the virtue of the active vulgar is the strength of the state."[20]

Smith's activities resulted in the organization in London in 1754 of a "Society for the Relief and Instruction of Poor Germans." Contributions from private sources were solicited in Britain and Holland, and six Pennsylvania trustees, including Franklin and Smith, were designated to oversee the establishment of schools. Instruction was to be offered in both English and German, and in bookkeeping, psalm singing, and the doctrines of Protestantism. By 1760, nine schools had been opened in the principal German communities of eastern Pennsylvania.[21] The Lutherans, German Reformed, and Moravians all endorsed and supported the schools, while the sectarians bitterly opposed them.

A critical issue was the nature of religious instruction. The sponsors proposed to teach the "uncontroverted Principles of Religion and Morality" shared by all Christians, while avoiding the "speculative and disputed Points" that separated the various denominations. The disputed points were, of course, precisely the matters most dear to the hearts of the sectarians, whose spokesman, the Dunkard journalist Christopher Sauer, correctly perceived the schools as agencies designed to undermine German culture.[22] The suspicions of the intended beneficiaries along with disputes among the trustees and a lack of adequate funds led to the dissolution of the Society and the closing of its schools in 1769.[23]

Although education was thus from the beginning called upon to play a central role in the Americanization process, it was also apparent that charity schools supported by private funds were wholly inadequate to the task. The Quakers, whose local meetings maintained some forty schools, were unsympathetic to an effort in the colonial legislature to provide public funds for the German schools.[24] Education for all children at public expense was still a century in the future.

I have found no evidence that those who were concerned about ethnic diversity held theories of innate racial superiority or inferiority. Their concerns were cultural: religious, linguistic, political, and economic. They had a not unrealistic sense of the practical problems that would arise out of social contacts between people of such diverse backgrounds, but they were confident that the process of assimilation would eventually erase these differences. They could contemplate with equanimity the prospect of ultimate intermarriage because they shared the environmentalist assumption, expressed succinctly by Hector St. John Crèvecoeur, that "we are machines fashioned by every circumstance around us."[25]

When one turns from the polemical literature of the Americanizers to a consideration of the political life of Pennsylvania in the mid-eighteenth century, however, a distinctly different impression of the assimilation process emerges. Thanks to Penn's farsighted provision for economic opportunities and political rights, the Germans were from the outset drawn into active participation in the political process. They were not, in fact, as culturally deprived as the propaganda of the Americanizers represented them to be. By focusing on certain clannish traits of the sectarians, the Anglo-Americans diverted attention from the Lutheran and German Reformed churchly tradition, with its educated clergy and devotion to parochial education.[26] Intraethnic differences between churchmen and sectarians would usually prevent the Germans from presenting a solid front in Pennsylvania politics. So also would the geographical distribution of the German population. Western frontiersmen often found themselves in conflict with the older established German communities in Berks or Northampton counties.

The structure of politics in the proprietary colony of Pennsylvania was comparable to that in the royal colonies, where the governor who represented imperial authority often found himself at odds with the local interests that dominated the elected legislative assembly. In Pennsylvania, the proprietary interest of the Penn family in income from rents, land sales, and other indirect revenues from commercial development came into conflict with the interest of the settlers in cheap land, military security, and low taxes. Thus the governor, a designee of the absentee proprietor, found himself the leader of a proprietary party perennially in conflict with a majority of the assembly. From the early years of their settlement, the German sectarians had been allied with the Quakers, their common religious principles furnishing a bond which, according to the proprietary party, often concealed divergent material interests. From the 1730s onward, it was a regular tactic of the proprietary party to attempt to detach the Germans from the Quakers, defending the continued immigration of Germans and criticizing the assembly for failure to provide defense for German settlers on the frontier.[27]

The proprietary government in Pennsylvania had from the beginning refused to deal with the Welsh, Swede, German, or Scotch-Irish settlers in a corporate capacity as ethnic groups, even when they were settled in compact communities. The so-called Welsh Barony, a settlement of some 6,000 Welsh Quakers who had hoped by establishing it to maintain their own language, culture, and customs, had been unable to persuade the Pennsylvania government to recognize and deal with it as an autonomous state. In keeping with this important precedent, the law continued to recognize only individuals and not ethnic groups. It was within that context that politics was able to play the important assimilative role ascribed to it here.

The rapid influx of Scotch-Irish settlers after 1717 further complicated the ethnic relationships in Pennsylvania. As Presbyterians, the

Scotch-Irish felt close churchly ties to the Dutch and German Reformed and to the Lutherans, among whom an ecclesiastical union was discussed in 1743. Although nothing came of the proposal, it was an early indication of an impending division between sectarian and churchly groups that would persist down to the Revolution.[28] Christopher Sauer understood very well that the Germans held the balance of power between the assembly and proprietary parties, and he urged them to exploit the situation for their own benefit. The sectarians refused to accept the charge that their pacifism was tantamount to disloyalty, or that the oath of naturalization obligated them to bear arms for the king in wartime. They continued to support the Quakers, who remained in control of the assembly.[29]

The capture of Fort Duquesne (Pittsburgh) by the French in 1754 and the defeat of Braddock's British expeditionary force in the following year opened the frontier to French and Indian incursions and brought about the division of the Germans into a frontier, predominantly Lutheran and Reformed group and an eastern, sectarian group. Westerners joined with the Scotch-Irish in a march on the assembly to demand military protection. Conrad Weiser, an Indian negotiator who had been largely responsible for stabilizing relations between Pennsylvania and neighboring Indian tribes, warned the sectarians to reexamine their pacifism in view of the precarious situation in which the colony now found itself. Born a Lutheran, Weiser was well known in the German religious community by virtue of his successive identification with the Lutherans, the Reformed, the Dunkards, and with Beisel's exotic Ephrata commune. With such credentials, Weiser did not hesitate to advise the sectarians that their pacifism, an originally appropriate response to persecution, was irrelevant in Pennsylvania, where the state had been good to them and where they now had something to fight for.[30] Although the sectarians were not persuaded to renounce their pacifism, they did consent to the enactment of a militia law and to the erection of a chain of eleven forts to protect the frontier from Indian depredations.[31] Such a flexible attitude toward public policy was an impressive indication of their assimilation.

During the decade between the end of the French and Indian Wars and the outbreak of the Revolution, the Lutherans and German Reformed were allied with the Scotch-Irish in support of the proprietary party, while the sectarians continued to support the Quakers in the Assembly party.[32] When the assembly failed to reach agreement with the proprietor on taxation and defense policy, Franklin led a movement to replace the proprietorship with direct royal government. To accomplish this, he attempted to build a new coalition of British, Scotch-Irish, and Germans, each of whom had had some experience of oppression at the hands of the proprietor. Franklin now lavishly praised the character and contributions of the German citizens, whose presence he had formerly deplored.[33] Although nothing came of the effort to replace the proprietor, Franklin did succeed in fashioning what was to become the nucleus of the Independence party in Pennsylvania.

This brief review does less than justice to the complexity of political maneuvering as it involved the Germans of Pennsylvania during the decades prior to the Revolution. But it should at least indicate that the Germans were playing an active role in colonial politics from the outset and that the concern of Anglo-Americans over the assimilation of German-Americans had less to do with culture than with politics.

Nationalist ideologies appeared in nineteenth-century Europe among ethnic groups sharing a language, traditions, and a sense of cultural identity. Political nationality and independence movements became the inevitable expressions of these sentiments. In British North America, however, the sequence was in reverse: political independence was achieved before a comparable philosophy of nationality had been articulated, thanks in part to the peculiar circumstances of the British colonial system, and in part to the universal terms in which the revolutionary objectives were phrased. The fact that the American rebellion was a colonial revolt against the government by people of the same cultural and ethnic background deprived the Revolution of an opportunity to play a role in stimulating ethnic consciousness. The non-British ethnic groups in America—Germans, Dutch, French—were if anything more loyal to the British connection than were the Anglo-Americans themselves.[34] An independent United States came into being without the sense of ethnic identity that underlay the later nationalist movements of Europe.

The American political vocabulary never developed the distinction Europeans made between the state as a political entity and the nation as a people. Here nation and state were and are both political terms, one referring to the federal union, the other to its constituent members. The sentiment of nationality had to be slowly nurtured through the processes of war, diplomacy, and politics, while the resisting local patriotisms of state and region lingered on well into the nineteenth century. As the sentiment of nationality developed, it came to be associated with political unity and the sovereignty of the federal union, not with ethnic unity.[35]

Perhaps for these reasons students of ethnic history have focused their attention on the nineteenth- and twentieth-century immigrant experience. During the long colonial and revolutionary eras an American national society had formed which could be regarded as ethnically neutral. Around this neutral core a fringe of recently arrived immigrants and their descendants constituted ethnic groups which could expect sooner or later to be assimilated into the larger society. This conception persists to the present day, and it has been incorporated into a recent interpretation of American ethnic history by John Higham in his book *Send These to Me*.[36]

Not all Americans are ethnics, according to Higham. There is an American "host society" composed of those who have lost all sense of ethnic identity, due to intermarriage or to the remoteness of their ethnic ancestry (a census survey of 1972 placed 37.6 per cent of the American population in this "host" category). Two factors account for the formation of the "host society." One is the distinction Higham makes between "settlers" and "immigrants": settlers were the first-comers who formed a new society and fixed the terms on which later-comers must establish themselves. Immigrants were the later-comers, subject to all the pressures of assimilation. Thus, the English colonists of the seventeenth century were settlers, not immigrants. Another factor enlarging the host society was the continuing process of assimilation among immigrants and their descendants. Ethnicity in America, as Higham conceives it, is a survival or residue of the immigration process, presumably doomed to eventual extinction by assimilation. Because Negroes and Indians were not voluntary immigrants, Higham excludes them entirely from his analysis.

My own interpretation differs in several respects from that of Higham. First, I do not believe that ethnicity is as closely tied to immigration as he does. Immigrants have often lacked ethnic consciousness, although it might develop later under the impact of American conditions (this was notably the case with the earlier Irish immigration). Second, I am not greatly impressed with Higham's distinctions between settlers and immigrants, and between host society and ethnics. The host society has often felt threatened by ethnics, not only in Pennsylvania in the eighteenth century, but at various times and places in the nineteenth.

But the principal objection to the concept of a host society is that it ignores the pervasive English traits of those Americans descended from "settlers." All American ethnic studies must begin, in my opinion, by recognizing the dominant position of the Anglo-Americans; they furnished the language, the value system, and the social institutions. Having said this, however, it also seems important to be prepared conceptually to recognize the signs of an emerging ethnic consciousness among Anglo-Americans. These signs were born out of the realization that Anglo-American dominance was threatened. A major ingredient of ethnicity in America is the sense of being in a minority status, of present or potential threat to ethnic survival. Anglo-American history is fraught with the kinds of fears that stimulate the growth of ethnic consciousness. Higham himself has earlier published a major study[37] examining the fear and hostility aroused among Anglo-Americans by the East European immigration at the turn of the twentieth century.

In recent years, several American historians have been using voting patterns as evidence for persisting ethnic identity. I have chosen the opposite path—using the same index of political participation as evidence for at least some measure of assimilation. Higham supports aspects of both views when he observes that ethnic voting often intensifies as ethnic identity becomes problematical.

The sociologist Milton Gordon has suggested[38] that it is useful to distinguish several major forms of assimilation: cultural assimilation, such as language, ideology, and other forms of nonmaterial culture; institutional assimilation, where individuals freely enter into the major forms of organized social activity; and social assimilation, the most intimate and personal forms of association out of which amalgamation (i.e., intermarriage) may result. In the United States today, cultural assimilation is far advanced for most ethnic groups, while institutional assimilation is now the focus of public laws on integration which are designed to assure equal access to institutional services and opportunities without ethnic discrimination. Ethnic survival in America clearly depends upon the will and ability of ethnic groups to perpetuate themselves by resisting social assimilation while sustaining their distinctive identity. Those observers who applaud the prospect of indefinite ethnic survival are called pluralists. But it cannot be too strongly emphasized that a pluralistic democracy would be wholly unacceptable—and doubtless undesirable as well—without the guarantees of equality extended in the policy of integration. And here again, as at the outset of ethnic history in America, a crucial role is being played by the political process in affirming the rights of ethnic minorities.

The experience of Pennsylvania, although unique in the colonial period, was to be frequently repeated during the nineteenth century. The coming of Catholic Irish and Italians, of Chinese, and of other immigrant groups elicited from Americanizers in the regions where the newcomers settled familiar demands for assimilation or exclusion. Attention invariably focused on cultural differences, while the assimilative role of political participation was ignored or deplored, especially in the cities, where ethnic-bloc voting could be readily identified. Formal education continued to be the principal tool of the Americanizers, although education was in fact probably more useful in assisting ethnic groups to perpetuate themselves, because it promoted a partial assimilation by teaching ethnics the English language and other practical skills, than it was in breaking down all ethnic distinctions. With the adoption of integration policies in the present generation, the political process has taken formal as well as informal control of American ethnic relations.

NOTES

1 G. B. Nash, *Red, White, and Black: The Peoples of Early America* (Englewood Cliffs, 1974), pp. 112–14.

2 A. T. Vaughan, *New England Frontier: Puritans and Indians, 1620–1675* (Boston, 1965), pp. 42–60; D. W. Hoover, *The Red and the Black* (Chicago, 1976), pp. 17–46; Nash, *Red, White, and Black*, pp. 76–87.

3 Ibid., pp. 134–39; Vaughan, *New England Frontier*, pp. 19–20.

4 J. C. Hurd, *The Law of Freedom and Bondage in the United States*, 2 vols. (1858; reprinted New York, 1968), vol. 1, p. 257.

5 J. Axtell, "White Indians of Colonial America," *William and Mary Quarterly*, 3rd ser., vol. 32 (January 1975): 55–88.

6 Hurd, *Law of Freedom and Bondage*, vol. 1, pp. 248, 260, 277–79, 258n.

7 S. V. James, *A People Among Peoples: Quaker Benevolence in Eighteenth-Century America* (Cambridge, Mass., 1963), pp. 128–40.

8 Hurd, *Law of Freedom and Bondage*, vol. 1, pp. 276–77.

9 E. S. Morgan, "Slavery and Freedom: The American Paradox," *Journal of American History* 59 (June 1972): 5–29.

10 D. B. Davis, *The Problem of Slavery in the Age of Revolution, 1770–1823* (Ithaca, 1975), pp. 213–54; W. D. Jordan, *White Over Black: American Attitudes Toward the Negro, 1550–1812* (Chapel Hill, 1968), pp. 269–311; D. J. MacLeod, *Slavery, Race, and the American Revolution* (Cambridge, 1974), p. 46.

11 Jordan, *White Over Black*, pp. 139, 168; Hurd, *Law of Freedom and Bondage*, vol. 1, pp. 236–37, 240, 249–50, 263, 290, 292, 295, 301; vol. 2, pp. 29, 77.

12 Ibid., vol. 1, p. 284.

13 *The Papers of Benjamin Franklin*, ed. Leonard W. Labaree et al., 18 vols. to date (New Haven, 1959–), vol. 13, p. 352; A. D. Graeff, *The Relations Between the Pennsylvania Germans and the British Authorities, 1750–1776* (Norristown, 1939), pp. 22–23.

14 A. E. McKinley, *The Suffrage Franchise in the Thirteen English Colonies in America* (Philadelphia, 1905), pp. 273–99; Graeff, *Pennsylvania Germans*, pp. 18–21; A. Dorpalen, "The Political Influence of the German Element in Colonial America," *Pennsylvania History* 6 (1939): 147–50.

15 *Franklin Papers*, vol. 4, pp. 120–21.

16 Ibid., vol. 4, pp. 483–85.

17 Ibid., vol. 4, p. 485.

18 Ibid., vol. 5, pp. 158–60.

19 Ibid., vol. 4, p. 234.

20 H. W. Smith, *Life and Correspondence of the Rev. William Smith, D.D.*, 2 vols. (Philadelphia, 1879), vol. 1, pp. 29–38.

21 Smith, *Smith*, vol. 1, pp. 41–42, 93; *Franklin Papers*, vol. 5, pp. 238–40, 204–5; Graeff, *Pennsylvania Germans*, pp. 44–46.

22 Smith, *Smith*, vol. 1, pp. 139–40.

23 *Franklin Papers*, vol. 8, p. 68n.

24 L. A. Cremin, *American Education. The Colonial Experience, 1607–1783* (New York, 1970), pp. 305–7; Graeff, *Pennsylvania Germans*, p. 30.

25 Hector St. John de Crèvecoeur, *Letters From an American Farmer* (1782) (New York, 1963), p. 92.

26 J. H. Dubbs, "The Founding of the German Churches of Pennsylvania," *Pennsylvania Magazine of History and Biography* 17 (1893): 260–62.

27 R. H. Shryock, "The Pennsylvania Germans in American History," *Pennsylvania Magazine* 58 (1939): 263; Graeff, *Pennsylvania Germans,* pp. 22–23.

28 Dubbs, *Pennsylvania Magazine* 17: 247.

29 N. S. Cohen, "The Philadelphia Election Riot of 1742," *Pennsylvania Magazine* 92 (1968): 306–19; D. Rothermund, "The German Problem of Colonial Pennsylvania," ibid. 84 (1960): 6.

30 C. Weiser, "Two Addresses of Conrad Weiser to the German Voters of Pennsylvania," ibid. 23 (1899): 519–21.

31 Graeff, *Pennsylvania Germans,* pp. 126–27, 131–39.

32 Rothermund, *Pennsylvania Magazine* 84: 18–19.

33 *Franklin Papers,* vol. 11, pp. 173, 505; Graeff, *Pennsylvania Germans,* pp. 239–46.

34 W. H. Nelson, *The American Tory* (New York, 1961), pp. 88–90.

35 Oswald Spengler observed that the common American expression "*this* country" indicated that subconsciously Americans were ambivalent in their sense of national identification.

36 J. Higham, *Send These to Me: Jews and Other Groups in Urban America* (New York, 1975).

37 Idem, *Strangers in the Land: Patterns of American Nativism, 1860–1925* (New Brunswick, 1955).

38 M. M. Gordon, *Assimilation in American Life: The Role of Race, Religion, National Origins* (New York, 1964).

THE LIMITS OF POLITICIZATION: AMERICAN WOMEN AND THE AMERICAN REVOLUTION
Linda K. Kerber, University of Iowa

> I have Don as much to Carrey on the war as maney that Sett Now at ye helm of government. . . . —*Rachel Wells*

> I can't help exclaiming now and then, dreadful fruits of Liberty. I confess I have not such romantic notions of the Goddess . . . you know that our Sex are doomed to be obedient in every stage of life so that *we* shant be great gainers by this contest.—*Margaret Livingston*

"Patriotism in the female Sex," wrote Abigail Adams as the American Revolution drew to a close, "is the most disinterested of all virtues. Excluded from honours and from offices, we cannot attach ourselves to the State or Government from having held a place of Eminence. Even in freest countrys our property is subject to the control and disposal of our partners, to whom the Laws have given a soverign Authority. Deprived of a voice in Legislation, obliged to submit to those Laws which are imposed upon us, is it not sufficient to make us indifferent to the publick Welfare? Yet all History and every age exhibit Instances of patriotick virtue in the female Sex; which considering our situation equals the most Heroick. . . ."[1]

We cannot know how widely these opinions—expressed in this private letter from wife to husband—were shared. Certainly they challenged much of the accepted wisdom of her generation; as Lord Kames had argued in his widely read *Sketches of the History of Man*, women did not seem to have a direct responsibility to national politics. Precisely because they were "excluded from honours and from offices"—that is, from the usual methods of attaching a subject's self-interest to the outcome of national policy—women's relationships to their nation seemed to be second hand; they experienced politics through husbands, fathers, and sons. Kames claimed they had "less patriotism than men."[2]

This distrust of the capacity of women to take politics seriously was present in the American colonies when the Revolution began, and it persisted long after it had ended. That many women shared this distrust is clear: it is found in Margaret Livingston's complaint that, however the war turned out, it would mean only inconvenience and trouble for women; it is found in the continued social correspondence of women from even the most political families—Jays, Livingstons, Pinckneys—during the worst of the war. It is implicit in the shrill insistence of the popular press both before and long after the war that American women were excessive in their consumption of British goods and books, and that by their indulgence in British products American women were undercutting the efforts of American men to develop a fully independent national culture. Despite anecdotal evidence of the economic and physical sacrifices of individual women, there persisted a folklore which distrusted women's political behavior, assumed that women were incapable of making reasoned and unbiased political judgments, and emphasized the hesitancy of women to sacrifice their creature comforts for higher national purposes.[3]

Could a woman be a patriot? If any experience ought to have provided unambivalent answers to that question, it was certainly the Revolution. But when it ended the answers in fact seemed only a little clearer—in part because memories of women who were patriots were counterbalanced by memories of women who were loyalists. That both sorts were active politically in ways that were sharply different from their prewar behavior was masked by the winners' scorn for the losers, and by the belief that neither group of women had made truly independent political choices but were boxed in by the political choices made by male relatives. Women were expelled from patriot-held territory, for example, not because of their own political persuasion, but because of their husbands': the burden rested heavily on the wife of a Tory to prove that she indeed did not share her husband's political opinions. Few were prepared to agree that a wife and mother could also be an independent political being. Those who, like Abigail Adams, thought women could be both faced a difficult task if they were to carry this idea past private conceptions. They would need to persuade a hostile public that expressive political behavior did not threaten the traditional domestic domain; they also would need to persuade a skeptical public that a mother could also be a patriot, and that what they would come to call a "Republican Mother" was not its own oxymoron.

Their task was made the more difficult by the liberal reluctance to believe that any propertyless person could make reasoned political decisions. But even unmarried women who did in fact hold property in their own name found no less resistance to women's political claims. Nevertheless, that women were not fully successful ought not blind us to the fact that they had begun to articulate a political ideology which blended the domestic and public spheres, and to offer the terms and rhetoric in which much of the nineteenth- and indeed twentieth-century debate on the proper dimensions of female patriotism and politics would be expressed.

The prerevolutionary colonial world antedated both the political and the industrial revolution. Circumscribed by the paucity of roads and lack of complicated market patterns, bounded by the strength of local traditions, limited by the constraints of preindustrial family life, most American men and women lived out their lives in a rural culture and an agricultural economy.

Like most women in preindustrial society, eighteenth-century American women lived in what is usually regarded as the traditional woman's domain. Their daily activities took place within a feminine domestic circle: infants were delivered by midwives, the sick were cared for by nurses, women who traveled would stay overnight at female-owned boarding houses. If daughters went to school, it was to female seminaries where the course of study rarely provided more than the rudiments of literacy, and where students apparently spent their time in needlework, music, and dancing.

The sharp disparity in literacy between colonial men and women has only recently begun to be measured. A standard feature of apprenticeship contracts for boys was that, by the completion of their term, they would have been taught a trade and have had some schooling, while girls' contracts rarely promised to teach them anything more than housework, rarely offering even informal instruction in reading and writing. Kenneth Lockridge, sampling signatures on New England wills, has shown that in the early eighteenth century, when perhaps 70 per cent of New England men were at least barely literate, only 40 per cent of the women who made wills could sign their names. By the eve of the Revolution, literacy among women in urban areas had substantially improved, but the gap between men and women remained as great as ever. "I regret the trifling narrow contracted Education of the Females of my own country," Abigail Adams complained. "You need not be told how much female Education is neglected, nor how fashionable it has been to ridicule Female learning." The *Royal American Magazine* put the matter squarely: "How many female minds, rich with native genius and noble sentiment, have been lost to the world, and all their mental treasures buried in oblivion?"[4] Of all the distinctions between the women's world and the "outside" world, this one is perhaps the most striking. Literacy, after all, is more than a technical skill: it makes competence possible in a broad variety of tasks; it promotes skepticism about received ideas. That is why it is used today as one of the primary indices of modernization in the developing nations.[5]

A second distinctive characteristic of the world in which women lived was that they rarely, if ever, were challenged to make political decisions. Unless they were Quakers or members of one of the rare Baptist groups that permitted older women to vote in church affairs, women never had *any* experience in voting or in the lobbying and discussion that go with it. The early revolutionary crises found most women (and a substantial minority of men) living lives of local isolation, political apathy, and rudimentary literacy. For the purposes of argument, it is useful to think of women as forming a traditional, underdeveloped nation within a larger, politically more sophisticated one.

The task of revolutionary activists and pamphleteers was to challenge Americans to change their habitual obedience to elites and to England, to emerge from a world of tradition and custom, and to behave as a serious political opposition. This task may well have been made easier because it was preceded by the sensitizing experience of the Great Awakening, which had pulled many men out of their private lives and their traditional deferential patterns of behavior, forced them to look skeptically and critically at a secular government that denied their religious demands, and led them to extend this skepticism to other aspects of governmental behavior. The prerevolutionary crises continued this political education.

But since the days of Anne Hutchinson, no secular group or institution had consistently sought to articulate the impact of imperial policy on the daily options of women. There were, of course, many individual exceptions: the crowds of women that fought the establishment of smallpox-inoculation centers too close to their homes, the women who had accompanied Braddock's troops as cooks and nurses, the women merchants and traders in each major port city, whose advertisements were to be seen in virtually every colonial newspaper, and whose most famous cooperative expression was the famous "petition" of New York's "she-Merchants."

For the most part, revolutionary activists and pamphleteers addressed themselves to men. It was men who passed resolutions in town meetings, and it was men who refused to try legal cases with stamped writs. But once economic boycott became a major mode of resistance to England, it became obvious that women would also have to be pulled out of the privacy of the traditional woman's domain and propelled into the public world and into making political decisions. If consumption codes were to be effective, women would have to participate in them; without their support, wrote Christopher Gadsden of South Carolina in 1769, " 'tis impossible to succeed." If women were to participate, they would have to be persuaded that their choices in the marketplace had real political effect. The politicization of women began with efforts to persuade them to run their homes in an "american" way; politics intruded on the woman's domain.

> Where is that hard hearted mother or wife to be found, [Gadsden challenged, who] when properly warned, that every farthing she lays out, even *unavoidably* and *necessarily*, for herself and family, in *European* goods, tends only to encrease a power, that is, at that very time, distressing herself, her family, her dearest friends and relations . . . and doing all it can to reduce them to the lowest infamy and disgrace. I say, where is that

woman to be found (I am persuaded not in *Carolina*) who, when informed of this by her husband, that will not . . . be . . . much grieved and distressed to find herself obliged, upon any occasion, to buy any the least article of British manufacture.[6]

The first stage in raised political consciousness would be to wear homespun, or *old* clothes of British cloth. But the latter was a fine distinction; Gadsden urged women to put off wearing even old British clothes lest they set a bad example. Women were being, in effect, asked to police themselves.

If purchasing was politicized, so was manufacture. In Newport, Rhode Island, Congregational minister Ezra Stiles played host to "ninety-two daughters of Liberty" who brought seventy spinning wheels at the break of day to his house and "spun and reeled, respiting and assisting one another" until 170 skeins were done.[7] Ordinary behavior suddenly became charged with political significance; political decisions might be ascribed where none was intended; and even those who wished to remain passive might find themselves accused of aligning themselves one way or another. If patriots wore homespun, could one wear an old silk dress? If "daughters of Liberty" brought their wheels to a communal spinning bee at the church, what did it mean to stay home? It might mean that ninety wheels whirring at once induced a headache. But it was also a way of identifying those with loyalist leanings.

The sharpest of these challenges came in the form of the tea boycott. Like the grape or lettuce boycotts of recent years, the tea boycott provided a relatively low-key way of identifying oneself with the patriot effect; it was easy to refrain from drinking tea. If one wished, one could be articulate about it, like the landlady with whom John Adams lodged briefly and who lectured him on the need to drink coffee, or the nine-year-old Susan Boudinot, daughter of a New Jersey patriot, who was taken to visit the Tory Governor, William Franklin. When she was offered a cup of tea she curtsied, raised it to her lips, and tossed the contents out the window. Doggerel verse appeared in newspapers:

> No more shall my teapot so generous be
> In filling the cups with the pernicious tea,
> For I'll fill it with water and drink out the same,
> Before I'll lose LIBERTY that dearest name,
> Because I am taught (and believe it is fact)
>   That our ruin is aimed at in the late act,
> Of imposing a duty on all foreign Teas,
> Which detestable stuff we can quit when we please.[8]

Occasionally the tea boycott became sharp enough to prompt a petition circulated and signed only by women. In the 1830s, women's petitions would be a familiar device, widely circulated by female antislavery societies. But they were, so far as I can tell, virtually unknown before the 1770s. For many women, signing such a petition was surely their first political act. The women's proclamation of Edenton, North Carolina, reads:

As we cannot be indifferent on any occasion that appears nearly to affect the peace and happiness of our country, and as it has been thought necessary, for the public good, to enter into several particular resolves, by meeting of members deputed from the whole Province, it is a duty which we owe, not only to our near and dear connections, who have concurred in them, but to ourselves, who are essentially interested in their welfare, to do everything as far as lies in our power, to testify our sincere adherence to the same; and we do therefore accordingly subscribe this paper, as a witness of our fixed intention and solemn determination to do so.

The dismay with which this sober and straightforward petition was received suggests its novelty. Arthur Iredell, who was living in England, wrote to his North Carolina relatives: "Is there a Female Congress at Edenton too? I hope not, for we Englishmen are afraid of the Male Congress, but if the Ladies, who have ever, since the Amazonian era, been esteemed the formidable Enemies, if they, I say, should attack us, the most fatal consequences is to be dreaded."[9]

The prewar boycotts initiated the politicization of the household economy and marked the beginning of the use of a political language that explicitly included women and offered them a mode by which they might make political choices. The politicization of the household economy continued and intensified during the war. The disruption of the British trade meant that consumption codes became self-enforcing; nonconsumption depended on national policy rather than on individual choice, and the burden on individuals diminished. But other demands were addressed to women and to housekeepers. They were asked to spin thread for cloth manufacturers; a good spinner could produce perhaps two-and-a-half pounds a day consistently. Sometimes the appeal to them was patriotic, sometimes commercial, sometimes quasi-religious, sometimes all three—as in a Philadelphia advertisement which, begging women to spin, emphasized that the "distinguishing characteristic of an excellent woman" was that she "seeketh wool and flax and worketh willingly with her hands. She layeth her hands to the spindle, and her hand holdeth the distaff." She ought to be strengthened by the sense that she was part of a long line of women stretching back to antiquity: "In this time of public distress, you have now, each of you, an opportunity not only to help to sustain your families, but likewise to cast your mite into the treasury of the public good."[10]

Women saved rags for papermaking and for bandages and collected the family urine for saltpeter.[11] And they undertook to police local merchants who hoarded scarce commodities. In May 1777, for example, a series of attacks was made on the Poughkeepsie, New York, home of Peter Mesier, a reputed loyalist who, it was rumored, was hoarding tea. His wife offered to sell it at four dollars a pound, but the twenty-two women, accompanied by two Continental soldiers, who demanded entry to her home, said they "would have it at their own Price, & brought a Hammer & Scales, & proceeded to weigh as much as they chose to take, untill they had taken near One hundred weight . . . for which they left about Seventeen Pounds in Money." The next day, when Peter Mesier was at home, one of the soldiers and fifteen women returned.

> . . . an Elderly woman desired the Dep^t [that is, Mesier] to weigh her a half pound, & she would pay him, then the Dep^t desired her to give him the money & she should have the Tea, which she refused, upon which the Dep^t offer'd to throw the Tea out of the Window, whereupon the said Elderly Woman Siezed the Dep^t by the hand, upon which . . . Rouse [the soldier] came in & Siezed the Dep^t by the Throat, & push'd him down, and offerd to strike him on the head with his Broad Sword.

Two days later the mob was back, this time augmented by some men; the other men "and a number of Women to the amount of bout 20" broke in without a warrant and searched the house, "Drew his Liquors & Drank of them, broke open every Cask in the Cellar and the case of his Clock. . . . After they had searched the house, they went into the yard and beat . . . [Mesier's] servants, threw Stones at & otherwise greatly abused him."[12] The following July, Abigail Adams reported that "a Number of Females, some say a hundred, some say more assembled with a cart and trucks, marched down to the Ware House" of an "eminent, wealthy, stingy Merchant" who was rumored to be hoarding coffee. When he refused to deliver the keys, "one of them seazd him by his Neck and tossd him into the cart . . . he delivered the keys . . . they . . . opend the Warehouse, Hoisted out the Coffee themselves, put it into trucks and drove off. . . . A large concourse of Men stood amazd silent Spectators."[13] Of course, women had been participants in crowds before the Revolution; the point is not to identify the "first" women's mob. It is to suggest that the war gave more obvious and more frequent opportunity for the aggressive enforcement of consumption codes, and for the display of aggressive political behavior by women. One measure of the difference in desperation between the French and American revolutions is that in France the comparable women's riots were more frequent and the issue was bread, not luxuries such as coffee or tea.

In wartime, women, like the majority of men, were civilians. Because the Revolution was a civil war, each adult had to assume a political identity and maintain it with sufficient clarity to satisfy the authorities who controlled the area in which he or she lived. Women had the advantage; because they were not being recruited into the conflicting armies, their political choices were less carefully scrutinized than those of men; they could even shift back and forth with some ease.

Patriots continually complained that women were moving into areas occupied by the British, bringing property and information behind enemy lines. "I have good reason to suspect," George Washington wrote, "that many persons (Women particularly) who obtain leave from the Executive Council of Pennsylvania to go and come to and from New York under the pretence of visiting their Friends, have, in fact, no other Business but that of bringing out Goods to trade with." Henry Livingston complained that the British "were informed of every thing that passed among us . . . and that Women were the most proper persons for that purpose."[14]

Women who were intercepted in circulating British proclamations or passing information about American troops were numerically few, but they were threatening enough to be taken seriously. In 1780, for example, some thirty-two women were brought to the attention of the Albany, New York, Commission for Detecting and Defeating Conspiracies, accused of being spies or sympathizers, along with well over four hundred men. Among the women were those who gave sanctuary in their homes to loyalists and to British soldiers; Rachael Ferguson was confined to jail in Albany "for harbouring and entertaining a Number of Tories" en route from Canada. She was released on the very high bail of £800. Lidia Currey was similarly jailed for "assisting in concealing and harbouring Persons from the Enemy." A Mrs. Henderson of Dutchess County, New York, smuggled a message from a husband who was fighting with the British to a wife who remained at home and publicly "expressed herself much in favor of the Superiority and Success of the British Arms and observed that She had no doubt but that finally they would subdue this Country and therefore that it would be best for all Persons to come in and submit."[15]

Wives of Tories, as a group, were regarded with hostility, especially if their husbands had actually joined the British. In patriot areas, their homes might be robbed and plundered with relative impunity. After the fall of Ticonderoga, insecurity ran especially high on the New York frontier, and it was suspected that Tories were hiding out in the woods, secretly provided with supplies by their wives, and readying themselves to assist in the expected attack on Fort Schuyler. "The Women of those Enemies is still living among us," wrote the chairman of the Tryon County Committee of Safety to Governor George Clinton, "some behave very rudely at present, and have proved very active to support and spirit up the opposite Cause."

The women saw their position rather differently. In a rare joint petition, which most signed with their marks, ten women complained that "being left by our Husbands and our Effects sold," they were "reduced to the greatest distress imaginable." They "humbly" asked that they be provided for, or that they be permitted to join their husbands, and eventually they got their request. In the summer of 1777, the Tryon Committee of Safety rounded up eleven women and placed them under house arrest; in October it gave them seven days notice to leave.[16]

Suspicion of Tory wives was not confined to Tryon county. The New York State Commissioners for Detecting and Defeating Conspiracies wrote to Governor George Clinton:

> From the frequent complaints which are exhibited to this Board that the wives of such disaffected Persons who are gone over to the Enemy daily harbour Persons who through fear of being punished for their Crimes against the State conceal themselves & their holding Correspondance with their Husbands it is conceived necessary that some mode should be adopted to prevent this evil.

They begged the governor to see to it that women whose husbands had joined the enemy were sent to the enemy themselves. By the summer of 1780, New York State had passed "An Act for the Removal of the Families of Persons who have joined the Enemy," justifying the removal on the basis of the "many and great Mischiefs" which "arise, by permitting the Families of Persons who have joined the Enemy, to remain at their respective Habitations, inasmuch as such Persons frequently come out in a private Manner, to gain Intelligence and commit Robberies, Thefts and Murders . . . and are concealed and comforted by their respective Families." It required the justices of the peace to give twenty days notice to the wives of persons who were with the enemy "that they depart this State . . . or repair to such parts of it as are within the power of the Enemy; and at their Discretion to take with them all or any of their Children, not above the Age of twelve Years."[17] When patriots reoccupied Philadelphia in 1779, they also assumed that wives' political loyalties were the same as their husbands', and that the wives had simply remained behind either to protect their property or to function as a fifth column should opportunity arise; in Philadelphia, too, wives of Tories were summarily expelled in 1780.

There was little room in the patriot position for the admission that women might make political choices that were distinct from—and at odds with—those of their husbands. The Albany Commission did permit one Tory wife to remain after the passage of the expulsion law on the grounds that "notwithstanding the Political Sentiments of her husband . . . Jane Moffit has always been esteemed a Friend to the American Cause." But in other cases, the woman's harmlessness and her willingness to promise that she would not be a burden on the public treasury were the major considerations. Tories' wives who petitioned to be allowed to stay brought certificates signed by their patriot neighbors to the effect that they had "behaved themselves in an unexceptionable Manner," and that permitting them to remain would not "be detrimental to the Freedom and independence of this and the United States."[18]

These pleas may not often have represented clearly political choices. The desire to remain in one's own home and in control of one's own property was of course very strong; few would choose to wander in the crowds of women who followed the British troops. Whether the woman who went behind the British lines would find the man she sought was unpredictable. But surely some women, like Jane Moffit, had political allegiances that differed from those of their husbands. If they did, they would find it difficult to persuade Committees of Safety to respect these distinctions. Robert Morris's wife, Mary, watched the expulsion of women from Philadelphia with misgivings:

. . . my feelings [are] . . . wounded for the sufferings of a Number of my Sex in this State, who are compeld to leave it, by that Cruell Edict of our Counsel: a resolve which Oblidges all the women whose Husbands are with the enemy, and Children whose parents are there, to repair to *them* Immediately; a determination like this which admits of no Exception; is unjust, and cruell . . . there is many whose conduct has not Merited it, tho there is others that have, yet why not discriminate between the Innocent and guilty. . . . Mrs. Furgerson is determined not to go, She says they may take her life, but shall never banish her from Her Country.
. . . there are others [who are] . . . rendered happier by the banishment of a worthless Husband and who by honest industry gains a Subsistence for themselves and Children to be torn from it to perish.[19]

The emergencies of the war pulled women into political relationships and forced them to make political choices. Patriot forces had employment to offer and new roles to suggest to sympathetic women who were willing to emerge, if only to a modest extent, from their traditional domain. Women represented a small proportion of those who came before Committees of Safety to testify against Tories, but that even these few women were taking the initiative by bringing their traditional private judgments of male political behavior into public tribunals testified to the intensity of wartime politics.[20] Occasionally, Committees of Safety had employment for "discreet Women, of known attachment to the American Cause" to search suspected women smugglers and Tories for illegal papers.[21]

The American army offered political uses for traditional domestic skills. Occasional military heroines such as Margaret Corbin represented the tip of an iceberg; they were among the thousands of dependents who drifted after the troops: wives and children who had no means of support when their husbands and fathers were pressed into service, and who followed after, caring for their own men, earning their subsistence by cooking and washing for troops in an era when the offices of Quartermaster and Commissary were run informally and inadequately.

The most common official position the American forces offered women was as nurse—an obvious extension of a domestic skill. Occasionally they could earn premium pay, but it is important to recognize that, two generations before Florence Nightingale and Clara Barton, the services offered by military nurses were largely custodial. Although Washington emphasized that if nurses were not found, "we are under the necessity of substituting in their place a number of men from the respective Regiments, [who are then] entirely lost in the proper line of their duty," most of the skilled tasks of nursing were throughout the war performed by male surgeon's mates. The official duties left to the nurse were closer to those of the modern orderly; only in the absence of the mates did nurses administer medicines. The formal job description suggests the menial role of the nurses, and, in its expression of fears that the nurses will be drunk or will steal the personal effects of the dead, their low status in the hospital staff:

> The NURSES, in the absence of the Mates, administer the medicine and diet prescribed for the sick accordingly to order; they obey all orders they receive from the Matron; not only to be attentive to the cleanliness of the wards and patients, but to keep themselves clean; they are never to be disguised with liquor [a stricture which is not placed on the males]; they are to see that the close-stools or pots are emptied as soon as possible after they are used, into a necessary house . . . they are to see that every patient, upon his admission into the Hospital is immediately washed with warm water, and that his face and hands are washed and head combed every morning . . . that their wards are swept over every morning or oftener if necessary and sprinkled with vinegar three or four times a day; nor are they ever to be absent without leave from the Physicians, Surgeons or Matron; they are to deliver the effects immediately of such soldiers as die in Hospital to the Ward-Master, who is to be accountable for the same; all attempt to steal from, conceal the effects of, or otherwise defraud the patients . . . will be severely punished.[22]

The pay scale that Congress established in 1777 for the hospital staffs also suggests the low status ascribed to women's services and the weakness of their bargaining position. Early in the war, Washington had begged for premium pay for nurses, and William Shippen had reported that, desperate for nurses for the hospital at Perth Amboy, New Jersey, he had "Been obliged to deviate from the regulation of the honorable Congress and allow them 10/per week instead of 3/9—the most ordinary woman here is able to earn much more, as there are so few women and so many men to work for . . . the sick must suffer much unless well nursed and kept clean." But as the hospital system was regularized, matrons and nurses were paid less well than stablehands. At a time when senior surgeons received four dollars per day and were entitled to six rations of food, matrons got only half a dollar, and nurses' pay ranged in fact from twenty-four cents to ninety cents and one ration each per day. Wartime inflation would drive up the salaries of physicians and surgeon's mates, but at the end of the war, when surgeon's mates got fifty dollars a month, a matron's salary remained at fifty cents a day.[23]

Had hospitals been staffed up to their full authorized strength, they would have provided employment for hundreds of women. The general plan for a coordinated military hospital establishment, which Shippen and Dr. John Cochran drafted and which was passed by Congress in April 1777, provided that one matron be hired for every hundred sick or wounded; she "shall take care that the provisions are properly prepared; that the wards, beds, and utensils be kept in neat order, and that the most exact oeconomy be observed in her department." Nurses were to be hired in a ratio of one to every ten sick or wounded, who were to be under the direction of the matrons.[24] (The plan for establishing military hospitals [27 February 1777] provides one nurse to every fifteen sick and wounded.)

Any coherence in this hospital system remained largely wishful thinking. Hospitals were usually dirty; the sick were not sufficiently separated from the wounded, who thereupon caught fevers and diseases. Convalescents wandered off the premises; the drunken disorder of convalescing men gave hospitals a bad reputation. And there never were enough staff. Lachlan McIntosh's report for the General Hospitals in the Pennsylvania area in 1778 claimed 571 men hospitalized and another 615 who had been admitted but had died or deserted in the course of the year. At the authorized strength, that would have meant a staff of seventy-nine nurses and ten matrons. But reports of personnel do not indicate that hospital staffs ever approached authorized levels. There was only one matron and one nurse to care for 133 patients at William Shippen's hospital in Philadelphia in 1779; four nurses cared for over one hundred sick at the general hospital in Hillsborough, North Carolina. When a tally of hospital staff was prepared at the end of the war, it listed only seven matrons and thirty nurses divided among seven hospitals.[25]

One of the readiest ways for women to earn money had long been to run a boarding house. It had the advantage of making use of the form of capital that the widow or spinster was most likely to control and requiring relatively slight domestic readjustment: one continued to live where one always had lived. It might imply a lowering of status, but perhaps not so radically as that implied by working for wages. It had the advantage of keeping the woman self-employed, while she did the work—housekeeping—which was traditional for women to do. There is no question that self-supporting women were frequently found to be landladies.[26]

And as landladies they were affected by the war. The influx of delegates to the Continental Congress meant a large number of respectable
boarders for the boardinghouse keepers of Philadelphia. Sometimes
they were paid for their services directly from the national treasury or
by local Committees of Safety, which rented rooms to house officers
and soldiers, employed them to cook meals for the militia, and com-
mandeered supplies from their cellars. The double purposes of the
medieval hotel—care for the sick as well as care for the traveler—had
not yet fully disintegrated. Sick and wounded might be sent to private
lodgings, and women were paid—on what appears to be a free-lance
basis—for their care.[27]

Jails were also scarce, and both British and Americans were likely to
place prisoners, especially officers, under loose house arrest. Thus,
Catherine Heydshaw was paid £114 "for lodging, firing, candles and
for dieting Hessian officers and soldiers" for a month in 1777, and Rachel Stille sent accounts for well over £300 to the Continental Congress
for boarding British officers who were prisoners. American officers
captured by the British were quartered with individuals on Long Island; when the war was over, those who had boarded the prisoners
refused to return them until the costs of their lodging had been paid.
The accounts of Abram Skinner, Commissary General of Prisoners,
report some £800 paid to twelve women who had boarded American
officers (perhaps five per cent of the total).[28]

Most of these civilian women who worked—sometimes voluntarily,
sometimes on a free-lance basis—for the American cause did so unofficially. It is difficult to retrieve them, except anecdotally. Perhaps one
of them, for whom the future Justice John Marshall and other officers
of the Virginia Continental Line organized a subscription, is as appropriate an epitome as we can find. The officers thanked

Mrs. Hay & her Daughter for their great attention and Tenderness to our Brother Officers, Prisoners in the City of Philadelphia . . . they have come out at different times
purely to serve the distressed at the risque of their Lives, & have actually assisted some
officers in making their escape, besides nursing the sick & takeing particular care of the
affects of the Deceased. Mrs Hay is a poor Widow, and any Little matter that Gentlemen
chuse to contribute, can't fail of being acceptable & will be considered as a greatfull
acknowledgement on their part for the Voluntary & Benevolent part she has acted.[29]

That women served the patriot war effort is clear. What these wom-
en thought of their actions and of the politics of the war is not. It has
come to be a commonplace assumption that the experience of commitment to the national military forces during the war was what we
would now call a "bonding experience" for many future political leaders, who came in the course of the war to widen their allegiance from
their colony to the nation, and who would go on to important political

roles in the early republic. It is by no means clear that shared hospital service performed this politicizing function for the women who were part of it. Moreover, most of the women who served the patriot's military purposes did not do so in an institutional context; as cooks, washerwomen, laundresses, private nurses, and renters of houses or of rooms they served as individuals, sometimes along with their husbands and children. They did not change their domestic identity (although they put it to a broader service); they did not seriously challenge the traditional definition of the women's domestic domain.

In a culture that refused women the technical machinery of political expression, there remained available a most archaic mode of political behavior. With the biblical Esther as role model and a strong English constitutional tradition for justification, women's relationship to political enterprise was most likely to be formulated as a petition. The petitioner may be a prepolitical being. The formulation of a petition begins in the acknowledgment of subordination; by definition the petitioner poses no threat. The rhetoric of humility is a necessary part of the petition as an art form; it may or may not be felt in fact. Occasionally the restiveness of the petitioner peeps out from the smothering rhetoric, and the petition approaches the broadside.

Women petitioned revolutionary governments and local Committees of Safety for permission to cross enemy lines—to join husbands or other family members, to reach ports from which they might embark for Europe, to claim property left behind. These petitions were often an irritant. The Committees of Safety which handled them often had far more substantive—sometimes desperate—concerns than the movements of individual civilians. But the Committees could not afford to ignore these petitions. If a petition was granted, they were at best contributing to the improvement of enemy morale by facilitating the reunion of families; at worst they might unwittingly be permitting the passage of a spy or a smuggler. If a petition was denied, they risked burdening their own charitable facilities with women and children who could not support themselves, and they missed an opportunity to rid themselves of a possible fifth column. As we have seen, there were many women who did not wish to leave and who were expelled by their neighbors. But if a woman had little or no property to protect *and* knew where her husband was, she might be better off, both psychologically and financially, with him.

Most petitions were from widows who had been left destitute. These were among the saddest artifacts left from the war. The real needs of the women—as well as the constraints of the rhetorical form—ensured that petitions would emphasize economic necessity, weakness, and despair. But many also testified to a strong belief that they had made real sacrifices to the state, and that the political system owed them something in return.

"To the Honorable Congress I, Rachel do make this Complaint," wrote Rachel Wells of Bordentown, New Jersey. "Who am a Widow far advanced in years and Dearly have occasion of ye Interest for that Cash I Lent the States . . . I was a sitisen in ye jearsy when I Lent ye Stats a considerable Sun of Meoney and had I justice don me it mite be suficant to suporte me in ye Countrey." She had temporarily moved away from Bordentown after her widowhood "to Phila to try to get a Living as I could Doe Nothing in Burdentown in any way"; but that move had apparently put her title to her bonds in jeopardy. "Now gentlemen in this Liberty. had it bin advertised that he or she that moved out of the state should Loose his or her Interest you mite have sum plea against me. But I . . . Suspected no trick I have Don as much to Carrey on the war as maney that Sett Now at ye helm of government."[30]

Elizabeth Gaudin's husband had died in Boston, "defending the rights of America," but his prize money had never been paid. "I am sorry to say I think myself ill-used," Elizabeth Gaudin wrote. "Shall a widow that Lost her Husband suffer and want[?]" Lydia Wallingford's husband died on the Continental ship *Ranger*, "exerting himself in the Glorious Cause of Freedom"; she petitioned for a widow's pension. And there was Ann Ledyard, whose husband died on the eve of Yorktown, defending Fort Griswold on the Connecticut coast; while everyone else in the nation was cheering, she "with her neighbors and Companions in misery had alone to lament Husbands and fathers . . . sacrificed."[31]

The litany of women's petitions fell on unresponsive ears. The only military group with any lobbying power to speak of was the Continental Line, and, when pensions were ultimately provided, they went only to the widows of Continental officers. Not until 1832, that is, fifty years after the close of the fighting, were the widows of enlisted men included in the pension legislation. The most obvious legislation benefiting women that the revolutionary generation might have provided would have granted pensions to war widows; that it had the lowest of priorities suggests one result of the exclusion of women from the political system.

The best-known organized political action by American women is the campaign of the patriot women of Philadelphia to collect funds for Washington's troops. Organized and led by Esther deBerdt Reed (in her role as wife of the president of Pennsylvania) and Benjamin Franklin's daughter, Sarah Franklin Bache, the leadership derived much of its publicity from the fact that they included "the best ladies" of the patriot side. "Instead of waiting for the Donations being sent the ladys of each Ward go from dore to dore and collect them I am one of those,

Honoured with this business. Yesterday we began our Tour of duty and had the Satisfaction of being very Successfull," wrote Mary Morris. Going door to door implied confrontation: "Of all absurdities," the loyalist Anna Rawle wrote to Rebecca Rawle Shoemaker, "the ladies going about for money exceeded everything; they were so extremely importunate that people were obliged to give them something to get rid of them."[32]

By 4 July 1779, Esther Reed was writing to George Washington that "the subscription set on foot by the ladies of this City for the use of the soldiery" had resulted in some 300,000 paper dollars. When Washington suggested that it be directly deposited in the Bank of the United States, and in that way be united "with the gentlemen," she replied coolly that it had *not* been the women's intention to give the soldiers "an article to which they are entitled from the public," but rather some special item that it would be obvious had come from an unusual source. The women wished to change the paper into hard specie and to give each soldier two dollars "to be entirely at his own disposal." Washington turned that down; "a tast of hard money may be productive of much discontent, as *we* have none but depreciated paper for their pay." In the end, the money was used to buy linen, and the linen to make shirts.

When Esther Reed died in the fall of 1780, the organization was taken over by Benjamin Franklin's daughter, Sarah Franklin Bache. In December, Sarah Bache sent Washington 2,200 shirts, with the wish that they "be worn with as much pleasure as they were made." If the women did not get their wish to provide each soldier with hard cash, they had at least managed to give them something that was identifiably from the ladies of Philadelphia. The women had not merged their money into the common fund. The subscription lists remain in the Reed family papers: they are long and detailed, dividing Philadelphia into districts, assigning districts to committees, and tallying all contributions, from the six thousand dollars in paper money of the Countess de Luzerne to the "Miss Somebody" who gave Mrs. Rush fourteen paper dollars.[33]

There has always been a tendency to overplay this project by those seeking to reconstruct the women's history of the Revolution. Benjamin Rush, whose wife was an enthusiastic participant in it, wrote "The women of American have at last become principals in the glorious American controversy." But they were not principals, of course; they were fund raisers, and only for a brief time and in a single city. Nor were they principals in the controversy to the extent that being a principal implies emergence from the women's private domain. They were not above teasing and flirting to get contributions, reminding those who were unenthusiastic that it was rude to refuse anything to pretty women.

The postwar years saw the initiation of a score of these women's societies, their constitutions roughly similar to the Philadelphia one of 1780, and their charity now directed at widows and orphan girls. There was the Female Association of Philadelphia for the Relief of Women and Children in Reduced Circumstance, the Newark Female Charitable Society, and the Boston Female Asylum. They, too, had their boards of manageresses and their treasuresses, and they often collected substantial sums of money. Because of the danger that property held by married women would be swallowed up into their husband's estates, the treasurers of these societies were often required to be single women—spinsters or widows. Separate women's charitable and reform organizations began as a wartime response to a wartime challenge. They became a common mode among abolitionists and nineteenth-century reformers. They represented, I think, a significant stage in women's political education.

These organizations provided a milieu for female collective behavior. Many were primarily religious in tone and closely associated with churches (it was common, for example, for the major fund-raising effort of the early ones to be an annual sermon by a sympathetic minister, at which the beneficiaries of the organization's charity would be lined up in the front pews as a demonstration of the worthiness of their cause); and some were primarily social (such as the Ladies Stocking Society of New York, which knitted stockings for soldiers in the War of 1812 and raised perhaps six hundred dollars for their uniforms, but did this in the flirting context of upper-class sociability), but in their own limited ways they could not help but enlarge women's political horizons. Within a generation, the woman who wished to communicate with government had developed a variant of the individual petition. The women's bazaars of the abolitionist campaign were a species of collective action hinted at by Esther Reed's fund raising, and the women's abolitionist petitions, which flooded Congress in the 1830s and forced the confrontation of the slavery issue, were the lineal descendants of Esther Reed's broadside.

"The Sentiments of American Women," circulated by women, embodied a justification for women's intrusion into politics that would become the standard model throughout the years of the early republic. They made the point that they were "born for liberty, disdaining to bear the irons of a tyrannic Government," and claimed that "if the weakness of our Constitution, if opinion and manners did not forbid us to march to glory by the same paths as the men," they would be found at least equal, and perhaps stronger, in their convictions and loyalty to the republic.

They pointed to a list of what we might call historical role models—examples of politically active women: Deborah, Judith, Esther.

> Rome saved from the fury of a victorious enemy by the efforts of Volumnia, . . . famous sieges where the Women have been seen . . . building new walls, digging trenches . . . Sovereigns . . . who have held with so much splendour the scepter of the greatest States . . . the Elizabeths, the Maries, the Catherines, who have extended the empire of liberty. . . . It was the Maid of Orleans who drove from the kingdom of France the ancestors of those same British, whose odious yoke we have just shaken off, and whom it is necessary that we drive from this Continent.

Finally, the place where this political consciousness was to be displayed would be, naturally enough, on their own turf, at home, in the woman's domain. We understand, they said, that if we live in safety, it is because the army protects us:

> The time is arrived to display the same sentiments which animated us at the beginning of the Revolution, when we renounced the use of teas, . . . we placed former necessaries in the rank of superfluities, when our liberty was interested; when our republican and laborious hands spun the flax, prepared the linen entended for the use of our soldiers; when [as] exiles and fugitives we supported with courage all the evils which are the concommitents of war.[34]

I think it needs to be said that, for all its limits, this is a novel formulation. Western political theory had provided no context in which women might comfortably think of themselves as political beings. Except for Condorcet—who had explicitly stated that republics were imperfect until they took account of the political claims of half of their people—the major theorists of the Enlightenment, the Whig Commonwealth, and the Republican Revolution had not explored what it might mean to include women as part of the people. The "man" of Enlightenment theory was literal, not generic. The only reference to women in *The Federalist Papers* is to the dangers that the private intrigues of courtesans and mistresses pose to the safety of the state. The image of the political women provided by the Philadelphia broadside of 1780, then, represents the beginning of the invention of a political role for women, one that sought to integrate the woman's traditional domain into the political world.[35]

This integration of domestic and political roles remained deep into the twentieth century the most widely accepted (although certainly not the most deeply radical) prerequisite for an ideology of women's political participation. It would continue to be used successfully by reformers; suffragists of the Progressive era, for example, found that their welcome was greatest when they stressed the obligations of women to ensure honesty in politics, efficient urban sanitation, pure food and drug laws—all as extensions of their responsibilities as mothers. It is possible to view the contemporary opposition to the equal-rights amendment as a continuing symptom of the incomplete integration of the political and domestic domains. A few women of the revolutionary generation began, haltingly, to express an ideology which justified that integration, but not fast enough to enjoy its benefits themselves or to establish securely a respect for women's patriotism and a faith in the reliability of their political commitment.

The shape of American women's patriotism has been thought to be different from men's precisely because it has had to be conditioned on the maintenance of the domestic world while fighting for political objectives. This integration of the woman's domain into politics is not fully accomplished, even yet. But the notion that a "Republican Mother" was not necessarily an oxymoron began to be articulated in the course of the Revolution, and a political ideology that republican women would find viable was—however haltingly—articulated.

NOTES

1 Abigail Adams to John Adams, 17 June 1782, *Adams Family Correspondence* (hereafter cited as *AFC*) (Cambridge, Mass., 1973), vol. 4, p. 328.
2 Henry Home, Lord Kames, *Sketches of the History of Man* (Edinburgh, 1778), vol. 2, pp. 85, 97.
3 Margaret Livingston [to Catherine Livingston?] 20 October 1776, Ridley Papers, Massachusetts Historical Society.
4 K. A. Lockridge, *Literacy in Colonial New England: An Enquiry into the Social Context of Literacy in the Early Modern West* (New York, 1974), pp. 38-44, passim; Abigail Adams to John Adams, 30 June 1778, *AFC*, vol. 3, p. 52; *Royal American Magazine*, January 1774.
5 See K. W. Deutsch, "Social Mobilization and Political Development," *American Political Science Review* 55 (1961): 493-514; J. Goody, ed., *Literacy in Traditional Societies* (Cambridge, 1968).
6 "To the Planters, Mechanics, and Freeholders of the Province of South Carolina, No Ways Concerned in the Importation of British Manufactures," 22 June 1769, in R. Walsh, ed., *The Writings of Christopher Gadsden* (Columbia, S.C., 1966), pp. 83-84.
7 *The Literary Diary of Ezra Stiles, DD., LL.D.,* ed. F. B. Dexter (New York, 1901), vol. 1, p. 59.
8 Verse reprinted in *American Heritage Cookbook* (New York, 1964), p. 145.
9 Arthur Iredell to James Iredell, 31 January 1775, in D. Higginbotham, ed., *The Papers of James Iredell* (Raleigh, 1976), vol. 1, pp. 282-86.
10 "To the Spinners in this City and County," August 1775, reprinted in W. Duane, ed., *Passages from the Remembrancer of Christopher Marshall* (hereafter cited as *Remembrancer*) (Philadelphia, 1839), p. 40.

11 *Archives of the State of New Jersey,* 2nd ser. (Trenton, 1906), vol. 3, p. 34; *Remembrancer,* p. 35n.; *Archives of Maryland* (Baltimore, 1892), vol. 12, pp. 427-28, *Minutes of the Provincial Council of Pennsylvania,* vol. 10, p. 633.

12 *Minutes of the Committee and of the First Commission for Detecting and Defeating Conspiracies in the State of New York* (New York Historical Society, 1924-25), vol. 1, pp. 301-03 (hereafter cited as *NYHS*).

13 Abigail Adams to John Adams, 31 July 1777, *AFC,* vol. 2, p. 295.

14 George Washington to Joseph Reed, 12 February 1779, *Papers of the Continental Congress* (hereafter cited as *PCC*) National Archives, M 247, roll 33, item 69, vol. 2, p. 129; Testimony of Henry G. Livingston, 5 February 1777, *NYHS,* vol. 1, p. 120. For fears that spies were hiding in women's clothes, see V. H. Paltsits, ed., *Minutes of the Commissioners for Detecting and Defeating Conspiracies in the State of New York* (New York, 1919), vol. 2, p. 563 (hereafter cited as Paltsits). See also *New Jersey Archives,* 2nd ser., vol. 1, p. 531.

15 Paltsits, vol. 2, pp. 445-46; *NYHS,* vol. 1, pp. 67-68. For interception of copies of Howe's *Proclamation* which had been sent to two women, see *NYHS,* vol. 1, pp. 64-65. See also Paltsits, vol. 1, p. 199; vol. 2, p. 751.

16 Peter S. Deygart to George Clinton, 25 August 1777; "Petition of Sundry women wives of tories for relief," n.d., Tryon County Committee of Safety Papers, New York Historical Society. See also Paltsits, vol. 2, p. 560.

17 Paltsits, vol. 1, p. 327; vol. 2, pp. 794-96, 799.

18 Jane Moffit's Petition is reported in Paltsits, vol. 2, pp. 619-20; for other petitions see vol. 2, pp. 619-20; 523, 528, 540, 541.

19 Mary Morris to Catherine Livingston, 10 June [1780], Ridley Papers, Massachusetts Historical Society.

20 Examples of women who testify against Tories are numerous; some can conveniently be found in *NYHS,* vol. 1, pp. 106, 264-65; Tryon County Committee of Safety Papers, February and March 1778, *NYHS;* and Paltsits, vol. 2, p. 508; vol. 1, p. 354; vol. 2, pp. 517, 519, 548; vol. 2, p. 475; vol. 1, pp. 290-94; vol. 2, p. 534; vol. 2, pp. 615, 717.

21 See *NYHS,* vol. 1, p. 103.

22 "Rules and Directions for the Better Regulating the Military Hospital . . .," 6 February 1778, *PCC,* National Archives, M 247, roll 103, p. 567. Matrons' jobs were not primarily medical; matrons were in effect the heads of housekeeping services, receiving supplies, supervising cooks, and seeing to it "that the Nurses do their duty."

23 William Shippen to Congress, 19 September 1776, *PCC,* National Archives, M 247, roll 102, vol. 20, pp. 55-58; ibid., roll 20, item 22, pp. 61-62. There was a little more flexibility in food supplies; women who had young children with them apparently drew more rations. See Revolutionary War Rolls, National Archives, M 246, roll 135, jacket 3, "Return of Officers belonging to the General Hospital Northern Department," 20 March 1780. I am indebted to George Chalou for this reference.

24 "Plan for establishing military hospitals," 27 February 1777, *PCC,* National Archives, M 247, roll 30.

25 "Report of the General Hospitals," 26 April 1778, Revolutionary War Rolls, National Archives, M 246, roll 135, jacket 3. Often the lists of personnel do not include matrons and nurses at all. Surgeon's mates handled the nursing duties, or women may not have been perceived as regular members of the staff. See also *PCC,* M 247, roll 46, vol. 3, p. 395; roll 102, item 78, vol. 20, p. 586; roll 30, item 22, pp. 61-62.

26 See E. A. Dexter, *Career Women of America,* pp. 116–38.

27 *Journals of the Continental Congress* (hereafter cited as *JCC*), vol. 11, p. 801; vol. 4, p. 237, vol. 8, p. 430; vol. 4, p. 294; *Archives of Maryland,* vol. 12, pp. 96, 234, 293, 534.

28 See Paltsits, vol. 2, p. 621; *Archives of Maryland,* vol. 11, passim; *JCC,* vol. 6, p. 877; vol. 4, p. 305; vol. 8, p. 479; ''Account of Debts incurred by sundry American officers during their captivity . . .,'' 5 August 1782, Revolutionary War Rolls, National Archives, M 246, roll 135, jacket 4.

29 Marshall contributed 15 shillings; the total amount collected was £50. See H. Johnson, ed., *The Papers of John Marshall* (Chapel Hill, 1974), vol. 1, pp. 13–14.

30 *PCC,* M 247, roll 56, item 42, vol. 8, p. 354.

31 *PCC,* M 247, roll 54, p. 301.

32 Mary Morris to Catherine Livingston, 10 June [1780?], Ridley Papers, Massachusetts Historical Society; Anna Rawle to Rebecca Rawle Shoemaker, 30 June 1780, *Pennsylvania Magazine of History and Biography,* vol. 35 (1911), p. 398. For a similar effort in Trenton, see *New Jersey Archives,* 2nd ser., vol. 4, pp. 486–88.

33 W. B. Reed, *The Life and Correspondence of Joseph Reed* (Philadelphia, 1847), vol. 2, pp. 264, 265, 270, 429–49.

34 ''The Sentiments of an American Women [*sic*],'' Broadside, Philadelphia, 10 June 1780.

35 L. K. Kerber, ''The Republican Mother: Women and the Enlightenment—An American Perspective,'' *American Quarterly* 28 (1976): 187–205.

REVOLUTIONARY CONSCIOUSNESS IN AMERICA AND EUROPE FROM THE MID-EIGHTEENTH TO THE EARLY NINETEENTH CENTURY AS A METHODOLOGICAL AND HISTORICAL PROBLEM

Jerzy Topolski, University of Poznań

I

The concept of revolutionary consciousness is an indispensable element in any description or explanation of revolutionary processes, but its significance has so far not been properly appreciated in the historical sciences. The consequences of this neglect become obvious when one begins to investigate the huge wave of revolutionary movements that took place in the late eighteenth and early nineteenth centuries — the first revolutions to occur on a scale sufficiently massive to require comprehensive analyses and complex explanations regarding their conceptual framework. Revolutionary consciousness is an essential term for a theory of revolution, particularly for one inspired by Marxism or developed within its framework. With no recourse to a theoretical framework subject to constant verification from empirical data, it is hard to imagine how any progress in the historical investigation of revolutions or of the images and mechanisms underlying the whole historical process can be achieved.

According to Marxist theory, revolutionary consciousness depends upon the existence of a revolutionary class. A class remains revolutionary so long as its consciousness — or more precisely, some aspect of it — shares the revolutionary structure with it. In the *Communist Manifesto* Marx and Engels point out that the first class to play a distinctly revolutionary role in history was the bourgeoisie, since wherever it assumed power, it destroyed feudal relations and "mercilessly" broke "all kinds of feudal knots."[1] It did not do so, however, until it came to power, i.e., until it had shaped its class consciousness to the point where its aims for an action could be clearly formulated. In the first half of the nineteenth century, however, the bourgeoisie lost its revolutionary character, a loss that was pointed out by Marx and Engels in the *Communist Manifesto*. The proletariat then became the "truly revolutionary" class that replaced the bourgeoisie.[2]

The link between revolutionary consciousness and a revolutionary class was not for Marx and Engels simply the possession of revolutionary consciousness by the members of that class. There is no unequivocal ordering. Marx, Engels, and Lenin all stressed the fact that the workers' class consciousness grew out of external circumstances that had been created by the intelligentsia. The same was true to some extent for the forming of the class consciousness of the bourgeoisie. What is essential to the theory of Marxism is the stress laid upon the presence of a definite type of social consciousness in some social group or class. If revolutionary consciousness is to grow, there must be a social class, or sometimes a very complex set of groups, whose interests are reflected and expressed in this type of consciousness. If this reference to social structure is absent, all ideas springing from the human mind either quickly become fiction or else "wait" for the appearance of a social force proclaiming a need for them. This situation of old ideas becoming topical, or antecedents for new ideas found in history, is a common one, and it is typical of the period under investigation. The changes in consciousness are clear symptoms either of transformations in social structure or of the appearance of new social classes and groups.

It follows from the above argument that one should be critical of Bernard Bailyn's claim that the American Revolution "was above all else an ideological, constitutional, and political struggle and not primarily a controversy between social groups undertaken to force changes in the organization of the society or the economy."[3] Although one can view ideology as an element that is to some degree autonomous and "travels" through time, one cannot assume an abstract struggle of political ideas unattached to any social basis. Revolutionary ideas can have a very complex genesis, and they usually do. The idea of revolution can penetrate the consciousness of classes, groups, or individuals from "the outside," but it is nevertheless wrong to speak of a struggle between revolutionary thought and nonrevolutionary or counterrevolutionary thought as being purely an intellectual one. It is hard to imagine a revolution consisting mainly, or solely, of a struggle between ideas. Ideas, consciousness, the spirit of the struggle, and revolutionary traditions are all significant, but they are not the only elements in the revolutionary process. The task is to locate them properly in that process.

If the concept of revolutionary consciousness is not introduced into the historian's store of knowledge, no valid analysis of a number of significant problems is possible. The problems referred to are those encountered by an investigator of the revolutions that took place at the turn of the nineteenth century.

The first of these problems, and one that is not restricted to that time period alone, can be called the dilemma of the sources of revolution. What matters is whether the sources are the correct ones, i.e., whether a given revolution can be explained in terms of the facts of history of a single country where the revolution occurred or whether it must include the facts of the history of some territories outside its boundaries.

Another problem is the frequent lack of symmetry between the level of social maturity of a given country and the occurrence of revolution there. Why, for example, did the revolutionary movements we are dealing with here appear in territories where the degree of reconstruction of the social structure, in terms of the growth of capitalism and of the bourgeoisie, was slight, while more mature areas were left uninvolved—as for example England and France, or England and America, in the eighteenth century? Another question is why did participation in the Revolution by the various social classes and groups not correspond better with their respective economic activities? We know, as Alfred Cobban[4] pointed out, that the most active groups among the bourgeoisie in the French Revolution were those least involved in the growth of the capitalist mode of production, while Poland, which promulgated the second constitution of the eighteenth century (the American was the first), did not belong among the countries with a fully developed model of society and economy.

This brings us to still another problem faced by the investigators of revolution: that of the common, if transitory, participation of very different social groups, with different social and economic interests, in a common revolution and in its preparation. As the history of the French Revolution demonstrates, the lines of revolutionary and counter-revolutionary activities often crossed social groups and classes in complex ways. Reality did not follow the rigid schemes that have often been constructed by historians, including the historians who have interpreted the Marxist theory of revolution in too simplified a way. The simplification lies, I think, primarily in neglecting the factor of revolutionary consciousness in the analysis of a revolution. This results in an inflexible linking of the concept of bourgeois revolution and the "spirit" of capitalism with the most mature aspects of the bourgeoisie. Such a simplified Marxist interpretation of the English Revolution of the seventeenth century is used, for instance, by Laurence Stone: he writes that Marxist theory does not explain the English Revolution because it was not a struggle between the rich and the poor, feudals and bourgeoisie, or enterpreneurs and hired laborers. Rather, it was a struggle between a new gentry and Parliament, on the one hand, and the aristocracy along with a merchant oligarchy and the king, on the other, while the rural masses remained passive.[5] It cannot be denied that some Marxist historians who interpreted the data using too simplified a model have contributed to this mistaken interpretation of the Marxist theory of revolution.

It is equally true that there have been no attempts to develop this theory using empirical material from the revolutions that occurred from the seventeenth to the early nineteenth centuries. One might note, for example, the similarity between the views on the driving forces of the English Revolution expressed by Stone and my own views, formulated under the influence of Marxism, in my study *The*

Birth of Capitalism in Europe from the Fourteenth to the Seventeenth Centuries.[6]

Another dilemma is whether to consider the events in the late eighteenth and early nineteenth century as a single revolution or as many different revolutions. Attempts have been made to introduce the concept of "a democratic revolution" covering all the ideological movements linked with the American and the French revolutions, but these have been opposed by many historians who want to preserve the "personalities" of the particular revolutions that occurred.[7] Reference to the factor of revolutionary consciousness can provide us with a tentative explanation. The sources of the revolution cannot be considered in too narrow a way. They are both internal and external because of the general dissemination of revolutionary ideas in the world at that time. Revolutionary consciousness is the main link between revolutionary movements, but it can never act "directly," causing revolution here or there. It has to act through human consciousness, the motive force for a human activity. Revolutionary consciousness can "travel" relatively easily from one country to another, and the more developed the means of communication are, the easier its dissemination becomes.

With regard to the lack of correlation between the growth of the material premises—the economic and social structures—and the localization of revolutionary consciousness also provides the key that explains why areas with relatively weak socioeconomic growth might witness a revolution. It is clear that without revolutionary consciousness, which can arise under the influence of specific internal factors in any given area, there can be no outbreak of revolution, and no revolution can survive.

The same holds true for an explanation of a complex revolutionary front line which crosses social classes and groups. The reference to the revolutionary consciousness which, as it turned out, could grow in the late eighteenth and early nineteenth centuries in countries with different levels of socioeconomic development provides the historian with an important analytical tool that allows him to adequately explain this frequently occurring phenomenon.

The same holds true when one seeks to answer the question whether the period witnessed one revolution or a number of them. There were, of course, many revolutions, but the sources leave no doubt that they all had similar results; thus, one general type of revolutionary consciousness must have been characteristic of all of them.

II

Historical research, both theoretical and empirical, has not yet accounted for the concept of revolutionary consciousness in a comprehensive manner. In some studies (e.g., those of François Furet) the concept is incidentally presented,[8] while in others (e.g., those of Hannah Arendt) it appears as a revolutionary "spirit." However, the role of this element in revolutionary processes is fully grasped by both these authors. This is what Arendt writes about the revolutionary spirit of the period in question:

> If we leave aside personal motives and practical goals, and identify this spirit with the principles which, on both sides of the Atlantic, originally inspired the men of the revolution. . . . We have mentioned these principles before, and following Enlightenment political language we have called them public freedom, public happiness, public spirit.[9]

Karl Griewank, who has dealt with the concept of revolution from the medieval period to the end of the eighteenth century, comes closest to my approach. He does not use the term revolutionary consciousness, but he does analyze the dissemination of the concept of revolution in the period and thus comes within the conceptual framework of revolutionary consciousness. It is for this reason that the results of Griewank's investigations should be considered vital for the understanding of revolutionary processes in the modern period.[10]

In a number of other works which deal with modern revolutions in a more general manner, we find no reference to the concept of revolutionary consciousness. Alfred Cobban's *Social Interpretation of the French Revolution* is characteristic in its point of view. The author fails to recognize the problem of consciousness in the process of revolution. He misinterprets Marxist theory, wrongly ascribing economic determinism to it. He writes that, on the basis of the Marxist theory, "if different responses occur in economically identical circumstances, the primacy of the economic factor is maintained by making the factors which produce the aberration into conditions on which the economic factor acts as a prime cause."[11] However, when Marxism is interpreted properly, the fact that a similar economic basis can and does cause different effects is explained by the factor of consciousness. Objective conditions do not influence human activity in a direct way, but through the prism of man's knowledge about those conditions and about his values. That knowledge and those values can differ from man to man and from class to class. In this way, the factor of consciousness becomes an important element in the explanation of an actual form the historical process takes.

Failure to take into account the concept of revolutionary consciousness in theoretical works and in studies on the revolutions of the eighteenth and the first half of the nineteenth centuries does not mean that the elements which make up this concept are totally ignored, but simply that no comprehensive approach has been used in the course of the explanation. It suffices to look through the lists of the causes of a revolution provided by any of these books to see the problem. For instance, when Jacques Godechot in his book on revolutions in the second half of the eighteenth century attempts to catalogue their common causes, he writes, ''Particular circumstances undoubtedly explain the outbreak of a revolution in each state, but a very general movement, such as the one we are seeking to define, should have common causes.''[12] Among these common causes, the following are enumerated by Godechot: social structure (leading to the tendency of the bourgeoisie to acquire power and the peasants to struggle against the remnants of feudalism), demographic changes (especially population growth leading to unemployment), economic circumstances (especially the crises caused by rising prices, new taxes, a series of bad crops, and an overproduction of wine in France in the period 1770–89), the ideas of the Enlightenment, and political events (e.g., the War of the Austrian Succession and the Seven Years' War), which acted as catalysts for revolutionary outbreaks.[13] Godechot says that changes in social structure, demographic pressure, and economic crises caused unrest, producing the need for definite ideas that would allow the formulation of a program. The philosophers of the Enlightenment furnished those ideas.

Other authors interested primarily in the intellectual and ideological causes of revolutions also hesitate at the threshold of the problem of social consciousness in general, and of revolutionary consciousness in particular. The classical works of Charles Hill, *Intellectual Origins of the American Revolution* (1967), and Daniel Mornet, *Les origines intellectueles de la révolution française (1715–1787)* (1954), are cases in point.

Revolutionary consciousness comprises more than simply philosophical ideas of a progressive nature, but less than all progressive intellectual or ideological thought. The concept of a progressive, and particularly a revolutionary, political ideology comes closest to the concept of revolutionary consciousness, for instance, in Bailyn's work. But even there they are far from being identical. Revolutionary consciousness is ''internal,'' while political ideology both influences the formation of revolutionary consciousness and is its indicator. The distinction between the two concepts is not essential here: it cannot bring us any closer to a definition of revolutionary consciousness in which definite philosophical, intellectual, or ideological contents are only some of its many distinctive features. The contents that are characteristic of revolutionary consciousness during our period will be discussed below.

In order to explain the concept of revolutionary consciousness more fully, it is necessary to state that not only the ideas themselves but also the way they function in social consciousness are of interest. Both must concern us insofar as they shape the attitudes that lead to a readiness to undertake some action and to the actions themselves. Although revolutionary consciousness can be investigated through an analysis of political brochures, such an analysis is no substitute for this discussion. The following more general matters correspond to the other aspects and configurations of social consciousness: (1) the nature of the components of revolutionary consciousness; (2) the mechanism that shapes revolutionary consciousness, along with the problem of its social background; (3) revolutionary consciousness as an element in attitudes, behavior, and action.

First of all one has to distinguish between individual and sociorevolutionary consciousness. Social consciousness is not the sum of individual minds, nor is it their "average"; it is some ideal magnitude, an abstraction, that is made up of all kinds of elements represented in individual revolutionary consciousness. It is, therefore, a plane of reference for individual minds that endows the individual with a conviction that a given view or attitude is some kind of social property, i.e., that is has, albeit limited, social reference.

A number of closely connected components of social consciousness should be pointed out. There are the sum of knowledge and the set of fixed beliefs about reality and about the values linked to social practice. There are also the intellectual and psychological attitudes toward radical change in the political sphere, as well as those in the social and cultural spheres that will result from it, and a willingness to undertake actions that might bring these changes about. When referring to changes in the political sphere we mean, of course, only those programs that will result in an increasing participation by society in power, i.e., including groups or classes that either had not participated in power decisions up to that time or whose participation was regarded by society as insufficient. The inclination toward change is obviously related to the conviction that the status quo is unsatisfactory, a feeling of deprivation or of injustice. Such a conviction is itself based on both subjective feelings and objective information pertaining to other domains and other social groups as well.

One significant component of revolutionary consciousness is the knowledge of previous revolutions, especially successful ones. This knowledge is a part of the foundation for the construction of the revolutionary program and to some extent supports it as well. That is important both in the self-definition of revolutionary nations and in the carrying out of revolutionary propaganda. Everybody familiar with the sources of the second half of the nineteenth century can only have been struck by the frequent references to previous revolutions by people advocating changes or bringing them about. In the consciousness of the people whose actions produced the American Revolution was, for in-

stance, an awareness of the Dutch Revolution in the sixteenth century
and the English Revolution in the seventeenth. Cromwell's Revolution
was referred to as well. The American Revolution then in its turn became a part of the revolutionary tradition for those who fought for
political and social changes in France, Poland, Russia, and elsewhere.
Knowledge about the French Revolution and other revolutionary
movements of the period was soon added, contributing to the gradual
enrichment and radicalization of the revolutionary consciousness. The
totality of this knowledge can be called, after Engels, the revolutionary
tradition. Writing the *Peasant War in Germany* in 1850, Engels pointed out that "the German people are by no means lacking in revolutionary tradition."[14] Evoking those traditions had stimulated the recent
revolutionary consciousness of German society. A "revival" of historical facts is accomplished by referring to revolutionary traditions. They
live on in the human mind even after their visible effects have disappeared.

We may characterize revolutionary consciousness as a syndrome
linking the feeling of injustice to knowledge, to a program of action,
and to a strong emotion. Revolutionary consciousness is always placed
in the totality of social or individual consciousness and is its most dynamic part if it occurs at all.

The emotional intensity and the conscious enrichment of the elements of consciousness, or of knowledge about the past and present
social reality, are most recognizable in the revolutionary elite, i.e., the
people who are particularly devoted to revolution, and are specific for
some historical periods—for example, the years 1770–99, some definite
years, months, or days. When these occur we are dealing with revolutionary "mood," revolutionary "feeling," revolutionary "enthusiasm," or revolutionary "fervor," to quote the terms of Marx, Engels,
and Lenin. The concept of revolutionary mood or feeling reflects primarily emotional attitudes. Engels, in his introduction to the *Class
Struggles in France (1848–1850)* by Karl Marx, wrote in 1895 that the
"revolutionary mood of the masses had almost always, and usually
very speedily given way to lassitude or even to a revulsion to its opposite, so soon as illusion evaporated and disappointment set in."[15] Similarly, Lenin stated that "experience has taught us the truth that revolutionary tactics cannot be built on a revolutionary mood alone."[16] Revolutionary enthusiasm has a more "stable" nature, according to Marx.
It includes a devotion to the Revolution and a readiness to undertake
actions and make sacrifices.[17] Revolutionary enthusiasm signals the
growth of revolutionary consciousness and its dissemination among
the masses.

These questions bring us closer to the problem of how revolutionary
consciousness is created. Revolutionary consciousness can only be ap-

plied to deprived or exploited classes or groups. Therefore, for example, we cannot call the activities of the opposition's Assembly of Notables in France in 1787 a revolution because it was done by the notables in a spirit of antiabsolutism, even though these activities did play an immense role as a prerevolutionary step toward the outbreak of the Revolution itself. As Vivian Gruder has pointed out, the fiscal discussions of 1787 "catalyzed and demonstrated their [i.e., the notables'] politicization."[18] The nobility tried to curb royal power, started speaking in the name of the "nation" or the "people," but did not think of providing the third estate with a share of the power.[19]

Lenin described the revolutionary situation as follows: "For a revolution to take place it is not enough for the exploited and oppressed masses to realize the impossibility of living in the old way, and demand changes; for a revolution to take place it is essential that the exploiters should not be able to live and rule in the old way."[20]

The nobility's opposition to absolutism should be included among the actions indicating the inability of the elite to rule in the old way. Here one should also place the ideas of Montesquieu, Voltaire, and many other philosophers seeking to transform the system without preparing a blueprint for revolution. However, as both groups, viz., the masses and the nobility aflame with the spirit of opposition, had a common enemy in the degenerate autocracy, there was, up to a point, a community of interests: the activities of the elite that influenced the formation of the revolutionary consciousness. In this way opposition was introduced into the consciousness of the masses along with an involvement in politics. This contributed to an awareness of their own situation and ultimately encouraged the growth of revolutionary consciousness. In the period of revolution there was barely room for anything except revolutionary or counterrevolutionary consciousness; while in the period before the Revolution, revolutionary consciousness, which was in the process of being formed, was inspired by the ideas, attitudes, and activities of the noble class that was striving toward reforms but not toward revolution.

Engels' discussion of the events that preceded the outbreak of the peasant war of 1525 is very helpful in considering the making of revolutionary consciousness. "About fifty years after the suppression of the Hussite movement," wrote Engels, "the first symptoms of a budding revolutionary spirit became manifest among the German peasants."[21] In the vicinity of Würzburg, in 1476, "in a country long impoverished because of the Hussite wars," the first peasant conspiracy was conceived. A group began to emerge that could be termed a revolutionary elite; it propagated chastity, penance, and plebeian asceticism: "Only a violent exertion, a sudden renunciation of all habitual forms of existence could bring into unified motion a disunited, widely scattered generation of peasants grown up in blind submission."[22]

These remarks should not be applied literally to the investigation of more "urban" revolutions, although general methodological directives can be extracted from them. A common element is undoubtedly a conspiracy that results from the activities of a limited number of people, that is, of the revolutionaries. Thanks to them a liberation of what Engels termed "revolutionary energy" followed. The conspirators were exposed to repression, which either stimulated a further liberation of revolutionary energy or retarded revolutionary activity. The latter occurred in Germany. It took new conspiracies (the *Bundschuh* and *Der arme Konrad*) to prepare the ground for the peasant war of 1525. In spite of repressive measures, peasant agitation steadily increased, and a program gradually developed. Believers appeared in growing numbers, and the social composition of the movement became broader. Apart from the peasants, the conspiracy included knights, priests, and craftsmen. Luther's emergence became a unifying factor for all the opposition elements in Germany. In his theses they found from the beginning a general expression of common beliefs that quickly became a unifying factor.[23] The unification of the strivings of the oppressed and the oppressing classes so characteristic of the prerevolutionary phase took place. The religious factor (analogous to the financial factor in case of the Assembly of Notables) contributed to the revelation of these strivings and at the same time influenced the growth of revolutionary consciousness.

But this very rapid growth of the movement was also destined to develop the seeds of discord which were hidden in it. It was destined to tear asunder at least those portions of the aroused masses which, by their very situation in life, were directly opposed to each other, and to put them in their normal state of mutual hostility.[24]

From what has been said so far, it follows that the mechanism that creates revolutionary consciousness—at least with respect to the revolutions in the sixteenth, seventeenth, and eighteenth centuries—includes an increasing awareness of deprivation, similarities to earlier revolutionary movements, the appearance of a revolutionary elite, and contradictory motives within the ruling class which surface during the prerevolution and stimulate growing numbers of people on both sides of the barricades to action, bringing about the revolutionary spirit and revolutionary feelings in a society. In order to complete this image, let us remember another very vital element that influences the growth of revolutionary consciousness, or at least the emergence and survival of the revolutionary feeling and enthusiasm. This is the struggle for independence that liberates attitudes of patriotism and national honor, and shapes the will toward action and commitment. The histories of the American, French, and Polish revolutions testify clearly to the importance of this factor.[25] In the American Revolution the Declaration of Independence ended the period of prerevolution. In the French Revolution, the war of independence of 1792–93, regarded as a revolutionary war against a dangerous counterrevolutionary coalition, got entangled with the radicalism and terrorism of the Jacobins, who found some support among the masses in the form of the *sans-culottes*. In Poland the activities of the Four-Years Diet of 1788–92 were undertaken in a political atmosphere which was favorable to the saving of the independent Polish state. However, until the mass action of the Kościuszko uprising in 1794 we cannot consider the frontiers of the prerevolution to have been crossed. Robert R. Palmer was right when he wrote: "If the rebellion was successful, democracy in America would be favored. If it failed, if Parliament and the loyal Americans had their way, development in America would move in an aristocratic direction. In this respect the American revolution resembled the revolutions in Europe."[26] It is clear that without revolutionary consciousness as an element of social action there would be neither victory for France in her revolutionary war, which meant a triumph of revolution, nor independence and democracy for America.

III

Revolutionary consciousness during the second half of the eighteenth century was a general, gradually growing phenomenon in both Europe and America. As was the case with the particular revolutions, revolutionary consciousness assumed different forms in different places, but some common features were evident and significant everywhere, although adapted to local conditions. There is no doubt that these conditions alone would not have sufficed to cause revolution. Revolutionary consciousness had to be fed from the outside before it could formulate clearly and express what was felt and strived for, and change these feelings and strivings into a more or less precise program. This external element also included historical experience, for the revolutionary consciousness of the second half of the eighteenth and the beginning of the nineteenth century not only traveled from one country to another but also had a genesis strongly linked to historical growth.

How was the revolutionary consciousness of the period born and shaped? Two currents can be discerned. The first took the form of an attack upon traditional ideas both with respect to a general world outlook and to the political systems. The attack was launched by various groups within the ruling class, mainly the "enlightened" nobility. We might call it the liberal mainstream. It reflected the willingness of an elite to abandon the traditional ways of living and thinking and to break the vicious circle which continually resulted in the same attitudes and actions. The second current comprised the revolutionary tradition of mass uprisings against social conditions. We might call it the plebeian mainstream. These currents did not, of course, develop in isolation from one another, but the history of the revolutionary movements of the eighteenth and nineteenth centuries demonstrates their basic divergences and different fortunes. Their development was strongly linked to progress in communication, as Palmer points out: "This growth of communication was obviously one of the fundamental preconditions of the whole revolutionary era."[27]

All these intellectual transformations and social, religious, and political movements which prepared the way for the ideology of the Enlightenment were the sources of the liberal current. The spirit of reform, the struggle against ignorance and intolerance, the concept of the natural rights of man, freedom of thought which required opposition to the church or at least a questioning of its role (the results of which were deism and atheism), freedom in general (although interpretations of what it was differed), and, finally, the idea of progress all contributed to this ideology. The denial of the sacred nature of royal power and the theory of the social contract, which resulted in the idea of democracy and bourgeois equality, must also be counted among the elements of this ideology. If we examine the sources for the ideas of the Enlightenment, and we do not have to go back very far, the Reformation looms large. The very term "reformation" was used in the political language of the medieval period to mark a striving toward the transformation of an existing state of affairs, although not in the name of progress, but in the name of a return to older, better times. Religious reformation resulted both in the discontents of the elite and those of the revolutionary plebeian mainstream. Luther codified the divergent hopes about the reformation of reality, making them palatable to those who held power as well. The effect—quite against his intentions—was an increasing laicization.

A further stage in the development of the elitist reform movement was English science and philosophy of the seventeenth and early eighteenth centuries (Hobbes, Newton, Locke, Bolingbroke, and others) which provided a deistic and rationalistic world outlook that was indirectly influenced by the thoughts of the Polish Socinians, producing the Glorious Revolution of 1688 which introduced—in a "bloodless revolution"—the supremacy of the Parliament over the monarchy. It is characteristic that this event was labeled a "revolution," while the truly revolutionary events of the years 1642–60 were not. The Glorious Revolution became an inspiration for the antiabsolutist nobility in Europe, and in England herself it became a point of reference in political discussions about social liberties and laws. "I seek for the liberty and constitution of this kingdom," said the Lord Chancellor of England, "no farther back than the [Glorious] Revolution."[28]

Voltaire's popularization of the ideas of Bacon, Newton, Locke, and the Deists, especially in his anonymously and secretly published *Philosophic Letters on the English* (1733), and references to English liberal institutions in Montesquieu's *Persian Letters* (published anonymously in Holland as was often the case among French political thinkers), as well as the generally broad influence of English ideas flowing into France contributed to the growth of intellectual ferment, which was nourished as well by native sources (Bayle, Fontenelle, and others).

English society also influenced the style of life among the upper and middle nobility in France, who began to pay more and more attention to education and intellectual pursuits. The death of Louis XIV (1715), which put an end to his reign of seventy-two years, was also the end of an absolutist epoch which provided the French nobility with the opportunity for change. Intellectual ferment encouraged by new forms of communication, especially the dissemination of books, gradually influenced increasing numbers of the nobility and third estate.[29] Even clergymen invited skepticism and a critical attitude toward religion. The church, still busy fighting the Jansenists, did not notice the dangers of skepticism. In 1751, when the first volume of the *Encyclopédie* appeared, Abbé Prades defended his dissertation in praise of natural religion at the Sorbonne.

Freemasonry played an important part in the forming of the new mentality among the upper classes. Freemasonry was revived in England as an expression of hostility toward Catholicism and the Bourbons. It spread to France, where a number of aristocrats (including the Duc d'Antin and the Comte de Clermont) and philosophers were attracted to it, and where it disseminated the ideas of English liberalism, parliamentarism, and deism. Gradually, along with the new ideas, Freemasonry spread all over Europe, acquiring local features in different countries (including France).[30]

There were many vast differences between England, France, Poland, Germany, and Holland. In England, "noblesse" referred to a way of life more than it did to a social and economic system, for as early as the sixteenth century the process of the making of capitalist society and bourgeois mentality had taken over in England. In France, where social and economic development was less advanced, sensitivity to new ideas resulted from the strivings of all social classes and strata arising from an atmosphere of social crisis. Apart from the nobility's struggle against absolutism, the political consciousness of the bourgeoisie called for legal and political equality, while growing dissatisfaction among the peasants reflected their exploitation by bourgeois owners or farmers in an increasingly capitalist manner.[31] Finally, there was a growing awareness of social injustice among the urban poor. The unification of refeudalizing and bourgeois tendencies further complicated both the situation itself and the awareness that it must be changed, and not only in France.

Criticism of the existing relations, according to Bailyn, surfaced occasionally in America by the end of the seventeenth century and was significant by the 1730s.[32] The philosophical and political ideas of the Enlightenment were spreading very rapidly. This young society, which had never known the pressures of feudal traditions, proved to be a particularly fertile soil for natural philosophy, i.e., for the concepts of natural law, of social control, and a contractual basis of government. Freemasonry became popular, there as in Europe, propagating the ideas of republicanism, English liberalism, civil liberties, and the spirit of liberty in general. The English radical political pamphlets became particularly popular in America. They evoked the revolution of the seventeenth century, and they criticized the court and called (e.g., J. Trenchard) for vigilance against royal schemes and aristocratic encroachments upon civil liberties.[33] The idea of a sovereign parliament opposed to a sovereign monarch was transformed in the minds of colonial Americans into the idea of a sovereignty with respect to England; this was a logical development, as the Americans had not been represented in the English Parliament.

At the same time, however, an influential group of merchants was, according to Arthur M. Schlesinger, "sensitive and articulate with regard to their interests as members of the British empire. They were ever on the alert to obtain the best terms possible from the home government."[34] If we consider all these factors and bear in mind this contradiction between the tradition of home administration and a colonial system of the governors in America, we should say that the prerevolution had already started by about 1760. At that point, the demands centered on stabilizing the system after the English patterns; no break with the crown was intended. Traditional colonial treatment that paid no attention to local aspirations was rejected by the Americans. No new taxes or custom duties were acceptable. The American elite began to support Benjamin Franklin when he called for a revolution against the tyrants. But the situation changed completely when the aspirations of the masses became public, when slavery was opposed, and when the traditional system of landholding was criticized. Then most of the elite chose life in England or Canada.

The plebeian mainstream which cooperated in preparing the growth of revolutionary consciousness in the eighteenth and nineteenth centuries—and we know that revolutionary consciousness was an indispensable factor in the revolutionary situation and in revolution itself—differed from its liberal counterpart in structure and dynamics. It was not a continuous, specific intellectual, scientific, philosophical, or political movement but rather a series of eruptions of human thought and emotion stemming from the feeling of having been wronged and from a willingness to fight which made a revolutionary tradition. The tradition was a historical achievement of the masses and was evoked whenever the oppressed groups and classes rose in revolt. Here again we should start our analysis with the Reformation, although this time we are not interested in Luther but in plebeian movements that referred back to the medieval radical religious sects and to the Hussite heresy. The writings of Joachim Fiore (or Pseudo-Joachim)[35] vere very popular in the period when this radical branch of the Reformation was born. Of the entire Reformation, the activities of Thomas Münzer especially deserve to be mentioned; they can be compared at least in some respects to the Jacobin mainstream of the French Revolution.

The movement of Münzer was still a revolutionary outbreak in the old style; i.e., it was couched in religious terms and had some utopian features.

With every larger movement of the bourgeoisie, wrote Engels, independent outbreaks of another class took place. It was a more or less developed predecessor of the contemporary proletariat. Therefore in the period of Reformation and peasant war in Germany we can notice the Anabaptists and Thomas Münzer, in the period of the English Revolution, the Levellers, in the French Revolution, Babeuf. These military revolts of an immature class were accompanied by theoretical propositions. In the sixteenth and seventeenth centuries, they assumed the form of a utopian image of ideal social systems, and in the eighteenth century, there was quite simply communist theory [Morelly and Mably].[36]

Let us add that in the case of the utopian-communist ideas of the second half of the eighteenth century—when the revolutionary consciousness of the bourgeoisie was already born—these utopian ideas were not the only symptom of revolutionary feelings. The concept of the plebeian mainstream became narrower than the concept of the revolutionary mainstream, which furnished the intellectual and emotional background for the growing revolutionary consciousness.

In the countries of Eastern and Central Europe, revolutionary traditions of the modern period were mainly connected with the peasant uprisings. The situation of the peasants became increasingly more burdensome as refeudalization gained momentum. The best known uprisings were the Dozsa campaign in Hungary (1514) and the Bolotnikow (1606–07) and Razin (1670–71) uprisings in Russia, but numerous other peasant movements of the eighteenth century can be added to this tradition, such as the great Pugachev uprising (1773–74). The uprisings reflected the specific situation of the peasant-serfs and constituted an autonomous plebeian movement. The liberal element was too weak in Russia to join in and create a revolutionary situation.

IV

A plebeian current alone could not give birth to revolutionary consciousness in the sense in which it is defined here for the period under consideration. There could be revolutionary feelings or even revolutionary enthusiasm, but there was no revolutionary class with a consciousness directed toward progress as opposed to a return to an earlier, better time. This situation would only occur later on. In Western Europe, the Paris Commune would be a symptom of that new situation. It evoked in 1871 the Jacobin-ruled Paris Commune of 1789–95. In Eastern and Central Europe the Revolution of 1905 would be an analogous symptom. Both these events were connected with the growth of the class consciousness of the proletariat, and the latter could not be formed if no ideological elements were brought in from the outside.

The question remains, however, whether it was possible for revolutionary consciousness to grow directly from the liberal mainstream. England, where the Glorious Revolution and the profits from colonial expansion wiped out the traditions of the Cromwellian Revolution, testifies to the fact that the bourgeois liberal mainstream, with its large aristocratic component, did not automatically cause a revolution. We notice some breaking with this mainstream and turning to revolutionary activities (i.e., identifying with some part of revolutionary class), but all this happened under the influence of specific events and the revolutionary feelings of the masses. The political and social content and intensity of feeling varied from one country to another and depended on what was supposed to be changed. Characteristic examples of "deserting" one's own class, of passing from prerevolutionary to revolutionary activities, were provided by Lafayette, Mirabeau, the families of Noailles and Rochefoucault, and Louis-Philippe of Orleans, but these examples refer to the French Revolution.

In Poland no "desertion" was possible, as there was no mature bourgeoisie. As Bogusław Leśnodorski has successfully pointed out, even the Polish Jacobins could hardly be identified with a real plebeian movement, since the latter did not acquire organizational forms and revolutionary consciousness at that time.[37] The same holds true, as French researchers have mentioned, for the relation between the French Jacobins and the *sans-culottes* with the other groups among the masses. In both cases the relation was maintained between a group of people with revolutionary consciousness and the masses which spontaneously acted upon limited, daily demands and felt that those demands had to be supported with violence. The masses represented a social force expressing a "demand" for definite ideas, but they were incapable of acquiring revolutionary consciousness in a spontaneous way. They produced revolutionary feeling; they were particularly sensitive to threats to national dignity and to political morality and religious concerns, but they formulated no programs. The programs were formulated, sometimes doctrinarily, by the revolutionary elite. It is sufficient to mention Robespierre's dislike of the clubs, which were the pressure groups of the poor, and the struggle of the Jacobins against the clubs' republican, i.e., anticentralist, tendencies.[38]

Only exceptional conditions made it possible for the liberal-aristocratic and plebeian currents to coincide and produce revolutionary consciousness. Revolutionary traditions and activization of the plebeian masses were indispensable elements in the general conviction that changes were inevitable, and liberty, equality, democracy, and happiness essential. This cooperation usually began during the transition from prerevolution to revolution, and it gradually bore fruit in the sphere of consciousness.

In the case of America, revolution was triggered by, among other things, the Stamp Act, which united the Americans in opposition to the crown and provided a foundation for the prerevolutionary actions of an elite that included Thomas Paine, Franklin, John Adams, and Jefferson. The British repression brought the same results, ending in conflicts that turned into the Revolutionary War and in the promulgation of the Declaration of Independence.

From the point of view of social content, the American Revolution had fewer aims to achieve than did the Revolution in France, densely covered with feudal forms and social contradictions, but its role in making revolutionary consciousness in Europe was immense. The American Revolution triggered the growth of revolutionary consciousness in Europe. The ideas of the American Revolution were dynamic elements in stimulating liberal-aristocratic movements in Europe toward revolutionary action.

The fortunes of the various revolutions in Europe differed. France alone managed to pass from the period of prerevolution to the period of revolution. The French example was then placed in the forefront as the prime example of revolutionary consciousness, but the example was far too radical for Central and Eastern Europe, which, with few exceptions, was still submerged in the movement of reform among the nobility.

In that movement, Poland took the lead as the country where no absolutism could grow. That and the fact that the struggle for independence had become all important made the American Revolution immensely popular in Poland.[39] The events of 1791, the May 3 Constitution, and the Insurrection of 1794, when the elements needed for a passage to revolution occurred, could still be placed within the liberal-aristocratic current. The Polish events of the year 1791 were very favorably commented upon by Edmund Burke, the father of English conservatism. Tadeusz Kościuszko, who was directly influenced by the

American Revolution, borrowed many ideas and slogans from it, and he tried to use them during the uprising of 1794.

The influences of the French and the American revolutions became distinct; the means of arousing revolutionary consciousness were very complex indeed. European revolutionaries preferred to use the French Revolution as their model. The American Revolution defeated the aristocracy and met, aside from the Negro question, almost all the requirements for the democratization of a capitalist society. In Europe many more problems remained unsolved. The periods of aristocratic reaction followed, occasionally stimulating, occasionally hampering the growth of revolutionary consciousness. The situation in Eastern and Central Europe was particularly complex; the forces of feudalism showed no signs of giving up and, at worst, tried to control the passage from feudalism to capitalism. It is in those regions that the most intense center for revolutionary action began to emerge.

NOTES

1 K. Marx and F. Engels, *The Communist Manifesto* [Polish edition] (Warsaw, 1945), p. 38.
2 Ibid., p. 48.
3 B. Bailyn, *The Ideological Origins of the American Revolution,* 3rd ed. (Cambridge, Mass., 1968), p. vi.
4 A. Cobban, *The Social Interpretation of the French Revolution* (Cambridge, 1964). F. Furet relies strongly on this source, cf. F. Furet, "Le catechisme revolutionaire," *Annales: Economies, Societés, Civilizations,* no. 2 (1971): 282.
5 L. Stone, *The Causes of the English Revolution 1529-1642* (London, 1972), p. 54.
6 J. Topolski, *Narodziny kapitalizmu w Europie* (Warsaw, 1965), p. 97ff.
7 Cf. J. Godechot, *Les Révolutions (1770-1794)* (Paris, 1970), pp. 6-9.
8 Cf., e.g., Furet, "Le catechisme revolutionaire": 286.
9 H. Arendt, *On Revolution,* 3rd ed. (New York, 1966), p. 223.
10 K. Griewank, *Der neuzeitliche Revolutionsbegriff,* 2nd ed. (Frankfurt a/M, 1973).
11 Cobban, *The Social Intrepretation of the French Revolution,* p. 13.
12 Godechot, *Les Révolutions (1770-1794),* p. 91.
13 Ibid., pp. 91-101.
14 F. Engels, *The Peasant War in Germany* [English edition] (New York, 1926), p. 33.
15 K. Marx, *The Class Struggles in France 1848-1850* [English edition] (New York, n.d.), p. 15.
16 V. I. Lenin, " 'Left-Wing' Communism—An Infantile Disorder," *Collected Works,* vol. 31 (Moscow, 1966), p. 63.
17 See an interesting discussion of the subject in H. P. Jaeck, "Die Menschenrechte und die französische bürgerliche Revolution von 1789. Historische Interpretation in Marx Aufsatz 'Zur Juden-frage,' " *Jahrbuch für Wirtschaftgeschichte,* vol. 12, p. 62ff.

18 V. R. Gruder, "Class and Politics in the Pre-Revolution: The Assembly of Notables, 1787" (in press).

19 See V. R. Gruder, *The Royal Provincial Intendents: A Governing Elite in Eighteenth-Century France* (Ithaca, N.Y., 1968). See also J. Egret, *La Pré-Révolution française 1787-1788* (Paris, 1962).

20 Lenin, " 'Left-Wing' Communism—An Infantile Disorder," pp. 84-85.

21 Engels, *The Peasant War in Germany,* p. 74.

22 Ibid., p. 75-76.

23 Ibid., p. 93.

24 Ibid., p. 93.

25 J. Ellis in *Armies in Revolution* (London, 1973) discusses the question of the influence wars and armies had upon the course of various revolutions.

26 R. R. Palmer, *The Age of the Democratic Revolution,* vol. 1 (Princeton, 1959), p. 202.

27 Ibid., p. 243.

28 Bailyn, *The Ideological Origins of the American Revolution,* p. 243.

29 See D. Mornet, *Les origines intellectuelles de la révolution française (1715-1787)* (Paris, 1954), where he writes that "dans le domaine des idées religieuses l'évolution est . . . plus marquee" (p. 21).

30 Cf. B. Fay, *La Franc-Maconnerie et la révolution intellectuelle du XVIIIᵉ siecle* (Paris, 1935).

31 Cf. Gruder, *The Royal Provincial Intendents,* p. 220.

32 Bailyn, *The Ideological Origins of the American Revolution,* p. vii.

33 T. G. Hall, "Jak rozumieć rewolucję amerykańską: nurt republikański w imperium brytyjskim," *Kwartalnik Historyczny* 83, no. 2 (1976): 316-28.

34 A. M. Schlesinger, *The Colonial Merchants and the American Revolution* (New York, 1918/1968), p. 31.

35 Griewank, *Der neuzeitliche Revolutionsbegriff,* p. 88.

36 F. Engels, *Socialism, Utopian and Scientific* [Polish edition] (Warsaw, 1946), p. 22.

37 B. Leśnodorski, *Polscy Jakobini* (Warsaw, 1960), pp. 25-27.

38 Arendt, *On Revolution,* p. 248.

39 See Z. Libiszowska, *Opinia polska wobec rewolucji amerykańskiej w XVIII wieku* (Łódź, 1962).

PART II

POLISH-AMERICAN RELATIONS IN THE REVOLUTIONARY ERA

THE AMERICAN REVOLUTION AND THE PARTITIONS OF POLAND

Piotr S. Wandycz, Yale University

This paper addresses itself to two questions which, given the vagueness of its title, have to be formulated with some precision. The first is: to what extent did the Partitions of Poland affect American thinking, attitudes, and policies toward the Polish nation? and the second: to what extent did the American Revolution—defined for our purposes as a successful bid for independence and the long-range achievements stemming from it—affect Polish attitudes about, and expectations from, the United States? The two questions need not necessarily be related, yet in a sense they represent the two sides of the phenomenon that may be called the essence of American-Polish political relationships over the last two hundred years. The emphasis of this paper will be on the first question, which appears to be less explored. Even so, the remarks that follow can only be viewed as a preliminary inquiry that raises problems rather than attempts to answer them. As such, the paper is intended to serve only as a preliminary exploration, hopefully delineating the area for extensive and exhaustive studies.

Seen from a pre-1918 perspective, the American Revolution and the Partitions could, and did, give rise to interpretations that were largely deterministic in character. The Revolution appeared as the logical climax to historical processes operating in the colonial era, the Partitions as the inevitable nadir resulting from the course of events in the preceding centuries of Polish history. The War of American Independence created a state and opened an era of success; the Partitions marked the fall of a state and seemed to end Polish history on a note of failure.

Visiting the new American Republic in 1783, Kajetan Węgierski wrote John Dickinson a letter that contained phrases crucial for our discussion here:

> When I think, Sir, that with three million people, and without money you have shaken off the yoke of such a power as England, and have acquired such an extensive territory—and that Poland has suffered herself to be robbed of five million souls and a vast country—I acknowledge, I do not understand the cause of such a difference. [Węgierski called on the Americans to preserve their newly won rights, and then he added:] If the state of my country remains always the same, if the gods will not show pity to her fate, I will say to my countrymen: Come, cross the seas, and insure to your children liberty and property![1]

The contrast of American achievement with Polish failure and the belief in a great future for America and a tragic one for Poland are illuminating, particularly since this letter was long believed to have come from the pen of Kościuszko himself. The shadow the Partitions threw on American attitudes toward Poland was already noted early in this century by the American pioneer of Polish history, Robert H. Lord, who, writing shortly after the Paris Peace Conference of 1919, commented:

> For most outsiders the partitions have overshadowed all the preceding period of Polish history. Such observers have fastened their eyes too exclusively upon the deplorable condition into which Poland had fallen just before her dismemberment and have concluded that her history is chiefly made up of a tissue of mistakes, sins and follies, interesting only as furnishing a terrible example of how a State ought not to be governed and of how badly a people can mismanage its national life.[2]

The impact of the American Revolution on its contemporaries in Poland has already been the object of several extensive studies,[3] and there is no point here in covering the same ground in detail. It should suffice to recall the great interest shown by the Poles in the events taking place across the ocean and the use made of American political ideas by both the Patriots and the Republicans during the debates in the Four Years' Diet. On the other hand, since Miecislaus Haiman wrote his pioneering work on the subject of the American reaction to the Polish Partitions,[4] no new exhaustive study has been made to gauge the precise nature of the response by prominent Americans and the press to the collapse of Poland. True, the young American historian K. A. Sutherland has attempted an interesting general survey of American views toward Poland since the Partitions;[5] R. R. Palmer's great synthesis on the eighteenth century "democratic revolution" offers us some enlightening remarks on the Partitions themselves. His comment "It has been the fate of Poland, more than of most countries, that outsiders have been mainly concerned to see in it a spectacular object lesson, hurrying on from interest in the Poles themselves to find evidence for general truths of wider application" has been cited many times. A fairly recent article by Janina Hoskins on Jefferson and Poland is truly illuminating and provides some new material.[6] Still, a great deal remains to be done before a study can be attempted comparable in scope to that of Henryk Serejski on Europe and the Partitions of Poland.[7]

On the basis of the limited material at our disposal, we can say that the Partitions were viewed by Americans from two angles: either as an injustice, calling into question Europe's international morality, or as the result of Polish mismanagement—the "terrible example" mentioned above by Lord. The moral, or should we say moral-legal, aspect was the more popular, which was not surprising given the Americans' own attachment to the moral-legal arguments used to justify their own Revolution.

In the interesting exchange between Thomas Jefferson and John Adams of 11 January–2 February 1816, Jefferson, commenting on the high level reached by European society in the eighteenth century, wrote: "A wound indeed was inflicted on the character of honor in the eighteenth century by the partition of Poland. But this was an atrocity of a barbarous government chiefly, in conjunction with a smaller one still scrambling to become great, while one only of those already great, and having character to lose, descended to the baseness of an accomplice in the crime." Jefferson added that the other great powers— France, England, and Spain—shared to some extent the responsibility for the event inasmuch as they permitted it to happen. Adams in his reply made clear that there was "no difference on opinion or feeling between us, concerning the partition of Poland."[8] These opinions, voiced some twenty years after the last Partition, did not substantially differ from those made immediately after the event. Haiman has cited an article written in 1797 by the lexicographer Noah Webster in the *Massachusetts Mercury,* which claimed that when Poland was partitioned an "outcry was raised by all lovers of freedom—and justly." Among the toasts drunk in Baltimore in 1795 was one directed against Catherine II: "Execration to the abominable tyrant—May the blood of Poland crying from the dust, bring down Heaven's vengeance on her."[9]

These statements, however, came after the May 3 Constitution and the Kościuszko Insurrection, which had gained much sympathy for Poland in America. There were apparently no similar criticisms after the First Partition except for Adam's use of the word "shameful" in 1779; if anything the criticisms were aimed at Poland. There were references to "miserable" Poland (Franklin), comments concerning Polish unfitness for self-government and self-defense (Hamilton and Madison), and statements that a country with twelve million inhabitants under an English or American type of constitution would not have allowed itself to be dismembered (Adams).

John Adams, in the two essays concerning Poland that appeared in his *Defence of the Constitutions of . . . the United States of America* (1787–88), invokes Poland as an example of "the effects of 'collecting all authority into one centre,' of neglecting an equilibrium of powers, and of not having three branches in the legislature."[10] Writing to Colonel William Duane more than twenty years later, Jefferson still referred to "the example of a country erased from the map of the world by the dissensions of its own citizens."[11]

The Partitions, as Lord rightly pointed out, have not only obscured most of Poland's past but for a long time have relegated to near oblivion the interesting parallels between the American and the Polish "Revolutions." Both Palmer and some recent Polish historians have brought out this aspect very clearly. The American Revolution was compared at the time with both the French Revolution and the two "revolutions" in Poland—the bloodless revolution culminating in the May 3 Constitution and the Kościuszko Insurrection. At the Harvard Commencement on 19 July 1792, a conference was held on the theme "Upon the Comparative Importance of the American, French, and Polish Revolutions to Mankind." The American press acclaimed the May 3 Constitution as a "most wonderful revolution," and an English journal declared that the Poles had caught the revolutionary spirit from the Americans.[12] Washington commented more cautiously, in his letter to David Humphreys on 20 July 1791, that Poland "appears to have made large and unexpected strides toward Liberty, which if true, reflects great honor on the present King."[13] The poet Joel Barlow, American envoy to France, who died in Poland in 1812, lauded the Polish King in the following lines:

> There Stanislaus unfurls his prudent plan,
> Tears the strong bondage from the eyes of man,
> Points the progressive march, and shapes the way
> That leads a realm from darkness into day.[14]

A comparison of the May 3 "Revolution" that seemed so contagious to the neighboring regimes of Eastern Europe with Polish revolutions of the nineteenth and twentieth centuries that provoked foreign intervention on similar grounds would be a fascinating study. It cannot, however, be attempted here. Nor can we engage in another discussion, namely about the inevitability of the Second Partition and the related question of the Polish-Prussian alliance.[15]

Contemporary analogies, explicit or implied, between American and Polish events, or at least opinions pointing to basic similarities, ought to be more fully explored. A clergyman writing to Washington in September 1794 hoped that the same Lord of Hosts who made Washington the instrument for the delivery of America had commissioned Kościuszko "to deliver the Poles from under slavery."[16] James Monroe wrote Jefferson about the 1794 Insurrection, "under the direction of Kosciusko [sic] who acted with us in America," and called it a "formidable head [that] has been raised against Prussia and Russia."[17] Other examples have been mentioned by Haiman and subsequent historians and need not be repeated here. They attest, to some degree at least, to the contemporaries' belief in a general revolutionary process in which the American, Polish, and French revolutions were related, making them striking phenomena.

Poland's obliteration from the political map of Europe produced a shock which made such Polish patriots as Czacki, Kołłątaj, and Wybicki speak of the end of the Polish nation. Its fate was compared to that of Carthage or Troy. Thus, it is hardly surprising to read in the *Columbian Centinel* on 23 November 1797: "Poland is no more. Its Stanislaus is dead—its nobles scattered abroad; and that it ever existed, will speedily only be remembered by the Historian, the Geographer, or the Newsmonger."[18]

The story of American success contrasted forcibly with the failure, albeit noble failure, of Poland. Those Poles—among them Kościuszko and Piotr Świtkowski—who had worried lest America, torn in the 1780s by internal dissension, survive, saw their worries to be groundless. Yet there were also some Americans who wondered if the United States would have survived had they found themselves in the same position as Poland. "The Polish constitution of 1791," Charles Adams (son and grandson of the two presidents) wrote:

. . . was immediately overthrown by the interference of neighboring powers interested to destroy it. The constitution of the United States has survived until now, and bids fair to last yet longer. But, if we could for a moment suppose the geographical position of the two countries to have been exactly changed, looking back at the nature of the political controversies which agitated America for many years, it is at least open to question, whether as marked disorders would not have been developed under the constitution of the United States, as were ever found in the worst of times in Poland.[19]

Subsequent American opinions about the Polish Partitions seemed to reflect little awareness of that view, nor is it likely that such a view appreciably affected the image of the Revolutionary War held by the average American. Was that Revolution closer to failure than Americans had traditionally been taught to believe? Was not outside aid, particularly from France, of crucial significance? Palmer draws attention to this question when he writes: "Could the revolutionary leadership in America . . . have accomplished its purpose of independence with the resources of America alone? Was the outcome of the American War of Independence only an event in American history taking place on American soil?"[20] One other, although indirect, connection between the American Declaration of Independence and the First Partition of Poland emerges from a recent article by James H. Hutson. While analyzing the reasons that prompted the Congress to adopt a formal declaration, the author points to the fears of a partition of North America between England, France, and Spain. In the spring of 1776, Philadelphia journals sounded alarm and spoke of the "partition spirit" prevailing in Europe. The press and Richard Henry Lee, among others, expressly referred to the Partition of Poland as a dangerous precedent that could be relevant for America.[21]

It is not my intention here to engage in a historiographical discussion concerning the changing views toward the American Revolution and its outcome. Suffice it to say that a deterministic view of history ascribing American success and Polish failure to immutable and necessary forces appears too facile. Yet this was precisely the view that colored much of the subsequent American and English thinking about Poland. It took its most extreme form on the tongue of Jan Smuts at the Paris Peace Conference of 1919, when he uttered the well-known judgment: "Poland was an historic failure, and always would be a failure, and in this Treaty we were trying to reverse the verdict of history."[22]

The fact that Poland had lost her statehood at the very moment when the United States had won theirs and thus gained entry on the international scene had far-reaching repercussions. The Partitions, as mentioned above, were largely condemned as a breach of international morality and not because they upset the balance of power in Europe. Further research might perhaps reveal that some Americans were impressed by Edmund Burke's penetrating remarks about the First Partition—Burke after all was widely read in America—but I have so far failed to come across any evidence for it. Burke's condemnation of the Partitions as a "very great breach in the modern political system in Europe" referred to the balance of power more than it did to international morality, and his remarks about the connection between the Partitions and the rise of Prussia were truly prophetic. So was his opinion that "to purchase present quiet, at the price of future security, is undoubtedly a cowardice of the most degrading and basest nature."[23]

True, there were a few American comments that seemed to show some awareness of the connection between the growth of Russian might and the collapse of Poland. Strongly anti-Russian articles appearing in *Niles' Weekly Register* for the years 1812–21 contained references to the Russo-Polish aspect of international relations. Russia was described at one point as consisting of "*conquered* countries, *usurped* provinces, and *ravaged* territories." The *Register* later spoke of Congress Poland as having been reduced to the status of a mere province of Russia. Still, these articles resulted more from domestic American polemics about the respective merits of a pro-French or a pro-English policy than from a criticism of the working of the international system in Europe. The anti-Federalist *Niles' Weekly Register* represented the pro-French stand, and this colored its attitude toward Russia and Poland. Whether its views were based on an appreciation of the balance-of-power aspects of the Polish Partitions is more than doubtful. An instinctive dislike of the concept that Wilson would so heatedly denounce a hundred years later was already having its impact on American thinking.

As a result of the Partitions, the United States did not confront a

Polish state during the nineteenth century; instead, they confronted "the Polish question." Louis Gerson commented that "since the Polish nation had not existed throughout most of the United States' history, no friction had arisen to impair the friendship of the two people."[24] This is a highly dubious assertion. The likelihood of American-Polish friction was not great; the "friendship" or sentiment which influenced American attitudes toward Poland was distorted by the absence of normal inter-state relations and was thus largely of a moral or moralistic nature, an extension of the revulsion felt when Poland had been partitioned. Gallant Polish patriots were subjects for sympathy and pity. Liberal American public opinion took the Polish side in the November 1830 Uprising, and among the many speeches and writings that appeared, the voice of moral rectitude predominated—the Poles deserved support because theirs was a just cause. Their struggle for liberty was dear to Americans, who invoked in their pro-Polish statements "claims of outraged humanity" that were said to be more important than "ordinary rules of diplomacy." References to the Polish contributions to the American War of Independence were also made; the surgeon Dr. Eve who went to serve in Poland during the Uprising referred to his repayment of the American debt owed to Pułaski's countrymen.[25] Attempts by leading Polish exiles—for instance, Gaspar Tochman—to argue the Polish case in geopolitical terms by pointing to the imbalance created in Europe by the Russian might apparently found little echo.

This pro-Polish outlook charged with indignation and moral rectitude clashed with purely political considerations during the 1863 Uprising.[26] Russia, previously denounced as Poland's oppressor, became an important asset, almost an ally, of Washington. Torn by the War of Secession—the outbreak of the January Uprising came twenty-one days after Lincoln's Emancipation Proclamation—the United States looked to Russia, whose potential conflict with England and France could only assist the cause of the North. Northern papers severely criticized the Poles for starting the struggle without "a reasonable prospect of success." The influential *North American and United States Gazette* wrote that it was no small matter to disturb the peace of the world. While it wished the Poles "another chance of becoming a nation," it also suggested that they make "a better use of their independence than they did when they were one."[27] The earlier view that the Partitions resulted purely from Polish misgovernment was once again in evidence. The American chargé d'affaires in St. Petersburg, Bayard Taylor, wrote brutally that history teaches us "there is no resurrection for a nation once dead."[28] In early 1864, one article went so far as to suggest that the extinction of Poland had been "truly a gain to the cause of civilization."

The Southern press and the Northern papers sympathetic to the Confederate cause used heavy sarcasm in commenting upon these views. Had the Polish rebellion, wrote the Boston *Daily Courier*,[29] broken out three years earlier, there would have been pro-Polish enthusiasm in the United States, praises for Kościuszko, and denunciations of the tsar. Now rebels were rebels, and they deserved to be hanged. The *New York Times,* in an article on 19 August 1863, struck an interesting note that would recur in the years to come: the Poles were surely unreasonable, the paper wrote, to demand that the tsar "submit to a dismemberment of his empire."

Seen in the context of our discussion here, the 1863–64 period was of tremendous importance. It showed that American sympathies for Poland fared badly when confronted with political realities. It showed that opposition to a "dismemberment" of the Russian Empire could win out over a condemnation of the Partitions of Poland. The Partitions were ancient history, and thinking in historic terms has never been an American forte—as Emily Hahn once put it: "We have never been overly fond of history. We always think that what we are experiencing is new." The parallels drawn between the secessionist South and the Poles struggling to be free, between the territorial integrity of the United States and that of the tsarist empire, appeared relevant and to the point. Concern about Poland, when it existed, belonged to a different realm of ideas. One John Harper of Philadelphia wrote his son in August 1863: "The Poles have our sympathies, *though* [italics mine], they rebel against Russia."[30]

None of the pro-Polish statements in 1863–64 showed any awareness of what role a resuscitated Poland could play in international politics. Marx's and Engels's insistence on Poland's rebirth within the borders of 1772, which had appeared in the pages of the *Neue Rheinische Zeitung* only fifteen years earlier, would have been virtually unthinkable in America in the 1860s.

The above-mentioned association of secession in America with a "dismemberment" of the Russian Empire, reinforced by a community of American-Russian interests, proved to be long lived. In his Fourteen Points, Wilson spoke of the Polish state that was to be "erected," not re-erected, a nuance that was not lost at the time on Paderewski and other Poles. It was the principle of national self-determination more than the undoing of a historical wrong that shaped Wilson's pro-Polish feelings in the years 1917–19. Interestingly enough, Wilson did not apply the same principle of national self-determination to the Russian Empire. Colonel House, for one, noted this as he remarked how effectively the principle had been used against the equally multinational Habsburg monarchy. The earlier parallel between the American and Polish revolutions was forgotten; in the twentieth century, a new parallel was occasionally drawn between the United States, a republic that was born in a monarchical world, and Bolshevik Russia, a regime that was born in a capitalist one. Among those who made this analogy was the powerful chairman of the Senate Foreign Relations Committee, William E. Borah.

A sympathy for oppressed Poles, a humanitarian feeling which only on rare occasions would coincide with political considerations after 1795, continued, of course, to exist. Its character was affected by many factors, among which the contacts with the large Polish immigration to the United States must naturally be included. From Anne Porter's novel *Thaddeus of Warsaw,* published in England in 1831 and read widely in America, to *The Trumpeter of Cracow* written by E. P. Kelly, the first Kościuszko Foundation scholar in Poland after the First World War, stories and poems appeared presenting the Polish past in heroic terms. Two *Sixth Readers,* published respectively in 1873 in Pittsburgh and in 1874 in Cambridge, included a moving poem entitled "The Polish Boy" by Ann S. Stephens. It told in a most dramatic, indeed melodramatic, form of a Polish child who chose death at Russian hands in preference to exile in Siberia. Robin Carver's *Stories of Poland,* meant for the young reader, contrasted the unhappy fate of Polish children with that of their more fortunate American counterparts.

American college students were not much exposed to European, much less to Polish, history. In fact, a systematic teaching of history did not begin until the late nineteenth century; Yale, for example, did not establish its first history chair until 1865. The history that was taught was heavily influenced by German scholarship, and its emphasis was almost exclusively West European. Among the first texts used, François Guizot's *General History of Civilization in Europe,* which went through nine American printings between 1838 and 1868, virtually ignored East Central Europe and Poland. Three major textbooks that appeared around the turn of the nineteenth and twentieth centuries did, however, deal with the Partitions, and it is instructive to look at the treatment Poland received.[31] The earliest, written by a Yale professor, George Burton Adams, and entitled *European History: An Outline of Its Development* (New York, 1899) approached the Partitions in the context of Russia's rise to power. Mentioning that conditions in Poland had for a long time invited interference by her neighbors, Adams wrote, "The destruction of Poland was a well-merited punishment of the selfish corruption of the ruling class, who would not allow reformation or abandon their privileges in the interest of the nation." At the same time, Adams noted that this state of affairs offered no justification for an "open violation of right and justice by those who destroyed the State" (p. 400). Under the heading "Poland at last destroyed," the Yale historian covered in a few sentences Polish attempts to reform the constitution, Kościuszko's struggles, and the Second and Third Partitions. The most important effect he saw of the disappearance of Poland, combined with the decline of Sweden and Turkey, was a weakening of France.

Ferdinand Schevill, who at that time still spelled his name Schwill and taught at the University of Chicago, authored a *History of Modern Europe* published in New York in 1900. Like his predecessor, he too placed the story of the Partitions in the Russian context and stressed Polish anarchy. Poland, he wrote, "has herself to thank in the first place for the ruin that overtook her in the eighteenth century." Like Adams, he went on to say that this "does not exempt from guilt the powers that . . . rent her asunder" (p. 228). A description of the Second and Third Partitions was followed by a reference to Kościuszko but none to the reforms and the Polish revival. Schevill concluded, "Poland ceased to exist as a state . . . but as a people, she exists to this day, and stubbornly nurses in her heart the hope of a resurrection" (p. 229).

The third textbook, *The Development of Modern Europe* (Boston, 1907) was the work of two Columbia professors, James H. Robinson and Charles A. Beard. Their relevant section bears the heading "Three Partitions of Poland." The authors provided a few pages of background to the events of the eighteenth century and thus, at least quantitatively, improved on their predecessors. Polish "feudal anarchy" figured prominently in their narrative, and Rousseau was cited for his view on Poland on the eve of the First Partition. Robinson and Beard condemned the Partitions in stronger terms than had the other two historians by calling it "this outrageous mutilation of an ancient Kingdom, which had once been one of the most important in Europe" (p. 77). The Polish revival culminating in the May 3 Constitution was discussed, as was Kościuszko's Insurrection.

It is likely that the short references to Poland in these three books provided some sort of simplified notion of the Partitions for the student, but in any case he had few other American books he could turn to. One may mention Nevin O. Winter's *Poland Today and Yesterday*, but this volume was hardly learned or sophisticated. It was not until 1893–94 that Archibald C. Coolidge introduced a course in Northern and Eastern European history at Harvard, much to the amazement of the academic community, and his student was none other than the Robert H. Lord we have already quoted. It is not surprising that Lord chose the topic of Poland's Partitions for his doctoral dissertation. The result was the great classic on the Second Partition (only recently translated into Polish) which challenged the previous facile and one-sided interpretations.

Occasional public references to Poland's Partitions continued to be made, although largely for the benefit of Polish immigrants. In 1908, William Howard Taft, speaking in Milwaukee, mentioned the Partitions as deserving "the most severe condemnation. . . . It is a historical fact lamented by nearly every heart."[32] It is difficult not to suspect that this was hardly more than a phrase useful for the occasion and devoid of any political meaning. As a writer commented in the *Nation* on 24 December 1914, "The partition of Poland a century and a half ago was long the favorite example for American orators of a great international crime."[33] Did the ordinary American still believe that all Polish misfortunes were largely of their own doing? Very likely. One cannot help but recall here Franklin Roosevelt's remark made at Yalta: "Poland has been a source of trouble for over five hundred years."[34]

Now let us turn very briefly to the second question—the Polish image of America as an outgrowth of the Revolutionary War. Admiration for the Americans struggling for liberty and democracy against oppression has been noted by several historians. During the Four Years' Diet debates, the names of Washington and Franklin were invoked, for instance in Niemcewicz's often-quoted phrase: "No one knows to whom Washington owes his birth, and no one knows who Franklin's ancestors were. Yet it is to these two famous men that America owes its liberty and independence." Polish expressions of admiration for American democratic institutions and her *élan* run through the entire nineteenth century. Such eye witnesses as Kościuszko, Niemcewicz, Węgierski, and later travelers down to Norwid and Sienkiewicz transmitted the image of American achievements back to Poland.[35] Even though some of the travelers were at times shocked by exotic American ways and customs and offered strong criticism of their treatment of the Negroes, their overall views were frequently enthusiastic. In the latter part of the nineteenth century, a Cracow liberal and member of the *Akademia Umiejętności*, Stefan Buszczyński, wrote a comparative study of America and Europe in which his rather pessimistic view of the old Continent contrasted with his picture of the United States as a model worthy of imitation by Europeans.

What attracted the Poles to America were largely those characteristics that can be associated with the Revolution: a quest for a national and individual freedom and independence. If we think in terms of political impact, America as the land of freedom took precedence over America as the land of opportunity. Węgierski's remark, cited at the beginning of this paper, and Niemcewicz's and Kościuszko's declarations that the United States was their second fatherland bear witness to this conception. Staszic's words of praise for Washington and Franklin in the *Ród ludzki* reflect the same attitude. Such criticisms as there are concern American materialism, the treatment of the Negro, and—a typically European complaint—the absence of "gracious living" in America.[36]

Could the United States have served, in the opinion of prominent Poles, as a model for Poland? A tentative answer, I think, would be negative: inspiration, yes, a model for practical reforms and policies. no. For all his interest in American constitutional developments, Stanislas Augustus did not really think them applicable to the Polish situation. The question to what extent Kościuszko drew on American military and political models during the 1794 Insurrection is still open. It would seem, however, that Haiman and some more recent Polish historians exaggerate in their attempts to establish American influences for Kościuszko's actions. True, the Kościuszko-inspired pamphlet *Can the Poles Fight Their Way to Independence? (Czy Polacy wybić się mogą na niepodległość)* has clear references to America and even envisages an institution patterned on the American Congress,[37] but later, American and Polish roads diverge so completely that even to speak of conscious imitation of American models seems unjustifiable. Paderewski's "United States of Poland" presented in the 1917 memorandum to Colonel House appears to be more an homage to American terminology than a realistic attempt to transplant the United States pattern of government to his homeland.

The question of the "American dream" serving as an inspiration is another matter. It is conceivable that the successes of the Revolutionary War did inspire some Poles. Haiman quotes a letter from the Polish camp in 1792, reprinted in the *Dunlap's American Daily,* to the effect that it was "the example of the Americans who sustained many defeats before they achieved the glorious conquest of liberty" that inspired the Polish troops.[38] I somehow doubt, however, that this letter is in any way representative of Polish soldiers in the late eighteenth century.

Did the Poles expect, given the view of America as the land of liberty, to receive help from the United States during the nineteenth-century uprisings? Thanking Fenimore Cooper for his activity in the Polish-American Committee in 1831, two Polish emigré leaders wrote, "May America, the model for all free countries, preserve the remembrance of our efforts and of our wrongs; the recollections of her spontaneous and generous sympathy will ever be dear to the Poles." The way in which this phrase is couched is fairly characteristic. Given the American determination to avoid entangling alliances in Europe—an unbroken tradition from Washington's *Farewell Address* through John Quincy Adams's speech and the Monroe Doctrine to the end of the nineteenth century—Polish politicians could perhaps count on some American sympathy but not on their active aid to the Polish cause. At one point during the Crimean War, the American minister in London, James Buchanan, dropped remarks which made Lelewel think that

America would not be inactive in the event of an uprising in Poland. The leadership of the Democratic Society was more sober in its evaluation of American policy. Manifestations of sympathy on the part of the United States "with the elements of the European future" were certainly to be welcomed, but one could not conceive that Washington would allow itself to become politically involved. The diplomacy of the 1863 Uprising did not take America into its calculations and was not unduly concerned by the Seward Note which refused to associate the United States with a Franco-British-Austrian *démarche* in St. Petersburg. Still, in 1864, a member of the insurrectionary government was appointed to represent Poland in Washington. Henryk Kałussowski, however, never stood the slightest chance of being officially received, much less recognized, by the United States government.[39]

The last decades of the nineteenth century contrast the rapid American rise to great-power status with the nadir of Polish post-1863 misfortunes. Manifest Destiny stands in stark contrast to the near obliteration of Poland in the nineteenth century. All that remained were the symbolic links between the American and the Polish revolutions represented by the names of Kościuszko and Puławski, but their status as symbols in American-Polish relations belongs to a different story.

As we said at the outset, the scattered examples given here can only be regarded as an introduction to further study. To attempt a systematic survey of the impact of the Partitions on American thinking about Poland, one would need to collect and examine references to the Partitions by American leaders in the White House, the State Department, and the Congress and analyze their context. The American press, whose reactions to the Polish Uprisings of 1830 and 1863 have already been studied in some depth, would have to become the object of another inquiry directed at different questions. Historical writings and textbooks would have to be scrutinized for the views they conveyed to the reader and student.[40] References to Polish Partitions in novels, poetry, music, and iconography would have to be collected. As arduous and difficult as this task might prove, its reward would be a clearer picture of American views on the Polish past and a refutation, or a confirmation, of the thesis implied in this paper.

What then is the thesis? The main point I have tried to make is that the Partitions affected both the American image of, and policies toward, Poland in the nineteenth century—and in the twentieth, although I have only touched on the latter. Condemnation of the Partitions, predominantly in moral terms, obscured the political significance of Poland and its place in international relations. Sympathy and pity mingled with condescension were present; an appreciation of Poland's potential or actual role in East Central Europe and its importance from the point of view of American global interests were generally absent. Only on rare occasions was Poland pictured as the "key to Europe"—the sub-title of Buell's book published in 1939.[41]

One has, of course, to distinguish between various periods. Up to the First World War, the verdict of the Partitions appeared final; as the British diplomat Sir Esme Howard put it, Poland was "like a closed and forgotten book."[42] The situation obviously changed during the First World War and in the interwar period, but the problem of Po-land's ability to maintain her independent existence rose again in American minds during the Second World War. Although we have con-centrated on the pre-1918 period, occasional references to the later decades of the twentieth century point to possibilities for fruitful inves-tigation of the last fifty years.

Looking at the Polish side, American identification with the univer-sal cause of liberty, independence, and "democratic revolution" tend-ed to make some Poles confuse expressions of interest in Polish free-dom with American willingness to involve itself on Poland's behalf. As already noted, this was not so visible in the nineteenth century, but it began to be apparent during the First World War, reaching its high point during the Second World War and its aftermath. Polish ex-pectations at times proved unrealistic precisely because they mistook American sympathy toward Poland or the Polish issue for American political commitment. It is at this point that the two questions raised in my paper converge; a closer scrutiny of both can provide us with addi-tional dimensions and depth of understanding.

NOTES

1 Cited in M. Haiman, *Poland and the American Revolutionary War* (Chicago, 1932), pp. 147-48.

2 Ch. H. Haskins and R. H. Lord, *Some Problems of the Peace Conference* (Cam-bridge, Mass., 1920), p. 165.

3 To mention only Z. Libiszowska, *Opinia polska wobec rewolucji amerykańskiej w XVIII wieku* (Łódź, 1962)—short English version, "Polish Opinion of the American Revolution," *Polish American Studies* 34 (Spring 1977)—and her "American Thought in Polish Political Writings of the Great Diet (1788-1792)," *Polish-American Studies* 1 (1976); I. M. Sokol, "The American Revolution and Poland: A Bibliograph-ical Essay," *Polish Review* 12 (Summer 1967): 3-17; M. M. Drozdowski, *The Ameri-can Revolution in the Polish Socio-Historical Literature* (Chicago, 1977)—a short but detailed survey—and relevant parts of R. R. Palmer, *The Age of the Democratic Revolution* (Princeton, 1959-64).

4 M. Haiman, *The Fall of Poland in Contemporary American Opinion* (Chicago, 1935).

5 K. A. Sutherland, "America views Poland: Perspectives from the Final Partition to the Rebirth of the Polish Nation," *Antemurale* 20 (1976).

6 J. W. Hoskins, " 'A Lesson Which All Our Countrymen Should Study': Jefferson views Poland," *Quarterly Journal of the Library of Congress* 33 (January 1976): 29-46.

7 H. Serejski, *Europa a rozbiory Polski* (Warsaw, 1970).

8 A. A. Lipscomb, ed., *The Writings of Thomas Jefferson* (Washington, 1903–05), vol. 14, pp. 394, 424.

9 Cited in T. A. Bailey, *America Faces Russia: Russian-American Relations From Early Times to Our Day* (Ithaca, 1950), p. 10.

10 Cited in Hoskins (cited above, note 6), p. 33; compare Palmer, *The Age of the Democratic Revolution,* vol. 1, p. 412.

11 Cited in Hoskins, p. 43.

12 See Haiman, *The Fall of Poland,* pp. 38–62 and Palmer, vol. 1, pp. 429–34.

13 J. C. Fitzpatrick, ed., *The Writings of Washington* (Washington, D.C., 1931–44), vol. 31, pp. 320–21.

14 "Conspiracy of Kings" published 18 August 1792, cited in Hoskins (cited above, note 6), p. 40.

15 See the highly stimulating and controversial J. Łojek, "The International Crisis of 1791: Poland Between the Triple Alliance and Russia," *East Central Europe* 2, no. 1 (1975): 1–63.

16 Cited in Haiman, *Poland and the American Revolutionary War*, p. 9.

17 On 7 September 1794, S. M. Hamilton, ed., *The Writings of James Monroe* (New York, 1898–1903), vol. 2, p. 53.

18 Cited in Haiman, *The Fall of Poland,* p. 260. At that time Stanislaus Augustus was not yet dead.

19 Ch. F. Adams, ed., *The Works of John Adams* (Boston, 1850–56), vol. 4, p. 374n.

20 Palmer, *The Age of the Democratic Revolution,* vol. 1, p. 209.

21 J. H. Hutson, "The Partition Treaty and the Declaration of Independence," *Journal of American History* 58 (March 1972): 877–96. My attention was drawn to this article by my distinguished colleague at Yale, Professor E. S. Morgan.

22 Cited in D. Lloyd George, *The Truth about the Peace Treaties* (London, 1938), vol. 1, p. 693.

23 Cited in P. S. Wandycz, "Partitions of Poland and the Diplomacy of the Partitioning Powers: Some Reflections on the Bicentennial of 1772," V. Erlich et al., eds., *For Wiktor Weintraub: Essays in Polish Literature, Language and History, Presented on the Occasion of His 65th Birthday* (The Hague, 1975), p. 559.

24 L. L. Gerson, *Woodrow Wilson and the Rebirth of Poland* (New Haven, 1953), p. 38.

25 On this topic, see especially J. J. Lerski, *A Polish Chapter in Jacksonian America: The United States and the Polish Exiles of 1831* (Madison, 1958) and J. W. Wieczerzak, "The Polish Insurrection of 1830–1831 in the American Press," *Polish Review* 6 (Winter-Spring 1961): 43–72.

26 See especially S. Bóbr-Tylingo, "The January Uprising and the American Civil War," *Antemurale* 20 (1976); J. Wieczerzak, *A Polish Chapter in Civil War America* (New York, 1967); J. J. Lerski, "The United States and the January Insurrection," *Polish American Studies* 30 (Spring 1973): 45–53; and A. P. Coleman and M. M. Coleman, *The Polish Insurrection of 1863 in the Light of New York Editorial Opinion* (Williamsport, Mass., 1934).

27 Cited in Wieczerzak, *A Polish Chapter in Civil War America,* pp. 47–48.

28 Ibid., p. 83.

29 Ibid., pp. 53–54.

30 Cited in M. Kaufman, "1863: Poland, Russia and the United States," *Polish American Studies* 21 (January-June 1964): 15.

31 The three books were reviewed in the *American Historical Review* at the time. H. B. Adams, *The Study of History in American Colleges and Universities* (U.S. Bureau of Education, Circulars of Information, Washington, 1887) provides valuable information on the general topic. See also American Historical Association *Annual Reports* for 1905, pp. 231–332. I am indebted to my distinguished colleague at Yale, Professor R. R. Palmer, for directing my attention to these publications.

32 Cited in J. A. Wytrwal, *Poles in American History and Tradition* (Detroit, 1969), p. 303.

33 Cited by K. A. Sutherland, "America views Poland" (cited above, note 5), p. 37.

34 Cited in W. S. Churchill, *Triumph and Tragedy* (Boston, 1953), p. 372.

35 The English edition of Niemcewicz's American diary is by M. Budka, *Under Their Vine and Fig Tree* (Elizabeth, New Jersey, 1965); a selection of Sienkiewicz's American correspondence was edited by Ch. Morley, *Portrait of America: Letters of Henryk Sienkiewicz* (New York, 1959). See also J. Svastek, "Polish Travelers in Nineteenth-Century United States," *Polish American Studies* 2 (January-June 1945): 38–45.

36 See among others the stimulating article by J. Jedlicki, "Images of America," *Polish Perspectives* 18 (November 1975); Drozdowski (cited above, note 3); and W. Weintraub, "Three Myths of America in Polish Romantic Literature," *Studies in Polish Civilization,* ed. D. S. Wandycz (New York, 1971).

37 See the 1967 edition prepared by E. Halicz as well as Halicz's *Partisan Warfare in 19th-Century Poland: The Development of a Concept* (Odense, 1975).

38 Cited in Haiman, *Kościuszko: Leader and Exile* (New York, 1946).

39 A collection of Kałussowski papers is in the archives of the J. Piłsudski Institute in New York.

40 An example of what I have in mind might be conveyed by my article "The Treatment of East Central Europe in History Textbooks," *American Slavic and East European Review* 16 (1957): 513–23.

41 L. Buell, *Poland: The Key to Europe* (New York, 1939). The book grew out of a report prepared for the Foreign Policy Association after a 1938 field trip to Poland.

42 Sir Esme Howard, *The Theatre of Life* (Boston, 1935–36), vol. 2, p. 312.

THE AMERICAN FOUNDING FATHERS AND POLAND

Anna M. Cienciala, University of Kansas

Why should we even expect the Founding Fathers of the United States to have known much, if anything, about such a distant country as Poland? Why should they have devoted any attention at all to Polish affairs? They were busy enough fighting for American independence and seeking the best form of government for the new state. Poland appeared somewhat exotic even to the English and French, both of whom were geographically much closer. In addition, Poland was a declining power just as the United States was emerging as a political entity onto the world stage. And finally, from 1789 onward, what attention the Americans did devote to European affairs was mostly given to the Revolution in France and the wars which followed, and to efforts to reestablish relations with Britain.

But despite all these factors, the Founding Fathers nevertheless did display some interest in Poland, and for two of them—John Adams and Thomas Jefferson—the interest was not merely a passing one. In the debates at the Constitutional Convention of 1787, the several references to Poland indicate an awareness of the anarchy that prevailed there before the First Partition. The explanations given for the anarchy reflected the Americans' own search for a viable constitution. But what were the sources for the Founding Fathers' information about Poland? How did they make use of it? And what were their interpretations of the reasons for her decline?

In colonial times, much as in our own days, Americans did not learn much of anything about Poland at school or in college. Today this is because history and geography have largely disappeared from the American school curriculum, while college history courses deal mostly with the United States and Western Europe (Eastern Europe is generally mentioned as an example of "a failure in democracy" in the interwar period and relegated to Communist studies after 1945). In colonial America, the educational system simply did not include any modern history at all, although geography was sometimes taught. Education followed the European model of the time. Boys learned Latin and sometimes Greek; the college curriculum still reflected the old *trivium* and *quadrivium* (logic, rhetoric, grammar, plus the classics, then mental, moral, natural philosophy, and mathematics), plus, at some colleges, astronomy, navigation, and land surveying. What history students learned, they learned through reading Homer and Thucydides. It was only in the curriculum of the College of Philadelphia, drawn up in 1756 by the educator William Smith, that we find history extending beyond the ancient world; this was Jean Le Clerc's *Compendium Historiae Universalis,* which reached the breathtakingly modern times of Charlemagne.[1]

Where, then, did educated Americans obtain their information about the contemporary world? They found it in newspapers, which reproduced it from papers printed in London, Paris, Leyden, and The Hague, and in books imported from Europe. Many of the Founding Fathers—almost half of the signatories of the Declaration of Independence—were lawyers, and they were voracious readers and library-builders. We know something about the libraries of John Adams and Thomas Jefferson, and they reflect the extensive and varied interests of those two men.[2] Finally, several leading American figures of this period spent time in Europe on diplomatic missions and maintained the contacts they developed there through active correspondence after their return home.

But it was at the Constitutional Convention of 1787 that we find references to Poland in numbers not matched before, or for a long time after in American politics. Since the debates concerned the best constitution for the new country, and since the Polish constitution and anarchy represented an obvious and contemporary negative example, the frequency is not surprising. Most of the references were made during the dispute on whether the chief executive should be elected by the legislature or by the people. Thus, James Madison—or Hamilton, since attributions vary—discounted fears that an election of the chief executive by the people need necessarily be accompanied by the upheavals that were so typical in Poland, because, it was argued, in Poland there were great rival princes who had the independent power and means to start them.[3] The same point was made by James Wilson, and Gouverneur Morris also denied that popular election of the president need necessarily be likened to a royal election in Poland. Madison also brought up the negative example of Poland in arguing his opposition to the proposal that the legislature should elect the chief executive. He warned that the ministers of foreign powers would intrigue and try to influence elections of that kind, for the great rival European powers who had American possessions would want a chief executive sympathetic to their interests. "Germany and Poland," he said, "are witness to the danger."[4]

Poland was also mentioned in debates on how Congress should vote. Hamilton argued in *The Federalist* in favor of a vote by two-thirds of the members present as against two-thirds of all members. Thus, he said, if the presence of two-thirds of all members was required for a vote, then the absence of some could be manipulated to achieve unanimity and hence recreate the impotence, perplexity, and disorder of the Roman Tribunate, the Polish Diet, and the States General of the Netherlands.[5] Some foreign observers mentioned Poland in their criticism of the system of government developing in America before the new Constitution was voted. Thus, the French chargé d'affaires, M. Otto, complained in June 1787 that the opposition of one state had, for the past four years, prevented the establishment of a duty of five per cent on imports. He remarked that encouraging a situation where one state alone could hinder legislation was as ruinous to the United States as the *liberum veto* had been for Poland.[6] In Poland itself, where American affairs were followed with great interest, there was disenchantment with American politics. After the first enthusiasm over the Declaration of Independence, doubts grew as to whether the United States would survive its anarchic system of government. The Constitution of 1787 met with general approval since it was seen as guaranteeing a strong central government—the goal of Polish reformers at that time.[7]

It is therefore no accident that the year 1787 saw the publication of the first brief account of Polish history and politics by an American. We find two chapters on Poland in John Adams's famous work *A Defense of the Constitutions of the Government of the United States*. The book, first published in London and Philadelphia in 1787, was republished the following year in London and Boston, and a decade later again in Philadelphia. In the meanwhile, it had also been expanded into a larger work, *History of the Principal Republics in the World,* which was published in three volumes in London in 1794. Adams was moved to write his *Defense* by an attack on the constitutions of the American states made by Anne-Robert-Jacques Turgot (1727–87), the famous French physiocrat and reformer, in a letter to Richard Price, an English clergyman who was well known for his support of the American cause, in his work *Observations on Civil Liberty and the Justice and Policy of the War with America,* published in 1776.[8] Turgot held that the system of checks and balances was useful in England to check the power of the crown, but that, in a republic, authority should repose in the nation. Adams believed in the absolute necessity of a government based on checks and balances, and his historical arguments and interpretations of history were founded on this belief.

In his book, Adams listed Poland together with England as "Monarchical Republics." For his major sources on Poland, he lists a book published in 1736, by the Abbé Desfontaines, a historian and an opponent of Voltaire;[9] he also quotes extensively from the work of an English historian, William Coxe, whose *Travels into Poland, Russia, Sweden and Denmark* had been published in three volumes in London in 1784, and from the writings of the Polish philosopher-king, Stanislas I

Leszczyński, the *Oeuvres du Philosophe Bienfaisant*, published in three volumes in Paris (1763) and Amsterdam (1764). Finally, he was also familiar with Rousseau's work on Poland.

Adams's chapters on Poland would justify a fuller discussion than is possible within the brief scope of this paper, for it influenced not only the views of his contemporaries but also of their descendants. He begins his account of Poland with a description of its society and government. "The peasants are slaves to the gentry. Having no property, all their acquisitions are made for their masters; they are exposed to all their passions, and are oppressed by them with impunity."[10] His source for this information was probably the work of King Stanislas I, although the power of the nobles and the state of the Polish peasantry were matters of general knowledge among educated Europeans, as witnessed by the account of the well-known lawyer and historian Samuel Puffendorf.[11] He then goes on to describe the Polish system of government (the Senate, general diets, royal elections—with their venality and corruption—and the *pacta conventa* and *liberum veto*) and to summarize Polish history up to the First Partition of 1772, basing his account mostly on Coxe.

Adams's interpretation of the reasons for Polish anarchy and decline rests on two main arguments. In the first place, there was no "balance," that is, checks and balances, in the Polish government, only the king and an assembly of nobles. Since there was no mediating power by the people, confusion and calamity were the results. The nobles were able to concentrate all power in their hands and reduce the king to the status of a "mere Doge of Venice, or avoyer of Bern."[12] The second argument is really an extension of the first: it is the abasement of the Polish people, that is, the peasantry, and here, citing long extracts from the works of Stanislas I,[13] he concludes: "It is not to be doubted that if there had been a people in existence in Poland, as there is in Holland, to have given that amiable prince [Stanislas Augustus] only the authority of a Stadholder, he would have said: 'I will die in the last ditch,' "[14] He then advances a syllogism to bolster his views: "If there should ever be a people in Poland, there will soon be a real King; and if ever there should be a King, in reality as well as in name, there will soon be a people."[15] Thus, Adams linked the absence of the people as a mediating power between the king and the nobles with the conclusion that the absence of checks and balances led to the partition of Poland, seeing it as the "consummation of all panegyrics upon a sovereignty in a single assembly."[16]

However, so far as the First Partition is concerned, Adams did not neglect forces other than those he had already stressed. He saw the impetus to the Partition in religious intolerance, a common view at the time. He rendered honor to King Stanislas Augustus for opposing the

use of torture in the treason trials that followed the revolt of the Confederation of Bar. He also thought the king had been unable to improve
the government because of the fetters placed upon him by the Polish
constitution and because of the alarms his efforts had aroused among
the neighboring powers.[17] He attributed the Partition to the king of
Prussia. He concluded his chapters on Poland with regret that he could
not translate all the works of the philosopher-king and wrote, "It is a
pity that the whole people whose misery he describes and laments,
were not equally sensible of the necessity of a less circumscribed royal
authority."[18]

John Adams may have mellowed in his old age, or perhaps Charles
Francis Adams, his grandson and editor, softened his judgment; for in
a footnote to this passage there is praise for the Polish Constitution of
1791, while the Third Partition of 1795 is attributed to the alarm the
constitution had aroused among Poland's neighbors, particularly Catherine II of Russia. Then he observes, first, that no constitution can
prevail if it does not reflect the character and principles of the community which adopts it, and second, that if the geographical situation of
Poland and the United States had been reversed, it is at least open to
question whether disorders would not have developed in the United
States similar to those that had occurred in Poland.[19] It is doubtful,
however, whether these comments had much impact on American
readers, for most people do not read footnotes, nor do they like having
one simple, clear-cut argument modified by others requiring more profound reflection. As it was, the picture of a greedy and ruthless nobility
exploiting a poor, ignorant peasantry came to dominate American interpretations of Poland's decline and fall for a long time to come, even
down to our own days.

Let us now pass to Thomas Jefferson. It is a pity he failed to write a
work on Poland, for, of all the Founding Fathers, he was the best informed on Polish affairs and the most sympathetically inclined to that
country. His library included the major contemporary works on Poland, indicating his lively and continuing interest.[20] During his stay in
Paris, where he represented his country from 1785 to 1789, he was in
close touch with Philip Mazzei, an Italian, who was also a citizen of
Virginia, and who was the agent of the King of Poland in the French
capital from 1789 to 1791. Indeed, Jefferson encouraged Mazzei to accept that post—overcoming his fears of displeasing his fellow Americans by telling him that "the King of Poland was better known in
America than in Europe, that he was the head of a Republic and not a
despot and that he was considered the best citizen of his kingdom."[21]
This was certainly an exaggeration, but what Jefferson may have had in
mind were the rather cool relations that had developed for some time

between France and Poland, due mainly to the French view of the King as a puppet of Russia.

In any case, it was Mazzei, along with another Italian in the Polish King's service, Abbé Piattoli, who kept Jefferson informed on Polish affairs between 1788 and 1792. A third source of information was Lewis Littlepage, a native Virginian who was more a typical eighteenth-century diplomat and soldier of fortune than a typical American. Littlepage finally opted for service under the King of Poland and became a royal chamberlain. His letters from Warsaw are of great interest, as are his memoirs published in 1797. Like Mazzei, he was finally able to collect the King's debts to him from the rulers of Russia, who had assumed them as part of the agreement that led to the King's residence in the Russian capital after the Third Partition.[22] It was on the basis of information supplied by these three men, and particularly, Mazzei, that Jefferson wrote on Polish affairs to John Adams, John Jay, and George Washington. The American consul in Paris, William Short, continued to send reports on Polish affairs, based on the same sources, after Jefferson had left Paris.[23]

As is well known, Jefferson developed a close friendship with Tadeusz Kościuszko when the latter visited America for the second time in the years 1797–98. He was in constant contact with the Polish hero and arranged for his secret departure for France in 1798, when he also gave him an unofficial mission to try to improve Franco-American relations. We also know that Kościuszko made him the executor of his will. There is a holograph letter from Kościuszko to Jefferson in the Pierpont Morgan Library in New York, written at the time of his departure, illustrating his anxiety as well as his English. It reads as follows:

Dear Sir,
     I lost the passage to Lisbon and I [am] afraid of this to Bordeaux and when you will go to Virginia my hopes are at an end. It may perhapes bee [be] found one going to Lisbon, do not fogget [forget] that jam [I am] under your protection, and you only my rescue in this country. Your humble and obedient
                                                                  servant Kosciuszko[24]

Two later references to Poland, written in 1811 and 1816, illustrate Jefferson's views on that country's fall. To William Duane in July 1811 he wrote:

The history of Poland gives a lesson which all our countrymen should study; the example of a country erased from the map of the world by the dissensions of its own citizens. The papers of every day read them the counter lesson of the impossibility of subduing a people acting with an undivided will. Spain, under all her sad disadvantages, physical and mental, is an encouraging example of this.[25]

Jefferson seems to have accepted the view that lack of unity was the principal cause of the fall of Poland. However, a later letter to John Adams, written in January 1816, puts the fall of Poland into the larger context of international morality and its violation by Russia while others stood by as passive observers:

> With some exception only, through the seventeenth and eighteenth centuries morality occupied an honourable chapter in the political code of the nations. Those who administered the governments of the greater powers at least, had a respect to faith, and considered the dignity of their goverment as involved in its integrity. A wound indeed was inflicted on this character of honour in the eighteenth century by the partition of Poland. But this was the atrocity of a barbarous government chiefly in conjunction with a smaller one still scrambling to become great, while one only of those already great, and having character to lose, descended to the baseness of an accomplice of the crime. France, England, Spain shared in it only inasmuch as they stood aloof and permitted its perpetration.[26]

Apart from Adams and Jefferson, the other major figures of American independence showed little interest in Poland after the debates at the Constitutional Convention of 1787. It is ironic that the two Americans who enjoyed the greatest popularity in Poland, Benjamin Franklin and George Washington, apparently lacked interest in Polish affairs. Apart from one brief mention of Poland in *Poor Richard's Almanac* for 1736, where Poland was rhetorically asked if she would be the floodgate for letting the infidel Turks into Europe,[27] and a note of 1770 that "horizontal windmills" were not in general use except in Poland,[28] we find only one statement on Poland, and a rather disparaging one at that. In a letter of 16 August 1764 to Colonel Henry Bouquet, Franklin wrote:

> Abroad, the Poles are cutting one another's throats a little, about their Election. But 'tis their Constitution, and I suppose reckon'd among their Privileges to sacrifice a few thousand of the subjects every interregnum to the Manes of the deceas'd King, or to Honour his Successor. And if they are fond of this Privilege, I don't know how their Neighbours have any right to disturb them in the enjoyment of it. And yet, the Russians have entered their Country with an Army to preserve Peace! and secure the FREEDOM of the Election![29]

It may be that Franklin had more profound things to say on Poland toward the end of his life, but as is also the case with Adams, Jefferson, and others, we cannot verify this until all his works have been published.

George Washington seems also to have had no more than a passing interest in Poland. He did, however, react favorably to news of the Constitution of 1791, for he wrote to David Humphreys on 20 July 1791, "Poland, by the public papers, appears to have made large and unexpected strides towards liberty, which, if true, reflects great honor on the present King, who seems to have been the principal promoter of the business."[30] Apart from that, we have on record, so far at least, nothing more than sincere good wishes to Poland. Thus, in reply to a note from Kościuszko, dated 23 August 1797, in which the latter complimented him as "a great man whose eminent virtues to his country rendered him dear to every feeling breast,"[31] Washington graciously replied:

> I beg you to be assured that, no one has a higher respect, and veneration for your character than I have; or one who more sincerely wished, during your arduous struggle in the cause of liberty and your country, that it might be crowned with Success. But the ways of Providence are inscrutable, and Mortals must submit.[32]

In June 1798, he wrote to Kościuszko's friend and companion, Julian Ursyn Niemcewicz, in reply to the latter's thanks for the hospitality extended to him at Mount Vernon:

> That your country is not as happy as your struggle to make it so, was Patriotic and Noble, is a matter which all lovers of national Liberty and the Rights of Man, have sorely lamented: and if my Vows, during the arduous contest could have availed, you would *now*, have been as happy in the enjoyment of these desirable blessings under your own Vine and Fig Tree, as the People of these United States may be under theirs.[33]

Of the remaining figures among the Founding Fathers, Alexander Hamilton and James Madison merit some consideration, while four others, Gouverneur Morris, James Wilson, John Jay, and Rufus King, seem to have had a marginal interest in Poland. In *The Federalist,* this time written by Madison, the longest statement on Poland is to be found in Number 29 of 8 December 1787. This passage reflects the debate on the election of the chief executive and is reminiscent of the statements on Poland at the Constitutional Convention of 1787. Discussing the examples of confederacies, the article mentions the German confederacy and the Polish as examples of weakness leading to foreign intervention:

> If more direct examples are wanting, Poland, as a Government over local sovereigns, might not improperly be taken notice of. Nor could any proof more striking be given of the calamities flowing from such institutions. Equally unfit for self-government and self-defence, it has long been at the mercy of its powerful neighbours, who have lately had the mercy to disburden it of one third of its people and territories.[34]

Aside from this, Madison appears not to have written anything important on Poland, while Hamilton referred to it either for its significance vis-à-vis American security or, again, as an example of the dangers of foreign intervention. Thus, in Number 11 of *Americanus,* on 7 February 1794, he commented:

> The new dismemberment of Poland will be another obstacle to the detaching of troops from Europe against this country. The fruits of this transaction can only be secured by Russia and Prussia by the agency of large bodies of forces kept on foot for the purpose within the dismembered territories.[35]

Two years later, in December 1796, Hamilton published in *Minerva* an "Answer" to the French decree against neutrals. He interpreted this step as designed to influence "timid minds" to vote for a president or vice-president amenable to France and asked what would happen if foreign agents interfered in the election. His answer was: "Poland, that was once a respectable nation, but is now a nation no longer, is a melancholy example of the dangers of foreign influence in the election of a chief magistrate. Eleven millions of people have lost their independence from that cause alone."[36]

Gouverneur Morris became acquainted with Polish affairs during his mission to Paris and London in 1789–94. In August 1790, he wrote to George Washington, "The King of Prussia has endeavored to obtain from Poland the Cession of Thurn and Danzig . . . and if he had succeeded or should succeed he will not only become at once a naval Power, but will hold in his Hand the Key to the great Granary of Europe."[37] A year later, he asked a Pole he had met at Mme. de Stael's whether there might not be an opportunity for Poland to regain the territory lying between Poland and the Baltic and then wrote, "He shews on this subject the Eagerness which I expected."[38] He approved of the Constitution of 3 May 1791, writing shortly thereafter:

> The Kingdom of Poland has formed a new Constitution which will I think change the political Face of Europe by drawing that Kingdom out of Anarchy into Power. The leading Features of the Change are an hereditary Monarchy, the Affranchisement of the Peasants and a Share of the Government given to the Towns. These are the great Means of destroying pernicious Aristocracy.[39]

He saw the Russian attack on Poland in 1792 as resulting from Catherine's desire to overturn the Polish constitution.[40] In December 1796, he noted that he had heard from St. Priest of Emperor Paul's visit to Kościuszko and from a Pole, M. Lanskorenski (i.e., Lanckoroński), of the emperor's release of ten thousand Poles from Siberia. Morris thought this act would do more than an army of twenty thousand men to secure the Russian part of Poland. Then he concluded his note as follows: "But yet the character of the Poles is not such as may easily be trusted; the great are too corrupt, and the body of the people too much abased."[41] Clearly, the stereotyped image of the Poles, as it then existed in Adams's work and contemporary European accounts, affected Morris's analysis of the situation.

Such was also the image of Poland of James Wilson, the great American legislator and teacher of law. In his law lectures given at Philadelphia in the winter of 1790–91, he referred to Poland while comparing the American Constitution to that of Great Britain. He traced the objections to a popularly elected chief magistrate to the example of Poland. The picture he painted of that country could have come straight out of Adams:

> And whence this strong antipathy to choice? Popular clamours, popular disturbances, popular tumults, and popular insurrections are ever present to their view. The unfortunate and fluctuating example of Poland dances perpetually before their eyes. They reflect not on the cause of this example. Poland is composed only of slaves, headed and commanded by a few despots. Those despots have private purposes to serve; and they head their slaves as the instruments for executing those private purposes. In Poland, we search in vain for a people. Need we be surprised, that, at an election in Poland, where there are only tyrants and slaves, all the detestable and pernicious extremes of tyranny should unite?

This danger, said Wilson, did not exist in the United States, where freemen and fellow citizens could be entrusted with the election of the chief magistrate.[42] One may well wonder how many generations of American law students have been, and perhaps still are, affected by this view of the decline and fall of old Poland.

We come now to John Jay and Rufus King. They seem to have had contact with Polish affairs only through the person of Tadeusz Kościuszko. Thus, Rufus King wrote from London on 10 June 1797, introducing Kościuszko and Niemcewicz to John Jay, who was then Governor of New York. He recommended them to Jay's esteem and friendship.[43] In Rufus King's papers, we find a letter from Kościuszko, written in French and dated 3 June 1797, thanking him for his help in procuring them passage on an American vessel sailing to the United States. Kościuszko wrote that Niemcewicz would call on King to express his thanks.[44] He thanked King again in a letter written two weeks later, this time in English. In the postscript, he also mentioned the "tender" treatment he had received from the family of the American consul in Bristol, Vander-Horst, and that he would soon sail for Philadelphia on the "Captain Lee" since that ship was "more comfortable for the Passage of a man in my Situation."[45] This was a reference to Kościuszko's inability to walk, which, it has been recently discovered, was feigned in order to facilitate his departure from Russia. His sudden ability to walk again, which he demonstrated on leaving America in 1798, was the result of the intensive, solitary exercises, kept secret even from Niemcewicz, that had enabled him to retain the use of his legs during the ruse.[46] The last reference to Kościuszko in King's correspondence is a letter from General John Armstrong, dated 9 January 1819, in which the latter asked whether the secretary of state's office had any evidence that Kościuszko was dead. If so, General Armstrong wished to claim the $3,700 Kościuszko had left to his son in a bequest he had made in the presence of the American consul in Paris and payable by Jefferson on Kościuszko's death.[47] As it happened, Kościuszko's will was also contested by his landlord in Soleure, Switzerland, Franz Xavier Zeltner, and his family, and by Kościuszko's relatives in Poland. The matter was finally settled in 1852, in favor of Kościuszko's descendants, the seven grandchildren and great-grandchildren of his sisters.[48]

Two conclusions seem to emerge from this brief study. First, an interest in Poland emerged in America during the Constitutional Convention of 1787, which was reflected in John Adams's *Defense of the Constitutions of the United States*, with its brief study of Polish history and institutions, published in the same year. Its source was obviously the heated debate for and against a strong central government, particularly the issue of an elective presidency. The proponents of a strong central government used the Polish example as an argument against the type of loose confederation that existed in America from 1776 to 1787. The proponents of a popularly elected president pointed to foreign interference in the Polish Diet, while the proponents of election by legislature pointed to the unrest that accompanied elections by the "masses," actually the nobility, in Poland. Second, insofar as the Founding Fathers and other educated Americans tried to interpret the causes of Poland's decline and fall, they saw them mainly in the phenomenon of an all powerful nobility combined with an enslaved peasantry. They were not deterred from this conclusion by the knowledge that there were also nobles and serfs in Prussia, Austria, and Russia, or rather, this did not seem to lead to any reflection. Abhorring both serfdom and nobility, they believed that a free people possessed the wisdom to choose its own government. In view of their own struggle and the structure of their society, it is not surprising that they should have fastened on the power of the Polish nobles and the misery of the peasantry as the major causes for the fall of Poland. While they were not unaware of the role of the partitioning powers, they tended to see this as the natural consequence of the evils of the Polish system of government and the structure of Polish society. In this view, they were seconded not only by the liberals of Western Europe but also by the emerging school of democratic thought among the Poles themselves, a school that exerted a strong influence on Polish views and attitudes (Polish Democratic Society).

A major controversy in Polish historiography over the causes of the

Partitions was carried on between those who held that noble anarchy and peasant enslavement led to Poland's fall and those who believed that it was due primarily to the greed of her neighbors. We now try, on the basis of our greater knowledge, to find a compromise between these views, but it is not surprising that the Founding Fathers preferred what we might now regard as the democratic interpretation. This preference and the successful development of American democracy, contrasted with the unsuccessful Polish bids for independence in the nineteenth century and the history of Poland in the twentieth century, have tended to preserve to this day a negative image of the Poles in explaining the causes of the Partitions.

NOTES

1 Jean LeClerc (1657-1736), *Compendium Historiae Universalis, ab Initio Mundi ad Tempora Caroli Magni Imp* (Amsterdam, 1698; Leipzig, 1713; London, 1735); see William Smith's proposed curriculum for the College of Philadelphia, 1756, in L. A. Cremin, *American Education: The Colonial Experience, 1607-1713* (New York, 1970), pp. 382-83. Some other useful studies on the subject are L. F. Snow, *The College Curriculum in the United States* (New York, 1907); J. J. Walsh, *Education of the Founding Fathers of the Republic. Scholasticism in the Colonial Colleges: A Neglected Chapter in the History of American Education* (New York, 1935); R. Middlekauff, *Ancients and Axioms: Secondary Education in Eighteenth-Century New England* (New Haven, 1963).
2 See J. Hoskins, " 'A Lesson Which All Our Countrymen Should Study,' Jefferson Views Poland," *Quarterly Journal of the Library of Congress* 33 (January 1976): 29-46; W. Peden, "Notes and Documents: Some Notes Concerning Thomas Jefferson's Libraries," *William and Mary Quarterly*, 3rd ser., vol. 1, no. 3 (July 1944), 265-72; there is a catalog of John Adams's library in the *Boston Public Library Bulletin*, vol. 1 (1926).
3 This passage is attributed to Hamilton in *The Journal of the Federal Convention Kept by James Madison*, ed. E. H. Scott (Chicago, 1898), p. 184; and to James Madison in *The Records of the Federal Convention of 1787*, ed. M. Ferrand, 4 vols. (New Haven, 1966), vol. 1, p. 290.
4 M. Ferrand, *Records*, vol. 2, p. 109.
5 *The Papers of Alexander Hamilton*, ed. H. C. Syrett (New York, 1962), vol. 4, p. 632.
6 M. Ferrand, *Records*, vol. 3, p. 41.
7 See Z. Libiszowska, *Opinia polska wobec rewolucji amerykańskiej w XVIII wieku* (Łódź, 1962), pp. 121-28; also M. M. Drozdowski, "Rewolucja amerykańska w polskiej myśli historycznej i społecznej," *Kwartalnik Historyczny* 82, no. 1 (1975): 69-73.
8 For Richard Price, see *Dictionary of National Biography*, vol. 16 (Oxford, 1967-68), pp. 334-37.

9 Pierre François Guyot Desfontaines (1685-1745), see *Dictionaire de Biographie Française*, vol. 10 (1965), where, however, the work on Poland is not listed.

10 *The Works of John Adams, Second President of the United States, by His Grandson, Charles Francis Adams*, vol. 4 (Boston, 1865), p. 360.

11 Samuel Puffendorf, *An Introduction to the History of the Principal Kingdoms and States of Europe*, English trans. 6th ed. (London, 1706), on Polish peasants, p. 369; nobles, 369-71.

12 *Works of John Adams*, vol. 4, p. 362.

13 Ibid., pp. 371-73.

14 Ibid., p. 369.

15 Ibid., p. 371.

16 Ibid., p. 368.

17 Ibid., p. 367.

18 Ibid., p. 373.

19 Ibid., pp. 373-74, n. 1; this note is prefaced by a quotation from Dufau et al., *Précis de l'histoire du Gouvernement de Pologne; Collection des Constitutions*, vol. 4, p. 24. The reference is to Pierre Armand Dufau, 1795-1877; the work in question was published in six volumes (Paris, 1821-23).

20 See n. 2 above.

21 *Memoirs of the Life and Peregrinations of the Florentine Philip Mazzei, 1730-1816*, trans. H. R. Marraro (New York, 1942), p. 302. See also Marraro's article "Philip Mazzei and His Polish Friends," *Bulletin of the Polish Institute of Arts and Sciences in America* 2 (April 1944): 757-822. Mazzei's letters to Stanislas Augustus for the period 1788-92 were published by R. Ciampini, *Lettere de Filippo Mazzei alla Corte di Polonia (1788-1792)* (Bologna, 1937). This was to be volume 1, but volume 2 has never appeared. See also J. Fabre, *Stanislas Auguste Poniatowski et l'Europe des Lumières* (Paris, 1952), pp. 4, 350-52, 371, 432-37, 507-22.

22 There are two biographies of Lewis Littlepage: C. C. Davis, *The King's Chevalier, A Biography of Lewis Littlepage* (New York, 1961), and N. H. Boand, *Lewis Littlepage* (Richmond, Va., 1970). While Boand was not a trained historian, her work is preferable to the rather popular study by Davis. Littlepage's *Mémoire politique et particulier* was published in Hamburg in 1797.

23 William Short, diplomat, 1759-1849. I do not cite this correspondence, since this was most ably done by J. Hoskins in the article cited in n. 2 above.

24 Holograph letter, Tadeusz Kościuszko to Thomas Jefferson, received 14 August 1798, now in J. Pierpont Morgan Library, New York.

25 *Jefferson Cyclopedia*, ed. J. P. Foley (New York, 1900; reprinted 1967), vol. 2, p. 697.

26 *The Adams-Jefferson Letters*, ed. L. J. Capon (Chapel Hill, 1959), vol. 2 (1812-26), pp. 458-59.

27 *The Papers of Benjamin Franklin*, ed. L. W. Labaree (New Haven, 1960), vol. 2, pp. 143-44.

28 Ibid., vol. 17, p. 105.

29 *The Writings of Benjamin Franklin*, ed. A. H. Smyth, 10 vols. (New York, 1905-07), p. 253.

30 *The Writings of George Washington*, ed. J. C. Fitzpatrick (Washington, D.C., 1939), vol. 31, pp. 320-21.

31 Tadeusz Kościuszko to George Washington, 23 August 1797, George Washington Presidential Papers, ser. 4, reel 114.
32 George Washington to Thaddeus Kosciuszko, 31 August 1797, *Writings of George Washington,* vol. 36, p. 22.
33 George Washington to Julian Ursyn Niemcewicz, 18 June 1798, ibid., p. 297.
34 *The Complete Madison,* ed. S. Padover (New York, 1953), p. 74.
35 *The Papers of Alexander Hamilton,* ed. H. C. Syrett, vol. 16, (1972), p. 15.
36 *The Works of Alexander Hamilton,* ed. H. C. Lodge, vol. 5 (New York, 1885), p. 349.
37 *The Papers of Thomas Jefferson,* ed. J. Boyd et al. 19 vols. to date (Princeton, 1950-74), vol. 18, p. 294.
38 *Gouverneur Morris: A Diary of the French Revolution,* ed. B. C. Davenport (Boston, 1939), vol. 2, p. 285.
39 Ibid., p. 188.
40 *The Diary and Letters of Gouverneur Morris,* ed. A. C. Morris (New York, 1888), vol. 1, p. 542.
41 *Gouverneur Morris Diary,* vol. 2, p. 238.
42 *The Works of James Wilson,* ed. R. G. McCloskey, vol. 2 (Cambridge, Mass., 1967), p. 318.
43 *Correspondence and Public Papers of John Jay,* ed. H. P. Johnston (New York, 1893), vol. 4, p. 223.
44 *The Life and Correspondence of Rufus King,* ed. Ch. R. King, 6 vols. (New York, 1894-1900), vol. 2, pp. 188-89.
45 Ibid., p. 189.
46 J. Dihm, *Kościuszko nieznany* (Warsaw, 1969).
47 *Life and Correspondence of Rufus King,* vol. 6, p. 188.
48 On this, as well as on the friendship of Jefferson and Kościuszko, see E. P. Alexander, "Jefferson and Kosciuszko: Friends of Liberty and of Man," *Pennsylvania Magazine of History and Biography* 92 (January 1968): 87-103.

TADEUSZ KOŚCIUSZKO, KAZIMIERZ PUŁASKI, AND THE AMERICAN WAR OF INDEPENDENCE: A STUDY IN NATIONAL SYMBOLISM AND MYTHOLOGY

M. K. Dziewanowski, University of Wisconsin, Milwaukee

This essay[1] will concentrate on the repercussions in subsequent Polish-American relations of the roles played by Tadeusz Kościuszko and Kazimierz Pułaski during the American Revolutionary War rather than on their activities in that war.[2] That role is often misrepresented on both sides of the Atlantic in election rhetoric and patriotic speeches. For instance, an American ambassador to Poland during the 1930s wrote, "The friendship of the U.S. toward Poland is based upon gratitude for the sacrifices of Pułaski and Kościuszko, and the scores of other noble Poles who during our Revolutionary War offered their lives in the cause of liberty, asking nothing in return."[3] Are such sweeping statements justified by the facts?

First of all, Kościuszko and Pułaski, in offering their services to the thirteen colonies, were not motivated primarily by the cause of liberty. As has been shown by Korzon and by Dihm, Kościuszko volunteered to join the American forces mainly to forget an unhappy love affair with Ludwika Sosnowska, whose father, a powerful magnate, governor, and senator, judged the impecunious squire unworthy of her and had married her off to Prince Joseph Lubomirski. Frustrated and humiliated, Kościuszko decided to leave his native country and find an outlet for his talents abroad. He first hesitated between Saxony and America. His choice of the latter might have been ideologically motivated, but we do not really know.[4] As for Pułaski, his desperate financial situation in 1777 in France, his desire "to restore the family's fortune," and his futile hope eventually to "engage in commerce" were strong motives for offering his services to Silas Dean and Benjamin Franklin.[5] Here, too, the idealistic and the practical after two centuries are difficult to disentangle.

Despite their original motives, once Kościuszko and Pułaski had come to America and espoused its cause they both did their best to serve their "second country" well. Since Kościuszko came before Pułaski, served longer, and was by far the more important of the two, we shall start our discussion with him. To begin with, he was one of the first foreign officers to join the army. He came in August 1776, a thirty-one-year-old captain of the Polish artillery. On 18 October, he was appointed colonel of engineers with a salary of sixty dollars a month. Kościuszko's first assignment was to fortify Philadelphia to make it secure against possible attacks by the Royal Navy. This he achieved by building two forts on the banks of the Delaware River: the first, Fort Mercier, on the New Jersey side, and the second, Billingport. For his good work, he was awarded fifty pounds.

In Philadelphia, Kościuszko befriended General Horatio Gates, who insisted on taking him to Ticonderoga as his engineer. Kościuszko immediately recognized that Fort Ticonderoga would be indefensible should the British place cannons on top of nearby Mount Defiance. His suggestion that this crucial peak be fortified was rejected, however, as too difficult to accomplish, although his views were vindicated when General John Burgoyne came from Canada and did in fact immediately drag his cannons to the top of the mountain, compelling the American commander of Ticonderoga, General Arthur St. Clair, to abandon the fort and retreat.

Instructed by General Gates to establish a new defensive position, Kościuszko, as chief engineer of the Northern Army, selected a field near the present Saratoga Springs. He protected its weak spots with formidable redoubts and crowned Bemis Heights with a powerful fort to face the advance of Burgoyne's troops.[6] The Battle of Saratoga was one of the important military encounters of the war; the surrender of General Burgoyne was particularly significant because it brought France actively into war as America's ally.

The efficient fortification of West Point was Kościuszko's third important contribution to the American War of Independence. This he accomplished during two and a half years of strenuous work (1778–80) by directing a labor force of some twenty-five hundred workers. According to an American expert, West Point "was the hub from which the spokes of the war radiated and returned," a "pivotal point of tactics and strategy," "the Gibraltar of America." Just two months after work was completed, Benedict Arnold attempted to deliver the fort to Major John André but fortunately failed. Later, it was Kościuszko who urged the selection of West Point as the site for a United States military academy. He planted with his own hands a flower garden there, which still bears his name. A monument was also erected by the Corps of Cadets in 1828 in commemoration of Kościuszko's contributions to the cause of independence.

His fourth contribution to the American Revolutionary War was in the ranks of the Southern Army under General Nathaniel Greene. Kościuszko organized the entire campaign up to the evacuation of Charleston, and fate preserved for him the honor of firing the last shots in the American Revolution at James Island on 14 November 1782. Throughout the southern campaign he made many operational surveys and planned, as well as executed, the transportation of troops. General Greene called Kościuszko a "master of his profession" and gave him a letter of commendation to General William Irvine, in which he thus described the Pole:

> Among the most useful and agreeable of my companions in arms, was Colonel Kościuszko. Nothing could exceed his zeal for the public service, nor in the prosecution of various objects that presented themselves in our small but active warfare, could anything be more useful than his attention, vigilance and industry. In promoting my views to whatever department of the service directed, he was at all times, a ready and able assistant. One in a word whom no pleasure could seduce, no labor fatigue and no danger deter. What besides greatly distinguished him was an unparalleled modesty and entire unconsciousness of having done anything extraordinary. Never making a claim or pretention for himself and never omitting to distinguish and commend the merits of others.[8]

Among his contemporaries, Kościuszko enjoyed considerable prestige and respect for his service in America. At the end of the war, he was accepted, one of only three foreigners, into the Society of the Cincinnati. He had many American friends, but contrary to a popular legend, George Washington was not one of them. It was after some difficulty that Congress rewarded Kościuszko by promoting him to the rank of brigadier general on 13 October 1783, for the "high sense of his long, faithful and meritorious services."[9]

His last military service rendered to his "second country" came in Paris in 1800, when, at the request of General William R. Davis, he wrote the first authoritative handbook for the United States artillery. Originally written in French, it was translated into English in 1808 under the title *Manoeuvres of Horse Artillery*[10] and became the official manual of the United States armed forces (which it remained for a long time to come).

Although Kościuszko's service was meritorious, it was not free of conflict. A great deal of research is still needed before some blank spots in his relations with his associates, especially George Washington, can be elucidated. Kościuszko's radicalism, especially his strong abolitionist views, and his openly manifested compassion for the slaves must have been distasteful to many of his comrades. After the completion of the West Point fortification, General Gates gave Kościuszko a Negro slave, Agrippa Hull, as a token of appreciation. Kościuszko immediately set Hull free and declared that slavery was repugnant and immoral. After his liberation, Hull settled on a farm near Stockbridge, Massachusetts. One wonders how that gesture of defiance was received by his colleagues, many of whom were southern planters. Some of them may well have regarded him as an eccentric do-gooder and an inconvenient man to have around.

In fact, Kościuszko's service with the southern command had a direct bearing on his attitude toward the Negroes. While waiting for his assignment, he visited a number of plantations, where he had his first direct contact with masses of Negro slaves and the abject conditions under which they lived. Those visits were never forgotten, and their memories would find their reflection in Kościuszko's last will.

After the war, along with his promotion to brigadier general, the Congress issued Kościuszko a certificate for $12,208.54 in unpaid salary including interest for the period 1 January 1793 to 31 December 1797. In 1798, although more often than not in dire need of money, he decided to leave this entire American sum, a considerable one in those days, for the purchase, liberation, and education of Negro slaves. He had had a chance to become a landowner and had rejected it. He designated Thomas Jefferson as executor of his estate, but legal complications, including the existence of other wills made later, frustrated his intentions. When Kościuszko died in 1817, Thomas Jefferson refused to become the executor of Kościuszko's American estate.

The full text of Kościuszko's principal testament reads as follows:

I, Thaddeus Kościuszko, being just on my departure from America, do hereby declare and direct that, should I make no other testamentary disposition of my property in the United States, I hereby authorize my friend, Thomas Jefferson, to employ the whole thereof in purchasing negroes from among his own or any others, and giving them liberty in my name; in giving them an education in trade or otherwise; in having them instructed for their new condition in the duties of morality, which may make them good neighbors, good fathers and mothers, husbands and wives; in their duty as citizens, teaching them to be defenders of their liberty and country, of the good order of society; and in whatsoever may make them happy and useful. 5th of May 1798. T. Kościuszko.[11]

These words were written sixty-five years before the Emancipation Proclamation of Abraham Lincoln. By drafting such a testament and entrusting its execution to Jefferson, Kościuszko was not only pleading the cause of emancipation of American slaves but also pointing to the necessity of having them "instructed for their new condition." He understood that emancipation without education would turn the Negroes into a proletariat, that training not only in job skills but also in citizenship was necessary. This, he stressed, was the only way of solving the problem of slavery in a satisfactory way. By the standards of his time, his testament was a bold, progressive abolitionist manifesto.

A foreigner, a pioneer of emancipation, a Polish nobleman as a spokesman for racial democracy and justice in eighteenth-century America is something to consider. Kościuszko, a man of vision, ahead of his time, must have been a challenge to his American contemporaries. It seems to me that herein lies one of the reasons behind the ambivalent relationship between Kościuszko and George Washington. The problem is worth investigating in contemporary documents, memoirs, and correspondence.

Already Korzon has pointed to the fact that Washington was rather cold and reserved toward the Polish engineer. It is interesting to note that Kościuszko, who started the war as a lieutenant colonel, ended it as only a colonel, despite his "meritorious service" of eight years. To get his promotion to brigadier general, he had to insist on it in a special letter. In turn, Washington's letter of thanks to him after the war was extremely restrained and formal, not to be compared with similar letters he wrote to other foreign officers.[12] On his return to the United States in 1789, Kościuszko brought Washington a package from Paris, but he sent it by mail from Philadelphia and never paid a visit to his former commander-in-chief at Mt. Vernon. He refused to do so despite Washington's invitation to come and see him.[13] This also does not indicate a particularly friendly relationship.[14]

All these facts do not detract from Kościuszko's contribution to the cause of independence for the thirteen colonies: it was substantial and solid. He served in the United States Army for eight years, 1776–84. His main achievements in America were those of an engineer and artilleryman, most notably the construction of five forts; two, Fort Mercier and Billingport, were on the banks of the Delaware River, three, Ticonderoga, Bemis Heights, and West Point, along the Hudson. Another was the handbook used by three generations of American artillerymen. Kościuszko's merits were hailed by his contemporaries and by posterity. When he died at Soleure, Switzerland, on 15 October 1817, the United States mourned his death, and an eloquent speech was made to the House of Representatives by the nation's ninth President, William Henry Harrison.[15] America's respect for Kościuszko is also attested by numerous monuments, the most important of them located in Washington, D.C., at Lafayette Square across the street from the White House.[16]

Pułaski's contribution to the War of Independence was superficially more dramatic and colorful; it involved organizing and training the first American cavalry units as well as active participation in front-line combat, including several spectacular cavalry charges and, in the end, a hero's death on the battlefield of Savannah. While Kościuszko came to America as a well-trained but unknown captain of modest military standing, Pułaski arrived with an established reputation as an unsuccessful, but extremely brave and resourceful, commander of significant units during the protracted (1768–72) guerrilla war against the Russians, the war led by the Confederation of Bar.[17] Pułaski's high military reputation was recognized by the immediate granting of the rank of brigadier general, a rank that Kościuszko did not receive until after the end of the war.

Pułaski distinguished himself in at least five military episodes, all of them involving active combat. The first, soon after his arrival, was on

11 September 1777, at Brandywine, where he volunteered to lead a daring counterattack against the British who were threatening to cut off a segment of the retreating American army. As one American historian concluded, "It was through his intelligence and activity that the army of Washington was saved from a surprise attack of the British at Warren Tavern."[18]

Four days after the Battle of Brandywine, on 15 September, during the Battle of Germantown, Puɫaski, who had been granted the title of Commander of the Cavalry, successfully covered the retreat of the revolutionary forces with a handful of horsemen. In February 1778, together with a cavalry detachment, he cooperated with General Wayne and defeated the British forces at Haddonfield, near Camden, New Jersey. Finally, he led the defense of Charlestown, Virginia, in May 1779. During the operations around Savannah, Georgia, in the summer and autumn of 1779, while cooperating with General Benjamin Lincoln and Admiral d'Estaing, he took part in the Battle of Savannah. There he was mortally wounded while covering with a bold charge the retreat of a French column. On 11 October, he died aboard the American frigate *Wasp*. He was thirty-two years old.

Puɫaski is remembered in this country not only for his reckless courage and his heroic death on the battlefield, but also for his organization of the first regular cavalry units in the revolutionary army. Before Puɫaski's arrival, it had no cavalry in the European sense of the term, although small groups of mounted infantrymen were attached to various infantry units to act as scouts. Puɫaski suggested organizing a cavalry brigade, an idea initially too bold for the Continental Congress; his plans were repeatedly rejected as impractical and too expensive, refusals that frustrated Puɫaski.

Having contributed greatly to the organization and training of the first regular cavalry units, Puɫaski commanded them with courage. Yet his service was full of conflict. He grumbled and criticized the decisions of the Continental Congress and quarreled with his associates. Unlike Kościuszko, about whose possible disagreements with Washington we know very little, Puɫaski's quarrels are well documented.[19] He was in constant and open conflict with his superiors, as well as with his comrades-in-arms, about recruitment, discipline and matters of prestige. He resigned his command twice: in March and in November 1778.

Puɫaski also had numerous clashes with the Treasury about funds and their use. There was no doubt about his honesty, but there was considerable doubt about the ways of conducting business and keeping accounts. These clashes were probably unavoidable between a former leader of the irregular detachments of the Bar Confederation, where everything was improvised, and the methodical and pennypinching revolutionary administration. In desperation, Puɫaski often distributed not only his own salary to his soldiers, but even money sent to him by his family in Poland. The paymaster of the Pułaski Legion stated that "Count Pułaski has laid out for the Legion at least $50,000 of his own money" without any expectation of repayment.

In spite of all the quarrels, as well as Pułaski's sensitivity and his excessive pride, his dashing, colorful, and intrepid personality fascinated his comrades-in-arms as well as his soldiers, who adored him. One of the minor controversial points of Pułaski's life abroad was over his use of the title Count, to which he had no right whatsoever.[20] The Pułaskis came from the ranks of petty nobility, recently enriched through the financial skill of Casimir's father, Joseph, a lawyer. One may assume that Casimir's use of the title was a reflection of his insecurity as well as his pride. "Pułaski is rash and proud, actually more proud than ambitious," said a French observer about him.[21]

Pułaski's participation in the American War of Independence was the beginning of his early popularity in this country, which soon surpassed that of Kościuszko. While the latter was a solid but unspectacular engineer, Pułaski's dash and his heroic death on the battlefield captured popular imagination and made him an American hero and an authentic symbol of Polish-American ethnic consciousness. His name, more easily pronounceable for Americans than that of Kościuszko, has probably had something to do with Pułaski's greater popularity in the United States. In 1825, Longfellow wrote his poem "Hymn of the Moravian Nuns of Bethlehem—At the Consecration of Pułaski's Banner." It referred to a ceremony during which the Moravian Sisters of Bethlehem presented a crimson pennant to Pułaski. There are numerous songs and verses written on this subject, but none of them equals Longfellow's poem.[22]

A few weeks after Pułaski's death in November 1779, the Congress voted to erect a monument in his honor, but it was not actually erected until 1910, and by then with financial assistance from various Polish-American organizations. In 1885, on his last battlefield at Savannah, a column with a bas-relief was erected. His memory is revered at the United States Military Academy at West Point, where his portrait as Father of the United States Cavalry hangs in an honored place. It would be difficult to count all the minor monuments, commemoration tables, stamps, streets, roads, counties, and towns named after Pułaski. Each 11 October, the American Poles celebrate Pułaski Day, and in many states the governors issue special messages for the occasion.

Kościuszko's path to the rank of an American folk hero has been more arduous. There is no Kościuszko Day, and he is rarely mentioned in speeches, no doubt in part because of his unpronounceable name. Gerald Ford, during his July 1975 presidential visit to Poland, found

Kościuszko's name a formidable obstacle. But when we turn to Polish history, Pułaski's influence cannot be compared with that of Kościuszko. For Pułaski, Savannah spelled the end of a brief and controversial career; for Kościuszko, the American adventure merely served to help his rise to national prominence in his native country. It is his role in Poland during the period 1791–94 that gave him the status of a major national hero.[23] Kościuszko is a major figure in the Polish national pantheon; there he overshadows Pułaski almost completely.

What is the significance of these two freedom fighters for the Polish-American relations?

Pułaski and Kościuszko were among the forerunners of those innumerable Poles who were to go abroad to continue their struggle for liberty begun in their native land. Those acting outside Poland strengthened the ties of the diaspora with the country of origin and thus created the concept of *Polonia*, the community of emigrants of Polish extraction who, despite their foreign citizenship and loyalty to their chosen country, preserve sentimental and cultural ties with the country of their ancestors. *Polonia*, about equal in number to one-third of Poland's present-day population, has been an important factor in the life of the Polish nation, especially during the period of the Partitions. Prior to 1918, so long as the three partitioning powers held the country under their authority, some Polish patriots went so far as to consider the Polish immigrants in America as constituting a "fourth province of Poland."[24]

For the Polish nation, the triumph of the American people in their struggle for independence was an important psychological boost in the fight against the partitioning powers. Since the American people had been successful in their struggle for independence, the Polish people tended to look up to them as an example and a source of inspiration. The participation of at least two of their number as prominent officers in the American Revolutionary War thus became a particular source of pride. On the other side, the American people viewed the Polish fight for independence with sympathy, but on the whole, with detachment. The policy of "no foreign entanglements," initiated by George Washington in his Farewell Address of 1796 and reemphasized by James Monroe, precluded any active expression of sympathy, an attitude that remained unchanged until the United States emerged momentarily from isolation during World War I.[25]

Woodrow Wilson's role in the rebirth of Poland is still a controversial subject, which has not yet been sufficiently investigated; it is certainly worth further research.[26] There can be no doubt, however, close of World War I and the sponsorship of the principle of national self-determination by the American government greatly helped the Polish people. Whatever the results of further investigation of the subject, one may now safely say that the legends of Kościuszko and Pułaski had very limited influence on President Wilson, if only because he knew so little about them. In his huge history of the American people, both the shorter five-volume, and the longer ten-volume, version, there is not much about either of them.[27] In both editions of this richly illustrated publication there is even a picture of a Hessian boot, but there is no portrait of Kościuszko. He is mentioned only once in passing. Pułaski's picture is reproduced, but without any mention of his role.[28]

Thus, Wilson's advocacy of an independent Polish state was dictated not by the achievements of Kościuszko and Pułaski nor even by Paderewski's friendship. The Fourteen Points were essentially an instrument of political warfare, and they were determined by the vital interests of the United States at that time. The main objective of the points was to destroy the danger of a German-dominated Central Europe. The reconstruction of an independent Poland, as well as of other states of East Central Europe, served this purpose. As a veteran American diplomatic historian put it, "The Fourteen Points were designed as a statement of war aims and as an instrument of propaganda, both at home and abroad."[29] The points were first drafted on the basis of suggestions submitted by the inquiry. How much Paderewski's memoranda and personal contacts affected Point Thirteen is still an open issue.

There were, however, three phenomena that may be legitimately interpreted as something of a repayment for the "debt of gratitude" contracted by Kościuszko's and Pułaski's participation in the American Revolution. One was Herbert Hoover's generous and effective relief activities in Poland during and after World War I; another found a reflection in the formation of the Kościuszko Squadron; the third was the participation of the Polish-American volunteers in the army of General Józef Haller.

Analyzing Hoover's action, while far from denying his humanitarian impulse, one has to bear in mind the broader political considerations that undoubtedly were strong in Hoover's mind during the years 1918–22. He also realized perfectly well that, at that time, the social structure of Europe, especially of its East Central segment, could be preserved from crumbling under the pressures of Communist Russia only by an extensive and timely relief program.[30] Wilson's and the Entente's sponsorship of the Polish cause was also made easier by the triumph of the Bolshevik Revolution, which had immediately changed the pro-Russian sympathies of the West and made Poland into a potential bulwark not only against Germany but also against communism.

The American Kościuszko Squadron was organized in 1919, after the end of the war in the West. It was composed primarily of American pilots who spontaneously and selflessly volunteered their services to the reborn Polish Republic in its hour of supreme need. The squadron gave significant aerial support to the Polish ground forces during the war of 1920.[31]

The participation of over twenty thousand Polish immigrants from America, who had volunteered for the army formed in France by the Polish National Committee during the last stages of World War I in 1917–18, is another deed that may be partially ascribed to Kościuszko's and Pułaski's contributions to the American War of Independence. These volunteers, often referred to as the "Army of Kościuszko," formed a considerable portion of those six divisions which, under the command of General Józef Haller, were transported through Germany to Poland in 1919 to play a significant role in the task of consolidating the old country's independence.[32] The volunteers were recent immigrants; they did not yet have American citizenship, did not have to serve in the American army, and were still moved by Polish patriotism. As one Polish-American scholar pointed out, only with the establishment of independent Poland could the bulk of the Polish-American community come to regard the United States as its permanent home. Only then could American Poles become, first, Polish-Americans and, finally, Americans of Polish descent.[33]

The misinterpreted experiences of World War I, when America's interest as a rising world power dictated the destruction of the nascent *Mitteleurope* as well as opposition to communism, and hence the support of the smaller nations of East Central Europe, had considerable impact on Polish expectations during World War II. There seems to be little doubt that the Polish Prime Minister, General Władysław Sikorski, was misled into believing the myth of the United States as a potential protector of Poland against both Germany and the Soviet Union. During his three visits to Washington, Sikorski made several valiant efforts to persuade President Franklin D. Roosevelt of the substantial identity of interests between the United States and Poland. Sikorski found a willing listener to his plans but no firm diplomatic support in Washington: all three of his visits to the United States ended in diplomatic failure. The attitude of the American leaders toward Polish war aims, especially their expected loss of the eastern provinces and territorial compensation for war damages, was reserved. Obviously General Sikorski overlooked the fact that for the American government the problem of Poland was a function of its policy toward Russia and Germany. The concept of Allied unity, restricted by Roosevelt largely to the good will of Stalin, was considered to be far more important to the United States than Kościuszko, Pułaski, and the alleged traditional friendship with Poland represented by the Polish government in London.[34]

The attitude of the Americans of Polish descent also disappointed the great expectations of General Sikorski. Although Roosevelt had granted him permission in March 1941 to raise a volunteer force for the Polish army in the then neutral United States, the drive yielded meager results, despite the considerable efforts of the Polish government in London. The legend of Kościuszko and Pułaski paid few dividends; a mere handful of American volunteers enlisted in the Polish army. Wrote an American friend of Poland, "General Sikorski overestimated the probable response of the younger Americans of Polish ancestry. These young men were perfectly willing to fight, but in the American army."[35]

Thus, during World War II, any illusions about "the American debt of gratitude" toward Poland received a powerful blow and gave birth to another concept, that of the "betrayal" of Poland by the United States. The most vocal presentation of this point of view can be found in the book by the first post-World War II American Ambassador to Poland, Arthur Bliss-Lane, entitled *I Saw Poland Betrayed*.[36] Later, Bliss-Lane, in an open letter, chided Polish-Americans for being too lenient in appraising their government's foreign policy toward the Communist government of Poland. He reminded the Americans of Polish ancestry that the United States had reason to be grateful to Poland because of Kościuszko and Pułaski's participation in the War of Independence.[37]

Another major issue in Polish-American relations was that of the mass immigration that resulted in the formation of a large group of American citizens of Polish descent maintaining links with their homeland. Kościuszko and Pułaski, of course, had little to do with the exodus of Poles to America. That was largely determined by socioeconomic considerations.[38] But to the already settled Americans of Polish descent, both heroes soon became a source of great comfort in an alien country. The early Polish immigrants needed ancestors who could emulate those who had traveled on the *Mayflower:* the controversial Jan z Kolna and the group of Polish artisans who landed in Jamestown, Virginia, in 1609, were never accepted as cofounders of the United States. The Polish-Americans were badly in need of some heroic father figures who could bolster their pride and self-confidence by stressing their native country's share in the establishment of the United States. The vague, but discernible, prestige that Kościuszko and Pułaski did enjoy among the dominant Anglo-Saxon Americans provided the Polish immigrants, overwhelmingly of working-class origin, with moral comfort and helped them to settle in the new world with a modicum of self-respect. Yet, lacking self-confidence, they have often tended to exaggerate the importance of their heroes by supporting such legends as the belief that Kościuszko and Pułaski were close friends of George Washington.[39]

Thus, for understandable reasons, both figures have enjoyed much popularity with Americans of Polish extraction: they are the patrons of many immigrant organizations. The first Polish political club organized in Philadelphia in 1871 was the Kościuszko Club. Innumerable Polish-American organizations, including the Polish Falcons of America *(Sokols)*, have Kościuszko as their patron; the most important of them is the Kościuszko Foundation of New York, established in 1926, which by now is playing an important role in cultural relations between the two countries. Thanks to the energetic and generous actions of Philadelphia industrialist Edward Piszek and the Polish-American Congress and other organizations, the Congress recently passed a bill establishing Kościuszko's last residence in Philadelphia as the Tadeusz Kościuszko memorial site.[40] Pułaski has been even more popular, as attested by the number of monuments and localities named after him— far greater than those named after his more important countryman.[41]

As is the case with most legends, the legend of the two Polish heroes was also used as a tool of domestic politics. Ambitious politicians exploited it as an electoral tactic to elicit Polish-American votes: "Encomiums of Count Pulaski . . . are the approved political approach to the favor of the Polish section of the American population."[42] A senator declared to an interviewing American historian, "Whenever I speak before a nationality group I have only to mention a Garibaldi, Piłsudski, Kościuszko, or a Kossuth to receive a tumultuous ovation."[43] In spite of this, Kościuszko and Pułaski are both relatively unknown among Americans of non-Polish extraction. They are, for instance, not mentioned in any edition of Thomas Bailey's standard work, *Diplomatic History of the American People,* and only twice in passing, and not for their role in the War for Independence, in Bailey's well-known book on American-Russian relations.[44] In such popular nineteenth-century works—on which many of America's soldiers and diplomats of the World War I era had probably been nurtured in their youth—such as W. C. Bryant and S. H. Gray's *Popular History of the United States,* there was no mention of either Kościuszko or Pułaski. In the more scholarly *History of the United States* by Edward A. Channing, Kościuszko is briefly mentioned once (in volume 3, p. 278). In Beard's history of the United States, there is no mention of either of them.[45] I have a strong suspicion that among most American people the names of Kościuszko and Pułaski are usually pronounced in one breath like the ancient legendary Slavic deity Lelum-Polelum, without knowing which is which. For instance, the American ambassador to Vietnam, Graham Martin, speaking on 2 March 1975 (Boston, Channel 2), compared American aid to South Vietnam with the assistance that the American colonists received from Europe; he mentioned the monuments erected by the grateful American people to four foreign generals: he faultlessly enumerated Lafayette and Rochambeau, the two French heroes, and von Steuben, but mistook Kościuszko for Pułaski.

The fact that there are several variants in spelling, and hence pronouncing, of their names is in itself a source of confusion. Criticizing the silences, omissions, or misrepresentations of Kościuszko's services in American textbooks and in the media, the President of the Polish-American Congress and Polish National Alliance, Aloysius A. Mazewski, said in a recent speech, "It is one of the ironies of history that had General Tadeusz Kościuszko been born with a name as easily pronounceable as that of General Andrew Jackson, Robert E. Lee, Thomas Stonewall Jackson, Ulysses Simpson Grant, John J. Pershing or Dwight David Eisenhower—his name would resound . . . as one of the great soldiers of American history."[46] Whatever the final judgment of history, both Poles deserve a far higher place in the American pantheon and greater recognition by people not of their own ethnic stock. This is especially true of Kościuszko, certainly one of the most able and creative military engineers of the revolutionary war, and a bold pioneer of the emancipation as well as education of the blacks.

Despite all these reservations, one could say that the records of Kościuszko and Pułaski in America are impressive. The conflicts they often had with their contemporaries do not detract from their overall creditable performance. Quite the contrary, our knowledge of their quarrels and weaknesses rehumanizes their stereotyped images so powerfully influenced by the bland banalities of official speeches. Historic facts speak for themselves and need no embellishment. Kościuszko came to this country and offered his services to its army in August 1776, one of the first foreign soldiers of note to volunteer to fight for America's freedom. He served for eight years (1776–84) with dedication and distinction. He was genuinely devoted to the United States. In a letter to General Gates, he called himself "more than half a Yankee."[47] He contributed an authoritative handbook that was used by three generations of American artillerymen.

Pułaski never did become adjusted to America: he did not master English, he quarreled, and he grumbled all the time. Nevertheless, he, too, served with devotion and zeal, doing many things beyond the call of duty. Despite his constant criticism of the American army, its soldiers as well as its commanders, Pułaski admired their enthusiasm.[48]

Kościuszko was an able, resourceful engineer and a man of unusual nobility, sensibility, charity, and courage. His stand on the slavery issue was remarkable. Pułaski's reckless courage, constantly displayed in combat, and his heroic death overshadow both his original motives and his constant quarrels, and the pride so often displayed by him, especially in relations with his peers and superiors. One brief characterization of Pułaski was given by his good friend La Hayes, who said that "he was a fearless and noble knight . . . better as a captain than a general *(intrepide et vertueux chevalier . . . meilleur capitaine que général)*."[49] They had dramatically different personalities and operated in different ways. Yet both were courageous and selfless individuals, sincerely devoted to the cause they had espoused.

The influence of Kościuszko and Pułaski on American foreign policy has been limited. In 1918–19, expediency, moral considerations, and historic justice, as perceived by Woodrow Wilson, coincided with his sympathy for Poland and for the musical genius of Paderewski. But the fame of Kościuszko and Pułaski played only a minor, marginal role.

What is, then, the balance sheet of the Kościuszko and Pułaski legends? On the whole it is positive. By fighting for American independence they created a bond of sympathy; the fact that Poland and the United States have shared these two national heroes has helped the flow of communication between the two countries and made the Poles more sympathetic toward America. Kościuszko and Pułaski thus bridged the gap between two distant and different peoples, helping to initiate a closer relationship and develop a modicum of understanding.[50] Yet their activities in America, so often invoked in patriotic speeches as a major and constant factor in the history of Polish-American relations, have indeed been a significant, if never decisive, element in the dealings between the two nations.

Historic symbols have their valid and honored place in human history. But the importance of such symbols should not be overrated in international relations: they can seldom be used as hard diplomatic currency. The political and economic gains that Poland derived from the activities of Woodrow Wilson and Herbert Hoover at the end of World War I were largely a result of a perception of American national interest and of the moral convictions of those two men. When that perception changed during World War II under a different leadership, Wilson's performance was not repeated. The attitude of the United States toward Poland has always been a by-product of America's broader view of European issues and not of any "debt of gratitude" or vague feeling of sympathy.

NOTES

1 This essay is based on a paper given at the Fourteenth International Congress of Historical Sciences in San Francisco, 21 August 1975.

2 The standard book on Kościuszko's and Pułaski's role in the revolution is M. Haiman, *Poland and the American Revolutionary War* (Chicago, 1932); see also idem, *Kościuszko in the American Revolution* (New York, 1943). The basic Polish biography of Kościuszko is T. Korzon's *Kościuszko . . .* (Cracow, 1894); although it is weak on the American side, it has not yet been replaced. Consult also A. M. Skał-

kowski, *Kościuszko w świetle najnowszych badań* (Poznań, 1924), and J. Dihm, *Kościuszko nieznany* (Wrocław, 1969); a popular English biography by M. M. Gardner is *Kościuszko* (London, 1942). The standard book on Pułaski is by W. Konopczyński, *Kazimierz Pułaski* . . . (Cracow, 1931); this scholarly work has been popularized by J. S. Kopczewski, *Kazimierz Pułaski* (Warsaw, 1973), and by C. Manning, *Soldier of Liberty* . . . (New York, 1945). See also W. Wayda, ed., *Pułaski w Ameryce* (Warsaw, 1930); S. P. Mizwa, "Tadeusz Kościuszko"; and V. I. Alski, "General Casimir Pułaski, the First Chief of American Cavalry," *Cavalry Journal* (May-June 1932); and H. Waniczek, "Casimir Pułaski, the Father of American Cavalry," in *Great Men and Women of Poland,* ed. S. P. Mizwa (New York, 1942).

3 John Cudahy in his foreword to M. Haiman's book *The Fall of Poland in Contemporary American Opinion* (Chicago, 1935), p. v.

4 For Kościuszko's motivation in first going to America, see Korzon, *Kościuszko,* p. 16ff, and Dihm, "In Praise of Kościuszko . . . ," *Kościuszko nieznany,* especially pp. 357, 384, and 401; see also Gardner, *Kościuszko,* pp. 34–51.

5 For Pułaski's motives, see his letters to his French friend in F. Pułaski, ed., *Correspondence du Casimir Pułaski avec Claude de Rullière, 1774–1778* (Paris, 1948); also Konopczyński, *Pułaski,* pp. 354–68; see especially Pułaski's letter of June 1777 to his sister (ibid., pp. 366–67), which is contrary to what he wrote to Colonel R. H. Lee on 13 August 1778: "Honor and a true desire of distinguishing myself in defense of Liberty was the only motive which fired my breast for the cause of the United States," and in his last letter to the Continental Congress, 19 August 1779: "I could not submit to stoop before the sovereigns of Europe, so I came to hazard all for the freedom of America"; quoted by Haiman, *Poland and the American Revolutionary War,* p. 27.

6 According to Woodrow Wilson, it was Kościuszko who had shown General Gates how to entrench on Bemis's Heights (*A History of the American People,* 5 vols. [New York and London, 1902], vol. 3, p. 282). A temporary marker in honor of Kościuszko was erected at the battlefield of Saratoga in 1930. The revolutionary poet Joel Barlow mentions Kościuszko in his description of the Battle of Saratoga (*Columbia* [London, 1809], p. 202):

> But on the centre swells the heaviest charge,
> The squares develop and the lines enlarge.
> Here Kosciuszko's mantling works conceal'd
> His batteries mute, but soon to scour the field.

For a warm tribute paid to Kościuszko for his fortification work at Saratoga, see G. O. Trevelyan, *The American Revolution,* 4 vols. (London and New York, 1899–1914), vol. 2, p. 147. "The credit of Saratoga belongs to Horatio Gates, and with him to Daniel Morgan, Benjamin Lincoln and Thaddeus Kościuszko." E. A. Channing, *A History of the United States* . . . (New York, 1918), vol. 3, p. 278. See also Haiman, *Kościuszko,* pp. 5–34. General Gates, in his official report of the victory at Saratoga, informed Congress, "Col. Kosciuszko chose and entrenched the position"; and to a friend congratulating him on the victory, he said, "The greatest strategists were the hills and woods which a young Polish engineer knew how to select with skill for my camp"; quoted by Korzon, *Kościuszko,* p. 136.

7 For an expert analysis of Kościuszko's role in securing the future military academy,

see the work of D. R. Palmer, *The River and the Rock: The History of Fortress West Point, 1775-1783* (New York, 1969), especially the chapter "An Engineer from Poland," pp. 154-69. One of the members of the committee entrusted with collecting the fund for the monument was Robert E. Lee, later commander-in-chief of the Confederate States Army. In the collections of the West Point Academy there is a sword of Kościuszko, which he presented to Colonel John Bayard of Pennsylvania on leaving America in 1784. The sword has two inscriptions in Spanish on its blade: "Do not draw me out without necessity" and "Do not put me in without honor." References to Kościuszko in American poetry dealing with West Point are quite numerous. S. L. Knapp published *Tales of the Garden of Kosciuszko* (New York, 1834); Haiman, *Kościuszko*, p. 98; "Kościuszko spent over twenty-eight months, almost without interruption, at West Point. When he came there in March, 1778, it was a wilderness, almost uninhabited and almost without any fortifications. Three months after his departure Marquis de Castelleux visited West Point and he was enraptured with the 'beautiful and well contrived works' which he inspected with the eye of an expert. Armstrong most aptly summed up his long services at this post when he added that Kościuszko 'had the credit of giving to it a character of strength which deterred the enemy from any new attempt at gaining the command of the highlands.' If West Point was the backbone of Washington's strategy, it was Kościuszko's merit that this backbone victoriously stood up against British attempts to break it" (ibid., p. 96).

8 Haiman, *Kościuszko*, p. 142. Kościuszko often surprised his comrades by his moderation and abstemiousness. As surgeon of the southern army, Dr. Read reports that Kościuszko "gave up all his rations to the hospital, never touching a drop of ardent spirits, but contenting himself with the slops and soups of that establishment, which fare was no luxury, and that he had invited him, as a companion, to do so" (J. Johnson, *Traditions and Reminiscences Chiefly of the American Revolution* [Charleston, S.C., 1851], p. 415). The extravagant Lafayette always traveled with seven horses and four servants (Palmer, *The River and the Rock,* p. 159).

9 For Kościuszko's difficulties with his promotion to the rank of brigadier general, see Haiman, *Kościuszko,* pp. 149-56. Another proof that he was never a close friend of the commander-in-chief was the correspondence between the two, which lacked warmth and intimacy. "Washington never could quite grasp the spelling of the Pole's name even though he tried every feasible way. Some other samples: 'Koshiosko,' 'Kosuisko,' 'Kosciouski,' 'Koscousko,' 'Kosciusko,' 'Cosciusko,' 'Koscuisco,' 'Koscuiszko.' Once, in apparent surrender, he used two different variations in a single letter" (Palmer, *The River and the Rock,* p. 133).

10 *Manoeuvres of Horse Artillery, Written in Passing, in the Year 1800 by General T. A. B. Kościuszko at the Request of General W. M. Davies, Then Envoy from the United States to France* (New York, 1808).

11 Haiman, *Poland and the American Revolutionary War*, pp. 21-22. For an analysis of Kościuszko's testaments from the legal point of view, see L. Ottenberg, "A Testamentary Tragedy: Jefferson and the Wills of General Kosciuszko," *American Bar Association Journal* (January 1958), and "Kosciuszko's Many Wills," *Polish Heritage* (Fall 1976). The estates were not settled until forty years after the general's death. Innumerable claimants appeared for all or part of the estate. One of Jefferson's administrator-successors embezzled most of the assets of the estate, then died insolvent. The recent work of F. M. Brodie, *Thomas Jefferson: An Intimate History* (New York, 1976), throws no light on the problem of Kościuszko's testament

and Thomas Jefferson's role as its executor. The author notes without explanation the curious fact that Jefferson, a prosperous man, owed money to the always impecunious Kościuszko: "The debt to . . . Thaddeus Kosciuszko dragging on for years, could not have been paid at all had he not sold his books to the Library of Congress" (p. 456). According to an American historian, Jefferson borrowed the sum of $4,500 at 8 per cent from Kościuszko (E. P. Alexander, "Jefferson and Kosciuszko," *Pennsylvania Magazine of History and Biography* 92 (January 1968): 93-98. The same author mentions further that "the Senate of the Free City of Cracow asked Jefferson in 1820 to collect money from the American friends of Kościuszko for a memorial being erected to him in Cracow. Jefferson declined because of his retirement and unsuccessfully urged President Monroe to take charge of the collection of funds to build the Kościuszko Mound atop a hill on the edge of Cracow" (ibid., p. 102). See also J. W. Hoskins, " 'A Lesson Which All Our Countrymen Should Study': Jefferson Views Poland," *The Quarterly Journal of the Library of Congress* 33 (January 1976): 29-46.

12 The main Polish biography of Kościuszko concludes that the dry, impersonal letter of Washington "excludes any legend about the friendship and even closeness" between them (Korzon, *Kościuszko,* pp. 169-70).

13 Korzon, ibid., pp. 354, 394, 489-90.

14 The only tangible proof of Washington's "friendship" for Kościuszko is the sword offered to him at the end of the war. The inscription on the sword ran, "America cum Vashington suo Amico T. Kosciusconi." He was also presented with a pair of pistols with the following inscription engraved on their barrels: "G. Washington 17 E Pluribus Unum 83 Th. Kosciuszko" (Haiman, *Poland and the American Revolution*), p. 8. Washington, however, gave many such swords to his former comrades-in-arms, and the engraving is obviously a formula.

15 *Congressional Globe,* House of Representatives, 20 January 1818. See also M. J. E. Budka, ed., *Under Their Vine and Fig Tree: Travels through America in 1797-1799, 1805 . . . by Julian Ursyn Niemcewicz* (Elizabeth, N.J., 1965), pp. 3-32. The esteem that Kościuszko enjoyed in this country in his time may be judged by perusing contemporary memoirs written by Americans as well as foreigners. For instance, a French observer who saw Kościuszko during his second visit to the United States writes in his diary under the date 20 January 1789: "I saw General Kosciuszko, who had come to Philadelphia. The Americans received him with great demonstrations of joy, unhitching the horses from his carriage and drawing it from the point where he had debarked to the lodging that had been reserved for him" *(Moreau de St. Mery's American Journey [1793-98]),* trans. and ed. K. Roberts and A. M. Roberts (Garden City, N.Y., 1947). See also Haiman, *Fall of Poland,* p. 27; for the reaction to the Kościuszko Insurrection, pp. 122-250; also Z. Libiszowska, *Opinia polska wobec rewolucji amerykańskiej w XVIII wieku* (Łódź, 1962), especially pp. 71-79, and her paper at the San Francisco International Congress of Historical Sciences, "American Influence on Polish Political Thought," August 1975; M. M. Drozdowski, "Rewolucja amerykańska w polskiej myśli historycznej i społecznej," *Kwartalnik Historyczny* 82 (1975): 66-99. For a broad background of the three revolutions of the eighteenth century, American, French, and Polish, see the relevant parts of R. R. Palmer, *The Age of Democratic Revolution* (Princeton, 1959-64). A revisionist view of Kościuszko and Pułaski's role in the American War of Independence was presented in another paper given at the Slavic section of the Fourteenth International Con-

gress of Historical Sciences in San Francisco in August 1975, G. Rhode's "Einige Aspekte zur Teilnahme von Tadeusz Kościuszko und Kazimierz Pułaski am amerikanischen Unabhängigkeitskrieg."

16 J. A. Wytrwal, *America's Polish Heritage* (Detroit, 1961), pp. 197-98. The act of presentation of the Kościuszko monument stated that the monument was "an expression of our loyalty and devotion to our adopted country, for the liberty of which Thaddeus Kościuszko nobly and gallantly fought, and for the welfare and safety of which we, the Poles in America, are at any time ready to shed our blood, as those two illustrious Poles and our predecessors, Kościuszko and Pułaski did" (R. Piątkowski, *Pamiętnik Kongresu Polskiego w Waszyngtonie* [Chicago, 1911], pp. 45-70).

17 Claude de Rullière, who knew about his reckless courage, wrote to him, "Il n'y a point de Spartiate in de Romain que ne s'honorait de vous resembler" (quoted by F. Pułaski, *Correspondence,* p. 7). See also J. Gurn, "Why We Honor Gen. Casimir Pulaski," *Columbia* (October 1929). Gurn writes, "He was an expert horseman, and not the most trivial of his contributions to the efficiency of Washington's cavalry was his knowledge of equestrianship which he imparted to it."

18 W. H. Gordon, "Count C. Pulaski," *Georgia Historical Quarterly* 13:184.

19 Haiman, *Poland and the American Revolutionary War,* pp. 29-30. For Pułaski's quarrels in America, see Konopczyński, *Pułaski,* pp. 379-93, and Manning, *Soldier of Liberty,* p. 206ff; see also P. Bentalou, *Pułaski Vindicated* (Baltimore, 1824; New York, 1903).

20 S. Konarski's scholarly *Armorial de la Noblesse Polonaise Titrée* (Paris, 1958) does not list the Pułaskis as counts; for Korzon's explanation of Pułaski's behavior, see *Kościuszko,* pp. 137-48. The author concludes that Pułaski had "no ability to adjust to circumstances." His failure to learn correct English was a major handicap in his post of commander.

21 "Report of Dumouriez about the leaders of the Confederation of Bar . . . ," in W. Konopczyński, ed., *Konfederacja Barska . . .* (Cracow, 1928), p. 113.

22 For the text and other examples of literary tributes, see Haiman's chapter on Pułaski in his *Poland and the American Revolutionary War.* For instance, an American poet, William McDonald, wrote in 1909 (ibid., p. 27):

> When Freedom raised her standard sheet,
> And drums the call to battle beat,
> When rose the din of conflict shrill
> From Concord field and Bunker Hill,
> Who heard the summons o'er the wave?
> Pulaski brave, Pulaski brave!

Another poet, William K. Palmer, wrote (*Poland* [June 1924]):

> Columbia! He died for thee—
> Cheerfully—and for Liberty!
> Honored forevermore—
> On this Atlantic shore
> Palms for Pulaski! Palms!

There are counties named after Pułaski in the following six states: Georgia, Illinois,

Indiana, Kentucky, Missouri, and Virginia. The twenty towns and villages are in Alabama, Arkansas, Georgia, Illinois, Indiana, Iowa, Kentucky, Michigan, Mississippi, Missouri, New York, North Dakota, Tennessee, Texas, Virginia, and Wisconsin (L. Siekaniec, "Pulaski, U.S.A.," *Polish American Studies* [January–June, 1950], p. 39).

23 See M. Haiman, "American Influence on Kościuszko's Act of Insurrection," *Polish American Studies* (January–June 1946). To what extent the Kościuszko Insurrection of 1794 was influenced by the American Revolution is a controversial problem. His American experience, however, must have had some influence on his political ideas: it was, for instance, reflected in his decrees and proclamations as well as in the military concepts governing the irregular war conducted by voluntary militia. What he saw in America provided a convincing example of free men fighting of their own free will. This may be observed in Kościuszko's system of organizing the armed forces and his emphasis on the concept of a citizens' army that should be drawn from the most numerous segment of the population—the peasantry (Korzon, *Kościuszko,* pp. 174–78). See also J. Kownacki, *Pospolite ruszenie w insurekcji 1794* (Warsaw, 1963). For an interesting study of the influence of the American experiences on the European military mind in general, see P. Paret, "Colonial Experience and European Military Reform at the End of the Eighteenth Century," *Institute of Historical Research* (May 1964).

24 Quoted by K. Symon-Symonolewicz, "The Polish-American Community—Half a Century After," *Polish Review* (Summer 1966). A satirical reflection of the broad concept of Polonia stretching well beyond the frontier of the mother country is to be found in one of the songs which Tadeusz Boy-Żeleński wrote for "Zielony Balonik":

Pełna wrzasku ziemia polska
Od Czikago do Tobolska.

25 For a study of such a sympathetic but platonic reaction to a major event in Poland and its aftermath, see J. J. Lerski, *A Polish Chapter in Jacksonian America and the Polish Exiles of 1831* (Madison, Wisconsin, 1958); for the period of the Civil War, J. W. Wieczerzak, *A Polish Chapter in Civil War America* (New York, 1967).

26 For preliminary essay, E. Kusielewicz, "Wilson and the Polish Cause at Paris," *Polish American Studies* (Winter 1956), and "Woodrow Wilson and the Rebirth of Poland," ibid. (January–June 1955). For a study in the allegedly decisive influence of the Polish-American minority group on Wilson's foreign policy, see L. L. Gerson, *Woodrow Wilson and the Rebirth of Poland 1914–1920* (New Haven, 1953); the book is an often biased presentation of the subject and of Wilson's attitude toward Poland. For the best-documented critical analysis of the book, see Z. J. Gąsiorowski's review essay in *The Polish Review* (Autumn 1957). For the polemic that followed, see ibid. (Summer 1958). Roman Dmowski was surprised when Wilson brushed aside his strategic justification for Poland's future western frontier by saying that "nobody after this war will talk about strategic considerations. We will have a League of Nations." For Dmowski's view of the United States, Woodrow Wilson and J. I. Paderewski, see *Polityka polska i odbudowa państwa,* 2nd ed. (Warsaw, 1926), pp. 388–402. For a critical appraisal of the role of President Wilson and the U.S. diplomacy toward Poland, see Marion Leczyk, *Komitet Narodowy Polski a Ententa i Stany*

Zjednoczone 1917-1919 (Warsaw, 1966); also K. Lapter, "Trzynasty Punkt Wilsona," *Sprawy Międzynarodowe,* no. 1/27 (1954).

27 W. Wilson, *A History of the American People,* 5 vols. (New York and London, 1902), and the expanded edition in 10 vols. (New York and London, 1918).

28 "French, and even German and Polish officers . . . volunteered for service in the American armies. It was the gallant Polish patriot, Tadeusz Kosciuszko, who had shown General Gates how to entrench himself upon Bemis Heights" (1902 edition, vol. 2, p. 283; 1918 edition, vol. 4, p. 100). This short sentence is more than counterbalanced by Wilson's derogatory remarks about immigrants from Poland, Hungary, and Italy (vol. 5 of the 1902 edition, pp. 212-13). For these remarks, smacking of racism, Wilson had to apologize repeatedly during the presidential campaign of 1912, when he tried to woo the immigrant vote.

29 T. A. Bailey, *A Diplomatic History of the American People,* 3rd ed. (New York, 1947), p. 649. For the role of the problem of self-determination as a competitive issue between the U.S. and Soviet Russia, see V. Mamatey, *The U.S. and East-Central Europe, 1914-1918* (Princeton, 1957), p. 174.

30 American relief activities were extensively described in H. H. Fisher, *America and the New Poland* (New York, 1928), pp. 78ff, especially pp. 126, 214, 292, and 298; for the role of the "Red Scare," pp. 161, 195, and 238. American aid was especially crucial for children; the total number of children fed in 1921-22, at the peak of the relief action, was 1,246,921 (ibid., p. 298). For more statistical data, see pp. 366-67. For the most recent study of the problem, consult G. J. Lerski, *Herbert Hoover and Poland: A Documentary History of a Friendship* (Stanford, 1977).

31 The Kościuszko Squadron originated from a chance meeting of two American pilots in a Paris café; one of them was Captain Meriam C. Cooper, later a major Hollywood film producer. These were joined by other pilots, some from the old Royal Flying Corps. The squadron flew unfamiliar German and Italian aircraft, worn out from war or unproven in combat. Two of the three American pilots who died crashed in test flights (R. F. Karolevitz and R. S. Fenn, *Flight of Eagles: The Story of the American Kosciuszko Squadron in the Polish-Russian War, 1919-1920* [Sioux Falls, S.D., 1974]). Major Cedric E. Fauntlery, first commander of the Kościuszko Squadron, received Poland's highest award for valor, the Virtuti Militari, and eventually became chief of aviation of the Second Polish Army. In addition to being intrepid airmen, some of the Americans were also talented men; three of them authored books. One of these, by K. M. Murray, *Wings Over Poland* (New York, 1932), gives an expert pilot's view of the squadron.

32 H. H. Fisher, *America and the New Poland,* pp. 104-5. For the reminiscences of the commander of the Polish Army formed in France, see J. Haller, *Pamiętniki* (London, 1964), chaps. 12-16. For a proposal to form a Polish government in the United States, see J. J. Sosnowski, *Prawda dziejowa* (Warsaw, 1925), p. 694, and S. R. Pliska, "The Polish-American Army 1917-1921," *Polish Review* (Summer 1965). Polish-Americans were once described as the best national investment Poland ever made and one which continues to pay "handsome dividends" (B. E. Schmitt, ed., *Poland* [Berkeley, 1945], p. 348).

33 K. Symons-Symonolewicz, "The Polish-American Community—Half a Century After," *Polish Review* (Summer 1966).

34 The U.S. did not initially favor giving Poland more than a fraction of what she eventually got; the Americans were ready to concede only East Prussia with Danzig,

Upper Silesia, and an additional slice of Eastern Pomerania (*Foreign Relations of the United States* [cited hereafter as *FRUS*], *Conferences at Malta and Yalta*, pp. 232–33 and 510. Sikorski's desire to enlist Roosevelt's support for the idea of a "reemergence of a strong and independent Poland . . . capable of effective defense and capable of economic development" brought a rebuff from Undersecretary of State Sumner Welles that the first implied "a program of rearmament which was entirely counter to the objectives of this Government." Welles even objected to the portion of Sikorski's proposal that mentioned the agreements of July and December 1941 as providing the basis for "a Polish-Soviet alliance . . . as one of the best guarantees of European peace," on the grounds that "the conclusion of military alliances of this character would have no valid basis if an effective international security were to be established" (*FRUS*, vol. 2 [1943], pp. 320–21, and *FRUS*, vol. 3 [1942], pp. 201–2). After Potsdam, until December 1970, the American stand concerning the Oder-Neisse line was formally one of leaving "final delimitation" to the peace conference. Michał Sokolnicki writes, "on the basis of personal conversation with General Sikorski in June 1943, in Beirut": "In the last months of his life General Sikorski was quite aware of the . . . uncertainty of Washington's support" (*Kultura* [June 1951]).

35 P. Super, *Twenty-Five Years with the Poles* (New York, 1951), p. 327.

36 A. Bliss-Lane, *I Saw Poland Betrayed* (New York, 1948).

37 *New York Times*, 13 July 1956.

38 Many poor and illiterate immigrants, born and brought up under a foreign rule, were slow to accept Kościuszko as their spiritual leader; it came only later, with the spread of education. According to one sociologist, many Polish immigrants changed their opinion of Kościuszko through contacts with Americans of Polish extraction (K. Duda-Dziewiarz, *Wieś małopolska a emigracja amerykańska* [Warsaw, 1938], p. 147). According to Wincenty Witos, many Galician peasants at the close of the century still considered Kościuszko "as a criminal who revolted against the authority established by God, and was for it severely punished" (*Moje wspomnienia*, vol. 1 [Paris, 1969], p. 133). Only gradually did education bring about the change that made Kościuszko a popular hero (vol. 1, pp. 201, 218; vol. 2, p. 150). For the motives of the immigration, see W. Thomas and F. Znaniecki, *Polish Peasant in America*, 5 vols. (Chicago, 1918–20), vol. 1, pp. 103–4, 321, 335; and vol. 2, p. 193; see also V. R. Green, "Pre-World War I Emigration to the United States: Motives and Statistics," *Polish Review* (Summer 1961).

39 According to an authority on mythology: "Every theological and mythological system stands for something, and helps the society believing it toward self-understanding, self-acceptance, pride in its past, and trust in what is and what will be" (G. Dumezil, *L'idéologie tripartiete des Indo-Européens* [Brussels, 1958], p. 91). For an attempt at sketching the Polish contribution to the discovery of America and its colonial beginnings, see M. Haiman, *Polish Past in America 1608–1865* (Chicago, 1939), pp. 5–19; the author gives (on p. 13) a facsimile of a paragraph from a manuscript of the court book of the Virginia Company in London, describing a victory of Polish settlers in a strike for equal suffrage in Virginia in 1619.

40 Edward Piszek's energetic campaign has been described by D. M. Jones in his article "The Struggle to Preserve a Slave," *Poland* (January 1976). The renovated home at 301 Pine Street, Philadelphia, was designated as the Kościuszko national memorial. It was to this house that distinguished visitors came to visit Kościuszko in 1797, including Thomas Jefferson, the Duke of Orleans (the future king of France), cabinet

members, senators, governors, and some diplomats from abroad.

41 J. A. Wytrwal, *America's Polish Heritage,* pp. 157, 186. For a sympathetic evaluation of Kościuszko's role in the life of Americans of Polish extraction, see S. P. Mizwa, *Great Men and Women of Poland* (New York, 1941), p. 143; see also A. Q. Maisel, "The Poles Among Us," *Readers Digest* (June 1955). For a highly critical approach to Kościuszko's, as well as Pułaski's, activities in America, see S. L. Sharp, *Poland: White Eagle on a Red Field* (Cambridge, Mass., 1953), pp. 6–9, 255–59. Americans of Lithuanian extraction also claim Kościuszko as one of their own. In 1930, the New York Post of the Lithuanian Legion of America was named after Kościuszko, "the first Lithuanian soldier in America"; see also A. Burdecki's "Thaddeus Kościuszko—Pole or Lithuanian," *Vienybe* (December 1975).

42 J. H. Wallis, *The Politician: His Habits, Outcries and Protective Coloring* (New York, 1935), p. 80.

43 Interview of a United States senator, 1958, quoted by L. L. Gerson, *The Hyphenate in Recent American Politics and Diplomacy* (Lawrence, Kansas, 1964), p. 242.

44 T. Bailey, *America Faces Russia* (Ithaca, N.Y., 1947, and nine subsequent editions between 1947 and 1970), pp. 10, 39.

45 C. A. Beard and M. R. Beard, *A New History of the United States* (Garden City, N.Y., 1968).

46 *Zgoda* (Chicago), 1 March 1974. Kościuszko's military talents are controversial. A nineteenth-century Polish historian evaluated them as follows: "God did not create [Kościuszko] a genius transcending contemporary knowledge, ideas, and perspectives; neither was he a transformer of society, nor a soldier who would revolutionize existing methods of combat; on the other hand, he was endowed with common sense, self-discipline, great sensitivity, and a conscience . . ." (L. Siemieński, *Żywot Tadeusza Kościuszki* [Cracow, 1866], p. 27). For a more generous evaluation of his talents, see E. L. Cueno, "General Thaddeus Kosciuszko: Master Military Mind of the American Revolution," *Saturday Evening Post* (October 1975). For recent Polish works on Kościuszko's military contribution, see L. Tyszyński's essay in *Studia i materiały do historii sztuki wojennej,* vol. 1 (Warsaw, 1954); B. Grzelonka and I. Rusinowa, *Polacy w wojnach amerykańskich 1775–1783* Cracow, 4 April 1976.

47 Quoted by S. P. Mizwa, *Tadeusz Kościuszko (1746–1817)* (New York, 1967), p. 12.

48 Korzon, *Kościuszko,* p. 138.

49 Ibid., p. 145.

50 As an American poet put it, Kościuszko belongs both to his native country and to the United States (William K. Palmer, Poland, June 1924):

His dust in Poland rests—
His urned Heart a Shrine!
Poland! He is Thy Son!
Columbia! Also Thine!

One of the recent symptoms of this "special relationship" between the U.S. and Poland is the fact that Poland, together with France and Britain, has been selected to display in Europe a bicentennial exhibition: "The World of Franklin and Jefferson."

PART III

POLITICAL AND SOCIAL ASPECTS OF THE
FRENCH REVOLUTION

THE STATE OF THE JACOBIN DICTATORSHIP: THEORY AND REALITY

Bogusław Leśnodorski, University of Warsaw

RÉVOLUTION—"UN PROCÈS OUVERT"

The words of our heading are borrowed from the opening statement of J.-R. Suratteau's concise and illuminating survey of the principal issues in recent historiography dealing with the French Revolution.[1] The *procès* referred to is both that of the investigation into the details of the drama and tragedy, the many people and problems, events and ideas that occurred in the period 1789–99 (although in some cases, the period shrinks to 1789–92 or 1789–94), and that of the successive trends and directions in this historiography, such as those exemplified in Godechot's *Un jury pour la Révolution*.[2] A reader of the relevant French literature will become aware that interest in the Great Revolution, while it never really disappears entirely, is periodically renewed with particular energy as a way of providing an introduction to an "understanding of the political wisdom of the French."[3] This is because studies of the Revolution, from whatever point of view, based on the numerous Parisian and provincial archival resources and ever more sophisticated research methods, provide a valuable laboratory for comparative analysis and for tracing the mechanisms of history.

New developments in the general approach to the Revolution in historiography and historical narratives are of tremendous significance. For example, in Soviet Russia, the decree of the Council of People's Commissars of August 1918 (signed by Lenin) initiated a wave of scholarly interest (as well as artistic and literary creativity, particularly in drama) and political propaganda dealing with the Revolution.[4] In Petrograd, Nikolaevskaia Street, named after the tsars, was renamed Marat Street, and in Moscow Robespierre's statue was unveiled in the Alexander Gardens near the Kremlin.

Soviet historical studies in this period concentrated primarily on the dictatorship of the Jacobins and its relations with the people. M. N. Lukin published a biography of Robespierre in a popular series entitled *To Whom is the Proletariat Building Its Monuments?* Their interests then shifted to ultra-radical trends, and they began to concentrate on Jacques Roux and other *enragés* and on Babeuf. But they also stressed the bourgeois character of the Revolution as a whole, and they questioned whether it was legitimate to call it the "Great French Revolution." Lenin had used the term both before and after 1917: it was "great" because "to protect its achievements it was capable of mobilizing the broad ranks of the people," because of the ideas and phrases it proclaimed, and because it was a "revolution of action."[5]

Another revival of interest in the French Revolution was aroused by the outbreak of war in the Soviet Union against the Nazi invader in 1941, with its war cry "la patrie en danger," strongly linked anew to national and universal traditions. The outstanding Soviet scholars V. P. Volgin and E. V. Tarle published in that year their joint work *The French Bourgeois Revolution of 1789–1794.* Finally, the last few years have witnessed the appearance of many Soviet monographs and treatises as well as collective works devoted to analytical and synthetic studies of many issues dealing with the Revolution. From among that welter of material the following publications deserve particular attention: the synthetizing studies of A. Z. Manfred; the monographic works of V. M. Dalin;[6] a collection of studies published in Odessa and featuring a minute analysis of Lenin's statement on the hegemony of the masses in 1793–94 and the supremacy or dictatorship of the Jacobins;[7] V. G. Revunenkov's work on Marxism, the Jacobin dictatorship, and the Parisian *sans-culottes;*[8] and finally, P. T. Dobroliubskii's work on 9 Thermidor.[9] The majority of these studies deal with questions first posed by Lenin: how did it happen that the Jacobins "sided with the people," and why did their dictatorship fall?

Soviet literature has also been enriched by the valuable works of M. N. Shtrange, who dealt with the attitude of the Russian society toward the French Revolution in 1789–94 and with the democratic intelligentsia in eighteenth-century Russia.[10] Similar studies have been made for the Ukraine.[11] When one compares these studies with those that have been done in Western Europe and the United States dealing with the origins of the Russian intelligentsia, the Soviet works yield broader conclusions with regard to the role and character of the intelligentsia.

In French literature a comparison of the attitudes and policies of the French Jacobins of 1793–94 and the Bolsheviks of the early phase of the Russian Revolution of 1917 has twice been undertaken, first by A. Mathiez in 1922,[12] and more recently, from the point of view of the formal and legal aspects of Jacobin and Soviet constitutionalism, in a study published in Paris in 1971.[13]

A shift in interest similar to that observed in the Soviet Union has also occurred in French Marxist historiography.[14] Prior to 1934, attention was focused on certain aspects of the Revolution, which was generally defined as a bourgeois revolution. But the program of the Popular Front brought about a revival in studies of the Revolution as a whole and, in particular, the popular movement, its defense of the country, and of the Revolution's achievements. In 1937, A. Soboul's book on Saint-Just was published; it continues to be its author's most important work. It was followed by a lengthy list of studies on this revolutionary as practitioner and theorist.[15] In 1939, a popular publication on *The Birth of the National Army in 1789-94*[16] was published, under the pseudonym Jules Laverrier, by the Polish Communist Julian Bruno-Bronowicz. Albert Mathiez, who died in 1932, left behind a series of well-known monographs, the Société des Etudes Robespierristes, which he founded and which continues to function under that name, and the meritorious *Annales Historiques de la Révolution Française*.[17] His follower, G. Lefebvre, attempted to draw a specific parallel between the Popular Front of the 1930s and the concentration of the popular forces under the Jacobins. He applied the concept of the Front to the Jacobin period even earlier, on the bicentennial of Robespierre's birth, celebrated in 1958.[18]

Modern research in France and particularly in Great Britain, the United States, Italy, and both East and West Germany has produced a never-ending supply of new materials and new approaches which have promoted stimulating discussion. The extreme revisionist approach to the Revolution now being promulgated can be described as nihilistic. Its adherents claim that the Revolution was superfluous; it simply created a myth which should now be dispelled. To this category belong the *Myth of the French Revolution* (1953) by the late A. Cobban and the polemics against his opponents that followed.[19] Of greater consequence are those recent studies that have sought to point out some positive changes in the economy and administration that preceded the 1789 upheavals, due, *inter alia*, to the efforts of the intendants in various regions of the country. Were it not for the torpor that pervaded the royal court, the Revolution—according to this line of reasoning—could have been avoided.[20]

Another controversial thesis was the one advanced by J. Godechot and R. R. Palmer at the International Congress of Historians held in Rome in 1955 of the so-called "Atlantic Revolution" that covered the coastlines on both sides of the Atlantic and penetrated further inland; a slightly modified version called it the "Western Revolution."[21] Contrary to its authors' intent, the thesis—although it aptly defined many similarities and the compatibility of certain ideas—tended, as it were, to obliterate the particular role and identity of the Revolution in France, particularly the period of the Jacobin dictatorship and the emergence of "Jacobins" in other countries. Both Godechot and Palmer, we should add, later modified their original concept.[22]

Many important conclusions were reached in research into the various revolutions *sensu largo* that combined to form the Great Revolution, with its many phases, various classes and milieus involved, and the different forms it assumed. One was called an aristocratic revolution—a *révolte nobiliaire*—which strove to rebuild the monarchical

form of government from the inside; another a revolution of the peasantry, another a revolution of the towns. A wave of controversy was
aroused by Fr. Furet and D. Richet's thesis formulated in their work
La Révolution Française, and in other treatises that appeared separately. They argued that the fundamental liberal revolution responsible
for the overthrow of feudalism and the emergence of the bourgeois
order in France took place in 1789–92 and then collapsed—its
dérapage threatening to destroy its achievements.[23] A. Soboul,[24] Cl.
Mazauric,[25] E. Walter, in his contributions to the valuable annual *Le
XVIIIe Siècle,*[26] and A. Gerard in her journalistic book *La Révolution Française: Mythes et interprétations* (1970) all challenged this
thesis.[27]

The discussion aroused by the question whether the Great Revolution on the Seine and in other parts of France should be considered as a
number of revolutions or whether it was, varying as it did in certain
aspects, one distinct process is of vital importance. Was there a "bloc"
of forces and aspirations embracing a multitude of people who still
could come under the common label of *les patriotes?* To Guerin the
Revolution was a premature class struggle on the part of the masses,
and in particular on the part of the urban *sans-culottes,* against the
bourgeoisie.[28] Soboul studied the question of the Parisian *sans-culottes*
in the Year II using extensive archival sources,[29] which was supplemented by an interesting study by K. D. Tønnesson on the defeat of
the *sans-culottes* in the Year III.[30] The urban plebeian movement received comprehensive coverage when Soboul presented the role the
sans-culottes played in the development of the Revolution, their part in
the seizure of power by the Jacobins, and the circumstances under
which the dictatorship severed its links with the masses, with the resulting tragedy of 9 Thermidor.

It seems, however, to be going too far to give the *sans-culottes* such
a prominent place, particularly to view them as a self-contained and
ideologically mature entity. Soboul himself points out that no more
than ten per cent of the Parisian *sans-culottes* or their leaders were
close to or identified with the Jacobins. A particularly controversial
point of Soboul's analysis, found also in Soviet literature, is his view
that the Revolution ended with the downfall of the Jacobins in 1794.[31]
Major works outlining the role of the masses in the Revolution were
produced by the Australian Rudé[32] and the Englishmen Hobsbawm[33]
and Cobb,[34] who studied the revolutionary people's armies and more
recently dealt with popular protest. That the term "crowd" was used
in Rudé's book where "mob" was employed in Cobb's recent publication is indicative of their differences in approach. Cobb has been
increasingly inclined to censure what he has viewed as the "mob."[35]

A number of leading personages of the period have been treated in depth. "The father of victory," Carnot, was the subject of an excellent monograph by Reinhardt.[36] Jacques Roux and his group were presented in fresh light by Markow of Leipzig. Markow described the tragedy of the Jacobins in their clash with the *enragés* who, in their endeavors to radicalize the Revolution, were in fact not at all hostile to the Jacobins.[37] Among a large number of valuable studies centering on Saint-Just one might single out a sympathetic study by the Polish scholar S. Salmonowicz.[38]

However, the greatest campaign and one frequently infiltrated by nonscholarly arguments continues to have Maximilian Robespierre as its target. The bicentennial of his birth produced a number of penetrating studies,[39] but the "process" mentioned at the beginning continues and blends with the whole image of the Revolution, and in particular with that of the period of the Jacobin dictatorship. The two passages quoted below illustrate the tendency, from various viewpoints, to vindicate the Jacobins against the still-prevailing opinion among historians. A meritorious student of the Revolution and the author of a concise and useful analysis of *La République jacobine*, M. Bouloiseau,[40] who is also an editor of Robespierre's writings, used as a heading for his popular selection of Robespierre's works the following quotation:

> Le ciel, qui me donna une âme passionnée, pour la liberté, m'appelle peut-être à tracer de mon sang la route qui doit coduire mon pays au bonheur. J'accepte avec transport cette douce et glorieuse destinée. . . .[41]

Somewhat surprisingly, Godechot chose the following quotation of Robespierre as a heading for his valuable collection of French declarations of law and constitutions down to the present:

> Depuis le moment où l' acte constitutionnel fut terminé et cimenté par l' adhésion générale, je me suis toujours borné à en réclamer l' exécution fidèle . . . comme un ami de la patrie et de l'humanité, convaincu que le salut public nous ordonne de nous réfugier à l'abri de la constitution pour repousser les attaques de l'ambition et du despotisme.[42]

One cannot fail to acknowledge here that the tragedy of the Thermidor was largely brought about by departures in practice—against the will of those concerned—from the proclaimed ideals, and for this not only Robespierre was to blame. Among the Polish historians, a monographic study of Robespierre by Jan Baszkiewicz, the discriminating author of a history of France, is soon to appear. In this new study, Baszkiewicz does not try to avoid facts in favor of or against Robespierre, although he tends to side with him.[43]

But perhaps the most interesting item in the Polish literature on Jacobinism is a treatise by the historian of philosophy M. Król, devoted to the Jacobins' historical consciousness (1793–94). This is, unfortunately, only a portion of his doctoral dissertation on "The Concepts of History and Utopia Held by the Jacobins," the rest of which remains unpublished. Despite their tendency to copy models, costumes, and gestures from the ancient patterns, the Jacobins made a point of breaking with history, entirely cutting themselves off from the past and its burden of inherited traditions in the name of future generations who would realize the aims and purposes of the Revolution. The future should differ not only from the past but also from current reality.[44]

Modern research has also yielded up some attempts at a typological approach to the French Revolution and other social revolutions and upheavals covering radical changes in political power. The most advanced of these was that attempted by the French author J. Beachler, who tried to cover *phénomènes révolutionnaires* in their entirety, including every variation, within the scope of the newly promoted science of staseology (from the Greek *stasis,* meaning "to oppose, to stand out against"). According to the author's typological definition, the Jacobin dictatorship comes under *révolutions prolongées,* those exhibiting a comparatively lengthy process of change. Linked with the theory of Max Weber, this typology can, however, be faulted on the grounds of its all-inclusiveness and the consequent incompatibility of many of the phenomena it combines.[45]

Among the authors of synthetic elaborations a place of distinction goes to R. R. Palmer as the author of the two-volume work entitled *The Age of the Democratic Revolution*[46] and for his use of that typological term, although the scale of the phenomena it covered was very broad indeed. Palmer's approach was disputed *in passim* by one of the leading Polish theorists and methodologists, Jerzy Topolski, who utilized most of the literature on the subject in his rebuttal. He presented six successive types of revolution that occurred from the seventeenth to the twentieth century in Europe and in the colonies that were later to become the United States. Starting with "revolutionary movements of precapitalist formations," he arrived at his sixth type, named the "socialist revolution." The eighteenth-century revolutions are classed as "bourgeois revolutions" (his third type, preceding the bourgeois-democratic revolutions).[47]

However, the state of the Jacobin dictatorship displayed many features typical of the bourgeois-democratic type, nor do I believe Topolski was right in holding that the eighteenth-century revolutions, except the American one, "already had no need for additional impulses," such as the struggle for independence. In France under the Jacobins, independence was also most clearly one of the leading motivations, and the same struggle for independence helped to deepen the revolutionary current in the 1794 Insurrection in Poland. Similarly, the unification of Italy was a strong motive in the endeavors among the Italian republics at the close of the eighteenth century.

REFORM OR REVOLUTION

An obvious question to ask is whether the period of the Jacobin dictatorship brought along sufficiently extensive changes in the class structure to have them labeled as truly revolutionary or whether it can be viewed solely as a period of reform (and the changes would still have been no less significant) realized by the First Republic of 1792.

There is a tendency to obliterate the differences between the Girondists and the Jacobins outside their competition for power and the form of terror they applied. In fact, no notable differences, sociologically speaking, can be detected in the social composition of the two groups. But the Jacobins' guiding ideas reveal some basic differences inherent in their social and political program and their notion that they represented the broader masses of the French society. That they represented various classes and interests is clearly seen from the draft of the Declaration of Rights prepared by Robespierre and drafts of the Constitution of 1793—not to mention those numerous drafts and proposals that flooded the convention. It is also clear from Condorcet's draft, presented by him on behalf of the Gironde, and from the bill proclaimed by the Jacobins, under pressure from the people, as well as from later Jacobin-drafted bills and decrees. The Jacobins refuted the notion that some citizens were passive, some active, and they adopted the principle of general suffrage; they held property to be based not on natural law but on contractual law, fixed by positive law and justified, according to Robespierre, as being a result of one's labor; they included rudiments of ''social law''—that is, of labor protection, public relief, and universal education—in the Declaration of Rights and the Constitution of 1793, as well as in later legislation; although they declared themselves against *loi agraire* and introduced capital punishment for anyone who would venture to propose a far-reaching reform of land ownership, they aimed at the eventual leveling of financial standing and certainly endeavored to fill the gap between the rich man and the pauper.

These attitudes persisted in France until the present century, when they found their way, through the constitution and the declaration of civil rights of 1793 to the first draft of the French constitution of 1946 which was voted down in a referendum. The last major referee of the draft was Pierre Cot, who was close to the Communists in his views. The 1946 draft not only invoked the general ideas of those documents but also used their concept of property rights as being a fundamental characteristic of the social and economic order.[48]

THE DOCTRINAL FACTOR: THE FUNCTION OF J.-J. ROUSSEAU'S IDEAS

Both the onset of the French Revolution and its further development were related to a variety of social, economic, and political factors; only gradually did the French public come to grasp the meaning of the Revolution that was beginning on its course, to comprehend its extent, its character, and its prospects. It is also clear that the French of that time were at first inclined to view the Revolution as a single event before they gradually came to realize both in internal strife and during front-line battles against the attacking armies that it was a process in the making.

The social understanding of the term "revolution" was maturing during this process. Previously it had been used to imply various types of change, but mainly violent change, a radical change of political power; only later did it include deep ideological transformations. As a historian of state institutions and ideas, I would like to deal with a doctrinal element in the source of this shift of meaning, particularly the impact of the ideas of Jean-Jacques Rousseau, an impact that can be clearly discerned in the writings, speeches, and constitutional bills of the time.[49]

The numerous editions of the *Contrat social* are indicative of its importance. Between 1762 and 1763 it had thirteen French reprints, one German, and one Russian, although numbers could be explained as a reflection of an attempt to saturate the publishers' market. But the decade 1789–99 saw thirty-two French, four English, four German, two Dutch, eight Italian, and four Spanish editions, along with one rendered into Latin for the Hungarians (presumably primarily for lawyers, who would be accustomed to that language).[50] In Poland, Rousseau was mainly read in French; only six early chapters translated into Polish appeared in print. Its popularity was, however, a world-wide phenomenon. In some states of America, portions of Rousseau's writings were incorporated into the texts of statutes; in Poland, Rousseau's "exposition of uninterrupted European peace" formed an integral part of a textbook on political history for schools under the Committee of National Education. In 1771, Rousseau also wrote a treatise devoted to *Le gouvernement de Pologne (gouvernement* standing here for the entire state system) and a utopia.

The vast literature about the author of the *Contrat social* continues to expand from year to year in every language. The trend of study that sees in Rousseau, as well as in the Jacobins, the harbingers of twentieth-century totalitarianism should be rejected.[51] I would turn rather to the generally acknowledged line of research (also represented in Poland, most recently in the works by K. Grzybowski and A. Burda[52]), and propose to consider the following ideas of Rousseau:

Nature provides man with an unlimited right to everything he is attracted to and everything he is capable of achieving ("un droit illimité à tout ce qui le tente et qu'il peut atteindre"). This is reminiscent of recurrent demands in France for general access to an enjoyment of both material and spiritual goods. It is only after he enters the social community that man gains civil liberty, as distinct from natural liberty and ownership of everything in his possession ("et la propriété de tous ce qu'il possède . . ."').

From human nature also springs—next to that "droit á tout ce qu'il tente"—equality before the law as well as a notion of justice that is also a product of human nature. It is interesting to observe that Rousseau failed to stress political equality; in his opinion, it did not have to embrace every man regardless of whether or not he is capable of taking part in governing.[53]

Rousseau made this characteristic appeal: "Bring the two extremities closer together: suffer neither rich nor poor. These two conditions, by nature inseparable, are equally disastrous for the commonweal; the one breeds adherents of tyranny and the other tyrants; between them they are trading in public liberty: the one is the buyer and the other is the seller. . . ."

Rousseau was strongly opposed to "patriotic bonds." The citizen should represent only his own opinion ("un avis particulier"). The splitting of the community into parties and factions wrecks the community and the state.

While one should not overwork the point, it should nevertheless be admitted that Rousseau was misinterpreted by many earlier historians, who placed insufficient emphasis on the fact that, although Rousseau professed the sovereignty of the general will *(la volonté générale)* and believed that "it is possible to transfer power, but not the general will" ("le pouvoir peut bien se transmettre, mais ne pas la volonté") and that it could be vested in a legislative body that could control the executive, at the same time, he had little preference for an executive. On the contrary, he was all for a strong and efficient one, although subject to supervision by a legislative body.

The model drawn up by Rousseau in his various writings is, nevertheless, a coherent whole, based on four premises: that there should be minimal differences of wealth among community members; that there should be dissemination and consolidation of a minimum body of practically homogenous opinion; that the community should be prevented from splitting into interest groups; and that the relation between the citizens and the state authority should be carried out through spokesmen of the general will within the state, thus avoiding the necessity of associations, unions, or parties.

The impact of Rousseau's ideas on the Jacobins and other members of the Convention, including a considerable number of lawyers, was further strengthened by other supporters of natural law—Grotius, Puffendorf, and Locke—whose writings Rousseau studied in translations made by the French translator and commentator Barbeyrac, as well as two writers born in Switzerland, Burlamaquie, who wrote *Principes du droit naturel* (1747), and Emer de Vattel, renowned for his *Droit des gens* printed in Leyden in 1758. Their influences crossed with those of Malby and Condorcet. The latter, who was Rousseau's pupil, was among the casualties of the Jacobin dictatorship.

Apart from these, one should mention a group of dissenters who broke off from the physiocrats and were known as the "economists." They were more interested in economic liberties than they were in liberty of thought. It was a hard task for the supporters of state interventionist policy among the Jacobins to deal with these ideas under the pressure of the people.[54]

Let us, however, return to the question of how Jacobin ideas were affected by Rousseau. The reader should be cautioned that Rousseau is regarded here as an embodiment of certain social and political tendencies and as a spur to thought as well, but hardly as an old-fashioned inspiration for text-copying.

The problem will be briefly reviewed from the vantage point of the ideas of Robespierre and Saint-Just, especially of those incorporated into the Declaration of Rights, proclaimed in 1793, which was a compromise version of Robespierre's draft.

Its Article 1 contains a reference to "general happiness," which was a slogan of the age but had not—in Saint-Just's words—begun to be realized until recently. Man's right to "enjoy the exercise of natural laws which would never expire" followed as a consequence.[55]

Article 2 names these rights: freedom (heading the list), security, and property. In the Declaration of 1789, property was listed second.

Article 3 strengthens, but also restricts, the function of equality by making clear that this is an equality before the law, ensuing from nature.

Article 16 defines the right of property as a "fruit de son travail et de son industrie."

Articles 23 and 24 introduce social safeguards *(la garantie sociale)* in the form of the obligation of all men *(action de tous)* to guarantee to every citizen the preservation of his rights. That warrant is grounded on national sovereignty (Article 23), and it will not exist "unless public functions are clearly defined by law and all officers are held fully responsible for their actions."

Articles 21 and 22 safeguard certain public welfare functions which are a sacred obligation of the community. They pertain to unfortunate citizens either by providing them with an opportunity to work or by assisting those who are no longer able to work. Here also belongs Article 22 which guarantees universal education: "La société doit favoriser de tout son pouvoir les progrès de la raison publique, et mettre l'instruction à la portée de tous les citoyens." Instruction in that understanding forms only part of a broader program—that is, continuing education, to use the modern term, and propaganda, another word coined by the Age of Enlightenment.

Article 27 has sinister undercurrents; it allows a new kind of terror: "Que tout individu qui usurperait la souveraineté nationale soit à l'instant mis à mort par les hommes libres." That article opened or rather encouraged attacks against the "enemies of the people." But the closing Article 35 repeated after Rousseau that "la révolte à l'opression est le plus sacré des devoirs," an article that provides a safeguard of a sort against a reign of terror in too extreme a form. However, this article is concerned with rights as well as duties which, if not named, are implied in the declaration. It should be remembered that the debates on successsive declarations of rights on 14 July 1789 featured Lafayette, who was the first to speak, and on 27 July 1789, Champion de Cicé, Archbishop of Bordeaux. Another speaker was Condorcet, whose speech, delivered at the very beginning of the Revolution, remained for a long time unknown; he then modified it in his other statements in 1793. The declaration was commented on by J.-J. Mounier and by J. Barnave on 1 August 1789. The famous priest Grégoire delivered his address on 4 August 1789 (he was perhaps the first to speak) pointing out the need for combining rights and duties so that they would complement each other.

The Girondists presented their draft on 15 and 16 February 1793, and its final revision was foreshadowed by Robespierre's speech in the Convention on 24 April. He dwelt on the necessity of safeguarding not only the rights but also the duties of public responsibility. Article 29 of his draft on the right and duty of insurrection in the face of extremes of injustice on the part of the government was incorporated *in extenso* in the proclaimed act. However, the final version did not include Robespierre's proposals concerning international matters such as a ban on wars, for example.

In considering the impact of Rousseau's ideas on the bills of 1793, we will confine our argument, so far as the Jacobin Constitution of 24 June 1793 is concerned, to its Article 7, which reads, "Le peuple française est l'universalité des citoyens français." The wording is not accidental. The article invites the entire community of citizens to participate in political action; it asks for their participation in the game of politics, without, however, departing from the concept that the state is a community of individuals. The nation, as a body of people, is not yet considered here as identical with the state.

STATE AND POLITICS

The Jacobins' gradual rise to power and their final success were accompanied by their proclaiming—in conformance with Rousseau's teaching—an enormously widened scope of political concerns. They took up the battle for a special type of state defined by them as to its form as well as its practical machinery for government: "The Jacobins sided with the people" to obtain that end. They engaged more and more furiously in combats with their adversaries, who seem to have been closing in on them from all sides; they waged war with the enemies of the country but also battled with their competitors for power.

At the same time, the role of politics was linked with the "state of virtue" by greater and lesser ideologists of Jacobinism.[56] Idealized as this state was, the Jacobins firmly believed in it, as did those who were later to become casualties of 9 Thermidor. That is why they reacted against the de-Christianization campaign in its most extreme manifestations, even if they risked losing some of their supporters by doing so. In deism and the cult of the Supreme Being which they tried to impose, they saw a means of strengthening public ethics, and ethics were considered indispensable in their political vision of the world. Maximum involvement in public affairs was regarded as one of the most important characteristics of the developing *mentalité révolutionnaire* (the subject is perhaps the most interesting of those now studied both in and outside France). This can be gathered from symbols employed by the Revolution, a never-ending sequence of *fêtes* or other manifestations of the revolutionary unity of the patriots and from the great importance attached to public oath-taking.

Apart from speeches and articles that appeared in the press, *feuilles volantes*, and theatrical performances, this state of virtue also left its impression in the fine arts: "L'artiste, le peintre éminemment, doit savoir penser," wrote Starobiński, having in mind David, but also Fuseli and Goethe.

Et penser, ce n'est pas seulement composer, c'est proposer au spectateur, des actions exemplaires, et c'est encore doubler l'exemplarité du sujet par une exécution assujettie au style d'un modèle exemplaire. Chez un David, nous l'avons vu, le tempérament pictural, le sens de la présence humaine, si manifestes dans ses admirables portraits, entrent en composition avec le *dessein discursif, civique et moralisateur* [emphasis added]. Malgré ce qui sonne faux dans certaines de ses grandes toiles "d'histoire," . . . il a été dans ses meilleurs moments, presque en dépit de lui-même, un peintre du sacré, de l' effroi, capable de conférer au visible sa présence la plus intense. . . . "Le Marat assassine," "piétà jacobine" [an admirable expression] énonce magnifiquement la solitude funèbre, pour la transmuer en communion selon l'impératif universel de la Terreur et de la Vertu.[57]

The Jacobins' line of development, which had started as a broad approach to the role and goals of politics in the new state and a general appeal to the people of every class, somehow dwindled into a sclerosis of dictatorship. How could it happen? I do not concur with that school of thought which finds, perhaps, its most striking expression in J. L. Talmon's *Origins of Totalitarian Democracy*. This Israeli scholar has argued that the Jacobins consciously aimed at totalitarianism *avant la lettre* as a single-party government. However, it will be remembered, they viewed their club as the link between the masses and communes, of which the Paris commune was only one, and the Convention, and as a forum for propaganda.

Saint-Just was the most prominent spokesman of their programmatic idea: "Je ne suis d'aucune faction, je les combattrai toutes. Elles ne s'éteindront jamais que par *les institutions* [emphasis added], qui produisent les garanties, qui poseront la borne de l'autorité et feront plonger sans retour d'orgueil humain sous le joug de la liberté politique."[58]

What immense confidence in law and public institutions, so typical of the Age of Enlightenment, that passage breathes! Of course, the wars they waged against their adversaries and competitors for power played no small part in their collapse along with their ever increasing distrust, extending even to their own organizations; they distrusted the meetings of the Parisian sections as well as popular associations in the provincial centers, even branches of the Jacobin Parisian club. But, in my opinion, the prime culprit among all these causes goes to their maddeningly rationalistic cult of institutions, so removed from genuine political life and providing no outlet for the discussion of competing and conflicting ideas and views. Many Jacobin ideas were turned against their advocates.

INSTITUTIONS

The term "institutions" is used here as it is defined by P. Robert in his *Dictionnaire alphabétique et analytique de la langue française:* "The entire set of forms and basic structures of social organizations as shaped by the law and customs of a group of people."[59] It is obvious that the subject matter of the history of institutions is disputed between historians and lawyers as much as it is between historians and social scientists. American sociologists, for example, consider an institution to be any organized mechanism that controls and shapes individual behavior within a group, i.e., has a distinct structure (an acknowledged leader and actions motivated by group interest).[60] There is no need to shuffle definitions and discuss their particular merits. What is important is that, to the French Jacobins and their followers in other countries, institutions served as points of reference both in principle and in each particular case. That tendency manifested itself in the mass elections of members of the Convention and the next legislative body, of judges, municipal governments, and priests until the separation of church and state, popular consultations in legislature, and public deliberations on other matters.

The draft of the constitution prepared by the Gironde in 1793 and that prepared by the Jacobins differed fundamentally in one respect. The Gironde believed that any question could be referred to the general public in a referendum. But according to the proclaimed constitution each draft of a bill *(loi)* was subject to popular consultation prior to its passing in parliamentary debate, except in minor questions, where the Convention could issue decrees, which were not subject to public scrutiny. The situation led, in practice, to a proliferation of decrees and confusion in terminology. The newly founded *Bulletin des lois* published between its covers a multitude of such decrees.

Robespierre's speech of 10 May 1793, dealing with the draft of the constitution submitted to the Convention, was truly inspired. In this speech he visualized an assembly hall large enough for twelve thousand persons attending the sessions (note that print was his sole means of mass communication). Robespierre was highly critical of previous solutions to the design of parliamentary halls and recent alterations in Parisian halls which were deliberately aimed at excluding a larger public from parliamentary sessions. His speech, not surprisingly, reflected the utopian schemes and demagoguery characteristic of speakers of the revolutionary period, when he claimed that working sessions could really be held under such conditions. Most probably, he was not so much concerned with dimensions and numbers as with an image that would emphasize popular involvement.[61]

Institutions of the new state had to express the very opposite of conservative inertia. They were expected to exhibit a specific dynamic innovation which has rightly been defined in our own time as an important social and civilizing characteristic, one that evolves in the course of the historical process. It does no harm, however, to help it along.[62] Elections, consultations—all the excitement was soon to lead to an appalling sham.

REVOLUTIONARY GOVERNMENT AND THE INSATIABLE DEMON OF BUREAUCRACY

The Jacobin Constitution was never instituted. The wars at the frontiers of the country and the civil war inside it were supposed to prepare the French for the application of the laws contained in the constitution as well as for the Declaration of Rights of 1793 in the peaceful period to follow.[63] Robespierre explained in the Convention that

. . . vaincre des Anglais et des traîtres est une chose assez facile à la valeur de nos soldats républicains; il est une entreprise non moins importante et plus difficile, c'est de confondre par une énergie constante les intrigues éternelles de tous les ennemis de la

liberté et de faire triompher les principes sur lesquels doit s'asseoir la prospérité publique. Tels sont les premiers devoirs que vous (i.e., citoyens représentants du peuple)
avez imposé à votre Comité de salut public.

The most pressing needs of the country, imperiled by external as
well as internal enemies, sketched in the speech, and the function of
the Comité de Salut Public vividly presented there dictated the basic
lines the government should take in the course of the Revolution and
the war. Robespierre and Saint-Just tried to define the principles of the
temporary government. "La théorie du gouvernement révolutionnaire
est aussi neuve," said Robespierre in the Convention, "que la Révolution qui l'a amené." It should be sought in books by political writers no
more than in old laws imposed by tyrants, or in the language of the
aristocrats for whom *la terreur* is a term of abuse:

La fonction du gouvernement est de diriger les forces morales et physiques de la nation
vers le but de son institution. Le but du gouvernement constitutionnel est de gouverner la
République: celui du gouvernement révolutionnaire est de la fonder. La Révolution est
la guerre de la liberté contre ses ennemis: la Constitution est le régime de la liberté
victorieuse et paisible.

In the subsequent passages of his speech dealing with the government of the period of the Revolution and the war, which he viewed as a
strong, efficient, and consequently highly centralized body, Robespierre confessed—as did Saint-Just—that the revolutionary government

. . . a besoin d'une activité extraordinaire, précisement parce qu'il est en guerre, il est
soumis à des règles *moins uniformes et moins rigoureuses* [emphasis added], parce que
les circonstances où il se trouve sont orageuses et mobiles, et surtout parce qu'il est
forcé de déployer sans cesse des ressources nouvelles et rapides, pour des dangers nou-
veaux et pressants.

These somewhat lengthy quotations contain the gist of the Jacobin
concept of *gouvernement révolutionnaire*, or at least that held by their
leaders, for the Jacobins never were a homogeneous group. Of course
recent legislation in every country has made use of the so-called state
of emergency or of martial-law by which, in keeping with constitutional
and other constitution-based norms, certain laws and civil liberties can
be suspended in a given territory and for a given span of time if a specific situation demands it. In the case under consideration, however, at
the close of 1793 and in early 1794, it was the whole of the Constitution
and the Declaration of Rights that were suspended. The theory of the
revolutionary government—as Robespierre had it—"in preparation for
victory and the future" was then developed. In his speech of 10 October 1793, which took up the subject even earlier, Saint-Just further

specified that the revolutionary government—apart from mobilizing the nation's maximum effort—should also care for war casualties and soldiers' families specifically during the immediate period it was in power and prior to the conclusion of the war.

In that speech he also attacked—and with what perspicacity—the bureaucracy:

> Everyone in governmental service is lazy: an official of higher standing does little and gets his work done for him by officials of lower standing, these in turn get their work done by those below them, and the Republic falls prey to twenty thousand fools who corrupt it, overpower it, suck it out. . . . A ministry is a paper world. . . . Verbose governmental orders and correspondence are signs of its inertia: you cannot rule if you cannot be concise. Representatives of the people, of generals, and of administrators circulate around offices as they once did around palaces; nothing gets done and expenditures are enormous. Officials have replaced monarchy: a pen-pushing demon is waging a war against us, and governing is out of the question. . . . Aristocracy, greed, indolence, thievery, and unsound methods all combine to distress the people and reduce them to misery. The government should be put straight *or it will tend toward the tyranny* [emphasis mine] that its enemies try to instill in it.[64]

Robespierre warned that the definition of a revolutionary government is not to be found in political writings but in life. Nevertheless, on 5 February 1794, when he spoke about sound policy, which should involve the entire nation, and when he connected the ideas of the revolutionary government with the principles of the new public morality, he was in fact referring to the ideas of his master, Rousseau. Bronisław Baczko interpreted Rousseau's thought, which, I believe, was also Robespierre's and others like him, when he said:

> In his view a political decision is an act of self-knowledge and moral self-determination, a confrontation of the "self" with "the general will," a continuous affirmation of one's moral identity with the people, with the entire community. . . . It would be ideal to have such a society, . . . where the social conditions and the spiritual frame of reference in which the individual exists would result in no disparity in the individual's attitude to the world. . . . A measure of the political liberty of a *citoyen* is not to be sought in increasing the real possibilities of choice among various policy alternatives, but in the ratio by which his own decision is in harmony with "the general will."[65]

Rousseau, like Robespierre, was aware that the people can be deceived by the ruling elite and by private enterpreneurs as easily as they can by one or another leader aspiring to autocracy.

I impute no aspirations to tyranny, no plots to gain power, or machinations for its preservation to the Jacobin leadership; nor will I criticize them for their utopian visions about a land of happiness; nor will I introduce psychotic or neurotic explanations, although this would not be difficult in Robespierre's case, and I am sure the psychohistorians could contribute to a discussion on that topic. Nevertheless, it was not only their own faults and the plots of their adversaries that were responsible for the fall of the Jacobins. There are also pathological processes that rot a dictatorship, typically when it either loses touch with the broad masses of the community—that is, the people—when its links with the people have been broken with a consequent loss of a basic understanding of the actual situation and the reality that surrounds it.

To return to the centralization and bureaucratization of the authority in France under the Jacobin dictatorship, these processes were rapid indeed. The ever-growing army of clerks reached several hundred thousand, and its growth seems to have been little affected by the purges effected by local revolutionary committees or by inspections of government envoys (or, to be specific, those of the Committee of Public Safety), two to each department. These actions merely resulted in some officials being replaced by others. Considering all central and municipal units, in Paris alone the army of white-collar workers numbered into the tens of thousands. The office of the Committee of Public Safety, for example, employed 418 persons in mid-1793 and seven times as many five months later.

After the reform that replaced the monocratically-run ministries by twelve governmental committees subordinated to the Committee of Public Safety, the number of their employees multiplied at an alarming rate. Add to that the well-developed police apparatus, including officials of the special police department of the Committee of Public Safety and the competing department of the Committee of Public Security. The mounting *paperasse* resulted in the Committee of Public Safety daily issuing over sixty decrees along with requirements for immediate implementation under supervision. Envoys of the Committee sent to various parts of the country reported that "unfortunately the patriots are numerous but little educated, and gifted people are either rather reserved or take no advantage of the confidence placed in them." Many of them did not embrace the cause of the Revolution early enough and by now are pushed aside. It is high time "to wake up all the depositaries of public authority." However, in mid-1794 it was too late to do that.

Let us once more quote the Saint-Just speech of 13 March 1794:

What more do you want, all you who are occupying high posts just to show off, so that you can be talked about: look, that man who speaks, he is the man who leads the others. Now, you no longer wish to pursue the trade of your father, who was perhaps a worthy artisan and whose modesty made a patriot of you; instead you want to become a public figure. You will perish, you who are so intent on making a fortune out of the state and looking for a bit of luck beyond that allotted to people.

His comments referred to the fact that capable persons committed to the work of the Revolution, mostly lawyers and other notables, were frequently being replaced by artisans, small traders, and journeymen. The summer of 1794 diverted farmers from their fields. "How long have we had too many clerks," continued Saint-Just, "and too few citizens, *le peuple y est nul*. It is not the common people that criticize the government, but clerks, associated with each other, ever striving to increase their influence and silencing the people." These "être artificiels" should be "driven out of the Temple of Equality, if Liberty is to survive."[66]

Not all the clerks were a burden to the state, nor were they all blameworthy. One must distinguish between the central and local administrations, which are indispensable for growth and for the day-to-day running of the country, and the bureaucracy. But the fact remains that federalism and the participation of the people were destroyed while excessive centralization combined with bureaucracy to bring about the collapse of the Jacobin dictatorship soon after the first benefits of the new system were reaped.

INSTITUTIONS; ADMINISTRATION: THE LASTING INHERITANCE OF THE DICTATORSHIP

That the Convention was looked upon, and referred to by the Jacobins, as a supreme, decision-making organ of the new state was as much a fact of life as a Jacobin tenet. The bill of 14 Frimaire of the Year II stated that the "la Convention nationale . . . est le centre unique de l'impulsion de gouvernement." That ruling put a stop to the vaulting ambitions of various groups and factions as well as those of other state institutions. This tenet was held in deep reverence by Robespierre and his associates. But was it really so? Was it not merely a formula?

A Polish historian will recall an impossibly far-fetched, elaborate piece of flattery with which the leading Polish statesman, writer, and reformer Hugo Kołłątaj addressed the *Sejm* when, as a member of the new government, he took the floor in a session in June 1791, shortly after the same *Sejm* proclaimed the May 3 Constitution. Expounding on the anticipated program of fundamental reforms, Kołłątaj compared the Polish *Sejm* to, of all things, the Creator. Just as the Lord had raised the universe out of chaos, so had the *Sejm* extricated the Polish-Lithuanian Commonwealth out of anarchy and inertia.[67] It is conceivable that Robespierre, as Kołłątaj before him, had begun to succumb to the idea that the parliament was truly the sovereign authority of a nation, delegated not only with legislative but with total power. There was a good reason why Montesquieu's bust, originally exhibited in the Convention, was removed. That political philosopher's idea of the separation of powers was becoming obsolete under the new regime.

The government, composed first of ministers and later of twelve committees, was the executive, subject to the Convention; two of its committees—Security and Public Safety—were contending with each other for power. Robespierre, who first served on the Committee of Instruction, moved to the Committee of Public Safety on 27 July 1793. After ridding itself of Danton and one other member by the guillotine, the Committee, comprised by then of twelve persons, renamed itself the Great Committee and became in fact the head of the revolutionary government. Theoretically, its members were to be elected each month, but somehow they remained in office the year round. Nevertheless, the Committee was responsible to the Convention, and in its every statement it stressed the supremacy of that body.

Based on the tribune of the Jacobin Club and its three million branches, and entrenched in the strongly pro-Robespierre commune of Paris, the Committee of Public Safety brought under its control the whole central government and the entire country. Striving to subdue any federalist tendencies, it minimized the role of the departments and their chiefs, and it turned for support to the more docile Jacobins and the *sans-culottes* in the districts and communes. The huge number of communes—even today there are in France almost thirty-five thousand communes with populations averaging around four hundred inhabitants—meant the fragmentization but also the politicization of the administration, which was an advantage to the centralized government.

In spite of its many weaknesses and problems, the achievements of the Jacobin dictatorship are likewise many and undeniable in their importance for France and the whole of Europe. A few of these contributions are suggested below.

1. Unlike the Girondists, and part of his own camp, Robespierre was as opposed to war as he was to generals; based on his French experiences, he distrusted the leader of the Polish Insurrection, Tadeusz Kościuszko, for being a general. Brissot wanted "to set Europe on fire"; Chaumette called for a new crusade covering "an area that separates Paris from Petersburg" that, he believed, would soon be "francisé, municipalisé, et jacobinisé"—not an unlikely prediction at the outset of the war. The war cries, which first referred to the "liberté de peuples" to have them "délivré du déspotisme," were later replaced by the "guerre des conquêtes" and demands for territorial expansion. The war was at first a defensive war, accompanied by condemnations of the invaders of "un sang impure," as they sang in the *Marseillaise*. The future was to prove that the same blood circulated in the veins of traitors and enemies within the country.

But in the situation that developed, the Jacobins did a great deed— they saved France, or to be more precise, they stood at the head of that war effort to which the common folk, soldiers, and scholars alike contributed; to all of them goes the credit for victory. They raised an army of 1,200,000 men, built a new, democratic cadre of officers, and despite great difficulties, fed the army and the city of Paris.

2. A social relief scheme, envisaged by the Declaration of Rights, was elaborated in the legislation of 1793 and 1794 to cover the entire country; despite its many shortcomings and inconsistencies it remains to the lasting credit of the Jacobins.

3. The development of the public school system was begun after much debate.[68]

4. State interventionist policies in the provisioning of the army and the towns, in price and wage fixing, in ensuring employment in manufactories were repeatedly attempted despite many difficulties of a practical and doctrinal nature that hindered them.[69]

5. Up-to-date methods were used in finance, including state budgeting and government spending. In securing financial resources, however, they did not go in Cabon's policy beyond primitive instruments such as the issue of banknotes, combined with inflationary measures, compulsory loans, differential taxation designed to place the burden on the rich, and confiscation of the property of traitors and fugitives.

6. Civil law and, in some respects, administrative law reforms— again in conformance with Rousseau's ideas—were introduced. They concerned the equality of the sexes, the introduction of divorce, and— what proved to be of major consequence—equality of inheritance rights extended to natural children (made retroactive to 14 July 1789), and finally, increased possibilities of deferred payment in the case of parcelled-out estates under temporary state supervision. The first steps were taken toward codifying legal and civil procedures. Not all of these innovations were included in the famous Napoleonic Code of 1804, which in some respects departed from the achievements of the revolution.[70]

THE TRANSFORMATION OF THE SOCIAL STRUCTURE: THE NATION AND THE STATE

Who and what were the leaders and makers of the Revolution? The Convention did not include a single worker; the Jacobins were recruited primarily from the intelligentsia. Professionally, they were lawyers, journalists, writers, and teachers; some were artisans and shopkeepers. Part of a changing society, they could hardly be identified as petit bourgeoisie or lower middle class. Of similar occupational composition and social background were the leaders and spokesmen of the *sans-culottes* of Paris, five hundred and several scores of whom are listed by Soboul. There were some day-laborers among them. The revolutionaries also included a number of defrocked priests. The majority of the Girondists were of similar class extraction.

Out of the Revolution emerged *la France bourgeoise*, and this is not only Ch. Morazé's opinion. His book of that title (1946) closes with the statement—much enhanced by Le Febvre—"Le rythme profond du monde est celui de l'esprit." Or was it not rather France which was created by *les bourgeois conquérants* (to use the title of another Morazé book [1957]) for their own use and benefit? In fact, the France of the bourgeois community had emerged. The Jacobins embraced the cause of *la France bourgeoise,* which they rationalized on the basis of human rights such as man's right to private property. Eventually they restricted it somewhat, however; there was freedom to invest in small enterprises, but anyone demanding the large-scale parceling out of landed estates *(loi agraire)* was liable to the death penalty. Despite their occasional lapses into interventionist policy and shifts of opinion under the pressures of circumstances, they stood as a rule for the freedom of trade and industry. They were opposed to people's associating in unions, including workers' unions.

Nevertheless, despite its break with the bourgeois and democratic tenets of the Jacobin dictatorship, the year 1795 did not merely bring back the norms of 1789 and continue them. Despite the collapse of the Jacobin dictatorship and the subsequent curtailment of the gains of the Revolution, the Revolution continued to be an inspiration for liberalism and individualism through its affirmation of equality, its dissolution of the barriers between estates, and its abolition of many inequalities. It became a social revolution, and it launched many initiatives. The Revolution was responsible for the emergence of the people of France into a great era in their national history. Their later actions could be suppressed, but never again could they be relegated to a minor position. The legacy of the Revolution continues to be theirs. If Napoleon could say "politics is today's tragedy," this politics would now be embraced by the entire nation. Both the war in which the French were the winners and the enormous popular involvement in politics, although it tended to be kept in check in the closing stage of the Jacobin dictatorship, resulted in increased national consciousness and the identification of nationality with belonging to a state, with having citizenship: *État-Nation*. It is difficult to agree with R. Remond, who considered it a misunderstanding to link the national and state holiday of France celebrated on 14 July with the capture of the Bastille. In his opinion, the national day of France should be linked with 14 July 1790, "the day of Federation," which crowned federationist tendencies that had surmounted local patriotism and regional distinctions.[71]

The Battle of Valmy in September 1792 is considered by Remond to be an appropriate symbol of modern French patriotism. The battle in which the revolutionary army defeated the united armies of Austria and Prussia was a turning point in that war. It was during that battle perhaps for the first time that soldiers advanced with the "Vive la nation." Goethe called it a landmark in the history of mankind. Nonetheless, it was the battle cry "la patrie en danger" used by the Jacobins and volunteers during the campaigns of 1793 that better reflected the nation under arms, organized by the state.

To return once more to the Jacobin institutions, their range of influence was to be wide indeed. It was not only the broadly conceived idea of political and ideological education, of which formal instruction—in the Jacobins' view—was but a part; it was not only propaganda; it was not only the debates during the meetings of the sections controlled by the Jacobins. It was not only the press, as freedom of the press was abolished and the number of journals and pamphlets greatly reduced; it was primarily the institutions that were expected to mould, and did mould, the new French nation. Both civil and military institutions were responsible for that moulding. "Ce sont les institutions nationales," wrote Rousseau, "qui forment le génie, le caractère, le goût et les moeurs d'un peuple, qui ce font être lui et non pas un autre, qui lui inspirent cet ardent amour de la patrie fondé sur des habitudes impossibles à déraciner. . . . " The Revolution identified the ideas of *état* and *nation* with each other.

Jacobin institutions proved no less a stimulus to radical groups and centers outside France than did their social and national ideas combined with their appeals to unite in a common struggle against despotic rulers. They also found reflection in political events and among political groups in other countries at the close of the eighteenth century.[72] Obviously, local references to "Jacobins" and "Jacobinism" should not be taken as implying that they could be considered as identical with, or even close to, the ideas, attitudes, and activities of the French Jacobins. These terms were more often than not applied to groups as a propagandistic ploy by the courts of Petersburg, Berlin, and Vienna. They were sometimes used by the "Jacobins" themselves to identify themselves as supporters of France and the Revolution active in other countries. They differed from the French Jacobins, however, as much in substance as in time.[73]

THE POLISH AND ITALIAN JACOBINS

The Jacobins in Poland and Italy attained some influence in the politics of their respective countries short of participating in the government. The term "Polish Jacobins"[74] refers to the left wing of those supporting the National Insurrection of 1794 (i.e., after the Second Partition) headed by Tadeusz Kościuszko, who had been vested with the authority of a commander-in-chief of the army and a dictator. Polish Jacobins were recruited from the lesser nobility and burghers; they also included a comparatively large number of Polish intellectuals, members of the emerging intelligentsia of Warsaw, Cracow, and Wilno. In the course of the Insurrection they launched a campaign to reform as extensively as possible the condition of the peasantry. They were a driving force behind a number of legislative acts from the bill of 7 May 1794 on the emancipation of the peasants or the abolition of the personal bondage *(poddaństwo osobiste)*, through the establishment of governmental offices for the alleviation of the plight of the rural population, to the bill of 20 October 1794, which was Poland's first act aimed at the abolition of serfdom, although here restricted to peasants partaking in the Insurrection. The equalization of rights between the bourgeoisie and the nobility was another goal of the group gathered around Hugo Kołłątaj, a member of the government and christened "the Polish Robespierre," with no slight exaggeration, by his enemies, particularly the police of the partitioning states.

The Jacobins called for a fundamental transformation of the entire system of government, even to the point of advancing utopian proposals to admit peasants to the state administration. They urged the Supreme National Council—the ruling organ of the Insurrection—to act in cooperation with the lower classes, especially in Warsaw. It was from Jacobin France that they imported the ideas they sought to plant on the Vistula and in Warsaw: that the Supreme Council should not only consider proposals and complaints presented by the people but put its own proposals, and its candidates for the civil service as well, before the people for consideration.

In the face of the impending danger of ultimate collapse (the state had only recently ceased to be a republic of the nobility), the Polish Jacobins attacked the apparatus of the Insurrection for its many defects, its inefficiencies, and indecisiveness.

Two popular revolts in Warsaw in May and June 1794, with their acts of terror in the form both of court verdicts and direct assaults meted out against the high state dignitaries found guilty of treason and collaboration with Russia, have to be attributed to the Jacobins. In an effort to save King Stanisław Poniatowski, who was being kept prisoner in his castle, Kościuszko, who kept shifting from the Right to the Left of the movement, finally gave in to the Jacobins' demand. An extraordinary court martial was instituted, and the Jacobins were entrusted with the administration of justice during a period that required a major military effort to defend Warsaw against the besieging Russian and Prussian armies. The Jacobins' policy, in this case unreservedly supported by Kościuszko, was to concentrate every effort to mobilize the country's military and material potential, to raise and arm a national army that would include the mass participation of peasants and burghers, to propagate the goals of the Insurrection in speeches and in print, to issue memorandums and print journals, and to employ teachers, patriotic clergy, and representatives of the Insurrection's authorities to propagandize the common people. The Jacobins controlled the Supreme Council's Department of Instruction, which was responsible for education and propaganda; the alleged "Polish Robespierre," Kołłątaj, served in the department.

The Polish Jacobins also professed and propagated the concept of the brotherhood of peoples. Apart from their kings and commanders, Russian and Prussian soldiers were addressed with conciliatory words in the name of the common goal—that the yoke of despotism be thrown off. The insurrectionists had a strong feeling of solidarity with revolutionary France, for which the outbreak of the Polish Insurrection in the rear of the Prussian armies had been of considerable assistance. In July 1794, a proclamation was issued from besieged Warsaw. Published in Polish and French, it appealed for joint action by all the peoples of Europe in the common struggle against despotism. Publications that appeared in Warsaw also included appeals for the unity and fraternity of the peoples of two continents: Europe and America.

The French text of the Warsaw proclamation addressed its appeal to soldiers of all countries: "Soldats de tous pays! Dites à ceux qui vous dirigent que vous ne voulez plus désormais être les instruments du despotisme. . . . Peuple d'Europe! Elève ta voix et non ton bras; il faut maintenant un soulèvement de fraternité et d'humanité, non pas soulèvement de fureur, d'incendies et de meurtres. . . ." A poem printed on a handbill read: "Let two halves of the Earth—Europe and America—be knit by some chaste force with a brotherly knot as befits offspring of the same parents."

All these ideas were collected in a pamphlet entitled *Are the Poles Capable of Winning Independence?* prepared by one of the leading Polish Jacobins, Józef Pawlikowski, in close collaboration with Kościuszko, and printed in Paris in 1800. The title question was answered in the affirmative, three conditions being stipulated: countrywide partisan warfare by the peasants; provision of education for the general population in order to draw it into the sphere of world civilization; and fraternity of the peoples.

And what about the Italians? The closing decade of the eighteenth century saw the emergence of sympathetic individuals and clubs in various parts of Italy; their way had been prepared by the intellectual ferment of the Age of Enlightenment in the Italian states in the first half of the century.[75] The arrival of the French armies in the war with Austria and especially their triumphs under Napoleon favored radical agitation on the eve of an attempt to divide up Italy once again and to establish new state regimes under the influence of the French. Next to social changes, the consolidation of Italy into one unified, independent state was the basic tenet of the nineteenth-century Italian Risorgimento, and this was true of both south and north Italy. In French-occupied Lombardy, a competition on the subject "Proposals for a New Regime Suitable for Italy," with Pietro Verri as chairman, netted thirty-seven solutions. In Milan, an elaborated scheme was advanced by Michele Laurora. "All'Italia nelle tenebre, l'aurora porta luce"; Italy should be "libera, una e indipendente."

To achieve that aim, the Papal State should be abolished: "Cristo non aveva un regno. Perchè allora i papi si sono impadroniti di dodici tra le più belle province de l'Italia?" "L'Italia sarà retta a republica, divisi in 80 dipartamenti [again after the French model], a loto volta ripartiti in cantoni, e i cantoni in municipalità." Its supreme body would be a senate composed of 500 members and residing in the Vatican. Its responsibilities were to include the election of a president. Laurora was aware that the implementation of his project would depend on the general transformation and pacification of Europe as a whole.

Matteo Galdi of Naples wanted "La Republica d'Italia si farà." In another work, *Dei rapporti politice-economici fra le nazioni libera*, he argued that unification was as necessary for Italy as for Europe, and a guarantee of good relations between Italy and France. The Italian republic, like the French one, would have to be "una e indivisible."

Of no less interest are the constitutions of the Italian republic, promulgated at the close of the eighteenth century as a compromise with French commands, and the republican institutions which they introduced. Drafted under specific conditions, it was required that the Bolognese and subsequently the Reggio Emilian, Genoan, Roman, Neapolitan, and other constitutions (in Naples undertaken by a group headed by the noted writer Mario Pagano) be based on the French Constitution of the Year III. But with some remarkable divergences from that model, they adopted the Jacobin-style general suffrage, and next to a consideration for the Roman Catholic creed as the state religion, they included the principle of toleration of all religious worship, especially for the Jews. A few of the constitutions favored an increase in state control of the economy. In the Roman republic the drafting committee went back to antiquity to rediscover certain models and terms. Naples repudiated the principle that property is "diritto sacre e inviolabile" and introduced two novel institutions: the censors, who were to guard the democratization of life and take care of public morals in the cantons, and the ephors, who constituted a sort of tribunal that would make sure that legislation and justice conform to the constitution.

In the Cisalpine republic special tribunals acting alongside the regular institutions to guard the implementation of the revolution were very developed compared with other republics. But a drafted civil constitution for the clergy and the separation of church and state were put off in view of the special situation in Italy. Partial agrarian reforms were introduced. Pains were taken to form a democratic national army with the Polish Legion being formed in that republic at the same time.

Polish and Italian efforts were for a time being frustrated by their enemies, whose strength contrasted with the weakness of the local Jacobin groups, which either had little popular support or were completely detached from the masses of the people. The social soil was not yet ready.

THE PRICE FRANCE PAID

The price France paid to conquer the invaders and to keep the fundamental achievements of the Revolution and even try to extend them was enormous in both human and material terms. The Jacobin dictatorship and the preceding early period of the Republic experimented, so the phrase went, "sur la peau" of the French.

Himself a later casualty of the dictatorship, Danton, as the minister of justice in the first republican government, was one of those guilty of the 1792 butchery in Parisian prisons when 1,395 persons, only some of them political prisoners, lost their lives.

The great number of people suspected of antirevolutionary feelings who could show no proof of their good citizenship and lived in constant danger of losing their lives was first estimated at 100,000 persons, increased later to 300,000 or, according to some estimates, even as many as 800,000 persons.

The administration of the Terror falls into two phases. In 1794, the Jacobins endeavored to have it channeled in the centralized Parisian Tribunal, to guard against its eventual abuse in the provinces. This may have minimized the ultimate number of victims. In his *Incidence of the Terror: A Statistical Interpretation,* which remains as indispensable a source of reference as ever, the American scholar D. Greer made up a balance sheet for the Revolution.[76] His list is incomplete, however. He based his analysis mainly on lists and rolls of death sentences published by the Paris tribunal, municipal tribunals, and extraordinary committees. He listed by name 17,000 condemned to death. The Vendée accounted for 52 per cent of that number, the southeastern departments for 19 per cent, and the capital for 16 per cent. He further distinguished departments—six of them—with no acts of Terror; 31 departments belonging to the group had less than 10 persons condemned to death. Eighteen departments belonged to the group with over 1,000 death sentences. The sentences in retribution for rebellions and treason made up 78 per cent of the entire number; for federalism, 10 per cent; for views and opinions held, 9 per cent; and for economic offenses, 1.28 per cent. The largest proportion was not by any means represented by the aristocracy, but by artisans, shopkeepers, and day laborers. Common folk accounted for 31 per cent of those condemned to death, followed by peasants with 28 per cent, and in some regions, by noblemen and priests. The latter were as a rule spared by the Revolution and were almost exclusively prosecuted by the Terror.

Greer's estimate included roughly one-third of the capital sentences. To his number must be added those not reflected in the records of court proceedings and the mortality rate among prisoners. When these are included, the casualties of the Terror amount to 50,000 persons, or .02 per cent of the entire population of the country. Some prisoners were set free after 9 Thermidor.

The accelerated rate of executions in the period of the Great Terror in mid-1794 gave rise to another wave of "great fear," an emotion shared by those imperiled by the Terror and those involved in it. This was the increasing fear that the Great Terror had departed from its original purpose of combating the counterrevolution and was being employed by those wielding dictatorial power to further their own ambitions and quiet their private apprehensions. The masses refused further sacrifices. Members and representatives of the dictatorship were more frequently attacked by the dissatisfied seeking to save their own skin, by the humiliated, by the corrupted. They appealed in vain to the Committee of Public Safety that "c'est surtout de la lassitude du peuple qu'il faut se garantir." At the frontiers of France, in Alsace, and in the area around Nice, the spirit of patriotism was abating.

Apart from Greer's analysis and a few French publications, a Polish publication of 1934 (a doctoral dissertation by a graduate of the department of law at the University of Warsaw named J. Macleod Machlejd) entitled *The French Revolution in the Light of Statistics* gave a list of 356 revolutionaries whose contributions to the Revolution, measured by the frequency and character of their pronouncements, were outstanding, as supported by documentary evidence. Of them he found that one-third had been killed in the internecine war by other factions and/or individuals. One exception was Sieyès, who, when asked what he did during the Jacobin dictatorship responded, "J'ai vécu."[77]

Robespierre is said to have remarked that the Revolution is not made with a code in hands. He was referring to a fixed penal law and legal proceedings. That opinion was corroborated not only by the Great Terror, but by some earlier evidence as well. It is troubling to realize how easily, under some circumstances in a complex sociopsychological situation, one is liable to contradict one's own words and character. No one was more against capital punishment and in favor of other humane laws at the outset of his career than Robespierre, who had also been a pupil of Beccaria:

Le bonheur de la société n'est pas attaché à la peine de mort . . . . Il faut croire que le peuple doux, sensible, généreux qui habite la France et toutes les vertus vont être développées par le régime de la liberté traitera avec humanité les coupables et convenir que l'expérience, la sagesse vous permettent de consacrer les principes sur lesquels s'appuie la motion que je fais que la peine de mort soit abolie.[78]

Even when one is aware of what seems to be a recurring and regular pattern in the struggle of revolution against counterrevolution, one cannot overlook the particularly acute forms the Terror assumed in France; even though facing the war, counterrevolution, and moral danger to the country, one cannot ignore the abuse of justice. Dramas dealing with Danton and his trial, especially those by Romain Rolland and, in Poland, by Stanisława Przybyszewska, reflect what really took place: the president of the tribunal and the public prosecutor, Antoine Quintin Fouquier of the Cordellier Club (who was to be guillotined in 1794), were warned that they would be arrested if they failed to engineer Danton's trial (even though it meant not granting him leave to speak in his defense) so that its outcome would suit his adversaries.

The year 1794, in particular, was marked by the adoption of regulations in contradiction to the hitherto accepted procedural norms, even those in earlier legislation, and the repudiation of the warrants contained in the Declaration of Rights. It may be added that Poland during the 1794 Insurrection displayed many features of a revolutionary war, but the rules of the humane school of penal law (Beccaria, Flangari) adopted in court procedure prior to the events continued as a rule to be regarded. The rights of the accused were not forgotten, although—it must be added—this was viewed by some among the left wing as a sign of weakness on the part of the authorities.[79]

Apart from the exhaustion of propaganda resources, apart from the misconceived decrees of Vantose in 1794 on partial agrarian reform and of 5 Thermidor on maximum wages (which, devised as a means of combating inflation, dealt a head blow to the *sans-culottes*), apart from the general exhaustion of the country caused by war both on the frontiers and in the hinterland, the reasons for the withdrawal of the involvement of the masses and their *mentalité révolutionnaire* are also to be sought in the excesses of the period of Terror. Voltaire once remarked, with his typical cynicism, repeating here Machiavelli, that an adversary should be dealt a brisk but decisive blow before one returns to the ordinary way of ruling. As if anticipating the endless purges of the Revolution, he remarked that no one but a saint could long stand maltreatment without losing patience.

The question was considered by Marx in the period of the Springtime of the Peoples, and it was then that he formulated his much quoted opinion that "der ganze französische Terrorismus" should be viewed only "als eine plebejische Manier, mit den Feinden der Bourgeoisie,

dem Absolutismus, dem Feudalismus und dem Spiessbürgertum, fer-
tigzuwerden." Marx intended to write a book on the Convention.[80] In
the years following, both Marx and Engels were to develop more cautious and sagacious opinions, and they drew attention to the excesses
of the Terror. In a letter of 4 November 1870 written to a friend, Engels
referred directly to the 1793 events and remarked that such excessive
forms of terror are usually the work of people who are themselves
frightened and do it to reassure themselves. Their fright is elicited by
the "Lumpenmob" that surrounds them, selfishly pursuing its own
ends.[81]

Under these circumstances, when the Jacobins parted company with
the masses of the *sans-culottes*, for which they were largely to blame
and were left with no support to back them, the Jacobin leadership,
Robespierre, Saint-Just, Couthon, and some other close associates,
overburdened by their huge load of personal responsibilities, found
themselves on the verge of breakdown in the decisive moment of the
night preceding 9 Thermidor. Their collapse could be explained by psychological processes; it could also be attributed to their legalism *à out-
rance* with regard to the Convention, the majority of whose members,
they believed, could be persuaded.

In his speech of 15 April 1794, Saint-Just was conscious that it was
the beginning of the end: "La révolution est glacée, tous les principes
sont affaiblis, il ne reste que des bonnets rouges portés par l'intrigue.
L'exercice de la terreur a blasé le crime," and he used a simile, peculiar under the circumstances—"comme liqueurs fortes blasent le
palais."

Robespierre and Saint-Just's last speeches, addressed to the Convention and the whole of France, and prepared but never delivered, are
surprisingly weak. Their intellectual and emotional resources were
running low. "La révolution fut glacée." Seeing the tragedy of the
revolution as it is, no man of sense would say today after Joseph de
Maistre "L'histoire de Neuf Thermidor n'est pas longue; quelques
scélérats firent périt quelque scélérats."

In the world of violence, cruelty, and menace that we live in, it is
hardly possible to fail to see that the excesses of the Terror and the
abuse by the Revolution of the same laws it had promulgated were in
part behind the collapse of the Jacobins. Roger Ferrer, who twice
wrote his book devoted to the problems of the second half of the twentieth century, *Les libertés à l'abandon*, used a formula which aptly
fits the period: "Elles ne sont ni détruites ni deniées: elles s'effilo-
chent."[82]

Albert Camus in his *L'homme révolté* was sympathetic to Saint-Just.
He repeatedly quoted Saint-Just's words, such as "Hors des lois, tout
est stérile et mort." He appreciated that the revolutionary effort "es-

sayait d'instituer la réligion de la vertu,'' although it was overcome by faults inherent in human nature.[83]

Nonetheless, it is not only from the vantage point of its achievements—primarily its success in mobilizing the nation's efforts in the struggle for independence and the preservation of the social revolution—that the period of the Jacobin dictatorship and the entire Revolution have continued to remain a ''procès ouvert.'' Studies of its great achievements and its great mistakes, studies of the mechanism of history and the confrontation of the ideas and their practical realization have continued to be a laboratory of experiences, approached, not incidentally, by French and non-French scholars alike—by historians and legal scholars, as well as by social and political scientists of many countries and continents.

NOTES

1 J.-R. Suratteau, *La Révolution Française: Certitudes et controverses* (Paris, 1973).

2 J. Godechot, *Un jury pour la Révolution* (Paris, 1974).

3 Cl. Mazauric, *Sur la Révolution Française: Contribution à l'histoire de la révolution bourgeoise* (Paris, 1970), p. 15.

4 A. Z. Manfred, ''Die Grosse Französische Revolution des 18. Jahrhunderts und die Gegenwart,'' *Studien über die Revolution* (Berlin, 1969), pp. 157ff.

5 V. I. Lenin, *Werke*, vol. 29 (Berlin, 1961), pp. 52, 360, 342ff.

6 Dalin is primarily an authority on Babeuf and Babouvist doctrine, ''Babeuf und der 'Cercle social','' *Studien über die Revolution*, pp. 108ff; also, ''Babeuf et les idées de Rousseau,'' *Au Siècle des Lumières* (Paris-Moscow, 1970), pp. 301ff.

7 V. S. Alekseev-Popov and J. J. Baskine, ''Problemy istorii iakobinskoi diktatury v svete trudov V. I. Lenina,'' *Iz istorii iakobinskoi diktatury* (Odessa, 1962), pp. 21ff.

8 F. G. Revunenkov, *Marksizm i problema iakobinskoi diktatury* (Leningrad, 1966); also, *Parizhskie sankiuloty epokhi Velikoi Frantsuzskoi Revoliutsii* (Leningrad, 1971).

9 P. T. Dobroliubskii, *Termidor* (Odessa, 1949).

10 M. M. Shtrange, *Russkoe obshchestvo i frantsuzskaia revoliutsiia 1789-1794, gg.* (Moscow, 1956); also *Demokraticheskaia intelligentsiia Rossii v XVIII veke* (Moscow, 1965).

11 K. O. Dzhedzhula, *Rossiia i velikaia frantsuzskaia burzhuaznaia revoliutsiia kontsa XVIII veka* (Kiev, 1972).

12 A. Mathiez, *La Bolchévisme et le jacobinisme* (Paris, 1922).

13 A. Mestre and Ph. Guttinger, *Constitutionnalisme jacobin et constitutionnalisme soviétique* (Paris, 1971), including an extensive bibliography.

14 Among other sources, the proceedings of the ''Symposium zur Vergleichenden Revolutionsgeschichte der Neuzeit,'' mimeographed (Leipzig, 1974).

15 A. Soboul [P. Dérocles, pseud.], *Saint-Just, ses idées politiques et sociales* (Paris, 1937; 2nd ed., 1946). One of the more important publications issued after World War II, and strongly reflecting the ideas of the French resistance movement, is A. Olli-

vier, *Saint-Just et la force des choses* (Paris, 1955), with a remarkable preface by André Malraux. Particularly interesting data and material are to be found in *Actes du Colloque Saint-Just* (Paris, 1968).

16 J. Laverrier [J. Bruno-Bronowicz], *La naissance de l'armée nationale 1789-1794* (Paris, 1939) (Polish trans., Warsaw, 1956).

17 A. Mathiez, *Études sur Robespierre*, introduction by G. Lefebvre (Paris, 1958).

18 The principal publication that appeared that year was *Maximilien Robespierre 1758-1794: Beiträge zu seinem 200. Geburtstag*, ed. W. Markov (Berlin, 1958). Official celebrations in Paris to mark the anniversary were not considered to be advisable, but two conferences were held: one by the Sorbonne, sponsored by Rector J. Sarraihl, and the other by the Society of Robespierrist Studies presided over by G. Lefebvre. Lefebvre's interesting article for the occasion appeared in *L'Humanité*, 2 May 1957. A valuable exhibit was organized by the Archives Nationales.

19 A. Cobban, *The Social Interpretation of the French Revolution* (Cambridge, 1964).

20 For instance, M. Bordes, *La réforme municipale du Contrôleur général Laverdy et son application (1764-1771)* (Toulouse, 1968). On the other hand, publications that tend to vindicate the prerevolutionary system are H. Grange, *Les idées de Necker* (Paris, 1974); and R. Mousnier, *Les institutions de la France sous la monarchie absolue*, vol. 1 (Paris, 1974).

21 P. Amann, ed., *The Eighteenth-Century Revolution: French or Western?* (Boston, 1963).

22 J. Godechot, *Les révolutions 1770-1799* (Paris, 1963); R. R. Palmer, *1789: Les révolutions de la liberté et de l'égalite* (Paris, 1968), published in English under the title *The World of the French Revolution* (New York, 1971); as well as other works by these outstanding scholars.

23 F. Furet and D. Richet, *La Révolution Française* (Paris, 1965-66). Cf. also the more popularly written L. Bergeren, F. Furet, R. Kosselleck, *L'âge des révolutions européennes (1780-1848)* (Paris, 1973).

24 A. Soboul, *La civilisation et la Révolution Française*, vol. 1 (Paris, 1970), introduction.

25 Cl. Mazauric, "Refléxions sur une nouvelle conception de la Révolution Française," *Annales Historiques de la Révolution Française* (cited hereafter as *AHRF*), no. 189 (1967).

26 In 1974, this periodical was devoted to the Revolution.

27 A. Gerard, *La Révolution Française, mythes et interprétations, 1789-1970* (Paris, 1970).

28 D. Guérin, *La lutte des classes sous la Ire République: Bourgeois et "Bras nus,"* *1793-1797*, 2 vols. (Paris, 1946; 2nd ed., 1968).

29 A. Soboul, *Les sans-culottes parisiens en l'an II* (La Roche-sur-Yon, 1958; 2nd ed., Paris, 1962).

30 K. D. Tønnesson, *La défaite des sans-culottes: Mouvement populaire et révolution bourgeoise en l'an III* (Oslo-Paris, 1959).

31 No less controversial is the promise of D. Woronoff, *La République bourgeoise (1794-1799)* (Paris, 1972).

32 G. Rudé, *The Crowd in the French Revolution* (Oxford, 1959); idem, *The Crowd in History, 1730-1848: A Study of Popular Disturbances in France and England* (New York-London-Sydney, 1964).

33 E. J. Hobsbawm, *The Age of Revolution: Europe, 1789-1848* (London, 1962).

34 R. C. Cobb, *Les armées révolutionnaires: Instrument de la terreur dans les départements, avril 1793 —floreal An II,* 2 vols. (Paris, 1961-63). It does not seem right to compare the struggle of republican France to the famous dragonnades of Louis XIV.
35 R. C. Cobb, *The Police and the People: French Popular Protest, 1789-1820* (Oxford, 1970).
36 M. Reinhard, *Le Grand Carnot,* vol. 1: *De l'ingénieur au conventionnel* (Paris, 1950), and vol. 2: *L'organisateur de la victoire* (Paris, 1952).
37 W. Markov, *Die Freiheiten des Priesters Roux* (Berlin, 1967); also, "Grenzen des Jakobinerstaates," *Grundpositionen der französischen Aufklärung,* vol. 1 (Berlin, 1955).
38 S. Salmonowicz, "Saint-Just—rewolucjonista romantyczny (1767-1794)," *Kwartalnik Historyczny,* no. 2 (1968).
39 *Actes du colloque Robespierre* (Vienna-Paris, 1965).
40 M. Bouloiseau, *La République jacobine, le août 1792-9 thermidor an II* (Paris, 1972).
41 Robespierre, *Discours et Rapports à la Convention,* ed. M. Bouloiseau (Paris, 1965).
42 *Les constitutions de la France depuis 1789,* ed. J. Godechot (Paris, 1970); see *La pensée révolutionnaire en France et en Europe 1780-1799,* ed. J. Godechot (Paris, 1964).
43 J. Baszkiewicz, "Maksymilian Robespierre" (forthcoming). Because of its unique approach to the question, this monographic study may be placed next to the best available biographical work, J. Massin, *Robespierre* (Paris, 1956), as well as the extensive two-volume publication of G. Walter, *Robespierre: Histoire d'une solitude* (Paris, 1968) (an attempt at psychological analysis). Among popular works, one should not fail to mention M. Boukoisseau, *Robespierre* (Paris, 1956).
44 M. Król, "Świadomość historyczna jakobinów (1793-1794)," in the collective publication *Archiwum Historii Filozofii i Myśli Społecznej* 18 (1972): 137ff.
45 J. Baechler, *Les phenomenes revolutionnaires* (Paris, 1970).
46 R. R. Palmer, *The Age of the Democratic Revolution,* 2 vols. (Princeton, 1959-64). Palmer overcame the language barrier, making him the first to provide wide coverage of the Polish question in Western literature, including the most recent Polish publications. See also his "Great Inversion: America and Europe in the Eighteenth-Century Revolution," *Ideas in History* (1965).
47 J. Topolski, "Rewolucje w dziejach nowożytnych i najnowszych (XVII-XX w.)," *Kwartalnik Historyczny,* no. 2 (1976).
48 J. Ellul, *Histoire des institutions,* 6th ed., vol. 5 (Paris, 1969); G. Sautel, *Histoire des institutions publiques depuis la Révolution Française,* 3rd ed. (Paris, 1974).
49 R. Derathe, *J.-J. Rousseau et la science politique de son temps* (Paris, 1950); B. Baczko, *Rousseau—samotność i wspólnota* (Warsaw, 1964); J. Starobiński, *L'invention de la liberté* (Geneva, 1964); also, *L'oeil vivant* (Paris, 1971); collected studies, *Rousseau et la philosophie politique* (Paris, 1965).
50 J. Godechot, "Le Contrat social et la Révolution Occidentale de 1762 à 1789," *Études sur le Contrat Social de Jean-Jacques Rousseau* (Dijon, 1962).
51 I. G. Crecker, "Rousseau et la voie au totalitarisme," *Rousseau et la philosophie politique, Annales de philosophie politique* 5 (1965); J. L. Talmon, *The Origins of Totalitarian Democracy* (London, 1952) (mostly concerned with "Robespierrism").
52 K. Grzybowski, *Historia doktryn politycznych i prawnych* (Warsaw, 1967); A. Burda, "Metoda i ogólny charakter doktryny politycznej J.-J. Rousseau," *Annales Univ. M. Curie-Skłodowska* 1 (1954), also "Idea praworządności w doktrynie politycznej J.-J.

Rousseau," *Państwo i Prawo,* no. 2 (1963).

53 R. Polin, "Le sens de l'égalite et de l'inégalité chez J. J. Rousseau," *Études sur le Contrat Social* (Dijon, 1962), p. 158. Robespierre was by no means for the rule of "la plus vile populace," but for the rule of "les hommes vraiment dignes de la liberté" as "membres du souverain."

54 J. Godechot, "La définition classique," *Chrestomatie des droits de l'homme, Politique,* no. 10–13 (1960), pp. 137ff.

55 Quoted from Godechot, *Les constitutions de la France.*

56 Among the ample literature on the subject, note M. A. Cattaneo, *Il concetto di Rivoluzione nella Scienza del Diritto* (Milan, n.d.); *La Republica fondata sulla virtù come esempio di stato di diritto* (Milan, 1963); *Il partito politico nel pensiere del'illuminismo e della Rivoluzione francese* (Milan, 1964).

57 J. Starobiński, "1789 et le langage des principes," *Preuves,* no. 203 (1968).

58 Quoted after, *inter alia,* A. Camus, *L'Homme revolte* (Paris, 1951); Saint-Just, *Wybór pism,* ed. I. Bibrowska [in Polish] (Warsaw, 1954).

59 P. Robert, *Dictionnaire alphabétique et analytique de la langue française* (Paris, 1960).

60 A. and R. Mucchielli, *Lexique des sciences sociales* (Paris, 1969).

61 Quoted after his selected speeches, edited by M. Bouloiseau.

62 J. Pajestka, *Determinanty postępu. Czynniki i współzależności rozwoju społeczno-gospodarczego* (Warsaw, 1975), pp. 174ff.

63 Mestre and Guttinger, *Constitutionalisme jacobin,* pp. 64ff.

64 Bouloiseau, *Republique jacobine,* pp. 64ff.

65 Baczko, *Rousseau,* p. 686.

66 Bouloiseau, *Republique jacobine,* p. 220.

67 *Kuźnica Kołłątajowska,* ed. B. Leśnodorski (Wrocław, 1949), pp. 160ff.

68 W. Sjøstrand's invaluable monograph (including the relevant bills and legislative acts), recently published in English, is concerned with the general problem (W. Sjøstrand, *Freedom and Equality as Fundamental Educational Principles in Western Democracy from John Locke to Edmund Burke* [Stockholm, 1973]).

69 The revolutionary armies or militia were used to enforce these reforms. In particular they exacted food provisions from the countryside, but they were also employed for various acts of terror. In the spring of 1794 they were disbanded.

70 A. J. Arnaud, *Les origines doctrinales du Code Civil Français* (Paris, 1969); also *Essai d'analyse structurale du Code Civil Français: La règle du jeu dans la paix bourgeoise* (Paris, 1973).

71 R. Remond, *Introduction à l'histoire du notre temps,* vol. 1: *L'Ancien Régime et la Révolution* (Paris, 1974), p. 192.

72 The "revolutionary achievements" were surveyed in, among other recent publications, G. S. Wood, *The Creation of the American Republic, 1776–1787* (Williamsburg, 1969), chap. 6. See also quotations by S. Berstein, "Amerikanische Freunde der Französischen Revolution," *M. Robespierre* (Berlin, 1958); also his "Subject of Revolution in Post-revolutionary America," *Studien über die Revolution* (Berlin, 1969). The terms "Jacobins" and "Jacobinism" were understood there in quite a different way from countries on the European continent.

73 Their response is presented, *inter alia,* in C. Brinton, *A Decade of Revolution* (New York, 1961); J. Godechot, *Les Révolutions; La Grande Nation: L'expansion révolutionnaire de la France dans le monde,* 2 vols. (Paris, 1956); essential data also

in *Occupants—Occupés, 1792-1815* (Brussels, 1968), including J. Godechot, "Les variations de la politique française à l'égard des pays occupés."

74 The Polish Jacobins have been this author's concern for a considerable time now. B. Leśnodorski, *Les Jacobins Polonais* (Paris, 1965); also, "Le nouvel État polonais du XVIIIe siècle: Lumières et traditions," *Utopie et institutions au XVIIIe siècle: Le Pragmatisme de Lumières* (Paris-The Hague, 1963), pp. 147ff. See also the issue of *AHRF*, no. 177 (1964), concerned with the question of Poland.

75 J. Godechot, *Histoire de l'Italie moderne [1770-1870]* (Paris, 1971), chap. 2; *Giacobini Italiani*, ed. D. Cantimori and R. de Felice, 2 vols. (Bari, 1964); C. Ghisalberti, *Le costituzione giacobine (1796-1797)* (Milan, 1957); J. Godechot, "Originalité et imitation dans les institutions italiennes de l'époque napoléonienne," *Annuario dell' Instituto Storico Italiano* (Rome, 1975). For the earlier period, see F. Venturi, *Settecento riformatore*, 2 vols. (Turin, 1969-76).

76 D. Greer, *The Incidence of the Terror during the French Revolution. A Statistical Interpretation* (Cambridge, Mass., 1935).

77 J. Macleod-Machlejd, *Rewolucja francuska w świetle statystyki* (Warsaw, 1934).

78 J. Godechot, "Beccaria et la France," and M. A. Cattaneo, "Beccaria et Robespierre: Contributo allo studio dell'Illuminisme giuridico," in *Atti del Convegno Internazionale au Cesare Beccaria* (Turin, 1966).

79 A. Lityński, *Przestępstwa polityczne w polskim prawie karnym XVI-XVIII wieku*, chap. 5 (Katowice, 1976).

80 J. Bruhat, "La Révolution française et la formation de la pensée de Marx," *AHRF* (April-June, 1966).

81 K. Marx, Fr. Engels, *Briefwechsel*, vol. 4 (Berlin, 1950), p. 451.

82 R. Errera, *Les libertés à l'abandon* (Paris, 1968; 2nd ed., 1975); J. Rivere, *Les libertés publiques*, vol. 1 (Paris, 1973), notice that the title of Errera's publication echoes the title of the prophetic *La décadence de la liberté* (1930) of D. Halevy.

83 A. Camus, *L'Homme révolté* (Paris, 1951), pp. 158ff. Cf. M. Collinet, "Le Monde fermé de la Vertu," *Le Contrat social* (March, 1958) (in particular on the plight of Condorcet). This French example indicates of what extreme interest it is to know a legal and political model for a given time and place but also how often that model—and the constitution and the declaration of rights—differs from actual reality. Cf. M. Duverger, *Institutions politiques et droit constitutionel*, 2nd ed. (Paris, 1970), pp. 43ff.

THE FRENCH REVOLUTION AND THE "NEW" ELITE, 1800-50

Robert Forster, The Johns Hopkins University

Was there a governing elite in France before 1789? Social vocabulary presents an immediate problem as we grapple with "orders," *corps, états,* and a royal administration that tended to mix occupational rubrics with wider social categories. The Revolution of 1789 introduced a new social vocabulary, partly to institutionalize the abolition of legal privilege, but mainly to identify economic activities more precisely for tax purposes. The words *noble* and *bourgeois* receded from the administrative nomenclature to be gradually replaced by *propriétaire; laboureur* to be replaced by *ménager,* and *journalier* to be replaced by *cultivateur.* The word *paysan* had never been precise enough for the royal administration; the local revolutionary clubs considered it demeaning as well. A popular society chairman in a rural department chided one of his colleagues for employing the term. "Citoyen," he said, "n'y ayant plus de seigneur, il n'y a plus de paysans."[1] Even before we attempt to impose our own twentieth-century social vocabulary on this complex preindustrial society, we are faced with a melange of contemporary, overlapping categories mixing precise occupational function with new status, sometimes reverting to the looser labels of the Old Regime.

Much has already been said about the pitfalls of the word "bourgeoisie."[2] What about the term "noble"? *Noblesse* was, of course, a juridical category, a bundle of legally defined privileges ranging from tax exemption to a special code of inheritance law. It included honorific rights, especially the right to bear a title, to have a coat of arms, and to claim, at least, an ancestry, a myth comprising "illustrious acts" performed by ascendants. It is difficult to identify the moment in French history when the aura and the myths of nobility, especially those that related special virtues to ancestry, became subordinate—in the minds of nobles themselves—to the newer notion that nobility was an award for public service, the capstone of a long career in the royal courts or in municipal government. By the end of the eighteenth century, there were so many *anoblis,* from the *échevins* at Lyon to the *trésoriers de France* at La Rochelle,[3] and so many robe magistrates in the sovereign courts and in the royal councils at Paris that the nobility as an "order" no longer had any professional cohesion or common code of behavior. This is not to say that large sections of the French public did not identify the French nobility as a recognizable target of animosity, increasingly associated with a cluster of undesirable habits such as idleness, *morgue, luxe,* licentiousness, and, in a more rural setting, peremptory seigneurialism, cupidity, and speculation. The moralizing in French society at the end of the Old Regime was prodigious. Widespread antiaristocratic feelings can not be blamed entirely on grain prices, dues, rents, and other purely material considerations. But neither can the moral attributes ascribed to a social group be considered a sufficient criterion for its definition.

Recently, the notions of a "fusion" of the nobility and of an "aristocratic reaction" have come into serious doubt.[4] Many social historians are again emphasizing deep fissures in the nobility: robe vs. sword, Paris vs. provinces, rich vs. poor, "new" vs. "old," and so on. Should we not go a step further and abandon "nobility" altogether as a social category? There are magistrates, municipal officials, army officers, intendants, and ministers of state. These individuals may or may not have titles of nobility. I am suggesting that their precise professional and occupational activities are more important in determining their impact on society and their own values and outlook than the fact that they were officially members of the Second Estate in 1789. Let us not be misled by the temporary common defense of "privilege" by the parlements and local estates in 1787 and 1788. This was a momentary reflex, not the culmination of a century-long "aristocratic reaction." Moreover, each component of this so-called "noble class" defended only those "privileges" that concerned its own professional group or local interest. The robe magistrates of the Paris Parlement were willing to give way on direct taxes if they could extend their political power, while the vast majority of *hobereaux* in the remote provinces fought for tax exemption as essential to their local standing and even livelihood. In any society, when a whole gamut of privileges is threatened, there is likely to be a striking impression of solidarity on the part of those who have them; it is no proof of their social and ideological cohesion.

But if there was no "noble class," only "noble privileges," there was a national elite, an establishment, which managed the state apparatus, owned the major share of the nation's wealth in fixed and liquid capital, controlled the cultural institutions, and set the approved style of life. The cohesion within this elite was not complete and indeed was undergoing important changes in the scale of values and virtues. Perhaps the most important part of this undercurrent was the growing professionalization of the elite, its greater emphasis on public service and on recognition of individual merit—not to the exclusion of family, patronage, wealth, or even birth, but added to those older virtues.

Consider the repesentation of the French elite given in Table I:

Table I
THE FRENCH ELITE IN 1789

Archbishops Bishops Abbots	Magistrates of Parlements	Fermiers-Généraux Royal bankers	Ministers Councillors of State Intendants	Marshals Admirals	Grands Seigneurs Important Provincial Seigneurs
CHURCH	LAW	FINANCE	ADMINIS-TRATION	ARMED FORCES	LAND

A Weberian functional model fits the situation in 1789 much better than a horizontal Marxist one; it displays in terms of contemporary institutions and social vocabulary the hierarchies of wealth, power, and status. Note that all categories, with the exception of "land," are related directly or indirectly to the royal administration. Even the "landed interest" had a political "influence" through its sinecures and positions at Court. Of course, there is some overlap among these hierarchies, especially between the last two, where the same person might perform both functions. Land was the preferred form of wealth in 1789 as it would be throughout most of the nineteenth century. All these sub-elites owned land (and usually houses), public bonds, and constituted *rentes* besides. Almost all of them spent most of their lives in Paris and Versailles, which greatly influenced their habits of consumption and style of life. The variety of intellectual distraction and *salon sociabilité* in the capital was sufficient to make any generalization about social and political ideas tenuous, but these families were likely to be exposed to a literary culture that went beyond the Church Fathers and the *terrier*, even beyond military *mémoires* and Corneille.[5]

But more than landed wealth, a Parisian style of life, and a common literary culture, it was the relation to the royal government that gave the elite cohesion. The royal administration, one of the most elaborate of its day, was not only supported by a permanent peacetime system of land and head taxes, but it was continuously funded by the accumulated savings of an apparently unlimited number of office seekers and *rentiers* who found public bonds and annuities very attractive. There is no question that the greatest concentrations of liquid wealth in the Old Regime were those in the hands of the tax farmers, who used public funds for private loans and speculative ventures that even a port merchant could not equal.[6] Was there ever an administration that could attract so much capital, dispense so much status, and parcel out so much borrowed power?

Nor should the more material and mundane attractions of the government be exaggerated to the exclusion of a more worthy motive — public service. We are so conditioned to view the apex of French society and government from the perspective of Versailles that we often forget the Machaults, Turgots, Ormessons, Trudaines, and the hardworking intendants in the provinces. The *Almanac Royal* is not limited to cataloguing pompous marshals and chamberlains of the princes; the Councils of State had large complements of young and energetic intendants of finance and *maîtres des requêtes* who did not spend all their time at backgammon boards or watering spas. Tocqueville labeled this a *bourgeoisie de robe* because he ascribed other "qualities" such as "honor" to his idealized "aristocracy." But the upper echelon of the royal administration with its close affiliates (by family connection as well as by professional interdependence) in the church, the law courts, and the world of finance was the core and the model for the French elite in 1789. It was not a parvenu *anobli*, but the scion of an old titled family, who wrote, "I who in my youth [in the 1780s] had looked upon an intendancy as the finest post a man of heart and intelligence could desire."[7] State service, broadly defined to include intendants, marshals, parlementary magistrates, tax farmers, and even bishops, was the career goal of any ambitious son of *bonne famille* at the end of the Old Regime. The accumulation of titles, seigneuries, privileges, an urban style of life, and a broad literary culture were accessories to this primary role and function.

To be sure, the accessory habits and privileges did much to undermine the prestige and respect this elite needed to perpetuate itself. A flamboyant Cardinal Rohan or a pretentious Duc de Saulx-Tavanes could depreciate the quality of service earned by a dozen Turgots. A farmer-general who dragged down a swarm of small creditors of the state in a speculative failure created an image that could not be rectified by the technical services his colleagues rendered to the financial solvency of the government. Corporative and institutional loyalties within the elite also tended to weaken its hold on the bureaucratic apparatus. There was an increasing "dysfunction" between the technical, operational branches of the "machine" (administration, finance, armed forces) and the law courts, infused with revived constitutional claims, while the church, too, blocked reformist policies by asserting its traditional "rights." In short, the administration—and the elite that drew substance from it—needed renovation. It needed to reconstruct its *cadres*, open its ranks more widely to newcomers, revamp the institutional framework, purge its ranks of the idle and nonfunctional, those who gave the *tutelle administrative* a bad name. The Revolution and Napoleon would perform this necessary renovation. Much of the same personnel—or at least their families—would reemerge after 1800. The prerevolutionary elite survived and prospered, as *fonctionnaires*, as ministerial bureaucrats, as high-court judges, as prefects, as army officers, as bishops, and as landlords, although not as courtiers, nobles, *grands seigneurs*, or as *non-actifs*.[8]

Have I defined the old elite too narrowly—four or five thousand families, most of them residing in Paris, directly or indirectly related to the central government? Was there not also a much larger elite of landowners, not restricted to those few hundred *grands seigneurs* at Versailles? Call them nobles, call them *rentiers*, call them *propriétaires*, it matters not; where are the two hundred thousand seigneurs of the Old Regime?

A few years ago, I questioned Alfred Cobben's rather startling assertion that "landowners, large and small" won the French Revolution. I was especially perplexed by his reference to large landlords, by which I assumed he meant the nobility. I mustered all the antiseigneurial and antinoble legislation of the Revolution, stressed the abolition of seigneurial dues, the confiscation of émigré property, the costs of emigration, the debts incurred to repurchase lost land, the stricter laws of contract (more unfavorable to debtors), the very incomplete compensation provided by the indemnity law of 1825, and the new egalitarian inheritance law that even Villèle failed to change. I concluded that, whoever "won" the Revolution, surely the noble landlords "lost" it.[9]

Noble landlords did "lose" the Revolution in the restricted sense that economically the revolutionary decade was a burden for them. "They did suffer," as Cobban put it in his spirited rejoinder to my article.[10] But "lose" in the broader sense of being swamped by the middling and small proprietors or of being undermined as a "landed class" does not seem consistent with the latest evidence. Even my earlier argument that the Revolution precipitated a decline in deference and the erosion of an "aristocratic hold" on rural society may have been exaggerated. In any case, large landlords of the Old Regime, noble or not, were not destroyed—nor even permanently hurt—by the Revolution.

In 1802, the Napoleonic prefects began to assemble the so-called *listes électorales* which were in fact careful surveys of the local "notables," men of wealth, family, and influence, who presumably guided the *esprit public*, and who might serve as reliable candidates for the growing central administration. The adjoining map from Louis Bergeron's excellent survey of the First Empire charts the distribution of noble landowners among the twelve richest landlords in each department in 1802. It demonstrates conclusively that most of the wealthiest landlords in France were nobles of the Old Regime. Among them were old families like the Choiseuls and Luynes, royal administrators like

Lefevre d'Ormesson and Amelot de Chaillou, a *fermier-général* like Le Gendre de Lucay, and many parlementary families from Rennes, Dijon, Aix, and Pau.

THE TWELVE RICHEST LANDLORDS IN EACH DEPARTMENT IN 1802

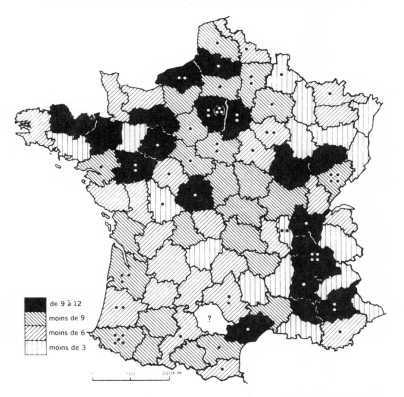

de 9 à 12
moins de 9
moins de 6
moins de 3

The darkest shadings indicate the larger proportions of noble landlords. The departments in black, for example, are those where from 9 to 12 of the most heavily taxed landlords were nobles, or 75 to 100 per cent of the twelve richest.
Reproduced from:
   L. Bergeron, *L'Épisode Napoléonien: Aspects Interieurs, 1799–1815* (Paris, 1972), p. 140, based on *Archives Nationales*, AF IV 1076.

It is perhaps not so surprising that the old nobility retained its position in rural areas such as Brittany, Normandy, North Burgundy, and the Rhône Valley. What is remarkable is their strong representation in the more commercialized and industrialized departments to the north and east of France and around the port cities. To be sure, one finds a few shipowners at Marseilles, ironmasters near the Belgian frontier, cattle merchants at Caen, and even a rich textile merchant at Amiens, but they are a minority among the richest landlords in their regions. Other sources such as the lists of the ''600 most heavily taxed'' and the ''most important notables of the department'' enlarge and substantiate these findings.[11]

Not only did the old landed families survive the decade of Revolution with their estates intact, but, thanks to tax equality, they were also now large contributors to the government coffers: they were no longer simply ornamental. Bonaparte considered them—at least potentially— reliable people, defenders of order, and ''opinion leaders'' in the countryside. Although some, like Villèle of Toulouse, refused to cooperate with the ''usurper,'' other old families recognized his merit, especially as a bulwark against ''confiscations'' and ''levelers,'' only too fresh in their memories in 1800. The loss of tax exemptions and the abolition of seigneurial dues were not negligible setbacks, but they were far from fatal. Cleansed of the stigma of ''seigneurialism,'' those noble landlords who accepted ''the new order of things'' were solicited by the Emperor as ''notables,'' from whom he would choose his administrators and advisers. For most aspiring provincial families, this was an improvement over the Court favoritism of the Old Regime, a clear recognition that land and local name would carry more weight than liquid wealth and intrigue at Paris. Among other effects, this policy anticipated the renaissance of the provincial squirearchy under the Restoration.[12]

Had anything changed in the occupational structure of France between 1789 and the establishment of the Napoleonic Empire? Consider the ''list of notables'' for 1810. In this project, the Napoleonic administration reached down deeper into each department in an expanded Empire of 110 departments to identify supporters and recruits for the civil service. Bonaparte instituted four to five electoral colleges in each department and had the prefects expand the number of notables to about one thousand per department, over one hundred thousand for the entire Empire. This was a very special kind of notability, one that included the *juge de paix* and local tax-assessor as well as the general and the magistrate. Neither tax requirement nor minimum landholding was prerequisite to being a member of an electoral college at the arrondissement level.

As a reflection of the social and economic structure of France in 1810, this ''electoral list'' must be treated with caution. But as a reflection of the kinds of people Bonaparte preferred and promoted, the list is revealing. The prefects were instructed to enter the occupation or public function of each notable, not only as of 1810, but ''before 1789'' and ''since 1789,'' along with age, marital status, landed revenues, and occasional special comments by the prefect. This permits us to see what proportion of this large group was upwardly mobile, benefiting from the revolutionary decade to change occupations and to improve its social position. Can we detect the "rise" of a new stratum in the society? If the French Revolution caused a *bouleversement* in the social structure, surely it would be reflected among the one hundred thousand beneficiaries of the regime, those handpicked by the imperial prefects.

Based on a sample of five departments, it appears that the new imperial regime relied on four occupational sectors in almost equal proportions—civil service (22.3 per cent), law (23 per cent), trade and industry (21.1 per cent), and agriculture (17.5 per cent). More interesting still is the inescapable conclusion that the occupations and careers of 2,425 local notables did not change very much from 1789 to 1810. Lawyers remained lawyers or became magistrates, farmers remained farmers, merchants remained merchants in overwhelming numbers. Only civil servants had a high rate of occupational change, and in many cases they simply moved into another branch of public administration—from the financial to the judicial sector, for example.[13]

It appears that the social and occupational structure of French society remained remarkably stable over the twenty "eventful years" between 1789 and 1810. We do not detect in this broader slice of "notables" any "classes" or occupational groups that differ from those of the Old Regime, nor many individuals who changed occupations because of the Revolution. It might be argued that the very fact that many of these people are mentioned at all on a list of "notables" indicates that the new regime had some awareness of a world of "little men," not the poor, of course, but the small proprietor, the notary, the village tax official, the *juge de paix,* the grain dealer, the wood merchant, the ironmaster, and even a small contingent of artisans and teachers. However, "awareness" does not mean social democracy. It may only reflect the growing efficiency of the Napoleonic administrative machine.[14]

With all his proclamations about "careers open to talent" and "a marshall's *baton* in every knapsack," Napoleon relied on men of independent wealth to serve and support the regime. Yet the various kinds of wealth were not all equally worthy in his view. "Who are the rich?" he once asked, "the purchasers of national property, the war contractors, the thieves. How can one build a notability on wealth acquired this way?"[15] Deeply suspicious of all forms of commercial wealth, especially high finance, Bonaparte turned to landed wealth for support: ". . . je n'emploierai plus que les gens qui auront 50,000 livres de *rente en terres.* Je ne suis pas assez riche pour payer tout le monde, et ceux qui sont le plus interessés au maintien de l'État le serviront gratuitement."[16] He would begin by appealing to those richest landlords in each department, whether they came from the nobility of the Old Regime or from a more recent vintage of landowner.

If the elite of 1800 was an elite of landed proprietors, it was also an elite of *fonctionnaires*. The French administrative state was not born in 1800, to be sure, but under Bonaparte it made a great leap forward, not only in sheer numbers, but also in the refinement of its organization, recruitment, and functions. It was this combination of expansion and professionalization, in addition to the promotion efforts of the new regime, replete with appeals to serve the "New France," that created a fresh *esprit de corps* and made the administration very attractive to recruits. A whole new set of officials was required to staff the new branches of the central government—financial and judicial as well as purely administrative. Moreover, the legal unification of France, consolidated by the Civil Code, meant that legal and administrative training could be standardized and that recruits drawn from anywhere in the Empire could be employed wherever a vacancy occurred. It was the dream of the old intendancies come true. Max Weber's bureaucratic apparatus was coming into its own.[17] There seems little doubt that at the turn of the century the French administration was the most "advanced," or at least the largest and most elaborate, of any state bureaucracy in the Western world.

From a central administration in the 1780s of a few thousand, the ministries and bureaux grew by 1810 to 25,000 in Paris alone. It would reach 250,000 by 1848.[18] What this meant in social terms is more easily grasped at the local level. In 1802, the new prefect of the department of Saône-et-Loire and his five subprefects had to find suitable candidates for the offices of mayor, assistant mayor, and *conseiller municipal* for each of 610 communes and 86 municipalities in a department with a population of 437,000, a large proportion of whom were only semi-literate. This was in addition to the prefect's task of finding another 1,400 candidates for six electoral colleges and the departmental *conseil général*. If the *cour d'appel* was in Dijon in the neighboring department, there were still the local tribunals to staff.[19] It may seem curious that Bonaparte, who had strictly forbidden the formation of political parties or any forums for political discussion outside Paris, encouraged such an elaborate apparatus of both functional administration and quasi-functional "colleges" of notables. One wonders if it was not partly motivated by a policy to keep every Frenchman of local importance occupied.

Difficult as it was at first to find sufficiently qualified recruits at the lower and intermediary levels of administration, there seemed to be an abundant supply of applicants at the upper level in Paris. In 1807, when the new *Cour des Comptes* created eighty-four new posts, in short order over two thousand candidates had presented themselves.[20] Of course, there was a world of difference between being elected a *chef de bureau* in a Parisian ministry and being chosen mayor of Villefranche-

Lauraguais or Mauriac. Salaries for *hauts fonctionnaires* were attractive, much improved over the Old Regime, and considerably more than
most annual earnings in the private sector. A prefect, for example, at
20,000 francs was earning six or seven times as much as the average
entrepreneur de bois or grain merchant, and forty times as much as the
average artisan. A scale of salaries was established and correlated with
a hierarchy of "grades"; it was intended to encourage performance
with suitable reward. (Tables II and III show the salary scales for the
Ministry of Interior and for a general sampling of government officials.)

Table II

SALARY SCALE IN THE MINISTRY OF INTERIOR

	1800	1809
Department Head	8,000	12,000 Fr.
Bureau Head: First Class	—	6,000
Second Class	5,400	5,400
Third Class	—	5,000
Assistant Bureau Head: First Class	—	4,500
Second Class	3,900	4,000
Third Class	—	3,500
Redacteurs: First Class	—	3,400
Second Class	—	3,000
Third Class	—	2,500
Commis: First Class	2,800	3,000
Second Class	2,200	2,600
Third Class	—	2,000

Table III

SALARY SCALE AMONG A SAMPLE OF OFFICIALS (1810)

Senator, Councillor of State	25,000 Fr. per annum
Prefect, Department of Allier	20,000
Archbishop, Member of *Tribunat*	15,000
Inspector, *Ponts et Chaussées*	12,000
Bishop	10,000
Councillor, Prefecture of Seine	9,000
Perpetual Secretary, *Institut*	6,000
Chief Engineer, *Ponts et Chaussées*	5,000
Sub-Prefect	4,000
Parish Priest*	1,500

*Recall that the new Concordat had added another 100,000 curés to the public payroll.
The parish priests were administrators in their way, as the First Consul well knew.

Sources for Tables II and III: Bergeron, *L'Épisode Napoléonien: Aspects Intérieurs,*
pp. 150-51.

To attractive salary one should add prestige. Social status in off ce-
holding did not end with the Old Regime; on the contrary, its importance is testified by an article in the "Declaration of the Rights of Man

and the Citizen." But under Bonaparte, office took on a quasi-military *élan*. Not only was there the saber, the *uniforme brodé*, and the sash, but also the opportunity to exercise borrowed power under the Imperial Eagle. Napoleon knew how to "caress self-love" with ribbons and "baubles" as well as with ample *traitements* and country estates. One should not underestimate the nationalist urge either, especially among the youth. Whether of "old" or "new" family, who could be completely unmoved by this circular letter to the new prefects from the Minister of Interior in 1800?

> The First Consul has given you, Citizens, the most honorable mark of his confidence in making you Prefect. This post imposes heavy duties, but it offers also great compensation in the days ahead. You are called upon to support the government in the noble purpose of restituting France to her former splendor, to resuscitate all that has been great and generous in her past, and to establish the magnificent edifice on the unassailable foundation of liberty and equality. You will appreciate, without any doubt, the nature of the mission confided to you.[21]

The flamboyance of the phraseology—at least to our ears—should not blind us to the emotional force of the appeal. Of course, the years would tarnish the glitter of such an exhortation, but they would never efface it completely. To this day, the prefects retain a certain sense of national mission.

Historians have exaggerated the extent of the "retreat of the old nobility" either to the quiet seclusion of their estates or to the social exclusivity of the Faubourg Saint-Germain. Eventually some young scholar will make an age analysis of the nobility in "voluntary exile" during the Empire, which will in all likelihood substantiate Louis Bergeron's view that they were overwhelmingly made up of the old and the retired. The liberal cartoonists of the Restoration have succeeded too well in identifying every noble family with the Duchess of Châtillon, hidden among her bird cages and clocks on the rue du Bac.[22]

The younger generation of Old Regime nobility, those born between 1770 and 1790, looked at the world with different eyes. For them, the Old Regime was at best a childhood memory; as young adults they knew only the Revolution and the Empire, especially the latter. Surely they felt their fathers' "principles" and "prejudices" less strongly. Chateaubriand observed about the youth in his circle, "To talk to them about the Bourbons is like reciting a list of the children of the Emperor of China." The Count de Moulivant reacted to talk of a Bourbon restoration "as if one were speaking about the resurrection of Louis XIV."[23] It is unnecessary to postulate some sort of generation conflict to surmise that ambition, boredom, and financial need would outweigh father's political principles in 1800, even if the family had emigrated abroad in the 1790s. Most of the old avenues for career advancement—

the selection of an *état* was customary even for the sons of the *rentier* type of *noblesse* or *anoblis*—were now closed. Venality of office had been abolished, ending at one stroke over a thousand posts of *secrétaire du roi* and *trésorier de France*, not counting the municipal offices. The sovereign courts from parlements to *cours des comptes* were also shut down. Even the Church offered fewer places and fewer attractions for the sons (and daughters) of *bonnes familles*, with the regular clergy only just emerging from a clandestine existence and bishoprics less remunerative and more demanding. Inevitably, a young man looked toward the new, expanding central administration.

Molé may have been exceptional in the rapidity of his advancement in the new regime—prefect at 26, minister at 32—but not in his decision to "rally" to the Empire. Edward Whitcomb's excellent quantitative study of the 281 prefects between 1800 and 1814 demonstrates that 110, or 40 per cent, of the entire corps were nobles of the Old Regime. Among these Napoleonic prefects one finds such family names as La Rochefoucauld, Chauvelin, Barante, La Tour du Pin, and, somewhat tardily, Rambuteau and Saint-Aulaire.[24] Although some contemporaries thought that the prefectoral corps was being taken over by "old families" and generals after 1810, the statistics indicate a fairly even 2:3 ratio of nobles to non-nobles over the entire period. More to the point, it appears that there were no "class tensions" within the corps: prefects and subprefects of different departments worked in harmony, recommending their colleagues without any special reference to rank in the Old Regime.[25]

Nor should this surprise us. The French bureaucracy—the prefectoral corps in particular—was molding its own "occupational type" with its own set of loyalties, values, and outlook. We need more biographies of prefects and other administrators to identify these professional or even personality traits precisely, but it is doubtful that differences of social origin, especially noble opposing non-noble, if present at all, played a determining role in the thinking or action of members of this corps. It may even be permissible to call the central administration a class, if we do not insist too strongly on economic criteria.[26] In any case, the prefectoral corps was an excellent example of the "Napoleonic amalgam" at work.

We know less about the occupational and status origins of other branches of the central administration—the ministries, for example. We need to know not merely the precise number of Old Regime nobles in the various *bureaux*, but how the "old" and "new" men functioned together as high officials and outside office hours. One thinks of men like Lebrun and Cambacérès, Fouché and Talleyrand, Chaptel and Ormesson, men of quite diverse social origins working together, if not always for the Emperor, at least for the administrative state. For those who still wish to make Talleyrand a "man of principle," this is the most promising route.[27] Of course, professional and especially social cohesion and harmony were not immediate, nor necessarily ever complete. When Étienne-Denis Pasquier, scion of an old robe family, was made Napoleon's prefect of police, he encountered Maury, a man of less distinguished origins, recently named Archbishop of Paris, at Fountainbleau one day. His Eminence was congenial and remarked, "The Emperor has just satisfied the two greatest needs of his capital. With a *bonne police* and a *bon clergé*, he can be sure of public tranquillity, because an archbishop is also a prefect of police." Pasquier was shocked by this remark which he said was in very "poor taste," especially coming from a high dignitary of the Church. But Maury had always been a man "devoid of tact," with "common habits," *de la dernière classe du peuple*.[28] But perhaps Pasquier was most disturbed by the basic truth of the remark—a parvenu cardinal and an illustrious magistrate of the old Parlement of Paris were both prefects now. They would get on.

That the new regime promoted and rewarded its civil servants needs no reiteration. Suffice it to say that 22 percent of the Napoleonic nobility of 1808 were *hauts fonctionnaires*, and 17 per cent more were notables, many of whom were local administrators.[29] Among the "Notables of 1810," a much larger group, 22 per cent were civil servants at all levels of the administration.[30] Just as Josephine and Talleyrand had acted as a discreet reception committee for returning *émigrés* in 1800, so Baron Pasquier, with his impeccable social credentials, was the ideal person to persuade (and warn) those old noble families who thought abstention from public service the way to "real importance." "The government appeals to the men of action, to those who by word or deed have the power and the means to render true (public) service, to those who have kept abreast of the times *[suivi le courant]* and not waited twenty years *en arrière*."[31] Join now gentlemen, tomorrow may be too late.

State service was more than a new career, more even than a source of social status and borrowed power, important as these were. It was becoming a profession with its own rules of recruitment and exclusion and, above all, with its own values—values which it was in a position to inculcate, sometimes only half-consciously, in the population at large. As Maurice Agulhon has remarked about the postrevolutionary administrative social vocabulary—that is, *propriétaire* replacing *bourgeois* or *noble* in ordinary official discourse—"Administrative practices are never without influence on the *administrés*."[32] At the same time, the administration reflected many of the mores of society at large, but none so much, I would argue, as those of the landlord and the lawyer. The Napoleonic amalgam was much more than an expanded civil service, but *le fonctionnaire*, especially the *haut fonctionnaire*, was the pivot of the regime, the elite within the elite, that would set the tone and standards of behavior for the long reign of the *notables*.

The *affiches* that covered the walls of public buildings might indeed invite all to apply to the civil service, but everyone knew that only a small minority of Frenchmen had the preparation or *formation* to be acceptable candidates. Apprenticeship for the attractive posts, as under the Old Regime, was long and costly, involving a good secondary education, a law degree, and a prolonged stay in a city, usually Paris, before being assigned to practical field work, such as the *auditoriat* for prefects.[33] In 1800, the *grandes écoles* that were to become the almost exclusive training ground for the top grades of the civil service had not yet been formed, but Napoleon's university was the beginning. The more one studies the history of education, the more it appears that fellowships were in fact easier to obtain in the Old Regime than in the new.[34] There was no *concours* or entrance examination; letters of recommendation, family connections, and personal contact with *bureau* heads still counted a great deal. There were family "dynasties" even in the department responsible for *Ponts et Chaussées*, where technical expertise would seem decisive. Patronage and nepotism still jostled with individual ability.

At the same time, in certain branches of government the *dossiers* of the candidates were very complete. The ministers—and Bonaparte himself—knew how to track down personal qualities as well as to review the formal facts of an official's performance.[35] And as the prefects improved their skills, the dossiers on the one hundred thousand notables of the Empire became very complete, noting the activities of the local personage before and since the Revolution. The *exaltés* of the early 1790s were seldom appointed to important posts, although this was as much the result of the decisions of local prefects as it was a policy of Bonaparte himself. Even after one had obtained a post, he was under the surveillance of his superior. More than one prefect was open to criticism of the minister, not only for his tardy or incomplete reports, but for the tone of his letters and even the inelegance of his style.[36] In short, to obtain an attractive post in the imperial administration required almost the same set of requisites as in the Old Regime— family, patronage, connection, wealth, education—*and* talent besides. It was a demanding forcing ground. No wonder the graduates were often officious with the *administrés*. And, like later graduates of the *grandes écoles*, they developed a strong sense of esprit de corps even before they began perusing reports and dispatches.

The peculiar qualities or traits of the bureaucrat, so well described by a Max Weber or a Michel Crozier (and satirized by a Honoré Balzac or a Herbert Lüthy), did not fail to leave their mark even on proverbial

French individualism. Conditions in 1800 were the result of a special legacy, of course, and one that was dissipated only slowly. The decade of the Revolution and the fears and anxieties it still evoked among so many were reflected again and again in ministerial circulars proclaiming that "the Revolution is now over," or as Lucien Bonaparte put it to the prefects, "A profound dividing line separates forever that which is from that which has been, . . . factions . . . have their place only in that deplorable chapter of human folly."[37] Administrative routine produces its own aversion to "disorder," but the memories and myths of '93 made the imperial regime especially wary of the fomentors of *tumulte*, those "ultra-democrats" or *réfractaires*, Jacobin or Royalist.

The fall of the Empire and the inception of the *régime censitaire* produced a somewhat different type of administrator and of local notable as well. The notables, or at least their wealthiest contingent, now became electors and deputies in a new parliament, which greatly increased their influence nationally and locally. At the same time, the ministries and prefects had to change their style of administration. Without openly abandoning political neutrality, they had to deal with an emerging political life, including political parties and public debate, however limited these may seem in retrospect. The imperial *préfet à poing* who leaned too exclusively on the "just but inflexible severity of the law" had to learn something about political tact and manipulation. The Napoleonic amalgam was undergoing an adjustment in the relative power of its components. The notables—the large battalions of landlords from the provinces—would no longer serve simply as national ornaments or recruits for the administration; they would share political power with prefect and ministry. Rémusat, noble deputy from Toulouse, observed how the prefects had bent with the times: ". . . sous le coup de vicissitudes rapides qui changeaient les positions du jour au lendemain, il fallut bien apprendre l'art de dissiper les préventions, de calmer les ressentiments, de ménager les opinions, de caresser les amours-propres."[38] In a larger sense, Georges Lefebvre saw "the regrouping of the notables under the protection of the emperor," and once "rid of the popular menace, [the notables] prepared to govern and restore liberalism."[39]

Until recently, historians of the Restoration and July Monarchy have been preoccupied with the political battle between Legitimists and Orleanists or between clericals and anticlericals and with the fate of the nobility. These issues, although not irrelevant, have tended to obscure the process of consolidation of the new elite of notables. Basic to that consolidation was the continued respect paid to the land by men of all political persuasions. As the journalist Fiévée said in 1816, "La propriété territoriale a toujours été et sera toujours aristocratique, bien que les propriétaires ne soient point nobles de naissance."[40] In fact, land was even more important after 1815 when it became the principal basis for tax assessment and hence for the right to vote. To be a *propriétaire* was now a mark of prestige, local influence, *and* political power, the label preferred by two-thirds of the notables of the July Monarchy. Of course, all the notables were landlords by definition, even those who came under the occupational rubric of *négociant, industriel,* or *avocat.*

Although a distinction should be made between the 200,000 electors (200 francs or more in taxes) and the 20,000 *grands notables* (1,000 francs or more in taxes) of the July Monarchy, the occupational composition of the two groups was remarkably uniform.

Table IV

OCCUPATIONAL LABELS OF THE NOTABLES

	All Electors (166,583) All Departments (1831)	Electors paying 1,000 Fr. or more (13,311) in 64 Departments (1840)
Propriétaires	59.1%	65.3%
Fonctionnaires	16.8	11.7
Professions libérales	4.8	5.9
Négociants and *Industriels*	18.9	15.9 (Industriels: 5.0%)
	99.6%	98.8%

Source: S. Kent, *Electoral Procedure under Louis-Philippe* (New Haven, 1937), pp. 10n, 26; A.-J. Tudesq, *Les Grands Notables en France, 1840-1849* (Paris, 1964), vol. 1, pp. 96-97.

The election lists of the Restoration and the July Monarchy are so complete that one is tempted to use them as an exact reflection of the occupational structure of France as a whole. This would be a mistake; they are an exact reflection of the notables only. Nevertheless, the available local studies indicate that the richer a *négociant, industriel,* or *avocat,* the larger the *percentage* of his fortune in rural property.[41] The pull of the land was enormous—for obvious economic, social, and political reasons—for anyone with a surplus beyond his immediate consumption needs. To be sure, in the absence of an advanced banking system, the textile-mill owner or ironmaster often invested in land to increase his collateral, his "credit-worthiness" for commercial borrowing, but the result was the same; he became a *propriétaire* as well as an *industriel,* and when he retired from trade, he usually dropped the less prestigious label.[42] That is surely one reason why there seems to be an increasing number of *propriétaires* on the election lists as the years passed. At first glance, one would think that France was deindustrializing. This is patently untrue, but the prestige of the land, and especially of the *propriétaire non-exploitant* or *propriétaire-rentier*, remained intact, even increased, from 1815 to 1850. It probably did not begin to wane until the 1870s when the price of land began to fall, and state bonds and railroad stock, although still not heavy industry, became more attractive.[43]

Aside from their new political role, were the notables—the *grands notables*—essentially *rentiers*—or *non-actifs*, to use another administrative category? Most notables preferred to think of themselves as *les capacités*, those for whom wealth was, if not the reward for their services to state and community, at least its *sine qua non*. Leisure, they argued, was essential for public service, and only the land provided it, in addition to other virtues of a psychological order. Merchants and manufacturers were disqualified because they were simply too busy with everyday affairs at the mill, apart from their tendency toward small-mindedness or downright cupidity. The notables, it seems, chose the narrow middle way between the dangers of idleness, on one side, and those of crass materialist ambition, on the other. The parliamentary Liberals were not alone in using the word "aristocracy" in a pejorative manner, that is, not as social category but as a cluster of undesirable character traits. "Aristocracy," said a deputy in the Parliament in 1821, "is a coalition of those who consume without producing, who live without working, who know everything without having learned anything, who assume all the honors without having the requisite merit, who occupy all the public offices without being capable *[en état]* of filling them."[44] Sièyes had used essentially the same words in 1789. The Duc de Broglie, in the debates on Villèle's new inheritance law in 1823, employed similar pejoratives in opposing a law which would reintroduce the inequalities of the Old Regime.[45] No, surely the notables were not like this. They saw themselves as an elite, but a functional, active, and meritorious one.

What was their economic role? Although the evidence is incomplete, it appears that the large landlords, Orleanists as well as Legitimists, began to make significant capital improvements on their estates after 1830. No doubt some credit can be given to the intensive labor of the small proprietor, but such indicators of agricultural change as we do have suggest that only the large landlord was in a position to implement agricultural innovations. The first marked decline in fallow land, the expansion of artificial meadows, increased grain yields, improvement in livestock, better drainage and irrigation, and the long-awaited, large-scale planting of the potato—all these developments began after 1830 and suggest that the larger domains (over one hundred *hectares*) were the leaders in agricultural improvement.[46] True, the difference in rates of growth between north and south remained, and local studies may confirm a marked social and psychological difference between the notables of Toulouse, for example, and those of the Loire Valley or the Paris basin. It may well be that appropriate forms of tenure (*fermage* in the north contrasted to *métayage* in the *Midi*) and a new type of *fermier* also played their role. Detailed studies of individual estates might tell us what portion of the credit for innovation and growth should be ascribed to the *propriétaire*. But he must have been more permissive than his noble counterpart under the Old Regime.[47]

The development in mining and metallurgy was closely associated with the land, especially forest land, still held in large tracts by the old nobility.[48] Here, too, one should like to know how much of the entrepreneurial talent can be ascribed to the *propriétaire* and how much to the ironmaster (*maître de forge*), who was often the *fermier* as well. Much depends on the lease contract, the provision of capital, the adjustment of rent, the cost of fuel, and so on.[49] Tudesq claims that, among all *chefs d'enterprise*, only the ironmasters had enough economic power (and land) to figure prominently among the notables.[50]

This did not mean that many *propriétaries* did not have investments in commercial companies. By 1848, 83 of 311 peers in the upper house were either board members (*conseillers d'administration*) or held shares in insurance companies, mines, and railroads, usually acting as silent partners.[51] One would like to know what portion of their income came from these investments, and, more important, how they affected their mentality or behavior. It is worth noting that 230 of the same 311 peers were either career officers (110) or *hauts fonctionnaires* (120), prompting the *Revue des Deux Mondes* to quip that "the peerage is a hierarchy of retired civil servants."[52] Balzac and Daumier would not hesitate to point a finger at the close relation between business investments and political power. But it is not clear, even for this section of the notables, which was more fundamental in terms of power and values—commerce, land, or administration.[53] Tudesq speaks of an "incessant osmosis between the world of commerce and that of *grande propriété*," but for him there is no doubt which world is preponderant: "*Le notable, dans la France de 1840, c'est d'abord le propriétaire.*"[54] In the area of values and social influence, this conclusion seems fully justified.

Identifying and weighing the elements of social control is not easy; quantification lends itself more readily to measuring categories of occupation, public function, and even social group than to calibrating such elusive things as influence and consideration. The intensity and durability of clientage habits no doubt varies from region to region, even from canton to canton. In the 1820s, villagers near Carcassonne petitioned their prefect, protesting that their mayor treated them as if he were their *ci-devant seigneur* armed with "feudal power," and they would not have it.[55] Not a hundred miles away, in the foothills of the

Pyrenees to the southwest, the Comte de Comminges commented on his father's relation to the local villagers in the same decade:

> Les paysans lui étaient très attachés, quoiqu'il les traitât comme des nègres. Malheur à qui ne lui parlait pas chapeau-bas, un revers de canne avait bientôt fait voler le couvre-chef recalcitrant. A cette époque, ces façons étaient supportées tout naturellement.[56]

The count's statement also says something about the decline of deference since his father's time.

In general, the gentry of the *Midi* from Toulouse to Aix-en-Provence held their *métayers* and *valets* in line; the phrase *mon maître* among the dependent sharecroppers and farm laborers lasted well into the second half of the century. Ironically, the very completeness of social control by the landlords in these unchallenged agricultural regions may have reinforced an ideology, which David Higgs does not hesitate to call a neurosis, that ultimately prevented the landlords from adapting to "new forms of economic activity."[57] But the history of deferential attitudes has still to be written. Perhaps the analysis of law cases, already begun for the eighteenth century, will prove the best way to begin.[58] There is no doubt, however, that Legitimist or Orleanist, landlord or *fabricant* saw no contradiction between the "competition of ideas" in a Paris academy and the essential need to "moralize" *la classe ignorante et pauvre* at the mill or on the *métairie*. For the latter task, *patronage*, patriarchy more than paternalism, was required. In 1836, the Academy of Metz organized a *concours* on the best means of exerting the beneficial influence of the *classe riche et eclairée* on the *classe ignorante et pauvre*. Among his other contributions, the winning contestant itemized the instruments of *puissance materielle, administrative, religieuse,* and *morale,* regretting that the last of these was still "unorganized."[59]

Because the July Monarchy owed so much to the anticlericalism of the 1820s, it has often been assumed that the regime was Voltairean, or at least that it dissociated itself from the Church. Although the government was careful not to present the blatant clerical image of its predecessor, the notables from parliamentary committee to provincial château were fully aware of the moralizing services of the clergy. Sunday mass in the village church was the main point of contact—and solidarity—between *châtelain* and isolated peasant.[60] Albert Soboul has pointed out how many of the nineteenth-century catechisms included the *seigneurs laiques* among those to whom the faithful owed obedience.[61] Local notable and parish priest knew how to get on.

The city was a more complex problem, but here the elector had potential favors to bestow—a new canal or railroad, a new primary school, a *maison de bienfaisance*—those local public agencies that most articulate constituents preferred to radical innovation. Given the extremely limited suffrage (about one adult male in thirty could vote in 1840), there was little fear of retaliation at the polls. Many of the departmental elections—in places such as Auriac or Vannes—must have resembled exclusive club meetings. In the more commercialized areas of the north and east, Lille or Mulhouse, for example, there were notables who were *maîtres de forges* and *fabricants* and who, while often differing with their more rural colleagues on national policies regarding trade, education, or religion, exerted the same kind of local influence, a mixture of paternalism and stern patriarchy. One thinks of Georges Dufaud, ironmaster from Nevers, who spent much of his time as *adjoint* to the prefect or as the "man behind the elector."[62] In any event, the notables held all the commanding heights of society, from the new primary school to the university and *Académie française*, from local tax assessment to *conseil des prudhommes*, and from Catholic catechism to *caisse de secours*.

Furthermore, the notables evolved their own social philosophy. Whatever Balzac might write or Daumier sketch, it was coherent and self-assuring. For, as Guizot never ceased to reiterate, his was the enlightened epoch of measured, rational progress where, under the *tutelle* of landlord and prefect, teacher and priest, lawyer and mill-owner, the vices of sloth *(paresse)* and licentiousness *(débauche)* would be overcome—or at least held in check—by the virtues of work and self-discipline.[63]

Nowhere do these virtues seem more explicit than in the attitudes of the notables toward the poor.[64] The best kind of charity or *bienfaisance* for the wage-earner was not indiscriminate alms-giving, private or public, but that kind of policy which inculcated a taste for economy and private property. Grivel, a mill-owner, was cited in Parliament, not only for providing housing for his workers, but especially for paying his workers each month instead of each week, so that they would save their wages and not squander them in the *cabarets*.[65] "L'épargne est avec la religion le plus grand moralisateur du peuple," to quote the Academy of Metz.[66] The notables of Catholic France needed no Protestant ethic to convince them that there was a self-evident affinity between wealth and enlightenment, as there was between ignorance and poverty. Was it not abundantly evident—empirically verifiable—from the inmates of the Paris asylums to the sick of the provincial *hospices*, from the marginal silk-workers of Lyon to the seasonally unemployed *colons* of Brittany or *journaliers* from Auvergne? All of the poor were not *vicieux*, to be sure, but even the *pauvres-malheureux* or *pauvres-honteux* were ignorant and, above all, improvident *(imprévoyant)*, a word regularly employed in discussions of the problem of pauperism.

By education and hard work, by sobriety and self-discipline, the *capacités* would, in the long run at least, rise to the top. They would be recognized by their functions and their wealth. Thus, the elites would be constantly renewed and the osmosis among their component parts facilitated. Shared virtues and a common outlook on society, more than shared occupation or a common economic base, formed the real cement of the society of notables in the first half of the nineteenth century.

This is not the place to explore in depth the whole complex of attitudes and values that characterized the notables of this half-century. They extend from formal tracks and maxims to a whole range of everyday habits: treatment of women and children, styles of clothing, food preparation, furnishings, forms of *politesse*, uses of leisure, and much else. But they deserve more than the simple label *bourgeois*, whatever that poor overworked word now means.

In two superb works, André-Jean Tudesq and Theodore Zeldin have begun to dissect this special mentality. Zeldin demonstrates from career guidebooks of the 1840s that rapid social and get-rich-quick schemes were neither expected of nor recommended to the educated children of well-to-do families. No one, from top to bottom of society, was encouraged to leave the occupation or profession of his father without careful reflection on the risks and dangers of such a decision. "An ambitious man is a sick man," reads one of these guidebooks. Wholesale commerce and industry, even in the 1840s, were too risky and too readily associated with reprehensible speculation. One must not confuse a few examples from the banking world—a Laffitte or a Perier—with the large batallions of *grands notables*. For them, *agiotage, trafic, profit* were the marks of cupidity and narrowness of mind; the new enterprises of the city, of Paris in particular, were suspect. Even engineering was considered in the guidebooks as a dubious career choice, unless it lead to the *Ponts et Chaussées*. The civil service and the liberal professions were much better choices, providing "public esteem" and a "regular life" with limited risk to one's future security and psychological equilibrium.[67]

There are some ambiguities in this tissue of values. One can escape poverty by hard work and self-discipline, but there should not be too much social and professional mobility. The importance attached to "moralizing the *peuple*" and the explicit awareness of the institutions of order and social control point not to a dynamic society, driven by "new forces of production" and a credo of enterprise, but to an elite that is very skeptical about rapid change of any kind, and whose credo might be described as 'the conservation of energy'—Max Weber's "secular ascetism" without Werner Sombart's "adventure capitalist." It is an ideology admirably suited to a society of landlords and *fonctionnaires*.

Even on the everyday level of operation, the procedures and habits of the large landlord and the civil servant have much in common. One cannot peruse the reports of a prefecture or the *états* of a private estate without being struck by the similarity of goals and techniques. Landlords—at least French landlords—did not seem to encourage entrepreneurial initiative among their tenants any more than ministers encouraged prefects to depart from directives from Paris. A man should be assiduous, *capable*, and full of *zèle* (a favorite quality in prefectorial correspondence), but this does not mean he should be creative, imaginative, or exert initiative on his own. The taxes and rents must be regularly assessed and transmitted, properly recorded and shelved for reference; the *régie* is orderly and regular, the *comptabilité* strict; it would seem to be a technique designed to supervise the official or *régisseur* rather than to facilitate cost analysis and explore reinvestment opportunities. At least this is how Michel Crozier characterizes the French bureaucracy today—a system of *contrôle* and *méfiance*, no matter what the civil-service manuals might say about *capacité créatrice*.[68]

A modern philosophical commentary on the French administration insists that *ménager* is a key word, reflecting the pervasive emphasis on prudence at all levels of the civil service. The bureaucrat makes an effort to *ménager les esprits, ménager l'argent, ménager les circonstances, ménager une ligne de retraite*, and so on.[69] One is rightly skeptical about single indicators, but a study of administrative vocabulary can be revealing. In this case, *ménager* nicely complements a better-known phrase of the July Monarchy—the *juste milieu*.

The elite that governed France after the Revolution and owed so much to the conscious policies of Napoleon was essentially a notability of landlords and *hauts fonctionnaires*, with smaller contingents of lawyers, merchants, and manufacturers—smaller in both number and influence. This elite was drawn from the old noble families as well as from newcomers, a successful amalgam of wealth, education, family connections, local influence, and political power. Without legal privileges and placing less weight on birth, it saw itself as a service elite, the rule of the *capacités*. Drawn from many of the same families who had administered France in the Old Regime, the new notables evolved a common set of social values and attitudes that were appropriate to their own time and place. They governed France, with a few brief interruptions, from 1800 to 1880 and even beyond.

NOTES

1 M. Agulhon, *La vie sociale en Provence intérieure au lendemain de la Révolution* (Paris, 1970), p. 248n.

2 A. Cobban, *A Social Interpretation of the French Revolution* (Cambridge, 1964).

Cobban's essay was the starting point for a brisk debate on the term *bourgeoisie* in France, England, and the United States.

3 For an effort to measure the impact of ennobling office in the Old Regime and its effect on social mobility, see D. Bien, "La réaction aristocratique avant 1789: Aristocratie et anoblissement au XVIIIᵉ siècle," *Annales: Economies, Sociétés, Civilisations* (cited hereafter as *Annales, E.S.C.*) 29 (1974): 23–43, 505–32. Bien concludes that there was no closing of offices to aspring non-nobles. The example of the *parlements*, often cited, was exceptional.

4 The question of whether there was an "aristocratic reaction" in eighteenth-century France has been raised by François Furet (1971), David Bien (1974), and Guy Chaussinand-Nogaret (1975) in the *Annales, E.S.C.*, and by William Doyle and Colin Lucas in recent issues of *Past and Present* (cited hereafter as *PP*). See also B. Stone, "Robe Against Sword: The Parlement of Paris and the French Aristocracy, 1774–1789," *French Historical Studies* 9 (Fall 1975): 278–303.

5 The pioneer work of Daniel Mornet on private libraries has now been enlarged to include a whole range of influences on a "group mentality." Associated with Ariès, Mandrou, Castan, and others, there is a growing corpus of *histoires des mentalités* in France. See also Bollême, Furet, Roche, et al., eds., *Livre et société en France au XVIIIᵉ siècle* (Paris, 1966) and the comments of Robert Darnton on the "social history of ideas" in *Daedalus* 100 (Winter 1971): 214–56.

6 The best recent works on the *financiers* are those by J. F. Bosher, Guy Chaussinand-Nogaret, and Yves Durand. See the excellent bibliography in Y. Durand, *Les Fermiers généraux au XVIIIᵉ siècle* (Paris, 1971), pp. 14–38. Bosher emphasizes the bureaucratic inefficiency of the tax-farming system; Chaussinand stresses the entrepreneurial function of the tax farmers.

7 Baron de Frénilly, *Souvenirs, 1768–1828* (Paris, 1908), p. 227.

8 M. Reinhard, "Elite et noblesse dans la seconde moitiê du XVIIIᵉ siècle," *Revue d'histoire moderne et contemporaine* (cited hereafter as *RHMC*) 3 (1956): 5–37. Reinhard was one of the first historians to stress the continuity of the French elite from the eighteenth to the nineteenth centuries.

9 R. Forster, "The Survival of the Nobility during the French Revolution," *PP*, no. 37 (July 1967): 71–86.

10 A. Cobban, "Debate," *PP*, no. 39 (April 1968): 170.

11 L. Bergeron, *L'Épisode Napoléonien: Aspects Intérieurs, 1799–1815* (Paris, 1972), pp. 137–66 and passim. See the special issue "La France à l'époque Napoléonienne," *RHMC* 17 (1970): 333–920, especially the articles in Section III *(Société)*; P. Bouyoux, "Les Six-Cents plus imposés du département de la Haute-Garonne en l'an X," *Annales du Midi* 70 (1958). For the Restoration, see Mme. Soutardé-Rouger, "Les notables en France sous la restauration, 1815–1830," *Revue d'histoire économique et sociale* 38: 98–110. For the July Monarchy, see A.-J. Tudesq, *Les Grands Notables en France, 1840–1849* (Paris, 1964), vol. 1, pp. 429–31 and passim. The "electoral lists" and the prefectoral reports on the *esprit public* are found in the *Archives Nationales*, F¹ C-III, arranged by departments.

12 For the Restoration, see N. Richardson, *The French Prefectoral Corps, 1814–1830* (Cambridge, 1966); D. Higgs, *Ultraroyalism in Toulouse from Its Origins to the Revolution of 1830* (Baltimore, 1972).

13 L. Bergeron, G. Chaussinand-Nogaret, R. Forster, "Les Notables du 'Grand Empire' en 1810," *Annales, E.S.C.* 26 (1971): 1052–75.

14 The larger study of all departments in 1810 is nearing completion by the École des Hautes Etudes en Sciences Sociales under the direction of Guy Chaussinand-Nogaret and Louis Bergeron.

15 J. Tulard, "Problèmes sociaux de la France napoléonienne," *RHMC* 17 (1970): 649.

16 Napoleon to Beignot, quoted in Bergeron, *L'Épisode,* p. 166 (italics mine).

17 R. Bendix, *Max Weber: An Intellectual Portrait* (Berkeley, 1978).

18 For the Old Regime, the figures are sketchy. See J. S. de Sacy, *Henri Bertin* (Paris, 1970), pp. 45–57, for an idea of the scope of operations and the small size of individual ministries. For the First Empire, see Bergeron, *L'Épisode,* p. 148; for 1848, Th. Zeldin, *France, 1848–1945: Ambition, Love and Politics* (Oxford, 1973), vol. 1, p. 114.

19 M. Rebouillat, "L'Établissement de l'administration préfectorale dans le départment de Saône-et-Loire," *RHMC* 17 (1970): 876–79.

20 Tulard, "Problèmes sociaux," p. 653.

21 Rebouillat, "L'Établissement," p. 860.

22 Bergeron, *L'Épisode,* pp. 145–46.

23 Chateaubriand and Vitrolles, both quoted from their memoirs by Richardson, *The French Prefectoral Corps,* p. 193.

24 E. A. Whitcomb, "Napoleon's Prefects," *American Historical Review* (cited hereafter *AHR*) 79 (October, 1974): 1095, 1098, and *passim.* In general, the noble prefects of the First Empire were from better-known families than were those of the Restoration. Seventy per cent of the prefects named during the Restoration were nobles (118 of 164), most of them from the "rural squirearchy" (Richardson, *The French Prefectoral Corps,* pp. 179, 186).

25 Whitcomb, "Prefects," pp. 1089–1118; P. Boucher, *Charles Cochon de Lapparent* (Paris, 1969), p. 264. The "aristocratic reaction" of the late Empire appears to be as much a "myth" as the one of the late eighteenth century.

26 G. Thuillier and J. Tulard, eds., *Histoire de l'administration française depuis 1800: problèmes et méthodes* (Geneva, 1975). These articles represent a pioneering colloquium on the history of administration. Thuillier and Tulard conclude with an *appel* for research that moves beyond institutional history in the formal sense.

27 Duc d' Audiffert-Pasquier, ed., *Mémoires du Chancelier Pasquier* (Paris, 1893), vol. 1, pp. 244–53. Pasquier's portrait of the first four of these men is itself an example of the process of "amalgamation."

28 Pasquier, *Mémoires,* vol. 1, p. 415.

29 Tulard, "Problèms sociaux," p. 655. The military represented 59 per cent, "academics" 1.7 per cent, and commerce and industry less than 1 per cent.

30 Bergeron, et al., "Notables du Grand Empire." Recall that these percentages are based on only five departments: Haute-Garonne, Côte d'Or, Yonne, Nord, Seine-Inférieure. However, these five do represent a variety of social structures and different stages of economic development.

31 Tulard, "Problèmes sociaux," p. 656.

32 Agulhon, *La vie sociale,* p. 249.

33 Richardson, *The French Prefectoral Corps,* pp. 132–33.

34 Like administration, education is moving beyond strict institutional history. See the recent articles by Harvey Chisick, Dominique Julia, and Paul Pressly in the *Annales, E.S.C.* 30 (1975): 1516–84. See also A. Prost, *Histoire de l'enseignement en France, 1800–1967* (Paris, 1968).

35 Tulard, "Problèmes sociaux," p. 653; Boucher, *Cochon*, pp. 224-25. Bonaparte to Cambacérès: "Un homme probe, infatigable, au courant des affaires . . . et il marchera." A negative comment of the First Consul: "brave homme, mais incapable de deviner ce qui peut être sur ce qui est."

36 Rebouillat, "L'Établissement," p. 869.

37 Ibid., p. 863.

38 Ch. de Rémusat, *Mémoires*, quoted in Richardson, *The French Prefectoral Corps*, pp. 131-32.

39 George Lefebvre, quoted in Bergeron, *L'Épisode*, pp. 146-47.

40 J. Fiévée, *Histoire de la Session de 1815* . . . (Paris, 1816), quoted in D. Higgs, "Politics and Landownership among the French Nobility after the Revolution," *European Studies Review* 1 (1971): 113.

41 Higgs, "Politics and Landownership," p. 112.

42 Bergeron, *L'Épisode*, p. 167; "A propos des biens nationaux: la signification économique du placement immobilier," *Annales, E.S.C.* 26 (1971-72): 415-19.

43 Zeldin, *France, 1848-1945*, vol. 1, pp. 60-62. This is not to exclude other changes of a noneconomic order in the 1880s, especially in local politics.

44 Richardson, *The French Prefectoral Corps*, p. 4.

45 Forster, "Survival of the Nobility," *PP* (July 1967): 84. "The right of primogeniture," said Broglie, "is the foundation of an inequality of condition; it is pure privilege. . . . It is a social and political revolution against the Revolution accomplished in France forty years ago." The impact of the revolutionary message of *legal* equality should not be underestimated.

46 One hesitates, however, to employ the term "agricultural revolution." See A.-J. Tudesq, *La France des Notables, 1815-1848* (Paris, 1973), vol. 2, pp. 22-23, 139, 152, 179, and passim; M. Morineau, *Les faux-semblants d'un démarrage économique* (Paris, 1969). Morineau concludes that grain yields did not increase between 1450 and 1840. Recent research by E. Le Roy-Ladurie and J. Goy on the *dîme* contests this pessimistic view without invoking an "agricultural revolution" before 1830.

47 R. Forster, "Obstacles to Agricultural Growth in Eighteenth-Century France," *AHR* (October 1970).

48 R. Forster, "Survival"; *House of Saulx-Tavanes* (Baltimore, 1971), chap. 5.

49 For nineteenth-century industrial growth, see the specialized studies listed in Bergeron, *L'Épisode;* D. Landes, *The Unbound Prometheus* (Cambridge, 1969). French historians have yet to produce a history of economic growth comparable to that of P. Deane in England. The data may not be sufficient for the task.

50 Tudesq, *Grands Notables*, vol. 1, pp. 430, 435.

51 A.-J. Tudesq, "Les pairs de France au temps de Guizot," *RHMC* 3 (1956): 272.

52 Ibid., pp. 265-66, 269n.

53 Relating economic interests to political behavior is no easy task. The work of William Aydelotte on the members of the English House of Commons is one example of the problems involved; see William Aydelotte's paper in W. Aydelotte, A. Bogue, R. Fogel, eds., *The Dimensions of Quantitative Research in History* (Princeton, 1972). This is not to say that a roll-call analysis of the French deputies in 1840 would not be worth attempting. But it must go beyond occupational identification.

54 Tudesq, *Grands Notables*, vol. 1, pp. 429, 475.

55 R. Descadeillas, *Rennes et ses derniers seigneurs, 1730-1820* (Toulouse, 1964), p. 199.

56 Comte de Comminges, *Souvenirs d'enfance* (Paris, 1910), quoted in Tudesq, *Grands Notables*, vol. 1, p. 122.

57 Higgs, "Politics and Landownership," pp. 120-21.

58 See the recent work of Nicole Castan on crime in Languedoc. Among her articles, see "La justice expéditive," *Annales, E.S.C.* 31 (1976): 331-61.

59 "Rapports sur le Patronage," *Mémoires de l'Académie Royale de Metz, XVIIIᵉ année (1836-37)* (Paris, 1837), pp. 159, and 99-169 passim.

60 Tudesq, *Grands Notables*, vol. 1, p. 143.

61 A. Soboul, "Les Survivances 'féodales' dans la société rurale au XIXᵉ siècle," *Annales, E.S.C.* 23 (1968): 965-86. Most of Soboul's examples date from the Restoration. An investigation of catechisms of the later years of the century might be fruitful.

62 A. Thuillier, *Economie et société nivernaises au début du XIXᵉ siècle* (Paris, 1974), chap. 9. Dufaud's "day at the office" (p. 275) appears "measured," to me at least. The phrases *"fonctions de régisseur"* and *"finesse commerciale"* (p. 269) suggest something less than dynamic entrepreneurship.

63 D. Johnson, *Guizot: Aspects of French History, 1787-1874* (London and Toronto, 1973).

64 Tudesq, *Grands Notables*, vol. 2, pp. 566-605.

65 Ibid., p. 581.

66 *Mémoires de l'Académie Imperiale de Metz, XLIIᵉ année (1860-61)*, 2nd ser., vol. 9, p. 311.

67 Zeldin, *France, 1848-1945*, pp. 88-99. The implications of these attitudes for French economic growth have been hotly debated. See E. Carter II, R. Forster, and J. Moody, eds., *Enterprise and Entrepreneurs in Nineteenth- and Twentieth-Century France* (Baltimore, 1976), introduction, and especially the essays by David Landes and Maurice Lévy-Leboyer.

68 R. Catherine and G. Thuillier, *Introduction à une philosophie de l'administration* (Paris, 1969), chaps. 8, 9, and passim; M. Crozier, *Le phenomène bureaucratique* (Paris, 1963), pp. 295-305, and passim.

69 Catherine and Thuillier, *Introduction*, p. 243n.

THE AMBIGUOUS HERITAGE OF THE FRENCH RESTORATION: THE DISTANT CONSEQUENCES OF THE REVOLUTION AND THE DAILY REALITIES OF THE EMPIRE

Alan B. Spitzer, University of Iowa

In his great work on the Mediterranean, Fernand Braudel has asked us to visualize ''a series of overlapping histories developing simultaneously.''[1] These are histories of various phenomena extending through varying lengths of time, the effects of which at any given period are conceptually distinct but actually simultaneous. Of course, many historians before Braudel had been aware that human destinies were limited, conditioned, and defined by intersecting developments of various durations and amplitudes, and that any present is the product of multiple pasts. For example, Ernest Labrousse, whose influence on two generations of French historians rivals that of Braudel, has shown how the effects of economic developments—of ''curves'' of various lengths and amplitudes—were experienced in the years before the Revolution: how the daily lives and expectations of various social and economic groups were simultaneously conditioned by the consequences of a century of rising agricultural prices, by a generation-long experience of a cyclical recession, by the catastrophic crop failure of the 1780s, and by the ''histories'' of many other economic phenomena.[2]

This paper will examine the consequences of two overlapping ''histories'' for the political destiny of the French Restoration. The first of these was the divisive legacy of the living memories of the French Revolution, especially the memories of the Revolution of 1793–94; the second, the actual process of transition from Napoleon's Empire to the restored Bourbon regime, which entailed a transaction with imperial elites. The political and social amalgam produced by this transaction constituted one of the foundations for the existence of the Restoration political system, but it could not withstand the corrosive effects of the memories of the Revolution.

No historian of the period after 1814 has ignored the effects of the years between 1789 and 1794, referring not only to the consequences of the fundamental legal and social transformations that no restored monarchy could reverse, but also to the persistence of collective attitudes, loyalties, myths, and symbols that Paul Bois has called *les survivances de la Révolution*.[3] It is commonly said that the Restoration died of those *survivances*.

My reference to the survivals of the Revolution as memories has to do with tendentious memories that identified and separated individuals according to their political pasts. On those rare occasions when politics

invade the entire space of a society, when political differences are perceived as irreconcilable moral choices, when political decisions are
matters of life and death, the results are seared permanently into the
consciousness of contemporaries and are often bequeathed to their political and biological heirs. The survivors of participation in public affairs are marked by the stigmata of their commitments for the rest of
their lives. And there is always someone to remember for them what
they would prefer to forget. Such reminders pressed heavily on the
fragile consensus that supported the constitutional pillars of the Restoration.

Indeed, the restored monarchy, whose very existence depended on
the revival of memories much diminished in the long exile of the Bourbon house, itself enacted forgetting as an organic law. Article 11 of the
Charte—the constitutional charter—decreed, "All investigations of
opinions held or votes cast prior to the Restoration are forbidden. The
same oblivion is required of courts and citizens alike."[4] No one believed that the King could legislate oblivion, but this remarkable piece
of constitutional law did imply commitments fundamental to the constituting of the regime. First, quite obviously, it expressed the intention
to proceed from the reconciliation of those divided by the Revolution,
rather than from the retribution for the sins of revolutionaries. Second,
it implied that past commitments were no bar to integration into the
reconstituted monarchy. In the event all explorations of the past could
not be suppressed by constitutional decree.

The *Charte* was widely accepted as the basis for the pragmatic resolution of old conflicts, but, as a brilliant passage in Pierre de la Gorce's
history of the Restoration remarks, the very meaning read into the constitution varied according to the political memories of the interpreter.
To some, the constitutional guarantees of an elected Chamber and the
right of public petition revived the nightmare of a menacing mob of
petitioners at the bar of the Convention. To others who could recall the
lost glories of the old parlements, the *Charte* was a rather inferior version of what their venerable corps had provided. Or for those whose
memories ran to the springtime of the Revolution, the *Charte* was to be
measured against the model of the Constitution of 1791. In addition to
the examples of incomprehension induced by nostalgia, there were the
misconstructions derived from the recent experience of former servants of the Empire. To them a legislature was a consultive body like
the *conseil d'état*. Obedience was the essence of government, and a
self-limiting monarchy was a self-contradiction.[5]

The differences over the theoretical implications and practical possibilities of the *Charte* were peculiarly embittered by the liberation of
political animosities long repressed, but never relinquished, under the
Empire. Napoleon's regime had also been founded on a presumed ob-

literation of the divisive past and a political reconciliation effected through the eclectic appointment of anyone willing to provide loyal and competent service to the state. Of course, many devoted Royalists and persecuted Jacobins had never been reconciled to the Empire. But the physical and moral authority of the imperial system during its years of success had enforced politically, and perhaps psychologically, the repression of vindictive memories devastatingly liberated at its collapse.

In some cases, the trauma of the collapse allowed the expression of resentments deeply felt and never forgotten; in other cases, it revived recollections attenuated almost beyond recall. To cite a rather modest example: during the last years of the Empire, the Breton students at the college of Vannes had scarcely an idea of the existence of the house of Bourbon and imagined no alternative to the regime they were being trained to serve. But on the fall of Bonaparte, their family histories of heroic service in the *chouannerie* took immediate possession of their political imaginations. They were transformed into implacable opponents of the usurper when he reappeared in 1815 and, during the last weeks of the 100 Days, marched off almost to a man to fight with the Royalist legions against the disintegrating imperial army.[6] Young men from the same region but with different antecedents—despite, as one remembered, his acceptance of the *Charte* and hatred of military despotism—rallied to the cry of "France and liberty," renewing "this federal pact of '89 consecrated by the signature and the blood of the Breton bourgeoisie."[7]

Among those who rallied to Napoleon's last desperate gamble in 1815, there were many inspired, not by devotion to the Empire, but by a determination to preserve the legacy of the Revolution that they had helped to create.[8] Indeed, the enthusiastic revival of revolutionary symbols and slogans among the lower-class volunteers for the renewed battle against the *ci-devants* and the crowned heads embarrassed a leader who had no intention of presiding over a Jacobin commonwealth.

The most dramatic and depressing example of the relevance of memories of the Revolution to the stormy transition from empire to monarchy was manifested in the selection of the victims of the Second White Terror in 1815. Down along the Rhone valley, in the regions of the south stained by the bloody reprisals of the Thermidorean reaction, in the department of the Gard where the ancient conflict of religious confessions assumed the aspect of political murders, the memories of the Revolution were recapitulated in the brutal actions of mobs and murder bands. While the White Terror was certainly directed against the hated representatives of Napoleon's regime, it also hunted down the remnants of a more remote revolutionary past.[9] Twenty-year-old scores were settled against surviving political enemies and their descendants. "Indeed," observes Richard Cobb, "a number of people were murdered in the Gard, the Bouches-du-Rhone, the Vaucluse, and the Lozère in 1815 mainly because their near relatives had been murdered in the previous White Terror. A number of the murderers, too, on both occasions, had lost parents to one or another of the Revolutionary Terrors."[10]

The spasm of the White Terror would pass, but, in some regions, past political conflicts would continue to be recapitulated with meticulous geographic precision. In 1822, when the secret societies affiliated with the French *Carbonari* (the *charbonnerie* and the *chevaliers de la liberté*) tried to raise revolutionary bands south of the Loire, they found their recruits in just those towns strung out along the border of the Vendée that had been the centers of resistance to the counterrevolution in 1793. As the news of the conspiracy spread through the Royalist hinterland, crowds gathered at the old rallying places of the counterrevolution, eager to take arms against the enemies of church and crown.[11]

Without the stimulus of the conspiracy, the old animosities along the edge of the Vendée might never have revived. There is a sense in which collective memories are latent, preserved perhaps in family traditions but lost to the historian's view until they are exposed by a dramatic shift in circumstance. The political memories of the counterrevolutionary peasantry of the Sarthe were lost to public view for years until a means of public expression was provided by the application of universal suffrage in 1848. Given that opportunity they cast their ballots where their grandfathers had planted their banners.[12]

The dramatic change in circumstance, the historical trauma which ineffaceably stamped the politics of the Restoration with the memory of old hatreds was the incredible, catastrophic adventure of the 100 Days. The spirit of claustrophobic mistrust briefly expressed at the grass roots in bloody reprisals would permanently poison the political relations in the narrow elite of notables who had assigned themselves the authority to share out the governance of France. Any hope for the pragmatic repression of political hatreds was lost when former servants of Bonaparte violated their newly minted oaths to the Bourbons, confirming the Ultraroyalist conviction that no one who had ever supped with the devil could be trusted at the table of the King. During the fifteen-year history of the Second Restoration, legal political debate in the press and on the floor of the Chambers of Deputies would be conducted with a sort of extraconstitutional ill-will and virulence, especially when differences over major issues evoked reference to the past.

When the Abbé Gregoire, ex-*conventionnel* who escaped the label of regicide only because he was absent during the fatal vote, was elected to the Chamber of Deputies in 1819, Royalist opinion was united in outraged opposition to the acceptance of such a mandate. The appeal of Constant, Manuel, and the spokesmen of the liberal opposition, to Article 11 and the constitutional repudiation of all investigations into past votes and opinions was answered by appeals to a higher law. "We must decide," intoned the Comte de Corbière, "if regicide has the right to appear in our midst trailing the entire Revolution behind it."[13] A crushing majority gave the answer—refusal to admit Gregoire to a seat in the Chamber. The opposition journal, *La Minerve Française*, identified the dangerous implications of this sort of appeal to the past. If one party could retroactively establish crimes of *lèse-majesté*, another could find plenty of evidence for the crime of *lèse-nation* in the past actions of those who had borne arms against their country and delivered it into the hands of its enemies.[14]

When a debate on the organization of the jury system elicited criticism of the Constituent Assembly, the predictable polemical exchange focused on issues outside the constitutional and temporal boundaries of the existing regime:

> *M. Pardessus:* I say that no one, within or outside of these precincts has the right to eulogize an Assembly that deposed its King, an Assembly that proclaimed the absurd and antisocial dogma of popular sovereignty. (Murmurs on the left.)
>
> *M. Manuel:* Don't think that I intend, Gentlemen, to try to add my feeble voice to those you have heard in order to defend the Constituent Assembly, that Assembly is sufficiently justified by its actions. With it, posterity was born, and if its well-earned tribute of respect and admiration can be refused in this spot, all France has accorded that tribute, and the entire world has not disavowed it. (Several voices on the Right: We disavow it!)[15]

When the Comte de Serre, brilliant Royalist orator with impeccable emigré credentials, made the mistake of conceding that the majority of the members of the revolutionary *Convention* were probably *saine* but constrained to commit atrocities by the pressures of the mob, he was treated by the orators of the extreme right and by the Ultraroyalist press as if he were an apologist for the Committee of Public Safety.[16] However, the same publicists would celebrate de Serre as the sword and buckler of the social order when he broke with his friends and political associates to support the revision of the electoral law which further stacked the electorate in favor of the wealthiest landowners.

It is difficult now to imagine the emotions released by the decision to manipulate the already miniscule electorate by giving the richest one-quarter of the electors a double vote—emotions that spilled out of the Chambers into the streets in demonstrations, riots, and fatal clashes between students and the police. The lessons drawn from the "battle of the elections" varied according to which precedents it was presumed to recall. Lafayette, who appeared to his fellow deputies as the incarnation of heroic or disreputable memories, treated them to a survey of the antecedents of the Revolution, characterized the tricolor as the banner of "liberty, equality, and public order," and warned them that a repudiation of the fruitful results of the Revolution would force the new idealistic generations "to take up the sacred fasces of the principles of eternal truth and sovereign justice."

The Comte de Serre's sensational answer is still savored by connoisseurs of legitimist oratory. Following Lafayette to the tribune, he said:

> The previous speaker has spoken to us of two epochs: The early days of the Revolution and the present moment. The first epoch belongs to history, and history which will judge it, will also judge the honorable member *(vive sensation)* . . . Hasn't that era left the honorable member with sorrowful experiences and useful recollections? He should have felt more than once, death in the soul and a blush on his brow, he should have felt, after having stirred up the masses, not only that they cannot always be checked on a criminal course, but that one is often forced to follow them and virtually to lead them *(très vive sensation;* cries of approval are heard from the right and center).[17]

In such debates we read whatever chances there were for any minimal consensus on the fundamental premises of the political system. In his invaluable history of the Restoration, Achille de Vaulabelle remarked with his characteristic acumen, "The Revolution cut an uncrossable chasm between the parties." What was a glorious event for the Liberals was a tragedy for the Royalists, virtue for one was crime for the other, "they had neither the same political *patrie,* nor the same religion, nor the same gods." They held these irreconcilable convictions with the same sincerity.[18]

Yet the Restoration did not fail because it could not reconcile de Serre and Lafayette, or the Protestants and Catholics in the Gard, or the *chouan* peasantry with the *bleus* of the Breton towns. It survived the conspiracies of the early '20s, the discontents of the discharged and demoted soldiery, and the anticlerical unrest of the regions subject to the visitations of the "missions to the interior," only to commit suicide over a conflict of its ruling elites. A full discussion of the causes of the Revolution of 1830 is beyond the scope of this paper, but I can at least suggest that French politics after 1815 were not completely determined by their revolutionary antecedents and that other problems confronted the Restoration which were gravely exacerbated by the memories of the Revolution but were not identical with them.

Some of these problems are suggested by the observation that, while Louis XVIII dated his reign from 1795, he ascended his throne in 1814. The restoration of the royal government did not entail the replacement of the Committee of Public Safety, or village watch committees, or representatives on mission, but the expropriation of the central and local apparatus of a well-established administrative state. The return-

214 ALAN B. SPITZER

ing emigrés did not seize power from Jacobin democrats or revolutionary demagogues but hoped to gain access to the corps of professional administrators, military chieftains, political *arrivistes*, and pragmatic noblemen who ran the Empire.

Most of the classic multivolumed histories of the Restoration (which still repay careful study) include a passage on the burden placed on the monarchy by unresolved conflicts carried over from the Revolution. Duvergier de Hauranne, who wrote one of the best of these, concludes such a passage with an additional insight, "In truth, between the old and new society, between the Revolution and the emigration, there existed a common need, but one which far from facilitating the task of the Restoration made it more difficult: the need to find public jobs."[19]

There are implications here that go beyond the familiar evocation of the universal desire to feed at the public trough. The government of Louis XVIII was eased into existence by way of a transaction with the elites in place. The negotiations which presented the Allies with a regime that could claim support among influential elements in the French population had to do not only with Louis's acceptance of irreversible social and legal reforms, but also with his reassurance of vested interests and acquired positions. In fact, the imperial Senate, which had granted itself the authority to conduct these negotiations, managed to discredit itself by the egregious self-interest displayed in its draft constitution demanding guarantees for the prerogatives and endowments of sitting senators. This behavior made it easier for Louis XVIII to reject an imposed constitution and to present the concessions and compromises imposed by reality as a free exercise of royal authority.[20]

The royal gift of the *Charte* did in fact contain reassurances for those whose status and property seemed threatened by the collapse of the previous regime. The most significant provision to this effect was the article guaranteeing the inviolability of the *biens nationaux*, the lands expropriated during the Revolution. Interest in that question extended far beyond the small circle of those concerned with preserving the high ranks and rich emoluments they had obtained under the Empire. This was also the case for the guarantee of the public debt. Quite specific guarantees of a different sort were listed under the sections of the *Charte* entitled *Droits particuliers garantis par l'État*. Article 69 stipulated that soldiers with the colors or *en retraite* retained their ranks, honors, and pensions; Article 71 recognized the titles of the new (imperial) nobility; and Article 72—as odd an organic law as Article 11—decreed: "The Legion of Honor is maintained."

Since the great majority of the members of the Legion of Honor were soldiers, the inclusion of Article 72 might simply be seen as another reassurance to the army, but the importance of the Legion in the general scheme of things is indicated by the legislative debates over the im-

plementation of the article in which the Legion of Honor was characterized as "the national award most appropriate to the French way of
life" and as "an essentially monarchist and constitutional institution."[21] The constitutional commitment to the Legion of Honor not
only promised that imperial military citations would be afforded the
same recognition as the Cross of Saint Louis but assured those who
had obtained status and emoluments in the gift of the state that these
would be retained, as would the system that sanctioned the status and
granted the rewards.

The spirit of the guarantees in the *Charte* seemed confirmed by the
policies of Louis XVIII during the First Restoration. Although he had
repudiated the self-serving pretentions of the imperial Senate, he did
send ninety-three of its members along with ten marshalls to the Chamber of Peers. The working draft of the *Charte* was submitted to a committee chosen from the imperial Senate and *Corps Legislatif* by three
commissaires, of whom one, Jacques-Claude Beugnot, had been a
trusted official of Napoleon. In April 1814, the provisional government,
attempting to reconstitute the authority of the central administration,
sent twenty-two *commissaires-extraordinaires* out into the provinces,
fourteen of whom had served the Empire, among them three marshalls
and other dignitaries of the previous regime.[22] The majority of the
members of the first full-fledged Royalist ministry appointed in May
1814 had held high office under the Empire.

The purge of the prefectoral apparatus—the spine of the national
administration—was remarkably moderate considering the circumstances. Nicholas Richardson's meticulous analysis of shifts in the personnel of the corps has qualified exaggerated estimates of the percentage of Napoleonic administrators installed during the First Restoration, but it does grant that a substantial proportion of the prefects
maintained in office or nominated between April 1814 and 15 March
1815 had been imperial functionaries. Richardson wished to emphasize
the mixed political and social background of the appointments, in
which imperial antecedents were often combined with noble birth and
even a stint as emigrés. He concludes, "The First Restoration movement [of prefects] was in some sense a compromise . . . if the newly
nominated prefects included a high proportion of imperial functionaries, these were often men who, if they had not themselves served the
Monarchy, offered a pledge in their name and family."[23]

This compromise, which Chateaubriand identified with distaste as a
politique of "fusion and amalgam,"[24] might be considered a continuation of Napoleon's first steps in the construction of a *nouvelle classe
dirigeante*.[25] Or one might characterize the attempt at an amalgam of
social class and political background as Louis XVIII's version of the
Victorian Compromise—that is,the coopting of wealthy and influential

commoners into an expanded governing class. The failure of the compromise was the failure of the regime.

Even at its best moments, the First Restoration was subject to immense pressures from exigent office seekers because there were so many candidates for each post. The expectation that the change in regimes would entail a vast turnover in personnel encouraged what Vaulabelle called a virtual "*levée en masse* of every ambition and every cupidity,"[26] when in fact the number of public offices had shrunk with the contraction of the Empire. The universal assumption that public employment was the most promising and desirable avenue to personal and family mobility was one of the most profound and permanent results of the Revolution. The manifest inability of the monarchy to satisfy all the ambitions unleashed by the fall of the Empire made it the target of the political resentments produced by the competition of famished emigrés and imperial functionaries for the limited number of offices.

Despite its efforts to maintain a certain continuity of administrative personnel, the new regime could scarcely placate all the seasoned servants of the great Napoleonic system who saw the coveted openings filled by the inexperienced, arrogant detritus of an obsolete aristocracy. The inevitable contraction of the army and the appointment of old Royalists to high military posts were special causes of resentment in a popular and dangerous segment of the population.

In the eyes of Royalists (and not merely frustrated job seekers), the apparent preference for supple careerists over loyal paladins of the legitimate dynasty was a moral outrage and a political issue of major significance. All their objections and warnings had received irrefutable verification, they believed, during the 100 Days, when so many people with a tainted past violated their oaths to the King to return to the service of the usurper. It became an item of faith that the corps of imperial functionaries constituted a conspiracy in the bosom of the monarchy, that it had successfully plotted its humiliating collapse before the last great gamble of the Corsican adventurer. This conspiracy theory was argued with striking effect in Chateaubriand's *Monarchie selon la Charte* in which all the ministerial blunders between May 1814 and March 1815 were assimilated into a conscious, deeply meditated scheme to bring down the Bourbons.[27]

Even those officials who had played crucial roles in the reestablishment of the monarchy were constantly reminded of their dubious antecedents. Jacques-Claude, Comte Beugnot, for example, a member of the inner circle of trusted royal advisers, one of the three commissioners representing the King in negotiations over the *Charte*, and the person entrusted by Louis with the direction of the national police, had to defend himself against malicious allegations that in the early days of the Revolution he had helped to desecrate the royal tombs.[28] None of his outstanding contributions to the consolidation of the monarchy would disarm those Royalist types for whom a career that began in a revolutionary assembly and reached a summit in the parvenu monstrosity of the Grand Duchy of Berg was *prima facie* evidence of unfitness.

Nor would Royalist suspicions be disarmed by Beugnot's reaffirmation of loyalty to the crown during the 100 Days. The "journey to Ghent" to share the fortunes of the unhappy dynasty might seem the ideal litmus-paper test for loyalty, but the *bona fides* of those ex-revolutionaries and Bonapartists who held fast to their oaths did not obliterate the vindictive memories of their original sins.

It is not simply that a sensible pragmatism regarding personnel was finally frustrated by the mindless intransigence of the Ultraroyalists. Chateaubriand, the inspired sloganeer of Royalist sentiments, struck a deeply felt chord with his insistence on *les choses politiques de la révolution, et non les hommes politiques de la révolution*[29]—the measures but not the men of the Revolution. This was the formula for the realistic acceptance of the irreversible reforms and the repudiation of the bloodstained reformers, the application of the spirit of rational compromise without the compromise of moral principle.

The application of any principle that purged the men of the Revolution, however, was far from simple, and not only because there were not enough competent emigrés to fill the jobs—an infuriating truth that Royalists such as Chateaubriand identified as a dangerous lie: "The truly false and dangerous system," said Chateaubriand, "the system which has cost us dear, is that which locates talent for the service of France only in the men of the revolution."[30]

It would be simple enough to dispense with certain "men of the revolution" regardless of talent. Talleyrand and Fouché, intolerable but indispensable contributors to the two restorations, were disposed of at the first convenient hour. The purity test could be applied, with a certain disregard for the letter and spirit of the *Charte*, in quashing the election of the Abbé Gregoire. The criterion of memory could be used to winnow out the residue of the revolutionary era from the prefectoral corps. But the criterion became much more problematic when applied to all of those who had served some illegitimate government between 1792 and 1814, especially because most of the competitors for office were too young to have earned much of a reputation during the Revolution. The Bonapartist journal, *Le Nain Jaune*, alleged that the emigrés around the King were so accustomed to quiz people about their behavior in 1793 that the Duc de Blacas, Minister of the Royal Household, inquired when introduced to a youth of twenty years "what monsieur had done during the Revolution."[31]

In *De le Monarchie selon la Charte*, Chateaubriand refers again and again to revolutionaries who are usurping all the offices, plotting to dominate the monarchy, and consorting with its enemies. But these "revolutionaries" were not Jacobin alumni of the Year II, or even constitutionalists of Lafayette's political vintage; most of them had made their careers in service to the Directory, the Consulate, or the Empire. Chateaubriand was appealing to the memories of the bloody heights of the Revolution to eliminate officials, or would be officials, who had directed a resolutely nonpartisan gaze on the occupational main chance during all those years when the Bourbon house had been hardly a memory. In fact, if not in political rhetoric, the diabolic image of the regicide had been replaced by the shabby portrait of the *girouette*.

A *girouette* is a weathervane—the term applied to a politician indicates what we would call a "turncoat." In 1815, *Le Nain Jaune* introduced the conceit of an *Ordre de la Girouette* as an honorable recompense for those who had "distinguished themselves by the variety of their opinions since 1789." The popularity of this approach to the recent history of France, especially after the immense contribution of subject matter during the 100 Days, was reflected in the publication of a series of *dictionnaires des girouettes*, the most successful of which ran through three editions in 1815.[32] The *dictionnaires* characteristically listed names of familiar figures over a brief relevant biography and awarded one *girouette* for each turn of coat. Here is a typical entry for one of the more venerable *girouettes:*

Barbé-Marbois. Former intendant for the colonies; member of the *conseil des anciens*; deported to Sinnamary as a consequence of the day of 18 fructidor an 5; named *grand-aigle* of the Legion of Honor by the Emperor the 13 pluviose an 13; Count of the Empire and president of the *cour des comptes* which he had reorganized.

"We offer our efforts to Your Majesty, as the surest expression of our fidelity and our love for his august person." [Discourse delivered 10 January 1808. See *Le Moniteur*.]

"Sire,

Your *cour des comptes* joins its felicitations to those of the entire corps d'état, of all the subjects of your empire. In your absence our bliss had fled, your presence renews all our hope and love; our zeal did not fade during your absence but it is redoubled beneath your gaze. We have celebrated your victories but above all we revel in the well-being guaranteed by your laws and your genius." [Discourse of the president of the *cour des comptes*, on 24 January 1809. See *Le Moniteur*.]

Maintained as first president of the *cour des comptes* by the King (May 1814); named peer of France, June 4 of the same year, and *conseiller honoraire de l'université royale de Paris* [*Journal des Debats*, March 1815].[33]

We could have cited examples from more distinguished careers. Talleyrand, who was a *girouette* to the point where it gave his life a sort of satanic consistency, was awarded twelve *girouettes*. All this undoubtedly exemplifies a brand of public humor, always popular in France, that still helps to sell such publications as *Crapouillot* and *Le Canard Enchaîné*. However the figment of the political *girouette* was something more than a *blague*—a malicious joke—in the context of post-revolutionary, post-Napoleonic France. It conveyed in Gallic form the legacy of the period of total politics that weighed so heavily on the process of accommodation necessary to the survival of the Restoration. The criteria that would exclude *girouettes* from the royal administration would prohibit any policy of political and social fusion and amalgam.

Such criteria, of course, are never consistently applied. The arch-reactionary Ultraroyalist was perfectly willing to make an exception for someone who had abjured an obnoxious past if he did it with sufficient extremism and vindictiveness against his old comrades. The Duc de Bellune, ex-drummer boy, volunteer of '92, Marshal of France in the Napoleonic army, was a suitably reactionary Minister of War in the Ultraroyalist ministries of the mid '20s. But those tarnished figures who had established positions anywhere near the middle of the road were twice damned and doubly suspect. No Jacobin, not even Fouché, would be the object of the visceral hatred and polemical venom that Royalists of the Right reserved for Louis XVIII's favorite and leading centrist minister, Elie Decazes.

Decazes was born in 1780, too late to have compromised himself in any sort of revolutionary activity, but he had managed to make his way in the world, as the Comte Molé remarked in a marvelously revealing passage, "thanks to the confusion of ranks caused by the Revolution."[34] By the end of the Empire he had arrived at the eminence of secretary to the imperial dowager mother, Letizia Bonaparte. He rallied to the Bourbons in 1814 and preserved his political chastity during the 100 Days. From that point, every step in his sure-footed ascent by way of the Prefecture and Ministry of Police to the position of Louis XVIII's personal favorite, and eventually president of the Council of Ministers, was interpreted as a move in a carefully planned scheme of subversion of the monarchy.

The assassination of the heir to the throne, the Duc de Berry, was seized on as the opportunity to destroy Decazes, not merely with reference to incompetent security measures, but in the spirit of Chateaubriand's predictable assertion that "the hand that struck the blow is not the most guilty." The most guilty were those who had governed the country for the past four years, introduced democratic laws, harassed religion, welcomed regicides—those who had "rewarded treason and punished fidelity" and "handed over public office to enemies of the Bourbons and to creatures of Bonaparte."[35]

According to the Royalist *Journal de Paris,* the Duc de Berry had been "foully murdered by a fanatic, driven on by *souvenirs révolutionnaires*."[36] Thus the line was drawn from the memories of the Revolution to the dagger of Louvel; and despite the fact that the most assiduous investigation turned up no accomplices, the dagger was pointed at the heart of the royal administration. Clausel de Coussergues, deputy of the Far Right, took the tribune of the Chamber of Deputies to demand that the Chamber "indict M. Decazes, Minister of the Interior, for complicity in the assassination. . . ."[37] This was too rich even for the blue blood of many ultras, but Decazes was finished, despite the affection of the King.

The assassination of the Duc de Berry opened the way for six years of Ultraroyalist government and the demise of the policy of political compromise and social amalgam. Now, it was not only a Decazes who was purged from the government of the *pur et dur* but even such a conservative aristocrat as Étienne-Denis Pasquier. Pasquier was a *girouette* professionally and by conviction, the incarnation of the ethic of service to the society rather than to a particular sovereign, highly respected in some circles for his lifelong commitment to the principle that the best people should rule regardless of regime. "If decent people stand aside," he was heard to say,

won't all power be surrendered to intrigue and chicanery? Doesn't the abdication of *la grande propriete, la grande industrie* compromise the conservative principle of a state? If moderate men refuse to speak out, doesn't influence fall into the hands of the peddlars of false nostrums and deplorable, dangerous utopias?[38]

But not altogether regardless of regime. As the quotation indicates, Pasquier took his stand on the narrow terrain occupied by *la grande propriété* and *la grande industrie*, on the grounds of government in the interest of *les Grands Notables*. But this allowed him to serve Napoleon as prefect of police, Louis XVIII as minister of justice, minister of the interior, and minister of foreign affairs, and Louis-Philippe as one of the chief dignitaries of the July Monarchy. It did not make him acceptable to the Royalists who dominated the last years of Louis XVIII's reign and guaranteed the demise of the reign of Charles X. In the course of the public debate and backstairs intrigue that led to the formation of the first full-fledged Ultraroyalist ministry in December 1821, Pasquier, the most eloquent defender of the increasingly illiberal policies of the previous ministries, was subjected to venomous abuse by the Ultraroyalists, who preferred to remember him as "an agent of the imperial police and a public critic of the Bourbons."[39]

The fact that Pasquier's antecedents lay in the great magistrate families of the old *noblesse de la robe* was no patent of political acceptability in Ultraroyalist circles. The criteria they explicitly applied were political first of all and social only secondarily; however, the results of applying the ideological litmus paper did have a latent social content. The Prince de Polignac, chief of the last doomed ministry of Charles X, had a wistful version of the way things should have been: "It may be difficult," he said, "but it is not impossible for us to return someday to a system which incorporates aristocratic principles and closes the door of the chamber of deputies to mediocre men driven by turbulent and revolutionary passions."[40] While waiting for that day, the various Ultraroyalist governments applied aristocratic principles in the sense of replacing bourgeois officials with descendants of the Second Estate. This is not to say that a policy of class bias was uniformly applied, but that a policy of excluding the imperial service elite in favor of authenticated Royalists transformed the class composition of the administrative apparatus.

Or to put it a slightly different way, as Richardson demonstrates in his analysis of the prefectoral corps, the *politique* of Center-Left Ministries (Talleyrand, Decazes) was to preserve "tried imperial methods and men"; that of ministers of the Right and Extreme Right (Vaublanc, Villèle, and Polignac) was to look to monarchist credentials. The consequence was a considerable difference between the social backgrounds of the prefects nominated by the moderate and by the ultra ministries. Although the largest shift in the social composition of the prefectoral corps took place at the First Restoration when the number of nobles in office almost doubled, the subsequent shifts in the corps revealed, as Richardson puts it, "the full extent of the dichotomy between the Centre Left and the Right during the Restoration. They recruited in two different societies." The result, according to Richardson, was "the evanescent triumph of the rural squirearchy."[41]

This characterization of the government of the Restoration as a system of (qualified) class rule is not far from the venerable view that the last Bourbon regime represented the political swan song of the French aristocracy in its long losing battle against the emerging bourgeoisie. In a recent version of that interpretation, Jean Lhomme located the fatal error of the Restoration in its unwillingness to admit the *grande bourgeoisie*, who were perfectly satisfied with a conservative constitutional monarchy, to a share of state power: "In a union with the aristocracy, the *grande bourgeoisie* could have supported the King and the regime. Its offers were rejected."[42]

Precisely what the term *grande bourgeoisie* might usefully denote in that context has been subject to considerable controversy. The actual contest for political power carried on within what Tudesq calls the *classe dirigeante* of rich bourgeois and aristocrats[43] had less to do with a conflict between a landholding aristocracy and an elite of bankers and industrialists than it had with a competition between a nobility with political-administrative ambitions and a *roturier* state-service elite. The latter were *bourgeois*, in the sense Reinhard ascribes to that term in the conclusion to his article on elite and nobility in the second half of the eighteenth century when he says, ''France has passed from an elite of race to an elite of function. . . . *C'etait sa façon de s'embourgeoiser.*''[44]

The political and social alignments that fractured the consensus of ruling groups in the Restoration are usually described as products of the past—on the one side, the remnants of the Old Regime; on the other, the new social and political interests developed between 1789 and 1814. As it is put in a recent manual of political history, the *Charte* was a paper barrier between two worlds, ''the world of the Old Regime and the world of the Revolution and the Empire. The profound solidarity uniting the Revolution and the Empire (to a considerable extent the same political personnel was involved) was manifested in opposition to the world of the Old Regime.''[45]

It is true that there had been a fusion of revolutionary and imperial personnel and that, especially after the 100 Days, there was a deeply felt opposition between those whose careers were made outside the monarchy and those who had never qualified their commitments to it. An emphasis on the ideological fusion of exrevolutionaries and servants of the Empire, however, loses sight of the genuine counter-revolutionary consensus that might have provided a basis for the sort of regime that was finally established in 1830.[46]

The notables of the Empire and the aristocrats of the Old Regime accepted certain of the fundamental consequences of the Revolution, more or less enthusiastically in the first case, reluctantly in the second. They were also at one in their repudiation of those aspects of the Revolution that we associate with the traditions of democracy and social justice. There was a memory of the Revolution shared by the various elements of the classe *dirigeante,* a memory incarnated in the universal repudiation of popular sovereignty. They read each other endless lessons from the past to demonstrate the dangers of allowing the masses to participate in the political process. In addition to their mutual antipathy to democratic politics, they shared assumptions about the role of the state in relation to the social order.

There was a considerable Royalist literature deploring the monarchy's application of the instruments and techniques of imperial despotism.[47] Despite the familiar polemics against overcentralization, the hypertrophy of Paris, the dead hand of the bureaucracy, and the abuse of police powers, the great administrative machine was not dismantled but redecorated; lilies painted over the bees, the machine operated in the same spirit, often for the same ends, if against different enemies. The despised consolidated sales tax, the *droits réunis,* would continue to be collected; the internal passport would be required of every traveler; the worker's passbook, the *livret,* required of every worker; and the immense apparatus of political surveillance and social control sub-sumed under the *police générale* rigorously applied to the actual and potential enemies of the realm.

A case can be made that the exigencies imposed by the enemies of the regime forced it to carry on a system of government which was its only available instrument of self-defense. But it is also true that the legal and administrative system forged under the Consulate and Em-pire corresponded to the inclinations of all the elites—aristocratic, grand bourgeois, or high functionary. A favorite tactic of the opposi-tion on the Left was to attack the governments of the Restoration for their application of the legal and practical restrictions of civil and politi-cal liberties inherited from the Empire. The characteristic Royalist re-sponse was to contrast the liberties granted by the King to the iron constraints of his predecessor. Another answer, heard less often, but closer I think to the instincts of all those in power between 1814 and 1830, was expressed in an unusually revealing speech in the Chamber of Deputies by that influential spokesman for constitutional con-servatism, the Comte de Serre:

> It is easy, but dangerous, to stigmatize the majority of existing laws by characterizing them as laws of the Empire. We should not forget that the era of the Consulate and the Empire followed years of anarchy and tyrannical demagogy, and if the imperial govern-ment unquestionably did a great deal to strengthen its despotism, it also made contribu-tions to order and the repression of anarchy.[48]

To the extent that "anarchy" was the anarchy of an effective politi-cal opposition, the attitude toward despotic practices varied according to the observer's position in or outside the government. But where anarchy was perceived as a threat to social order, a firm consensus could be found regarding the appropriate techniques of social control. No one was heard to object to those Napoleonic decrees that repre-sented a repudiation, not so much of the abstract conception of liberty, as of the concessions to simple humanity introduced by the Revolu-tion. The tentative efforts to enlarge the social space and recognize the dignity of women, the young, and the poor had been revised by Napo-leon's legists to guarantee the supremacy of males, property-holders, and the heads of families. A similar conception of the social order was manifested in the legal and practical treatment of the collective aspira-tions of the workers as a police matter.

In the light of this consensus, one can see considerable merit in Nich-olas Richardson's remark that "even in 1814 the question had been less how to govern France than who should do the governing."[49] But the question of who should do the governing did bear on how France was to be governed. Chateaubriand was wrong to think that it was possible to preserve all the necessary *choses politiques de la révolution* while dispensing with the *hommes politiques*. The tendentious memories of the Revolution that so exacerbated the question of who should do the governing also affected the policies of the Ultraroyalists in power—to the point where Chateaubriand himself went into the opposition. Even before the accession of the ultra ministries, the emigré mentality was expressed in the various manifestations of aggressive clericalism, in the paranoid handling of the university (which greatly contributed to the alienation of emerging elites), in the nervous harassment of a critical press, and in the inability to accept an electoral victory of the opposition.

J. P. T. Bury supposed that if Louis XVIII had accepted the draft constitution of the Napoleonic Senate, "on paper France would have had her 1830 peaceably sixteen years sooner."[50] Something like the July Monarchy's system of political and class rule was possible in 1814, and it was implicit, I believe, in Louis XVIII's version of the Victorian Compromise. In the event, the fusion and amalgam of the notables was only completed in response to the menace of the Revolution of 1848; before that it was aborted by the memories of the Revolution of 1789.

NOTES

1 F. Braudel, *The Mediterranean and the Mediterranean World in the Age of Philip II*, trans. Siân Reynolds, 2 vols. (New York, 1972–73), vol. 2, p. 829.

2 C. E. Labrousse, *La Crise de l'économie française à la fin de l'ancien régime et au début de la Révolution* (Paris, 1944).

3 P. Bois, "Reflexions sur les survivances de la Révolution dans l'ouest," *Annales historiques de la Révolution Française* 31 (April–June 1961): 177–86.

4 For the text of the *Charte Constitutionelle*, see L. Duguit, H. Monnier, and R. Bonnard, *Les Constitutions et les principales lois politiques de la France depuis 1789* (Paris, 1952), pp. 168–74.

5 P. de la Gorce, *Louis XVIII* (Paris, 1926), pp. 22–25.

6 A. F. Rio, *La Petite Chouannerie, ou Histoire d'un collège breton sous l'Empire* (Paris, 1842), p. 52; Pierre Bainvel, *Souvenirs d'un écolier en 1815, ou vingt ans après* (Paris, 1874), pp. 73–74; J. J. Mauricet, *Le Collège de Vannes en 1812: Souvenirs d'un vieux collégien* (Vannes, 1876), pp. 1–6.

7 Manuscript journal of Paul-François Dubois, *Archives Nationales, Archives privées*, Papiers de Paul-François Dubois, 319 AP 3.

8 See, for example, J. Chaumié, "Les Girondins et les cent jours," *Annales historiques de la Révolution Française* 43 (July–September 1971): 329–65.

9 D. P. Resnick, *The White Terror and the Political Reaction After Waterloo* (Cambridge, Mass., 1966).

10 R. Cobb, *The Police and the People* (Oxford, 1970), p. 109.

11 A. B. Spitzer, *Old Hatreds and Young Hopes: The French Carbonari Against the Bourbon Restoration* (Cambridge, Mass., 1971), pp. 286–88.

12 Bois, "Survivances de la Révolution dans l'ouest," p. 184.

13 *Archives parlementaires*, 2nd ser., vol. 25, p. 734.

14 J. P. Pagès, "Session des chambres," *La Minerve Française*, vol. 8 (1819), p. 287.

15 *Archives parlementaires*, 2nd ser., vol. 29, p. 704.

16 B. Combe de Patris, *Le Comte de Serre* (Paris, 1932), p. 140.

17 *Archives parlementaires*, 2nd ser., vol. 28, pp. 152–55.

18 A. de Vaulabelle, *Histoire des deux Restaurations*, 4th ed., 8 vols. (Paris, 1858), vol. 5, p. 258.

19 P. Duvergier de Hauranne, *Histoire du gouvernement parlementaire en France*, 10 vols. (Paris, 1857–71), vol. 2, pp. 190–93.

20 J. P. T. Bury, "The End of the Napoleonic Senate," *The Cambridge Historical Journal* 11 (1948): 165–89.

21 *Archives parlementaires*, 2nd ser., vol. 29, pp. 45–46, 112.

22 H. C. Payne, "The Bourbon Restoration's *Commissaires-extraordinaires du roi* in 1814," *French Historical Studies* 9 (Spring 1975): 38.

23 N. Richardson, *The French Prefectoral Corps, 1814–1830* (Cambridge, England, 1966), p. 54.

24 [François de Chateaubriand], *Oeuvres de Chateaubriand*, 20 vols. (Paris, 1857–58), vol. 15: *De La Monarchie selon la Charte*, p. 188.

25 L. Bergeron, *L'Épisode napoléonien, Aspects interieurs, 1799–1815* (Paris, 1972), p. 146.

26 Vaulabelle, *Histoire des deux Restaurations*, vol. 2, p. 67.

27 Chateaubriand, *De La Monarchie selon la Charte*, p. 182.

28 There is a copy of a letter from Beugnot to the King dated 23 June 1814, which denies the slanders and presents a justification of his entire career, in the *Archives Nationales, Archives privées*, Papiers Beugnot, 40 AP 16; see also [Jacques-Claude Beugnot], *Mémoires du Comte Beugnot*, 3rd ed. (Paris, 1889).

29 Chateaubriand, *De La Monarchie selon la Charte*, p. 222.

30 Ibid., p. 193.

31 *Le Nain jaune*, 25 March 1815.

32 *Dictionnaire des girouettes ou nos contemporains peints d'après eux-mêmes* (Paris, 1815); my citations are from the second edition. This *dictionnaire* was probably the work of César de Proisy d'Eppe.

33 Ibid., p. 30.

34 [Louis Mathieu Molé], *Le Comte Molé, 1781–1855: Sa Vie—ses mémoires*, 3rd ed., 6 vols. (Paris, 1922–30), vol. 2, p. 21, "Decazes . . . se poussa dans le monde de la confusion des rangs causée par la Révolution, et surtout a l'aide d'une belle figure, de manières agréables et d'un esprit élevé."

35 *Le Conservateur*, 18 February 1820.

36 *Journal de Paris* quoted in *Le Moniteur Universel*, 18 February 1820.

37 *Archives parlementaires*, 2nd ser., vol. 26, p. 195.

38 L. Favre, *Éstienne-Denis Pasquier, Chancelier de France, 1767–1862: Souvenirs de son dernier secrétaire* (Paris, 1870), pp. 59–60. The same passage is quoted in the suggestive note by Jean Tulard, "Un Nomination de Préfet sous l'Empire: Le Baron Pasquier à la Préfecture de Police," *Revue de l'Institut Napoléon*, no. 70 (January 1959): 14–17.

39 *Archives parlementaires*, 2nd ser., vol. 33, p. 660. For the atmosphere of ferocious hatred for Pasquier, see the reminiscences of the Duc de Richelieu, "Ma retraite du pouvoir," *Revue de Paris* 24 (November–December, 1897): 203–4.

40 Quoted in V. Beach, *Charles X of France* (Boulder, Colo., 1971), p. 297.

41 Richardson, *The French Prefectoral Corps*, pp. 75–77, 186.

42 J. Lhomme, *La Grande Bourgeoisie au pouvoir (1830–1880)* (Paris, 1960), p. 29.

43 A. J. Tudesq, *Les Grand Notables en France (1840–1849)*, 2 vols. (Paris, 1964), vol. 1, p. 8.

44 M. Reinhard, "Élite et noblesse dans la seconde moitié du XVIIIe siècle," *Revue d'histoire moderne et contemporaine* 3 (1956): 37.

45 J. J. Chevallier, *Histoire des institutions et des régimes politiques de la France moderne (1789–1958)* (Paris, 1967), p. 180.

46 Cf. Bergeron, *L'Épisode napoléonien*, p. 144, on social structure under the empire:

. . . il convient de souligner, par-delà la rupture des barrières de caste imposée par la Révolution, la continuité des structures sociales en France, plutôt que d'opposer globalement deux sociétés, l'une feodale et l'autre bourgeoise—séparées par le fossé infranchissable, en apparence, des inimitiés et des rancunes, creusé depuis le Quatre-Août jusqu'aux condamnations à la guillotine.

47 See C. H. Pouthas, "Les Projets de réforme administrative sous la Restauration," *Revue d'histoire moderne* 1 (1926): 321–67; J. J. Oechslin, *Le Mouvement ultra-royaliste sous la Restauration* (Paris, 1960), pp. 181–87.

48 *Archives parlementaires*, 2nd ser., vol. 29, p. 702.

49 Richardson, *The French Prefectoral Corps*, p. 67.

50 Bury, "The End of the Napoleonic Senate," p. 189.

PART IV

REVOLUTIONARY TRADITIONS IN
EAST CENTRAL EUROPE

THE *HAIDAMAK* INSURRECTIONS AND THE OLD REGIMES IN EASTERN EUROPE

Jaroslaw Pelenski, University of Iowa

The challenge of the Ukrainian *haidamak*s in the eighteenth century to the Old Regimes in Eastern Europe—directly in the form of insurrections against the Polish sociopolitical system in the Ukrainian provinces of the Polish-Lithuanian Commonwealth, and indirectly as an insurrectionist model against the Russian Empire—may be regarded as the final phase of the intricate triangular Polish-Ukrainian-Russian relationship that had lasted since the mid-sixteenth century.[1] From the time of the emergence of the *haidamak*s in the early eighteenth century to their final repression in the early 1770s,[2] their history coincided chronologically with the international demise and internal decline of Poland and with Russia's rise to prominence as the major power in Eastern and Northeastern Europe. Russia's ascendance was accompanied by a series of bureaucratic reforms that aimed at centralizing and streamlining the autocratic imperial system. This paved the way for the elimination of the non-Russian autonomous sociopolitical entities within the Empire and their forceful incorporation into the imperial framework.

The word *haidamak*, or its Ukrainian equivalent *haidamaka*, corresponded to the Serbian *hajduk*, the Bulgarian *xajduk*, and was derived from the Turkic words *hada*, "to harass," and *hajdemak*, "to pursue," "to persecute," "to victimize." The term *hultajstwo hajdamackie* is first attested in the Ukraine in a document dated 22 February 1717,[3] although the *haidamak*s, or at least their predecessors, had been roaming the Volhynian, Braclavian, and Kievan provinces for a decade before that date.[4] In any case, they first appeared sometime between the Battle of Poltava (1709), which had sealed the fate of the Cossack Ukraine's political independence, and the *sejm* "*niemy*" (the "Dumb Diet") of 1717, which had so glaringly revealed the extent both of Russia's interference into Poland's internal affairs and of Poland's political and military weaknesses. The repression of the *haidamak*s occurred just before the First Partition of Poland, in response to their last major insurrection, the *koliivshchyna*, which took place in 1768.[5] Two possible etymologies of the term *koliivshchyna* have been offered: according to one, accepted by contemporary Soviet Ukrainian historiography, the term was derived either from the word *kil*, meaning "stake," "picket," "bludgeon," or from the word *koloty*, meaning "to thrust," "to pierce," "to stab," [the enemy].[6] The second etymology connects the word *koliivshchyna* with *kolej, po kolei, kolejno,* terms which were associated with *służba kolejna,* meaning the "rotational service" and referring specifically to the Ukrainian Cossack militia serving on the estates of Polish magnates in the Right-bank Ukraine.[7]

The *koliivshchyna* insurrection took place four years after the abolition of the Ukrainian Hetmanate by the Russian imperial government in 1764, and seven years before the liquidation of the Zaporozhian Host in 1775 by Russian military authorities acting under instructions from the government. These two events represented the end of the independent political power centers and autonomous institutions in the Ukraine.

The *haidamak* activities were concentrated in the Right-bank Ukraine and had two major aspects. First, there were the countless attacks themselves, both major and minor, on the estates and other property belonging both to the Polish magnates and nobility and to others working for them in the system of the magnate-nobility economy in the Right-bank Ukraine. Secondly, there were the major sociopolitical, ideological-religious, and national concerns that underlay these attacks and raids and which assumed dangerous dimensions for the Polish state and the Polish ruling elite, particularly when large-scale revolts and insurrections broke out in situations already made critical by domestic problems and foreign intervention.

The *haidamak* attacks on landed property were caused by the social relations and economic conditions of the Right-bank Ukraine where the process of concentrated accumulation of the latifundia economy had reached its peak in the eighteenth century. The latifundia in the Ukraine belonging to the leading Polish magnate families were particularly vast. For example, the Potocki family, that is, the estate of Franciszek Selezy Potocki which was inherited by Franciszek Szczęsny Potocki, in 1768 possessed 8 cities and 173 villages in the Uman' territory alone. Its annual income from the Mohyliv estate in the years 1777–78—1792–93 fluctuated between 109,000 and 209,000 *złotys*. The Ukrainian estates of the Potocki family included approximately 125,000 dependent subjects. The estates of other prominent magnate families, such as the Czartoryskis, Lubomirskis, Mniszechs, Poniatowskis, Branickis, and Jabłonowskis were of comparable size.[8] The process of concentrated accumulation of the latifundia economy was accompanied by a corresponding impoverishment of the lesser Polish and Ukrainian nobility, and by the further pauperization and enserfment of the Ukrainian peasants and of those Cossacks who continued to live in the Right-bank Ukraine. The *haidamak*s were recruited primarily, although not exclusively, from these two social groups, that is, peasants and Cossacks, including lower-class, run-away Cossacks who had fled from the territory of the Zaporozhian Host. They raided, robbed, and plundered the estates of the Polish landlords and the properties of the real, or assumed, intermediary exploiters such as service people and merchants. In these raids, the dividing line between legitimate economic struggle and defiant criminal greed was often conveniently overlooked, or simply ignored.

The broader sociopolitical, ideological, and national ramifications of the *haidamak* movements became particularly apparent in connection with the three major and separate waves of insurrections, each of which comprised a series of intermediary and minor revolts, partisan operations, and local outbreaks of violence. Two of these insurrections shook the very foundations of the Polish order in the Right-bank Ukraine and were repressed only with the help of the Russian army. The first of the three began with the insurrection of 1734 and continued in the form of sporadic rebellions until 1737. These outbreaks were connected with the succession struggle between Stanisław Leszczyński—supported by the patriotic elements of the Polish ruling elite and the society, as well as by France—and August III of Saxony—supported by Russia and Austria. The Russian military intervention on behalf of August III, and the appearance of Russian troops in the Ukraine, were viewed by certain Ukrainian elements as an ideal opportunity to abolish Polish rule in the Right-bank Ukraine. The second major *haidamak* insurrection took place in 1750, apparently in reaction to accumulated socioeconomic grievances among the Ukrainian populace. It coincided with a period of acute political and financial difficulties in Poland. The third and the most violent insurrection, the *koliivshchyna* of 1768, broke out mainly as a result of another major Polish crisis, namely the formation of the Bar Confederation of 1768 and the subsequent Russian military intervention in Poland. Aside from highlighting the perpetual socioeconomic problems of the Polish state, the *koliivshchyna* insurrection, for the last time in the history of the old *Rzeczpospolita,* also dramatized the military, political, religious, and national aspects of the complex Russian-Polish-Ukrainian relations.

The relevant sources for the insurrections of the 1730s and the *koliivshchyna* provide evidence that allows us to revise some established notions regarding the social profile of the *haidamak* movement and to reevaluate the relationship between the Cossack leadership groups and its predominantly peasant following.[9] Basing their views, at least, to some extent on old populist assumptions, most historians have tended to agree that the *haidamak* insurrections were basically antifeudal peasant uprisings.[10] Similarly, it has been thought that the vast majority of the participants were peasants (mostly serfs) from the Right-bank Ukraine, i.e., from the lands under the sovereignty of the Polish crown. Other participants in the *haidamachchyna* recruited themselves from among free men, such as Cossacks (both those in Polish service and the Zaporozhian Cossacks), lower-class burghers, service people and sons of lower Orthodox clergy. Although Antonovych and Shulhyn mentioned in passing the participation of individual Ruthenian/Ukrainian noblemen in the *haidamak* movements, they did not provide sufficient explanation for it.[11] The view that the *haidamak* uprisings were ''peasant insurrections'' represents a too simple conclusion to a complex problem. While it is possible to say that the majority of the participants in the *haidamak* movements were in fact peasants, it is equally important to try to establish what proportion of the participants came from other social strata.

The Kodna Book of Criminal Cases (Kodens'ka knyha sudovykh sprav), a collection of materials pertaining to the activities of the Polish Military Tribunal acting on behalf of the Ukrainian and Podolian detachments of the Polish army in the years 1769–72, can be regarded as one of the most important documentary sources on the *koliivshchyna*. It provides information about the numbers and sometimes the names of the people who were tried, found guilty, and executed for participating in the *koliivshchyna*.[12]

According to the register of the *Kodna Book*, the total number of participants who were executed between 1769 and 1771 was 317.[13] In addition, others were tried, found guilty for minor transgressions, and punished by mutilation, and still others were found not guilty. However, the number in the last two categories was relatively small (not more than a few dozen) since those brought to Kodna or other places where military authorities held court were almost always executed.

The *Kodna Book* also contains materials pertaining to the interrogation and trials of 3 noblemen who were charged with involvement in the *haidamak* movement, but it does not mention the final disposition of their cases.[14] Among the 317 executed, the *Kodna Book* register mentions the names of 9 individuals who were executed for *haidamak* activities, 3 of whom are specifically referred to as ''noblemen''[15] and 6 of whom can be classified as noblemen on the basis of their surnames.[16] These 9 executed noblemen constitute 2.83 per cent of the total number executed. If we take the 12 noblemen involved and compare it with the approximately 360 listed as being involved (317 executed and a few dozen who were tried but not executed), then the ratio of the noblemen to non-noblemen who appeared before the Polish Military Tribunal amounts to 3.33 per cent, a significant figure because it approximately corresponds to the proportion of the Ruthenian/ Ukrainian nobility to the total population living in the territories of the Right-bank Ukraine at that time. Although the *Kodna Book* provides only limited insight into the social composition of the participants (we do not have, for example, any materials on those who were executed without trial either on orders of Polish Hetman Jan Branicki [approximately 700 people] or Commander Józef Stępkowski [several thousand people(?)]), we are justified in concluding that in general terms it corresponded much more closely to the social composition of the population inhabiting the Right-bank Ukraine than has heretofore been assumed.

The testimony of the Ruthenian nobleman Jan Gradowski who was charged with *haidamak* activities deserves to be quoted here because it reveals some of the complexities of Ukrainian-Polish relations not only during the *koliivshchyna*, but also later, persisting throughout the nineteenth and into the twentieth century. During his interrogation, Jan Gradowski made the following statement about his familial background:

> . . . I was born in Jabłonówka Białocerkiewska, the child of Andrzej and Zofia (nee Burkowska-Dunin) Gradowski; [my] father was a Pole and [my] mother a Ruthenian. Following [my] mother's rite, I was baptized in the Ruthenian rite, and my younger brother and sister were baptized in the Polish rite; this was decided by my grandfather, who was of the Ruthenian rite, so that I, as the first born grandson, should be destined by my parents to the Ruthenian rite.[17]

The organization and the military and political leadership of the *haidamak* insurrections were provided by the Cossacks of Ruthenian/ Ukrainian ethnic background, who also formulated the objectives of the insurrections. The Cossacks who initiated and led the first and last of the three major insurrections, that is, those of 1734 and 1768, were recruited from among two different Cossack groups. One was the Cossack militia, i.e., Cossacks in the service of the Polish magnates. The officers and regulars of the militia were free men and relatively conservative and traditionalist in their views. Verlan, the self-appointed colonel and a leading figure of the insurrection of 1734, was a *sotnyk* (''captain'') in the militia, in the service of the Potocki family; he also owned a village.[18] Ivan Gonta, one of the leaders of the *koliivshchyna*, was a protégé of the same family and a captain of the Uman' service Cossacks; he held two villages in tenure. He wrote Polish well, and he could pass for an *obywatel* (''citizen-nobleman'') according to hostile contemporaries.[19] Men such as Verlan and Gonta were not ordinary freemen, but members of a group which, for lack of a better term, might be categorized as service nobility.

The second group consisted of impoverished, highly unstable, mobile Cossacks, who were socially, politically, and religiously more radical, and who were sometimes collectively referred to as the *siroma* (''the poor,'' ''the wretched,'' ''the dispossessed'').[20] They included former serfs, Cossacks threatened by enserfment, artisans, *chumaks* (''carters''), and other socially marginal elements from the Left-bank Ukraine and the Zaporozhian Host. Their most prominent representative was the principal leader of the *koliivshchyna*, the elected colonel,

Maksym Zalizniak.[21] These Cossack elements can most properly be regarded as the real *haidamak*s in a broader sociopolitical sense. It deserves to be noted that Russian political and military authorities made a very clear distinction between the peasant followers and the *haidamak*s themselves.[22] The role of the latter in these eighteenth-century insurrections was similar to that of the registered and Zaporozhian Cossacks in the great Ukrainian rebellions of the late sixteenth and seventeenth centuries, particularly the Revolution of 1648–54. The ratio of Cossacks to peasants participating in the major *haidamak* insurrections varied between 1:5 and 1:10. At its height, Verlan's insurrectionist force included several dozen service Cossacks from his own detachment, a company of Uman' service Cossacks numbering approximately 100 men, a detachment of some 100 Zaporozhian Cossacks, and approximately 1,000 peasants. Russian military authorities in July 1768 captured 65 Zaporozhian Cossacks and 780 peasants when they liquidated the insurrectionist camp near Uman'. After the completion of the Uman' operation, the Russian military commanders reported 87 Zaporozhian Cossacks and 851 peasants captured.[23] According to the reports of Major-General Petr N. Krechetnikov, the Russian troops operating in the Right-bank Ukraine turned over approximately 878 peasants and service Cossacks to Branicki and approximately 250 Zaporozhian Cossacks to the Russian authorities in Kiev.[24] One can assume that a considerable number of Zaporozhian Cossacks managed to escape. Thus, by a conservative estimate, the number of active participants in the *koliivshchyna* can be put at approximately 500–600 Cossacks and roughly 4,000–5,000 peasants.

Peasants usually joined the insurrections either under the prodding of *haidamak* Cossacks or following some obvious Cossack-*haidamak* success. The participation of peasants in the insurrections frequently added to their chaotic nature. While peasants joined the *haidamak* detachments in great numbers, accompanied them in their campaigns, and participated actively in some military operations, their military value was small since their goals were often limited. They were easily satisfied with seizing property, destroying estates, or sacking a town or city. Occasionally, they would kill whatever personal, social, or religious enemies were about and then simply depart to their villages. The only significant ideological step such a peasant might take would be to return to his original, Orthodox, faith. Lower-class Ukrainian burghers demonstrated similar behavior: they would be sympathetic to the *haidamak*s and join their ranks following a takeover of the town or city in which they lived (in Uman', for example). The peasants and lower-class burghers played the role of "mass following," but it was the Cossack *haidamak*s who were the decisive elements both in the insurrections of the 1730s and in the *koliivshchyna* later on.

The sociopolitical programs of the two major *haidamak* insurrections were remarkably alike.[25] In both cases the goals were the liquidation of the political and economic systems based upon magnate latifundia and Polish nobility landownership, and the abolition of serfdom. Both aimed at the expulsion or destruction of the Polish nobility, the Jews, those in the service of the nobility and the Ruthenian/Ukrainian Uniates, and the removal of all non-Orthodox religious institutions and their adherents from the Right-bank Ukraine. Beginning in the late 1730s and early 1740s, the *haidamaks* first began to direct their hostility toward Polish Roman Catholic and Ruthenian/Ukrainian Uniate clergy and to commit extraordinary acts of cruelty against them.[26] Their contempt and hatred for all but the Orthodox Eastern Slavs were reflections of a xenophobia that assumed its most obscurant and drastic forms in the *koliivshchyna* insurrection as a reaction to the religious intolerance of the Polish ruling elite that had accompanied the decline of the Polish-Lithuanian Commonwealth in the eighteenth century.

The *koliivshchyna* originated as a movement against the Confederates of Bar, who, the *haidamaks* believed, intended to destroy all the Orthodox. Zalizniak's detachment began its campaign in the vicinity of the Motrenin Monastery, and sufficient evidence can be found to maintain that a number of monks, as well as of Orthodox lower clergy, sympathized with the objectives of the *haidamaks* to extirpate both Roman and Uniate Catholicism and Judaism. These ecclesiastics seem to have provided religious and ideological guidance to the *haidamaks*, and some of them instigated religious excesses similar to those that occurred during the Uman' massacre. The question of the relationship between Melkhisedek Znachko-Iavors'kyi, the Archmandrite of the Motrenin Monastery, and the *haidamaks* and their excesses has yet to be settled. Znachko-Iavors'kyi was accused by his Polish and Ruthenian Uniate contemporaries with having incited the *haidamaks* and peasants to undertake the *koliivshchyna* insurrection and with having been the chief ideologue and principal architect of a campaign to reconvert the Ruthenian/Ukrainian Uniates to the Orthodox Church.[27] His involvement in reconversion activities can in fact be fairly well proved, but it is more difficult to establish his direct connection with the *haidamaks*. In his Pastoral Epistle of 1768, Znachko-Iavors'kyi advised his compatriots not to participate in *haidamak* activities but instead to use legal channels in their struggle for religious rights:

. . . Orthodox Christians do not join the *haidamaks*, because by doing so you will offend the Lord, and no one will come to your defense; Russia will not intercede on behalf of the lawless, namely, the *haidamaks*, and will not open her boundaries to them. Even if someone flees there, he will not be able to hide. We should obtain justice for our cause through the courts, by legal means, and by suffering. . . . The whole world should know that you are not *haidamaks*, thieves, or bandits, and that you do not shed the blood of others.[28]

It deserves to be noted that, while Znachko-Iavors'kyi did condemn the killing of Jews, he never specifically discouraged the annihilation of Uniate or Roman Catholic fellow Christians.[29]

The principal sociopolitical objective of the leaders of the two major *haidamak* insurrections was the return to the "ideal" social conditions that allegedly had prevailed before the enserfment of the peasantry and the social degradation of certain groups of Cossacks, conditions that were now projected as being an utopian ideal for the future as well. This ideal historical model and the ideal projected for the future were later formulated in the nineteenth century by Taras Shevchenko and the Ukrainian populists in their credo *[Ukraina] bez kholopa i bez pana* ([a Ukraine] without serfs and without lords) suggesting the hope for some vague and undefined classless society.

In political terms, the *haidamak* leaders sought to restore the traditional Cossack system which represented a combination of a military caste system and rudimentary participatory democracy. Verlan, Zalizniak, and Gonta attempted to reestablish, and to a certain extent succeeded in reestablishing, military discipline and to appoint Cossack officers as junior-level commanders to exercise authority in the conquered areas and to expand the insurrection. In spite of their violent attacks upon the established order and their professed claims that they were removing both lords and social distinctions, the *haidamak* leaders immediately reintroduced the traditional Cossack registers[30] and organized military units according to a decimal system patterned on the Mongol-Turkic model.

The Cossack register automatically created a new elite among the insurrectionists which, according to the precedents of the seventeenth century, would eventually have acquired a privileged position in Ukrainian society. The reinstitution of the register can thus serve as an additional argument to bolster the hypothesis that almost every insurrectionist or revolutionary movement, regardless of its ideology and its claims to represent the "lower classes" or the "people," has a tendency even in its incipient stages to develop an elite which then strives for a dominant and privileged position in the newly formed society.

The Cossack leaders of the insurrections also followed Cossack traditions when it came to the creation of offices and assumption of titles and ranks. Verlan himself was referred to by his subordinates as an "appointed colonel," reflecting his claim that his appointment came directly from the Russian Empress Anne.[31] Similarly, Maksym Zalizniak, in his interrogation, stated that "he was a colonel elected to this rank by Zaporozhian Cossacks."[32] Zalizniak signed his *universaly* ("charters") either as "Colonel of the Zaporozhian Army" or as "Colonel of the Zaporozhian Army and the Entire Host."[33] Both titles were taken verbatim from the military and administrative titulature of the Zaporozhian Cossack Host. According to reliable accounts, Zaliz-niak established an administrative residence (similar to that of the *koshovyi*, the highest military and administrative official elected by the Cossack Assembly in the Zaporozhian Host) from which he exercised authority over both the city and the entire province of Uman'.[34] The allegations that Maksym Zalizniak acquired the titles of Hetman and Prince of Smila and that Ivan Gonta was referred to as Governor of Rus' and Prince of Uman' appear to be either misconceptions by con-temporaries or later inventions.[35]

In sum, the sociopolitical program of the *koliivshchyna haidamaks* represented an amalgamation of traditional Cossack political ideas, based primarily on the experience of the Zaporozhian Host, and the most radical social and ideological concepts developed both in the Left- and Right-bank Ukraine in the third quarter of the eighteenth century.

Since the last major *haidamak* insurrection occurred at the very end of the *ancien régime* of the Polish-Lithuanian Commonwealth and on the eve of the First Partition of Poland, it now becomes necessary to ask ourselves whether the *haidamak* insurrections, and particularly the *koliivshchyna*, hastened the decline of Poland. It is, first of all, safe to assume that the *koliivshchyna* contributed to the defeat of the Bar Con-federates in the Ukraine, where this Polish political movement origi-nated and where it had its most significant power base. More impor-tant, however, was the general impact the *haidamak* insurrections had on the Polish state, its political system, and the fortunes of at least part of its ruling elite.

By the eighteenth century, the majority of this elite had abandoned the Jagiellonian policy of relative religious toleration with respect to non-Catholic denominations and had also deviated considerably from the traditional Polish open constitutional system. Both traditions—tol-eration and the traditional constitutional model—had made the Polish-Lithuanian state an attractive option for those Ruthenians/Ukrainians who distrusted or feared the alternative of oppressive Russian autoc-racy and consequently had helped Poland to acquire and to incorpo-rate the Ukrainian lands of the Old Rus' into Crown Poland at the time of the Union of Lublin in 1569.[36] In the eighteenth century, however, one important segment of the Polish ruling elite, determined to sup-press the Orthodox religion in the Ukraine, invited the disasters of in-ternal violence and foreign intervention.

Although the *haidamaks* represented both politically and militarily a far more minor problem than the great seventeenth-century Cossack rebellions, especially the Khmel'nyts'kyi Revolution, Poland's admin-istrative and military resources were nevertheless insufficient for the task of coping with them. In the years 1717–64, the Polish army was maintained at approximately 12,000–16,000 men, although, according to the agreements concluded with Russia in 1716 and ratified in 1717, it was entitled to a standing army of 24,000 men. The military reforms inaugurated after the election of Stanisław Poniatowski did not increase these numbers substantially. The army had not been modernized, and its combat ability certainly could not compare with that of the Polish armies of the sixteenth and seventeenth centuries. The various auxiliary troops, including the Cossack militia and the security detachments in the service of Polish magnates, were unreliable—their members often defected to the *haidamaks*. In contrast to the Polish forces, the *haidamaks* were highly mobile and experienced in partisan warfare; they operated among a populace sympathetic to their activities— and they had nothing to lose. Jędrzej Kitowicz, an astute eighteenth-century commentator on Polish affairs, observed that in order to defeat "fifty *haidamaks*, two or three hundred, or even more [Poles] were necessary, and [the *haidamaks*] had never been defeated by an equal, or even slightly larger, number [of their enemy]."[37] Beginning with the insurrection of 1734, Polish regular troops and auxiliary forces could no longer hold off the *haidamak* detachments. In that year, Verlan's troops fought a pitched battle against the Poles which resulted in a draw and in which 170 Poles perished. In 1737, Polish cavalry troops fought another battle against 250 to 300 *haidamaks*. Out of 224 Polish participants, only 16 escaped alive. Even Russian military forces were often incapable of defeating *haidamak* detachments, as can be seen in the events of the summer of 1750. Most embarrassing for the Polish state was its inability to prevent the *haidamak* units from capturing towns and cities in the Right-bank Ukraine. In the course of all these uprisings, the *haidamak* forces revealed themselves as able to take cities with relative ease, at times in the fashion of regular troops, at other times resorting to trickery. In 1734–37, they took and sacked Zhvanets', Zbarazh, Brody, Pavoloch, Chyhyryn, Uman', and other towns. In 1750, Uman', Vynnytsia, Chyhyryn, Fastiv, and Korsun' fell into their hands. In 1768, they occupied Zhabotyn', Smila, Korsun', Bohuslav, Lysianka, and Uman'. Even after the liquidation of the hard core of the Zalizniak-Gonta forces, approximately 600 *haidamaks* fought a hard battle against combined Polish-Russian forces, during which approximately 300 of them were killed and close to 150 captured.

The *haidamak* movements, including the *koliivshchyna*, had disastrous consequences for Polish-Ukrainian relations since they deepened the already existing Polish-Ukrainian antagonism. The Uman' massacre in which approximately 2,000 people had perished[38] and the subsequent Polish pacification action (under the leadership of Józef Stępkowski, the commanding officer of the Polish troops in the Ukraine) which resulted in the execution of approximately 5,000–7,000 peasants[39] contrituted to the brutalization and demoralization of both the victors and the conquered. The physical devastation of the Right-bank Ukraine, the material losses, and, even more, the psychological scars left by those upheavals on both the Ukrainian and the Polish society were a frightening epilogue to the Ukrainian-Polish relations in the old *Rzeczpospolita.*

The *haidamaks*, and in particular the participants of the *koliivshchyna*, indeed contributed to the continuing decline of Poland. However, their Ukrainian compatriots did not profit from her misfortunes and ultimate fall. In his celebrated poem and political testament entitled "To the Dead, the Living and the Unborn," Taras Shevchenko, with his unerring historical instinct, sensed the tragic consequences of the Polish-Ukranian struggle and addressed his fellow countrymen in these words:

> And you boast because we once
> Brought Poland to destruction. . . .
> It is true, yes, Poland fell,
> But in her fall she crushed you.[40]

The three major *haidamak* insurrections were finally suppressed only with the help of Russia. Requests from the Polish government and the Polish nobility living in the Ukrainian palatinates for the Russian government to protect them against *haidamak* attacks and to reimburse them for the losses sustained at *haidamak* hands provided convenient opportunities for the Russian imperial government to interfere into the internal affairs of the Polish-Lithuanian Commonwealth.[41] These requests represent manifestations of the Polish nobility's extreme selfishness. Russia, not surprisingly, eagerly accepted their invitations to intervene, thus creating a complex situation. The Polish government, and particularly the Polish magnates who had their estates in the Ukraine, became more and more dependent on Russia, not only concerning their relations with foreign powers and major domestic political crises, but also with regard to internal social and religious problems. The Russian authorities exploited Poland's difficulties as a means of keeping the country in a perpetual state of disorder. Officially, the Russian government cooperated with the Polish authorities in the repression of the *haidamaks* and even agreed to the creation of a joint border court with jurisdiction over cases resulting from *haidamak* activities (beginning in 1735, this court held its sessions for fifty years in the town of Motovylivka, the border station of the Kievan Palatinate).[42] Russia also chose to support the Orthodox dissidents through appropriate diplomatic and political channels. The Russian government was interested in subordinating, and eventually in absorbing, a weakened but still un-

divided Polish state, including its Ukrainian and Belorussian territories, through political arrangements, but not as a consequence of social upheavals and religious-national revolts from below.

While the challenge of the *haidamaks* to the Polish state has received
a good deal of attention in scholarship, their relationship to the Russian
ancien régime still awaits a balanced account. Ia. Shulhyn, a Ukrainian
populist historian of the *koliivshchyna,* was the first to address himself
to the problem. He stressed the negative role of Catherine II and the
leading Russian officials in the suppression of this insurrection and
maintained that Russia's policy was opportunistic and her defense of
the Orthodox dissidents a pretext to expand the sphere of Russian supremacy.[43]

On the other side, some Polish historians tended to search for proofs
that the Russian authorities were actually behind the *haidamaks,* encouraging them to rise up and to commit brutal acts against the Polish
nobility.[44] An assessment of relationship between the *haidamaks* and
Russia is further complicated by claims attributed to *haidamak* leaders
and even references in the sources that they were granted Russian imperial charters. During the insurrection of 1734, Verlan asserted that he
had received a charter of appointment from Empress Anne and that
"the whole Ukraine and Rus' as far as the rivers Zbruch and Sluzh
already belong to her Majesty, the Empress."[45] The charter he received was apparently a circular memorandum sent by the Russian
Colonel Polianskii to all Polish military units and Cossack militia forces
with orders to side, in the Polish succession crisis, with Russian troops
against the supporters of Stanisław Leszczyński.[46] Verlan used the
document for his own purposes, however, and, in order to encourage
his followers, simply led them to believe that his actions were in accord
with Russian political objectives.

Zalizniak's *haidamaks* also attempted to convince the population
that they were acting on behalf of Catherine II; one of Zalizniak's charters even invokes her name.[47] However, the "Golden Charter" which
she allegedly granted to Znachko-Iavors'kyi and Zalizniak, a charter to
which some contemporary sources refer, is evidently a forgery.[48] Apparently, the *haidamak* leaders simply invented stories about Russian
support to create the impression that they enjoyed the backing of a
strong and established power. It can be argued that, in reality, they
sought to unify parts of the Right- and Left-bank Ukraine and to establish an autonomous Cossack polity, or to incorporate the conquered
territories into an expanded Cossack military republic of the Zaporozhian Host, in which the leaders of the *koliivshchyna* would assume the
highest offices. Since the Zaporozhian Cossacks played such an influential role in the *haidamak* movement, it is difficult to imagine that
the *haidamaks* would have favored permanent unification with Russia.

Traditionally, the Zaporozhian Host had been the most anti-Muscovite Ukrainian Cossack organization, and it remained committed to an anti-Russian policy until the end.

From its first encounters with the *haidamak* problem, the Russian imperial government took a thoroughly negative attitude toward the *haidamak*s. Beginning in the early 1730s, Empress Anne and her Russian officials began referring to them as thieves, robbers, bandits, and killers who should be apprehended, punished, and executed.[49] On 13 February 1750, Empress Elizabeth issued an order to Mikhail Leont'ev, the Governor-General of Kiev, instructing him to deal firmly with the *haidamak*s.[50] The outbreak of the *koliivshchyna* came to Russian officials as a complete surprise. They, as well as their Empress Catherine II, immediately undertook all the necessary measures to suppress it. Their correspondence and, especially, the manifesto of Catherine II of 9 July 1768 to the Orthodox inhabitants of Podolia, Volhynia, and Kievan land reveal that the imperial government was determined to crush the *haidamak* movement altogether. Then, it was expected, the peasants would submit to Polish authorities and the existing social conditions.[51]

Among the Russian officials who were involved in the suppression of the *koliivshchyna*, at least one made a serious attempt at searching for the causes of the insurrection. Petr A. Rumiantsev, the chief imperial administrator of the Left-bank Ukraine, in his correspondence with other Russian officials, tried to explain the *koliivshchyna* in terms of religious and, by implication, national conflicts between the Orthodox peasant population of the Right-bank Ukraine and their Roman Catholic and Uniate protagonists. Rumiantsev's interpretation of the *koliivshchyna* insurrection as being grounded in religious antagonisms deserves mention not only because it represented the first serious attempt to explain the *koliivshchyna* in broader conceptual terms, but also because some of his statements reflect ideas of denominational neutrality.

> Simple zeal [Rumiantsev wrote] for the pious [Orthodox] faith and the hostility toward it shown by the Roman [Catholic] clergy and spread by them with ferocious inhumanity have undoubtedly been the two extremes that have incited the peasants under Polish [rule] to rebellion. . . .
> And when the hearts of those who suffered from these cruel persecutions were full of hatred against their oppressors, it was not difficult under such conditions for the so-called *haidamak*s to convince the unenlightened minds of the common people [to commit] their well-known [acts of] impudence.[52]

In his correspondence, Rumiantsev also defended the Zaporozhian Host against charges of complicity in the *koliivshchyna* and requested the removal of Stępkowski's punitive expeditionary forces from the Right-bank Ukrainian territories. Rumiantsev revealed himself as an expert on Ukrainian affairs as well by suggesting, eleven years after the insurrection, that the Orthodox in the Polish Ukraine would experience a "terror of extreme destruction," and that "so long as [Orthodox] piety is not extinguished in this land, the hearts of Orthodox inhabitants will always be inclined toward us [the Russians]."⁵³ Rumiantsev's isolated position and even his apparent sympathy for those involved in the *haidamak* movement may, however, have been prompted by his desire to appear as a lord protector of the Ukraine and of her people.

In general, the Russian imperial government treated the *haidamaks* as dangerous criminal elements and acted in accordance with the wishes of both the great Polish magnates and the lesser nobility. As the extensive report of the Chancery of the Kiev Governor-General indicates, the *haidamak* participants who came from the Ukrainian territories under the Russian sovereignty escaped death sentences, although they were severely punished by the Russian authorities.⁵⁴ Maksym Zalizniak, for example, was condemned to death on the wheel, but his sentence was commuted to "150 lashes with a whip, tearing out of the nostril, branding on the forehead and the cheeks, deportation to Nerchinsk in Siberia, and hard labor for life."⁵⁵

The Russian government had no intention of tolerating either the destabilization of the established sociopolitical order or the forceful abolition of existing property relationships: both represented serious threats to the institution of serfdom. The Russian authorities were apparently also concerned lest the social turmoil spread from the Right-bank Ukraine into the Ukrainian territories under Russian sovereignty, or even into Russia proper. The great Russian rebellions in which usually Russian Cossacks, peasants, lower-class burghers, and non-Russian nationalities participated tended to follow chronologically Ukrainian precedents established in the Polish-Lithuanian Commonwealth. The insurrection under the leadership of Ivan Bolotnikov (1606–07), for example, followed the Ukrainian Cossack and peasant rebellions under the leadership of Kryshtof Kosyns'kyi, Hryhorii Loboda, and Nalyvaiko in the 1590s. Stenka Razin's rebellion (1667–71) followed the great Ukrainian Revolution of 1648–54 led by Bohdan Khmel'nyts'kyi, and the subsequent "Ruin" in the Ukraine. The insurrection under the leadership of Kondrat Bulavin (1707–09), who had established close relations with the Zaporozhian Host, followed major antitsarist activities in the Ukraine and occurred simultaneously with Hetman Mazepa's break with Peter I and the Russian Empire. Finally, the rebellion led by Emelian Pugachev (1773–75) began only five years after the *koliivshchyna*. Interestingly enough, not a single peasant insurrection worth mentioning against the Polish magnates or nobility occurred on ethnic Polish territories in early modern history. So far, historians have been unable to explain this absence of popular upheavals in Poland proper.

Finally, the Russian imperial government was apprehensive about any sociopolitical movement that would encourage the continuation or expansion of the Ukrainian Cossack autonomy, whether in its hetmanite (military-aristocratic), Zaporozhian (military-democratic), or *haidamak* (military-plebeian) form. Following the abolition of the Ukrainian Hetmanate in 1764, seven years after the outbreak of the *koliivshchyna*, and just prior to the final repression of the Pugachev rebellion, the Russian government, in June of 1775, abolished and destroyed the Zaporozhian Host.[56] Russia had accomplished the absorption of the Ukraine and had thus eliminated her autonomous and potentially independent political forces.

NOTES

1   The most important source materials directly pertaining to the Ukrainian *haidamak*s have been published in "Akty o gaidamakakh 1700-1768," *Arkhiv Iugo-Zapadnoi Rossii* (cited hereafter as *AIuZR*), part 3, vol. 3 (Kiev, 1876); [P. N. Krechetnikov], "Zhurnal general-majora Petra Nikiticha Krechetnikova, . . . o dvizhenii i voennykh deistviiakh v Pol'she v 1767 i 1768 godax," *Chteniia v Obshchestve istorii i drevnostei rossiiskikh pri Moskovskom universitete* (cited hereafter as *ChOIDR*), book 3 (1863), pp. 1-205; [N. Kostomarov], "Materialy dlia istorii Koliivshchiny ili rezni 1768 g.," *Kievskaia starina* (cited hereafter as *KS*), no. 8 (1882): 297-321; "Perepiska gr. P. A. Rumiantseva o vosstanii v Ukraine," *KS*, no. 9 (1882): 523-51; no. 10, 89-118; *KS*, nos. 9-10 (1883): 254-86; [A. Andrievskii], "Reliatsii kievskogo general-gubernatora za 1768 i 1769 gg.," *Chteniia v Istoricheskom obshchestve Nestora-letopistsa*," book 7 (1893), pp. 73-211; [A. Kryzhanovs'kyi and M. Hrushevs'kyi], "Materialy do istorii Koliivshchyny. I. Vasylyians'ki zapysky i lysty pro Koliivshchynu," *Zapysky Naukovoho Tovarystva im. Shevchenka* (cited hereafter as *ZNTSh*) 57 (1904): 2-24; *Kodens'ka knyha sudovykh sprav, Ukrains'kyi Arkhiv*, vol. 2 (Kiev, 1931); and most recently in I. L. Butych and F. P. Shevchenko, eds., *Haidamats'kyi rukh na Ukraini v XVIII st.* (Kiev, 1970). For the related source materials on the religious and socioeconomic aspects of the *haidamak* movements, cf. "Arkhimandrit Mel'khisedek Znachko-Iavors'kii, 1759-1771 g.," "Materialy do istorii pravoslaviia v XVIII v.," *AIuZR*, part 1, vols. 2-3 (1864); "Akty o ekonomicheskikh i pravovykh otnosheniiakh krestian v XVIII veke (1700-1799)," *AIuZR*, part 6, vol. 2 (1870).

The memoirs of contemporaries, folklore, and literary materials represent other types of sources. From among the Polish memoirists, the following ought to be mentioned: Jan Lippoman ("Bunt hajdamaków na Ukrainie r. 1768"), Weronika Krebs (nee Młladanowicz) ("Opis autentyczny rzezi humańskiej. . . ."), Paweł Młladanowicz ("Rzeź humańska czyli historya rewolucyi zrobionej przez Żeleźniaka i Gontę") which, together with other materials, were published by H. Mościcki, ed., in *Z dziejów hajdamaczyzny*, parts 1-2 (*Dzieje porozbiorowe narodu polskiego w żywym słowie*, vols. 5-6 [Warsaw, 1905]). These memoirs have to be treated with caution because Weronika and Paweł Młladanowicz, the children of Rafał Młladanowicz (the governor of Uman'), were minors at the time of the insurrection of 1768 and wrote down their accounts long after the event. The treatise of Paweł Mładanowicz cannot be regarded as "history" but rather as a literary and ideological work aimed at eulogizing the Polish nobility in the Ukraine in the face of the tragedy that befell them. It has already been suggested that the Mładanowicz "memoirs" were written in the 1820s (H. Iu. Khraban, "Pro spohady Pavla Mladanovycha [do 200-richchia povstannia 1768 r.]," *Istorychni dzherela ta ikh vykorystannia,* issue 4 [1969], pp. 47-65, especially pp. 48-49, 52-55, 58-59).

The work of Jan Lippoman, which was completed only in 1830, falls into a similar category of literature. Lippoman's memoirs have not yet been studied for their ideological content. For some tentative observations on the Polish "memoirs," as well as on other Polish literary works, see V. Shchurat, "Koliivshchyna v pols'kii literaturi do 1841," *ZNTSh* 97 (1910), and separately; S. F. Ivanytskii, "Pol'skie memuary o krest'ianskom vosstanii 1768 g. (Koliivshchina)," *Uchenye zapiski Leningradskogo gosudarstvennogo pedagogicheskogo instituta* 11 (1938): 119-47; H. Iu. Khraban, "Memuary iak istorychne dzherelo vyvchennia narodno-vyzvol'noho povstannia 1768 r.," *Koliivshchyna 1768 (Materialy iuvileinoi naukovoi sesii prysviachenoi 200-richchiu povstannia)* (Kiev, 1970), pp. 134-46. The memoirs of Adam Moszczeński (*Pamiętnik do historyi polskiej w ostatnich latach panowania Augusta III i pierwszych Stanisława Poniatowskiego,* ed. H. Mościcki [*Dzieje porozbiorowe narodu polskiego w żywym słowie,* vol. 4] [Warsaw, 1905]) and Karl Chojecki ("Zapiski Karla Khoeckogo 1768-1776," ed. V. Antonovych, *KS,* no. 1 (1883): 145-60; no. 3: 630-46; no. 11: 433-51; no. 12: 593-608) belong in a different category of memoir literature. The Polish and Ukrainian folklore materials have not yet been adequately studied, nor have the relevant literary works, such as the anonymous Polish poem about the Uman' massacre ([I. Franko], "Materialy do istorii Koliivshchyny. III. Pols'ka poema pro umans'ku rizniu," *ZNTSh* 13 [1904]: 1-40), and the famous work by Taras Shevchenko, "Haidamaky" (1841). For a relatively satisfactory account of Shevchenko's views on the *haidamaks,* confer M. I. Marchenko, *Istorychne mynule ukrains'koho narodu v tvorchosti T. H. Shevchenka* (Kiev, 1957), pp. 80-118. Regarding other relevant source materials, see the bibliography on the *haidamaks* in *Haidamats'kyi rukh na Ukraini v XVIII st.,* pp. 567-74.

2 Surprisingly enough, the monographic literature on the *haidamaks* is not very extensive. The most important studies on the *haidamaks* are: M. A. Maksymovych, "Skazanie o Koliivshchine" (1839), in *Sobranie sochinenii,* vol. 1 (1876), pp. 623-53 and "Izvestiia o gaidamakakh" (1845), ibid., pp. 572-94; A. Skal'kovskii, *Naezdy gaidamakov na Zapadnuiu Ukrainu v XVIII st. 1733-1768* (Odessa, 1845); V. Antonovych, *Issledovanie o gaidamakakh po aktam 1700-1768 gg.* (Kiev, 1876), and his *Predislovie* to "Akty o gaidamakakh (1700-1768)," *AIuZR,* part 3, vol. 3 (Kiev, 1876), pp. 1-128, and "Umanskii sotnik Ivan Gonta (1768 g.)," *KS,* no. 11 (1882): 250-76; Ia. Shulhyn, *Ocherk Koliivshchiny po neizdannym i izdannym dokumentam 1768 i blizhaishikh godov* (Kiev, 1890); Shtajnshnaider, *K istorii Umanskoi rezni 1768 g. (Materialy i issledovaniia po istorii evreev v Pol'she i Iugo-Zapadnoi Rossii),* issue 1 (Kiev, 1908); Fr. Rawita-Gawroński, *Historya ruchów hajdamackich (w. XVIII),* 2 vols. (Brody, 1913); O. Hermaize, "Koliivshchyna v svitli novoznaidenykh materialiv," *Ukraina,* books 1-2 (1924); V. Grekov, "Bunt siromy 1768 r.," *Zapysky istoryko-filolohichnoho viddilu Vseukrains'koi Akademii Nauk* 11 (1927): 226-32; N. Polons'ka-Vasylenko, "Do istorii povstannia na Zaporizhzhi 1768 roku" (1942), in her

Zaporizhzhia XVIII stolittia ta ioho spadshchyna, 2 vols. (Munich, 1965-1976), vol. 1, pp. 107-26; V. O. Holobuts'kyi, ''Gaidamatskoe dvizhenie na Zaporozhe vo vremia 'Koliivshchiny' i krest'ianskogo vosstaniia pod predvoditel'stvom E. I. Pugacheva,'' *Istoricheskie zapiski* (cited hereafter as *IZ*) 55 (1956): 310-43; O. P. Lola, *Haidamats'kyi rukh na Ukraini (20-60 rr. XVIII st.)* (Kiev, 1965); W. A. Serczyk, *Koliszczyzna (Zeszyty Naukowe Uniwersytetu Jagiellońskiego* 113, Prace historyczne, Zeszyt 24) (Cracow, 1968), as well as his popular survey of the history of *haidamaks (Hajdamacy* [Cracow, 1972]); *Koliivshchyna 1768*, including ten articles of interest to the historian; H. Iu. Khraban, ''Z istorii haidamachchyny,'' *Ukrains'kyi istorychnyi zhurnal* (cited hereafter as *UIZh*), no. 6 (1968): 96-103; V. V. Hrabovets'kyi, ''Vidhuk haidamats'koho rukhu na zakhidnoukrains'kykh zemliakh,'' *UIZh*, no. 6 (1968): 104-110; I. O. Hurzhii and V. M. Kulakovs'kyi, ''Vyznachna podiia v istorii ukrains'koho narodu (Do 200-richchia Koliivshchyny),'' *UIZh*, no. 7 (1968), 58-67; F. P. Shevchenko, ''Pro mizhnarodne znachennia povstannia 1768 r. na pravoberezhnii Ukraini,'' *UIZh*, no. 9 (1968): 11-23; P. Mirchuk, *Koliivshchyna (Haidamats'ke povstannia 1768 r.)* (New York, 1973). For a review article of the more recent literature on the *haidamaks*, see Z. E. Kohut, ''Myths Old and New: The Haidamak Movement and the Koliivshchyna (1768) in Recent Historiography,'' *Harvard Ukrainian Studies* 1, no. 3 (1977): 359-78. Concerning additional literature, consult the bibliography on the *haidamaks*, albeit incomplete, in *Haidamats'kyi rukh na Ukraini v XVIII st.*, pp. 567-74.

3 *AIuZR*, part 3, vol. 3, pp. 22-24; *Haidamats'kyi rukh na Ukraini v XVIII v.*, pp. 25-27, especially p. 26.

4 Antonovych, *Izsledovanie o gaidamakakh po aktam 1700-1768 g.*, pp. 6-9.

5 For the sources and the literature on the *koliivshchyna*, see above notes 1 and 2.

6 For the latest restatement of this interpretation and the relevant literature, cf. K. I. Stetsiuk, ''Koliivshchyna—velyke narodno-vyzvol'ne antyfeodal'ne povstannia na Ukraini XVIII v.,'' *Koliivshchyna 1768*, p. 72, n. 2.

7 V. Shcherbyna, ''O proiskhozhdenii slova 'Koliivshchina','' *KS*, no. 2 (1893): 356-58. Shcherbyna's explanation of this term has been accepted by Serczyk (*Koliszczyzna*, p. 7, n. 1).

8 Serczyk, *Koliszczyzna*, pp. 25-26; *Hajdamacy*, p. 158. For a discussion of the latifundia economy of the Polish magnates, see his *Gospodarstwo magnackie w województwie podolskim w drugiej polowie XVIII wieku* (Wrocław-Warsaw-Cracow, 1965), as well as an earlier work by A. I. Baranovich, *Magnatskoe khoziaistvo na Iuge Volyni v XVIII v.* (Moscow, 1955).

9 The foundations for the study of the social composition of the *haidamak* movements have been laid by V. Antonovych, *Issledovanie . . . / Predislovie*, and Ia. Shulhyn, *Ocherk Koliivshchiny*. Little progress has been made on the subject since the publication of these studies. Holobuts'kyi's study on the *haidamak* movement in the Zaporozhian Host (*IZ* 55 [1956]: 310-43) can be regarded as an exception to this general observation.

10 Typical examples of this approach can be found in articles by D. I. Myshko, ''Borot'ba trudiashchykh mas Pravoberezhnoi Ukrainy na peredodni Koliivshchyny za svoie vyzvolennia i vozz'iednannia z Rosiieiu (30-50-ti roky XVIII v.),'' *Koliivshchyna 1768*, pp. 45-56, and by K. I. Stetsiuk, ''Koliivshchyna—velyke narodno-vyzvol'ne antyfeodal'ne povstannia na Ukraini XVIII v.,'' *Koliivshchyna 1768*, pp. 66-80.

11 Antonovych, *Issledovanie . . . / Predislovie*, pp. 21–22.

12 *Kodens'ka knyha sudovykh sprav (Ukrains'kyi Arkhiv*, vol. 2 [Kiev, 1931]) (cited hereafter as *KK*).

13 *KK*, pp. 383–92.

14 Their names were Marcin Ostrowski, Jan Gradowski (interestingly enough, referred to as a "nobleman-Ruthenian") and Jan Stromenecki (*KK*, pp. 114, 116–22, 189–91).

15 Stanislaw Rogowski and the brothers Bazyli and Piotr Obornicki.

16 Jan Boiemski *(ritus graeci)*, Tymofei Czopowski, Iwan Wiśniowski, Jan Biliński, Stefan Ilnicki, Antoni Bukowski.

17 *KK*, p. 117.

18 For his activities, see "Akty o gaidamakakh 1700–1768," *AIuZR*, part 3, vol. 3, pp. 68–75, 95, 96, 111, 176; and *Haidamats'kyi rukh na Ukraini v XVIII v.*, p. 575.

19 V. Antonovych's classical biographical essay on Gonta is still unsurpassed ("Umanskii sotnik Ivan Gonta 1768 g.," *KS*, no. 11 [1882]: 250–76).

20 For a good analysis of the *siroma*, consult the informative study by V. O. Holobuts'kyi, *IZ* 55 (1956): 310–43.

21 For a biography of Zalizniak, see V. O. Holobuts'kyi, *Maksim Zhelezniak* (Moscow, 1960).

22 Krechetnikov, "Zhurnal . . . ," *ChOIDR*, book 3 (1863), pp. 178, 180.

23 Serczyk, *Koliszczyzna*, pp. 122, 124.

24 Krechetnikov, "Zhurnal . . . ," *ChOIDR*, book 3 (1863): 183–203.

25 Antonovych observed, quite correctly, that the *haidamak* movement began to have clear social and political aims only around 1734 (*Issledovania . . . / Predislovie*, p. 11).

26 For some names of the Uniate priests who were killed, and the description of the attacks on the Uniate clergy, see the petition by the Uniate clergy of the Kievan archdiocese ("Skargi i zażalenia xięży unitów obrządku greckiego archidyecezyj kijowskiej," *Z dziejów hajdamaczyzny*, part 2, pp. 16–29). The *Kodna Book* contains revealing materials pertaining to the case of Semen Falinowski, the son of Mikołaj Falinowski, an executed Uniate priest, against the Orthodox priest Jan Starzewski, who was accused of persecution and complicity in the killing of the Uniate priest on Zalizniak's orders (*KK*, pp. 74–75, 85–93).

27 For contemporary accusations, see the instruction for the deputies to the Diet of the Kievan Palatinate of 1768. The relevant excerpt from the instruction (located in the Central State Archive of the Ukrainian Soviet Socialist Republic in Kiev, F. 11, ob. 1, manuscript 53, p. 741) was published by W. A. Serczyk in his informative study entitled "Melchizedek Znaczko-Jaworski i monaster motreniński przed wybuchem koliszczyzny," *Studia Historyczne* 11, no. 3 (1968): 297–322, especially 297. Similar charges were made by Lippoman and the authors of the Uniate petition (*Z dziejów hajdamaczyzny*, part 1, p. 52; part 2, pp. 23–28).

In his classical work on the domestic history of Poland in the last third of the eighteenth century, T. Korzon attributed the outbreak of the *koliivshchyna* to the Orthodox fanaticism of Mel'khisedek Znachko-Iavors'kyi, who allegedly incited the uneducated local population (*Wewnętrzne dzieje Polski za Stanislawa Augusta, 1764–1794*, vol. 1 [Cracow-Warsaw, 1897], p. 200). Korzon was also extremely critical of Ia. Shulhyn's work on the *koliivshchyna* ("Nowa książka o koliwszczyźnie," *Kwartalnik historyczny*, no. 3 (1892): 527–40). For Ia. Shulhyn's reply, see "Pravda o Koliivshchine pol'skogo istorika g. Korzona," *KS*, no. 1 (1893): 126–60.

246 JAROSLAW PELENSKI

28 "Arkhimandrit Mel'khisedek Znachko-Iavors'kyi, 1759–1771 g.," "Materialy dlia istorii pravoslaviia v Zapadnoi Ukraine v XVIII st.," *AIuZR*, part 1, vol. 3 (1864), p. 716.

29 Ibid., p. 715. For the most recent evaluation of the activities of Mel'khisedek Znachko-Iavors'kyi, see Serczyk's article cited above n. 27 and his *Koliszczyzna*, pp. 50–68.

30 An almost complete register of a Cossack company under the leadership of Stefan Kifa, with an appendix specifically enumerating the subofficers in charge of squads of ten men, is available from the period of the insurrection of 1734. This register was originally written in "Ruthenian script" and translated into Polish by Polish military authorities conducting interrogations of *haidamaks* captured in the insurrection of 1734 (*AIuZR*, part 3, vol. 3 [1876], pp. 74–75). Interestingly enough, Stefan Kifa is referred to in this register as "his grace, Lord . . . ." Apparently there were other registers of the insurrectionists, but they were lost in the course of the military activities (ibid., p. 75).

31 *AIuZR*, part 3, vol. 3 (1876), p. 68.

32 *Haidamats'kyi rukh na Ukraini v XVIII st.*, p. 361.

33 Ibid., pp. 349, 351.

34 Ibid., p. 373.

35 Khraban, "Memuary . . . ," *Koliivshchyna 1768*, p. 143.

36 For the most recent discussion and literature on this problem, see J. Pelenski, "The Incorporation of the Ukrainian Lands of Old Rus' into Crown Poland (1569), (Socio-Material Interest and Ideology—A Reexamination)," *American Contributions to the Seventh International Congress of Slavists* (Warsaw, August 21–27, 1973), vol. 3: *History* (The Hague–Paris, 1973), pp. 19–52; idem., "Inkorporacja ukraińskich ziem dawnej Rusi do Korony w 1569 roku: Ideologia i korzyści—próba nowego spojrzenia," *Przegląd historyczny* 65, no. 2 (1974): 243–62; idem., "Pravni ta ideologichni obgruntuvannia vkliuchennia ukrains'kykh zemel' do Koronnoi Pol'shchi (1569)," *Iuvileinyi Zbirnyk Ukrains'koi Vil'noi Akademii Nauk v Kanadi* (Winnipeg, 1976), pp. 1–14.

37 J. Kitowicz, *Opis obyczajów za panowania Augusta III* (Wrocław, 1951), p. 342.

38 Zalizniak stated in his interrogation that approximately 2,000 people were killed in the Uman' massacre (*Haidamats'kyi rukh na Ukraini v XVIII st.*, p. 361). For the first analysis of the figures attested in the sources and a critical evaluation, see [Franko], "Materialy . . . ," *ZNTSh* 13 (1904), pp. 33–35.

39 For another assessment of the figures, consult Serczyk, *Koliszczyzna*, p. 167.

40 T. Shevchenko, *Povne vydannia tvoriv*, 2nd ed., vol. 2 (Chicago, 1961), p. 115.

41 The decisions and instructions of the Diets of the Braclav and Kiev Palatinates by themselves provide for the years 1735–1750 ample evidence for the continuous attempts on the part of the Polish nobility to involve the Russian imperial government in affairs connected with the *haidamaks* (*AIuZR*, part 3, vol. 3 (1876), pp. 167–82, 220–25, 290–95, 297–301, 317–21, 443–47, 447–50, 479–90, 490–93, 493–508. See also Antonovych, *Issledovanie . . . / Predislovie*, pp. 56–57.

42 Antonovych, *Issledovanie . . . / Predislovie*, p. 91.

43 The principal Russian officials involved in the decision that led to the suppression of the *koliivshchyna* were: Major-General Petr N. Krechetnikov, in charge of the Russian military operations in the Right-bank Ukraine, 1767–68; Fedor M. Voieikov, the governor-general of Kiev; Petr A. Rumiantsev, the president of the second Little

Russian College, the governor-general of Little Russia, the chief Russian administrator of the Left-bank Ukraine and the supervisor of the Zaporozhian Host; Nikolai V. Repnin, the Russian envoy to Poland; and Nikita I. Panin, in charge of Russian foreign policy at that time. For Shulhyn's comments, see his *Ocherk,* pp. 185–87, 190–91, 196.

44 For example, T. Morawski gave the *haidamak* chapter of his multivolume history of the Polish people a title that can be translated "Moscow Unleashed the *Haidamaks*" (*Dzieje narodu polskiego,* vol. 5 [Poznań, 1877]).

45 *AIuZR,* part 3, vol. 3 (1876), p. 70. For a similar statement, see ibid., p. 71.

46 Antonovych, *Issledovanie . . . /Predislovie,* p. 107.

47 *Haidamats'kyi rukh na Ukraini v XVIII st.,* p. 347.

48 Not a single copy of this falsified document has been found by scholars so far. It is not clear from what document its French translation was prepared in the nineteenth century. The French translation of the document was republished by Rawita-Gawroński, *Historya ruchów hajdamackich (w. XVIII),* vol. 2, pp. 105–6.

49 *Haidamats'kyi rukh na Ukraini v XVIII st.,* pp. 41, 55–56.

50 Ibid., pp. 141–42.

51 Ibid., pp. 376–77.

52 See Rumiantsev's letter of 24 August 1768 ("Perepiska gr. P. A. Rumiantseva . . . ," *KS,* no. 10 (1882): 101–2).

53 See Rumiantsev's letter of 17 September 1779 ("Perepiska gr. P. A. Rumiantseva . . . ," *KS,* nos. 9–10 [1883]: 283–84).

54 *Haidamats'kyi rukh na Ukraini v XVIII st.,* pp. 431–58.

55 Ibid., pp. 444–45.

56 For the text of Catherine's most interesting *ukaz* on the abolition of the Zaporozhian Host, see *Haidamats'kyi rukh na Ukraini v XVIII st.,* pp. 560–64.

THE MODEL OF REVOLUTION IN EAST CENTRAL EUROPEAN POLITICAL THOUGHT DURING THE NAPOLEONIC ERA

Jerzy Skowronek, University of Warsaw

At the turn of the nineteenth century, the term "revolution" gained wide currency, accompanied, as is often the case, by a diversification in the functions and connotations concealed behind the word as it was applied to different situations and sociopolitical structures in individual countries. This diversification was perhaps most apparent in East Central and Southeastern Europe. Most of the countries in that region experienced a rapid increase in contacts with the external world, especially with Western Europe at the turn of the nineteenth century. While this was often simply a matter of renewing long neglected relationships (as was the case of Poland, Hungary, Greece, and, to some extent, Russia as well), it was sometimes also a question of initiating new contacts that had not existed before, chiefly in the form of ideology and propaganda (as was the case among the Bulgarians, Greeks, Romanians, and Southern Slavs).

The fundamentally distinct nature of the region meant that neither ideas nor ideologies were accepted there *in toto*, but only piecemeal and rather passively. They underwent profound modifications and adaptations as they confronted the sociopolitical situation in each country. Even enlightened representatives of the most developed societies of East Central Europe (for example, the Czechs and Poles), although enthusiastic about the ideas of the Enlightenment and some of the slogans of the French Revolution, found them unsuitable for a practical program of political and social action.[1] In those countries under Habsburg rule, the attractiveness of the program advocated by the moderate current of the French Revolution in the sphere of social reform had been attenuated by the thorough-going reform of administration, law, and in part even social relations, which had been carried out by Maria Theresa and especially her son Joseph II during the second half of the eighteenth century. These reforms went some way toward defusing the threat of social unrest within the Empire by improving the condition of some nationalities—particularly in education—and limiting the domination of the Magyars. This strengthened pro-Habsburg sentiments among the first generation of Slav nationalists in the Austrian Empire.[2] The full-fledged French model of radical revolution encountered counterproposals in the shape of a program of reforms that had either already been introduced or had been expected and that was recognized by the majority of nationalists as being adequate.

248

This situation applied particularly to the countries of Southeastern Europe. For centuries they had been subjected to foreign (Austrian, Hungarian, or Turkish) rule, they were dominated by feudal, often very backward and semideveloped, social structures, and the low level of social consciousness prevailing in them made the conduct of large-scale political and propaganda campaigns rather difficult. In this situation the influence of the American and, later, the French Revolutions on the political aspirations of those countries was minimal. Society—or rather its politically and intellectually active elements—was at that time beginning a struggle for minimal reforms along the lines of the demands of the moderate current of the Enlightenment, above all for a distinct linguistic and cultural, but very rarely political, identity. These were the aims set by the still weak national movements among the Bulgarians and the Slovaks, and, to some extent, the Romanians and Albanians as well.

Stray fragments of information concerning the French Revolution occasionally reached the leaders of these movements, generally via the German, Austrian, or Russian press, or some other publication in German or Russian. Sometimes the role of intermediary in the transmission of this information was played by participants in the Polish and Greek national liberation movements. The Poles performed this service for the Romanians, the Greeks for the Bulgarians, Albanians, and Romanians.[3] Unfortunately, it is not known whether news of the American Revoltuion was similarly transmitted. It is possible that some account penetrated to parts of the Balkan countries (e.g., to the Romanian provinces) together with the popularization of the figure of Tadeusz Kościuszko as a hero of revolutions on two continents. But it can be assumed that the American Revolution was very little known and had no impact on the theories and practice of political movements in the Balkans around the turn of the nineteenth century, even though as a classic combination of struggle for independence with fundamental internal sociopolitical reforms, it was the American Revolution which should have played an incomparably greater role than the French one.

That it was so and not otherwise was due to the great geographical distance of the American events and to the very sketchy knowledge of the affairs of that continent, limited to what could be gleaned from the German and Russian press. Equally important was the understandable view that the French Revolution and its consequences were influencing change in the various countries of Central and Southeastern Europe, while the American Revolution could play no such role. The total absence of propaganda in that part of Europe by representatives of the American Revolution or the young American republic contrasted with the fairly widespread and variegated propaganda provided by the French Revolution, and this also had its effects.

The slogans of the Revolution—derived from the popularization of the ideas of the French Enlightenment in previous decades—were promulgated during the period under consideration in émigré communities in France, chiefly among Poles and Greeks, but sporadically among small groups from other countries as well. Propaganda work of this kind was carried out by Revolutionary and, later, Napoleonic France through official and unofficial representatives in Greece and the Romanian provinces, and, in the years 1806–12, also among the Serbs and Croats.[4] However, only in the pre-Napoleonic period did this become a classic case of "exporting revolution" in the sense of proposing that the model of revolution as it arose in France in the years 1789–95 be recreated elsewhere. In the periods of the Consulate and the Empire, the propaganda campaigns were aimed at encouraging individual nations of that part of Europe to collaborate politically and militarily with France as the best avenue for regaining independence or for substantially improving their situation.

This propaganda found a favorable reception in countries where the desire for freedom was strong. There a peculiar model of revolution— or revolutionary activity—was born: the model, if one may call it that, of "national revolution." Within the confines of Southeastern Europe this model was elaborated by representatives of the nations most advanced in their aspirations to gain freedom. It was done in the years 1793–94 by one of the leaders of the so-called Hungarian Jacobins, Ignazius Martinovics, a revolutionary of Serbian extraction who was founder and leader of the Liberty and Equality Society. In his draft constitution, drawn up in the fall of 1793, he demanded a revolutionary struggle for democratic civic rights, including universal suffrage, participation of citizens in deciding affairs of state, and abolition of censorship and of the secret police. The future state embracing the Habsburg lands—or at least a substantial portion of them—was to be a constitutional monarchy with a representative government answerable to the people. National problems were to be solved by granting territorial autonomy to every nation and by introducing a state structure approximating a federation of equal nations. Other Hungarian Jacobins demanded, in addition, a bicameral parliament, the abolition of the aristocracy as a privileged social group and the confiscation of its estates, the confiscation of the estates of the church and of the enemies of the Revolution,[5] and even the introduction of a republican system. They intended to accomplish this by means of a revolutionary coup d'état, carried out with the aid of small groups of Jacobins in the army. Only a few envisaged any broader participation by the masses.

The above model of revolution—the most radical in that part of Europe—combined elements of both eighteenth-century revolutions. The bicameral parliament and broad territorial autonomy were in keeping with the American model, while the social demands had their source in the French Revolution, although one can find a few analogous elements in the American one as well.

A similar, though different in some respects, model of revolution was created by the first generation of modern Greek patriots headed by Rhigas Velestinlis. His movement arose in 1798 in an atmosphere of considerably more explicit cooperation with France, and perhaps even with Bonaparte, at least in the period when hopes connected with the Egyptian expedition of the future ruler of France were at their peak. The factors determining the content of Velestinlis's project were the models of the French Revolution and an idealized picture of the past, especially the period of the waning of the Byzantine Empire, combined with a conviction regarding the inevitability of fundamental changes in the Ottoman Empire.

In his *Revolutionary Proclamation* and draft of a future constitution, Velestinlis considered the main aim to be the founding of a democratic state that would embrace all the Balkan peoples under the rule of the sultan and would even extend to Asia Minor. It was to be based on the principles of the Declaration of the Rights of Man and the Citizen, and especially on that fundamental slogan of the French Revolution: Liberty, Equality, Fraternity. The author of the draft did not concern himself with a more detailed discussion of principles and social reforms but instead concentrated his whole attention on the political structure of the state. He wanted above all to ensure the equality, freedom, and unification of the Balkan peoples within the framework of a single state, where, alongside a strong, centralized executive power, there would be a decentralized legislative power.[6] He thought that in this way he could combine the unity of the state with considerable freedom and separate identity for the nations comprising it, while at the same time avoiding antagonisms between them.

The most elaborate models of revolution at the end of the eighteenth century were the work of groups of radicals, the so-called Polish Jacobins, in the Polish patriotic camp during the Four-Year *Sejm* and the Kościuszko Insurrection (i.e., in the years 1790–95).[7] In many speeches, especially during the Kościuszko Insurrection, we find demands similar to those in Martinovics's program, sometimes even more radical, but in any case more detailed and specific. Here the models of the French Revolution dominated, despite the interest in, and sympathy for, the American Revolution, which was much greater than in other countries of the region.[8] The Polish Jacobins attempted to derive maximum benefit from the example of the most radical Parisian leaders regarding tactics and revolutionary propaganda for reaching the broad masses of the people, concentrated almost exclusively in the largest towns, and skillfully organizing them for specific purposes.

Some publicists, chiefly those who had traveled in the United States, painted a similar vision of revolution on the basis of their observation of American realities. They did this with the purpose of utilizing the American experience for the benefit of their own people, but the scanty acquaintance with reality that superficial observation can produce meant that the picture of the American Revolution became in fact just one more model. The best example of this is the account of the young Polish poet and advocate of progressive ideas, Tomasz Kajetan Węgierski (1756–87), who traveled in America in 1783. His picture of the Revolution was dominated by the conviction—typical of the Enlightenment—that it would initiate a return on the part of man and society to a life in harmony with nature and, at the same time, would bring about the national integration of very heterogeneous, and even mutually hostile, ethnic groups by guaranteeing everyone maximum freedom, independence, and opportunities to achieve prosperity.[9]

All the above-mentioned models of revolution created before the Napoleonic period had a number of features in common. A very minor place—especially in comparison with the French models—was allotted to social problems, to demands for radical social reforms. This was a result partly of the dominant role played by the privileged feudal strata in most of the societies of East Central and Southeastern Europe (with the exception of the Greek), but primarily it was caused by the aims, which were different from those in the West, of the political movements that created these models of revolution.

In this part of Europe revolutionary demands or programs were drawn up by the most radical activists of the national movements, above all those who had set the goal of independence for themselves. The principal and most urgent task was to win complete freedom for one's own people, to guarantee it the best conditions for development. The chief functions of social reforms were to strengthen and modernize the nation, thereby increasing its chances of victory. In Southeastern Europe the national problem was further complicated by the necessity of preventing antagonisms among the various peoples striving toward liberation. The universal slogans of the French Revolution were translated into concrete sociopolitical demands, although without altogether losing their universal character. Proposals concerning agrarian reforms, the extent to which feudal rights should be abolished and the methods of abolishing them, and the structure and powers of government varied not only from country to country, but even within the left wing of the same national movement. Radicals everywhere, however, demanded equal rights for all, the extension of public influence on government, the proclamation of a constitution, and the introduction of a parliamentary system of government.

In the moderate wing, the dominance of national demands was even more marked. The intensified struggle for legislative powers by the Hungarian Parliament, the demands for the independence of the Kingdom of Hungary, and the increased efforts of the Croats to achieve separate political status and the unification of their country within the framework of the Habsburg Empire can serve as examples.[10] Only in the initial period of the French Revolution did Hungarian pamphleteers, who wrote with particular sympathy of events in France, step up their attacks on the "usurpative feudal system" and call for the overthrow of all feudal privileges, the introduction of real equality of rights, and the establishment of a republican system.[11]

The Napoleonic period saw a fundamental modification of earlier models of revolution, and in many cases their complete collapse. As time went on, interest in the American Revolution waned to the point where the model of state and society it had created was of interest only to the small number of people who had been in America. On the other hand, the Jacobin terror had compromised the French Revolution in the eyes of those who had initially supported it with enthusiasm, the representatives of the moderate current of the Enlightenment, while, at the same time, the consolidation of the power of the bourgeoisie and, especially, the reign of Napoleon were sources of profound disappointment to the radicals.[12] These sentiments were intensified in some countries—especially in Poland and Greece—by the collapse of the hopes of immediate aid from France and, even more, of their own aspirations for national liberation.

The activity of the radical groups in most of the national movements dwindled to nothing, and where it was continued there was a drastic scaling-down of the model of revolution elaborated by the organizing groups. To a greater degree than before, the program of struggle for freedom and bourgeois social reforms was bound up with French successes and hopes of French help. During times when these hopes were running particularly high, some radicals continued to demand the implementation of basic social reforms and, at the same time, the creation of strong state power. This was what the Polish Jacobins did in 1806–07 by starting a peculiarly national discussion in the press of the prospects for development of the Polish state, society, and nation.[13] The Hungarians did the same in 1809 when Napoleon was achieving his last great success in that part of Europe and encouraging the Hungarians to act.[14] In both cases the main demands were held in common and included the abolition of feudal privileges, even the *corvée* and other duties binding on the peasant. The Hungarians wanted to implement this program with the aid of a strong central authority, while the Poles thought that the main role should fall to an efficient and highly qualified state apparatus with the maximum participation of all society in clearly defined tasks that genuinely involved the entire nation.[15] In neither case was any form of revolutionary struggle envisaged.

This profound modification, or rather destruction, of the model of revolution that had existed before the 1796–99 period was most glaringly evident in Polish political thought. This was because Polish political ideas and programs were the most closely bound up with events in France and the policy of Napoleon, as they constituted the one real chance to realize Polish hopes of national liberation. Following the impact of the destruction of the Polish state and the checking of the further radicalization of the Revolution, people began to lose faith in any swift and complete victory of a rational, enlightened, and humanitarian program and its concomitant resolution of all national problems.

The first conspiratorial groups to carry on the struggle for independence immediately after the Third Partition did not postulate any revolutionary social or political changes. All their attention was concentrated on a strong, organized, patriotic, nationwide conspiracy and on the preparation of an uprising to be launched when the international situation was favorable. The model of revolution was reduced to that of a national uprising combined with a declaration of readiness to collaborate with France and a vague general acceptance of a political system approximating the French model in exchange for explicit support of the Polish struggle for independence. The matter of a radical liquidation of feudal relations in the countryside, i.e., the abolition of serfdom, was passed over in silence. Emissaries were sent to win peasant support for the national movement, but no revolutionary agrarian program was formulated.[16]

Only the Jacobin Franciszek Gorzkowski, a surveyor by profession, undertook some action among the peasants. His propaganda consisted of radical phraseology and a vague, muddled, antifeudal agrarian program. His actions were essentially guided by the desire to rouse the peasants against the Austrian partition authorities, who represented the existing order and the imposition of burdensome obligations, especially the drafting of recruits.[17] Thus one can discern in Gorzkowski's propaganda an effort to exploit radical slogans for the cause of the national movement. This was the first clear attempt to manipulate the elements of social revolution to achieve the political goal of independence, and it marked the virtual abandonment of the model of revolution in favor of a nationwide uprising, in which only some concrete elements of the model would be used.

This interpretation of Gorzkowski's program (which came to be known as the Gorzkowski conspiracy) is supported by his links with the moderate national movement (the so-called Lwów Centralization) and especially by the fact that Gorzkowski's propaganda omitted any mention of who the movement's overall leadership would be or what precise sociopolitical program would be implemented after victory. Nevertheless, the very existence of an organized political propaganda campaign that was actually reaching the peasants undoubtedly constituted a new and important revolutionary element, and it was to add depth to revolutionary programs and ideologies in later decades, especially in the 1840s.

A further evolution can be observed in the program of the Society of Polish Republicans, a democratic independence organization active in the years 1798-1807, but effective only to 1801, whose ranks contained a large proportion of Polish Jacobins. In the very title of their program, *Presocial Statutes,* and its explanation in Article 4, the organization's leaders established a clear distance between themselves and the earlier model for revolution. They questioned the role of the leaders of the Revolution in the creation of a new reality. They stressed the importance of democratic activity, which assumed organized legal—almost legalistic—forms:

The Society's statute is called presocial because it arises from the will of a few secretly gathered citizens, and not from the will of society as a whole, which cannot manifest itself at a time when the community is dissolved. A government arises as a result of a statute passed by representatives of the people. Such a government has a real existence, whereas when there is no such statute, there is no such government.[18]

In this way the Society justified its lack of competence and its total silence regarding future social reforms. It declared its solidarity only with "the rights of man and the citizen in the French Constitution of the Year III of the Republic [1795]" and alluded to the propagation of those rights. At the same time, it saw their basis in the postulate of harmony with nature, in "two natural truths" formulated almost in the spirit of Christian morality: "1. Do not do unto others as you would not have them do unto you; 2. Always be as good to others as you would have them be to you."[19]

No doubt these formulas arose from a desire to guarantee everyone personal freedom and equal rights, but the fact remains that the question of agrarian reforms—fundamental to the model of revolution in that part of Europe—was passed over. The authors of the statutes postulated "the restoration of the fatherland with a republican-democratic representative government" (Art. 1), the bringing of enlightenment to the peasants with the principal aim of awakening national consciousness in the countryside, and the drawing of the most enlightened and active peasants into the organization.[20] The virtual elimination of any social program most probably arose from the conviction that the French model of revolution could not be applied to the different conditions of Poland, and, most important, it would not guarantee all members of society genuinely equal rights and full, harmonious development.[21] An awareness of their own weakness after the collapse of the Kościuszko Insurrection and of the fact that there were no social forces that would support a program of radical revolution might also have determined the attitude of the leaders of the Society of Republicans.

These modifications of program were linked with a considerable increase in emphasis on the role of national problems. The nation, and not the society, became the main focus of action. Even the internationalist links that were maintained with progressive or revolutionary forces elsewhere were not presented as being a joining together of kindred social or ideological forces, but as cooperative action among "free peoples," and, to a lesser degree, as an expression of concern about the "fate of humanity"[22]: "The nation comes before everything, it is the beginning of everything. Its will is always law, and over it there is only the law of nature. . . . The nation cannot cede its rights to a tyrant."[23] Thus, in the revolutionary model, Rousseau's doctrine of the social contract was extended to the nation, which has become identified with society. The abstract and unifying Enlightenment concept of society has been replaced by the national society, a notion that diluted the universal model of revolution.

For the time being this notion was limited to the thesis that in the absence of complete national freedom, i.e., independence, the existence of a genuine society was impossible, and the people inhabiting the country in question were thrust back into a presocial phase; the winning of national freedom was therefore a primary and necessary condition for the work of building a society. This thesis, developed much further by Romantic thinkers in subsequent decades, put into question the universality of a uniform, concrete program of revolution.

A new element in the model of revolution created by the Polish Left was the replacement of social mass action by extensive organizational and educational programs, the discussion of which takes up over sixty per cent of the texts. Under the influence of the ideology of the Enlightenment and the experiences of the French Revolution, actions became more institutionalized, serving to organize the whole of society for precisely defined national campaigns both for the immediate and the more distant future. They were, in a way, to make up for the absence of the normal organization of society, in conditions of complete national freedom, i.e., the nation's own state.[24]

A similar function was fulfilled by the educational program, which included both raising the educational level of the population, especially of the peasants, and, particularly important, preserving and popularizing the native culture and history, which were to be the foundation for the development of a national consciousness and the will toward independence in the society as a whole. The elaboration of this program required that national revolutionary struggle itself be relegated to the indefinite future—the first time such a possibility was envisaged in the revolutionary model. In the absence of external help, e.g., from France, the Revolution was left for future generations, when "through the spread of enlightenment the citizens of Poland will in the course of time enter the epoch in which the rule of reason will establish the rights of man on the ruins of tyranny."[25]

Thus, added to the model of revolutionary struggle were postulates concerning legal or quasi-legal cultural, educational, propagandistic, and, later, economic activities (the last was called "organic" work in Poland, as it involved working within the existing sociopolitical organism). The model contained no revolutionary ideas, but the long-term aim—preparing for the day when the revolutionary struggle would break out, and working to bring it closer—ennobled its activities by conferring upon them the dignity of revolutionary work.

The realization that the prospect of revolution was distant and the organized and conscious social forces necessary for speedy initiation of a struggle were lacking added to the importance of the role of individuals and of ethical problems. Instead of a concrete program of future social and political change, the leaders of the Society drew up a lengthy *Collection of Moralities,*[26] and in the *Presocial Statutes* themselves they devoted a fair amount of space to this problem. The moral worth of the individual—"sincere friend, good husband, tender father, just, mild, human, manly, daring, modest, forgiving, forbearing, graceful, decent, sober"—were the criteria applied in recruiting new members for the organization.[27]

Alongside this idea of implementing a program of revolutionary struggle for independence in the remote future, the victorious struggle for independence and radical reforms in the immediate future continued to be of concern. The leaders of the Society of Polish Republicans considered unreserved assistance from France an indispensable condition for its realization. Thus, despite what some earlier historians have maintained, the radicals clearly recognized the importance of external conditions in hastening or retarding the revolutionary struggle. However, they did not regard this help as a function of diplomacy of foreign policy in the classical sense; instead they viewed it as arising out of "a general plan for other nations" rather than as being dictated by the interests of France as a great power.[28]

Thus there was added once again, and even more emphatically than at the beginning of the French Revolution, the task of "exporting revolution," not in the form of introducing a single, unified model, but of supporting all political movements that were attempting to overthrow or modify the *ancien régime,* or, better yet, attempting to liberate nations from foreign domination. The elimination, therefore, of some of the manifestations of evil in the world—or at least in Europe—was once again made the overriding aim of revolution. At the same time, the struggle against injustice shifted from the social sphere, or from the framework of a single society, to that of international relations.

The importance of these external factors was sometimes questioned once the international situation and the policy of Napoleon had ruled out any hope of French assistance. On those occasions, another model of revolutionary struggle was produced which found its fullest expression in the famous political pamphlet written in the winter of 1799–1800 by Tadeusz Kościuszko and his secretary, Józef Pawlikowski, under the title *Are the Poles Capable of Winning Independence?* In it the two representatives of the moderate democratic current in the Polish independence movement attempted to prove that only by relying on their own strength would the Poles be "capable of winning independence." Here the models of the American Revolution, the experience of the Dutch and Swiss struggles for independence, and the native uprising of 1794 all played a substantially larger, not to say a fundamental, role.[29] On the basis of the outcome of the American Revolution, the pamphlet's authors were convinced that victory was possible if the struggle would take on a genuinely mass, popular character. The struggle for independence had to be transformed, however, into a large-scale, partisan, people's war. At the same time, it had to be a social revolution, social relations in the countryside especially having to be revolutionized, since the peasants, being the most numerous part of the population (about eighty per cent), would be the decisive force in the struggle. The slogans urging a modification of feudal relations in the countryside were also expected to have an influence on neighboring countries and to paralyze or weaken the military forces sent by the three partitioning powers against the Polish revolutionary uprising.[30]

But despite their awareness of the importance of a program of social revolution, the authors reduced theirs to a demand for the abolition of serfdom and some generalized libertarian phrases. Like the authors of the *Presocial Statutes*, they allotted a large role to moral character, although what they demanded of participants in the future national revolution was "civic virtues," ardor, endurance, and, above all, sincere commitment to the ideas of democracy and freedom.[31]

They did not devote much attention to the question of political reforms. On the basis of a few sentences, the most one can conclude is that the authors of this model of revolution were probably advocates of the organs of power similar to those that had functioned during the Kościuszko Insurrection, possibly somewhat modified to conform with the model of the American Revolution.[32]

This faith in the nation's own strength and its powerful, single-minded desire for freedom as the basis for a "national revolution" already contained something of the Polish political thought of the Romantic period; it showed a spiritual affinity with the Romantic conviction that right ideas would be automatically victorious, summed up in the slogan of the young Romantics: "Feeling and faith speak more eloquently to me than the eye and lens of the scholar" (Mickiewicz).

At the same time, the model proposed by Pawlikowski and Kościuszko did not involve a total denial of the role of external influences in revolutionary activity; here, too, we encounter the idea of the "export of revolution" in the shape of a conviction that the peasants in neighboring countries would be roused and take part in the revolutionary struggle, and the hope that, in the event of major successes that would demonstrate the ability to hold out militarily for a long time, external help might eventually be counted on.[33] However, this concept involves active, autonomous creation and exploitation of an external situation, a situation auspicious for one's own revolutionary struggle and determined by it, and not simply a passive waiting for favorable circumstances. These were correct, but wholly theoretical, declarations made by one part of the left wing of the Polish independence movement.

The months and years to follow were to expose the unreality of these hopes, as both in Poland and abroad, in the wake of the universal pacification of the Continent following the French treaties with Austria, Russia, and Britain in 1801–02, the activity of all democratic and independence groups and organizations gradually faded. The Left, despite its declarations, turned out to be so weak as to be unable in the new international situation—and in the face of the prevailing mood among the Polish upper classes—to continue any kind of national or independence activity. And this, perhaps, marked the total and final destruction of the revolutionary models elaborated over the previous decade by the generation of Polish activists who had grown up in the atmosphere of enthusiasm surrounding the ideas of the Enlightenment and in the years of the rise and fall of the great French Revolution. The brief period of the Duchy of Warsaw did bring about the activation of a small group of Polish Jacobins in the years 1806–07 and 1809–10, it is true, but in the last analysis, it was not they who directed the implementation of the fundamental principles of the bourgeois legal and political system in the part of the Polish territories liberated from Prussian and Austrian rule. The guarantee of the abolition of serfdom and the admission of commoners to participation in government meant the virtual realization of the sociopolitical elements of the Polish model of revolution, and consequently this model was outmoded as a basis for further action. It was necessary to seek out and formulate new goals and a new program.

Someone who underwent an analogous, if not so radical, evolution toward the end of his life was Stanisław Staszic. He was a burgher who, next to Hugo Kołłątaj, was the most outstanding intellectual representative of the radical current of Polish sociopolitical thought during the Enlightenment. In his fundamental historical and philosophical work entitled *Ród ludzki (The Human Race)*, written at the beginning of the nineteenth century, he criticized the "excesses of the revolution" while praising its fundamental achievement. The latter he considered to lie in the implementation of the main postulates of the Enlightenment, and for that reason he declared his opposition to a continuation of the Revolution.[34] Thus the model of a moderate revolution proposed by Staszic—an intellectual and theoretician, not a politician totally involved in actual events—did not collapse but gradually died away as it was implemented.

It is significant that Staszic, too, transferred the focus of attention from problems of internal reforms to changes in international relations, in the "law of nations." He proclaimed the need for a united Europe and presented concrete proposals concerning the creation and functioning of an international, suprastate organization ("an assembly of nations") which would watch over universal peace and security and maintain the freedom of nations.[35] The realization of this idea was to be an immediate consequence and consummation of the revolutionary changes brought about in the societies of many European countries. It would consolidate these changes while at the same time guaranteeing further progress, justice, and happiness for people in every country.[36]

In the Napoleonic period, the Emperor's bitterest opponents also modified their ideas about revolution. The most varied models of this kind arose in feudal circles, above all in Vienna and St. Petersburg, the chief anti-Napoleonic centers. The overwhelming majority of those who belonged to the privileged strata viewed Napoleon's internal and external policies negatively, even with hatred, and dubbed advocates of the most moderate reforms "Jacobins."[37] At the same time, following the overthrow of the Jacobins, and later on the Directorate, an increasing number of people advocated seeking some kind of compromise, or rather *modus vivendi,* with the new social and political system that had established itself in France and its neighboring countries.

As this process of stabilization advanced and as it became clear that the French Revolution was going to go no further, its original somber aspect was somewhat brightened. Visions of chaos, permanent anarchy, and "the unleashing of the mob" were replaced by observations concerning the functioning of the new society and state. Those who took this view were generally enthusiastic supporters of the moderate ideas of the Enlightenment and in some cases had been advocates of the French Revolution in its early phase up to the overthrow of the

monarchy. They were rationalist politicians, advocates of liberal gestures, either from inner conviction or from a belief in their necessity.

Among the most outstanding representatives of this group were
Count Stadion and the Archduke Charles in Vienna, and Alexander I's
group of young advisers known as the Unofficial Committee in St. Petersburg.[38] Their vision of revolution had a dual nature. On the one
hand, they continued to fear the powerful forces, difficult or impossible
to control, that Napoleon might unleash by drawing upon the traditions
of the French Revolution, and this inclined them to carry out liberal
political and social reforms as the best way of forestalling that threat.[39]
On the other hand, they launched broad propaganda campaigns in
which, by attacking Napoleon, they tried to undermine sympathy for
the Revolution. They argued that he had betrayed the aims of the Revolution, that he was driven exclusively by his own unlimited ambitions
and lust for power, which were the sole reasons for the continuing
wars. They considered that his assumption of monarchical power compromised the Revolution which had led to it and ended with it.

In this way, they replaced the model of a revolution having a developed sociopolitical program with a vision of the expansionist policy of
Napoleon, whom they compared to Attila. Despite all the formidable
power and successes of the ''modern Attila,'' such a conception of the
Revolution was optimistic and more convenient for those who regarded the Revolution and Napoleon as enemies. It made it possible to
thrust matters of revolution into the shade and to show that the forces
and heroes it had produced were acting in a way that was blind, ele-
mental, and despite current successes, impermanent.[40] Some representatives of this group stressed the negative features of the policy and
personality of Napoleon, which they considered the quintessence or
consequence of the Revolution.[41] They attempted to compromise the
very essence of revolution and, to this end, compared the figure of
Napoleon ''the usurper,'' ''the cold egoist,'' grasping for untrammeled
power in France and in Europe, with an idealized portrait of the young
Tsar of Russia, Alexander I.[42] The model of revolution, reduced for
propaganda purposes to the figure of Napoleon presented in appropriate guise, was all but identified with the great-power policy of France
or her emperor. This meant a questioning of the universal character
and value of the Revolution and of Napoleon's activities. This latter
aim was also served by contrasting the French Revolution and Napoleon with the American Revolution and Washington.

The liberal-conservative camp presented the American Revolution
as a struggle for independence and a harmonious realization of many
lofty ideas of the Enlightenment within the framework of a new independent state built from the foundations. This revolution did not destroy—as did the French—fundamental social and political institutions

with centuries of tradition behind them; it did not introduce changes in neighboring countries as a result of victorious wars. The events on the North American continent made possible the development of "the power of an enlightened and astute man, supported by a wisely understood freedom and liberated from the bonds of despotism," but also free from "the impartially destructive disorder, wantonness, and anarchy" which in the opinion of these people had characterized the French Revolution.[43] But even in these positive opinions the negative aspects of the new society and state were also noted—excessive concern for the freedom of the individual to the detriment of community interests, the exploitation of official functions for private interests, and especially "bad economy and unnecessary administrative outlays" and the plight of the Negroes.[44] Moreover, opponents of the Revolution pointed out that it had not eliminated inequalities and injustices, as the sources of these phenomena were to be found in social prejudices, and those would never disappear.[45]

The above model of revolution has almost completely lost its aggressive ideological character. The only motor for further political changes it contained was the expansionist policy of Napoleon. It was therefore against that policy that opponents of revolution now directed their main attack. Next to propaganda campaigns aimed at compromising Napoleon, they considered their most effective weapon to be the slogan of national freedom and the proposal to create a loose federation or an international organization of states. They treated this as a counterproposal to Napoleon's total subordination to his will of each successive state he controlled, and his imposition of identical or similar sociopolitical systems on all of them. They tried to oppose the demands for the freedom and sovereignty of nations, which were also intended to make further changes in Europe in Napoleon's favor impossible, to the revolutionary principles of the freedom and sovereignty of the people of a given country.[46]

In moments of decisive political or military confrontation with Napoleon a substantial section of the antirevolutionary camp was fully aware that their great rival embodied many permanent elements of the Revolution and, in making use of these elements, was establishing them on a firm basis.[47] Further successes strengthened the pessimistic conviction of the more enlightened opponents of revolution, that many of the changes brought about by the French Revolution and upheld by Napoleon were becoming permanent. This realization that it would be impossible to ever return totally to the *ancien régime* was particularly characteristic of the group of young advisers around Alexander I in the years 1801–07. One of them gave succinct expression to this feeling in a letter addressed to the Tsar during the war of 1806–07:

La révolution qui a changé la face de la France . . . portera bientôt jusqu'aux derni-
ères limites du monde civilisé, n'est pas un de ces fléaux passagers, qui répandent pen-
dant qualques instants la désolation et la mort et laissent ensuite aux lieux qu'ils ont
dévastés la liberté de reprendre leur ancienne physionomie et leur ancien éclat. . . . Des
trônes se relèvent, des empires se rétablissent. . . . Mais le institutions, mais les moeurs,
mais les principes fondamentaux et les traits caractéristiques ne se rétablissent jamais.
Et telle est la nature et tels doivent être les résultats des événements dont la Providence
a voulu que nous fussions témoins! Nous avions été jetés dans une de ces époques
fatales où l'ancien édifice social attaqué et ébranlé dans chacune de ses bases fond-
amentales, s'écroule de toutes parts pour faire place à de nouvelles créations. Nous
sommes trop faibles pour arrêter les progrès de cette décomposition générale.[48]

The above tentative and still very incomplete analysis of the models
of revolution in the progressive and liberal-conservative currents of
political thought in East Central and Southeastern Europe testify to the
rapid evolution of these models, especially during the reign of Napoleon. It comes as something of a shock to notice that these models underwent analogous, sometimes parallel, modifications in both progressive
and conservative thought. The representatives on both sides down-
played the importance of the social elements in the program of revolution. The first with enthusiasm, the others out of necessity and often
tacitly, approved the changes introduced; the former recognized the
impossibility of withdrawing them, the latter declared themselves
against adding new and more progressive goals to the revolutionary
program. Both the proponents and the opponents of revolution and
progress attributed an increasing role to the national question in both
the model of revolution and in the most effective way of combating it.
They advocated the organization of international relations on completely new and better principles and emphasized the importance of
ethics in individual as well as international affairs.

The struggle between supporters and opponents of the new order of
things intensified. It polarized all Europe and even extended beyond
the boundaries of the old continent. But at the same time, the conviction was born, although often expressed inconsistently and mostly
in favorable circumstances—in short, not always sincerely—that a sensible compromise for coexistence was needed.

NOTES

1 J. Dobrovský, *Spisy a projevy*, vol. 22 (Prague, 1941), p. 81.
2 V. I. Freidzon, ed., *Natsional'no-osvoboditel'noe dvizhenie slavianskikh narodov
Avstriiskoi imperii (konets XVIII-70-e gody XIX v)*. An example of the similarity, not to
say identity, of language and even of attitude toward some social phenomena which
linked the moderate current of the Enlightenment and the officials implementing Jo-

sephine policies may be seen in the opinion expressed on the occasion of the annexation by Austria of those lands of former Poland known as Galicia: "The monarchical government must fight against the demoralization and selfishness of an oligarchy deprived of its privileges, against its villainy even, especially if it desires that the laws should correspond to the wishes of the discriminated or oppressed parts of the nation. . . . It would be difficult to find a country in which disorder and political corruption had reached a higher degree." ("Beschreibung der Königreichen Galizien und Lodomerien nach dem Zustand, in welchem sie sich zur Zeit der Revindizierung durch Ihre K. K. Majestät und besonders im Monat Julius 1773 befunden haben.") MS. in the Library of the Ossoliński Institute, no. 525, pp. 1–3, published in M. Tyrowicz, ed., *Galicja od pierwszego rozbioru do Wiosny Ludów 1772–1849*, pp. 119–20.

3 N. Todorov and V. Traĭkov, *Bălgari uchastnitsi v borbite za osvobozhdenieto na Gărtsia 1821–1828: Sbornik dokumenti* (Sofia, 1971); N. Todorov, *Filiki eteriia i bălgarite* (Sofia, 1965); N. Botzaris, *Visions balkaniques dans la préparation de la révolution grecque 1789–1821* (Geneva, 1962), pp. 31, 71–73; the paper given by N. Ciachiri at the International Conference of Historians in Štip, Yugoslavia, on 17–19 May 1976 contained interesting information concerning the role of the Poles in propagating the French Revolution in Moldavia and Walachia. The proceedings of this conference are to be published.

4 Besides the earlier works of E. Driault, see N. Botzaris, *Visions balkaniques*, p. 32; A. M. Stanislavskaia, *Russko-angliiskie otnosheniia i problemy sredizemnomoria 1798–1807* (Moscow, 1962), pp. 204–7, 245–47; G. L. Arsh, "Iz istorii natsional'no-osvoboditel'nogo dvizheniia v Gretsii v kontse XVIII-nachale XIX v," *Voprosy Istorii*, no. 12 (1962): 174; the major role played by the national problem in the ideology and political propaganda in Hungary at the end of the eighteenth century is shown in *Tsentral'naia i iugovostochnaia Evropa v novoe vremja* (Moscow, 1974), pp. 21–26; Ap. Daskalakis and R. Velestinlis, *La Révolution française et les préludes de l'indépendence hellenique* (Paris, 1937), pp. 7–22, 104–18; Georgii Dimitrevich Motsenigo, Russian consul in the Republic of the Seven United Ionian Islands, to Adam Jerzy Czartoryski, 17 December 1803; *Vneshniaia politika Rossii v XIX i nachale XX vv.*, vol. 1 (Moscow, 1960), p. 727.

5 More details about this in B. Kalman, *A magyar jakobinus mozgalom története* (Budapest, 1957); V. Tibor, *A magyar jakubinusok köztársasági mozgalma* (Budapest 1968), quoted from *Natsional'no-osvoboditel'noe dvizhenie*.

6 N. Botzaris, *Visions balkaniques*, pp. 23–27; Ap. Daskalakis, *Révolution française*, pp. 94–104, 119–30; for a different assessment of Velestinlis's program, see N. Danova, "Grătskoto vastaniie ot 1821 i 'Megali ideia' " in N. Todorova, ed., *Sto i petdeset godini ot grătskoto vastanie 1821–1828* (Sofia, 1973), p. 77.

7 Their views and activities are described extensively and with profound knowledge of the subject by B. Leśnodorski in *Polscy Jakobini* (Warsaw, 1960), and *Les Jacobins polonais et leurs confrères en Europe* (Wrocław, 1964).

8 Z. Libiszowska, *Opinia polska wobec rewolucji amerykańskiej w XVIII wieku* (Łódź, 1962), pp. 44–116, 125–28; an interesting paper on this subject was presented by Irena Sobol at a conference of historians in Warsaw in the spring of 1976, "Echa rewolucji amerykańskiej w polskiej publicystyce lat 1776– 1794."

9 Account by Kajetan Węgierski in *Ameryka w pamiętnikach Polaków*, ed. B. Grzeloński (Warsaw, 1975), pp. 23–24.

10 N. Petrovič, "O temišvarskom saboru i njegovom istorijskom značaju," *Temišvarski sabor 1790* (Novi Sad, 1972), p. vii.

11 P. F. Sugar, "The Influence of the Enlightenment and the French Revolution in Eighteenth-Century Hungary," *Journal of Central European Affairs* 18, no. 4 (1958): 338; I. Sotér, *L'Esprit français en Hongrie* (Budapest, 1946), pp. 47–49.

12 J. Skowronek, "Jan Potocki—polityk konserwatywny czy liberalny?" *Przegląd Humanistyczny*, no. 6 (1972): 19; M. Handelsman, "Ideologia polityczna Towarzystwa Republikanów Polskich 1798–1807," *Rozwój narodowości nowoczesnej*, vol. 1 (Warsaw, 1973), pp. 114–15, 142–43; A. J. Czartoryski, *Mémoires*, vol. 1 (Paris, 1887), pp. 285, 380.

13 *Korrespondencya w materyach obraz kraiu i narodu polskiego roziaśniających* (Warsaw, 1807); an analysis of the program of the Jacobins during the period of the Duchy of Warsaw is to be found in B. Leśnodorski, "Jakobini wobec zagadnień wzrostu wspólnoty politycznej w Księstwie Warszawskim," *Studia Historyczne* (a *Festschrift* presented to Professor Stanisław Arnold) (Warsaw, 1965), pp. 260–72; W. Tokarz, *Ostatnie lata Hugona Kołłątaja 1794–1812*, vol. 1 (Cracow, 1905), pp. 331, 334–35.

14 K. Domokos, "Napóleon és Magyarország," *Századok*, nos. 3–4 (1971): 579–81.

15 "Valiant nation! I warn you to make the most of time. . . . Strive all of you to arm yourselves as heavily as possible so that, if worst comes to worst, you will be able by force of arms to ensure yourselves, if not of a complete political entity, at least of your nationality, language, national rights and offices." S. Staszic, *O statystyce Polski. Krótki rzut wiadomości potrzebnych tym, którzy ten kraj chcą oswobodzić i tym, którzy w nim chcą rządzić* (Cracow, 1809), p. 47.

16 "Akt konfederacji z 6.I.1796 r. w Krakowie z deklaracją działalności celem odzyskania niepodległości Polski . . . ," *Wybór tekstów źródłowych z historii Polski w latach 1795–1864* (Warsaw, 1956), pp. 62–63; "Instrukcja Zgromadzenia Centralnego we Lwowie dla Ludwika Trzecieskiego z 6 III 1797 r.," ibid., p. 64.

17 A. Orchowski, "Związek Gorzkowskiego 1796 r. między ludem założony," *Wybór tekstów*, pp. 58–60.

18 E. Halicz, ed., "Ustawy przedspołeczne, 1.X.1798," *Nurty lewicowe w dobie polskich powstań narodowych 1794–1849: Wybór źródeł* (Wrocław, 1961), pp. 101–2; the original manuscript is in the Czartoryski Library (National Library in Cracow) (cited hereafter as Czart), MS. no. 3929, pp. 91–128; a general description of this document is to be found in M. Handelsman, "Ideologia polityczna," pp. 145–49.

19 Ibid., p. 102.

20 Ibid., pp. 101, 118–19, 124.

21 Letters of Józef Kalasanty Szaniawski to Andrzej Horodyski, 18 May 1807, in *Korrespondencya w materyach*, p. 34; letter of Dominik Krysiński, ibid., p. 93; J. K. Szaniawski to the Main Committee of the Society of Polish Republicans of 5 October 1799, in M. Handelsman, "Ideologia polityczna," p. 191.

22 Ibid., pp. 102, 118.

23 Ibid., p. 108.

24 Ibid., p. 118. In the introduction to the Statutes, it was affirmed that "in making the greatest efforts to sustain the public spirit and to take the place of a community dissolved by anarchy and violence" a group of people was calling into being the

present organization which would be ''a school of future defenders of a free government'' (ibid., p. 101).

25 Ibid.

26 Ibid., pp. 105-12.

27 Ibid., pp. 102, 106. ''Laziness and idleness'' were listed as causes for dismissal before such reasons as ''departure from the republican system,'' ''breach of oath and contempt for the aims of the Society,'' and ''defamation of the Society'' (ibid., p. 112).

28 Ibid., p. 101; cf. the viewpoint of J. K. Szaniawski in M. Handelsman, ''Ideologia polityczna,'' pp. 141-42 and 193.

29 *Czy Polacy wybić się mogą na niepodległość?* ed. and with an introduction by E. Halicz (Warsaw, 1967), pp. 70, 74-77.

30 Ibid., pp. 88-89, 102-16. An extensive analysis of the military and social elements of this concept has been given by E. Halicz in his *Partisan Warfare in 19th Century Poland: The Development of a Concept* (Odense, 1975), pp. 38-44.

31 *Czy Polacy wybić się mogą na niepodległość?* pp. 79, 85, 93, 98: ''A Polish general should not only be an instrument of the art of war, but also a citizen. . . . A leader must animate the people with liberty, and how can he speak of her if he does not love her in his soul?'' (ibid., p. 96).

32 Ibid., p. 120.

33 Ibid., pp. 109, 117.

34 S. Staszic, ''Ród ludzki,'' *Pisma filozoficzne,* vol. 2 (Warsaw, 1954), pp. 156-58; an interesting, if in part questionable, discussion of Staszic's concept is contained in B. Szacka, *Teoria i utopia Stanisława Staszica* (Warsaw, 1965), pp. 68, 94-96, 149-52.

35 S. Staszic, ''Ród ludzki,'' p. 133; idem, ''Myśli o równowadze politycznej Europy,'' ibid., pp. 305-20.

36 Ibid., pp. 172-74.

37 Cf. Feodor Rostopchin's letter to Semeon Vorontsov, 15-27 February 1802, *Arkhiv kniazia Vorontsova,* vol. 8 (Moscow, 1875), p. 297. Even among the youth of St. Petersburg he saw ''hundreds of young people who could have been the adopted children of Robespierre or Danton.''

38 M. Rauchenstein, *Kaiser Franz und Erzherzog Carl* (Munich, 1972), p. 85; J. Skowronek, *Antynapoleońskie koncepcje Czartoryskiego* (Warsaw, 1968), pp. 10, 20-29 passim.

39 ''Notatki pamiętnikarskie A. Czartoryskiego,'' Czart. MS. no. 1308, p. 48; session of the Unofficial Committee on 3 November 1803; M. I. Bogdanovich, *Istoriia tsarstvovaniia imperatora Aleksandra I i Rossii v ego vremia,* vol. 1 (St. Petersburg, 1869), p. 91.

40 Skowronek, *Jan Potocki,* pp. 28-29; Viscount Vargemont, ''L'Homme et son siècle,'' Czart. MS. III 2093, vol. 2, pp. 267-73; Vargemont, ''Voeu pour la tranquillité de l'Europe,'' ibid., MS. III 5469, p. 73.

41 ''Fragment tiré du mémoire de Mr Pozzo di Borgo'' (1804), Czart. MS. IV 5220, pp. 139-40.

42 Skowronek, *Jan Potocki,* pp. 24-25, 29; Kajetan Koźmian, *Pamiętniki,* vol. 3 (Wrocław, 1972), p. 53; A. J. Czartoryski, *Mémoires,* vol. 1, p. 348; ''Mémoire sur le danger de temporiser dans l'état présent des intérets politiques de l'Europe'' (May 1805), Tsentral'nyi Gosudarstvennyi Arkhiv Drevnikh Aktov (cited hereafter *TsGADA*), stack 15, Part 15, vol. 507, pp. 5-10, 35-37, 54-55.

43 *Ameryka w pamiętnikach Polaków,* p. 35 (the diary of the Polish poet and political

activist Julian Ursyn Niemcewicz of his journey through the United States in the fall of 1797); Koźmian, ibid., p. 52. A similar contrast between the American and French Revolutions is drawn by S. Staszic in "Ród ludzki," p. 156. Much later an outstanding representative of the Czech national movement, Leo Thun, saw in the American Revolution an example of the disintegration of an artificial political community when the links of material and moral interests between its parts were broken (*Prelog, Slovenska renesansa* [Zagreb, 1926] p. 179).

44 *Ameryka w pamiętnikach Polaków*, pp. 39, 44–45, 50.

45 The distinguished Czech scholar of the Enlightenment Josef Jungmann wrote that "the French proclaimed liberty and equality only in words and not in reality" and at the same time declared that the full realization of this slogan is impossible, being contrary to nature (*Zapisky* of Josef Jungmann, "*Časopis Musea Kralovstvi českeho* [1871], pp. 263–64, 270).

46 J. Skowronek, "Le programme européen du prince Adam Jerzy Czartoryski en 1803–1805," *Acta Poloniae Historica* 17 (1968): 141–58; idem, *Antynapoleońskie koncepcje*, pp. 316–28; F. Červinka, *Český nacionalismus v XIX stoleti* (Prague, 1965), p. 19; E. Chalupny, *Jungmann* (Prague, 1909), p. 153; Th. Schiemann, *Geschichte Russlands unter Kaiser Nikolaus I*, vol. 1 (Berlin, 1904), p. 266; A. J. Czartoryski, *Mémoires*, vol. 1, pp. 374–75; Matija Nenadovič, *Memoari* (Belgrade, 1968), pp. 11ʾ, 163 (for the statement that the people enjoyed French support and that Russia wantɛ to work together with the people and its organized representatives!); Memorial by N. N. Novosiltsov, 13–25 October 1803, Istoricheskii Muzei, Moscow, MS stack 316, vol. 1, pp. 66–68; "Aperçu politique sur la descente des Français en Grèce," St. Petersburg, November 1803, Czart. MS. V 5214, pp. 21–36; General Comnène, "Idée sur les moyens de conserver notre influence dans les Principautés de Valachie et Moldavie" (before 1805), Czart. MS. V 5214, p. 469.

47 "Son usurpation n'a changé ni les choses, ni les personnes; tout l'ouvrage de la révolution reste intacte, il acquiert une nouvelle force dans l'unité que va le consolider et le rendre plus que jamais un instrument de désolation et de ruine contre les autres nations. . . . L'ombre de Robespierre va reçevoir son apothéose, les souverains de l'Europe seront confondus avec la monarchie révolutionnaire, d'autant plus dangereuse, que malgré son origine, elle se presentera revêtue de formes augustes de la souveraineté légitime . . . les rois sont constitués sur les limites terribles d'une ruine certaine ou d'une résistance honorable" (Pozzo di Borgo [?], "Réflexions politiques sur le titre d'Empereur dans la personne de Napoléon Bonaparte" [mid 1804], *TsGADA*, stack 15, part 15, vol. 505, p. 12).

48 Unsigned epistolary memorial for Alexander I (1806), Czart. no. 1039ᶜ; very similar in tone and viewpoint were the "Réflexions: Mémoire du prince Czartoryski," 20 June 1810, *TsGADA*, stack 1278, vol. 58.

THE REVOLUTIONARY NOBLEMAN: AN EAST EUROPEAN VARIANT OF THE LIBERATION STRUGGLE IN THE RESTORATION ERA

Stefan Kieniewicz, Polish Academy of Sciences

The political system established at the Congress of Vienna was to last in its main outlines for nearly a hundred years. Between 1815 and 1912, Europe experienced few wars and few border changes; throughout it was guided by the firmly established principle of the balance of powers. Successive generations of revolutionaries did denounce the system and did their best to overthrow it; today, after two world wars, a worn-out Europe looks back on those times with nostalgia, and some people even recommend the system that governed them as a model worthy of emulation. While abstaining from an evaluation for the present, we should stress that, on the contrary, the first decades following the famous Congress did not seem as peaceful to its contemporaries as they are described in our textbooks today.

The first half of the nineteenth century witnessed in Western Europe the triumph of the Industrial Revolution, the political advance of the middle classes, and the birth of a labor class. The same phenomena occurred, somewhat later, in Central and Eastern Europe, but there they were conjoined with other problems, such as the emancipation of the peasants and the rise of nationalism. All these changes did not develop without political unrest, particularly between 1820 and 1871, and most auspiciously in the revolutionary year of 1848.

Two European countries managed to survive these disorders without great damage by adjusting their political structures to the requirements of the time through deliberate reforms and compromises. These two were England and Prussia; reforms in both countries were far-reaching enough, but not so radical that the continuity of political tradition could not be preserved. Elsewhere, from Lisbon to St. Petersburg, governments were challenged with imminent, even if not always erupting, revolution. Even in Russia, where revolution long seemed a hopeless case, the ineptitude of the *ancien régime* to cope with new ideas placed its continued existence in jeopardy.

The territories endangered or swept by revolution in the twenties, thirties, and forties of the last century were far from homogeneous. One can distinguish two revolutionary zones and is even tempted to designate them the Latin and the Slavic zones—assuming that linguistic families have anything at all to do with specific political conditions. What does differentiate the French, Italian, and Iberian revolutions in the first half of the nineteenth century from those that broke out simultaneously in Austria and Russia? The level of economic development was certainly not the cause: southern Italy and Spain were in fact lagging behind Bohemia and Silesia in this respect. Nor was it a question of political structure: the Russian government under Nicholas I and the Austrian regime under Metternich actually had their counterpart in Naples. What seemed to be crucial were the differences in social base between the revolutionary movements. In France and Italy, the leading revolutionary force came from the middle classes supported—at least until 1848—by the bulk of the urban population. But in Central and Eastern Europe, the middle classes had no political power.

Who, then, headed the Revolution? Here again the answer is not the same for every country or region. In all societies deprived of an upper class as a result of prolonged subjugation, the role of pioneer and leader in national and class movements was taken on by the intelligentsia. Its exact composition varied, but usually the leadership of a national movement was assumed by that group from among the intelligentsia who represented the highest social status in that country for the nationality on the rise.[1] Sometimes they were civil servants or liberal members of the professions, as in Bohemia; clergymen, as in Ukrainian Galicia and Lithuania; village schoolteachers, as in Upper Silesia and Belorussia. National movements slowly began to acquire a political character—after 1830 in the Habsburg Monarchy, although a revolutionary outbreak did not actually occur until 1848. Bulgarians, Eastern Ukrainians, Lithuanians, and Belorussians started to be active in the political sense still later, in the second half of the century. Thus, some nations (which were later rather misleadingly categorized as "unhistorical") were not touched by the revolutionary wave that in the course of the 1820s assaulted the Holy Alliance. But other countries of central and Eastern Europe—those which possessed a native upper class while lacking a sufficiently developed (or assimilated) middle class—were involved. In those countries, namely, Russia, Poland, and Hungary, the opposition movements of the 1820s were nobility movements in their social composition. It seemed a strange thing to government circles in St. Petersburg, Warsaw, and Vienna that members of privileged rank should behave like the French Third Estate. Old Count Rostopchin, when told of the events of 14 December 1825 remarked sarcastically: "I understand why cobblers and coachmen made the French Revolution. They wanted to secure the rights reserved to marquesses and viscounts. But why leading Russian aristocrats—among them descendants of the house of Rurik? Do they want to become cobblers and coachmen?"[2]

This paradox was stressed by Lenin when he coined the term "revolutionary noblemen" to denote this group.[3] An effective and convenient term indeed, for it emphasizes the contrast between the noun and its modifying adjective, while denoting the basic contradiction inherent in the movement in question. Its revolutionary character undermined the privileges of the nobility, while its noble composition could only hamper the revolution's impetus. No wonder that Lenin's term was readily adopted even outside Marxist historiography. While using it, however, we must bear in mind that it is an ahistoric concept—none of the revolutionaries of the 1820s would have called himself by such a name—and that Lenin, when he spoke about "revolutionary noblemen," alluded solely to Russia. If we are to apply the term in other countries, such as Poland or Hungary, we must begin by ascertaining whether we have really to do with analogous processes.

Hungary must be left aside for the moment. The Hungarian political movement, which arose in the 1820s from the self-governing assemblies of the counties and forced its way into Parliament from 1825 on, in many ways resembled parallel phenomena in Poland and Russia. It was a movement based on the middle, or lower-middle, nobility. This was a rather numerous class, opposed to the conservative aristocracy, but at the same time conscious of its fundamental class antagonism to the peasantry. Friendly contacts between Hungarian and Polish patriots were frequent, as shown by the events of 1831 and after. Here, however, similarities come to an end.

In the period under consideration, the Hungarian movement remained a legal one, and it concentrated exclusively on national problems. It was able to retain this character, as it had the means at its disposal for forcing the Vienna government gradually to make concessions. The Magyar nobility did not start its revolution until 1848—and then, of course, they were also compelled to deal with social problems. In many ways, the Hungarian Revolution of 1848–49 is reminiscent of the earlier Polish Insurrection of 1830–31, to the extent that both were predominantly revolutions by noblemen. But Europe, in 1848, no longer resembled the pattern of the 1820s, and it would be hazardous to compare the two groups; they do appear, it is true, in similar guise, but they act in totally different sceneries. We are therefore obliged to limit our considerations to a comparison of the revolutionary noblemen in Russia and Poland.

At first sight, the similarities are striking. Conspiracies start in both countries at the same time, almost immediately after the Congress of Vienna. Both movements involve an elite; both are led by officers of noble descent. They soon come into contact and are involved in the same disaster. Nonetheless, most historians, beginning with the first of them, Maurycy Mochnacki, when comparing the Russian Decembrists and the Patriotic Society in Poland, are struck by the differences, rather than the similarities, of the two movements: "A most peculiar thing!" says Mochnacki. "While Poland after the partitions seeks only the means . . . of reuniting her disrupted members, Moscow starts a movement aimed at the dissolution of the state." And, indeed, "the Muscovite conspirators had a different aim than the Polish ones. They entered agreements against a common oppressor, but with the former, the nature of government was the prime consideration, while with the latter, it was their existence and their land."[4]

Let us reach the primary cause: the Poles were a nation deprived of its independence. Hence, for a majority among the politically conscious classes, the main task was to rescue their endangered nationality, if possible, by regaining an independent state. Revolutionary tactics and slogans of social reform were intended as expedients leading to a national goal. Russia, on the other hand, was at the time already a world power, although under an autocratic government. Russian revolutionaries rebelled against their lack of freedom; they contemplated a remodeling of the state and society that would ensure liberty for all its citizens.

The next generation of Polish revolutionaries, when they entered agreements with their Russian partners in 1862, stated this difference of aims in almost identical terms: "The Russian movement is agrarian; ours is national. In Russia, the social upheaval will bring political freedom; among us, social reconstruction can only follow liberation and the reconstruction of our independence."[5] This divergence of goals could only lead to further differences, already visible in the 1820s. Two of them merit particular attention.

The idea of national independence was more popular among the Polish educated classes than the idea of social upheaval was among comparable groups in Russia. The Polish conspirator of the 1820s felt much less alienated among his fellow countrymen than did his Russian counterpart. Consequently, the Polish revolutionary could assume the understanding and support of patriotically minded countrymen, even of those generally unsympathetic to revolution, and he was therefore inclined to modify his views on social matters and to conform to the habits and prejudices of those more moderate circles—always on the assumption, of course, that he could win them over, when necessary, to the national cause. That the Russians could not entertain such hopes is perhaps the reason why Russian revolutionaries, less numerous and more isolated, were inclined to develop far more advanced ideas.

Nor does the contrast end there. The Kingdom of Poland, united with Russia since 1815, enjoyed a rather liberal constitution, at least superficially. On the central and provincial levels, authority rested in the hands of wealthy landowners. They were satisfied with the state of affairs; even if they complained, they hesitated to risk their substantial advantages in an uneven struggle against powerful Russia. On the whole, the landowners of the Congress Kingdom kept their loyalties even after 1820, when the major part of those constitutional guarantees were shown to be merely an illusion.

The attitude of the Polish provinces of the former republic differed somewhat. These provinces did not enjoy constitutional liberties, and they had already lost hope that they would ever be joined to the Congress Kingdom, an arrangement that had once been promised by Alexander I. Hence, it was more likely for a gentleman of the eastern provinces to become a revolutionary, albeit a moderate one, than for his relative, seated within the Congress Kingdom. But on the whole it was possible, in Poland, to be a patriot without becoming a revolutionary, whereas in Tsarist Russia, any sincere liberal was bound to become a revolutionary, at least from the moment when the granting of a constitution to Russia proved a dream.

In Congress Poland, as well as in the Polish provinces under Prussian rule, serfdom had been abolished since 1807. It persisted, in a milder form and under state control, in the Austrian province of Galicia. The revolutionary nobleman in Poland could under these conditions close his eyes to the still unsolved problem of peasant claims to the land. He could delude himself into believing that the social question would solve itself in Poland through the interplay of economic forces. A Russian revolutionary—even one of noble descent—could not ignore the agrarian problem, which had swollen with the misdeeds of centuries.

Let us search deeper still: when comparing Russian and Polish revolutionary noblemen, we cannot lose sight of the structural differences between the nobilities in the two countries. In Russia, the *Dvorianskaia Gramota* (Charter for the Nobility) of Catherine II (1785) circumscribed the nobility as a closed order of hereditary owners of land and of the peasant serfs who tilled it. It was expected, in return, that the same nobility would serve the state in the officer corps or in the civil service. In the immense empire of the tsars, the nobility formed a tiny group: 1.5 per cent of the whole population, comprising 140,000 families: of those, about 20,000 belonged to families of magnates and wealthy landowners.[6] The vast majority of Russian nobility were either already impoverished or on the verge of ruin and therefore compelled to enter government service. Nonetheless, even the poorest and most heavily indebted noble family possessed some peasant serfs, if only a dozen or so, and consequently, they remained interested in maintaining the *krepostnoe pravo* (the institution of serfdom) with all its abuses.

At the same time, the constitutional Congress Kingdom counted four million inhabitants, among them 300,000 members of the *szlachta* (nobility) (60,000–65,000 family heads according to some statistics), amounting to 7.5 per cent of the population. Among them were about 4,000 large landowners, 5,000 tenants on large farms, 32,000 small, independent farmers, 13,000 estate agents, stewards, overseers, and the like, and at least 8,000 families of the urban intelligentsia.[7] Similar proportions were to be found in other provinces of the former republic, with the exception, perhaps, of Poznania and Pomerania. For centuries, the Polish *szlachta* represented a highly differentiated society from the point of view of wealth, social rank, manners, and culture. They were aware, nevertheless, that they belonged to a privileged estate, and that realization could only influence their political attitudes. In other words, within the nobility the landed element counted for much less in Poland than in Russia, at least in number. This circumstance was bound to affect the character and scope of a revolutionary movement based, in both countries, on the nobility. If we compare the fate of that movement in Russia with that in Poland, we shall see that the military demonstration at the Senate Square in St. Petersburg lasted one day, the rebellion of the Chernigov Regiment in the Ukraine, five days. After their suppression under the reign of Nicholas I, thirty years of dead silence prevailed in the Empire. Meanwhile, in Poland, four years after the crushing of the Patriotic Society, an insurrection broke out which affected the whole of Russian Poland, a movement obviously provoked by the revolutionary noblemen. The insurrection collapsed after ten months, but the struggle for independence continued: conspiracies proliferated in the 1830s and 1840s in Poland, all the while becoming more numerous and more radical.

To the contrast between the one-day drama of the Decembrists and the decades-long Polish struggle for independence let us oppose another paradox. The historical literature concerning the Decembrist movement is much more extensive in comparison to that devoted to the revolutionary noblemen in Poland. Russian bibliographies of the Decembrist movement already registered over eight thousand entries sixteen years ago; since that time new books and smaller contributions probably number another thousand or more.[8] Polish historiography can, of course, claim an ample literature dedicated to the November Insurrection. But if we lay aside the works concerning the war, diplomacy, and the politics of the Conservative party in 1830–31, we shall be left with scarcely a thousand items devoted to the history of the 1830 Insurrection.[9] Serious works devoted to the problem of the revolutionary noblemen are still not very numerous in Poland.[10]

It is not my task to stress the differences between the revolutionary noblemen in the two neighboring countries. On the contrary, I intend to call forth those characteristic features that would entitle us to give a common name to the conspiring elements in Russia and in Poland. These different elements include, in Russia, the Northern and Southern Societies as well as the Society of United Slavs. In Poland, apart from the National Freemasonry and its extension, the Patriotic Society, other organizations existed mainly at the universities. The most important of them was the Union of Free Poles. Far-reaching differences of program and tactics can be found between these various groups. It seems to me that the common denominator among them lies neither in the attribute *revolutionary*, nor in the noun *noblemen*, but precisely in the internal contradiction between those two words.

Let us therefore suggest a definition: we shall treat a political movement in Eastern Europe during the 1820s which intended to overthrow the existing social and political order without the participation of the masses—who were, however, to be liberated. By insisting on the word *overthrow*, we are excluding from our discussion any kind of enlightened conservatism or liberalism that aimed at improving unsatisfactory political and social conditions through reforms from above. The expression "without participation" is bound to stress the differences between revolutionary noblemen and the earlier Jacobins or later revolutionary democrats, both of whom did, or intended to, appeal to armed popular masses. This definition may also help us understand why such a political trend had to develop at that time in that place. Just then, in the decade following the Congress of Vienna, those reforms from above that were characteristic of the Enlightenment came to a halt in Central and Eastern Europe. That region, however, lacked a politically active middle class capable of leading the masses, as it had done in France, in an assault on the *ancien régime*.

I am unable to deal with all the details of the problem in question here. I must limit myself to three points: the number and social composition of the organizations; their most far-reaching ideological conceptions; and what I shall term the heritage of the revolutionary noblemen.

"How many were they? Several score, maybe several hundred. Only a small minority of the nobility, a handful of brave men, knew how to rise above the interests of their own class to engage in an uneven struggle with the colossus of autocracy." This is the opening sentence of a recent monograph dedicated to the Russian Decembrists.[11] These words testify to the difficulty of measuring the scope of the movement in question. The official "list of members of former criminal secret societies and other persons connected with the inquest opened up by Imperial Order on December 17, 1825"[12] included 456 officers, 72 members of the civil service, and 51 persons not connected with government service. This list may have some omissions, but not exceeding a dozen names, and it does not include private and noncommissioned officers involved in the rebellion, who numbered about 2,500. Among the 579 persons called to account, 23 were Poles; the Court of Inquiry liberated 290 persons as "not suspected." It is possible, of course, that some of those exonerated had nonetheless had connections with the conspiracy; and some others might have escaped arrest. All in all, it

would be hazardous to estimate the actual number of Russian conspirators at more than 500, presumably 400 of them officers. This last figure
would represent 2.2 per cent of the Russian officers corps of those
days.[13]

Civilian sympathizers were far less conspicuous, although they included among them some eminent intellectuals, such as Pushkin and
Griboedov, for example. The social composition of the conspiracy was
almost exclusively noble; some *raznochintsy* (individuals of mixed social origin) enrolled in the Society of United Slavs do not change the
general picture. Wealthy and titled persons were not lacking in the
Northern and Southern Societies; the majority, however, came from
middle or poorer (but not *déclassé*) landowning families. The older
generation of future Decembrists entered the army in the first years of
the nineteenth century; the younger, just before the campaign of 1812.
Ten years later, a large percentage of leading Decembrists held higher
officer ranks.[14] Lieutenants or lower were initiated rather exceptional-
ly, in any case, not on a massive scale. Crack guard regiments were
amply represented. Generally speaking, the Decembrists were an elite,
at least judged on the basis of intellect and character.

A comparison of the membership of clandestine organizations in
Russia and Poland presents difficulties because of the differences in
their functioning. There were officer conspiracies in Poland, similar to
those in Russia, as well as distinctly civilian—mainly student—organizations. Their composition cannot be established exactly because the
inquest was conducted much more superficially in Poland than in Russia, and it left many participants out of the case. In the trial of the
National Freemasonry (1819-21), 68 officers and 15 civilians were involved, but it is thought that the actual membership of that organization could well have reached 200. A list of members of the Patriotic
Society (1821-26) compiled from different sources contains 239 names,
among them 42 former members of the National Freemasonry.[15] The
civilian element seems far more numerous in the latter organization,
but this may be because the Grand Duke Constantine, as commander-
in-chief of the Polish army, tried his best to exculpate as many of his
subordinates as possible. The list of 239 is far from complete; the figure
of 500 affiliated members advanced by some historians seems, however, exaggerated.

As for student organizations,[16] about 50 have been reckoned between 1815 and 1825 in various universities and colleges. These were
for the most part tiny groups of several, seldom a score of, members. It
is all the more difficult to reach a total figure because many members
crossed from one group to another. It would be commendable to omit
from the score some smaller groups confined to scholarly interests, as
well as the ephemeral attempts at mass student organization that were

immediately suppressed by the academic authorities. Around 600 civilians would be left who had belonged, as students, to clandestine organizations that could be categorized as "revolutionary nobility." Many of these were to sympathize with or participate in the movement after leaving school. Of the 600, about 200 came from Warsaw and other smaller towns of the Congress Kingdom; 200 from Wilno; 100 from Cracow; 70 from the German universities, and 30 from Lwów. These are not small numbers at all for a period of about five years, if one considers that the University of Warsaw counted at that time not more than 700 students, Wilno and Lwów, 1,000 each, and Cracow, about 200. All these organizations disappear between 1823 and 1826, even those not uncovered by the police. The climate in the high schools rendered any clandestine activity too dangerous, so there were no such groups there to begin with.

The next phase of the conspiracy begins in 1828–29, with Piotr Wysocki of the Cadet Infantry School. His group at first numbered less than a hundred junior officers; later, on the eve of the November Night, there were about 200, including some civilians. A number of student groups (at least 40 in all) were also connected with Wysocki's conspiracy. This group formed the nucleus of the Insurrection of 1830.

What was the social background of the Polish conspirators of the 1820s? In a majority of cases, it was, of course, nobility. Among the 239 members of the Patriotic Society known by name, men of plebeian descent numbered about 15—slightly more than 6 per cent. Among student conspirators, if we restrict ourselves to the activists, we can find around 15 plebeians. Among the leaders of some student groups, middle-class names do appear: Köhler, Mauersberger, Szreder, and Gudrajczyk. Tadeusz Krępowiecki, one of the leaders of the Free Poles, was, strictly speaking, a nobleman, but his was a family of recent ennoblement and of Jewish descent.[17]

Let us describe some characteristic examples: Jan Nepomucen Janowski, son of a peasant, graduate of the Warsaw University Faculty of Law, librarian of the Scientific Society, a radical journalist during the Insurrection, and, later, a democratic leader in France, did not belong, before the Insurrection, to any clandestine group. After all, he could hardly be classed as a "revolutionary nobleman." The same is true of the brothers Darasz: sons of a doorkeeper of peasant descent, both graduates of the University of Warsaw, one, a lawyer, the other, a physician, both democratic leaders in the Emigration; we do not find them, before 1830, in the ranks of the conspiracy.[18] The same is true of Jan Czyński, a lawyer of Jewish descent, very active during the Insurrection, but only after its outbreak. As an emigrant, Czyński became an adept of Fourierism; there is nothing in common, in his case, with nobility revolutionaries.

Obviously it can be said that the Polish conspirators of the 1820s were about as apt to be nobility as were their Russian counterparts. It was, however, by and large a much poorer nobility than the Russian one; a large percentage of the families no longer possessed land. Among 45 members of the Union of the Free Poles (1819–21), two belonged to aristocratic families, two were sons of wealthy landowners, one was the son of a higher official, and the rest were sons of tenants, surveyors, and lower clerks. The best-known leaders of the Philomaths, the Free Poles, and the National Freemasonry were not landowners' sons; they belonged to the intelligentsia, they lived on their officer's pay, or they earned their living as teachers or civil servants; they did not derive profit from the peasant's compulsory labor. One person does resemble, in social status, the Russian Decembrists: he is Lieutenant Colonel Seweryn Krzyżanowski, Łukasiński's successor in the leadership of the Patriotic Society. His family possessed a middle-size estate in the Ukraine. Two of his nearest collaborators, Andrzej Plichta and Wojciech Grzymała, descended from well-to-do landowning families; both functioned, however, in the civil service. It must be stated that, in its last phase, the Patriotic Society enlisted a large number of landowning nobility and even of aristocrats. But it was also a phase of slackening activity, when the Society and its leadership on the whole were less radical, less revolutionary. Nevertheless, the average Polish revolutionary of that time was less apt to have landed property than was his Russian counterpart.

Wysocki's conspiracy of 1830 centered on the Infantry Cadet School. Eighty-four per cent of the cadets belonged to the nobility—"and good nobility"[19]—albeit not well off. As a matter of fact, service in that school presented no great prospects of a career and thus was not very attractive even for the younger sons of landowning families. One-sixth of the Cadets had bourgeois backgrounds and German names—showing themselves, nevertheless, to be Polish patriots. Civilian members of Wysocki's organization were young journalists, men of letters, lawyers, almost exclusively of noble descent. Among the conspiring students we do find one bourgeois, Leonard Rettel, who took part in the assault on the Belvedere Palace, the residence of Grand Duke Constantine.

The November Insurrection was thus a deed of revolutionary noblemen; they managed, however, to enforce the participation in the struggle for national independence of all or almost all the nation. More or less openly, with more or less conviction, the Polish landed classes eventually acceded to the Insurrection: the aristocracy (with some exceptions), the generals, the bishops, and the bourgeoisie. As for the masses, the urban proletariat, especially in Warsaw, artisans, craftsmen, and journeymen supported the movement with much patriotic

enthusiasm. The peasants were more restrained, but they did not oppose the Insurrection; and when they were enrolled into the army, they
fought most gallantly. "At Stoczek, the troops were capturing guns/
Their hands still black from the plough . . .," said a verse in the middle
1830s,[20] thus perpetuating a democratic legend.

Various political parties came to life during the Insurrection: the revolutionary Left, the counterrevolutionary Right, and the Liberal Center. It is obvious that not all the November insurgents can be reckoned
among revolutionary noblemen. One should even question whether the
November Insurrection belongs to the "revolutionary nobility" period
at all. Most historians think it does; they consider that decisive ideological changes did not appear on the Polish Left until after the defeat of
1831—and as a consequence of that defeat. Later democratic leaders of
the Emigration were beginning to realize their aims only during the
Insurrection. One can consider the years 1830–31 as a turning point
between the period of nobility revolutionism and the period of conscious democracy. It seems more accurate, however, to treat the November Insurrection as the culmination of the story of revolutionary
noblemen: a moment when their ideology, confronted with hard realities, proved inadequate and met defeat.

In any case, during the November Insurrection only left-wing politicians can be considered as having belonged to the revolutionary nobility
current. The left wing was active mainly in Warsaw, with less important groups in some provincial towns. Their center was the Patriotic
Club, founded the day following the outbreak, and functioning as a
formal organization from the end of January 1831 under the name of the
Patriotic Society—a name inherited from a clandestine organization
dispersed five years earlier. The official list of 486 members[21] included
active members as well as individuals who payed only occasional visits. It has often been claimed that the Club consisted of several ring-
leaders and a dozen zealots, while the other participants were only a
passive throng. This was, of course, a line of defense adopted by many
members during the Russian inquest after the defeat. It is a fact that the
usual attendance at the Society's meetings were rather small, not exceeding fifty persons except in moments of political tension, when it
mounted sharply; then several hundred members and guests might be
present.

The composition of the Patriotic Society in 1831 differed from that of
earlier clandestine organizations. The majority was now, of course,
civilian; the officers were with the army, and their headquarters did not
care to have them mingling with leftist politicians. A large number of
radical hotheads considered it a point of honor to enlist as volunteers
into the army and to shed blood on the battlefield. Only toward the end
of the campaign, when the blockade by Russian forces began to tighten

around the capital, did its garrison become more numerous; many young officers, especially the supernumeraries, joined the Club as members or guests.

The great majority of members belonged to the intelligentsia. I have been able to ascertain the social status of 165 members of the Patriotic Society, 34 per cent of the total. They are distributed as follows: 40 officers, 30 civil servants, 21 landowners (some of them bearing titles), 15 magistrates, 13 journalists, 11 men of letters, 6 tradesmen, businessmen, and the like, 6 professors and teachers, 6 physicians, 6 clergymen, 6 students, and only 3 artisans—one tailor, one cobbler, and one goldsmith. It is certain that there were no representatives of the working classes. The intelligentsia, which forms the bulk of the Society's membership, belonged for the most part to the nobility: the list mentioned above of 486 members contains about 70 names which are obviously plebeian (3 of them Jewish). This estimate may be low since many people of humble origin adopted more elegant nobility names; but even with this correction, the general picture would not change much. There were relatively more people belonging to the middle classes in the Patriotic Society of 1831 than in the conspiracies of the previous period. The open political life during the Insurrection, the bitter fight against the Conservative party, resulted in an influx of non-nobility elements into the leftist organizations. This tendency was checked after the defeat, so far as clandestine life was concerned. The conspiring circles of the 1830s were again almost exclusively of nobility descent. The same phenomenon can be observed in Russia in the first two decades after the catastrophe of 14 December.

Since active participants in the clandestine movement of the 1820s were about as numerous in the Kingdom of Poland, which counted four million inhabitants, as they were among the forty-five million subjects of the Russian Empire, one might perhaps draw the conclusion that Poland at that time was more revolutionized than Russia. However, if we compare not numbers of conspirators but their ideologies, we shall get quite a different picture.

It is known that in the Russian as well as in the Polish underground there was no uniformity of opinion with regard to ideology or political program. The majority of the Northern Society of later Decembrists favored Nikita Murav'ev's constitution; that is, they were partisans of a constitutional monarchy, a parliament elected under a franchise limited to property owners, and the emancipation of peasants, without granting them rights to the land. The Southern Society, on the other hand, accepted Pestel's *Russkaia Pravda* (first version) in 1823, which called for a republican system with full democracy and the popular vote. According to Pestel, half the arable lands were to be given over to the peasants through rural communes; the other half were to be left to

the landlords, with some curtailment of the bigger latifundia. Pestel
eventually introduced further amendments to his project; but time ran
out, and this second version was never formally adopted.[22] In any
case, the *Russkaia Pravda* proposed a total and violent transformation
of Russian society along modern, bourgeois lines. As to the third component of the Decembrist movement, the Society of the United Slavs,
historians still do not agree upon the essence of their ideology. Some
specialists are willing to call them the forerunners of future revolutionary democrats; others treat them as belated utopians of the Enlightenment.[23]

A comparison of the Russian and Polish programs of the nobility-
revolutionary period presents serious difficulties because the Polish
conspirators paid so little attention to ideological matters. The claims
of the moderate wing of the Decembrists provided for only those
changes that had already been granted by Alexander I to the Kingdom
of Poland. Nikita Murav'ev's revolutionary program was equivalent, *in
merito*, to the legal program of Polish liberals, who wanted to constitu-
tionally defend more or less the same privileges that the Northern Society in St. Petersburg meant to secure by fighting. It is true that the
Polish underground movement also had its moderate wing, which did
not care to tamper with the status quo either in social or constitutional
matters. These moderate conspirators differed from the liberals in that
the latter would limit their opposition to parliamentary procedure and
print,[24] while the conspirators (even the moderate ones) regarded an
armed response to any threat against the constitution as necessary.
The difference between these "revolutionaries on the defense" and
legal oppositionists was rather theoretical. The so-called *Kalisz*, or
Liberal party, kept some contacts with the underground, and it acceded to the Insurrection of 1830 after having opposed the outbreak—
thus, willy-nilly, joining the national cause.

In the present paper, we are more interested in the radical current
within the Polish "revolutionary nobility" movement. There is not
much to say on that subject regarding the National Freemasonry and
the Patriotic Society of the 1820s. The originator of both those conspiracies, Łukasiński, defined the aim of the former as "the maintenance
of nationality" and of the latter more explicitly as "the recovery
of independence." Both formulas were conceived as defensive ones—
it was a question of mobilizing public opinion in case of a Russian
threat against the constitution, or of readiness for military action
given a favorable international situation. Prospective constitutional
changes, either in the republican or in the democratic sense, were
not contemplated at all. The same was true of social problems.
Łukasiński personally had more than once expressed his compassion
for the downtrodden peasantry. One of his closest collaborators, the

lawyer Szreder, pronounced himself in favor of "stirring all the peasantry to insurrection with the promise of some liberty or other."[25]
Łukasiński, however, considered such projects premature, the more
so as he did not foresee an outbreak of insurrection in the very near
future. In the Congress Kingdom, peasants were personally free; it
could be assumed that an improvement of their material condition
might be achieved through agreements between them and the gentle-
man-landlords.

The most important of the Polish clandestine organizations of the
1820s did not oppose the tsar on ideological, but only on political,
grounds. Here lies one of the causes (although perhaps not the most
important one) of the difficulties in arriving at an understanding between the Patriotic Society in Poland and the Russian Decembrists.
More radical tendencies did appear, however, in the Polish underground, especially among the students. The *Panta-Kojna* (Everything
in Common) Society in Warsaw derived its democratic convictions
from Rousseau's *Contrat social;* its members criticized in their clan-
destined discussions the exploitation of the people by parasitic nobles.[26] The Union of Free Poles combined the slogan of national independence with the postulate of "spreading and generalizing liberal
principles." In their propaganda, they referred to Carbonari ideals,
while glorifying the Spanish and Italian revolutions of 1820. More generally, they advocated the necessity of improving the material conditions of the peasants and the proletariat.

The student organizations were more interested in ideological deliberations than in actually preparing political or social rebellions. The
most famous of these student groups—because of the part played in it
by Mickiewicz—was the Philomaths of Wilno, who entered the field
of politics only in their final phase. From the very beginning, the Philomaths' program combined patriotic and liberal ideas. They were also
determined to convince public opinion of the necessity of peasant
emancipation (serfdom continued to exist in Lithuania as a consequence of her incorporation into Russia). The Philomath movement
collapsed, however, before it was able to elaborate a program of social
reform.

It must be emphasized that the Polish secret societies of the 1820s
labored to loosen the ties between Poland and Tsarist Russia. To that
extent they *did* serve the cause of progress in Europe by helping to
undermine the principal partner of the Holy Alliance even if they did
not profess republican, democratic, or, still less, socialist opinions.
There existed, therefore, a community of interests between Polish and
Western conspiracies of the time, which was reinforced, at least to
some degree by sporadic contacts between the Patriotic Society and
Carbonari *venta*s in France and Italy. The international importance of

the Polish independence struggle became clear to every eye in 1830, when the November outbreak actually did paralyze the proposed intervention of Nicholas I in the revolution in Belgium.[27]

In contrast to the Patriotic Society of 1821–26, the Cadets' Conspiracy of Piotr Wysocki[28] was an unmistakenly revolutionary group, planning a call to arms in the near future. This organization, however, did not intend to seize power, but only to force the patriotic elements of the Conservative party to break with the tsar and to take the lead in the struggle for independence. As a consequence, Wysocki and his partners did not give much thought to the future political or social status of the country they intended to liberate. They discussed, it is true, the necessity of establishing a revolutionary government and of defining a political program; the opportunity of abolishing compulsory peasant labor was also mentioned as a means of winning over the rural masses. Suggestions of the kind, however, did not find any support among the leaders of the Insurrection.

The outbreak of the Insurrection threw open the door in Warsaw to a lively political life, which expressed itself in press polemics, pamphlets, epigrams, meetings, and parliamentary debates. The left wing was also given the opportunity of openly advocating its opinions. There were two circumstances that speeded up the radicalization of the Movement party. First was the necessity of counteracting the conservative policy of the National Government and the Headquarters, which, according to the patriots, was leading the country to disaster. Then there was the necessity, now clearly realized, of social reform that would gain the wavering peasants to the national cause. Thus, in the course of the year 1831, the Left's organs, *Gazeta Polska* and *Nowa Polska,* started to advocate a republican regime, a democratic franchise, equal rights for the Jews, and, even more far-reaching, Saint-Simonian slogans, such as limiting the rights of inheritance, and introducing a progressive income tax. As for the peasants, the Left fought to commute their compulsory labor into cash annuities and to grant full property rights to peasants volunteering for the National Army, as well as to the families of fallen soldiers. Less frequently voiced were postulates of granting property to all peasant landholders and against indemnization of the landlords by the state. These were not ultraradical, much less socialist, postulates, but they went far beyond any pronouncement of the Polish conspiratorial circles before the November uprising.

Voices of this kind, however numerous, still did not amount to a coherent, revolutionary program of the Polish Left. That program did not exist in 1831; the same publicists in the same columns could utter divergent and vacillating opinions on constitutional and social subjects, and they did not conceal their doubts about the appropriateness of coming out with one slogan or another. A fragment of the left *Nowa Polska* may give some idea of the vagueness of their argumentation.

> No one thinks of a republic. A republic may be excellent for America, but it could be most damaging in Europe—infested as it is with . . . feudalism, with castes, with Roman Catholicism, it has therefore to be monarchical. But whether republic or monarchy is not of great concern to us. . . . Theories do not ensure happiness. . . . The state of Ohio is rich, flourishing with science, trade, and industry; therefore we deduce that Ohio's government is excellent, beneficial, and salutary. . . . Let us pass to England. The English government pays their King 40 million [pounds?]; the American government pays their president 180,000 [dollars?]. On the other hand, there are no beggars in America, while in England there are asylums, poverty, and destitution. . . . We call that government the best one that secures the greatest fortune for the largest number of its citizens.[29]

One of the most recent monographs devoted to the political history of the November Insurrection provides the following verdict on the "second" Patriotic Society:

> The Patriotic Society, in spite of its well crystalized political form, did not evolve a unified political program, nor did it produce consistent revolutionary tactics capable of overthrowing the conservatives in power. . . . In the course of the Insurrection, the Patriotic Society did not transform itself into an efficient and vigorous organization of revolutionary noblemen.[30]

The reason for that failure, according to the author, lay in the fact that the Society's membership remained confined to the intelligentsia, a class deprived of any effective contact with the masses, even the patriotic proletariat of the capital.

Lenin similarly defined the root of the weakness of the Russian Decembrists, saying that they remained "terribly far from the people." He acknowledged, nevertheless, their lasting, historic role, namely that they "awakened Herzen" and set an example for the next generation of champions of liberty—those we today call "revolutionary democrats." As a matter of fact, between the revolutionary noblemen, defeated on 14 December 1825, and the conspiracy of Petrashevskii almost twenty years were to elapse. There were no secret societies during the intervening period, only small circles of young intellectuals from whom some famous adversaries of the regime would eventually emerge, such as Herzen, Ogarev, and Bakunin. These intellectuals still belonged to the nobility, but, in contrast to the Decembrist generation, they were solitary and apparently not dangerous, at least so long as they remained in Russia. They would become famous abroad after 1848. The influence of the Decembrist tradition on Herzen has been emphasized by Herzen himself; he describes in his memoirs the solemn divine service of thanks celebrated in Moscow on the very day of the execution of the five "rebels." "As a fourteen-year-old boy," writes

Herzen, "lost in the crowd, I attended this service, and on that spot, before the blood-stained altar, I swore to myself that I would avenge the executed victims, and I sentenced myself to fight that throne, that altar, and those cannons."[31] In fact, Herzen did eventually become one of the most redoubtable adversaries of the Russian autocracy.

Herzen is commonly ranked with revolutionary noblemen—accurately enough, strictly speaking, since he was the son (illegitimate, but recognized) of a magnate and senator. Considering his ideology and way of dealing, however, he transcended by far the Decembrist tradition. Their heroism and their martyrdom did inspire him—but he himself belonged to another epoch.

One can perceive a curious parallel between the moral and intellectual inheritance of nobility revolutionism in Russia and in Poland. Their great defeat in Poland occurred in 1831. The next phase of the ideological revolution—that of the revolutionary democrats—begins around 1843 (including conspiracies in Poland herself). In the intervening period some of the former revolutionary noblemen gradually cross over to more democratic positions.

There is, however, an essential difference between the processes in the two countries. The Russian Decembrist movement was thoroughly crushed, most of its members sent to Siberia, and those who escaped kept silent. The mission of the fallen victims was taken over by the next generation, by those who were still children at the time of defeat. Things went otherwise in Poland. The nobility revolutionary movement had its martyrs in that country as well: Łukasiński, Krzyżanowski, Wysocki, and many others. But a large fraction of the November insurgents, and among them the most compromised leftist politicians, went abroad and eventually created in France and in England a vital center for political discussion. The most distinguished among the revolutionary noblemen, Lelewel, Mochnacki, Mickiewicz, and Krępowiecki, joined in these discussions on the causes of the defeat and on the means of reprisal. The chief ideologues of the Polish emigration in the 1830s are consequently the same as those in the 1820s, only now enriched by recent experiences and acting in a different environment. These ideologues of nobility revolutionism did educate those among the younger participants of the last Insurrection, the first echelon of emissaries who were to carry into Poland the new democratic slogans. The most famous of these, Szymon Konarski, was to be executed in Wilno in 1839. He was also the first to make a try at reestablishing contact with the revolutionary underground in Russia after fifteen years.

The revolutionary noblemen did not play any decisive role in the history of either Poland or Russia. Theirs was a rather narrow elite movement, rather inconsistent, and, one might say, doomed to failure.

But they left an immensely important heroic and romantic legend. Mickiewicz's poetry engraved this legend on Polish hearts, and Herzen's *Kolokol* on the Russian ones. In both cases, literary genius was at work. But genius alone could not fix in the public memory the image of the Russian Decembrists and of the Polish heroes of the November night. Two more conditions were necessary: the historicity of the fact itself and the persistence of the objective conditions. Both were needed to revive the resistance to despotism.

NOTES

1 See M. Hroch, *Die Vorkämpfer der nationalen Bewegung bei den kleinen Völkern Europas: Eine vergleichende Analyse zur gesellschaftlichen Schichtung der patriotischen Gruppen* (Acta Universitatis Carolinae Philosophica et Historica, Prague, 1968).

2 S. S. Landa, "Rytsari pravdy i svobody," *Komsomolskaia Pravda*, 26 December 1975.

3 The term appears for the first time in Lenin's writings in 1906, designating the first phase of the revolutionary movement in Russia, the second one being called *raznochinskii*, and the third, and last, proletarian. This theme eventually evolved into the well-known paper of 1912, *To the Memory of Herzen*.

4 M. Mochnacki, *Powstanie narodu polskiego w r. 1830 i 1831*, 3rd ed. (Berlin, 1863), vol. 1, pp. 7, 13.

5 Letter of the Polish Central National Committee to the editors of *Kolokol*, 20 September 1862, published in *Kolokol* on 10 October. Quoted in *Współpraca rewolucyjna polsko-rosyjska* (Moscow, 1963), vol. 1, p. 526.

6 S. Askenazy, *Rosja-Polska 1815–1830* (Lwów, 1907), p. 32.

7 Statistics on the nobility and their family heads in the Duchy of Warsaw and in the Congress Kingdom are found in H. Grynwaser, *Pisma* [Works] (Wrocław, 1951), vol. 1, pp. 225–27.

8 N. M. Chentsov, *Vosstanie dekabristov: Bibliografia* (Moscow-Leningard, 1929); R. G. Eimontova, *Dvizhenie dekabristov: Ukazatel' literatury* (Moscow, 1965). The fundamental monograph still remains M. V. Nechkina, *Dvizhenie dekabristov*, 2 vols. (Moscow, 1955).

9 S. Płoski, ed., *Bibliografia historii Polski XIX wieku*, vol. 1, 1815–31 (Wrocław, 1958), supplemented by the annual volumes of the *Bibliografia historii Polski*.

10 The monumental work of S. Askenazy, *Łukasiński*, 2nd ed., 2 vols. (Warsaw, 1929), maintains its value up to the present. This paper owes much to the book by J. Szacki, *Ojczyzna, naród, rewolucja* (Warsaw, 1962); R. F. Leslie's *Polish Politics and the Revolution of November 1830* (London, 1956) may be also consulted. Other items are quoted below.

11 S. S. Landa, *Dukh revolutsionnykh preobrazovanii* (Moscow, 1975), p. 7.

12 Published in vol. 8 of the series *Vosstanie dekabristov: Materialy* (Leningrad, 1925).

13 The Russian army counted, in 1825, 500 generals, 18,000 officers, and 730,000 privates. Askenazy, *Rosja-Polska*, p. 11.

14 Among the Decembrists sentenced by the High Court were 3 generals, 12 colonels, 10

lieutenant colonels, 3 majors, 22 captains, 26 lieutenants, 23 second lieutenants, 9 cornets, and 8 civilians. Thirty-five officers belonged to guard regiments; 76 defendants were under 30; and 5 were over 40 years of age.

15 H. Dylągowa, *Towarzystwo Patriotyczne i sąd sejmowy 1821-29* (Warsaw, 1970), pp. 332-35.

16 A. Kamiński, *Polskie związki młodzieży 1804-1831* (Warsaw, 1963).

17 W. Łukaszewicz, *Tadeusz Krępowiecki* (Warsaw, 1954).

18 J. N. Janowski, *Notatki Autobiograficzne* (Wrocław, 1953); W. Darasz, *Pamiętnik emigranta* (Wrocław, 1953).

19 W. Tokarz, *Sprzysiężenie Wysockiego i Noc Listopadowa* (Warsaw, 1925), p. 17.

20 From a poem by Gustaw Ehrenberg, coupled with the ironic refrain: "O cześć wam, panowie magnaci!" [Hail, my lords!] Adopted as an anthem by the Polish Populist movement since the end of the nineteenth century.

21 Published by W. Smoleński in *Przegląd Historyczny* 8 (1909): 91-105; see E. Oppman, *Warszawskie Towarzystwo Patriotyczne 1830-1831* (Warsaw, 1937), pp. 89- 92.

22 Nechkina's introduction to *Vosstanie dekabristov*, vol. 7 (Moscow, 1958).

23 An analysis of this polemic in S. S. Landa's book cited above, n. 11, pp. 251-61.

24 See H. Więckowska, *Opozycja liberalna w Królestwie Kongresowym 1815-1830* (Warsaw, 1922).

25 Łukasiński's letter of 17 October 1825, quoted by Dylągowa (n. 11), p. 48, See Łukasiński's *Pamiętnik*, written in prison (Warsaw, 1960), p. 70.

26 A. Kraushar, "Panta-Kojna: związek tajny młodzieży polskiej w Warszawie i Berlinie 1817-1822," *Biblioteka Warszawska*, vol. 1 (1907).

27 I do not have to enter into the controversy among historians over the question of whether the Polish conspirators took to arms in November 1830 at the summons or command of the Paris Carbonari. Contradictory opinions are voiced by M. Kukiel, *Uwagi i przyczynki do genezy rewolucji listopadowej i wojny 1831 r.* (London, 1958), and W. Zajewski, "Prądzyński, Lelewel i mit o karbonarskim podziemiu," *Kwartalnik Historyczny*, no. 1 (1964).

28 See T. Łepkowski, *Piotr Wysocki* (Warsaw, 1972).

29 J. Dutkiewicz, *Wybór źródeł do dziejów powstania listopadowego* (Wrocław, 1967), p. 93; ibid., passim, other excerpts of similar pronouncements.

30 W. Zajewski, *Walki wewnętrzne ugrupowań politycznych w powstaniu listopadowym 1830-1831* (Gdańsk, 1967), pp. 34-35.

31 A. Herzen, *Byloe i dumy* [Polish edition, 1951], vol. 1, p. 69.

THE PROBLEM OF REVOLUTION IN
POLISH THOUGHT,
1831-1848/49
Andrzej Walicki, Polish Academy of Sciences

I. INTRODUCTORY REMARKS

The period of Polish history between the defeat of the November Uprising (1830-31) and the Springtime of the Peoples saw numerous revolutionary conspiracies and abortive revolutions—most notably, the
Cracow Revolution of February 1846 that was drowned in blood by a
jacquerie skillfully encouraged and directed against the Revolution by
the Austrian government. The significance of this period for the Polish
revolutionary and national tradition lies in its flourishing pre-Marxian
revolutionary Polish thought and, simultaneously, its intense identification of the Polish national cause with that of a universalist, all-European revolution. Never before, and never afterwards, was the conviction of the inseparability of the Polish cause from the cause of revolution so strong and so widespread among the Poles. It seemed quite
natural that a nation heroically struggling against the Holy Alliance of
the reactionary monarchs, a nation constituting (as Engels put it) "the
revolutionary part of Russia, Austria and Prussia,"[1] had to be part—
and a most important part—of the Revolutionary Alliance of the Peoples. The "overturning of the old order" in Europe was its only hope
and, in its turn, depended on the fulfilling of this hope. The famous
words from Mickiewicz's *Litany of the Polish Pilgrim*, "For a universal war for the freedom of the nations,/ We beseech Thee, oh Lord,"[2]
expressed the mood of the Polish patriots in exile. It is also fair to say
that the mood of the majority of Polish patriots actively committed to
the struggle for independence (Mickiewicz included) would have been
expressed even better if emphasis had been given to the *revolutionary*
character of this ardently invoked universal war.

The awareness of the revolutionary character of the Polish cause—of
the fact that the Partitions of the Polish Commonwealth were the basis
of strength, mutual solidarity, and external influence of the three main
pillars of European conservatism—was equally strong among the
people of the Right. Both right-wingers and moderates concurred with
the classical diagnosis of Marx and Engels that "Poland must either be
revolutionary or perish,"[3] and that is why a hard-boiled conservatism
was often seen as incompatible with Polish patriotism. It was precisely
that diagnosis which led Count Henryk Rzewuski, the most consistent
Polish disciple of De Maistre, to abandon and condemn any struggle for

the independence of Poland and to recognize that, for the victory of conservative values, Poland could only exist as a province of Russia.

For the same reason, or rather, from the same logic, the right wing of the Polish independence movement, represented by the followers of the "king de facto," Prince Adam Czartoryski, contributed to the revolutionary ferment in Europe. And it did so in spite of its firm decision to do everything possible to avoid social revolution in Poland and to collaborate with the liberal governments rather than with revolutionary peoples. This explains the curious paradox that Michael Bakunin was willing to collaborate with them. In spite of the Polish democrats' violent attacks on Czartoryski's "aristocratic party," the Russian revolutionary, looking at that party from the point of view of an all-European revolutionary strategy, saw in it an important, well-organized progressive force.[4] Metternich was certainly right when he rebuked Prince Adam for espousing the cause of "Polonism" and, by doing so, betraying his own class interest.[5]

In the present paper I shall deal with various kinds of revolutionary thinkers. First of all, there are, of course, the ideologists and leaders of the large and politically most important revolutionary-democratic movement. This movement, very numerous for that time and internally differentiated, included both the powerful Polish Democratic Society in exile (which was, as Peter Brock has indicated, the first democratically run centralized and well-disciplined political party in the history of East European peoples)[6] and also some more moderate and less stable groups. The latter as a rule regarded as their ideological leader the eminent democratic historian Joachim Lelewel. Almost all the Polish democrats of that time came from the middle or petty gentry (although there are some very important exceptions to this rule), and this was not without consequences for their ideological as well as their practical points of view (the latter were usually more moderate than their theories).

In spite of this, however, attempts to divide the Polish democrats of the time into two distinct groups—the gentry revolutionaries and the true revolutionary democrats (i.e., genuine followers of a radical "bourgeois-democratic" and revolutionary program in the agrarian question)—seems to me both artificial and sterile. Gentry revolutionism, in the sense of a nostalgia for the ancient liberties of the gentry or a defense of aristocratically constituted bodies against the encroachments of absolutism (a defense of the *old*, but making use of the *modern*, constitutional language, as was often the case in the Hungarian opposition to the Hapsburgs),[7] was something very different from Lelewel's idealization of the ancient Polish republic. Lelewel's idealization of the petty gentry was bound up with the most severe accusations against aristocracy; it harked back to the equalitarian and libertarian principles of the ancient Slavonic communes.

Closer to the political experience of the Polish democrats was the gentry revolutionism of the Decembrists, although generally the Decembrist movement represented a stage through which the Polish revolutionary movement of the 1830s and 1840s had already passed. After the defeat of the November Insurrection, the Polish democrats, even the most moderate among them, never identified revolution with a military coup d'etat (as the Decembrists did). Nor did they think it possible to solve the peasant question without enfranchisement or (as Nikita Murav'ev had finally conceded) with giving to the peasants as freeholds only a small part of the land which under serfdom they had cultivated for their own usage.

We are often reminded that the Polish democrats of the time did not demand a full expropriation of gentry lands and did not provide an adequate solution for the landless peasants. True—but they also demanded that the lands be given to peasants without compensation to the gentry for their loss. It was precisely this that was the main feature of a truly democratic agrarian program (as opposed to a liberal-conservative one),[8] according to Nikolai Chernyshevskii whose statements are often quoted as typical for revolutionary democratism.

In their political thinking, the Polish Democratic Society and other Polish democratic organizations of the epoch were in favor of a radical political ("bourgeois") democracy; their economic programs, although not always consistent, favored the development of a free and independent peasantry; their ideal (to quote again from the excellent article by Peter Brock) "was the Jeffersonian kind of agrarian democracy, where the independent yeoman farmer predominated but in which the landed gentlemen continued to exist."[9] Therefore it seems proper to treat them as more or less consistent, more or less radical revolutionary democrats—keeping in mind, of course, that some features of their ideology can be explained by, or related to, their gentry background.[10]

Less important as an active political group, but very important for their contributions to Polish thought, were the revolutionary Christian socialists. They were violently critical of the "individualistic" ideology of the democrats, and they appealed to the peasants through their religious vocabulary and millenarian visions. Somewhat similar was the place of revolutionary Messianism in the history of revolutionary ideas in Poland. In spite of Mickiewicz's Legion, fighting in 1848–49 for the freedom of Italy, the role of the revolutionary Messianic poets (Mickiewicz and Słowacki) in Polish politics was in fact rather marginal. Their ideas, however, as the purest and most extreme expressions of the political romanticism of the epoch, are, I think, of great importance to Polish intellectual history.[11]

Attention should also be drawn to the fact that, in the 1840s, which were a truly "philosophical epoch" in the history of Polish thought, the problem of revolution was of utmost significance for the philosophical speculations about the dialectics of history. Three outstanding leaders of the revolutionary democratic movement, Karol Libelt, Henryk Kamieński, and his younger cousin, Edward Dembowski (who was killed at the age of 24, as the virtual leader of the Cracow Revolution), were enthusiastic and full-fledged philosophers, steeped in Hegelian dialectics and trying (in accordance with the general trends in Polish philosophy of the time) to transform it from a contemplative wisdom into a practical "philosophy of action." The importance of their thought also derived from the fact that it was developed, not in the emigration, but in partitioned Poland; thanks to its abstract philosophical language, it was able to pass censorship and find its way to numerous readers throughout the country.

Within the scope of a short paper it is impossible to present all the richness of our topic. In the pages that follow I have tried to give, not a comprehensive and detailed analysis, but rather a brief outline of the main levels on which the problem of revolution was discussed and a characterization of the main varieties of revolutionary thinking during the period in question.

II. THE NATIONAL AND UNIVERSAL AIMS OF REVOLUTION

The problem of revolution in an epoch striving to produce a peculiar "Nationalist International" ("The Holy Alliance of Peoples") necessarily involved the problem of the relationship between national and international tasks and between national and universalist values. The most widely accepted solution to this problem was the concept of romantic progressivism, developed in many countries (in France it was represented, among others, by Mickiewicz's friends Michelet and Quinet), but most clearly articulated in the writings of Mazzini and of the Polish thinkers. The latter even claimed that it was originated in Poland, along with the famous slogan of the November uprising: "For our freedom and yours."

When the Polish insurgents were still fighting, Kazimierz Brodziński, in an address on the anniversary of the May 3 Constitution, credited the Poles with being the first to realize that the principle of national egoism had to be replaced with an awareness that the central position in the world of nations belonged to all mankind: "Formerly each nation regarded itself as the goal and center of everything in the same way as the earth was regarded as the center of the universe. . . . Copernicus discovered the system of the material universe; the Polish nation alone (I say it boldly and with a patriotic pride) could have a foreboding of the true movement of the moral universe. It has recognized that every nation is a fragment of the whole and must roll on its orbit and around the center like the planets around theirs."[12]

In fact, the origins of romantic progressivism should be traced back to the emergence of romantic universalism, as opposed to the rationalistic universalism of the Enlightenment. While the latter found its ideal in the uniform, universally valid norms of enlightened reason, romantic universalism professed the principle of "diversitarianism" (Lovejoy's expression),[13] and it identified universality with variety and fullness, thus sanctifying the pluralism of national cultures as unique and irreplaceable individualities of mankind. Romantic progressivism was simply a temporalization of romantic universalism. The Enlightenment and post-Enlightenment conception equated progress with the achievements of reason and universal civilization. It measured these achievements by standards set up by "laws of nature" that were unchangeable and, consequently, leveled the differences between nations. At its beginning the Polish Democratic Society based its program upon this conception and was rebuked by Lelewel for "having emigrated from the national cause to an ethereal cosmopolitanism."[14] The romantic conception of the history of mankind saw it as a wonderful symphony, with each nation in it representing a single sound. At the same time, each nation was appointed to its own historical mission, serving the universal goal in accordance with its individual character. Although the national was subordinated to the universal, yet the realization of specific national tasks came to be recognized as the only possible way of attaining universal progress. The Democratic Society espoused this conception, describing its ideological evolution as a transition from "foreign faith" to "national faith," from the slogan "through mankind for Poland" to its reverse, "through Poland for mankind."[15]

The idea that each nation has its own individual task in the international division of labor was interpreted, of course, in such a way as to allot to the Poles an important, *revolutionary* task. In the "Act of Foundation" (1832) of the Polish Democratic Society, this task is formulated as follows:

> The free Polish people, but only the Polish people as a whole [i.e., not reduced to the old notion of the "nation of the nobility," but uniting in active citizenship the entire population of Poland], can inspire even the Russians to strive for enlightenment, freedom, and true social life, because Poland's one calling, her only duty to mankind, is to bring to the farthest reaches of the East true enlightenment and an understanding of the rights of man. This is why the existence of Poland is essential to the civilization, happiness, and peace of Europe.[16]

This formulation is characteristic of Polish democratic thought in the first half of the 1830s, revealing its roots in the Enlightenment tradition and, at the same time, its commitment to a secularized version of the ancient Polish idea of *antemurale Christianitatis*. This conception of what Poland's task was gained enthusiastic support among the contemporary European Left, who saw in the Poles (to quote Engels) "twenty millions of heroes" defending Europe from the Asiatic despotism of Tsarist Russia.[17] On the other hand, the Polish democrats sincerely acknowledged that the Russians could not be excluded from the brotherhood of nations. That this was not merely lip service to an abstract ideal was shown by the fact (largely unknown in the West) that the Polish democrats (especially Lelewel) repeatedly pointed to the existence of a democratic-republican tradition in Russia (Novgorod and Pskov, the ancient self-governing Slavonic communes). They alone in contemporary Europe commemorated the anniversaries of the Decembrists' uprising and of the death of its five leaders.[18] In the later period, this tradition of revolutionary brotherhood with the Russians was manifested in the generous help given by the Poles to the first Russian revolutionary émigrés—both minor (Golovin and Sazonov) and great (Bakunin and—first and foremost—Alexander Herzen).[19]

In spite of all this, with the passing of time this formulation of Poland's mission began to be viewed as neither sufficiently important nor as sufficiently universal. First, in the middle of the 1830s, the program of the Polish Democratic Society was violently attacked by the newly emerged socialist organizations. They felt that the doctrine of the "rights of man" led to the egoism of private property, that the bourgeois West was not worth defending, and that the mission of the Poles had to be truly universal—that it was nothing less than the struggle to establish the perfect and final social order—the true Kingdom of God on earth. In spite of many obvious differences, similar motifs could be found in Messianism: Mickiewicz (like Mazzini)[20] also condemned the individualistic ethos of the "doctrine of rights" and called for it to be replaced with the ethos of heroic self-sacrifice in fulfilling the supreme duty. He also saw the West (except France) as a decaying civilization. Finally, he preached the imminent total regeneration of mankind—the Poles (leading the other Slavs and in alliance with France) were seen by him as a chosen instrument of this earthly salvation. True, he was more concerned with the "national idea" than were the early Polish socialists. It must be remembered, however, that at the beginning of the 1840s his *national* Messianism became transformed into a *religious* Messianism, preaching the new religious dispensation and completely subordinating the Polish national cause to the universal revolutionary spiritual and material regeneration of mankind. As the prophet of a "new revelation,"Mickiewicz could say, "Poland must initiate a new world, otherwise it makes no sense to struggle for her restoration."[21]

The imminent revolutionary transformation, as Mickiewicz saw it, would bring about the collective salvation of all suffering nations by the Christianization of political life. The revelation of Christ had heretofore been confined to the sphere of private life, whereas the new revelation would extend the rule of Christian ethics to the sphere of social and political relationships. This was not a new idea: we can find it in Saint-Simon, in Fourier, and even in De Maistre, who expressed the hope that the *société des individus* would be elevated to the *société des nations*.[22] Nevertheless, it seems worthwhile to emphasize that in no other country did this idea become as popular as it did in Poland. It was embraced not only by Messianists and revolutionaries, but even by Prince Adam Czartoryski. His *Essay on Diplomacy*,[23] written in connection with the Greek uprising on the eve of the November Insurrection, sounded the most eminent protest against the immorality of politics.

The concept of universal regeneration was developed most systematically by August Cieszkowski, a firm opponent of revolutionary methods of struggle, but at the same time a philosopher of history who saw his epoch as one of profound revolution (in the sense of a irresistible overturning), comparable only to the "palingenetic" crisis of the ancient world out of which the new Christian world had been born. In his major work, *Our Father*,[24] he outlined a vision of the future Kingdom of the Holy Ghost in which three supranational institutions would guard peace and secure justice in political relations: a Central Government of Mankind, a Universal International Tribunal, and a Universal Council of the Peoples.

The most important factor influencing the atmosphere in which these Polish revolutionary ideologies were being developed was, certainly, progressive romantic nationalism. The word "nationalism" in this case should be understood in its broadest sense: romantic thinkers, combining an ardent patriotism with an equally ardent condemnation of national egoism, cannot be called "nationalists" in the modern, narrower sense of the term. In the writings of Mazzini "the spirit of nationality" is also often contrasted with "the narrow spirit of nationalism" that is incompatible with the ideal of the brotherhood of nations.[25]

However, instead of indulging in terminological problems it would be more useful to summarize the motifs that underlay the romantic conception of what the nation was. First, there was the idea of universal historical progress which was inextricably involved in the conception of the nation as the individualization of mankind and the principal agent of progress. Then, there was the idea of a national mission, and a conviction that that mission, and not inherited traditions, constituted the true essence of the nation. From this came the possibility of espousing the idea of revolution, and a readiness to accept a radical break with the immediate past, if that past were seen as a deviation from the national calling. Third, the ethos of activism and moral perfectionism and the recognition of the ''spirit of sacrifice'' were recognized as the highest national virtues. Finally, a belief in the active brotherhood of nations was promulgated and the egoistic principle of nonintervention—the principle of *chacun chez soi, chacun pour soi,* so much despised by Mickiewicz—was indignantly condemned.

It is obvious that such a set of ideas was incompatible with *conservative* romanticism—that romanticism of tradition which saw history as a slow, organic development and rejected not only revolution but any kind of deliberate social engineering, condemning the very spirit of conscious, purposeful activity. It was also obviously difficult to reconcile it with the heritage of the Enlightenment. The rationalism, utilitarianism, and hedonism of the Enlightenment were rejected with equal force by the Messianists and the socialists; the bourgeois individualism of a Voltaire or a Bentham was condemned both from the collectivist standpoint (the socialists) and, no less strongly, from the point of view of the charismatic individualism of hero worship (the Messianists). More complicated, or rather more eclectic, in this respect was the ideology of the Democratic Society, but even this organization, at the beginning so strongly committed to the values of the Enlightenment, was, on the whole, moving away from this initial commitment.

One of the reasons for this evolution was the fact that the tradition of the ''Polish eighteenth-century revolution'' (as it has been called by the American historian Robert R. Palmer)[26] was monopolized by the monarchists from Prince Czartoryski's camp. The democrats reacted to this with a severe—sometimes too severe—criticism of the May 3 Constitution (as a concession to aristocracy and monarchism). Equally characteristic was their very critical attitude toward Kościuszko, whom they accused of being not radical enough, tamed, as it were, by the aristocrats who surrounded him.[27]

Even more important, however, was the general disappointment with postrevolutionary, bourgeois Europe and the growing awareness that the Enlightenment had, in fact, paved the way for contemporary European capitalism with all its evident evils. Naturally enough (as was later the case with Herzen and the Russian populists), the growing disappointment with the capitalist West led to a more or less consistent abandonment of Westernism. It is no exaggeration to say that in the 1840s Westernism, proclaiming the need for a strong bourgeoisie in Poland, had influential followers among the liberal-conservative monarchists, but it was already something almost completely alien to the democrats. An isolated exception was the Fourierist Jan Czyński, who, because of this, had no other choice but to sympathize with Prince Czartoryski's party. The other democrats were by then vying

with each other in anti-Westernism. The Democratic Society cut itself
off from the Westernism of the monarchists but was in its turn accused
of Westernism by the Lelewelists. They criticized it, among other
things, for imitating the centralist leanings of the French Revolution, so
alien to the spirit of the ancient Polish Commonwealth.

Still more anti-Western were the socialists, who accused the democrats of an uncritical attitude toward "merely political" freedom, sanctifying the principle of unconditional private property. Mickiewicz extolled the Slavs as people "unspoiled by industrialization";[28] the socialist Communities of the Polish People saw Western capitalism as a
worse social evil than feudalism, and declared, "We are ready to cover
Poland with our corpses in order to free her from the plague of industry
and trade, in the sense of contemporary commercial exploitation."[29]
The Democratic Society, accused by the Communities of a desire to
Westernize Poland by replacing her nobility with a "new aristocracy of
money, potatoes, and cheese,"[30] rejected this charge with indignation.

It is difficult to deny that the socialists were right when they claimed
that the agrarian program of the Democratic Society could lead only to
the "fragmentation of individualism" and not to its liquidation. This,
however, cannot change the fact that the Society's leaders were thoroughly convinced that the road chosen by them for Poland was in accordance with ancient Slavonic communalism and had nothing in common with repeating the errors of the West. The assertion that Poland
needed a strong bourgeoisie of her own aroused them to vigorous resistance; General Mierosławski claimed that the lack of a native bourgeoisie was a peculiar privilege of Poland, enabling her to skip the tran-
sitional phases of development and to introduce at once an unlimited
sovereignty of the people.[31] Later, under the influence of the multiple
disappointments during the Springtime of the Peoples, Polish democrats became more skeptical of the revolutionary, regenerative po-
tentialities of the Western nations. This, of course, could only strength-
en their anti-Westernism.

Anti-Westernism, however, did not mean giving up the universalist
ideal. Polish democrats and socialists of the 1840s never ceased to expect a universal revolutionary change and never confined their tasks to
the narrowly national one. They simply ceased (like the Russian populists would later) to conceive of "universalism" as tantamount to
Westernism."

III. REVOLUTION AND RESTORATION

The word *revolution* originally meant a "restoration," "a reversion
to a state of affairs similar or equivalent to an earlier one."[32] After the
French Revolution this meaning fell into disuse, although we can still
find it in the writings of Maurycy Mochnacki, a leader of the patriotic

Left during the November Insurrection for whom "revolution"—in the Polish case—meant an overturn in order to *restore* independent Poland.[33]

After the defeat of the Insurrection, "revolution" (in contradistinction to "insurrection") became firmly associated with solutions to *social* questions, and the relationship between "revolution" and "restoration" became less simple, more dialectical. I have already touched on this problem in connection with the ancient Slavonic communes providing an inspiration for revolutionary visions of the future. This was in fact the Polish variant of "the second reaction against the French Revolution and the period of the Enlightenment," described by Marx as follows: "The first reaction against the French revolution and the period of Enlightenment bound up with it was naturally to see everything as medieval and romantic. . . . The second reaction is to look beyond the Middle Ages into the primitive age of each nation, and that corresponds to the socialist tendency."[34]

The only reservation I have to make is that, in the Polish case, "looking beyond the Middle Ages into the primitive age" was a characteristic feature of a broad current of democratic thought, and not only of "the socialist tendency." Dembowski—a convinced socialist—was not the only one to hark back to the mythical times of "pre-Christian Slavdom"; the ideologists of the Democratic Society also "looked for light in the pre-national epoch" and claimed to have found in Polish "pagan antiquity" the key to the Polish future.

The source of these ideas can easily be found in the historical and archeological studies inspired by the Slavophile atmosphere in Polish thought during the reign of Alexander I. First of all, I should mention Lelewel's theory of ancient Slavonic communalism and Chodakowski's famous essay "On Pre-Christian Slavdom."[35] Both were bound up with the characteristic Enlightenment motif of a "return to origins," but they reinterpreted it in the spirit of a romantic understanding of national individuality and a romantic idealization of the common people. In fact "dialectics of retrospection" were inherent in the structure of romantic progressivism and its idea of nationality. An interesting analysis of these dialectics has been made by Kazimierz Kelles-Krauz, a pioneer of Marxist sociology in Poland.[36] He pointed out that striving for a radical renovation of society implies, of course, breaking with the present and with the *recent* past, but that, at the same time, it often draws inspiration from a more remote past—the more remote, the more radical the ideal of renovation.

Polish revolutionary thinkers of the romantic epoch provide good examples of this. They knew perfectly well that nationality—in the modern sense of national consciousness—was something new, that the national awakening of the masses was a task to be fulfilled rather than

an accomplished fact. They agreed, therefore, with Tadeusz Krępowiecki (a radical of the Enlightenment type, a co-founder of the Democratic Society) who claimed that feudal institutions were necessarily a
negation of nationality.[37] Dembowski saw clearly that Poland before
the Partitions was merely a "nation of one caste," that a more comprehensive conception of the nation became widespread only at the beginning of the nineteenth century;[38] Kamieński in his *Democratic Catechism* went so far as to accuse "the nation of the nobility" of lacking
true patriotism;[39] Libelt, in his philosophical analysis of the love of the
fatherland, put emphasis on the prosaic fact that the economic emancipation of the peasantry was a necessary precondition for a strong self-
conscious national feeling.[40] At the same time, however, the "primary" nation (the nation "in itself") was considered to be of ancient,
prehistoric origin. Therefore, in order to become nationally conscious—"to recognize oneself in one's essence" (Mochnacki's expression)[41]—one had to look back to prehistoric times and search there
for a pure, although unconscious, national substance, which the emerging modern nation had to rediscover in itself and raise to the level of
self-consciousness.

The aim of the revolutionary, nation-building transformation of Poland
was thus seen as a *restoration*—on a higher level, of course—of ancient Slavonic democracy. For Lelewel (and the moderates who followed him) it also meant a rehabilitation and a partial restoration of the
best features of the Polish "gentry republic." Although under this "republic" only a part of the population had enjoyed civil and political
rights, it was nonetheless, in its best times at least, incomparably better
than the absolute monarchies of the West. Some essential features of
ancient Slavonic freedom had been preserved in it, and these could be
developed into modern republicanism, skipping the phase of royal absolutism. The ideologists of the Democratic Society accepted this conception, but they tried to avoid any idealization of "gentry republicanism," thus corroborating Kelles-Krauz's assertion that a *more radical*
ideology idealizes, as a rule, a *more distant* past. They did not deny the
alleged casual relation between ancient Slavonic communalism and the
Polish gentry's love for freedom. They also agreed to regard the "gentry republic" as a society relatively better than the Western absolute
monarchies. At the same time, however, they saw it as a deep dis-
tortion of right principles and refused to praise and to continue any
traditions specific to the gentry. The moderates treated this standpoint
as a complete break with the national tradition and imputed to the
Democratic Society a desire to create on the shores of the Vistula an
entirely new nation, preserving only the name of the former one.[42]

The most unbridled idealization of the "gentry republic" is to be
found, naturally enough, in the writings of the Messianic poets. They

saw it as a state based upon enthusiasm and exaltation, enjoying the fullest possible freedom, but, unfortunately, lacking great charismatic leaders with an irresistible power to command. Only such leaders are able to discipline freedom without recourse to compulsion by virtue of their spiritual superiority. In the coming revolutionary upheaval they believed that a great, divinely inspired leader would appear and that, therefore, the ancient Poland would be reborn in a new Poland, with her freedom disciplined in enthusiastic obedience and her republican virtues strengthened by Messianic zeal.[43]

Let us now turn to the Christian socialists. Since the ancient Slavonic communes represented not only the principle of democratic self-government, but also the principle of common ownership, the socialists might be expected to look backward to "pre-Christian Slavdom" and to see the coming revolution as a restoration (again on the higher level) of the archaic collectivism of the Slavonic communes. In fact, however, it was not so: the majority of the Polish socialists of the romantic epoch looked backward to the evangelic spirit of early Christianity and were repelled by the anti-Christian leanings of the democrats, expressed, among other things, in their idealization of the pagan institutions of the ancient Slavs. The theme of "Slavonic community" was too closely associated with the enthusiasm for pre-Christian times. For this reason Polish socialists in exile—Stanisław Worcell, Zenon Świętosławski, Ludwik Królikowski—treated this theme with suspicion and preferred to keep themselves aloof from it.

Nevertheless, there is an inner logic to the development of these ideas, and consequently Polish thought could not escape a phase of "populist socialism." Some populist-socialist motifs were not unknown to Lelewel, and it is quite possible that Bakunin became interested in the Russian village commune under his influence.[44] In Mickiewicz's "Paris Lectures on Slavonic Literature," the Slavonic village commune was compared to Fourier's phalanstery.[45] Later, in the revolutionary year 1848, the idea of communal ownership of the land was introduced to the "Set of Principles" of Mickiewicz's Legion.[46]

Most important, however, was the gradual assimilation of socialist ideas by the democrats—a process that bridged the initial gulf between the two ideologies. Dembowski was a socialist, and yet an emissary of the Democratic Society. His socialism was not Christian, but it was bound up with admiration for "pre-Christian Slavdom." Under the influence of Mierosławski and J. K. Podolecki,[47] in the 1840s the Democratic Society itself began to appreciate the ancient Slavonic commune, not only as a prototype for political democracy, but also as a model for agrarian socialism. In 1846 Worcell joined the Society; he, of course, made it even more susceptible to socialism. The events of the Spring-

time of the Peoples brought discredit to the bourgeois radicals and, by
the same token, contributed to the further popularization of socialist
ideas among the Polish exiles. Characteristically, the Democratic Society did not embrace the idea of the nationalization of all the land (an
idea set forth in the 1830s by the Communities of the Polish People).
Instead, they embraced Podolecki's conception of an agrarian socialism
organized as a federation of self-governing cooperatives, i.e., in the
spirit of ancient Slavonic communalism.

To conclude: when Alexander Herzen started to proclaim and to
propagate (with the help of the Polish democrats) the populist ideas of
his "Russian socialism" a very similar ideology had been already elaborated and widely accepted by the democratic wing of the Polish emigration.

IV. REVOLUTION AND THE DIALECTICS OF HISTORY

Let us turn now to the problem of revolution in the philosophical
thought of the epoch. From the end of the 1830s until the events of the
Springtime of the Peoples (which, as Engels put it, everywhere "thrust
the whole of philosophy aside"),[48] Polish intellectual life was the scene
of ardent philosophical debates which would be called a controversy
over Hegelianism.[49] In this speculative controversy, two important
practical problems were involved: the first was nation-building; the
second, a thoroughgoing (revolutionary or nonrevolutionary) social
and political transformation. Both were in fact two aspects of a concern about a future which, it was felt, depended upon the unbending
will of patriots to persist and persevere. Therefore, it is easy to understand why Polish thinkers could not remain consistent, orthodox Hege-
lians. The stateless existence of the Polish nation alongside the conviction that nations (in contrast to states) are "divinely constituted"—
alive and indivisible in spirit in spite of oppression and regardless of
any artificial political divisions—was incompatible with Hegel's apotheosis of the state and of the growing rationalization of social life realized through it. This is why in Poland romantic progressivism was usually more influential than Hegelian historicism (although the latter did
shape the views of the revolutionary philosophers Dembowski and Kamieński).

The romantics saw historical progress as being accomplished
through nations— nations not reduced to the role of mere instruments
of the universal "reason of history," but nations that felt, suffered, and
loved, nations endowed with will and consciously fulfilling their individual callings. Hence, the glorification of the present, a characteristic
feature of Hegelianism, had to be replaced with a concern for the future, and Hegelian contemplativeness had to be criticized in the name
of "action." The emphasis placed on the necessity of progress had to

be supplemented with an appeal to heroic will and ethical duty, since the actual situation the nation was in rendered impossible a complacent, optimistic confidence in anonymous laws of history. Hegel's "autocracy of reason" had to be limited for the sake of feeling; the recognition that the existing state of the world was necessary had to be opposed by the belief that the will could change it and actively mold the future. It was taken for granted that the goal of history did not consist in attaining self-consciousness of the absolute, as Hegel chose to see it, but in the welfare and happiness of mankind, as was claimed by the progressive thinkers of France.

All these motifs, including an appeal for the synthesis of Hegelianism with French socialism (especially the teachings of Fourier), were contained in Cieszkowski's *Prolegomena zur Historiosophie* (1838), the first book within the Hegelian school to set forth a "philosophy of action" *(Philosophie der Tat).*[50] The critique of the onesidedness of the Hegelian "panlogism" was later developed by Karol Libelt, a disciple of Hegel, who, however, ended up rejecting Hegelianism almost completely and in his own "Slavonic philosophy" tried to combine a Schellingian type of romantic criticism of rationalism with a romantic-populist idealization of the common people and a democratic political program.

The most interesting conceptions concerning the problem of revolution were developed by Dembowski and Kamieński. Not satisfied with a mere theory, they embodied the idea of "philosophy in action" by becoming—together with the more moderate Libelt—the main leaders of the revolutionary movement in the lands of partitioned Poland (as opposed to the revolutionary movement in exile).

The most original and valuable of Dembowski's contributions to philosophy is probably his conception that development takes place through the struggle of opposites; it was set forth in an article entitled "A Few Thoughts on Eclecticism" (1843). Following the radical Hegelian Left, especially Bruno Bauer and Michael Bakunin (whose article "Reaction in Deutschland" was known to him),[51] the young Polish thinker postulated a revolutionary reinterpretation of Hegelian dialectics, bringing out the concept of negation and rejecting the idea of mediation between the two opposites in the name of their higher synthesis. The other Polish philosophers—Cieszkowski, Bronisław Trentowski, and even Libelt—more faithful in this respect to the orthodox interpretation of Hegelian notions of *Vermittelung* and *Aufhebung,* put emphasis just on the mediation between the negating and the negated, on their reconciliation in a higher unity, preserving the "truth" of the negated moment as an inalienable, although subordinated, component of a new dialectic totality.[52] Practice, as postulated by them, was to be not "negative" and "critical," but "positive" and "organic." For Dembowski, such a conception was tantamount to a philosophical justification of the "eclectic" position of the *juste-milieu* liberals, trying to reconcile the irreconcilable. In the struggle of opposites, he maintained, only the negating force represents the truth of the future. All attempts at softening the struggle by an "eclectic" mediation between the opposite principles can only weaken the dynamics of progress, thus playing into the hands of reaction more effectively than the extreme reactionaries, who, unconsciously, help the revolution by bringing about a clear-cut polarization of social forces.

The most important part of Dembowski's philosophy—called by him "the philosophy of creativity" (*filozofia twórczości*)—was the philosophy of history, interpreting the past in order to deduce from it an image of the future. His article on "Creativity in Social Life" (1843) presented a vision of a socialist society in which the people would be free, not only from physical compulsion, but also from economic and intellectual subjugation (thanks to the liquidation of private property and equal access to education). In another article, "On Progress in the Philosophical Interpretation of Being" (1844), Dembowski gave an outline of a theory of "individualization," i.e., a theory of development consisting in the movement from the primitive undifferentiated unity, through its disintegration into autonomous ("individualized") and conflicting elements, to a new higher unity, complicated enough to comprise—and to transcend—all the positive results of "individualization." In the development of society the first stage was primitive theocracy, and the final goal was the fullest possible democracy, i.e., the people ruling itself, enjoying unity in its isocial life and in its convictions.

The last work of Dembowski's "philosophy of creativity" was his "Thoughts on the Future of Philosophy" (1845), which set forth a program for a Polish "national philosophy" that would unite German "thought" with French "deed." In fact what this article proposed was not a revision and a further development, but rather a radical transcending of Hegelianism. "Creativity" became identified with "creating," which, in turn, became a process of development in the "sensual substance," i.e., in material reality. Hegelianism was discussed as a philosophy developing the idea only in the sphere of logic, thus making it "only the law of life and not the living law." The inspiration behind these thoughts was obviously Feuerbach's criticism of Hegel—his "rehabilitation of matter," leading, consequently, to a rehabilitation of "sensuality," "heart," and "passions," and, in this respect, easily harmonizing with a romantic criticism of Hegelian rationalism. From the point of view of the problem of revolution the importance of Feuerbachian inspiration consisted in giving Dembowski a theoretical justification for seeing dialectics—interpreted by him in a revolutionary way—as an immanent living law of *material* reality, and not only as a dialectic of the absolute (Hegel) or of the human mind (B. Bauer).[53]

Henryk Kamieński, Dembowski's older cousin, also called his philosophy a "philosophy of creativity," summarizing it in the slogan "I create, therefore, I am."[54] This understanding of creativity was, however, very different from Dembowski's—almost completely free both of romanticism and of Hegelian idealism. Because Kamieński's philosophical views do not fall within the scope of this paper, it will suffice to point out only a few of the more essential features of his thought. First of all, Kamieński presented a philosophical expression of radical anthropocentrism reminiscent of Feuerbach's anthropologism.[55] Kamieński made a sharp distinction between two Absolutes—the divine cosmic Absolute and the "Absolute of all things human," that is, "man's being." The first Absolute exists, but it is completely inaccessible to the human mind. In order to penetrate its mysteries, man would have to acquire divine cognitive power, and this is impossible without his becoming God himself. Man can deal only with the finite manifestations of the cosmic Absolute, i.e., with the phenomena of nature. First, he gets into contact with them through his empirical receptive "power of comprehension"; then he starts to exercise within the world of his experience his "power of creativity." From this moment he raises himself above nature and acquires the significance of a true "being," that is, something that exists by force of its own activity. This activity, although necessarily limited, resembles and continues the divine work of creation.

Second, Kamieński's philosophical activism was bound up with a pronounced sociologism and historicism. When he praises man's creativity, he means not the individual, but the collective man. For him society is "a collective entity in mankind, living a complete and perfect life." In contrast to this, the individual is seen as only "a particle, an atom, incomplete in itself and having no significance of its own."[56] He is convinced also that man's creative activity is governed by historical laws, immanent to it and independent of individual desires. These laws can be violated, but to do so is always harmful to genuine progress.

Finally, in conscious opposition to German idealism, Kamieński's "philosophy of creativity" was based upon naturalistic assumptions. Man was placed by him in the objective, resistant, material world. His most important, pivotal activity was economic, conquering nature to make it obedient to the human creative spirit. Kamieński's main philosophical work bears the title *Philosophy of the Material Economy of Human Society* (Poznań, vol. 1, 1843; vol. 2, 1845). "Material economy" (i.e., political economy), he claims, is the science of development conceived of as a "progress of human activity in its struggle with matter."[57] Therefore, it is the most important science of human deeds and the key to the understanding of history. Its connection with history is evident and direct: history is subject to the laws of progress, and "material economy" is nothing else than a study of the universal, objective progress of mankind. It is thus a philosophy of history and a philosophy of action, or, rather, the only true philosophy of creative action. The "material economy," as Kamieński put it, realizes the *summa* of philosophy, that is, "the passing of knowledge into collective, practical life."[58]

It follows from all this that revolution is not necessarily a romantic struggle on the barricades. The name *revolution* should be given to any important, qualitative changes in economic relations, regardless of whether or how much revolutionary violence may be involved. Revolution, according to Kamienski, "is an organic social function which the nation exercises within itself in order to recast its inner organism; everything which fulfills this condition is a revolution, irrespective of the superficial forms which it may assume and of the source from which the change takes its beginning."

Another consequence is the question of timing. Progress, Kamieński maintains, consists in unity increasing among men. This unity, however, must correspond to man's successes in the struggle with matter. In other words, the goals of revolution should be in accordance with the level of economic development already achieved. No wonder, therefore, that, in contrast to Dembowski, Kamieński appreciated the progressiveness of capitalist development and discussed socialist teachings as they applied to Polish conditions as mere utopias. He was fully aware that the prime mover of capitalist progress is "individual interest," but he did not see in this anything morally wrong. "Individual interest" was not identified by him with antisocial egoism; on the contrary, it was seen by him as a socializing factor. Interest, he wrote, "is a social tie, and not a solvent"; it is "an expression of man's individuality, and this expression cannot be antisocial since the individuality itself is a creation of society."[59] Exploitation of men by men is a by-product of the social division of labor and therefore cannot be completely eliminated. It should be limited, but not at the cost of hampering economic progress and, by the same token, weakening mankind in its struggle with matter.

In the second volume of *Philosophy of the Material Economy* we find Kamieński somewhat modifying this standpoint. He recognizes the theoretical possibility of an "ideal moment" in social development in which the phenomenon of exploitation would disappear. Private interest as a stimulus to work would then give way to work viewed as a calling; wealth would be distributed according to need and the necessary division of labor would be based, not on a social hierarchy, but on

free choice governed by a universal desire to be useful. However, Kamieński emphasized an important reservation: the only way to achieve
this social ideal is a spontaneous evolutionary process in which "interest itself gives way to higher motives." It was to be a *natural* process,
not "a violation of the principle of interest by means incapable of replacing it," but "its natural disappearance."[60] Any artificial accelera-
tion of this process by a centralized political power could only result
"in destroying human society, not in bringing about its progress."[61]

From this discussion, it seems justified to conclude, then, that both
Dembowski and Kamieński should be placed within the body of post-
Hegelian philosophy that paved the way for Marxism. Dembowski's
contribution was primarily his revolutionary reinterpretation of Hegelian dialectics and his bold attempt at uniting German philosophy with
French socialism. Kamieński's contribution lies in his understanding
of the philosophical significance of the economy and in his reinterpretation of Hegelian historicism, economic and activist at the same time.

V. THE METHODS OF REVOLUTIONARY STRUGGLE

An important part of the Polish revolutionary writings of the epoch
were devoted to the technical problems of revolutionary conspiracy
and the purely military problems of revolutionary war. These discussions usually began with a critical analysis of the failure of the November Uprising: the conspiracy which started the uprising had refused
to appoint its revolutionary leaders from its own ranks, thus leaving its
leadership to people of moderate or conservative persuasion, many of
whom lacked ability and even faith in its ultimate success. Maurycy
Mochnacki drew the conclusion that the November Uprising had been
defeated because of a lack of "revolutionary absolutism." The next
revolution, he wrote, should not repeat this error. It "will be a system,
and this system will be despotic or will fall to the ground together with
the cause of the peoples. Who fights against kings should know the
kings' methods."[62]

To the majority of Polish exiles this conclusion seemed unavoidable—it was accepted, in fact, both by the monarchists (to whom
Mochnacki himself gave his support) and by the members of the Democratic Society. The first interpreted it as a program for an uprising under the strong leadership of a king (Adam Czartoryski) who would be
proclaimed as the founder of a national dynasty. They argued, among
other things, that only the authority of a king—as opposed to the leadership of the gentry—could secure for the revolutionary government
the allegiance of the peasants.[63] The democrats, in their turn, made
Mochnacki's conclusion a stepping stone to a theory of revolutionary
dictatorship. A peculiar solution to the problem was provided by the
Messianists who extolled strong leadership but, at the same time, de-

spised and rejected all rationally institutionalized "systems" as inimical to the "holy fire" of revolutionary enthusiasm. Their solution was presented in the vision of a great charismatic leader, a powerful "King-Spirit" (Słowacki), a divinely inspired man who (as Mickiewicz put it) would combine "the spirit of Christ" with "the spirit of Napoleon."

The most consistent variant on the theory of revolutionary dictatorship was elaborated—within the Democratic Society—by General Ludwik Mierosławski. Its importance is increased by the fact that it was the result of a polemic against an alternative theory elaborated by Kamieński. During the revolution, Mierosławski argued, the principle of the sovereignty of the people has to be suspended. The people can exercise its sovereignty only when revolution has been victorious, and not before, i.e., not before its physical and moral emancipation. The only true plenipotentiary of the general will is the successful revolutionary organization. Its very success is the best proof that the revolutionary conspirators have acted in accordance with the authentic general will of their nation. Therefore, the revolutionary executive—either a collective (if possible under existing conditions) or exercised by one man—should be given unlimited power. The revolutionary government must have all rights, the nation only unlimited obligations. No freedom of the press, no activities of revolutionary clubs can be tolerated, since the final victory depends solely on discipline and "blind obedience."[64]

Kamieński's book *On the Vital Truths of the Polish Nation* (Brussels, 1844)[65] set forth a very different theory. Its basic assumption was the historicist conviction that social life is governed by laws and that the "universal reason" of the masses is more trustworthy than the reason of a revolutionary elite. In the theory and practice of revolutionary conspiracies, Kamieński saw the danger of voluntarism. Conspirators, he asserted, always want to impose upon society their own will, not taking into account that society, "like the physical world, is subject to inevitable and unflinching laws."[66] Similarly, he criticized different variants of the "faith in persons," such as Mochnacki's "revolutionary absolutism," Mickiewicz's hero worship, and the exaggerated hopes that many democrats had begun to put in Mierosławski. He went so far as to deny the émigrés' claim to leadership: emigration, he argued, is necessarily a detachment from the concrete, real conditions of national life, exposing people to the danger of an uncritical acceptance of foreign theories and thus giving birth to illusions and "impractical" solutions.

The same theoretical assumptions served as justification for a broad program of propagandist activity, seen by Kamieński as a necessary preparation for revolution. The masses, he maintained, must be *prepared* to understand the revolution. The revolutionaries, on the other hand, must have the opportunity unceasingly to confront their ideas with the real needs and strivings of the masses. Thus, the emphasis put on propaganda was, in Kamieński's case, not a testimony to an idealistic belief in a magic power of words, but, rather, the result of a clear awareness of the dangers of revolutionary elitism, stemming from an absolutization of conspiratorial methods of struggle.

In Kamieński's account of his discussions with Tomasz Malinowski, an emissary of the "Centralization" (Central Committee) of the Democratic Society,[67] Malinowski accused Kamieński of "anarchy," arguing that the success of revolution depended, above all, on good conspiratorial organization, based upon the principles of centralization, hierarchy, and unconditional obedience. Kamieński, in his turn, accused the Centralization of a patronizing attitude toward the patriotic majority of the nation, neglecting "universal reason," and pushing the country to actions that would only increase sacrifices and repressive measures without benefiting the cause. Revolution, he claimed, must have time to ripen; conspiracy can achieve its aim only if *the masses* are prepared and willing to act. One should try to accelerate revolutionary maturity, but one should not try to pluck unripe fruit.

On the Vital Truths of the Polish Nation contained a whole chapter devoted to the problem of revolutionary terrorism. This chapter so much shocked and frightened the conservative poet Zygmunt Krasiński that he engaged in a rather lengthy antirevolutionary polemic against it in his famous *Psalms of the Future*, which in turn evoked a splendid poetic reply from Słowacki.[68] Regardless of Krasiński's exaggerated reaction, however, Kamieński's advocacy of terror was in fact rather moderate—more moderate than the position of the "Jacobin" left wing of the Democratic Society. True, he did not hesitate to state bluntly that terror, i.e., revolutionary justice, would be turned, not only against individuals, but against whole classes as well, if they chose to behave like a counterrevolutionary mass. Nevertheless, at the same time, he expressed his deep conviction that the Polish revolution would entail only very little bloodshed. He based this conviction on the educational influence of the Polish tragedy which, he thought, had cured the Polish gentry of its class egoism, thus making it capable of understanding and fulfilling its patriotic duty.

Kamieński's optimism regarding the possibility of avoiding a civil war in future revolutionary insurrection in Poland enabled him to develop in detail (in a separate part of *On the Vital Truths*) an interesting theory of the "People's War"—a war in which the peasant masses were expected to join the revolutionary gentry. This war, as Kamieński conceived it, was to be waged by a mass guerilla army of peasants, organized by militarily trained revolutionaries, and gradually transforming itself into a more regular army. Looking for historical precedents, Kamieński paid particular attention to the war waged against the Poles by the Ukrainian peasants and Cossacks under the leadership of Khmel'nyts'kyi and to the guerilla warfare waged by the Spaniards against the Napoleonic invasion. He also discussed the role of the revolutionary clubs which he, unlike Mierosławski, saw as necessary instruments for shaping an adequate revolutionary consciousness.[69]

Kamieński's theory of a "People's War" was without doubt an important achievement of Polish revolutionary thought, in some ways anticipating the phenomenon of the "militarized mass insurrection" that was to be fully developed only in the twentieth century.[70] The leaders of the Polish Insurrection of 1863 tried (mostly in vain) to make practical use of Kamieński's thought, and three-quarters of a century later, a translation of Kamieński's treatise on the "People's War" was used in France under the Nazi occupation to serve the needs of the French resistance movement.[71] The importance of Kamieński's theory was fully recognized by Polish Marxist historians in the 1950s, but because no serious attempt at reinterpretation has appeared since that time, I would like to add a few words concerning the relation between Kamieński's and Mierosławski's views.

According to the interpretations of the 1950s, Mierosławski's belief that the revolutionary process should be totally controlled by a centralized revolutionary government and that the revolutionary war should, insofar as it was possible, resemble a regular war, waged by regular, disciplined army units, simply expressed his fear of peasant masses and his wish to use the "revolutionary dictatorship" to support the interests of the gentry.[72] This interpretation, however, is not entirely convincing. It can easily be reversed—as was done in Mierosławski's polemic with Kamieński. There Mierosławski claimed that "revolutionary dictatorship" was necessary to prevent the counter-revolutionary activities of the gentry as well as the growing influence of the gentry within the revolutionary movement. Kamieński's conception, he maintained, would in practice give the gentry too much freedom of action. The theory that the bitter experience of Poland had had an educational influence was for him an illusion, since no social class could reasonably be expected to commit collective suicide.[73]

What is actually revealed by these two views on the methods of revolutionary struggle can be grasped, I think, not by trying to establish which of them was "more to the left," but, rather, by classifying them according to the classic problem of "spontaneity versus organization" in the revolutionary movement. Seen from this perspective, the revolutionary general represented a combination of *blanquism* (revolutionary elitism, absolutization of centralized political power) with the traditional attitudes of a professional soldier. Kamieński's views, in their turn,

appear as an attempt at a vindication of the legitimate role of spontaneity—not "anarchic" spontaneity, as his opponents claimed, but law-
governed spontaneity of the "universal reason" of society, more worthy of confidence than "the reason of Centralization."

VI. REVOLUTION AS UNIVERSAL REGENERATION

So far, the discussion has focused on the ideas of men for whom
revolution was a practical and more or less limited task. Both Kamieński and the democrats in exile thought of revolution in terms of a
simultaneous solution to two problems which were inseparably bound
up in their thinking—the agrarian problem and the problem of national
independence. Although this task was treated by them as part of a general all-European revolutionary transformation, they were far from
seeing their political activity in eschatological perspective, as an instrument for final universal regeneration.

Quite different were the revolutionary hopes of the Messianic poets
and revolutionary Christian Socialists who, unlike Dembowski, had
separated themselves from the broad democratic movement. For them,
the imminent revolution was nothing less than the realization of the
chiliastic dream of total earthly salvation for mankind. The Messianists, however, were concerned mainly with religious and philosophical
problems (the examination of which would lead us too far astray from
our subject).[74] Our attention will therefore be directed instead to the
ideas of the socialist millenarians. While they did not represent an important political force, their ideas seem nonetheless worthy of attention, if only to make us aware that an intellectually well-articulated
leftist opposition to the revolutionary democratism of the period existed.

Revolutionary Christian socialism—represented by the Communities of the Polish People, by Królikowski's journal *Christ's Poland* in
the emigration, and by the clandestine organization of Father Piotr
Ściegienny in Congress Poland[75]—was in fact very different from the
socialism of Dembowski. The latter had no sympathy for Christianity:
his socialism looked backward to "pre-Christian Slavdom"; essentially his political program (minimal program) was in accordance with
the program of the Democratic Society, and his literary and historical
views were permeated with that romantic idealization of the peasantry
so characteristic of revolutionary democratic populism. Revolutionary
Christian socialism differed from Dembowski's on all these points. Its
peculiar quality (which allowed it to avoid that excessive idealization
of the peasantry) lay in its deliberate attempt to create a genuinely
peasant ideology. Ludwik Królikowski and Piotr Ściegienny were
peasants themselves. The leaders of the Communities of the Polish
People—Stanisław Worcell and, later, Zenon Świętosławski—were

typical representatives of the "penitent gentry" (Mierosławski's expression),[76] willing to pay off their "debt to the people."[77] But their utmost concern was to create an ideology that would adequately express the needs and values of the majority of their organization: the simple, illiterate peasants who had been the soldiers of the November Insurrection, who had refused to accept the tsarist amnesty, and who had, after a long series of ordeals, finally been allowed to settle in England.

In some respects there is more romanticism in the Christian socialism of the Communities of the Polish People than in the ideology of the Democratic Society. The Communities accused the Democratic Society of bourgeois rationalism; against the "scribblings" of philosophers and economists, they, just as Mickiewicz, set their teachings "coming from the heart, from revelation."[78] They did not hesitate to proclaim that human reason was the source of antisocial egoism and the cause of all the misfortunes of Poland. Correcting the error of the Jacobins (whose tradition they otherwise wanted to continue), they rejected the Enlightenment doctrine of the "law of nature" (accepted by the Democratic Society). This doctrine, they claimed, sanctified and justified social inequality, deified man, endorsed individualism and private property, relativized morality, and denied the very notion of moral progress. However, this violent criticism of the eighteenth-century intellectual heritage went hand in hand with an espousal of the anti-individualistic, equalitarian tradition of eighteenth-century communism—the tradition of Babeuf's "Conspiracy of Equals," which had its living embodiment in the person of Filippo Buonarrotti. It was easier to reconcile this tradition with Christian millenarianism than it was with romantic individualism, including the romantic conception of a collective individuality of each nation.

The peculiar features of the Christian-socialist conception of the nation should not be reduced solely to their radical denunciation of all forms of social solidarism and to their constant repetition that "our fatherland, that is the Polish people, had always been separated from the fatherland of the gentry."[79] The same views can easily be found in Dembowski's writings as well. Theoretically, the most important objective was the replacement of romantic universalism, sanctifying and comprising within itself the individuality of the various nations, with a "Christian" universalism that was opposed to rationalistic universalism but was equally insensitive to the value of differences between nations. For the Communities of the Polish People, and for Królikowski and Ściegienny as well, the moral essence of the Polish people was identical with universal Christian truth.

The "Christianity" of the Communities was, of course, of an extremely heterodox variety. In spite of a certain sympathy toward Ca-

tholicism (which because of its opposition to Protestant individualism
was highly appreciated by Saint Simonians and Buchez), they proclaimed that since the Roman Church had betrayed the principles of
Christ, Christianity had its church and its pope in the people. Christ,
they believed, advocated "violent revolution"; the day upon which
Robespierre established the cult of the Supreme Being was to be celebrated as the return to true Christianity, with revolutionary Paris as the
new Apostolic See.[80]

Królikowski and Ściegienny reinterpreted Christianity in a similar
spirit. Both of them—peasants from the same poor region around
Kielce—represented in their writings a classical millenarian reading of
the Gospel. It seems justified even to say that millenarianism appeared
in their teachings in a simpler and purer form than in the richer and
more complicated theories of the Communities of the Polish People.

The sociologists of religion define millenarianism as a "religious revolutionism," a "religion of the oppressed," as an archaic form of social
protest.[81] In European nineteenth-century intellectual history, Królikowski and Ściegienny are, perhaps, among the best examples of a
direct fusion of the nascent socialism with the old tradition of millenarian plebeian heresies. Both of them preached (using the same quotations from the Scriptures) that true salvation was collective salvation
on earth, that Christ's ideals had been falsified by the official Church,
and that his mission would end only with the establishment of the ter-
restrial Kingdom of God—that is, a social order based on common
ownership and universal brotherhood. Both—in sharp contrast to most
of the French socialists—opted for revolution, continually repeating
that Christ had brought to the people, not peace, but the sword. Both
used the sharp, violent language of the prophets and based their
preaching on a Manichean vision, sharply contrasting the redeemed
with the condemned, the Kingdom of God with the Kingdom of Satan
(the latter embracing the whole of the evil "old World").

The revival of these millenarian beliefs harmonized with the messianic atmosphere of Polish romanticism. Królikowski's ideas (those of
Father Ściegienny were practically unknown to his contempories)
struck a sympathetic chord in Mickiewicz, Słowacki, and Libelt, while
both Królikowski and Ściegienny took inspiration from Mickiewicz's
Books of the Polish Nation and of the Polish Pilgrims. Nevertheless,
the ideology of the two socialist millenarians was very far from romantic Messianism. They believed in the anonymous masses and not in
personal messiahs. National messianism was also alien to them. Some
elements of it can be discovered in Królikowski's ideas, but a closer
analysis makes it evident that his "Christ's Poland" had nothing in
common with historical Poland. Finally, they had little understanding
of romantic mysticism: their ardent religious faith was utterly rational-

ized, stripped of supranatural mysteries, reduced almost to evangelical morality transformed into a revolutionary message. This is why Królikowski was able to exert an important influence on Étienne Cabet, becoming his right-hand man in the Icarian movement.[82]

Among the most characteristic features of Królikowski's and Ściegienny's socialism, one should also mention antihistoricism, antiindividualism, and retrospectiveness. It was unhistorical because all past history was renounced as the Kingdom of Satan; and the radical opposition between the Kingdom of Satan and the Kingdom of God eliminated the conception of historical progress as a mediation between absolute Evil and absolute Good. Królikowski made it clear that his God ``is not the God of progress, but the God of absolute Truth.''[83] It was antiindividualistic because both thinkers (just as the theorists of the Communities) violently condemned all manifestations of ``separatism'' (including the striving for individual salvation), because the beginning of the process of individualization was seen by them as the Biblical Fall, and the process itself as one of an increasing inequality among men and a growing dependence on ungodly, arbitrary political power. Finally, it was retrospective because the desired revolutionary upheaval was to be a return—although a return, to be sure, not to a pre-Christian national past, but to primitive Christianity, which, in its turn, had been nothing else than the restoration of the original paradisaical state of mankind. Historians of social thought will agree that all these features are typical of equalitarian ideologies of a precapitalist peasantry.

In contradistinction to Królikowski, the theorists of the Communities of the Polish People accepted historical progress, and they tried to unite an appeal to the eternal truths revealed in the Gospel with a conception of the laws of social evolution. Stanisław Worcell, in his most interesting treatise, *On Property*, set forth a theory of the historical development of property governed by laws essentially different from the laws of nature.[84] The institution of property, he argued, is not ``natural.'' Property is a relation among men, and not a relation between men and things. It has historical origins and has undergone a long series of historical transformations, entailing appropriate changes in the whole fabric of social life. Worcell himself treated this theory as a historical and ``scientific'' one. Nevertheless, he did not commit himself to historical relativism; in value judgments he remained an absolutist, opposing ``Christian'' (i.e., common) property to ``pagan'' (i.e. individual) property and unreservedly condemning the latter.

The opposite pole of the ideology of the Communities—a purely utopian mode of thought in quasi-religious form—was represented by Zenon Świętosławski. His *Statutes of the Universal Church* was a utopia in the classic sense—a detailed project of a future ideal society, set against the present nadir of human degration.[85] The Universal Church of the future—a union of nations with its capital near Suez, welded by one religious faith and a strong, centralized political power—was to be a truly militant *Church:* a *Church* unremittingly waging wars with "pagans" and converting them by the sword. Its inner organization was to be based upon political centralization and a consistent nationalization of all forms of property, including communal and corporate property. Political authority was to be a religious authority as well—a new theocracy, establishing and defending the true and obligatory interpretation of the Divine Word. The Church's people were to be paragons of the most demanding and severe morality. Any transgressions of moral norms were to be punished, and open disobedience to the *Church* was to be atoned for by death. Economic development was to be planned in detail and to provide not only for the economic but also for the aesthetic needs of the population (Świętosławski put special emphasis on building spacious and beautiful apartments). The official language of the *Church* was to be Polish. The Polish nation, however, was not to be privileged in any other way—all nations of the *Church* were to enjoy complete equality, and the division into nations was to be established for the needs of an effective administration rather than for preserving cultural or ethnic differentiation. The rulers of the Church were expected to do everything possible, to develop means of communication, build tunnels, level precipices—in a word, remove everything which divides people. In such a way the Christian ideal of "one fold and one shepherd" was to become a reality.

The "Statutes," officially, although not unanimously approved in 1844 by the Communities, were thus a peculiar manifesto of a revolutionary totalitarianism. It should be stressed that their totalitarian tendencies were completely alien to Worcell. Being aware of the growing danger of sectarianism, he left the Communities in 1840 and became a member of the moderate Union of the Polish Emigration. In 1846, as mentioned earlier, he joined the Democratic Society and was assigned to work on its Centralization.

VII. CONCLUSION

It seems justified to say that the flowering of Polish revolutionary thought which took place between the November Uprising and the Springtime of the Peoples was not without significance for Europe generally. There are, I think, at least three different, but complementary, perspectives from which this significance can be seen and assessed. First of all, Polish revolutionary movements and revolutionary thought of that time were important both as a continuation of the Western (particularly French) antifeudal revolutionary tradition and as an effort to complete the so-called bourgeois-democratic transformation of Europe. Seen from this perspective, Poland was trying to perform the same role in the European East as France had performed in its West.

The Poles, as Marx and Engels repeatedly pointed out, were by then the most revolutionary nation in East Central Europe—"the [very] words 'Pole' and 'revolutionary' have become identical."[86] In retrospect, the importance of the Polish revolutionary thinkers lay in their being the first to proclaim the necessity for agrarian revolution in Transelbian Europe:

The large agrarian countries between the Baltic and the Black Sea [wrote Engels] can free themselves from patriarchal feudal barbarism only by an agrarian revolution, which turns the peasants who are enthralled or liable to labour services into free landowners, a revolution which would be similar to the French Revolution of 1789 in the countryside. It is to the credit of the Polish nation that it was the first of all its agricultural neighbours to proclaim this.[87]

Second, Polish revolutionary thought of the epoch provided an important step toward the fusion of revolutionary democratism with romantic nationalism. Full-fledged revolutionary democratism appeared in Poland during its most intense struggle for national independence, and it appeared in all the oppressed or dismembered nations of Europe (in the Italian Risorgimento, among the Slavs under Austrian and Turkish rule, during the rise of German nationalism in their periods of national awakening). By then it was difficult to believe simply and solely in the eighteenth-century declarations of rights. The democratic individualism of the Enlightenment was replaced by romantic discovery of *collective* national individualities and collective national missions, with the ethos of supreme duties, heroic self-denial, and sacrifice. The exaltation of national feeling, however, did not at that time lead to a betrayal of the universalist revolutionary message in favor of a narrowly, "realistically" conceived "national interest," let alone brutal national egoism. Polish revolutionary ideologies, perhaps Polish Messianism (as represented by Mickiewicz and his Italian Legion) in particular, were in this respect at least as important for the understanding of this phase in the history of European revolutionism and nationalism as was the Italian Messianism of Mazzini. The spirit of "the Holy Alliance of the Peoples" was represented by the Poles, both in theory and in practice, as well as, indeed much better than, it was by any other European nation of that time. Engels spoke for the entire European Left when he acknowledged this in admiration: "In Paris and in Vienna, in Berlin, in Italy, and in Hungary the Poles have fought alongside in all revolutions and revolutionary wars, unconcerned whether they were fighting against Germans, against Slavs, against Magyars—indeed, even against Poles."[88]

Finally, the importance of the Polish revolutionary experience of that epoch lies in its relevance to the problem of revolutionary ideologies in underdeveloped countries, especially those which, although economically underdeveloped, have a strong intellectual elite participating in the intellectual life of the developed countries and painfully aware of its inalienable responsibility for the freedom and progress of its own nation. Polish revolutionary democratism emerged and developed at a time when purely "bourgeois" revolutionism had already been discredited by the "demonstration effect" of the results of the French Revolution, which was felt to be deeply disappointing. This is why the Polish revolutionaries often combined Western revolutionary ideas with a more or less profound criticism of the West, anticipating the ideas of the Russian populists. Polish democrats and socialists, like the Russian populists of the second half of the century, looked back to the old Slavonic communes and saw in them an embryo of the social regeneration they were looking for. The vocabulary was also similar: Polish revolutionaries spoke of the "debt to the people," of the "penitent gentry," and of the necessity of "going to the people." Even the word *intelligentsia*, widely believed to have appeared for the first time in Russia in the 1860s, was in fact being used by the Polish democrats in the 1840s.[89] This populist aspect of the Polish democratic movement of the 1830s and 1840s is usually overshadowed by the national question—so important for the Poles and so unimportant for the Russians. Nevertheless, it was already noted by Stanisław Brzozowski, the Polish philosopher and literary critic of the beginning of our century, for whom the traditions of Russian revolutionary populism were just as dear as the heritage of the Polish romantic epoch.[90]

NOTES

1 K. Marx and F. Engels, *Werke*, vol. 5 (Berlin, 1959), p. 355.

2 A. Mickiewicz, "Litany of the Pilgrim," *Selected Poetry and Prose*, ed. S. Helsztyński (Warsaw, 1955), p. 116.

3 Cf. Marx, Engels, *Werke*, vol. 18, p. 526.

4 See M. Handelsman, *Adam Czartoryski*, vol. 2 (Warsaw, 1949), pp. 279–80. As late as 1863, Bakunin was willing to collaborate with the Hotel Lambert, the headquarters of Czartoryski's party. See A. Leśniewski, *Bakunin a sprawy polskie w okresie Wiosny Ludów i powstania styczniowego 1863 roku* (Łódź, 1962), pp. 115–21.

5 See Handelsman, *Adam Czartoryski*, vol. 2, p. 155, and J. Feldman, *Bismarck a Polska* (Warsaw, 1947), p. 201.

6 P. Brock, "The Political Program of the Polish Democratic Society," *The Polish Review* 14 (Summer 1969): 20.

7 Cf. P. F. Sugar, "External and Domestic Roots of Eastern European Nationalism," in P. F. Sugar and I. J. Lederer, eds., *Nationalism in Eastern Europe* (Seattle and London, 1969), p. 26.

8 Cf. the estimation of the Russian peasant reform of 1861 by Volgin, the author's *porte-parole* in Chernyshevskii's novel *The Prologue*.
9 Brock, "The Political Program . . .," p. 5.
10 Some Polish Marxists of the 1950s tried to define "revolutionary democratism" so narrowly that they eliminated the Democratic Society as not "deserving" that classi-fication. This was tantamount to reducing the number of "revolutionary democrats" among the Poles to so small a number that they became the exception rather than the rule in the Polish (as distinct from the Russian) democratic movement; it also denied by implication the undisputable fact that Poland was the first East European country in which revolutionary democratism, that is, a movement proclaiming the agrarian revolution, became a significant social force, a development that was significant also for all-European revolutionary strategy. This was, by the way, the diagnosis of Marx and Engels, and also the reason for their consistent support of the Polish cause.
11 I have tried to show this importance in three articles: "The Paris Lectures of Mic-kiewicz and Russian Slavophilism," *The Slavonic and East European Review* 46 (January 1968); "Two Polish Messianists: Adam Mickiewicz and August Ciesz-kowski," *Oxford Slavonic Papers*, New Series, vol. 2 (1969); "The Conceptions of Nation in the Polish Romantic Messianism," *Dialectics and Humanism* 2 (Winter 1975).
12 Quoted from H. Kohn, *Panslavism. Its History and Ideology* (Notre Dame, Indiana, 1953), p. 38.
13 Cf. A. O. Lovejoy, *The Great Chain of Being* (New York, 1960), p. 294.
14 Quoted from W. Łukasiewicz and Wł. Lewandowski, eds., *Postępowa publicystyka emigracyjna 1831–1846. Wybór źródeł* (Wrocław-Warsaw-Cracow, 1961), p. 67.
15 Ibid., pp. 485–87.
16 Ibid., p. 201.
17 K. Marx, F. Engels, *The Russian Menace to Europe*, ed. P. W. Blackstone and B. F. Hoselitz (Glencoe, Illinois, 1952), p. 108.
18 See A. Baumgarten, *Dekabryści a Polska* (Warsaw, 1952). The first manifestation honoring the Russian Decembrist was organized by the Patriotic Society in January 1831 in connection with an act of the Diet depriving Nicholas I of the Polish throne.
19 See W. Śliwowska, *W kręgu poprzedników Hercena* (Wrocław, 1971), especially the chapters on Golovin and Sazonov.
20 Among the European thinkers of the time, Mazzini was certainly the closest to the spirit of the "political romanticism" of the Polish Messianists. His ardent belief in the unifying mission of the "Third Rome" is bound up with the firm conviction that nations, although "sacred and divinely constituted," are never ends in themselves, that the egoistic principle of nonintervention should be rejected in favor of a Holy Alliance of the Peoples. Like the Polish romantics, he condemned the rationalism, utilitarianism, and hedonism of the Enlightenment, extolling the spirit of heroism and self-sacrifice. His Messianism was not merely national, but religious as well; he felt deeply that "every social revolution is essentially religious," because only faith, "authoritative truth," can regenerate the people (G. Mazzini, *The Duties of Man and Other Essays* [London, Toronto, New York, 1915], p. 146, 214). On the other hand, however, one has to admit that, in comparison with Mickiewicz, Mazzini's religion seems rather to be a quasi-religion, secularized and devoid of a supranatural element, lacking the authentic, irreducible experience of "the sacred."
A good summary of Mazzini's views is to be found in G. Salvemini, *Mazzini: A*

Study of His Thought and Its Effect on 19th Century Political Theory (Stanford, 1957).

21 A. Mickiewicz, *Dzieła wszystkie*, vol. 16 (Warsaw, 1933), p. 341.

22 J. de Maistre, *Soirées de Saint-Pétersbourg*, vol. 2 (Paris, 1821), pp. 17-18.

23 *Essai sur la diplomatie; Manuscrit d'un philhellène publié par M. Toulouzan* (Paris-Marseille, 1830).

24 A. Cieszkowski, *Ojcze Nasz*.

25 G. Mazzini, *Essays* (London, 1887), with an introduction by W. Clarke, "Preface to Faith and Future," p. 5.

26 Cf. R. R. Palmer, *The Age of the Democratic Revolution: A Political History of Europe and America, 1760-1800*, vol. 1 (Princeton, 1959), pp. 429-35.

27 See especially W. Heltman, "Powstanie 1794 roku. Kościuszko" (Poitiers, 1838), reprinted in W. Heltman and J. N. Janowski, *Demokracja polska na emigracji*, ed. H. Rzadkowska (Warsaw, 1965), pp. 212-29. The series of articles, of which this article was a part, was given the apt title of *Półśrodki* (Palliatives).

28 Cf. A. Mickiewicz, *Dzieła*, vol. 10 (Warsaw, 1955), p. 315; vol. 11, p. 279.

29 *Lud Polski: Wybór dokumentów*, ed. H. Temkinowa (Warsaw, 1957), p. 71.

30 Ibid., pp. 70, 116.

31 L. Mierosławski, "Demokracja jako warunek bytu Polski," *Demokrata Polski*, vol. 5, part 2 (1842).

32 K. Griewank, "The Emergence of the Concept of Revolution," *Revolution: A Reader*, ed. B. Mazlish, A. D. Kaledin, and D. B. Ralston (New York, 1971), p. 14. See also H. Arendt, *On Revolution* (New York, 1963), pp. 34-40.

33 Cf. J. Szacki, *Ojczyzna, naród, rewolucja* (Warsaw, 1962), pp. 147-205.

34 Marx's letter to Engels of 25 March 1868, quoted from K. Marx, *Pre-Capitalist Economic Formations*, ed. E. J. Hobsbawm (London, 1964), p. 140.

35 Reprinted in Z. Dołęga-Chodakowski, *O słowiańszczyźnie przed chrześcijaństwem*, ed. J. Maślanka (Warsaw, 1967), p. 19-39.

36 See K. Kelles-Krauz, "La Loi de la Rétrospection révolutionnaire vis à vis de la théorie de l'imitation," *Annales de l'Institut International de Sociologie* 2 (1896), pp. 315-37 (reprinted in Polish in K. Kelles-Krauz, *Pisma wybrane*, vol. 1 [Warsaw, 1962]).

37 T. Krępowiecki, "Narodowość (Centralizacja)," *Postęp*, 29 July 1834 (reprinted in *Wiosna Ludów, Teksty i materiały źródłowe*, ed. N. Gąsiorowska [Warsaw, 1953], pp. 69-81).

38 E. Dembowski, *Pisma*, vol. 4 (Warsaw, 1955), p. 108.

39 F. Prawdoski [H. Kamieński], *Katechizm demokratyczny, czyli opowiadanie słowa ludowego* (Paris, 1845), pp. 17-21, 28-29.

40 K. Libelt, "O miłości ojczyzny" (1844), reprinted in K. Libelt, *Samowładztwo rozumu i objawy filozofii słowiańskiej* (Warsaw, 1967).

41 Cf. M. Mochnacki, *O literaturze polskiej w wieku* XIX (Cracow, 1923), p. 12.

42 See *Postępowa publicystyka emigracyjna*, p. 374.

43 The idealization of ancient Poland was most pronounced in Słowacki's mystical writings. In opposition to Lelewel and other Polish democrats, who saw the ancient Polish republic as a prototype of modern democracy, Słowacki glorified ancient Poland from an entirely different point of view—as a society most favorable to the spiritual elite, least resistant to the legitimate rights of spiritual superiority. For him the famous *liberum veto* was a precious device enabling the superior spirits to avoid the rule of inferior ones, even if the latter constituted an overwhelming majority.

44 Cf. B. P. Hepner, *Bakounin et la panslavisme révolutionnaire* (Paris, 1950), p. 228. See also Leśniewski, *Bakunin a sprawy polskie*, pp. 17–18.

45 Mickiewicz, *Dzieła*, vol. 8, p. 82.

46 Ibid., vol. 12, pp. 7–8.

47 See J. K. Podolecki, *Wybór pism*, ed. A. Grodek (Warsaw, 1955).

48 F. Engels, *Ludwig Feuerbach and the End of Classical German Philosophy* (Moscow, 1949), p. 18.

49 The most comprehensive presentation of Polish philosophy (as well as religious and political thought) of the 1840s is to be found in the collective work *Polska myśl filozoficzna i społeczna*, vol. 1 (1831–63), ed. A. Walicki (Warsaw, 1973).

50 Cf. an interesting analysis of Cieszkowski's "philosophy of action" in N. Lobkowicz, *Theory and Practice: History of a Concept from Aristotle to Marx* (Notre Dame and London, 1967), pp. 193–206.

51 See H. Temkinowa, "Edward Dembowski i Michał Bakunin," *Polskie spory o Hegla 1830–1860* (Warsaw, 1966).

52 It is worthwhile to add that Trentowski was by no means doctrinaire: a "reconciliation" of the two opposites was for him the best solution in principle, although it might not always be possible in practice. He made a distinction between the philosophy of politics (where the principle of reconciliation reigned supreme) and the practical art of politics, which he called "cybernetics." From the "cybernetic" point of view, revolution was for him an acceptable means of action, not the best, but sometimes unavoidable. See B. F. Trentowski, *Stosunek filozofii do cybernetyki oraz wybór pism filozoficznych z lat 1842–1845*, ed. A. Walicki (Warsaw, 1974). The first edition of Trentowski's book *Stosunek filozofii do cybernetyki* was published in Poznań in 1843.

53 Cf. A. Śladkowska, *Poglądy społeczno-polityczne i filozoficzne Edwarda Dembowskiego* (Warsaw, 1953), pp. 268–72.

54 H. Kamieński, *Filozofia ekonomii materialnej ludzkiego społeczeństwa*, ed. B. Baczko (Warsaw, 1959), p. 148.

55 This was pointed out by a Russian revolutionary Nikolai Speshnev, a member of Petrashevskii's circle. His two letters to Edmund Chojecki, probably written in 1847, contain an interesting analysis of Kamieński's views. See *Filosofskie i obshchestvennopoliticheskie proizvedeniia petrashevtsev*, ed. V. E. Evgrafov (Moscow, 1953), pp. 447–502.

56 Kamieński, *Filozofia ekonomii materialnej*, p. 37.

57 Ibid., pp. 39–40.

58 Ibid., pp. 347–48.

59 Ibid., p. 109.

60 Ibid., pp. 324–25.

61 Ibid., p. 325.

62 M. Mochnacki, *Dzieła*, vol. 4 (Poznań, 1863), p. 269.

63 Cf. *Kraj i Emigracja. Zbiór pism politycznych i wojskowych*, vol. 1 (Paris, 1835), pp. x–xii.

64 Cf. L. Mierosławski, "Przemówienie z dn. 29 listopada 1845," in *Postępowa publicystyka emigracyjna*, pp. 538–47.

65 F. Prawdoski [H. Kamieński], *O prawdach żywotnych narodu polskiego* (Brussels, 1844).

66 Ibid., p. 21.

67 Cf. H. Kamieński, *Pamiętniki i wizerunki*, ed. I. Śliwińska (Wrocław, 1951), chap. 3.
68 On this poetical polemic concerning revolution, see M. Janion, *Dialektyka historii w polemice między Słowackim a Krasińskim*, in M. Janion, *Romantyzm: Studia o ideach i stylu* (Warsaw, 1969).
69 F. Prawdoski [H. Kamieński], *O prawdach żywotnych*, pp. 143–48.
70 Cf. Ch. Johnson, *Revolution and the Social System*, Hoover Institution Studies 3 (Stanford, 1964), pp. 56–57.
71 This rare edition appeared in 1943 under the title *Insurrection est un art*, trans. by J. Tepicht.
72 Cf. W. Łukaszewicz, introduction to *Postępowa publicystyka emigracyjna*, p. lxxviii.
73 [L. Mierosławski], "Uwagi nad dziełem: O prawdach żywotnych narodu polskiego," offprint from *Demokrata Polski* (Brussels, 1844), p. 12.
74 I have already had the occasion to present their ideas elsewhere. See above, n. 11.
75 The ideas of the Socialist wing of the Polish emigration are discussed by A. Sikora in *Polska myśl filozoficzna i społeczna*, vol. 1, pp. 105–49. The most comprehensive monograph on Ściegienny is a recent book by the Soviet historian W. Diakow, *Piotr Ściegienny i jego spuścizna* (with editions of the archival sources) (Warsaw, 1972). See also P. Brock, *Z dziejów Wielkiej Emigracji w Anglii* (Warsaw, 1958); H. Temkinowa, *Gromady Ludu Polskiego* (Warsaw, 1962); J. Turowski, *Utopia społeczna Ludwika Królikowskiego* (Warsaw, 1958).
76 Cf. P. Brock, "Polish Nationalism," *Nationalism in Eastern Europe*, p. 324; L. Namier, *1848: The Revolution of the Intellectuals* (London and Oxford, 1971), p. 14.
77 Świętosławski's expression; see *Lud Polski w emigracji 1835–1846* (Jersey, 1854), pp. 215, 338–39, 356, quoted in Brock, *Z dziejów Wielkiej Emigracji w Anglii*, p. 65.
78 *Lud Polski: Wybór dokumentów*, p. 108.
79 Ibid., p. 58.
80 Ibid., pp. 204–6.
81 Cf. E. J. Hobsbawm, *Primitive Rebels: Studies in Archaic Forms of Social Movement in the 19th and 20th Century* (Manchester, 1963); V. Lauternari, *The Religions of the Oppressed* (London, 1963); Y. Talmon, "Millenarian Movements," *Archives Europeennes de Sociologie* 8 (1966).
82 Ch. H. Johnston, *Utopian Communism in France* (Ithaca and London, 1974), pp. 93–94; Królikowski's articles, published in *Le Populaire* in the summer of 1842, were "the beginning of a new doctrinal thrust that played an important role during the middle years of the Icarian movement and culminated in the publication of *Le Vraie Christianisme* early in 1846" (ibid., p. 94).
83 L. Królikowski, *Wybór pism* (Warsaw, 1972), p. 402.
84 See *Lud Polski: Wybór dokumentów*, pp. 135–59.
85 See ibid., pp. 230–315.
86 Marx, Engels, *The Russian Menace to Europe*, p. 81.
87 K. Marx and F. Engels, *The Revolution of 1848–49; articles from the Neue Rheinische Zeitung* (New York, 1972), p. 98.
88 Marx, Engels, *The Russian Menace to Europe*, pp. 80–81.
89 It was used by K. Libelt (*Samowładztwo rozumu*) and B. Trentowski (*Stosunek filozofii do cybernetyki*, p. 549). For other usages, see F. Pepłowski, *Słownictwo i frazeologia polskiej publicystyki okresu Oświecenia i romantyzmu* (Warsaw, 1961), pp. 166–67.

90 Brzozowski drew a parallel between the Russian Populists and the Polish democrats of the romantic era in his article "Russkaia revoliutsiia i pol'skie natsional-demokraty," *Russkoe Bogatstvo*, no. 11 (1906).

REFORM TRIUMPHANT: HUNGARY'S SELF-ASSERTION DURING THE SPRINGTIME OF THE PEOPLES (MARCH-APRIL 1848)*

Istvan Deak, Columbia University

This is the story of six weeks in Hungarian history, from 3 March 1848, when Louis Kossuth, leader of the nationalist opposition, made his celebrated speech at the Pressburg Diet demanding that the country's ancient constitution be restored, to 11 April, when Emperor-King Ferdinand ratified the constitution. Between those two dates, Hungary's political and administrative structure was largely overhauled, a number of feudal restrictions on the freedom of the individual and of the market were abolished, and legal equality was guaranteed to every citizen of the state. All this was accomplished by representatives of the old ruling class, the nobility, seeking to secure the continued predominance of their estate by winning over the masses to their cause.

Of course, these reforms could not have been introduced had the revolutions then occurring elsewhere in Europe not taken place, nor without the revolutionary agitation that was manifest within Hungary itself. What distinguished the Hungarian from the other revolutions was that the changes took place peacefully. The Hungarian leaders of the nobility profited from the barricades in Paris, Milan, Berlin, and Vienna, without allowing barricades to be set up in Buda-Pest.

It all began in January 1848 when revolution broke out in Sicily. Soon, most of the peninsula was in turmoil, and Austrian troops had to be sent to Lombardy to defend the territorial integrity of the Monarchy. Everyone in Vienna knew that the Italian revolt was only a beginning: the international and domestic situations were terrible, the Treasury could clearly not afford a war; the Habsburg Court was depressed, the liberals everywhere elated. A Prussian diplomat wrote from Vienna on 29 February:

Every day the Italian mail brings news of constitutions, rebellions, and assassinations. To see Metternich, weak, deaf, reduced to a shadow, senile, is to realize that he will not have the strength to brave the storm. I saw the Emperor lately at a Court ball: I could not believe the terrible condition he was in. The Empress spends all her time with her confessor, but she cannot pray away the trouble. Archduchess Sophie cries the whole day. It seems that she is the only one to sense the danger. . . . Bankruptcy is upon us. The thirty million [gulden] sent by the Russians is a drop in the bucket. No one buys tobacco or plays the lottery, and this has caused a deficit of ten million gulden in the Italian provinces alone. The army in Italy costs three million gulden monthly. . . . Today everyone is talking about the resignation of Louis-Philippe. Will this bring peace? Only a war can save Austria and Germany now.[1]

On the same day, Metternich wrote to a Prussian general: "We antici-
pate the most catastrophic events. . . . The world is being taught a
grave lesson."

News of the latest Paris revolution reached Vienna on 29 February
and the Hungarian Diet at Pressburg the next day. Henceforth,
changes were to follow upon each other in bewildering succession,
with the events in each large city in the empire acting as a catalyst on
the others. Reformers and revolutionaries in Vienna, Milan, Prague,
Pressburg, and Buda-Pest goaded one another on in a brief outburst of
national and international solidarity. In the drama, the two Hungarian
capitals—Pressburg and Buda-Pest—played a major role, and in both
places Louis Kossuth's influence was greater than anyone else's. Because Hungary had her own parliament and administration; because
the Hungarian liberals were organized and represented the interests of
a large and powerful social class; because Hungary had a tradition of
political independence; and because Kossuth was a Hungarian, that
country was to decide, in March 1848, the future of the dynasty and of
the monarchy's peoples.

The rise of Hungary in less than a quarter-century had been phenom-
enal. Although legally always in an exalted position, after 1815 she was
politically and economically almost inconsequential, completely overshadowed by Austria. With her parliament unconvoked, her political
life retrenched in the counties, her national tongue unused except in
colloquial speech, her agriculture medieval, her trade in crisis, her society old-fashioned and rigid, Hungary could with justice have been
described as one of the more backward and less influential provinces of
the prestigious and victorious Habsburg Monarchy.

But change came, at first gradually, then rapidly. On the Austrian
side, starting with the Greek Revolution of the early 1820s, which Metternich wanted to suppress but could not, the Monarchy suffered one
diplomatic humiliation after the other—nor was the court greeted with
any more success in its domestic policy. The Hungarians, in the meantime, were forging ahead relentlessly. By the 1840s, the Diet was almost continually in session, an exciting forum for debate and reform;
political parties had been constituted, and by now they were combating
the central government as well as each other; newspapers poured out
social criticism and political programs; the country's internal bureaucracy had become almost entirely Magyar; Hungarian literature was
thriving; assimilation into Magyardom was progressing, at least in the
cities; the Catholic Church and education were becoming Hungarian;
the social structure had become less rigid; the vestiges of feudalism
were on the verge of disappearing forever; and Hungary was getting
ready to impose her modernistic ideas on the other provinces of the
Monarchy, as well as to wrest a new constitution from the Court.

Meanwhile, the Slavic and Romanian inhabitants of Hungary were also in political and cultural ferment. In part spontaneously, in part inspired by the Western European example, this agitation was very often in direct response to the Hungarian developments. Thus, quite unwittingly, the Magyar nobility was helping these other nationalities to prepare for the same national rejuvenation that the Hungarians were achieving for themselves in those years.

But Hungary's newly found greatness was built on a shaky foundation. Created not by a rising industrial bourgeoisie, but by the landowing nobility, Hungarian progress lacked solid economic backing. Despite some modest successes, her economy was falling behind that of the western parts of the Monarchy. For the time being, Kossuth and his fellow reformers could hide the country's economic weakness behind the façade of progressive slogans and efficient political organization, but this cover-up could last only as long as neither the court nor the Austro-German (and Czech) ruling circles were in a position to use the same weapons. The rise of Hungary can be attributed mainly to Metternich's inactivity and conservatism; it would have to face powerful odds shortly after his fall. This year 1848 would give the Hungarians virtual independence within the empire, but it would also teach their opponents to counter Hungarian modernism with their own modernistic propaganda and political institutions. In the confrontation that developed in 1848–49, Hungary was inevitably the loser.[2]

The great Hungarian reformer Count István Széchenyi was right and Kossuth was wrong: Hungary ought not to have embarked on so ambitious a political venture without having first developed economic strength and a bourgeois society. On the other hand, once the empire had shown signs of falling apart, as it did in 1848, it is hard to see how the Hungarians could have abstained from trying to secure the greatest advantage from its weakness. Yet, in her understandable reach for independent development, Hungary helped to bring about the great crisis of the empire.

THE FIRST HUNGARIAN "JOURNÉES"

The Austrian revolutions of 1848 began in Hungary as the result of a financial panic. The public's rush on the state exchange counters to convert paper bills into specie prompted a deputy in the Lower Table at Pressburg to demand that Vienna finally issue an official statement on monetary policy. Kossuth, who, unlike the deputy in question, had not yet heard of Louis-Philippe's fall in Paris, but who knew about the precipitous decline of government bonds in Vienna, jumped to the occasion to announce that, instead of fussing over such piddling matters, he would now discuss all the major issues confronting Hungary. Two days later, on 3 March, at an unofficial "circular" meeting of the

Lower Table, he delivered what was thus far the most important speech of his career, and one that would lead directly to upheavals in Vienna and in Hungary. In it, Kossuth put all the blame on the imperial government for the financial ills of the Monarchy; he demanded a separate Hungarian financial system, the taxation of the nobility, the suppression of feudal dues and services with compensation to be paid to the landowners, political rights for the urban middle class and the peasants, the reorganization of the imperial army to fit Hungarian national interests, a Hungarian ministry responsible to a newly elected parliament, and the revision of Hungary's relations with the Austrian hereditary provinces. The Austrian half of the monarchy was to get the same constitution that Hungary was about to fashion for herself. Kossuth's speech contained an ultimatum to Vienna: "The dynasty must choose between its own welfare and the preservation of a rotten system."[3] This "inaugural address of the revolution," to use C. A. Macartney's phrase,[4] was translated by sympathizers into German the next day and distributed in Vienna, creating extraordinary excitement.

On 4 March, Kossuth's propositions were acclaimed at the official meeting of the Lower Table and were adopted as an Address to the Throne. The text of the Address was then sent to the Upper Table, but there it was stalled for a while—Archduke Stephen, Palatine (Viceroy) of Hungary and a young cousin of the emperor, was away in Vienna, as were his deputies, so there was no one in Pressburg legally entitled to convoke the Lords. This was almost certainly no coincidence; the high officials had undoubtedly left precisely to prevent the calling of such an emergency meeting. Assembled at Court, the greatest dignitaries of the realm, with a vehemently anti-Kossuth Széchenyi among them, swore not to let the seditious Address reach the throne. But it was difficult to stop Kossuth. Moved by his oratory, the deputies in the Lower Table issued a threat: they would send the Address directly to Vienna without waiting for the Lords. Had they carried out the threat, it would have been the first illegal act they had committed.

But there was no need: on 13 March, revolution broke out in the imperial capital, forcing the government to make immediate concessions to the Hungarians. A detailed description of the Vienna upheaval does not belong here; it is enough to remember that, on that single day, the already highly agitated meeting of the Lower Austrian Estates was invaded by Vienna university students, causing the Estates to send a mass delegation to the imperial palace with a petition for reform. In the suburbs of Vienna, workers revolted, destroying their hated machines and setting fire to the factories of unpopular owners; demonstrators clashed with imperial grenadiers, both inside and outside the city walls, leaving behind forty-five victims; the arming of the burghers and the students was authorized by a cowed court, and, in a veritable palace coup, the archdukes dismissed Metternich, whom they hoped to be able to turn into the scapegoat for these alarming developments. Also dismissed were Sedlnitzky, the Police Minister, and Apponyi, the Hungarian Chancellor. All these tumultuous events had begun with the repeated reading of Kossuth's 3 March speech to delighted crowds in the streets of Vienna and the aula of the university.[5]

After that day, the revolutionary fever infected one Central European city after another. On 14 March, the Viennese obtained arms from the imperial arsenal for their student legion and their burgher-dominated National Guard; censorship was lifted, and Emperor Ferdinand offered to grant something resembling a constitution in the near future. On the same day, in Berlin, there was a bloody clash between demonstrators and the Prussian soldiers, and in Pressburg the Diet took further forceful action.

Duly impressed by the Vienna revolution, Archduke Stephen had hastened back to Pressburg to convoke the Lords. Meeting on 14 March, the Upper Table accepted Kossuth's proposed Address to the Throne without debate. It also accepted Kossuth's request that a mass deputation bring the Address before the King. On the same evening, there was a torchlight parade for Kossuth during which he presented his friend and protector, Count Lajos Batthyány, as the future minister-president of Hungary.

The fifteenth of March was to become the revolutionary *journée par excellence* of Central Europe. In Vienna, new demonstrations erupted because the Emperor's vague promises had satisfied no one. The terrified archdukes now promised, through the mouth of Ferdinand, to grant a real constitution; the Viennese were jubilant and cheered the good Kaiser. In Prague, a hastily constituted Czech National Committee felt so exalted over Metternich's fall that it voted to increase its demands with regard to civil rights and a Bohemian constitution. The Czech petition was to be brought to Vienna by a mass delegation. Also, on 15 March, the Pressburg Diet decided to raise its own demands, and, simultaneously, a revolution broke out in Buda-Pest.

In Pressburg, the Diet voted to institute all Kossuth's reform proposals. It also decided, at Kossuth's request, that the parliamentary delegation to Vienna should now ask for the immediate appointment of a Hungarian minister-president, and that the King should make the pliable and seemingly pro-Hungarian Archduke Palatine Stephen his plenipotentiary in Hungary.

All this haste would have been inconceivable without alarming news from Buda-Pest. So far, Pressburg had experienced only vigorous parliamentary action and a few noisy street meetings; reports from Buda-Pest spoke of an intoxicating, but dangerous revolution.

The February events in Paris had infected Buda-Pest as well, and, ever since early March, the legislative and the executive capitals of Hungary had vied with each other in political agitation. As Buda-Pest was more radical than Pressburg, the first city spurred the second city on, while the second maneuvered to control and restrain the first. And as Kossuth was in Pressburg, not in Buda-Pest, it was natural that the second city should emerge victorious from this contest.

Buda-Pest (the two cities did not unite until 1873, but it was already customary to write the names together or to join them with a hyphen) was not only Hungary's official capital, but also her administrative, cultural, and business center. Buda, the seat of the Vice-Regency Council and of many other governmental institutions, and once the seat of the kings, had not changed much in the preceding decades: it was a pleasant, rather quiet place, built on hills and in valleys, and populated mainly by German burghers. In 1848, Buda had about 35,000 inhabitants.

Pest, on the left bank of the Danube, was on the edge of the Great Hungarian Plain: its expansion met with no natural obstacles, and it was rapidly becoming a boom town. In the 1780s, Pest had 25,000 inhabitants and was in fourth position behind Debrecen, Pressburg, and Buda. By the 1830s, with 70,000 people, it was well ahead of the other Hungarian cities. By 1848, the population had grown to 110,000. Even more important, Pest was becoming a Hungarian city through the assimilation of its German citizens and the influx of Magyar nobles and peasants. Pest had Hungary's only university, her Academy of Sciences, her National Museum and Library, her National Theater, her largest publishing houses, and her most important newspapers and journals. Its artisans (masters, journeymen, and apprentices) numbered over 11,000; its brand new factories employed about 900 people, by far the greatest concentration of factory workers in this otherwise agricultural country.

Finally, Pest had many professionals and artists—more often than not living in abject poverty. What indeed was this fledgling business center to do with its legions of lawyers, twice the number of all those in Bohemia, Moravia, Galicia, Styria, and Dalmatia combined,[6] or with its poets, journalists, dramatists, and actors who, even when they worked, were paid next to nothing by their struggling employers? No wonder that these intellectuals constituted Hungary's most subversive element. For years, they had met in the Pest cafés, passing along forbidden literature and debating the arts, politics, and the future. These young intellectuals were, regardless of their religious, ethnic, or social origin, culturally avant-garde, religiously indifferent, politically Magyar nationalist, and socially progressive, although their social progressivism ranged from advocating mild liberal reforms to republicanism and even communism. By 1848, their undisputed spokesman was Sándor Petőfi, a twenty-five-year-old poet of lower-class Slavic origin.[7] Petőfi was Hungary's greatest lyricist, her foremost patriot, and one of her most radical politicians. He hated the feudal system, the kings and aristocrats, the bureaucrats, and burgher philistinism. He loved the "people," by whom he meant the Magyar peasants, whose life he knew well, rather than the mostly foreign-speaking urban journeymen and workers, of whom he knew little. In 1846, Petőfi formed the Society of Ten, a club of young democratic writers who called themselves "Young Hungary" and dreamed of a revolution. A part of the "Young" movement in Europe, Young Hungary saw itself as creating a free, democratic, and thoroughly Magyarized nation, one that would live in perfect harmony with the other progressive nations of the world. It had occurred to no one in the group to seek to contact radical movements outside Hungary, however: the revolution would come by itself; it would arise simultaneously everywhere, and it would be met with immediate success. The month of March in the year 1848 was the moment of truth for Young Hungary.

Following his 3 March speech, Kossuth had turned to the Pest branch of the party of opposition with the request that they reformulate his program and submit it to the Diet as a "grassroots" petition. The Pest "Oppositionary Circle" knew where the talent was, and on 9 March it asked the Society of Ten to draw the petition up. Petőfi and his friends obliged in haste, for there was to be a popular fair in Pest at which some 40,000 peasants were expected, and Young Hungary hoped to put pressure on Pressburg by organizing a reform banquet and on that occasion to rouse the peasants. These 40,000 peasants were to become a decisive factor in the coming political events. Even though in fact the fair was not held until 19 March, and the peasants, when they came, were mostly interested in buying and selling, the political leaders in Pressburg and Vienna were convinced that they had arrived earlier, that they were armed, that Petőfi was their leader, and that the rustics were in an ugly mood. The chimera of a Petőfi-led jacquerie drove the Court and the Diet to make concession after concession to the popular-nationalist cause. Kossuth alone kept cool: he used the threat of the peasant uprising to further his political goals, but he never gave in to fear.

Young Hungary's program was ready for presentation by 11 March but it was not the petition that had been asked for; rather it was called the "Twelve Demands," and it included several radical postulates that had not even been suggested by Kossuth. Aside from Kossuth's reform proposals, it requested freedom of the press, an independent Hungarian ministry residing in Buda-Pest and responsible to a popularly elected parliament, the setting up of a National Guard, complete civil and

religious equality, trial by jury, a national bank, a Hungarian national
army, the withdrawal from Hungary of foreign, i.e., Austrian, troops,
the freeing of political prisoners, and union with Transylvania. Typically, not even this radical program proposed to do anything for the
landless or contractual peasants, or for the workers and journeymen—
although it did help the landholding (urbarial) peasants by omitting any
mention of compensation to be paid to the noble landowners—or for
Hungary's non-Magyar nationalities.

On 14 March, the Danube steamship brought news of the Vienna
revolution to Buda-Pest. Young Hungary decided to abandon the idea
of circulating the Twelve Demands for mass signature, or of submitting
them to the Diet; rather, they were to be acted upon immediately. This
revolutionary step was taken on the morning of 15 March, when, in the
Café Pilvax, they were read aloud, after which Petőfi recited a poem he
had just written for the occasion. The refrain of his "National Song"
was simple and effective:

> We swear by the God of Hungarians
> We swear, we shall be slaves no more.

Having gathered courage in the café, the young radicals went to the
university, there to be joined by the students. Thousands of ordinary
Pest citizens were also aroused. Petőfi and his friends then seized the
largest printing shop in the city, printed leaflets containing the Twelve
Demands and the National Song on the spot, and distributed them to
the multitude—in effect, establishing freedom of the press by that one
peaceful move. At three in the afternoon, Petőfi spoke to some ten
thousand demonstrators in front of the National Museum. It was a
rainy day, and instead of the fondly-hoped-for weapons, Petőfi faced
an arsenal of umbrellas. Still, the Pest burghers, caught up in the spirit
of the times, celebrated the poet whom they would have ranked as no
better than a circus performer a few days earlier.

From the Museum the crowd marched on the Pest city hall, invaded
the chamber of the council in session, climbed upon chairs and tables,
and ordered the council to endorse the Twelve Demands. Then and
there, a Committee of Public Safety was formed to govern the twin
cities, to spread the good word, and to set up a National Guard. Although this was a most revolutionary move, at the same time the composition of the Committee presaged the rapid decline of Young Hungary. Realizing that they represented only themselves, the radical intellectuals limited their membership on the Committee to four, Petőfi
included. The rest of the membership was made up of six liberals from
the Pest City Council, all functionaries or master craftsmen, and three
noblemen, all political friends of Kossuth. Young Hungary managed to

dominate the Committee of Public Safety for a few days, but thereafter it was Kossuth's colleagues who had the final say. It soon became clear that Kossuth was going to allow the Pest radicals to push the revolution only as far as he, Kossuth, wanted it to go.

But for that day all was success and joy. In the evening of 15 March, 20,000 people crossed over to Buda on the pontoon bridge connecting the twin cities (Széchenyi's permanent bridge was not yet complete), and the Committee of Public Safety invaded the chamber of the Vice-Regency Council. This high body capitulated immediately, ordering the garrison not to meddle in the affairs of the citizenry, abolishing censorship, and signing a release for Hungarian political prisoners. Of the latter, there turned out to be only one in the entire capital: Mihály Táncsics, a nationalist radical political pamphleteer of Slavic peasant origin, was carried in triumph across the city. The day ended with a gala performance in the National Theater in celebration of freedom.

Why had the Vice-Regency Council capitulated so easily on 15 March? Because 20,000 demonstrators in a city containing 150,000 inhabitants was an unheard-of multitude, even though the people had no arms; because the 7,000-man garrison, composed mostly of Italians, could not be counted on; and because the old order was frightened, as it seemed to be in those days everywhere in Europe. Petőfi was to write of the event that, while the demonstrators shouted outside the palace, and while the spokesman of the Committee of Public Safety (one of Kossuth's friends) presented the demands of the revolution "stammering in all humility and trembling like a pupil before his teacher . . . Their Magnificences, the Vice-Regency Council, turned pale and were graciously pleased to tremble also. Within five minutes, they consented to everything."[8]

The fifteenth of March was to become a national holiday in Hungary. Every regime, left or right, celebrated it as its own. But 15 March was also to become the traditional day for voicing opposition to any regime.

With 15 March, the first Hungarian *journées* temporarily came to an end, not to be renewed until the end of the month. In the intervening weeks, the Diet and the Pest radicals worked sometimes together, sometimes at cross purposes, to consolidate the gains of the revolution. On the very afternoon the demonstrators had taken over Buda-Pest, the delegation of Pressburg parliamentarians, accompanied by hundreds of young jurists, boarded two steamships to carry the Address directly to the throne. The time had come for the customary hard bargaining that had always marked compromise negotiations between crown and nation in critical periods—but on this occasion the nation was the stronger.

VIENNA SUCCESS AND CROATIAN CONTRETEMPS

To get from Pressburg to Vienna on a steam packet took only a few hours, time enough for the Hungarian leaders to rethink their strategy. Clearly, the Address to the Throne composed by Kossuth less than two weeks earlier was now outdated, requesting as it did a separate Hungarian cabinet only as a pious wish and not as an immediate need.[9] Yet the Diet, on the morning of 15 March, had instructed the delegation to press for an immediate appointment.[10] Now it was resolved to create a *fait accompli* by drawing up in advance the King's reply. His Majesty would merely have to sign. This royal rescript was drafted by Kossuth himself on the night of his arrival in Vienna.[11] If the King had signed the document as it stood, he would have instructed Count Batthyány to form a cabinet, appointed Palatine Stephen as royal plenipotentiary in Hungary, and promised to ratify any and all bills adopted by the Diet under the leadership of the Palatine. This was the first—but not the last—instance when Hungarian reformers, in particular Kossuth, drafted a royal rescript for Ferdinand's signature. That they dared to do so and that their drafts were sometimes accepted by the Court testify both to Hungary's sudden strength and to the near-collapse of the old regime.

Resplendent in gala dress, richly studded swords, and egret-feathered caps, the arriving Hungarian nobles presented the Viennese with an unforgettable sight. Kossuth looked somber and dignified in his simple black national garb. The reception given the Hungarian "Argonauts"—as the press referred to them—went beyond their fondest dreams. The crowd may have numbered one hundred thousand. Masses of armed students and national guardsmen lined the streets; a myriad hand-held lamps illuminated the dusk; weeping women rushed forward to touch Kossuth's cloak; his carriage was unhorsed, pulled by citizens, and forced to stop again and again so he could make yet another speech.

What struck most observers was the virility and elegance of the man. At forty-six years his brown hair was now lightly flecked with white; his beard, full and wavy (and thereafter so much in vogue in Hungary), lent dignity and enhanced the handsomeness of his face. He was frail, and when he began to speak, he always acted as though he were about to collapse. Then as if overcoming with a superhuman effort his weakness, his exhaustion, and his many illnesses (of which he complained constantly), his voice gradually rose until it rolled into a rumbling storm. Kossuth was not only a brilliant speaker—alternately majestic, dignified, fearsome, mellow, flattering and humble, refined and direct in simplicity—but his voice carried farther than anyone else's, an indispensable attribute in those days for someone addressing a crowd.

While the Champion of Liberty and Hero of the People was thus being celebrated as no one before in living Viennese memory, the imperial palace, locked and barred, was being protected by several companies of soldiers. The members of the imperial family were virtual prisoners. Writing in exile ten years later, Kossuth recalled with bitterness the events of the day:

> As I arrived in front of the imperial residence, behind whose dark and mute windows the offspring of proud emperors trembled, awaiting the verdict of fate, it flashed through my mind: what would become of the bungling masters of the Burg . . . what would become of them, within one-quarter of an hour, if I were to thrust the spark of the living word into the gaping mouth of the gunpowder keg which surrounded me from all sides? This on the very spot where even the written word [the German translation of Kossuth's 3 March speech] had sufficed to ignite a flame that had consumed the centuries-old edifice of absolutism. But I, who had come merely to seek justice for my fatherland, was not even tempted by the opportunity.[12]

Kossuth's claim that, on 15 March, he was master of Vienna and that, had he wanted, he could have put a sudden end to Habsburg rule, is not quite borne out by historical evidence. Remember that only a few hours in advance of his arrival, the Kaiser had promised a constitution to Austria and the Viennese had applauded him for it: in the exaltation of the moment, Ferdinand and Kossuth were both popular. In any case, however, the temptation for Kossuth to do away with the House of Austria did not loom large. Obviously, he enjoyed the adulation of the crowd, and he knew how to turn it to his own, and to his country's, advantage. But he had no desire to dissolve the Monarchy, nor to end the rule of the Emperor-King. On the contrary, he had come to Vienna to establish Hungary's preeminence in the Empire, and to repossess the Monarch for his country.

If 15 March was the *journée* of revolution, 16 March was the day of frantic bargaining. Early in the morning, Archduke Stephen hastened to Court to inform his relatives that, unless there was accession to Hungarian demands, the country would secede and proclaim itself a republic. What the Palatine failed to mention was that there was also a movement afoot in Hungary to make him king. Around noon, Ferdinand received the Hungarian delegation and, in response to flowery speeches, mumbled a few words of acknowledgment. Besieged for days by councillors, delegations, and petitioners, the Kaiser was at the end of his strength: his face a deathly pale, his head lolling, he was almost unable to understand what was happening, "Peinlicher Anblick," Széchenyi noted in his diary, while Kossuth was to write later, "Once the official procedure was over, Emperor-King Ferdinand V turned to Archduke Stephen and, folding his hands as in prayer, begged the Archduke with childish simplicity that now that the latter had become his vice-regent [in Hungary], he should remain vice-regent and not take away his throne (i' pitt' di', nim mir meinen Thron nit!)."[13]

Soon thereafter the State Conference met in the Hofburg. With brief intermissions, it was to remain in session until dawn. The participants—the Archdukes Louis and Francis Charles, the aged *Feldmarschalleutnant* Windisch-Graetz (Commander in Chief in Bohemia and an archconservative), a few Hungarian high officials, and a number of ministers of state as well as lesser councillors—were aghast at the arrogance of the Pressburg Diet, but as the day advanced, and alarming reports kept coming in of turbulence everywhere (the 40,000 Pest peasants loomed large here), they agreed to consider Kossuth's draft reply. The royal rescript, issued on the morning of 17 March, was a verbatim rendering of the Hungarian text, but with two crucial omissions: the name of Count Batthyány, and the promise of an unconditional ratification of the bills to be adopted by the Diet.

This was not good enough for the Hungarian leaders; now not only did Batthyány and Kossuth resist, but Széchenyi himself was adamant. The Palatine thereupon rushed to his imperial uncle and obtained his verbal consent to the appointment of Batthyány. Immediately thereafter, as Royal Plenipotentiary for Hungary, Archduke Stephen wrote a note to Batthyány, appointing him minister-president of Hungary and instructing him to submit a list of cabinet members.[14] The Hungarians had won a great victory, but there could be no doubt that the King's consent had been achieved by the Palatine going behind the back of the State Conference. This was to constitute the grounds on which the Court would later repudiate the entire Hungarian constitution, send Archduke Stephen into exile, and condemn Count Batthyány to the gallows.

The events of 16–17 March had clearly shown that the highest governing circles of the Monarchy were not united in their Hungarian policy. Naturally, they all wished to save the Monarchy and their own privileged positions in it, but they were at odds on tactics and strategy. For years, the Hungarians had been insisting that the Vienna Court was dominated by the ''Camarilla,'' an infamous conspiratorial clique that was as obscurantist and reactionary as it was anti-Hungarian. The existence and absolute power of the Camarilla, allegedly led by the fiendish Archduchess Sophie, mother of Francis Joseph, was an article of faith with Kossuth, and one that he refused to abandon to his dying day. There was literally no political speech or writing in which he did not refer to the ''murderous,'' ''infamous,'' or ''accursed'' Camarilla as the dedicated enemy of everything that was good and noble in the world. Kossuth and his compatriots saw themselves as innocent victims of Camarilla machinations: they, the Hungarians, had law and legality on their side, while the Camarilla violated the law. Revolutionary

Hungary's Paris envoy, Count László Teleki, assured the Polish Prince Adam Czartoryski in 1849, "Nous n'avons pas pris les armes que pour la défense de notre constitution légalement garantie et . . . c'est la Camarilla qui est en état de révolte contre nous."[15] Both nationalist and left-wing Hungarian historiography later unconditionally embraced the same view, and as recently as the late 1950s, Hungarian Marxist historians were still fervently reiterating the accusations of Kossuth.[16] What neither Kossuth nor the nationalist *cum* radical historians ever made clear was precisely what the Camarilla was: some Hungarians use the term interchangeably with State Conference; others distinguished between a "civilian" and a "military" one; still others a bit cavalierly identify the term with the entire Vienna Court, including the Austrian government.

Historical evidence does not support the Hungarian thesis. It is true, of course, that following Ferdinand's accession to the throne in 1835, a group of archdukes and imperial bureaucrats had been making all decisions in the name of the feeble monarch. It is also true that the secrecy surrounding all high-level deliberations fostered the creation of legends. But the fact remains that there was no conspiracy, and that there were many factions at court which were formed and reformed on important political issues. Of the twenty-five-or-so persons who usually attended meetings of the State Conference, at least ten were Hungarian aristocrats; the rest were of diverse nationality, often Germans from outside Austria. By 1848, nationalist sympathies had begun to influence these people, and so had diverse ideologies. Some members had pro-Magyar or pro-German or pro-Slav leanings; others showed aristocratic-federalist or bureaucratic-centralist inclinations; some put their faith in a quick military solution of the Monarchy's problems; others favored temporary or lasting concessions to the liberal cause. The imperial family itself was divided: Archduchess Sophie, "the only man in the Hofburg," but naturally not a member of the State Conference, was willing to introduce reforms and, even more, to dump both Metternich and Ferdinand; Archdukes Louis and Francis Charles were generally rigid, as was Archduke Albrecht, a tough militarist; Archduke John had German liberal leanings, and Archduke Stephen, not a regular participant of State Conference deliberations, yearned to be both a loyal Habsburg and a loyal Hungarian. As for the Hungarian high officials, their opinions ranged from absolute political orthodoxy to mild sympathy with Batthyány and the Diet, if not with Kossuth.

The strongest opposition to Hungarian demands on 16 March had not come from the conservative-aristocratic camp, but from the camp of German-Austrian bureaucrats who had pointed out, with some justification, that the Emperor's 15 March promise of an Austrian constitution clashed directly with the King's 16 March concessions to the Hungarians. Those functionaries saw the 15 March rescript as the first step toward the creation of an all-Austrian cabinet supported by a soon-to-be-elected all-Austrian parliament. How would Hungary's separate constitution fit into such a scheme?

Hungary's later defeat lay in this German-Austrian opposition to a separate Hungarian development. Conceivably, the Hungarians could have dealt with their conservative opponents alone: Habsburg traditionalists, such as Windisch-Graetz, had always recognized at least some of Hungary's historic rights. It proved to be much more difficult for the Hungarians to combat a coalition of conservatives and bureaucratic centralists, especially as the latter came increasingly to be supported by German-Austrian liberal-nationalist opinion, with only a few Vienna democrats remaining staunch supporters of the Hungarian cause. Finally, when the Czechs, Croats, and other Slavs joined this mighty coalition for reasons of their own, the fate of Hungary was sealed.

Why had the politically inexperienced Stephen, then thirty-one years of age, overruled the State Conference? No doubt because he enjoyed his popularity in Hungary, and because this was his way of saving the Monarchy. From that time on, all major Austrian leaders, whether archdukes, generals, or politicians, endeavored to save the Monarchy in their own way, and sometimes in violation of imperial-royal decrees. In the end, it was the generals who saved the throne, often in defiance of the expressed wishes of the Crown. But, unlike the generals, Archduke Stephen was not to earn royal pardon and gratitude.

In the next days, the roof seemed to collapse on the Monarchy. On 17 March, while the Hungarian Palatine pleaded with the King, revolution broke out in Venice. On the eighteenth, it moved to Milan, while—as if to show the Habsburgs that succor could not be expected from anywhere—violent clashes occurred in Berlin as well between revolutionaries and Prussian royal troops. On that day also, the State Conference ruled that Stephen had overstepped his authority, but by then it was too late. Bowing to the inevitable, the Conference "temporarily" upheld the appointment of Count Batthyány. The Hungarian success was complete.

On 19 March, the Czech delegation came to Vienna to present its demands. Two days later, the Austrian commander in Venice capitulated to the rebels without having fired a shot: a republic was proclaimed there, with Daniel Manin as President of Venice and, it was hoped, soon also of Italy. One-third of the Austrian land forces in Venice, and the majority of the Austrian fleet—manned mainly by Italians—declared a united Italy. The rest of the fleet fled to Trieste. On 22 March, the little Austrian garrison in Milan, with Field Marshal Radetzky, Austrian commander in Italy, at its head, evacuated the city.

The Milan revolutionaries formed a provisional government and asked for brotherly help from the Kingdom of Piedmont-Sardinia. On 23 March, the King of that country, Charles Albert, ordered his army into Lombardy: Austria was now at war with a foreign country. All Italy was in revolt; client princes of Austria had to flee their capital; even the Pope promised to send troops against His Catholic and Apostolic Majesty. Radetzky had by then withdrawn to the Quadrilateral: four great fortresses protecting the Alpine passes between Italy and Austria.[17] Meanwhile, there were demonstrations in Galicia and a revolt in Cracow.

The State Conference tried to save what it could. Troops and a little money were dispatched to Radetzky. In Vienna, a further step toward consolidation was taken on 20 March with the formation of an Austrian cabinet, the first in the country's history. It consisted of old and trusted servants of the Crown, but it was not at all clear whether this ministry, headed by Kolowrat, an old-regime figure, would command any authority. Windisch-Graetz was sent back to Bohemia to keep order there, and on 23 March, a Croat colonel, Josip Jelačić, was appointed *Ban* (Governor) of Croatia. That proved a fatal move, destined to lead to war with Hungary.

For nearly seven hundred years, the Kingdom of Croatia had been associated with the Kingdom of Hungary: both formed integral parts of the Crown of St. Stephen. Although theoretically equal, small and very backward Croatia had less than one and a half million inhabitants to Hungary's more than ten million (not counting Transylvania), and she was definitely in a subordinate position. Her deputies at the Pressburg Diet were hopelessly outnumbered by the deputies from Hungary. Moreover, ever since Turkish times, Croatia had been divided into two parts: Croatia proper, or Civil Croatia, and a much larger and more populous "Military Border." Originally established as a line of defense against the Turks, the Military Border was not administered, as Civil Croatia was, by the Hungarian Chancellery in Vienna, but by the Vienna War Council. Thus, the Military Border, while legally part of the Crown of St. Stephen, had nothing to do with either the Hungarian or the Croat authorities. The Military Border, incidentally, extended well beyond the boundaries of historic Croatia into Hungary proper and into Transylvania, thus infinitely complicating matters to contemporary legists and, presumably, to readers of this study. Still, the bulk of the Border was in historic Croatia, and its peasant-soldiers were either Croats or Serbs. These were the famous *Grenzer*, similar to the Cossacks of Russia, and the pride and joy of the Habsburg army.[18]

Civil Croatia was a small country with, however, her own Diet (the *Sabor*) and landed nobility, and with some measure of autonomy. Relations between the Hungarian and Croatian nobility, once most propitious in common opposition to the centralizing and reforming endeavors of Vienna, had lately become venomous. Hungarian nationalism was seen in Zagreb, capital of Croatia, as a mortal danger to the historic rights of their country. Naturally, the Croats were also divided among themselves. Some—mainly young middle-class intellectuals—belonged to the Illyrian movement that had sprung up as the result of the Napoleonic invasion. They dreamed of the unification of all South Slavs into one sovereign country, perhaps under the nominal rule of the Habsburg dynasty. Other Croats, mostly from the nobility, simply wished to strengthen Croat rights under the Crown of St. Stephen. Still others, especially a distinct group of Croat peasant-nobles, were ardent followers of Kossuth.

Now, in March 1848, both Civil Croatia and the Military Border were in a state of turmoil that greatly worried Vienna. There were some 30,000 Croat and Serb soldiers under Radetzky in Italy, and they constituted the best part of that army. If the Hungarians were satisfied but the Croats not, there was real danger that the latter would refuse to fight for Austria. In order to avoid giving the impression to the Croats that they had been delivered over to the whims of their Hungarian overlords, it was imperative that the governorship of Croatia be offered to a man whom both the Croats and Vienna could trust. This man was Jelačić.

The son of a two-star general in the Habsburg army, Jelačić was an officer himself by 1819. He counted as a Croatian patriot because of the heroic poems he wrote and read aloud to his soldiers in camp; he was the commander of a Croat regiment; he was a conservative; his loyalty to the throne was absolute; and, finally, he hated the Hungarian liberals. His appointment was passed in a hurry, since there was some danger that the Hungarian government, once constituted, would be able to prevent it. After all, the *Ban* of Croatia was legally one of Hungary's highest dignitaries. It was characteristic of the disunity in imperial circles that while most officials saw Jelačić's appointment as a peaceful measure and an inevitable consequence of the great concessions made to Hungary, at least one imperial official, not a member of the State Conference, wrote to Jelačić, "Austria will have to reconquer Hungary, and therefore you must at all costs retain the loyalty of the Military Border."[19] Within two weeks, Jelačić was promoted to two-star general and, in an unprecedented move, the new Governor of Civil Croatia was also put in charge of the armies of both Civil Croatia and the Croatian section of the Military Border. In September 1848, he was to invade Hungary, precipitating the war between the Habsburgs and Kossuth.[20]

From the point of view of Vienna, Hungary still posed a serious

problem, but for the time being it was not one of catastrophic proportions—the country would probably remain in the Monarchy, something
that could not be said of northern Italy. Nor could it be said of German-
Austria proper, where agitation was growing for unification with the
rest of Germany at any price, even, if necessary, that of discarding the
Habsburg dynasty. Thus the Hungarians were left to their own devices
for a few days, and they took advantage of the lull to create a new
country. In this effort the leadership was again taken by Kossuth.

MAKING A NEW CONSTITUTION

The delegation's dazzling success in Vienna swept the Magyars
(aside from the archconservatives) off their feet. Now even the cautious reformer Ferenc Deák bothered to remove himself from his estate
in order to attend the Diet, while the cynic and eternal worrier, Széchenyi, appeared uncommonly elated. Early in March, when he had
still been advising firmness to the government, he had written his secretary:

> We must decide what is more important: *gentle treatment to Louis* [Kossuth] or the
> *welfare of fatherland:* I believe it is high time to imitate the French—not *in proclaiming
> the republic* but in kicking our own Louis in the ass.[21]

But by 17 March, Széchenyi had changed his tune:

> My friend, we lived through miracles! Our national destiny hung by a thread. Act One
> of the drama was a magnificent success! I am full of the greatest expectations . . . I
> cannot doubt that things will develop for the best of our nation; and since I am only
> delighted by the tremendous roles played by Batthyány and Kossuth and since, as God
> sees my soul, I entertain not the slightest envy towards them, I indulge in the sweet
> conviction that the sole motive force of my politics is "devotion"! . . . As far as I am
> concerned, I shall serve Batthyány and Kossuth most sincerely! . . . My policy was cer-
> tain but slow. Kos[suth] staked everything on one card, and already had won as much for
> the nation as my policy could have produced over perhaps 20 years![22]

In the afternoon of 17 March, Pressburg celebrated the returning
Hungarian Argonauts: Kossuth was again the main speaker, and this
time he sounded a law-and-order note. Next day, the Diet sat down to
work—in haste, for the lawmakers were as worried about the further
radicalization of the public as the Court was about the radicalization of
the lawmakers. Fear of extremism was as much a mark of the times as
was exuberance and drive. March 1848 saw a multitude of inter-
connected, overlapping, and feverishly busy political groups, each
trying to put pressure on the group to its right and to neutralize or co-
opt the one to its left. Reactionary Court aristocrats were pressured by
moderate conservatives, the latter by liberal nobles, these again by
radical nobles, and the latter by plebeian radicals. Each group was di-

vided into many factions; all believed that those to their left were going dangerously far, and all attempted to mellow "the extremists" by calculated concessions and by luring them into their own camp. The Court suspected Archduke Stephen but was willing to work with him because it was better to have a Habsburg as palatine of Hungary than to have someone else, or to have a republic, or to see the Archduke proclaimed King of Hungary. The Palatine suspected Batthyány but made him minister-president because Batthyány was less dangerous than Kossuth. Batthyány feared Kossuth but supported his election to the Diet in 1847 so that Kossuth would become part of the noble establishment rather than a demagogue at large; now Batthyány was preparing to entrust Kossuth with a responsible but not too influential cabinet post. Kossuth despised the radical intellectuals, but he encouraged their activities because he needed their support; he also endorsed the Committee of Public Safety—and infiltrated it with his own friends—because it burdened the intellectuals with the responsibility of maintaining order in Buda-Pest. Finally, Petőfi and his colleagues had little respect for the peasant agitator Táncsics, but they supported him so as to secure the loyalty of peasants to the radical and national cause.

In this nerve-racking situation, the noble Diet, or rather its liberal majority, set itself the task of drawing up in rough outline the maximum number of reforms it was ready to adopt, lest more extreme measures be imposed on it by the street, before quickly dissolving itself. The new Hungarian government, it was hoped, would then execute the reform laws as it saw fit and would also restrain the radicals with the might of the state. For the next two weeks, seven days a week, there were daily meetings of both houses with unofficial "circular" sessions preparing the work of official ones, with incessant debate and voting, and with almost all important bills originating from Kossuth.

On 18 March, Kossuth proposed, and the Lower Table accepted, equal voting rights to be given during the remainder of the session to the hitherto practically voteless town representatives and clerical chapter delegates. On the same day, both houses voted in favor of a number of other Kossuth proposals, among them those on general taxation and the abolition of urbarial relations. Now that the landowning noble estate had made such a supreme sacrifice, it was high time for the members of clerical estate to give up something also. All eyes were turned toward them, but the delegates of the chapters kept silent. In one of his reminiscences, Kossuth tells us what happened next:

The emancipation of the serfs having been voted in . . . I stole quietly to the stand where the deputies of the chapters were sitting and, addressing them in a gentle low voice, I said: "Gentlemen: the tithe of the landlords has just ceased to exist; it is natural, therefore, that the tithe of the clergy cease also. Secure for the Hungarian Catholic clergy the glory of surrendering it yourselves; do not wait for me to make the proposition for you. You must take the initiative." Thereupon one of them replied: "Thank you for the warning: I shall do so immediately." . . . I can still laugh when I recall how some of the most reverend colleagues of this gentleman tugged at his cassock. "Per amorem dei," he should not be a fool. But the good man wanted to be. He announced, in the name of his chapter, that he would renounce the tithe, on behalf of the people, in perpetuity, and without any compensation. His example was followed by his colleagues, all making enthusiastic statements; not one spoke against it, not even the cassock-tuggers. . . . Such was the genesis of the eternally glorious Law XIII of 1848 [on the abolition of tithes due the clergy]. [23]

To reassure the worried priests, Kossuth immediately guaranteed state financial support to the lower clergy, a promise he kept as long as he was in power.[24]

With the Batthyány-Kossuth faction somewhat left of center in the political spectrum, it was inevitable that clashes would occur with opponents on both the Left and the Right. The first of these confrontations took place on 19 March, when delegates of the Buda-Pest Committee of Public Safety appeared at the circular meeting of the Lower Table to present the Twelve Demands and to request that the Diet immediately locate itself in the nation's capital. Széchenyi happened to chair this meeting and with all his loathing for hotheads, he could not help but admire these young revolutionaries, particularly twenty-two-year old Pál Vasvári, a historian and one of Hungary's few revolutionary theoreticians, who was to die at the hands of Romanian guerrillas a year later. "Charmant garçon," Széchenyi noted in his diary, adding that Vasvári reminded him of Saint-Just.

Less sensitive souls remained unimpressed by the beauty of youth. Delivering the reply of the House, Kossuth mixed flattery with threats. Neither then nor after did he refer to 15 March in Buda-Pest as a revolution: it was for him simply another manifestation of the "national movement." He told the youth delegation that the Diet would not budge: not with a few weeks of urgent work left; the Twelve Demands were laudable but unnecessary, as most of them were already included in the Diet's program. Kossuth then stated:

I recognize the inhabitants of Buda-Pest as inexpressibly important in this fatherland; I recognize Buda-Pest as the heart of the country, but I shall never recognize it as [this country's] master . . . just as the word "nation" cannot be arrogated by one caste, so it cannot be arrogated by any one city; the 15 million Hungarians [sic], as an entity, constitute the fatherland and the nation. . . . This nation is so strong in the awareness of its rights, its vocation, and its mission that it can crush anyone who entertains the notion of indispensability to the nation.[25]

Kossuth's message was clearly understood by everyone, especially by the moderate-conservative elements in Pressburg to whom the speech was really addressed. Their newspaper bannered Kossuth's threat to the youth as a headline. There was to be no second revolution in Hungary; Buda-Pest would not be allowed to play the role of Paris; commoners ought not to try to wrest power from the nobles; all changes would be made by the legally constituted Diet, and not by plebeian revolutionaries.

Through this address, Kossuth achieved two things: By simultaneously complimenting and warning Young Hungary, he made it clear that they were to remain loyal to him; they had, after all, no one else to whom they could turn. But by not advocating the dissolution of the Committee of Public Safety, he also served notice on the conservatives. Without Kossuth in the cabinet, there could be no peace in Hungary.

The following days saw feverish activity on the part of the Diet. On 20 March, the annual convening of the new national assembly was decided on, together with the creation of a national bank. On the same day, the new press bill was presented, abolishing censorship but setting strict limitations on the freedom of the press by severely punishing press delicts and by requiring publishers to put up security before starting a newspaper. The youth in Pest later burned the bill in public, and, in its final form, the press law was somewhat less stringent. On 21 March, decisions were made, among other things, on charters for the cities. This gave the opportunity to some urban elements to demonstrate their own interpretation of freedom. The bill would have granted voting rights for municipal elections to every city inhabitant otherwise qualified, without regard to religion—in other words, it would have granted suffrage to financially secure Jews. Members of the guilds, both masters and journeymen, had long resented the illegal immigration into the cities of Jewish shopkeepers and artisans. On the very day the city bill was debated in the House, Jewish shops were broken into and Jews beaten up in Pressburg. (The pogrom spread rapidly to other cities and did not reach its culmination until April.) Anti-Semitic outbursts were a disaster for the Hungarian reformers because they caused dissension among their ranks and because they provided another excuse for the imperial authorities to intervene in Hungary.

Kossuth condemned the pogrom in the House, but as the government, not yet formed, had practically no means of controlling the mob, the majority of liberals favored delaying the emancipation of the Jews. The city bill was modified—over the lukewarm protestations of Kossuth—to deny suffrage to the Jews.[26]

The twenty-second of March ushered in the bill on the National Guard system. Guards were in vogue during the Springtime of the Peoples: no revolution was considered complete without these armed and uniformed civilians, charged with defending property and the new regime. In Hungary, the first guard companies had sprung up on 15 March in Pest; from there, the movement spread rapidly to other cities and even to the countryside. The formation of the guard companies was unavoidable, but also dangerous: what if the armed peasants should turn against the landowners or, as one deputy put it, become "the tools of emissaries heralding communistic doctrines"? It was decided to set rather high property qualifications for entry into the guards; for instance, no peasant owning less than half a serf section was allowed to serve, and this effectively excluded most of them. Speaking on the issue, Kossuth again struck out in two directions: he sparred with the conservatives by declaring that "whatever the people have acquired cannot be taken away from them; rather, one must legalize and organize it,"[27] and with the radicals by categorically rejecting the idea that guard officers above the rank of captain should be elected democratically.

As it turned out, the guard companies blithely ignored the Diet's decision with regard to property qualifications. After the national minorities revolted, the government needed all the men it could get anyway. In any case, the Diet's initial fears would prove unwarranted: the guards became the willing, though inefficient, tools of the new regime.

On 23 March, the Lower and Upper Tables adopted no less than seven major laws, among them one on the abolition of entail and one on compensation to be paid the landowners who through the reforms had lost feudal dues and services. It was a major tribute to Kossuth that the deputies, unlike himself, almost all landowners, consented to wait for compensation without a deadline and without any better guarantee of payment than that "the compensation of private landowners will be placed under the protective shield of national honor."[28] True, no one could reasonably expect the peasants to pay, nor did anyone have the slightest notion where the state would get the money from in the near future.

On the same day, Batthyány had submitted his list of proposed cabinet members to the House, and thus Kossuth, when he spoke on the issue of compensation, was already addressing his audience as future Minister of Finance. Unlike the constitution, the first Hungarian government was not Kossuth's brainchild but Batthyány's. Two days earlier, Kossuth had been invited to Batthyány's house, there to be told who the ministers would be and to be offered the portfolio of finance. Formally, he had shown himself reluctant, but there could be no doubt about his accepting the nomination: all knew that if he insisted on a crucial post such as that of minister of interior the King would reject the cabinet list, and if he refused to enter the government the Diet and the people would turn against Batthyány. And Kossuth had also suffered an outright defeat on that day, for he failed to get either one of his two close collaborators, Count László Teleki and Pál Nyáry, anywhere on the list.

For the first time, but certainly not for the last, during their friendly rivalry, Batthyány emerged stronger than Kossuth. As a result of Kossuth's defeat, or magnanimity, the first Hungarian government became durable; unlike the weak Austrian cabinet, whose composition was to change constantly, Batthyány's ministry truly governed Hungary for the next six months. Yet Batthyány had started under very bad auspices: Court circles tended to regard him as a radical revolutionary, an egomaniac, a tool of Kossuth, and a fool; Hungarian radicals saw in him an enemy of Kossuth and a cunning agent of the Camarilla.

Batthyány was neither a radical nor a reactionary; least of all was he a fool or anybody's tool. He was a fine statesman, next to Kossuth the most remarkable political product of the revolutionary year. Unfortunately, relatively little is known of him, for he still awaits his biographer; nor have his papers yet been collected. Two valuable historical works, dedicated to his memory by the reliable and highly sympathetic Árpád Károlyi, deal mainly with his activities in 1848, not with his life or personality.[29]

At forty-one, Batthyány was one of Hungary's richest landowners and the bearer of an illustrious name. His ancestors had been, like those of Széchenyi, good Catholics and good Habsburg loyalists: for this they had been rewarded with the title of count and at various times with archbishoprics, palatinates, and chancellorships. Batthyány himself began as a soldier, then returned to govern his estates, traveled to Western Europe, and later helped create the liberal opposition among the Lords. He had participated in Kossuth's nationalist-economic undertakings, and in October 1847 he had secured Kossuth's election to the Diet. Handsome and elegant, Batthyány enjoyed luxurious living and women; he was intelligent, though indifferently educated, and while he was a poor speaker, he proved to be a first-class administrator and political organizer. If he failed, in the end, as minister-president, it was because his task was impossible: no one could have reconciled the interests of the House of Austria with Hungary's aspirations, nor the nationalism of the Slavs and Romanians with that of the Magyars. Batthyány wished to build a Hungarian empire within the Habsburg Empire or, if the latter disappeared, without it, though still, he hoped, with Ferdinand as King. He intended to act legally but did not hesitate to impose the law on the King or to bend it in a national emergency. In social and economic questions, he was close to Kossuth; in politics, the major differences between the two were that Batthyány was less inclined to take risks vis-à-vis Vienna and that he refused to resort to open rebellion against the ruler. In foreign policy, both the well-traveled aristocrat and the poor country lawyer proved to be naïve: neither could understand that all foreign powers would display total indifference to the independence and greatness of Hungary.

Batthyány's cabinet list comprised the brightest stars on the Hungarian political firmament, with ideologies ranging from the very conservative to the very liberal, but with the pre-1848 liberal opposition forming a six-member majority over two conservatives and one without party affiliation.

Prince Pál Esterházy, chosen to represent the government at the Court as "Minister Near the Person of His Majesty"—whether this was meant to be a foreign minister of a sort or a high commissioner no one could tell at the moment—was an outright conservative. He was also the wealthiest man in Hungary and the head of the country's greatest family. At sixty-two, he was the doyen of the new government. A professional diplomat, he had worked with Metternich and had been for many years Austrian ambassador to the Court of St. James. Although Batthyány had offered him the post in order to reconcile the aristocracy with the lesser nobility, and the Court with Hungary, Esterházy agreed to serve only at the solicitation of his own friends at Court. He conceived of his role as being that of a mediator between King and country, or as a substitute Hungarian court chancellor. Within the cabinet he hoped to "neutralize that deadly poison: Kossuth." Yet even this dynastic aristocrat perceived Buda-Pest as "the future and natural center of gravity in the Empire,"[30] and, in the course of his activities, he proved to be as loyal to Batthyány as he was to the King.

Széchenyi was made Minister of Public Works and Transport. More depressed than ever, he accepted the portfolio because he could not bring himself to say no to his friend Batthyány, and because he, too, hoped to neutralize Kossuth in the cabinet. On 23 March, when he accepted the post, he noted in his diary, "I have just signed my death sentence! My head will certainly land on the block!" To this he added, "I shall be hanged with Kossuth," a dire prospect for Kossuth's bitterest enemy.[31] But even Széchenyi was to do his best as Minister, until madness clouded his mind early in September 1848.

One more cabinet member stood outside the liberal opposition in the Diet, the Minister of War, Colonel Lázár Mészáros. Batthyány himself had not been able to find a suitable candidate for the post, all the imperial-royal generals of Hungarian origin being either indifferent or hostile. It was Kossuth who remembered this fifty-two-year-old colonel of the hussars. He had been a former subscriber to Kossuth's journal, the *Pesti Hirlap*, and had been in the habit of submitting his own pieces to it, principally on the growing of silkworms. Mészáros was assigned the portfolio *in absentia*, for he was at the moment fighting His Majesty's Italian enemies.

Mészáros had spent all his life in the army where, for a very minor

Hungarian nobleman, he had achieved a respectable career. Now the King reluctantly released him from service, and the "Old Man," as Mészáros came to be called, entered the cabinet as a moderate liberal and loyal soldier. Distressed by the growing conflict between the King and the country, he was to send in his resignation again and again, but his entreaties were always rejected. Out of discipline and patriotism, he shouldered various important tasks even after the ousting of the dynasty in April 1849. At the end, he went into exile with Kossuth. A dutiful administrator, Mészáros may very well have been a good regimental commander in the old army; as a general in the Hungarian revolutionary forces, he proved to be uninspiring, uninspired, and a steady loser.[32]

The other ministers came from the liberal camp in the Diet: Batthyány as Minister-President, Kossuth as Minister of Finance, Baron József Eötvös as Minister of Cults and Education, Ferenc Deák as Minister of Justice, Bertalan Szemere as Minister of Interior, and Gábor Klauzál as Minister of Agriculture, Industry, and Trade. In age they ranged from thirty-five (Eötvös) to forty-six (Kossuth); politically they were all experienced. All had been trained in law; all had once served as county administrators; with the exception of Batthyány and Eötvös, who because of their titles sat in the Upper Table, all had been, or were at that time, deputies in the Lower Table. Relative to the Court, Kossuth was the most militant, Eötvös the most moderate. In domestic policy, Eötvös was theoretically a radical; all the other liberals favored the cautious reforms of Kossuth. Again with the exception of Eötvös, all believed firmly in the supremacy of the nobility.

Eötvös, a poet, journalist, and Hungary's first successful novelist, was the leader of the Centralist movement that wished to destroy the rotten counties, unconditionally emancipate all peasants, and build political democracy on the basis of communal self-government and a strong central executive. In his novels, Eötvös lambasted the nobles, the cruel county jails, the corrupt county administrators, and everything else that was antiquated and feudal in the country. He was a true humanitarian, and in 1867, when he would again become Minister of Cults and Education, he was to create an excellent state school system and give an enlightened nationalities law to Dualistic Hungary. Before 1848, he had been Kossuth's friend and ideological opponent and, like Deák, he had reluctantly sided with Kossuth against Széchenyi. Now he entered the cabinet, very much against his better judgment, for he was persuaded that, in order to save the political and economic supremacy of the nobility, Kossuth was driving Hungary to war. Still, he agreed to serve out of loyalty to his colleagues. Only after war had broken out did Eötvös seek, in September 1848, more peaceful pastures.[33]

Bertalan Szemere seemed ideologically closest to Kossuth, although he often spoke like a "centralist" and his convictions were difficult to fathom. He was to prove an energetic, petulant, and ruthless wartime administrator; like Mészáros and Kossuth, he would not quit with the other ministers in September 1848. Rather, he would carry on till the end of the conflict, finally as minister-president. Thereafter, he, too, would go into exile.[34] Of the two other liberals, Klauzál belonged to the moderate faction, and the well-known Deák, no less a moderate, was another one who accepted his post only reluctantly.

This, then, was the first constitutional cabinet of Hungary: four titled and five untitled nobles and, with the exception of Mészáros, all well known political figures. Unlike the new Austrian cabinet, made up mainly of bureaucrats, the Hungarian ministry included only one servant of the Crown. Unlike the French revolutionary government, which consisted of middle-class lawyers, journalists, and businessmen, and one worker, this was almost entirely a government of noble landowners. In fact, Kossuth alone owned no land. The cabinet faithfully reflected the opinions of the Hungarian ruling class; it also bore witness to the fact that the lesser nobility was now stronger than the titled nobility. Of all these men, only two closely resembled the Western bourgeoisie—Eötvös in his political convictions and Kossuth in his need to work for a living. Yet this government of the nobility became the great hope of all the revolutionaries in Europe.

THE APRIL LAWS

The drastic reform bills of the Diet caused agony at the Court, especially since no one in Vienna knew what to do about them. In a confidential memorandum to the King, dated 24 March, the Palatine explained that there was, for the time being, no way to stop the Hungarians. This famous note (a copy of which the Hungarians were to find following the Palatine's resignation and departure from the country in September 1848, causing the parliament to brand the Archduke a traitor—in Habsburg eyes he was a traitor already) outlined three alternatives open to the King. First, he could order his troops out of Hungary, abandoning the nobility to the tender mercy of the peasants. "One could then," the Archduke wrote, "look on passively while the country is burned to the ground." Second, the King could deal with Batthyány, make compromises, and "save whatever can be saved." Third, the King could dismiss the Palatine, appoint a royal commissioner (with power over life and death), send an army into Hungary, disperse the Diet, advance on Pest, and place the country under martial law. The first alternative the Palatine found immoral; he also knew well what a sobering effect such a proposition would have on the Magyar aristocrats at Court. The third alternative he considered unfeasible in view of the Monarchy's multiple military commitments. There remained the second alternative, namely, collaboration with Batthyány; this the Palatine considered "the sole guarantee of the preservation of the province," adding that, "with the arrival of a more favorable time, much can be changed which at present would cause secession."[35]

Archduke Stephen was no traitor to Hungary or to anyone else. He was an embattled leader trying to mediate, as was almost everyone else in those days, between two hostile camps. Naturally, when he talked to the Hungarians, he emphasized the benefits of moderation, and when he talked to the Court, he held out the possibility of later improvements. What counted was that he had managed to persuade the State Conference to agree with him; for the time being, one had to negotiate with Batthyány. And, in truth, when the Palatine's second alternative was finally abandoned late in the summer of 1848, the court adopted his third alternative, complete with an army of invasion, a royal commissioner, and a state of siege.

Of course, the Palatine did not mean for the King to surrender without tough bargaining. A golden opportunity to weaken Kossuth's position presented itself with the hue and cry arising in Hungary over the bill on the abolition of serfdom. Unfortunately for the Court, it was to link a politically very promising campaign against peasant emancipation with a politically disastrous campaign against the separate Hungarian government, thus repeating the old mistakes of Metternich. As a result, the noble landowners, who could have been won over on the peasant question, rallied to Kossuth when Hungary's sacred national rights were threatened.

The abolition of serfdom, which Kossuth had driven so easily through both houses of the Diet on 18 March, exasperated the landowners, and not only those of conservative persuasion. It was an open scandal that there had been only seventeen members present when, in a surprise meeting, the bill had been introduced in the Upper Table. Without immediate redemption payments, how were the landlords to hire workers to cultivate the suddenly abandoned demesne land? What would become of the countless small nobles, especially in northern Hungary, who owned no demesne land and were entirely dependent on income derived from feudal dues? Count Antal Szapáry, a well-known liberal, turned on Batthyány at a meeting of the Upper Table: "If there is no compensation, I shall shoot you dead." To this the Minister-President replied "That won't be necessary because if that happens I shall shoot myself."[36] Estimating his annual losses at over half a million gulden, Prince Pál Esterházy was prepared to ask the assembly of the county of which he was lord lieutenant to petition the King not to sign the bill that Esterházy's own cabinet had submitted.[37]

Most of the Emperor's advisers did not personally object to the emancipation of the peasants; it had been part and parcel of Metternich's own program. But, in order to exploit dissension in Hungary, the State Conference decided, on 26-27 March, to request that the Diet suspend the bill until means were found to compensate the landowners. Simultaneously, it expressed its very understandable satisfaction with the taxation of nobles.[38]

A day later, without waiting for Vienna's rejection of the peasant bill to take effect in Hungary, the State Conference issued a second royal rescript attacking the bill on the separate Hungarian government.[39] While that bill was in fact far more dangerous to the unity of the Monarchy, still, by too suddenly adding a nationalist issue to a socioeconomic one, the Court defeated itself. In the ensuing tumult, the peasant question was nearly forgotten, especially as Kossuth wisely combined the two problems into one great national cause.

The royal rescript of 28 March stipulated: (1) that the Hungarian court chancellery should be preserved, with powers of supervision over the government; (2) that during the King's absence from Hungary—which the Austrians hoped would be permanent—plenipotentiary powers would be exercised by the present Palatine only, and not by all palatines, the danger being very real that future palatines might not be of Habsburg blood and might even be rebels; (3) that all royal revenues would flow into the central treasury from where, after deducting all royal expenditures, they would be redirected to Hungary (in essence, this meant that there would be no need for a Hungarian ministry of finance, and that the Hungarians would not be permitted to dispose of their own revenues); (4) that the King would not be deprived of his monopoly over the commissioning of army officers and the employment of troops, and that such rights would not be exercised by the Palatine even during the King's absence from Hungary (this meant that there was no need for a ministry of war either, and that the Hungarian government would have no say over wars); and finally (5) that Hungary should assume part of the state debt.

The royal rescript was read aloud at a joint meeting of the Diet's two houses on 29 March, creating great consternation.[40] The second major confrontation between King and nation had begun. Batthyány, who felt personally cheated by the Court, announced his resignation but then changed his mind, trusting that the Palatine would take immediate action with the monarch. There was general bewilderment: "Terror panicus an vielen Gesichtern," Széchenyi noted in his diary.

The storm erupted at the ensuing circular meeting of the Lower Table where, free from the Palatine's august presence, Kossuth "raised his thundering voice: more thundering and forceful than ever before." Already at a morning meeting Kossuth had threatened revolution; "It seems that God will not grant us the joy and pleasure of realizing our transformation without our citizens having to shed their blood." Now he announced that the Hungarian government was "no toy, no puppet, no useless post office," and that the royal rescript should be rejected *in toto*. This the House then proceeded to do, in two fiery resolutions, repeating verbatim what Kossuth had said.

In reality, Kossuth's fury was as calculated as it was political; in the same two speeches where he had asked for revolution and for the indictment of the King's evil Hungarian councillors as traitors, he had urged the Palatine to see to it that the King kept his word. Thus relations with the Court were not to be broken off; rather, the bargaining was to continue.

Now it was up to the street to help out the Diet. As early as 27 March, the Buda-Pest Committee of Public Safety had held a mass meeting where Petőfi and others had demanded the immediate convocation of a national convention, the repudiation of the Batthyány ministry, and the proclamation of a republic, and where the two ministers-designate, Klauzál and Szemere, had had a hard time controlling the crowd.

In the ensuing days, the second set of Pest *journées* continued. It is certain that Kossuth encouraged these manifestations by his passionate speeches and by stressing to the delegate from the Pest radicals that the "March Youth" ought to "risk everything for the fatherland." But it is also very probable that the *journées* would have occurred even without Kossuth. On 29 March, the agitation in Pest reached its crescendo with a massive march on the city hall to demand arms and with barricades erected in the streets, no one quite knew against whom. On the same night, the acting chairman of the Vice-Regency Council, Count Ferenc Zichy, sent an urgent message to Vienna: "If, within a few days, favorable decisions are not taken, especially with regard to the ministries of war and finance, Hungary is lost to the dynasty."[41] On 30 March, 22,000 people assembled in front of the Pest National Museum to hear Petőfi proclaim the coming of a world revolution.[42]

By then, the Pest commotion had achieved its desired effect, the more so as news from the capital had arrived in Pressburg and Vienna in a tremendously exaggerated version. On 30 March, the State Conference urgently summoned the Hungarian leaders to Court and, following an all-night debate, dropped almost all its restrictions on Hungarian self-government. What remained was the not-so-important reservation that inviolability apply only to the person of the present palatine, and not to all palatines, and the soon-to-be-very-important reservation that the King alone be empowered to commission officers as well as to employ the Hungarian army abroad. The King was left with his ancient privilege of appointing the Catholic prelates and the—often titular—high dignitaries of the realm. The matter of Hungary's participation in servicing the state debt was left to the next Hungarian parliament. For all this, the Palatine had secured the personal consent of Kossuth.[43]

On 31 March, this drastically modified royal rescript was read in the Diet amidst tumultuous cheering. Kossuth spoke again, "reaching one of the highest summits of his oratorical career," and then, when victory was complete, sounding a conciliatory note. He promised a generous civil list to His Majesty, all the while reminding the Monarch that he was on the throne only through the courtesy of Kossuth:

> Gentlemen! I am a simple citizen. I had no other power, no other influence in this world than that which justice, instilled by God in my soul, gave me. And yet, such are the ways of Providence that I, the simple citizen, one of the fatherland's lowest, was—because of the munificence of circumstances—in such a position, during a few hours [on 15 March], that this hand of mine was able to decide whether the House of Austria should stand or not stand.[44]

Thus the Hungarians had won again, or rather Kossuth had won because it was he who had taken the greatest risks: he alone had dared call the bluff of the Court and had mobilized the street. Whether the price ultimately paid by Hungary was not too high is another matter. Poor Pest radicals who, unlike the Court, remained permanently powerless, and whose bluff had been called earlier by Kossuth, now celebrated "Citizen Kossuth." Forgetting about a second government, a national convention, a republic, and a war, the radicals built bonfires in Pest to hail their hero. Only Petőfi and one or two of his friends knew that not only the court, but they, too, had been defeated. Petőfi wrote on 1 April, "No, the revolution is not over: this was only the First Act. Au revoir." But there were to be no new Buda-Pest *journées* until 10 May, and then the scenario of March would be repeated.[45]

It remained only for the Court to accept Batthyány's cabinet list. Kossuth's name was a bitter pill to swallow, but the argument prevailed that his appointment was inevitable and that, as minister of finance, he would have little power and a lot of responsibility. And truly, no portfolio could have been less enviable than his: while the peasants were no longer paying taxes and the nobles not yet, he was expected to balance a still nonexisting budget, send an annual three-million-gulden stipend to the King, pay the ministers, the administration, the army in Hungary and, *horribile dictu,* contribute to the Austrian debt payments. For the time being, Kossuth was satisfied. He summed up his views of past events in an address on 1 April to the Palatine: "The nobility, this first-born of the fatherland, has decided to share with all others the treasury of rights and liberty. Instead of privileged classes, Your Highness is now surrounded by a free nation, one that has become master of its fate and its future."[46]

The King having set 9 April as the closing date of the Diet, the fever-ish activity began again. On 31 March, the day the King's modified rescript was read aloud and celebrated, the legislators finally settled the question of suffrage reform which they had debated ever since the fall of 1847. Drafted by several people, the bill again bore Kossuth's imprint. Providing for an annual parliament in Buda-Pest, the bill con-firmed the rights of those who already possessed the franchise, that is, noblemen and the burghers of free cities, and extended the franchise to all those who were born in Hungary, were at least twenty years old (for the passive franchise the age limit was set at twenty-four), were free from the control of parents or master, had never been convicted of a major crime, belonged to a "received" religion, and met specific prop-erty, residence and employment qualifications. As to the latter, fairly substantial property and a secure income were required of the in-habitants of free cities, and possession of at least one-fourth of a servile "section," with corresponding income, was required of the inhabitants of towns and villages. Manufacturers, shopkeepers, and master arti-sans had also to be solidly established, with the latter employing at least one worker. This meant in practice that, aside from dependent children, domestics, servants, and other wage earners, the law ex-cluded all the landless and contractual peasants, as well as many of the urbarial peasants (thus extending voting rights to about one-third of the entire peasantry) and the urban poor. As the "Mosaic faith" was not yet a "received religion," the law also excluded the Jews. On the other hand, specifically included were the *honoratiores:* scholars, artists, surgeons, lawyers, engineers, teachers, ministers, in brief, all educated people of a commoner background. The ballot remained open (but sev-eral cities were eventually to resort to secret balloting), and the Upper Table was left unchanged (which would not prevent it from steadily losing influence). One slap administered at the minority nationalities: knowledge of Magyar was made obligatory for all legislators, "the lan-guage of legislation being exclusively Hungarian."

The most controversial issue, ending in a resounding defeat of the radical deputies and the allied "centralists" by Kossuth and his friends, was the nobility's continued franchise. No matter how desti-tute or uneducated, the nobles preserved their ancient rights, and they would succeed, through sheer numbers and, even more, through pres-tige and force, to maintain their hegemony in parliament. For even though Hungary was now divided into 377 electoral districts (Transyl-vania's 69 districts would be added following union with that prov-ince), thus guaranteeing the election of an identical number of deputies (as opposed to the hundred-odd deputies and fifty-odd votes of the county deputies in the old Diet), the new "House of Representatives" elected in June was to consist almost exclusively of noblemen, which is precisely what the March legislators had in mind. Ironically, this new "popular assembly," to remain in session until the end of the war in August 1849, would accomplish infinitely less in terms of social and economic reforms than the old feudal Diet accomplished in these three weeks. But this too was the legislators' wish as well, for the great reform age was to come to an end with them, and the age of consolidation was to begin. Then, too, the old Diet was not presiding over a war-torn country, as the new National Assembly would have to do.

All in all, the franchise provisions were very progressive, raising the proportion of qualified voters to about six per cent of the population, or one-fourth of all adult males, a proportion not to be surpassed in Hungary until after the First World War. It was more progressive than the French electoral law of 1830 had been; or the British Parliamentary Act of 1832, which had increased the proportion of voters to about five per cent of the population; or the famous liberal Belgian constitution of 1831, which had set the lower age limit at twenty-four and was in other respects more stringent as well; or the Austrian constitution of 25 April 1848, with its provisions for indirect voting. And while the Prussian law of April and the French electoral decree of March were definitely more democratic, the Prussian Assembly turned out to be not much more popular than the Hungarian, while the French National Assembly, elected on the basis of almost universal suffrage, became disastrously reactionary.[47]

The debate on the national electoral law was followed by a debate on the reform of the county system. Kossuth wished to extend the national suffrage system to the counties, with the proviso that the elected county assemblies would then choose the county officials, but, surprisingly, on this question he was defeated. Now that the political emergency was over, an unlikely alliance of conservatives, centralists, and radicals came into being, with the conservatives wishing to save noble privilege and the left wing hoping to destroy the counties through the rejection of reforms. Despite all his eloquence and his insistence that his whole purpose was to guarantee the economic and political hegemony of the nobility, Kossuth was voted down on 2 and 3 April. Finally, nothing was changed: the nobles alone had the franchise in the counties, and the problem was passed on to the new parliament which, in turn, would prove unable to deal with the issue. There would be no new county elections, and during the war, power over the counties would pass gradually into the hands of government commissioners, similar to Metternich's much hated "administrators," who were to exercise near-dictatorial power.[48]

One more major clash with the Court occurred before ratification of all the bills, but, as this took place behind closed doors in Vienna, not even the legislators heard much about it. At issue was the inclusion of the Military Border into the national electoral law and thus into the new parliament. Correctly understanding that this was the first step toward the reincorporation of the Border into the Hungarian administrative and military systems, Archduke Francis Charles categorically refused his consent. The danger to the Court was indeed enormous, for it would have meant subjecting the Monarchy's best and most reliable soldiers to the whims of the Hungarian minister of war and risking an anti-Habsburg revolt of the Croatian and Serbian *Grenzer*. Even though Batthyány and Kossuth immediately rushed to Vienna offering major concessions, nothing had been achieved by 8 April. Then, suddenly and inexplicably, the Archduke gave in, in exchange for a written promise that, for the time being, the Border's military system would not be changed.

It was all over. In the final days before the closing of the Diet, the State Conference approved a whole series of bills virtually without argument, and on 10 April, the King arrived in Pressburg in the company of Francis Charles and young Francis Joseph. On the following day, the King solemnly closed the Diet: "I wish from the depths of my heart the happiness of my loyal Hungarian nation, for I find therein my own. . . ."[49] Soon thereafter the deputies went home with printed copies of the thirty-one "April Laws" in their luggage. It seemed to them that a miracle had happened.

THE NEW CONSTITUTION: AN END OR A BEGINNING?

As the Hungarian liberals saw it, theirs had not been a revolution at all, but a peaceful adjustment to the times and the legal reconquest of Hungary's historical freedoms. Their actions had been forceful, dignified, and magnanimous. His Majesty's ancient rights had not been curtailed; rather, the dual sovereignty of king and nation under the Crown of St. Stephen was now reconstituted. The King could still appoint and dismiss the prelates and the high officials of the realm, commission officers, make war, suspend or dissolve parliament, veto legislation, grant pardon, and create nobles. He was given a generous civil list; the right of his family to succeed to the throne was not questioned, and his person remained sacred. The very law guaranteeing freedom of the press made it a crime to incite against the King, to agitate against the ties linking the nation with the crown, against those linking Hungary with the other parts of the Monarchy, and against the hereditary rights of the Habsburgs.

Such extra-legal institutions as the Court Chancellery, the Vice-Regency Council, and the Court Chamber having been abolished, Hungary now possessed her own government, responsible to a triennially elected, annually meeting popular parliament; she also had—as she always should have had—her own army, militia, administration, and judiciary. The counties and the cities were free; all citizens enjoyed equality before the law, and almost all enjoyed religious freedom; taxation was proportional and general; all privileged estates, churches, nations, and corporations had ceased to exist; the franchise was given to all who, because of their profession, position, or income, had a stake in ordinary progress and the stability of society; all peasants were free, and former serfs were granted full ownership of their tenure; patrimonial jurisdiction, labor services, the tithe to the church and to the landowner, as well as payments in kind and cash on former servile lands were abolished; entailment and other feudal restrictions on the free flow of goods and labor were suppressed; citizens could live where they wished and engage in any profession; the university was placed under state control; provisions were made for the establishment of a national land-credit institution, as well as for the building of canals, highways, railroads, and harbors; arbitrary arrest and detention were forbidden; jury trial for political crimes was introduced; and the state guaranteed the security of life and private property. In brief, theirs was now a free and modern country where dedication, talent, and patriotism were the sole avenues to career and prestige.

Moreover, Hungary was finally on her way toward unification. The *Partium*, those small districts on the Transylvanian border until now illegally administered from there, were finally returned to the mother country. The same could be expected of Transylvania proper, although in this case Hungary had generously consented to wait for the Transylvanian Diet to pronounce for unification and to adjust its antiquated political and social legislation to those of progressive Hungary. The Military Border remained under Austrian military control, but it too, would have to be placed, eventually, under the legal authority of Hungary. Last but not least, Croatia-Slavonia was guaranteed her traditional liberties, but the new *Ban* would be watched, lest he attempt to defy his own government.[50]

Writing from post-revolutionary exile, Bishop Mihály Horváth, a companion of Kossuth and the Revolution's first great historian, summed up the events of March-April 1848:

> This nation, so full of healthy, youthful and sparkling energy; so full of enthusiasm and of fervent yearning for all that was good, beautiful, and just, accepted these magnificent reforms with complete satisfaction and exuberant joy. Having been, through the practice of centuries, accustomed to freedom, it knew how to live with freedom. In political sophistication and in constitutional experience, it incomparably surpassed all the other peoples of the Monarchy.[51]

Seen from Vienna, or through the eyes of the Jews, the poor, the radicals, or the non-Magyar nationalities, the picture looked a bit more complicated. The King's privileges were gravely threatened by the special status granted the Palatine, and by the necessity of a ministerial counter signature to all royal or palatal decrees; the competences of the Minister near the Person of His Majesty, the Minister of Finance, and the Minister of War were ill-defined or not defined at all. The responsibilities of the Hungarian Minister of War were particularly obscure: was this minister to control the imperial-royal troops stationed in Hungary, or the regiments originating from Hungary no matter where they happened to serve, or was he to control both? How was he to coordinate his functions with his Austrian counterpart? Did he have authority over the Hungarian regiments now fighting in northern Italy? What would become of the *General-Militär-Commandos* into which the Empire was divided, with five out of a total of twelve finding themselves in lands under the Hungarian crown. What was the precise meaning of that ominous sentence in Law III of the Constitution: "The employment of the Hungarian army beyond the frontiers of the country will require the counter-signature of the responsible Hungarian minister"? This sentence went directly against another clause in the same law granting sole rights to the King over the deployment of the Hungarian army beyond the frontiers of the country. What was the Hungarian army anyway? Did "beyond the frontiers" include the other provinces of the Monarchy? What if the Hungarian government chose to disapprove of a domestic or foreign military action of the King? Would the Minister of Finance help pay for it? And what about the state debt? Clearly, even if the Hungarian government would wish to observe its own laws, and chances were that it would not, it could interpret them in a way fatal to the unity and greatness of the Monarchy.

So far as the Jews were concerned, nothing good had happened. To the contrary, things had become worse, with Romanian-speaking Greek Orthodox peasants having the franchise, but Hungarian-speaking wealthy Jewish businessmen being denied it; with city authorities suddenly cracking down and expelling "illegal residents," and with the mob thirsting for the blood of "Yids." Still, chances were that the situation would improve soon. The sympathies of Batthyány and Kossuth could not be doubted; in Buda-Pest, where Jews had volunteered *en masse* for the militia, only to be thrown out bodily by their Christian fellows, no lesser heroes than Petőfi and Vasvári had since created their own all-Jewish National Guard company. No wonder that the Jews rallied to the new Hungarian tricolor, the red, white, and green.

There is little evidence that the peasants saw great progress in their emancipation; rather, it seems that many peasants saw little progress or no progress at all. The same law that granted full ownership to urbarial peasants also confirmed the validity of all former seizures and forced enclosures effected by the landlords. The tithe on vineyards was not abolished, nor were any of the so-called regalia: the noble land-owner's exclusive right to sell wine and other produce at certain times of the year, as well as to hold fairs, to hunt, to fish, and to fowl. Peasants were still required to do public work for the county and to pay county dues. And as for the hundreds of thousands of peasants who held parts of demesne land in private contract, nothing was done for them, nor anything for the landless cotters, the homeless, the day laborers, and the estate servants. Demesne lands were considered private, and not feudal, property: their distribution among the poor was unthinkable to the nobility or, for that matter, even to the peasantry. But since there were so many disputed rights and so many disputed lands, the outbreak of peasant disturbances could be taken for granted and would, in fact, follow shortly.

The radicals resented the lack of complete national independence, the hegemony of the nobles, the restrictive suffrage, and the militia laws, but mainly they resented the punitive law controlling the press. The urban workers missed the regulation of wages and working hours, and, finally, the non-Magyar nationalities—for the moment mildly sympathetic—could not help but notice that their existence had gone unrecognized in the April Laws or was recognized only negatively in the stipulation that Magyar be the language of legislation and administration.

The Habsburg problem, the Croat problem, the Jewish problem, the peasant problem, the worker problem, the radical problem, and the nationality problem—the Hungarian cabinet would have to face them all, inextricably intertwined as they were, and face them simultaneously. The result was to be the failure of Hungarian policy. There would be many more triumphs, both political and military, but the liberals' policy as a whole was not to bring its promised results. Kossuth's dream that a better age would follow, now that everyone from king to beggar had been given his just rights, would prove precisely that—a dream.

Hungarian historians have never ceased to question whether, in March 1848, the nobility acted out of idealism, fear, or economic self-interest. The historian Mihály Horváth was the first to formulate clearly the idealistic interpretation:

> The former noble class, even though it had lost its privileges and urbarial benefits, . . . not only shouldered, with dignified resignation, the sacrifices made to justice and to the common good, but, with a few exceptions, was genuinely pleased with the fact that the walls separating social classes had fallen into dust and the nation now molded into one big and sturdy whole.[52]

The "fear" theory was best explained by the early-twentieth-century radical critic of Dualistic Hungary, Ervin Szabó, who wrote that "not revolutionary enthusiasm, but fear of the revolution coalesced the hitherto acrimoniously fighting parties in the Estates' Diet into that 'selfless' unity, of which the nobility has never since ceased to boast,"[53] an interpretation ironically corroborated by the great inter-war conservative historian Gyula Szekfű, who affirmed in his classic *Hungarian History* that not magnanimity, but "the pressure of foreign news" had driven the nobles to embrace laws "that cast a doubt on the future of their families."[54] Finally, the theory of economic motivation was best propounded by the Marxists, first by József Révai, who stated that economic circumstances—the superior productivity of the large estates—drove the market-producing, medium-landowning nobility to cast away the feudal system and to opt for the bourgeois-capitalist reorganization of Hungary. Thus, far from casting doubt on the future of the nobility, Révai argues, the April Laws saved the middle and lower nobles from economic decline and, consequently, political extinction.[55]

It is hard to see how one can determine the motives that governed the large and disunited body that was the nobility. Kossuth himself was so unsure of what the nobles wanted, or wanted to hear, that he appealed simultaneously to idealism and to patriotism, ambition and the thirst for power, fear and the instinct for survival, rational economic self-interest and greed, common sense and emotionalism. Nor can it be argued that Kossuth said one thing in public and another in private: everything that issued from his mouth or his pen was designed for public consumption. Even the delightfully candid and hesitant Széchenyi used a rich variety of arguments to convince himself, and those more conservative than himself, that the April Laws were a good thing. It is an easy answer—but not necessarily a wrong answer—to say that a great variety of motives lay behind the nobility's willingness to submit to the new constitution. Ervin Szabó writes in his revisionist history of the Revolution that, after an auspiciously radical beginning in the 1830s, Kossuth became more and more conservative in the 1840s, until there was no significant difference between his social program and that of Metternich.[56] József Révai says exactly the contrary, and so do all modern Marxist historians: it is an article of faith with them that Kossuth considered the April Laws only a first step toward the complete democratization of Hungary. Kossuth alone understood, Révai argues, that the interests of the nobility and of the peasantry had to be "equalized." "The equalization of interests . . . was the only possible program for the national unity front." Thus, according to Révai, Kossuth's seeming moderation was in reality a revolutionary act, national independence being a must for the establishment of democracy.[57]

It is difficult to agree with Szabó on Kossuth's gradual retreat toward conservatism. To the contrary, he moved from an old-fashioned "estates'' nationalism in the 1830s to modern liberal nationalism in the 1840s, a stand that was energetic enough and progressive enough to allow the establishment of the most significant reform laws in Hungarian history. Many of these laws were not immediately translated into reality, nor does legislation alone ever change society, but the April Laws did become a basis for later progressive developments. And while it is true that there was no fundamental difference between Kossuth's and Metternich's socioeconomic programs, the fact remains that Metternich did not dare to introduce these changes, whereas Kossuth dared.

But Révai's view that, for Kossuth, the April Laws were only a beginning does not stand up to historical scrutiny either. By the early 1840s, Kossuth's *Weltanschauung* was firmly established, and he was not to change it to his dying day. There is no evidence that, after April 1848, Kossuth had any intention of going still further to win over the lower classes. To the contrary, all signs indicate that he wished to stay put. For him, as for most other nobles, the great reform age had come to an end in April 1848.

After April, only a few radicals wished to extend the reform measures. Further progressive legislation was widely seen as dangerous to the stability of society, and the last thing Kossuth and his friends wanted was to endanger that stability. History, measured not in years but in decades, proved Kossuth successful. Neither war, nor defeat, nor the subsequent Habsburg absolutism was able to dethrone those who had consolidated their rule in March–April 1848. The National Assembly, elected in June, was made up almost exclusively of nobles, and so was the officer corps of Kossuth's national army; the list of rebels sentenced by Austrian military courts after the war reads like the Almanach of Gotha for the Hungarian (and the Polish and the German) nobility; Czech and German-Austrian commoners, whom the Bach regime imported in the 1850s to administer subjugated Hungary, were gotten rid of in the 1860s; and the parliament of 1867, the one of the Compromise Agreement between king and nation, consisted entirely of the traditional elite. The only victims of 1848 were those who had sided too closely with Metternich, or who, in the summer of 1849, had failed to desert Kossuth. Yet, even from among these loyal fools a good many eventually returned to the political stage.

Hungary was led by noblemen, or by ennobled commoners, until almost the middle of the twentieth century, and even though Kossuth died in exile he had realized his dream of a country modernized under the guidance of the noble estate.

The historic significance of the Hungarian Spring was enormous: it guaranteed the economic and political survival of the landowning class; it opened the way to spectacular economic and cultural development;

and it provided the Magyar nation with an eternal romantic legacy. Since agreement has never been reached as to what exactly happened in March–April 1848, short of a national consensus that it was something magnificent, Hungarians of all persuasions—extreme nationalists, fascists, orthodox conservatives, liberals, democrats, even communists—have looked back at the Hungarian Spring with pride and have derived from it a profound source of inspiration. The Hungarian Spring has become all things to all people in that country.

NOTES

*The editor wishes to acknowledge the permission of the Columbia University Press to publish in this book a revised version of Chapter II, entitled "Reform Triumphant," of Istvan Deak's *The Lawful Revolution: Louis Kossuth and the Hungarians, 1848–1849* (New York and London: Columbia University Press, 1979).

1 Letter of Count Karl Vitzthum, Secretary of the Prussian Legation, to his mother, Vienna, 29 February 1848; first printed in *Berlin und Wien in den Jahren 1845–1852: Politische Privatbriefe* (Stuttgart, 1886), reprinted (in Hungarian) in L. B. Szabó, ed., *Adatok gróf Széchenyi István és kora történetéhez, 1808–1860*, 2 vols. (Budapest, 1943), vol. 2, p. 641. (Hereafter, Budapest will be abbreviated Bp.)
2 The standard histories of the Monarchy before 1848 are C. A. Macartney, *The Habsburg Empire, 1790–1918* (London, 1968); A. J. P. Taylor, *The Habsburg Monarchy, 1809–1918* (London, 1941); V.-L. Tapié, *Monarchie et peuples du Danube* (Paris, 1969); and R. A. Kann, *A History of the Habsburg Empire, 1526–1918* (Berkeley, 1974). On the Monarchy's economic, social, and financial conditions in the pre-March period, see Macartney, pp. 255–278; M. Bach, *Geschichte der Wiener Revolution im Jahre 1848* (Vienna, 1898); A. Beer, *Die Finanzen Oesterreichs* (Prague, 1877); and, for a brief summary, W. Pollak, *1848: Revolution auf halbem Wege* (Vienna, 1974), pp. 34–39 and 85–90.
3 Kossuth's 3 March 1848 address can be found in all the major documentary collections dealing with the period. The most reliable version is in I. Barta, ed., *Kossuth Lajos az utolsó rendi országgyűlésen 1847/48* (Bp., 1956), pp. 619–28. Barta's work forms vol. 11 of *Kossuth Lajos összes munkái* (cited hereafter as *KLÖM* 11). The specific quotation is on p. 624.
4 Macartney, *Habsburg Empire*, p. 323.
5 The best description of Vienna's first revolutionary *journée* is in R. J. Rath, *The Viennese Revolution of 1848* (Austin, Texas, 1957); Macartney, *Habsburg Empire*, pp. 325–30; R. R. Lutz, "The Aula and the Vienna Radical Movement of 1848" (Ph.D. diss., Cornell University, 1956); and L. C. M. Bernstein, "Revolution and Response: Radical Thought in Vienna's Free Press in 1848" (Ph.D. diss., Columbia University, 1972).
6 See E. Szabó, *Társadalmi és pártharcok a 48-49-es magyar forradalomban*, 2nd ed. (Bp., [1945]), pp. 44–45.
7 Literature on Petőfi would fill libraries, but unfortunately almost nothing is available in a Western European language. A recent collection of essays, A. Tamás and A.

Wéber, eds., *Petőfi tűze. Tanulmányok Petőfi Sándorról* (Bp., 1972), contains a selected bibliography of scholarly work on the poet. For an introduction to Petőfi's life in English, see J. Reményi, *Hungarian Writers and Literature* (New Brunswick, N.J., 1964), pp. 84–105; see also *Sixty Poems by Alexander Petőfi*, trans. E. B. Pierce and E. Delmar (New York, 1948), with an introduction by J. Reményi.

8 The 15 March 1848 events in Buda-Pest have been described many times. Most useful, in a Western European language, is the abundantly documented G. Spira, "Le grand jour (le 15 mars 1848)," *Études historiques 1970*, 2 vols. (Bp., 1970), vol. 2, pp. 333–62; also, H. Incze, *Die Geschichte des 15. März in Buda-Pesth* (Bp., 1900), and L. Deme, "The Committee of Public Safety in the Hungarian Revolution of 1848," *Canadian Slavic Studies* 5 (Fall 1971): 383–400. The quotations from Petőfi's writings are in *Petőfi Sándor összes művei* (Bp., 1956), vol. 5, pp. 83, 141; quoted in French translation in Spira, "Le grand jour," p. 360.

9 The Address to the Throne is contained in Kossuth's 3 March speech; it passed through both chambers of the Diet in its original form. See *KLÖM* 11, pp. 625–28; see also D. Pap, ed., *Okmánytár Magyarország függetlenségi harczának történetéhez, 1848-1849*, 2 vols. (Pest, 1868), vol. 1, pp. 1–4.

10 The Diet's 15 March instructions to the delegation are published in *KLÖM* 11, pp. 658–60.

11 See Á. Károlyi, *Az 1848-diki pozsonyi törvénycikkek az udvar előtt* (Bp., 1936), p.14 (hereafter cited as Károlyi, *1848*). This volume, half of which consists of documents, thoroughly analyzes the Hungarian negotiations in Vienna. The draft reply is printed on pp. 207–9, together with the final reply signed by the King. The latter document is also published in *Németújvári gróf Batthyány Lajos első magyar miniszterelnök főbenjáró pöre*, 2 vols. (Bp., 1932), vol. 2, p. 604 (hereafter cited as Károlyi, *Batthyány*).

12 Kossuth, "Császári hála: császári forradalom és annak céljai," speech delivered in 1858 in England; published in L.K., *Irataim az emigráczióból*, 3 vols. (Bp., 1880–81), vol. 2, pp. 186–205; the specific quotation is on p. 187.

13 Széchenyi on 16 March 1848; reprinted in G. Viszota, ed., *Gróf Széchenyi István naplói*, vol. 6 (1844–48), p. 749, which is vol. 15 of *Gróf Széchenyi István összes munkái*. The Kossuth reminiscences are from notes written in exile; reprinted in *Irataim az emigráczióból*, vol. 2, p. 265.

14 The Palatine to Batthyány (Vienna, 17 March 1848); published in Károlyi, *Batthyány*, vol. 2, p. 605; also in I. Deák, ed., *1848: A Szabadságharc története levelekben* (Bp., [1942]), pp. 30–31. The Palatine's apologetic letter to Ferdinand, written on the same day, is in ibid., pp. 31–32.

15 Teleki to Czartoryski (London, 26 July 1849); published in E. V. Waldapfel, ed., *A forradalom és szabadságharc levelestára*, 4 vols. (Bp., 1950–65), vol. 4, p. 244.

16 See, for instance, G. Spira, *A magyar forradalom 1848–49-ben* (Bp., 1959), p. 92 and passim.

17 The March 1848 Italian events are best described in R. Kiszling, *Die Revolution im Kaisertum Österreich, 1848-1849*, 2 vols. (Vienna, 1948), vol. 1, pp. 86–122.

18 See G. E. Rothenberg, *The Military Border in Croatia, 1740-1881: A Study of an Imperial Institution* (Chicago and London, 1966).

19 Baron Franz Kulmer, Lord Lieutenant of Zagreb County, to Jelačić (Vienna, 30 March 1848); Jelačić Papers; quoted in Rothenberg, p. 145.

20 On the March events in Croatia, see Kiszling, *Die Revolution*, vol. 1, pp. 79–82. On

Reform Triumphant: Hungary's Self-Assertion 359

the origins of the Croat problem, see G. Miskolczy, *A horvát kérdés története és irományai a rendi állam korában*, 2 vols. (Bp., 1928), with most of the volume devoted to documents. On Jelačić, see F. Hauptmann, *Jelačić's Kriegszug nach Ungarn 1848*, 2 vols. (Graz, 1975). Ferdinand's letter of appointment to Jelačić (Vienna, 23 March 1848) is published in E. Andics, ed., *A nagybirtokos arisztokrácia ellenforradalmi szerepe 1848–49-ben*, 2 vols. (Bp., 1952-65), vol. 2, pp. 35-36.

21 Emphasis is Széchenyi's. Széchenyi to Antal Tasner (Pressburg, 6 March 1848); published in B. Majláth, ed., *Gróf Széchenyi István levelei*, 3 vols. (Bp., 1889-91), vol. 1, p. 600.

22 Széchenyi to Tasner (Pressburg, 17 March 1848); ibid., p. 602. Also in Deák, ed., *1848: A Szabadságharc*, p. 32. The English translation is borrowed from G. Spira, *A Hungarian Count in the Revolution of 1848* (Bp., 1974), pp. 31-32. Spira's work, published originally in Hungarian in 1964, is a thorough analysis of Széchenyi's erratic but fascinating doings in the revolution.

23 Cited in Spira, *Szabadságharc*, p. 95; documents on the 18 March 1848 meetings of the Diet are in *KLÖM*, 11, pp. 667-73.

24 For the Catholic Church's less than enchanted reaction to the unexpected magnanimity of its representative in the Diet, see E. Andics, "Az egyházi reakció 1848-49-ben," in A. Mód et al., *Forradalom és szabadságharc, 1848-1849* (Bp., 1948), pp. 324-28. This very biased Marxist account ought to be compared with the pro-Catholic account of A. Meszlényi, *A magyar katholikus egyház és állam 1848/49-ben* (Bp., 1928), pp. 63-87.

25 Kossuth in the Lower Table, 19 March 1848; published in *KLÖM*, 11, p. 675. For relations between the Diet and the Pest radicals in the Spring of 1848, see L. Deme, *The Radical Left in the Hungarian Revolution of 1848* (Boulder, Colo., 1975).

26 On Kossuth's defeat in the Lower Table over Jewish voting rights, see *KLÖM* 11, pp. 684-85.

27 Kossuth in the Diet on 22 March 1848; printed in *KLÖM* 11, p. 688.

28 On the "compensation" debate in the Lower Table, see *KLÖM* 11, pp. 689-91. For the whole issue of peasant emancipation, see J. Varga, *A jobbágyfelszabadítás kivívása 1848-ban* (Bp., 1971), and the documentary collection by G. Ember, ed., *Iratok az 1848-i magyarországi parasztmozgalmak történeténez* (Bp., 1959).

29 Károlyi, *1848*, and idem, *Batthyány*.

30 See Esterházy's memorandum to the court, Vienna, May 1848; published in Andics, *Nagybirtokos arisztokrácia*, vol. 1, p. 86.

31 Quoted in Spira, *A Hungarian Count*, p. 67.

32 On Mészáros, see V. Szokoly, ed., *Mészáros Lázár emlékiratai*, 2 vols. (2nd ed., Bp., 1881); also, Z. Sirokay, *M. L. tábornok az első magyar hadügyminiszter* (Mátészalka, 1928).

33 The best approach to Eötvös, a fascinating personality, is through a fine recent monograph written by the American-Hungarian historian P. Böch, *Joseph Eötvös and the Modernization of Hungary, 1840-1870: A Study of Ideas of Individuality and Social Pluralism in Modern Politics*, Transactions of the American Philosophical Society, ns., vol. 62, part 2 (Philadelphia, 1972). Many of Eötvös's own writings were published in German, for instance: [N.N.], *Über die Gleichberechtigung der Nationalitäten in Österreich* (Pest, 1850); his complete works appeared in Hungarian as *Báró Eötvös József összes müvei*, 2 vols. (Bp., 1904).

34 Some of Szemere's reminiscences appeared in Western European languages, for in-

stance, *F. m. Gr. Ludwig Batthyány, Arthur Görgey, Ludwig Kossuth,* 3 vols. (Hamburg, 1853), and *La quéstion hongroise, 1848–1860* (Paris, 1860); see also his *Összegyüjtött munkái,* 6 vols. (Pest, 1869–70).

35 The Palatine's letter, dated Vienna, 24 March 1848, appeared, with slight variations, in many collections of published documents. There is a very free English translation in the famous work of the American chargé d'affaires in Vienna, W. H. Stiles, *Austria in 1848–49,* 2 vols. (New York, 1952; reprinted by the Arno Press and the *New York Times* in 1971), vol. 2, pp. 396–97. The German original is printed in L. B. Szabó, ed., *Adatok gróf Széchenyi István és kora történetéhez, 1808–1860,* 2 vols. (Bp., 1943), vol. 2, pp. 664–66. The Hungarian version is in Pap, *Okmánytár,* vol. 1, pp. 28–30, and Deák, ed., *1848: A Szabadságharc,* pp. 45–46. For a good analysis of the letter's contents, see Károlyi, *1848,* pp. 66–71.

36 A. S. Thosz, "Emlékezések múltamra," *Budapesti Szemle,* vol. 27 (1881), pp. 287–88; quoted in Spira, *A Hungarian Count,* p. 62.

37 Undated financial statement from the Esterházy estates prepared during the Spring of 1848, published in Andics, *Nagybirtokos arisztokrácia,* vol. 2, pp. 76–79; see also Spira, *A Hungarian Count,* p. 63.

38 See Károlyi, *1848,* pp. 34–44; documents relative to the debate and resolutions of the State Conference on general taxation and the abolition of urbarial statutes are in ibid., pp. 216–25.

39 The debates and resolutions of the State Conference, together with the text of the Royal Rescript, are published in Károlyi, *1848,* pp. 226–43; for an analysis of the problem, see ibid., pp. 71–79.

40 On the 29 March events at Pressburg, see *KLÖM* 11, pp. 700–703; also, Károlyi, *1848,* pp. 79–84.

41 Zichy to Vice-Chancellor László Szögyén-Marich (Buda, 29 March 1848), published in Deák, ed., *1848: A Szabadságharc,* p. 54.

42 On the second Buda-Pest *journées,* see Deme, *Radical Left,* pp. 40–43; A. Degré, *Visszaemlékezéseim,* 2 vols. (Bp., 1883), vol. 2, pp. 10–15, and passim. The 31 March proclamation of the Pest Committee of Public Safety demanding that people prepare for war, "without regard to language or religion," is in Pap, *Okmánytár,* vol. 1, pp. 45–47. The reports of Klauzál and Szemere to Batthyány on the Pest disturbances of late March are in the Hungarian National Archives, Budapest. Országos Levéltár. Miniszterelnökség, Országos Honvédelmi Bizottmány. Kormányzóelnökseg. 1848–49. Általános Iratok, 1848:171. Klauzál, Szemere and Pulszky to Batthyány (Pest, 1 April 1848).

43 The revised Royal Rescript is reprinted in Károlyi, *1848,* pp. 244–57. The final Hungarian bill on the "responsible Government," modified by Kossuth himself in accordance with the Royal Rescript, is in ibid., pp. 248–50.

44 Kossuth at the plenary meeting of the Diet, 31 March 1848; printed in *KLÖM* 11, pp. 706–10; the particular quotation is on p. 709.

45 See G. Spira, "Petőfi kardja," in A. Tamás and A. Wéber, eds., *Petőfi tüze* (Bp., 1972), pp. 369–71.

46 Kossuth's address to the Palatine, Pressburg, 1 April 1848; published in *KLÖM* 11, pp. 712–13.

47 A fine monograph on the 1848 electoral law is A. Csizmadia, *A magyar választási rendszer 1848–1849-ben* (Bp., 1963); most of the data on the subject have been culled from that source; see also J. Beér, ed., *Az 1848/49. évi népképviseleti országgyûlés*

(Bp., 1954); the Diet's debates on the reform of the electoral law are printed in *KLÖM* 11, pp. 678-79, 703-4, and 711-12. The text of Law V, 1848, is in Csizmadia, pp. 311-21.

48 The debate on the reform of the county structure is printed in *KLÖM* 11, pp. 716-26.

49 The King's declaration to the joint meeting of the two houses of the Diet, 11 April 1848, is published in Szeremlei, ed., *Magyarország krónikája az 1848. és 1849. évi forradalom idejéről*, 2 vols. (Pest, 1867), vol. 1, p. 67.

50 The April Laws were published as *1848dik évi Magyar Országgyűlésen alkotott törvénycikkelyek* (Kassa, [1848]); there seems to be no modern edition of these crucial thirty-one laws. Contemporary liberal views of Hungary's achievements in March-April 1848 are sympathetically summed up in M. Horváth, *Magyarország függetlenségi harczának története 1848 és 1849-ben*, 3 vols. (Geneva, 1865), vol. 1, pp. 3-15.

51 Horváth, *Magyarország*, vol. 1, p. 19.

52 Ibid., p. 29.

53 Szabó, *Társadalmi és pártharcok*, p. 96.

54 Gyula Szekfű, in B. Hóman and G. Szekfű, *Magyar történet*, 5 vols. (Bp., 1936), vol. 5, p. 394.

55 See, especially, J. Révai, *Kossuth Lajos*, 2nd ed. (Moscow, 1944; Bp., 1945), and *Marx és a magyar forradalom* (Moscow, 1932); reprinted in *Válogatott történelmi írások*, 2 vols. (Bp., 1966).

56 Szabó, *Társadalmi és pártharcok*, p. 32.

57 Révai, *Kossuth* (Bp., 1945), pp. 12-14, and passim; the particular quotation is on p. 13.

PART V

ART AND POLITICS IN THE
REVOLUTIONARY AGE

ART AND POLITICS: 1770-1830
Jan Białostocki, University of Warsaw

Any attempt to discuss the complex problem of the interactions between the domain of art and that of politics in an age of social and
national revolution depends, of course, on how broad a concept of politics one adopts. In the sixty years between 1770 and 1830, political
beliefs and actions and their consequences affected all European civilization, an influence that is understandable when one considers that
the whole structure of European society was transformed during that
time from an old order based on the privileges of birth and on an irratio-
nal hierarchy of values to a new order based on economic and social
forces determined, and dominated by, the middle class.[1]

In dealing with the influence of these new middle class values on the
art of the period, I shall turn first to artistic representations of important contemporary political events—commemorations taking the form
sometimes of allegorical, sometimes of realistic depictions. I shall also
discuss what I call "politics in disguise," that is, historical subjects
expressive of specific contemporary events and political situations,
distinguishing between the view of those events as seen from above—
from the vantage point of those in power—and the same events as seen
from below. I shall, finally, attempt to describe the new imagery that
was devised to express the new political currents in that age of social
and national struggles—from Spain to Poland and from America to
Greece.

I

In 1938, Edgar Wind published an important study entitled "The
Revolution of History Painting,"[2] in which he found that literal representations of contemporary events in academic history painting did not
appear until the seventies of the eighteenth century, and that their appearance, when they finally did come, was facilitated by the practice of
showing events that had occurred in distant places—the geographic
distance substituting for the lack of a temporal one. Wind especially
stressed the importance of the use of American events for the introduction of contemporaneous events and people into the solemn category of "history painting." Reynolds's verdict had been that Benjamin West's *Death of General Wolfe*, painted in 1770 (see Fig. 1),
"will occasion a revolution in art."[3]

Contemporary events were, it is true, almost never represented in painting before the last quarter of the eighteenth century; the official Salons were full of pictures representing classical events, drawn not only from Ovid and Virgil, who had already been sources for a long time, but also from the Roman historians and from Homer,[4] but none from historical occasions of more recent vintage. Nevertheless, it is still difficult to agree altogether with Wind's thesis, and in fact scholars have already taken exception to some of his points.[5] Contemporary events, especially those drawn from military history, had of course been represented by painters earlier, but they were not treated as subjects for history painting in the grand style. Cycles of paintings of famous battles occasionally included representations of some quite recent battles,[6] for example, in the sixteenth century, the Battle of Pavia was depicted several times. The important battle between Polish and Russian forces at Orsza in 1514 was commemorated a few years later (sometime after 1518) in a large panel, now in the National Museum in Warsaw,[7] executed by an unknown master in the style of Cranach. The Masaniello uprising in Naples became a popular subject among the Neapolitan painters soon after it took place.[8] The most famous, the *Surrender of Breda* by Velázquez, was painted only ten years after that defeat, although temporary, of the Dutch Republic.[9]

In most of these cases we are dealing with works of art commissioned by victorious monarchs or their subordinates, and all of them were meant to fulfill the functions of triumphal commemoration and propaganda. Defeats were not commemorated: between 1625, the date of Breda's surrender, and 1635, the year in which Velázquez started painting his picture, the Spanish troops were, it should be recalled, defeated in the Netherlands more than once.

The concept of history that lay behind the art of the Renaissance and Baroque was very different from the modern idea of history as a scholarly discipline. History painting was an artistic genre the purpose of which was to instruct through the portrayal of moral example, and certainly not to present events as they actually happened. This latter documentary function was occasionally fulfilled, but usually in other genres and techniques. In the graphic arts, for instance, historical events were shown in realistic and accurate detail. Prints were intended to show things as they happened, and, in general, they are, as a result, much more reliable so far as topographic and historical accuracy are concerned.

Prints did not always express the point of view of the authorities, as did historical pictures in the grand style, or even simple pictorial recordings of military events. While it is true that prints, like paintings, commemorated splendid entrances and triumphs, unlike paintings, they could also include mutilated soldiers or the dead remaining on the battlefield. It was in his prints—in his famous series *The Miseries of*

War—that Callot, for example, formulated the first powerful criticism of war to be found in the visual arts. But works such as these belong to a moralistic tradition rooted in late-medieval graphic art: they were probably considered a kind of secularized dance of death; they were not intended to carry any definite political message, but only the general moral lesson that war was a calamity.

Apparently it was not until the period from the 1770s to the 1840s and as a result of the events of this period—namely the social revolutions and wars for national independence—that painting began to represent political events and to convey them not only from the point of view of those groups struggling against the powers of oppression, but also to do it in such a way as to affect the ordinary men involved in the events and the small nations in danger of oppression from the imperialism of the great powers. For such an evolution to occur, it was necessary for the artists to become sufficiently independent to paint subjects of their own choosing. For the most part, they undertook to represent scenes of oppression only after the danger was over, as did Goya, or to paint scenes of a war for independence only after the final victory, as did Trumbull. Total independence among artists remained rare even in this period. There were great artists, such as Goya, who expressed in pictures their own independent point of view, but there were also outstanding masters who followed the vacillations of the political situation, serving whatever party was in power. Jacques Louis David first served the royal art administration in some capacity, then the democratic and revolutionary authorities, in which he himself had a considerable role, and finally produced visual propaganda for the autocratic dictator. Others, such as Canova, worked almost concurrently for the two hostile political powers: Canova not only made statues of Napoleon, his mother, and other members of his family, but also designed the tomb of Nelson for St. Paul's Cathedral—until patriotic criticism in England finally forced the authorities to give the commission to Flaxman.[10]

To erect a statue or a tomb need not, of course, be considered a political act by everyone. The artist's profession was to make statues, and it was not for him to reject orders simply on the grounds of the moral qualifications or the political ideas of his sitter. It might be fruitful, then, to take into consideration those works of art which are more obviously to be considered expressions of political attitudes. During the years from 1770 to 1830, authorities, regardless of their political character, continued in principle to act in accordance with the traditional program of political propaganda in the visual arts; namely, they commissioned or encouraged works of art that were to commemorate important events seen as triumphal or to express through allegory the political ideas of the commissioning authorities.

Revolutionary leaders both in America and in France did not consider allegory to be a reactionary form of artistic expression. Their public ceremonies and pageants were full of symbols and allegories. American coins and official papers were adorned with emblematic conceits, which survive to this day in the design of some of its currency. In 1792, Samuel Jennings painted *Liberty Displaying Arts and Sciences*, quite in the old allegorical tradition.[11]

Revolutionary allegory in French painting is well illustrated in a picture by Jean Baptiste Regnault, of which only a smaller version, now in the Kunsthalle at Hamburg, is preserved; the whereabouts of the larger version is unknown.[12] This larger version, entitled *Liberty or Death* (see Fig. 2), was exhibited at the Salon de l'An IV (1795); above the globe a youth who personifies *le génie de la France* hovers between the personification of the Republic and that of Death. The beautiful girl embodying the Republic is shown with her attributes signifying *Liberté* (a Phrygian cap), *Égalité* (a level), and *Fraternité* (fasces). The picture is an allegorical representation of the maxim of the French constitution promulgated on 10 August 1793: *Liberté, Égalité, Fraternité ou la Mort*.

Regnault had painted his picture too late. It expressed the stern ideology of the times of the Terror, but it was shown in 1795, just before the Directoire. Regnault, who painted the picture on his own initiative, was criticized, not, however, for having chosen the allegorical form, but for being ideologically too close to Robespierre and his group, out of power since July 1794. But the painter learned his lesson only too well, and a few years later he exhibited an enormous painting representing *Napoleon's I Triumphal March to the Temple of Immortality*. After some years Regnault substituted a figure symbolizing France for that—already politically outdated—of Napoleon, and he soon greeted the Bourbon return with an appropriate allegory called *Heureux événement*.[13]

However significant and interesting, such works introduced nothing new so far as the mechanism of artistic representation is concerned. More important was the fact that, at the same time, works were being painted, and even commissioned, that were intended to commemorate significant actual events. Some precedent for this kind of art had been established by three pictures painted by Americans working in England: Benjamin West's *Death of General Wolfe*, painted in 1770, John Singleton Copley's *Death of Earl of Chatham*, in 1779–81, and the same artist's *Death of Major Pierson*, in 1782–84. These and other similar pictures depicted recent occurrences by carefully reconstructing not only the course of events, but also the natural or architectural settings, and the costumes; although, of course, they also subordinated this documentary realism to the rules of heroic composition, and—a very important point—these pictures expressed no revolutionary ideas. West and Copley, although Americans by birth, commemorated heroic devotion to the British monarch and British patriotism.

It was John Trumbull who "applied West's and Copley's innovations to American subjects, and reintroduced the accomplishments of these American artists into the mainstream of American art," to quote Jules D. Prown.[14] Trumbull was actually the first to depict important events in the American War of Independence, starting with the *Death of General Warren in the Battle at Bunker Hill* (1785–87) (see Fig. 3), continuing with the *Death of General Montgomery at Quebec* (1786), the *Declaration of Independence* (1787–95), and several other topics.[15] That introduction of revolutionary subjects was accomplished by substituting the dying heroes of the Revolution for the generals of the king. But it was always the supreme *exemplum virtutis*, the heroic death, that raised all those actual subjects to the elevated status of historical pictures. They recorded recent happenings but at the same time fulfilled the traditional function of history painting—they instructed and provided a great moral example.

Trumbull—although he mostly painted portraits—remained devoted to revolutionary subjects throughout his life and depicted the same events several times. These works were also engraved, and they enjoyed a considerable popularity. Trumbull, as a president of the American Academy of Fine Arts, initiated a project of federally sponsored historical paintings in his letter to the president of the United States in 1827:

I would propose [we read in that most interesting document] that whenever an event, political, moral or military, shall occur, which shall be regarded by the Government as of sufficient importance to be recorded as matter of History, the most eminent painter of the time, be ordered to paint a picture of the same, to be placed in some of the national buildings—that an artist of secondary talent be employed to make a copy of the same, which shall be given to the Minister, Admiral, or General under whose direction or command the event shall have taken place, as a testimony of the approbation and gratitude of the nation. . . . I would next propose, that the most distinguished engraver of the day should be employed to engrave a copperplate from the painting so executed, and that one thousand impressions, first printed from this plate, be reserved by Government. . . . Every Minister of the United States, going abroad on a mission should be furnished with one (or a set) of these reserved engravings as an article of his outfit: they should be handsomely framed and hung in the most public and elegant apartment of his foreign residence. . . . Every Minister of a foreign nation returning home from a residence among us, should also receive one (or a set) of those prints, in a handsome port-folio.[16]

II

France followed America in the recording of the glorious happenings of her Revolution. Because of the rapidity with which events followed upon each other, not many of these projects resulted in finished works of art. One of the most important would certainly have been David's *Tennis Court Oath (June 20,1789)* commissioned from him by the Société des Amis de la Constitution on the anniversary of the event. David's multifarious duties prevented him from taking the composition beyond the preparatory drawing and painted sketch stages.

Some pictures were painted to commemorate the heroes and martyrs of the Revolution, such as the *Heroism of the Young Désilles* by Jean-Jacques-François Le Barbier,[17] the *Death of Bara (Viala)* (1794) by David, and, the most famous of all, the *Death of Marat* (1793), also by David, a terrifying reportage from the site of the crime, noble and powerful, and still not devoid of allegorical overtones. But prints reporting actual occurrences were more numerous; they depicted the celebrations of the Revolution, the destruction of the Bastille, the *Removal of Voltaire's Remains to the Panthéon*, and so on. Many events were commemorated by drawings which did not reach the print or painting stage, as the *Tenth of August, 1792* by Baron François Gérard, a preliminary study for a picture never painted.[18] Medals, such as those by Dupré, commemorated important events of the Revolution. But such graphic works, coins and medals, only continued the traditional functions of commemoration they had always fulfilled.

In the following periods, those of the Directoire, the Consulate, and the Empire, art was to play a significant role in the powerful propaganda system of the dictatorial state. All the gifted French artists of the period had to work for the glory of Bonaparte, and most of them did it with an enthusiasm that recalled the court artists of the *ancien régime*. David soon forgot his severe revolutionary style of the *Oath of the Horatii* (1784) and of the *Death of Marat*, and he created pompous and noisy pictures such as the *Distribution of Eagles* (1810) or *Le Sacre*. The figure of the dictator appeared in flattering compositions, such as the allegory by Jean-Pierre Franque, *France before Napoleon's Return from Egypt*, in which the nation is shown awaiting with impatience, distress, and anticipation the reappearance of the savior.[19]

The corresponding events in Polish history merge with allegory in Marcello Bacciarelli's commemorative picture, unfortunately lost, and known from a sketch and from reproductions, representing *Napoleon Giving the Constitution to the Duchy of Warsaw* (1807) (see Fig.4).[20] The emperor is shown as a legislator (as in Annibale Carracci's Dresden picture *Genius of Glory*), but, although Bacciarelli's painting pretends to depict an actual scene, it is an idealization for the simple reason that such an event in fact never happened. Somewhat later, Napoleon rose up in Polish eyes to become the messianic prophet and saint who hovers in mid-air in a picture by Walenty Wańkowicz;[21] in French popular art, the dictator became simply *St. Napoleon the Patron of Warriors*.[22]

Bonaparte's extraordinary interest in Ossian caused Girodet to paint, for the former's country house in Malmaison, an allegorical picture, *Ossian Welcoming to Walhalla the Generals of the Republic* (1802), which was in fact a glorification of the French army and a celebration of the Continental Peace of 14 June 1801 between France and England.[23]

The flattering allusion was an essential element of the themes taken from Roman history used by the artists who decorated the Quirinal Palace in Rome for the residence of Napoleon. Paul Duqueylar painted *Trajan Distributing Scepters of Asia*, while Pelagio Pelagi contributed *Caesar Dictating Orders to Several Secretaries at the Same Time*. Napoleon, however, never came to the Quirinal to see these cheap compliments.[24] Numerous pictures were commissioned to adorn the residences of the dictator with representations of his victorious battles. In 1801, a competition was organized for a picture commemorating the Battle at Nazareth. The competition was won by Gros, but he was prevented by the Emperor from painting the picture because it would be a glorification of the Republican General Junot, the actual hero of the story.[25] On 3 March 1806, eighteen pictures were commissioned to record the German campaign. In 1808, several pictures were ordered to adorn the Gallery of Diana in the Tuilleries[26] that were to depict Napoleon's battles. Again great and minor masters participated. In the spring of 1807, after the Battle at Eylau, twenty-six painters were invited to enter a competition to commemorate it, one of the bloodiest and most terrible battles in Napoleon's career. Vivant Denon prepared the program: the picture had to show the day following the battle with the Emperor in the role of "good father" visiting the battlefield on horseback, distributing encouragement and help both to the French and to the enemy soldiers wounded and freezing in the snow.[27] Even the general scheme of the composition was determined by Denon, with the result that the sketches submitted by the various painters closely resemble one another. The jury gave the prize and entrusted the execution of the composition to Gros.

When the sketches were exhibited in the Apollo Gallery at the Louvre, the police protested those many works in which naked and mutilated corpses were shown in the foreground of the composition. The police report expressed dismay at the possible psychological and political effects elicited by pictures presenting war as disgusting and horrible.[28] Was this premeditated on the part of the artists? I do not think it likely. It was enough to show naked reality to be accused of acting against the interests of the state.

After Waterloo, new commissions went to artists; this time they were supposed to commemorate the heroes of the Counterrevolution. Beginning in 1816, Louis XVIII commissioned a series of portraits of generals in the Vendée Army to adorn the palace at Saint Cloud.[29] Pictures were also painted to recall the virtues of the deposed king and his family. This was certainly the idea behind *Louis XVI Distributing Alms to the Poor During the Winter of 1788* (1817), by Louis Hersent, or *Madame Elizabeth of France Distributing Milk*, by Richard Fleury.[30]

In the meantime, among the nations in the anti-Napoleonic coalition, art was following a similar course. In Britain, the heroes of the war against France were still being commemorated during Napoleon's rule. The most dramatic event, the death of Nelson in the very moment of his victory at Trafalgar, inspired several works of history painting in the grand style.[31] In those by Benjamin West showing, with due decorum, the event as it should have occurred (see Fig.5), and by Arthur William Devis, representing it more truthfully but with strong suggestions of Christian iconography (see Fig. 6), the theme of the death of Nelson found two realizations of a very different character. William Blake expressed in his allegorical compositions *Spiritual Form of Nelson* and *Spiritual Form of Pitt* his strong criticism of British imperial policy.[32]

After the war the British Institution organized (in 1816) a competition for an allegorical representation of the British victory. The winner was James Ward with his *Triumph of the Duke of Wellington*, showing the ''genius of Wellington on the car of war, supported by Britannia and attended by the Seven Cardinal Virtues, commanding away the Demons, Anarchy, Rebellion and Discord, with the Horrors of War'' (1822).[33] Luke Clenell chose a more realistic style in his picture *Decisive Charge Made by the Lifeguards at the Battle of Waterloo;* he also recorded the great reception given in Guildhall, London, in honor of the allied sovereigns, nobles, and generals who participated in the Battle of Waterloo.[34]

In Germany, Heinrich Olivier's allegorical representation of the three sovereigns of the Holy Alliance depicted in the guise of the patron saints of their respective nations, clad in armour, and shown inside a neo-Gothic church, is perhaps the best example of the new reactionary, religious, and neo-medievel spirit, as opposed to the revolutionary, secular, and neoclassical one of the Revolution and the Empire.[35]

These works of art, resulting mostly from official—or at least public—commissions constitute what may be called ''open politics'' in art. They are either statements of fact seen from the point of view of the commissioning authority, or proclamations of ideological programs, or obvious political propaganda (as is the case with *France Before Napoleon's Return from Egypt*). One can say this is ''art and politics from above.'' But what interests us perhaps more is what might be called ''art and politics from below'': I mean those works of art that express the ideas and feelings of the social classes or nations struggling for their independence and freedom.

In the period under consideration, art became, for the first time on a large scale, not only an instrument to commemorate victories, but also to depict injustice, cruelty, humiliation, defeat, and social and national calamities. The motifs of martyrdom originating in religious iconography were adapted to the history of nations and social groups. Some of them had already appeared much earlier in the graphic arts: in the awkward broadsheets of the Reformation, in the representations of the Peasant War in Germany,[36] in the Dutch engravings of the seventeenth century,[37] in the British political caricatures of the eighteenth century,[38] in a word, in all those moments when the middle class acquired some political importance. With Goya, Delacroix, and the other Romantic painters occurred an important change in the concept of history in art: political heroes were no longer necessarily victorious, they could also be defeated. The *exemplum virtutis* of Stoic origin was, it is true, a heroic *topos* known from earlier times. It appeared in Poussin's *Burial of Phocion,* as well as in innumerable representations based on Roman history in French painting of the pre-Revolutionary decades.[39] Such pictures, however, were usually intended to convey general moral significance. They were not political, i.e., they did not take a definite position in some political conflict.

Now, in the time span between 1770 and 1830, certain classical examples cited in a specific historical moment acquired political significance. French painting in the years immediately preceding the Revolution is full of pictures that may be called "political in disguise."[40] David's *Horatii,* his *Death of Socrates* (1787), and his *Brutus* (1789) are only the best known of them. *Horatii* proclaims fidelity to common patriotic ideals, but in such general terms that it could have been a perfectly suitable acquisition for the crown; *Socrates* shows the moral triumph of an ideological martyr in his heroic hour of death, and *Brutus* illustrates a most terrible "personal sacrifice to political belief," the hero "being able to suppress natural feelings considering only the welfare of the Republic," to quote Plekhanov's analysis of this picture.[41] *Brutus,* conceived before the outbreak of the Revolution, but not exhibited at the Salon until 25 August 1789, when the Bastille had already been taken, soon became a political picture *par excellence,* to be reinterpreted by public opinion according to the situation of the moment (as recently shown by Robert Herbert and Christopher Sells).[42]

To pass now to political history as seen "from below," it begins to appear in the major arts toward the end of the eighteenth century. The war's disasters and calamities were expressed for the first time in ways revealing a violent political passion—as opposed to the moralistic criticisms of Callot—in Goya's prints, but also— and this is a new departure in the early nineteenth century— in his historical paintings, especially that commemorating the Madrid rising of *2 de Mayo* (1808) and its subsequent cruel suppression by the French that ended in the executions of 3 May. While Paul Revere's *Boston Massacre* of 1770 (see Fig.7) anticipated important aspects of that masterpiece, it remained, just as the British anti-Napoleonic prints adduced by Gombrich as having been possible Goya sources, in the broadsheet category. Identical acts of brutality by the French in Russia inspired in 1813, just one year before Goya's painting, a Russian picture which has been attributed by some to V. K. Sazonov, and others to M. Tikhonov, now in the Russian Museum in Leningrad.[43]

In such works defeat seen as a martyrdom received artistic honors that until then had been reserved for triumphs. If we compared the *2 de Mayo* with Girodet's *Cairo Riots of 1798*,[44] aside from the obvious differences in artistic quality, the character is essentially the same. It is the vantage point that is the opposite. Instead of glorifying the conqueror, perhaps for the first time in painting in the grand style, Goya's pictures accuse him by showing his cruel deeds. To show martyrdom and to monumentalize its image have, of course, a long tradition in Christian art, the most popular images of which celebrate precisely the spiritual victory of those physically vanquished by a secular power. But Goya's images were secular. They did not promise eternal bliss to the martyrs; rather, they accused the invaders and murderers by exposing for posterity their inhuman and brutal deeds.

The French defeats became attractive to French painters only after sufficient time had elapsed to allow sentimentality and a picturesque approach. Napoleon's retreat from Russia became one of those romantic subjects that combined memories of bygone splendor and glory with reminders of present misery. As such, the theme was not political; it depicted the changing favors of fortune—again a subject with a long iconographic tradition. Exhibited in 1835 and 1836, the pictures by Jean François Boissard de Boisdenier and by Nicolas Toussaint Charlet (see Fig. 8) coincided with the period preceding the triumphal return of Napoleon's ashes in 1840, and with the publication of the memoirs of generals, such as Ségur's records of the retreat from Russia. They belonged to the retrospective and picturesque revival of Napoleonic times, seen from a quarter-century distance and by a generation well trained in romantic attitudes. For the Polish painter Michałowski, scenes which he revived in his pictures from the Napoleonic era were charged with additional meaning, painted as they were after the defeat of the Polish uprising of 1830–31; he revived in them the heroic period of the great political hopes that Polish leaders had connected with Napoleon.[45]

Horace Vernet had already represented in 1826 a *Scene of the French Campaign of 1814*.[46] Popular graphic art produced many prints commemorating the defense of France in the last period of the Napoleonic dictatorship, when the war brought by the French to all the European countries was returned to their own motherland. This time French popular artists such as Adam and Raffet showed the disorderly and brutal behavior of foreign armies in France, especially of the Cossacks. A direct look "from below" on a Napoleonic battle scene was first given in French art by Géricault, whose *Wounded Cuirassier* of 1814 is considered to be one of the first pictorial French criticisms of the blood battles which eventually brought France, not to glory, but to chaos and final defeat. Géricault insisted on displaying this picture in the Salon of 1814 together with his *Charging Chasseur*, first shown two years earlier. The two pictures exhibited side by side symbolized the original enthusiastic faith in victory, on one side, and the final disaster of the Napoleonic rule, on the other.[47]

In England, the period corresponding to that of the Revolution and Empire in France saw the development of political caricature in popular broadsheets. However, essentially no new attitudes or techniques were used. To ridicule enemy leaders had been traditional for prints from the period of the Reformation on. Gillray inherited many of his motifs from Hogarth. Less common was Blake's criticism of the leaders of his country. In those allegorical compositions he made Nelson and Pitt the focus of his analysis.[48]

III

The situation was very different in Germany, where the French invasion and strong censorship of publications elicited national feelings that found expression not only in literature and philosophy but also in the visual arts. One artist—Friedrich—and one statesman—vom Stein—are prominent examples.

Caspar David Friedrich, born in Greifswald in Swedish Pomerania, was a landscape painter—at least that was what he considered himself to be, and so did his contemporaries.[49] His contribution to our subject is therefore especially interesting and original, for he was, perhaps, the first to find ways of expressing political ideas in landscape pictures. Representative of the metaphysical attitude of German Romanticism, the elements of nature he represented in his pictures were for him always symbols. Death is omnipresent in his art, symbolically represented by tombs, cemeteries, dead trees, church ruins, crosses, and ravens. But death opens new life in Friedrich's conceptions: it is a boundary between the two worlds.

During the Napoleonic occupation of Germany, Friedrich joined in the general patriotic enthusiasm. He was a friend of the poets Körner

and Kleist and an admirer of Scharnhorst. He had contacts with Freiherr vom Stein and with Ernst Moritz Arndt. (Born on the island of
Rügen and for some time a Privatdozent in Friedrich's town of Griefs-
wald, Arndt, an historian and politician, was Stein's secretary during
his stay in Russia.)[50]

Friedrich's painting, usually poetical and metaphysical, turned for a
short time political and patriotic. But he did not abandon his favored
genre, and he remained essentially a landscape painter. He introduced
an element of historical analogy, including political allusions, into his
views of natural scenery. Like the Dutch artists of the seventeenth
century who glorified Claudius Civilis and the rising of the Batavians
under his leadership against the Roman Empire, in this way presenting
the ancient model for the contemporary struggle of the Dutch Republic
against the Habsburg Empire,[51] so Friedrich—following Kleist—revived the ancient Germanic hero, Hermann or Arminius, the leader of
the Germanic Rising and conqueror of the Romans in the Teutoburg
Forest. In 1808, Kleist wrote a drama called *Hermannschlacht;*[52]
Friedrich, the landscape painter, who had for some time been representing prehistoric stone tombs as memorials to the ancient national
past, painted two pictures with heroic tombs, one called *Arminius'
Tomb* and the other, *Tombs of the Freedom Fighters* (see Fig. 9). In the
first of them, a French chasseur is contemplating the glorious tomb, as
if confronted with the heroic tradition of German history.[53] It is not
impossible that the tomb was actually meant to be that of Scharnhorst,
who died of his wounds in June 1813 in Dresden.

The inscription of the sarcophagus says: "May Your Faithfulness
and Invincibility as a Soldier Be for Us a Perennial Example." We
know from a letter Friedrich wrote on 12 March 1814 to Arndt that he
intended to paint an imaginary town with a Scharnhorst monument in
its center. He remarked with the bitterness typical of all German patriots in the period of reactionary restoration that no monuments were in
fact erected to commemorate either the great causes of the nation or
the magnanimous deeds of its individuals, and he added, "As long as
we remain *Fürstenknechte* [lackeys to the princes] in art as well nothing great will happen."[54]

The other picture[55] shows several tombs at the foot of a steep rocky
cliff (suitable for the tombs of heroes as indicated in Hirschfeld's land-
scaping theory). Some tombs are inscribed, so we know with certainty
that one of them was meant to be Arminius'. It is one of those painted
in dark colors. In contrast an obelisk is shown in a bright light, decorated with crossed swords and an angel. The inscription says, "Noble
Youth, Fatherland's Savior." Similar inscriptions are to be found on
the other tombs. The identities of the heroes are not disclosed, and it
may be they were meant as allegorical tombs for the young German

patriots who had fallen in the war for national freedom against Napoleon.

The oak tree was, in German Romanticism, a symbol of virtue and heroism.[56] In a sentimental and allegorical form, oak trees appeared in a picture by Friedrich's friend Kersting, which shows a girl binding wreaths of oak leaves to adorn the tombs of dead heroes. Their names are inscribed on the trunks of the huge oak trees under one of which the girl is sitting on a rock (the symbol of heroism). Körner, Hartmann, and Friesen, young writers who died as members of the Lützow army, are commemorated in this way.[57]

In 1813–14, Friedrich painted a picture called *Chasseur in Forest*. A lonely man, seen from behind in the uniform of a French chasseur, is standing in a forest of snow-covered fir trees. He seems to be overwhelmed by the powerful nature of the north. The picture was considered to be a symbol of the French defeat. On 8 December 1814, the *Vossische Zeitung* said of it: "A raven sitting on an old tree trunk is singing a death song to the French *chasseur* who is going alone through the forest in the snow."[58] It is possible that Friedrich's imagination was moved by the records of the French retreat from Russia, but it is characteristic of his art that it always remains in the poetical realm of nature that allows for any number of interpretations. People were looking for patriotic meanings in his works. His friend, the Norwegian landscape painter Johann Christian Dahl, reported that during the German wars of independence people were buying Friedrich's pictures "and finding [in them] a specific—one might say—political-prophetic meaning, hints at an almighty, invisible hand which intervenes in the intricated history of mankind and the liberation of Germany from the foreign yoke."[59]

Friedrich also made plans for monuments which were never erected. Beginning in 1806, he designed a monument to Blücher, and several of his drawings are known with motifs of weapons and armour intended for heroic monuments. In these designs, that most romantic of the German romantic artists applied forms which may be called classical; he probably considered them as suitable for heroic designs.[60] Otherwise not classical but Gothic forms became symbolic of patriotic ideals. The Gothic revival in Germany was to a great extent fed by patriotic feelings, since Goethe, in his essay *On German Architecture* (1772–73), identified Gothic style with German artistic expression.[61]

A special interest in Gothic, considered as German, art found its expression not only in Friedrich's paintings, not only in Schinkel's architectural activity, not only in attempts at the restoration of medieval castles, but also in what was called by Eimer "the patriotic artistic program" of Freiherr vom Stein.[62] The great project organized by vom Stein and the Boisserée brothers to complete the construction of the

Cologne Cathedral was a political undertaking intended to awaken national feelings. The Gothic cathedral in Cologne assumed the role of a national monument.[63]

Freiherr vom Stein, the organizer of the German army in Russia to fight Napoleon's troops in Germany, and a statesman contemplating great projects of political reforms, was under the Restoration reduced to political inactivity. He busied himself by conceiving some artistic projects as monuments and symbols of the patriotic upheaval of the years 1811–14. In his castle at Nassau in the Rhineland he had erected a neo-Gothic tower by Johann Claudius Lassaux with an archive room on the ground floor, a study on the second floor, and a memorial room on the top floor. The rooms had an abstract, somewhat octagonal shape. The decoration pertained to contemporary history: on the pilasters outside, the carvings showed the four patron saints of the nations belonging to the great anti-Napoleonic coalitions: St. Aleksander Nevskii for Russia, St. Adalbert for Prussia, St. George for Britain, and St. Leopold for Austria. In the memorial hall were busts of victorious monarchs.[64] Stein conceived the tower not only as a symbol but also as a functional structure. In the study he intended to work on his great projects for political reform, and to use the memorial hall on anniversary days, decorated with oak leaves for patriotic festivals. The center of the radially decorated floor was formed by the pattern of the Iron Cross, the German military order, designed in 1813 by Schinkel.[65] Somewhat similar ideas were expressed in the so-called Tempelhof Monument in Berlin of 1818–26, designed by Schinkel with statues of Victories and Genii portraying members of the triumphant dynasties.[66]

Stein tried to initiate some other artistic projects, but only a few of them were brought to conclusion. The most interesting was a representation of the Tirol Rising of 1809 under the leadership of Andreas Hofer, painted on vom Stein's commission by the Tirolean-born Joseph Anton Koch in 1819–20. The picture shows a kind of triumph of Hofer, who is depicted on horseback, with symbolic allusions to the corruption of the politicians involved with the activities of the Vienna Congress (*die heiligen Bündler und Kongressler*, as Koch called them).[67]

IV

By 1820 the vivid memories of Napoleonic times were fading away under the impact of new political events. The hopes for independence, which had brought the Polish people under the banner of Napoleon's army, disappeared in the frigid atmosphere of the Holy Alliance and the Vienna Congress, but there appeared in Greece a new center for the struggle toward national independence. In 1824, Eugene Delacroix devoted his first monumental and his most famous work to the dramatic event of that war: the *Massacre at Chios*. By that picture he promoted the representations of the sufferings of a nation fighting for its independence to the high rank of history painting. Byron rushed to share the destiny of the Greeks defending Missolonghi, as did the French painter Constantin Guys, as well. After that tragic defeat, Delacroix again took up the subject—this time in allegoric form—showing *Greece on the Ruins of Missolonghi* (not, however, "expiring," as it was later misinterpreted, but "hopeful"), and he exhibited the picture in 1826 "au profit des Grecs."[68] The sincere feelings of the painter for the Greek people were probably mixed with his personal attachment to Byron, who had died on 9 April 1824 in the besieged town. The picture is both a monument to the Greek struggle for freedom and a memorial to the great romantic poet.[69]

Soon it was Poland's turn again to attract attention, this time because of the unhappy November Uprising of 1830. A gloomy and strange picture by the Edinburgh painter David Scott, inspired by a newspaper account, was completed on 16 January 1832, a few months after the final defeat of the Polish army (see Fig. 10.) It is a wholly unconventional image that does not fit into any stereotype of battle painting. Scott gave it a long descriptive title: *The Poles Did Nobly, and the Russian General Craved for an Armistice to Bury His Dead*.[70] In France the uprising and its tragic end were given particular attention. The famous answer of General Sebastiani in the Chambre des Députés, when asked about the situation in Warsaw, "L'ordre le plus parfait régne à Varsovie," inspired the artistic imagination of Grandville and Traviès.[71] Léon Cogniet depicted the dramatic desolation and destruction of the burning Praga, a suburb of Warsaw, in an idealized way, with a disarmed Polish officer facing the beholder, his arms crossed and his face expressing the tragic awareness of the disaster *(Praga, 1831)*.[72]

V

We have reached the chronological limit of our survey. It is justified now to ask a more general question: had those most essential changes, which between 1770 and 1830 affected the social and political order and ways of thinking, also transformed the imagery used by the artists depicting political events or giving expression to political ideas? In the beginning of the period discussed here, when Benjamin West, Copley, Trumbull, and others introduced contemporary events in pictures, such as the *Death of General Wolfe*, they attempted to give them a noble character by borrowing compositional patterns from religious or classical iconography. The dying Wolfe is shown like Christ in depictions of the Lamentation. Similar religious associations appear in the much later and much more realistic representation of the other famous death of a hero, that of Nelson by Devis. In other cases it was the

classical tradition that was used to justify the glorification of contemporary heroes. Using the death of a hero for representation was in itself a
traditional decision, connected both with martyrdom scenes and with
the heroic themes of classical antiquity in which death was a final trial
of virtue and a guarantee of eternal glory. Napoleon on horseback visiting the wounded at the battlefield of Eylau also harks back to representations known in classical art, namely, to those of the Emperor Trajan found on sarcophagi; other details of Gros's picture seem to be
borrowed from the historical reliefs on Trajan's column.[73]

The *Massacre at Chios* may be compared to traditional depictions of
the Massacre of the Innocents, if we want to look for a traditional
framework in iconography. Goya's *The Third of May, 1808* (see Fig.
11) is, like similar compositions which we have mentioned earlier, a
secularized Triumph of Death, or, again, a scene of martyrdom.[74] The
Spanish master "gave new national and social content to the old moral
and religious allegory. In transforming it in such a profound way, Goya
inaugurated, as it were, a new iconographic type characteristic for the
19th century," which may be described as "the freedom fighters versus tyranny; . . . that image was not to disappear from artistic imagery
until at least Picasso's *Massacres at Corée*."[75]

Romantic images were partly based on the time-honored repertory of
classical or religious themes, but they also constituted a new set of
types. Years ago I tried to describe that process in the following
terms:[76]

Although numerous encompassing themes of Christian and humanistic art endured the
rupture [which occurred in the time of Romanticism], they were filled with new content
and often they even basically transformed their character. . . . Romanticism did not
create, and could not have created, a compact and consistent iconographic repertory,
because its attitude to symbols and themes was free, individual, and subjective [suffice it
to recall Caspar David Friedrich] since it strove for originality and distinction of individual vision. But Romanticism introduced into art new heroes and martyrs: instead of
religious, they were secular and, instead of historical, they were contemporary, and particularly they were national, social, and even artistic heroes.

In the period of Romanticism, new images and iconographic stereo-
types were formed which expressed conflicts typical of many political
situations at the time, namely, struggles between the powerful and the
dependent nations. It was said that freedom was invented in the eighteenth century, but the political reality of the following century was in
many countries in glaring contrast to the idea of freedom. The explo-
sions of violence expressive of extreme despair continued throughout
the entire period. From the American Revolution to the Polish Uprising of 1830, the struggle for freedom in Spain, in Germany, in Greece,
in Poland, and in Hungary was accompanied by ideas and images crys-

tallizing in new visual archetypes, as it were, often based on traditional patterns, but sometimes born of the new experience of reality.

Here are some of the new images, or new encompassing themes, of the nineteenth century as they appear in art and politics:

1) *The oath:* A solemn declaration of fidelity to a great good cause uniting a group of people, it may have a military or an ideological character. Its roots obviously go back to David's *Horatii*. It reappears in a more historical guise in Henry Fusely's *Oath on the Rütli* (1778–1781). As a representation of a contemporary event, the oath image is shown by John Trumbull in his *Declaration of American Independence*, painted from 1786 to 1797: a group of people aware of the importance of the moment are gathered in common devotion to a single idea.[77] Next is David's composition, which remains only in the form of a drawing and a sketch, immortalizing the memorable event that took place in the Tennis Court in 1789. Jean Pierre Norblin's drawing contributes a Polish counterpart, for it depicts the *Voting for the Polish Constitution of May Third, 1791* (1792) (see Fig. 12). Three years later, the leader of the Polish Uprising of 1794 and the veteran officer of the American War of Independence, Tadeusz Kościuszko, took an oath in the Cracow marketplace to direct Poland's fight for independence. Franciszek Smuglewicz portrayed that moment in a famous picture (see Fig. 13), and it was subsequently represented by several others.[78]

2) *The uprising or revolution, the upheaval:* Together with the phenomenon itself, the image was born. Although upheavals had taken place sporadically before the late eighteenth century, they became a typical phenomenon for political history in the nineteenth and twentieth, in a world liberated from many traditional barriers and inhibitions. To limit our examples to the Polish scene, we should mention Norblin's drawings recording the Warsaw uprising of 1794, the picture by Marcin Zaleski showing the *Taking of the Warsaw Armory in 1830* (1831) (see Fig. 14),[79] and much later drawings by Grottger inspired by the uprising of 1863.[80] Goya's masterpiece and Delacroix's *Liberty Leading the People* (1830) are better known examples.[81]

3) *The triumph of evil, of oppression, the execution, the massacre:* To this category belong the well-known pictures by Goya, Delacroix's *Massacre at Chios*, the print by Paul Revere of the *Boston Massacre*, the Russian representation of the shooting of the Moscow patriots by the French, and in Poland Norblin's *Massacre at Praga* in 1794.

4) *The leader defeated:* He may be a military commander defeated, taken prisoner, or killed, but he no longer dies heroically in the very moment of victory, as he did in such British and American pictures as those presenting the heroic death of West, or Nelson, or Warren, or Mercer. These were triumphal pictures. Polish history abounded in de-

feated leaders who survived their defeat and therefore did not present a subject for triumphal iconography. The defeated hero was something new in art. Benjamin West depicted one of them—Kościuszko, a hero of the American war, now wounded and defeated but at least secure in London (the dome of St. Paul's in the background lends a more optimistic note to the picture) (see Fig. 15).[82] A somewhat later painter, Henryk Rodakowski, erected what may be called a painted monument to General Henryk Dembiński, a commander of the Polish army during the tragic Uprising of 1830–31. Rodakowski's picture shows Dembiński gloomily meditating past events (see Fig. 16).[83]

A specific case is the very abundant and popular iconography of Prince Józef Poniatowski, one of Napoleon's generals. His jump on horseback to death in the Elster River as he secured, with his Polish corps, the retreat of the great army at the Leipzig battle became a very popular image both in France and in Poland; to classically trained artists, it must have recalled Marcus Curius jumping into the crevasse opened in the Roman Forum to save the Roman people.[84]

5) The iconography of *political deportation, of prisons and exiles:* Introduced with Napoleon on St. Helena, it develops in Polish and Russian art somewhat later (beyond the period of our present interest). Especially Polish art in the second half of the nineteenth century abounds in representations of deportations, prisons, and labor camps in Siberian exile.[85] The unexpected return home of a political prisoner was also a frequent subject in Poland as well as in Russia, a late example being a popular picture by Repin, *They Did Not Expect Him* (1882).[86]

VI

The experience of hard reality was vivid in this period of violent conflict. Sometimes all the patterns and conventions of art broke down. If one compares the unforgettable drawing of *Marie Antoinette on Her Way to the Guillotine* by Jacques Louis David—who had voted for her death—with the idealized image made under the Restoration in 1817 by Lordon *(Marie Antoinette in the Conciergerie Prison),* we may easily measure the human and artistic power of that experience expressed by a great master.[87]

In the course of the nineteenth century, both contemporary history and "history seen from below" became current subjects. In the time of Daumier, the journalist illustration brought everyday news in visual form into the hands of everybody who cared to look for it. Daumier himself contributed both to reporting and criticizing the political scene. But when that excellent draftsman and graphic artist, who in his lithographs commented on political events of his time, wanted to create enduring symbolic images summarizing the essential features of con-

Figure 1. Benjamin West. *Death of General Wolfe*. 1770. Oil on canvas. National Gallery of Canada, Ottawa. Photo: after reproduction.

Figure 2. Jean Baptist Regnault. *Liberty or Death* (small version). 1795. Oil on canvas. Kunsthalle, Hamburg. Photo: Kunsthalle, Hamburg.

Figure 3. John Trumbull. *Death of General Warren in the Battle at Bunker Hill*. 1785–1787. Oil on canvas. Yale University Art Gallery, New Haven.

Figure 4. Marcello Bacciarelli. *Napoleon Giving the Constitution to the Duchy of Warsaw*. 1807. Oil on canvas. Muzeum Narodowe, Warsaw. Photo: Muzeum Narodowe, Warsaw.

Figure 5. Benjamin West. *Death of Nelson*. 1806. Oil on canvas. Walker Art Gallery, Liverpool.

Figure 6. Arthur William Devis. *Death of Nelson*. 1807. Oil on canvas. National Maritime Museum, Greenwich.

Figure 7. Paul Revere. *Boston Massacre*. 1770. Engraving. Library of Congress, Washington.

UnhappyBoston! see thy Sons deplore,
Thy hallow'd Walks befmear'd with guiltlefs Gore.
While faithlefs P—n and his favage Bands.
With murd'rous Rancour ftretch their bloody Hands;
Like fierce Barbarians grinning o'er their Prey.
Approve the Carnage and enjoy the Day.

If fcalding drops from Rage from Anguifh Wrung
If fpeechlefs Sorrows lab'ring for a Tongue.
Or if a weeping World can ought appeafe
The plaintive Ghofts of Victims fuch as thefe;
The Patriot's copious Tears for each are fhed,
A glorious Tribute which enbalms the Dead.

But know Fate fummons to that awful Goal.
Where Justice ftrips the Murd'rer of his Soul:
Should venal C—ts the fcandal of the Land.
Snatch the relentlefs Villain from her Hand.
Keen Execrations on this Plate infcrib'd.
Shall reach a Judge who never can be brib'd.

The unhappy Sufferers were Meff! Sam.! Gray, Sam.! Maverick, Jam.! Caldwell, Crispus Attucks & Pat.! Carr
Killed. Six wounded two of them (Christ.! Monk & John Clark) *Mortally*

Figure 8. Nicolas Toussaint Charlet. *Return from Moscow*. 1835. Oil on canvas. Musée des Beaux-Arts, Lyon. Photo: Musée des Beaux-Arts, Lyon.

Figure 9. Caspar David Friedrich. *Tombs of the Freedom Fighters*. 1812. Oil on canvas. Kunsthalle, Hamburg. Photo: Kunsthalle, Hamburg.

Figure 10. David Scott. *The Poles Did Nobly, and the Russian General Craved for an Armistice to Bury His Dead*. 1832. Oil on canvas. University Art Museum, Glasgow. Photo: University Art Museum, Glasgow.

Figure 11. Francisco Goya. *The Third of May, 1808.* 1814. Oil on canvas. Prado, Madrid. Photo: after reproduction.

Figure 12. Jean Pierre Norblin de la Gourdaine. *Voting for the Polish Constitution of May Third, 1791.* 1792. Drawing. Muzeum Narodowe, Warsaw. Photo: Muzeum Narodowe, Warsaw.

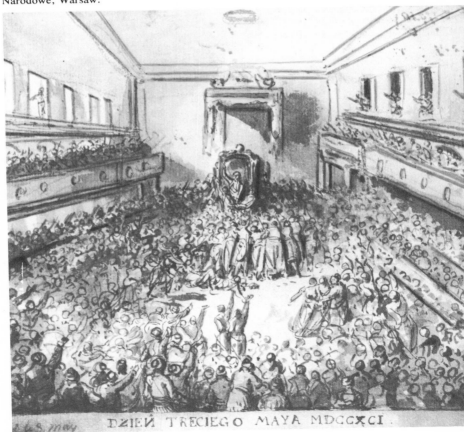

DZIEŃ TRECIEGO MAYA MDCCXCI.

Figure 13. Franciszek Smuglewicz. *Oath of Tadeusz Kościuszko on the Cracow Market Square*. 1797. Oil on canvas. Muzeum Narodowe, Poznań. Photo: Muzeum Narodowe, Poznań.

Figure 14. Marcin Zaleski. *Taking of the Warsaw Armory in 1830*. 1831. Oil on canvas. Muzeum Narodowe, Warsaw. Photo: Muzeum Narodowe, Warsaw.

Figure 15. Benjamin
West. *Kościuszko
Blessed in London*.
1797. Oil on canvas.
Allen Memorial Art
Museum, Oberlin
College, R. T. Mill-
er, Jr., Fund, 46.46.
Photo: Allen Memo-
rial Art Museum.

Figure 16. Henryk
Rodakowski. *Gen-
eral Henryk Dem-
biński*. 1852. Oil on
canvas. Muzeum
Narodowe, Cracow.
Photo: Muzeum
Narodowe, Cracow.

temporary history, he turned to painting and he knew how to transform the observation of typical events into new symbols of lasting value. In his *Revolution* and in his *Refugees*,[88] Honoré Daumier formulated images that have not lost their dramatic currency up to our own days.

NOTES

1 General studies of the problem are F. Antal, "Reflections on Classicism and Romanticism," *Burlington Magazine* (cited hereafter as *BM*) 66 (1935): 159–63; 68 (1936): 130–39; 77 (1940): 72–80; 77 (1940): 188–92; 77 (1941): 14–22; reprinted in idem, *Classicism and Romanticism* (London, 1966); J. A. Leith, *The Idea of Art as Propaganda in France: 1750–1799* (Toronto, 1965); R. Rosenblum, *Transformations in Late Eighteenth Century Art* (Princeton, 1967); K. Scheinfuss, *Reden und Dekrete*, vol. 1: *Von Brutus zu Marat. Kunst im Nationalkonvent 1789–1795* (Dresden, 1973).

2 E. Wind, "The Revolution of History Painting," *Journal of the Warburg Institute* 2 (1939): 116–27.

3 Quoted in Ch. Mitchell's article (see below, n. 5), p. 21.

4 L. Hautecoeur, *Rome et la Renaissance de l'Antiquité au XVIIIᵉ siécle* (Paris, 1912); D. Wiebenson, "Subjects from Homer's *Iliad* in Neoclassical Art," *Art Bulletin* 46 (1964): 23–37.

5 For this discussion, see Ch. Mitchell, "Benjamin West's 'Death of Wolfe' and the Popular History Piece," *Journal of the Warburg and Courtauld Institutes* 7 (1944): 20–33; E. Wind, "Penny, West, and the 'Death of Wolfe,' " ibid., 10 (1947): 159–62.

6 N. von Holst, *Das Ereignisbild* (Berlin, 1935).

7 J. Białostocki, "Zagadka 'Bitwy pod Orszą,' " *Biuletyn Historii Sztuki* 17 (1955): 80–98.

8 For the relation of artists to Masaniello and his political movement, see F. Saxl, "The Battle Scene Without a Hero: Aniello Falcone and His Patrons," *Journal of the Warburg and Courtauld Institutes* 3 (1939–40): 70–87.

9 W. Hager, *Die Übergabe von Breda von Velázquez* (Stuttgart, 1956); O. Cederlöf, "Källorna till 'Las Lanzas,' " *Konsthistorisk Tidskrift* (cited hereafter as *KT*) 26 (1957): 43–61.

10 *The Age of Neoclassicism* (London, 1972) (hereafter quoted as *London 1972*), p. 206. Catalogue.

11 Jennings's picture is in the Library Company of Philadelphia, reproduced in S. Kaplan, *The Black Presence in the Era of the American Revolution: 1770–1800* (Washington, National Portrait Gallery, 1973), p. 2, fig. 1. For revolutionary symbolism in France, see R. Herbert, cited below, n. 42.

12 *De David à Delacroix: La peinture française de 1774 à 1830* (Paris, 1974) (cited hereafter as *Paris 1974*), no. 150 (interpretation by J. Villain).

13 J. P. Cuzin in *Paris 1974*, p. 570.

14 J. D. Prown, *American Painting from Its Beginnings to the Armory Show* (Geneva, 1969), p. 47.

15 Prown, *American Painting*; A. Neumeyer, "John Trumbull," in *Kindlers Malerei Lexikon* (Zürich, 1968), vol. 5, pp. 573–76.

16 J. Trumbull, *Letters Proposing a Plan for the Permanent Encouragement of the Fine*

Arts by the National Government, Addressed to the President of the United States (New York, 1827), p. 3-4.

17 Rosenblum, *Transformations*, p. 91, fig. 93.

18 *London 1972*, no. 611, fig. 88a.

19 *Paris 1974*, no. 61, p. 26, fig. 137.

20 A. Ryszkiewicz, *Polski portret zbiorowy* (Warsaw, 1961), pp. 72-75; *Portrety osobistości polskich znajdujące się w pokojach i w galerii Pałacu w Wilanowie* (Warsaw, 1967), pp. 262-65.

21 *Romantyzm i romantyczność w sztuce polskiej XIX i XX wieku* (Warsaw, 1975) no. 91. Catalogue.

22 M. Levey, *Painting at Court* (London, 1971), p. 173, fig. 146.

23 G. Levitine, "L'Ossian de Girodet et l'actualité politique sous le consulat," *Gazette des Beaux-Arts* (cited hereafter as *GBA*) 6/48 (October, 1956): 39-56.

24 D. Ternois, "Napoléon et la décoration du Palais impérial de Monte Cavallo en 1811-13," *Revue de l'Art* (cited hereafter as *RA*) 7 (1970): 68-89, especially pp. 70, 74.

25 J. Lacambre in *Paris 1974*, pp. 464-65, no. 88, fig. 99.

26 *Paris 1974*, no. 173. See also Ch. O. Zieseniss, "Le décor pictural de la Galerie de Diane aux Tuileries sous le premier empire," *Bulletin de la Société d'Histoire de l'Art Français* (cited hereafter as *BSHAF*)(1966): 199-235.

27 *Paris 1974*, pp. 540-41 (J. P. Cuzin). See also Ch. O. Zieseniss, "Napoléon à Eylau, une esquisse de Charles Meynier," *Revue des Arts*, nos. 4-5 (1960): 213-20; P. Lelièvre, "Napoléon sur le Champ de Bataille d'Eylau, par Gros," *BSHAF* (1955): 51-55.

28 *Paris 1974*, p. 541.

29 *Henri de la Rochejaquelein* by Pierre Narcisse Guérin may be an example (*Paris 1974*, no. 95, fig. 157, p. 475, interpretation by J. Villain). That whole group is discussed by J. Bottineau, "Les portraits des généraux vendéens: Commande et critique. Diffusion et destin," *GBA* 6/85 (1975): 175-91. See also G. and J. Lacambre, "La politique d'acquisition sous la Restauration: les tableaux d'histoire," *BSHAF* (1972): 331-44, especially p. 340. For the political function of historical subjects under the Restoration, see R. Kaufmann, "François Gérard's 'Entry of Henry IV into Paris': The Iconography of Constitutional Monarchy," *BM* 117 (1975): 790-802.

30 *Paris 1974*, no. 180, fig. 252, p. 233ff; Rosenblum, *Transformations*, fig. 107, p. 101ff.; and *Paris 1974*, no. 155, fig. 154.

31 Ch. Mitchell, "Benjamin West's Death of Nelson," *Essays in the History of Art Presented to Rudolf Wittkower* (London, 1967), pp. 265-73. For the *Apotheosis of Nelson* by West of 1807, see G. T. Noszlopy, "A Note on West's Apotheosis of Nelson," *BM* 112 (1970): 813-17, and *London 1972*, no. 273. The picture is illustrated in D. Irwin, *English Neoclassical Art* (London, 1966), fig. 146.

32 *William Blake, 1757-1827* (Hamburg, Hamburger Kunsthalle, 1975), p. 6. Both pictures in the Tate Gallery, London (about 1805-08 and about 1805).

33 *Romantic Movement*, London 1959, p. 233, no. 370. Exhibition Catalogue.

34 Ibid., p. 333.

35 The picture of 1815 is in the Staatliche Galerie in Dessau; reproduced in P. Feist, "Romantik und Realismus," *C. D. Friedrich und sein Kreis*, Ausstellung im Albertinum (Dresden, 1974), p. 14, fig. 3.

36 *Deutsche Kunst und Literatur in der frühbürgerlichen Revolution: Aspekte, Probleme, Positionen* (Berlin, 1975).

37 H. van de Waal, *Drie eeuwen vaderlandsche geschieduitbeelding* ('s-Gravenhage, 1952).

38 F. D. Klingender, *Hogarth and the English Caricature* (London and New York, 1945); J. V. Kuyk, *Oude politieke spotprenten* ('s-Gravenhage, 1940).

39 Rosenblum, *Transformations*, pp. 50–106.

40 The degree to which they were even meant as political expressions is the subject of controversy. H. Honour, *Neoclassicism* (Harmondsworth, 1968), pp. 69–80, opposed the popular opinions about the political character of the prerevolutionary David production. But Rosenblum, *Transformations*, and the authors of the *Paris 1974* catalogue support, at least to some extent, the traditional view.

41 Rosenblum, *Transformations*, p. 78; A. Humbert, *Louis David, peintre et conventionnel; essai de critique marxiste*, 2nd ed. (Paris, 1947), pp. 53–66.

42 R. Herbert, *David, Voltaire and the French Revolution*, Art in Context Series (London, 1972); Ch. Sells, review of this book in *BM* 117 (1975): 811–13; L. D. Ettlinger, "Jacques-Louis David and Roman Virtue," *Journal of the Royal Society of Arts* 115 (January, 1967): 105–23, is critical of political interpretations.

43 F. D. Klingender, *Goya in the Democratic Tradition* (London, 1948); H. Thomas, *Goya: The Third of May 1808* (London, 1972). The Paul Revere print was copied by him after an engraving by Henry Pelham, who accused Revere of plagiarism. See *American Painting and Historical Prints from the Middendorf Collection: A Catalogue of an Exhibition* (Baltimore-New York, 1967), no. 60a-b; for the Russian picture, see N. Molieva and E. Belutin, *Russkaia khudozhestvennaia shkola pervoi poloviny XIX veka* (Moscow, 1963), fig. 45; for the connection between Goya and the British broadsheets, see E. H. Gombrich, "Imagery and Art in the Romantic Period," *Meditations on a Hobby Horse and Other Essays in the Theory of Art* (London, 1963), pp. 125–26.

44 Painted in 1810, *London 1972*, no. 108, fig. 12, p. 72.

45 For Boissard de Boisdenier and Charlet, see *Romantic Movement*, no. 31 (Salon of 1835) and no. 52 (Salon of 1836). For Michałowski, idem, nos. 248–49.

46 *Paris 1974*, no. 188, fig. 191, p. 647.

47 L. Eitner, "Géricault's Wounded Cuirassier," *BM* 96 (1954): 237–41; *Paris 1974*, no. 74, fig. 149, pp. 443–44.

48 A. M. Broadley and J. Holland Rose, *Napoleon and Caricature 1795–1821* (London, 1911); *Napoléon: Caricatures et dessins humoristiques de 1800 à nos jours*, Exposition, Boulogne, Catalogue by B. Foucart and N. Villard 1975. For Blake, see note 32 above.

49 The basic work H. Börsch-Supan and K. W. Jähnig, *Caspar David Friedrich: Gemälde, Druckgraphik und bildmässige Zeichnungen* (München, 1973). Important are catalogues of both Friedrich exhibitions, in Hamburg and in Dresden, in 1974.

50 Friedrich's political ideas and attitudes were first studied by A. Aubert, *C. D. Friedrich: Gott, Freiheit, Vaterland* (Berlin, 1915). Recently an interesting political interpretation was presented in the dissertation by P. Märker, *Geschichte und Natur. Untersuchungen zur Entwicklungsvorstellung bei C. D. Friedrich* (Kiel, 1974).

51 H. van de Waal, "The Iconographical Background to Rembrandt's Civilis," *KT* 25 (1956): 11–25, reprinted in *Steps Towards Rembrandt* (Amsterdam-London, 1974), pp. 28–43.

52 R. Kühnemund, *Arminius or the Rise of a National Symbol in Literature from Hutten to Grabbe* (Chapel Hill, N.C., 1953); L. Kerssen, "Das Hermannsdenkmal als Aus-

druck der Anknüpfung an den Cheruskerfürsten Armin,'' in his *Das Interesse am Mittelalter im Deutschen Nationaldenkmal* (Berlin-New York, 1975), pp. 78–85.

53 Börsch-Supan and Jähnig, *Casper David Friedrich*, no. 206; *Friedrich* (Hamburg, 1974), no. 106.

54 S. Hinz, *C. D. Friedrich in Briefen und Bekenntnissen* (Berlin, 1968), p. 25.

55 Börsch-Supan and Jähnig, *Caspar David Friedrich*, no. 205; *Friedrich* (Hamburg, 1974), no. 107.

56 F. Möbius discusses the political symbolism of the oak tree in a paper read at the Greifswald Friedrich conference in 1974. Its publication in the Proceedings of the conference is forthcoming.

57 In the National Galerie, West Berlin. Reproduced in *Patriotische Kunst aus der Zeit der Volkserhebung 1813* (Berlin, 1953), p. 9.

58 Quoted by K. Kaiser, "Patriotische Kunst,'' in the publication quoted in note 57 above, p. 13. The Fürst of Puttbus described the picture in the catalogue of his collection in the following words: "Es ist eine Winterlandschaft, der Reiter dessen Pferd schon verloren ging, eilt dem Tod in die Arme, ein Rabe krächzt ihm das Totenlied nach.'' W. Geissmeier, *C. D. Friedrich* (Leipzig, 1973), p. 45, sees in the picture the reflection of the annihilation of Napoleon's army in Russia.

59 The words of Dahl quoted by A. Aubert in *Kunst und Künstler* 3 (1905), p. 198, and Hinz, *C. D. Friedrich*, p. 217.

60 *Friedrich* (Hamburg, 1974), no. 100–15.

61 N. Pevsner, "Goethe and Architecture'' (1951), *Studies in Art, Architecture and Design* (New York, 1968), pp. 165–73; P. Frankl, *The Gothic* (Princeton, 1960), pp. 417–28. The best general account of the Gothic Revival in Germany is W. D. Robson-Scott, *The Literary Background of the Gothic Revival in Germany* (Oxford, 1965).

62 G. Eimer, "Zum patriotischen Kunstprogramm des Freiherrn vom Stein,'' in his *C. D. Friedrich und die Gotik* (Hamburg, 1963), pp. 39–49.

63 H. Lützeler, "Der Kölner Dom in der deutschen Geistesgeschichte,'' *Der Kölner Dom: Festschrift zur Siebenhundertjahrfeier* (Cologne, 1948), pp. 195–250; Kerssen, *Das Interesse*, pp. 16–48.

64 Eimer, *C. D. Friedrich;* P. Bloch, "Der Freiherr vom Stein und der Kölner Bildhauer Peter Joseph Imhoff,'' *Anzeiger des Germanischen Nationalmuseums* (1967), pp. 89–116.

65 C. von Lorck, *K. Fr. Schinkel* (Berlin, 1939), p. 26.

66 See P. Bloch, "Sculptures néo-gothiques en Allemagne,'' *RA* 21 (1973): 70–79.

67 Eimer, *C. D. Friedrich*, pp. 45f. The existing second version is preserved in Cappenberg Castle. O. V. Lutterotti, *J. A. Koch* (Berlin, 1940), pp. 91–96. Illustrated in Eimer, *C. D. Friedrich*, fig. 35.

68 G. Lacambre, in *Paris 1974*, pp. 376–77, no. 39, fig. 192, who stresses that the subject of the Greek independence was not popular, and that there were no more then twenty pictures using that subject exhibited at the Salons during the Restoration.

69 G. H. Hamilton, "Delacroix Memorial to Byron,'' *BM* 94 (1952): 257–61 (not quoted in *Paris* 1974).

70 *Romantic Movement*, no. 329, fig. 63. The picture is in the Glasgow University Museum.

71 P. Guinard, "Les thèmes polonais dans l'art français du XIXe siècle,'' *Art Polonais. Art Français. Études d'influences* (Paris, 1939), pp. 73–103, especially pp. 84–96.

72 Ibid., p. 88; A. Ryszkiewicz, "Jean Gigoux i romantyczny typ portretu wodza zwy-

cięźonej armii," *Biuletyn Historii Sztuki* 23, no. 1 (1961): 57–62; *Katalog wystawy powstania listopadowego* (Warsaw, 1931).

73 J. W. McCoubrey, "Gros' *Battle of Eylau* and Roman Imperial Art," *Art Bulletin* 43 (1961): 135–39.

74 J. Białostocki, "Encompassing Themes and Archetypal Images," *Studi in Onore di G. N. Fasola (Arte Lombarda* 10 [1965]), pp. 275–84.

75 J. Białostocki, "Romantische Ikonographie," *Stil und Ikonographie* (Dresden, 1966), p. 165.

76 Ibid., pp. 176–77.

77 J. D. Prown, *American Painting*, ill., p. 36.

78 M. Porębski, *Malowane dzieje* (Warsaw, 1961), pp. 27–42. A. Ryszkiewicz, *Polski portret zbiorowy* (Warsaw, 1961), pp. 97–98.

79 *Katalog, Malarstwo polskie od XVI do początku XX wieku,* Muzeum Narodowe w Warszawie, 2nd ed. (Warsaw, 1975), no. 1148.

80 M. Porębski, *Interregnum* (Warsaw, 1975), pp. 129–92.

81 Most recent contributions are G. H. Hamilton, "The Iconographic Origins of Delacroix' 'Liberty Leading the People,' " *Studies in Art and Literature for Belle da Costa Greene* (Princeton, 1954), pp. 55–66; G. Busch, *Delacroix: Die Freiheit auf den Barrikaden* (Stuttgart, 1960); S. Ringbom, "Guérin, Delacroix, and 'The Liberty,' " *BM* 110 (1968):270–74; W. Hofmann, "Sur la 'Liberté' de Delacroix," *GBA* 6/86 (1975):61–70.

82 Ch. Hamilton, "A Portrait of General Kosciusko by Benjamin West," *Allen Memorial Art Museum Bulletin* 9 (1952):81–91.

83 A. Ryszkiewicz, *Henryk Rodakowski, 1823–1894* (Cracow, 1954), pp. 16–17.

84 Z. Żygulski, Jr., paper read at a conference devoted to the iconography of the period 1750–1850 *(Ikonografia romantyczna)* (Nieborów, 1975), to be published in the Proceedings.

85 Porębski, *Interregnum,* passim.

86 Repin's picture in the Tretiakov Gallery, Moscow, reproduced, among other places, in G. H. Hamilton, *The Art and Architecture of Russia* (Harmondsworth, 1954), pl. 165A.

87 David's drawing in the Louvre, reproduced in H. Honour, *Neoclassicism* (Harmondsworth, 1968), fig. 29. Lordon's picture (after a print) is reproduced by Rosenblum in *Paris 1974,* p. 233.

88 Daumier's *Refugees* in *Romantic Movement,* no. 102, fig. 30, and no. 103. The sculpture in plaster, same catalogue, no. 475 (it is a late work, but the dating is not certain—either 1848 or 1871). The *Revolution* is in the Phillips Collection, Washington, D.C. (W. Hofmann, *Das Irdische Paradies, Motive und Ideen des 19. Jahrhunderts,* 2nd ed. [Munich, 1974], fig. 236).

NOTES ON CONTRIBUTORS

JAN BIAŁOSTOCKI is professor of the history of modern art at the University of Warsaw and curator of the Gallery of Foreign Paintings at the National Museum in Warsaw. His fields of interest include Renaissance and Romantic art in both Eastern and Western Europe, and art theory. Among his publications are *Spätmittelalter und beginnende Neuzeit* (Propyläen Kunstgeschichte, vol. 7, Berlin, 1972), *Pięć wieków myśli o sztuce* [Five Centuries of Thought on Art] 2nd ed. (Warsaw, 1976), and *The Art of Renaissance in Eastern Europe: Hungary, Poland, Bohemia* (Ithaca, N.Y., 1976).

ANNA M. CIENCIALA has been professor of history at the University of Kansas since 1971. She was educated at the University of Liverpool, McGill University, and Indiana University (Ph.D., 1962). Her specialty is modern Western and Eastern European history. She has published *Poland and the Western Powers, 1938-1939: A Study in the Interdependence of Eastern and Western Europe* (London, 1969), and numerous articles and reviews.

ISTVAN DEAK has been professor of history at Columbia University since 1971, and the director of the Institute on East Central Europe, Columbia University, since 1968. He specializes in the history of East Central Europe, particularly of Hungary. His principal publications are *Weimar Germany's Left-wing Intellectuals* (Berkeley, 1968), and *The Lawful Revolution: Louis Kossuth and the Hungarians, 1848-1849* (New York, 1979).

M. K. DZIEWANOWSKI is professor of history at the University of Wisconsin, Milwaukee. He received his education at the University of Warsaw, and Harvard University (Ph.D., 1951). His main fields of interest are modern East European and Russian history. His principal publications include *The Communist Party of Poland*, 2nd ed. (Cambridge, Mass., 1976), *Joseph Piłsudski: A European Federalist 1918-1922* (Stanford, 1969), and *Poland in the Twentieth Century* (New York, 1977).

ROBERT FORSTER has been professor of history at The Johns Hopkins University since 1966. He was educated at Swarthmore College, Harvard University, and The Johns Hopkins University (Ph.D., 1956). He specializes in the social history of France in the eighteenth century. His principal publications are *The Nobility of Toulouse in the Eighteenth Century* (Baltimore, 1960), and *The House of Saulx-Tavanes: Versailles and Burgundy, 1700-1830* (Baltimore, 1971).

SYDNEY V. JAMES has been professor of history at the University of Iowa since 1967. He was educated at Harvard University (Ph.D., 1958), and specializes in the history of colonial America. His publications include *A People among Peoples; Quaker Benevolence in Eighteenth-Century America* (Cambridge, Mass., 1963), and *Colonial Rhode Island: A History* (New York, 1975).

LINDA K. KERBER has been professor of history at the University of Iowa since 1975. She received her education at Barnard College, New York University, and Columbia University (Ph.D., 1968). She has published *Federalists in Dissent: Imagery and Ideology in Jeffersonian America* (Ithaca, N.Y., 1970), *Women of the Republic: Intellect and Ideology in Revolutionary America* (Chapel Hill, N.C., 1980), as well as numerous articles and reviews.

S T E F A N K I E N I E W I C Z is professor emeritus of history at the University of Warsaw, chairman of the Committee of Historical Sciences of the Polish Academy of Sciences, and editor-in-chief of the *Przegląd Historyczny* [Historical Survey]. He received his education at the University of Poznań and the University of Warsaw (Ph.D., 1934). He specializes in nineteenth-century Polish history. His principal publications include *Konspiracje galicyjskie (1831-1845)* [The Galician Conspiracies, 1831-1845] (Warsaw, 1950), *Sprawa włościańska w powstaniu styczniowym* [The Peasant Question in the January (1863) Insurrection] (Warsaw, 1953), and *The Emancipation of the Polish Peasantry* (Chicago, 1969).

B O G U S Ł A W L E Ś N O D O R S K I has been professor of the history of political and legal institutions at the University of Warsaw since 1950. He was educated at the University of Cracow (Ph.D., 1938; habilitation 1947). He specializes in the history of state and law. His principal publications include *Dzieło Sejmu Czteroletniego, 1788-1792* [The Achievements of the Four-Years Diet, 1788-1792] (Wrocław, 1951), and *Les Jacobins Polonais* (Paris, 1965).

J A R O S L A W P E L E N S K I has been professor of history at the University of Iowa since 1971. He received his education at the University of Munich (Ph.D., 1957) and at Columbia University (Ph.D., 1968). He specializes in the history of Russia, East Central Europe, and the Ukraine. He has published *Russia and Kazan: Conquest and Imperial Ideology (1438-1560s)* (The Hague–Paris, 1974), and numerous studies and reviews.

S T O W P E R S O N S has been professor of history at the University of Iowa since 1950. He received his education at Yale University (Ph.D., 1940) and specializes in American intellectual history. His principal publications are *Free Religion: An American Faith* (New Haven, 1947), *American Minds: A History of Ideas* (New York, 1958), and *The Decline of American Gentility* (New York, 1973).

J E R Z Y S K O W R O N E K has been docent of history at the University of Warsaw since 1976. He was educated at the University of Warsaw (Ph.D., 1966; habilitation 1976). He specializes in modern history of East Central and Southeastern Europe. His publications include *Antynapoleońskie koncepcje Czartoryskiego* [Anti-Napoleonic Conceptions of Czartoryski] (Warsaw, 1969), and in collaboration with K. Groniowski, *Historia Polski, 1795-1914* [History of Poland, 1795-1914] (Warsaw, 1977).

A L A N B. S P I T Z E R has been professor of history at the University of Iowa since 1963. He was educated at Swarthmore College and Columbia University (Ph.D., 1955) and specializes in modern French history. His principal publications include *The Revolutionary Theories of Louis-Auguste Blanqui* (New York, 1957), and *Old Hatreds and Young Hopes: The French Carbonari Against the Bourbon Restoration* (Cambridge, Mass., 1971).

J E R Z Y   T O P O L S K I is professor of history at Poznań University and a member of the Polish Academy of Sciences. He specializes in the social and economic history of early-modern Poland and Europe, and the methodology and theory of history. His principal publications include *Rozwój latyfundium arcybiskupstwa gnieźnieńskiego od XVI do XVIII wieku* [The Development of the Latifundia of the Gniezno Archbishopric from the Sixteenth to the Eighteenth Century] (Poznań, 1955), *Narodziny Kapitalizmu w Europie* [The Birth of Capitalism in Europe] (Warsaw, 1965), and *Methodology of History* (Warsaw-Dordrecht-Boston, 1976).

A N D R Z E J   W A L I C K I is professor of philosophy at the Institute of Philosophy and Sociology of the Polish Academy of Sciences in Warsaw. He was educated at Warsaw University (Ph.D., 1959; habilitation 1964) and specializes in Russian and Polish intellectual history. His principal publications include *The Controversy over Capitalism: Studies in the Social Philosophy of the Russian Populists* (Oxford, 1969), *Filozofia a mesjanizm* [Philosophy and Messianism] (Warsaw, 1970), and *The Slavophile Controversy* (Oxford, 1975).

P I O T R   S .   W A N D Y C Z is professor of history at Yale University. He was educated at Cambridge University and the London School of Economics and Political Science (Ph.D., 1951). He specializes in the history of modern Europe, particularly of Poland. His principal publications are *France and her Eastern Allies: 1919–1925* (Minneapolis, 1962), *Soviet-Polish Relations, 1917–1921* (Cambridge, Mass., 1969), and *The United States and Poland* (Cambridge, Mass., and London, 1980).